CHILDHOODS

Rethinking Childhood

Gaile S. Cannella
General Editor

Vol. 42

PETER LANG
New York • Washington, D.C./Baltimore • Bern
Frankfurt • Berlin • Brussels • Vienna • Oxford

CHILDHOODS

A Handbook

edited by
GAILE S. CANNELLA & LOURDES DIAZ SOTO

PETER LANG
New York • Washington, D.C./Baltimore • Bern
Frankfurt • Berlin • Brussels • Vienna • Oxford

Library of Congress Cataloging-in-Publication Data

Childhoods: a handbook / edited by Gaile S. Cannella, Lourdes Diaz Soto.
p. cm. — (Rethinking childhood; v. 42)
Includes bibliographical references and index.
1. Child development. 2. Child psychology. 3. Child care.
4. Early childhood education. I. Cannella, Gaile Sloan.
II. Soto, Lourdes Diaz.
LB1115.C516   305.231—dc22   2010005305
ISBN 978-1-4331-0451-0 (hardcover)
ISBN 978-1-4331-0450-3 (paperback)
ISSN 1086-7155

Bibliographic information published by **Die Deutsche Nationalbibliothek.**
Die Deutsche Nationalbibliothek lists this publication in the "Deutsche
Nationalbibliografie"; detailed bibliographic data is available
on the Internet at http://dnb.d-nb.de/.

The paper in this book meets the guidelines for permanence and durability
of the Committee on Production Guidelines for Book Longevity
of the Council of Library Resources.

© 2010 Peter Lang Publishing, Inc., New York
29 Broadway, 18th floor, New York, NY 10006
www.peterlang.com

Printed in the United States of America

Table of Contents

Introduction

GAILE S. CANNELLA

For the past 20 years, many scholars, educators, and cultural workers have examined dominant discourses of "childhood" using critical, feminist, and other postmodern perspectives. Located in a variety of disciplines, these poststructural, deconstructive, and even postcolonial critiques have challenged everything from notions of the universal child, to adult/child dualisms, to deterministic developmental theory. The purpose of this handbook is to acknowledge the profound contributions made by this body of literature, while demonstrating that critical analyses can be used to literally generate avenues/actions that increase possibilities for social justice for those who are younger (while, at the same time, avoiding determinism). In this time of globalization, hypercapitalism, and discourses that would control and disqualify through constructions like accountability, we believe that projects such as this are of utmost importance.

The authors approach their topics in different ways. Some focus on childhoods in their specific location, while integrating the local context with global issues. Others problematize universalized discourses of childhood by revealing the complexities of constructions as well as the ways in which universals mask oppressive power, which is harmful to both those labeled "adults" and those labeled "children." All generate perspectives through which critical forms of social justice for those who are younger can be maintained. The handbook is divided into four major sections to reflect multiplicity of human voices and perspectives (Section I), contemporary circumstances and dominant discourses within which we all attempt to function (Sections II and III), and the generation of new possibilities for constructing relationships together (Section IV). Finally, a voice from the "heart" within a "reconceptualist" social science agenda for early childhood studies is presented.

Diversity, Multiplicity, and Childhoods

Ariès's (1962) *Centuries of Childhood* certainly resulted in our considering that childhood is a social construction, created differently dependent on space, time, and the positions of "those" involved in the construction. In the half-century since, multicultural perspectives, cultural studies, and critical theoretical examinations of dominant views of the world have revealed human multiplicities, diversality (Kincheloe, 2008), and even the ways in which universalist constructions have privileged particular groups of human beings and disqualified/oppressed others (Cannella, 1997; Burman, 1995/2008). The authors in Section I continue this conversation while inviting the reader to go behind the critical practices that have informed a critical social science of childhood(s) thus far by introducing unique analytical perspectives and voices of history and/or oppression that our traditional forms of science do not often hear, and worse, often attempt (however unintentionally) to discredit.

In Chapters 1, 2, and 3, Burman, Saavedra and Camicia, and Nsamenang introduce transformative research methods and perspectives that acknowledge the harm inflicted by our modernist theories while constructing a commitment to countering that devastation. Recognizing that positivist science (even in its postpositivist forms) has constructed "childhood" as text, Erica Burman discusses an antipsychology approach that would use feminist critique to challenge the damage to younger human beings (labeled as children) through the imposition of developmental psychology. Cinthya Saavedra and Steven Camicia use descriptions of their own transnational childhoods to employ counterdiscourses of resistance for childhoods wounded within discourses of accountability, individualism, and assessment. A. Bame Nsamenang proposes a transformative Africa-centric form of early childhood care and education, demonstrating that modernist scientific methods can be used to reveal knowledge that is multiple and consistent with "life-journeys" of children.

In Chapters 4, 5, and 6, Kennedy and Bloch, Collins, and Miller focus on those life-journeys that are often marginalized, discredited, and even made invisible. Devorah Kennedy and Marianne Bloch focus attention on the case of American Jewish childhoods caught within shifting constructions of the child, while at the same time struggling to be acceptably different. By directly including the voices of African Americans, Donald Collins explores four generations of childhood education in the United States, asking questions like: What has changed? Are there forms of contemporary educational racism (e.g., assessment, new re-inscriptions of the deficit "retardation" paradigm)? Finally, Melinda Miller focuses on the strengths (and often denied knowledges) of children at home and at school, a perspective that is entirely disqualified by those in positions of influence who would test universalist, skill-oriented, narrow forms of education and knowledge.

Corporatized Childhoods, Neoliberalism, and Critical Policy Perspectives

For at least the past 50 years, the dominant world (those of us who are generally white, socioeconomically privileged, and often from the northern hemisphere) has engaged in discourses that allege "progress." This notion of progress has been used to legitimize intervening into the lives of "others" (most often those labeled as children) in order to "save" those others from whatever "we" deemed to be a problem. Generally, there has been no recognition that these "problems" are products of the inequitable power conditions in society that literally privilege those of us who would, most often, "identify" the problems. As examples, rather than addressing societal conditions that result in the imposition of poverty, we would intervene to "save" children whose parents are poor and therefore judged as intellectually lacking and/or lazy, and as a result do not understand how to "raise" their children. Or, although our educational practices impose particular cultural forms of knowledge and regulatory assessment on all children (not actually a democratic practice of education), we judge those with different knowledge and strengths as slow, or lacking, or their teachers (who are mostly female) as incompetent or lazy. Additionally, although always embedded within dominant constructions of childhood, most recently an imperialist hypercapitalism that interprets all human activity using the lens of a "free" market has gained strength as the avenue through which this progress can be attained. This hypercapitalist discourse is grounded within the neoliberalism framework proposed by Milton Friedman and his students at the University of Chicago and accepted (to some extent) by past and present federal government administrations in the United States but also around the globe. Neoliberal capitalism privileges competition, profiteering, and privatization and is using interventionist notions of progress to construct and privatize new forms of profiteering in the name of ("saving," "educating") the children.

The authors in Section II of this handbook address the ways that childhood has become (and is becoming) literally a site of capitalist profiteering legitimated through discourses of intervention. From within this contemporary circumstance, younger human beings are increasingly excluded from sites of power as the influence of poverty in their lives escalates. Technologies of neoliberalism are discussed that range from protective coercion displayed in discourses of welfare to the erosion of democratic possibilities masked in neoliberal illusions of educational choice. Neoliberal technologies that result in corporatized forms of childhood representation and the unquestioned acceptance of cyber technologies that reproduce social and economic inequities are discussed.

The first few chapters draw attention to the evolution of neoliberal societies as capitalist states. In Chapter 7, Michel Vandenbroeck, Rudi Roose, and Maria De Bie use a Foucaultian framework to analyze contemporary discourses of child welfare like "children's rights" and "active citizenship" that would (as purpose) construct autonomous, entrepreneurial citizen children and parents. I-Fang Lee, in Chapter 8, uses the Taiwan and Hong Kong preschool voucher movements to further examine the ways that neoliberal constructions of freedom, equality, and choice rework the public's image of concepts like justice and equality, resulting in dangerous and oppressive mentalities as "desirable normative knowledge." Neoliberalism is discussed historically and contemporarily by Michelle Salazar Perez and Gaile Cannella in Chapter 9 as a (perhaps "the") dominant discourse impacting those who are younger both locally and globally. These authors explain how childhood policy practices like school choice and No Child Left Behind (NCLB) in the United States are created as mechanisms of control and privatization (of public resources and services) that are then further facilitated through practices of disaster capitalism (Klein, 2007). Finally, in Chapter 10, Sue Books calls our attention to the most obvious, yet most denied components of neoliberal world views—that our market perspectives literally construct and maintain conditions of poverty for those caught in its "mechanics of unfairness." The ways in which childhood public policies (e.g., child care support, school funding, economic segregation in educational environments) are sustained and how they increase economic inequities and new vulnerabilities, and contribute to an increased exclusion are demonstrated.

The remaining chapters in the section illustrate the widespread embeddedness of neoliberal power within everything from the media, to new forms of science, to the arts and entertainment. Examining the reactions in Australia to the publication of *Corporate Paedophilia: Sexualisation of Children in Australia* by Rush and La Nauze in 2006, Sue Grieshaber (Chapter 11) discusses various interpretations of the neoliberal vocation, including the belief that it is a form of governmentality. Moral panics and the neoliberal discourse of tolerance/intolerance are just two of the practices that, when analyzed, illustrate the contradictory and paradoxical performances of neoliberalism. In Chapter 12, Nicola Yelland and Greg Neal discuss a research study through which low-income children were provided computers. This research can generate an awareness of the ways in which new neoliberal technologies (in the form of communication and information sciences) increase societal inequities and forms of domination and/or exclusion for particular groups of children. In the last chapter in the section (Chapter 13), Sandra Chang-Kredl calls attention to the positioning of adult spectators who use film as a site for the construction of childhood. This site reinscribes neoliberal notions of innocence, idleness, purity and freedom, constructing the "in-between" for the privileged "adult" viewer as one who has been child, who has the power to represent child, and as the legitimate regulator of childhoods for neoliberal (and other) purposes.

Unquestioned Discourses and the Universalization of Childhoods

While much has been written that examines the range of unquestioned technologies constructing and controlling "childhoods," critical forms of social science have often been ignored, placed under erasure, and/or dismissed by those who fear the loss of their own power positions (whether academic, economic, gendered, or otherwise). Further, although exalted as creating greater freedom and possibilities for human beings (at least in neoliberal, free market discourse), contemporary conditions of globalization result in circumstances that facilitate reinscriptions of old forms of power from within "new" discourses. The authors contributing to Section III discuss the new forms of reinscription as well as technologies of childhood that have remained generally unquestioning even within the critical social science that has been practiced over the past 20 to 30 years.

The first four chapters of the section clearly demonstrate the intersections between globalization and the reproduction of modernism and imperialism upon/within the bodies of younger human beings through linguistic exclusions, imperialist practices, and research conceptualizations and forms of representation. Addressing linguistic silencing in Chapter 14, Lourdes Diaz Soto, Sharon Hixon, and Clare Hite explore the ways that childhoods are muted and restrained, from the continued use of gendered perspectives that disqualify the voices of females and/or diverse cultural ways of knowing, to educational policies that linguistically exclude individuals and the countries in which they reside by denying linguistic human rights. Second, although, the construction of child development has been critiqued from a range of locations (Walkerdine, 1988; Cannella, 1997; Burman, 1995/2008), the discourse of developmentally appropriate practices (DAP) as a regulatory power imposed by the National Association for the Education of Young Children (in the United States) has become the dominant technology of "quality" around the globe. In Chapter 15, Sadaf Shallwani conducts a textual analysis of the DAP position statement illustrating how the technology reproduces imperialism and is a racist form of regulation that privileges the white subject. Critical social science has also implicated research in the perpetuation of intellectual imperialism. Yet, standardized and high-stakes testing as measures of intellect and technologies of comparison and regulation have never been more accepted as appropriate forms for "judging" children, their teachers, and their schools. Children of color, children who are linguistically diverse (read: non-English speakers), and children who are poor continue to be the victims of this "measurement," "accountability" research. Using a Foucaultian framework in Chapter 16, Araceli Rivas conducts a postcolonial examination of the positioning of young Mexican American children in the research conducted on/about them. Finally, Veronica Pacini-Ketchabaw and Radhika Viruru (in Chapter 17) use critical research perspectives to demonstrate how early childhood citizenship discourses are embedded within citizen-subject value structures that are racialized, gendered, and colonialist. They ask questions like: "What does it mean to speak of citizenship in the age of empire?" and Are discussions of citizenship in early childhood education appropriate from within the contemporary "transnational nature of participation in the world"?

The final two chapters in Section III address technologies imposed on younger human beings that have generally not been examined as part of the emerging critical social science of childhood(s). These disciplinary discourses are (a) the personification of younger human beings as heterosexual, and at the same time innocent and physically asexual and (2) the discourse of play that reproduces and continually reconstructs modernist "utopian longings for the rational subject." Corrine Wickens, in Chapter 18, discusses the cultural struggle for the bodies and minds of "children" that has led to the denial of childhood physicality, an unquestioned (hetero)narrative of childhood, and the use of censorship through discourses like developmentally appropriate practice that deny the physiological and sexual selves of younger human beings. In Chapter 19, Liz Jones, Rachel Holmes, Christina MacRae, and Maggie MacLure use the presence of playfulness, and our interpretations of play as construct, in four early childhood settings to consider how it represents both a hunger for living and the shadowy discourses of the past that envelop, entomb, and normalize. Play is considered as dualistic, creative, and freedom-oriented, while at the same time political and embedded within histories, cultures, and forms of domination.

Childhoods and Unthought Struggles for Social Justice

The chapters in the final section of the volume demonstrate the possibilities that are generated through a critical social science of childhood. From new directions for teaching young children to reconceptualizations of research, the authors shed light on the potential for antioppressive and decolonial constructions of work with/for children.

The first two chapters demonstrate the complete reconceptualization of the early childhood curriculum toward forms that reject determinism and engage with criticality and multiplicity. Beginning with Chapter 20, Iris Duhn describes the work of an early childhood classroom teacher concerned about climate change as she constructs a curriculum embedded within an ethics of care combined with environmental sustainability. The work illustrates the importance of recognizing the forces of globalization in order to redirect the impact of those forces through curriculum practices. Second, Reggio Emilia early education is put forward by some as the ideal early childhood education curriculum model and by others as the newest representation of a modernist belief in deterministic and rational definitions of educational quality (especially if interpreted as a curriculum model). Harold Gothson (in Chapter 21) addresses the problem with creating "cults of imperialism" out of curriculum practices and, rather, suggests ways that his own "telling" of Reggio Emilia is that of inspiration to look at one's own context and to develop one's own didactics.

The final three chapters focus on our potential for rethinking the dominant, including research and observation practices in early childhood studies. Maggie Maclure, Liz Jones, Rachel Holmes, and Christina MacRae partially deconstruct the ways researchers frame children in research in Chapter 22. Questions like the following are addressed: What is produced and concealed in the practices through which children become "data" and "text"? In Chapter 23, Liselott Mariett Olsson argues for the use of material politics in early childhood education that would avoid placing so much attention on everything as linguistic. She explains the importance of revisiting the nondiscursive aspects of political practice played out daily in classrooms. Finally, Jenny Ritchie and Cheryl Rau (Chapter 24) propose a counter colonial theory, a re-narrativization that offers all children a "sense of possibilities, of validation, of affirmation of their histories and trajectories."

Constructing Critical Futures: Projects from the Heart

Inspired by the multiple perspectives from which the authors of this volume have exhibited critical commitments to those who are younger, in "Constructing Critical Futures: Projects from the Heart," Lourdes Diaz Soto uses Chicana feminism to challenge us all to construct the collective *third* space

(Soto, Cervantes-Soon, Villareal, & Campos, in press), a location that would raise concientization and embrace hybridity. This *third* space would support unity and solidarity in the name of decolonization and the elimination of oppression. Finally, this *third* space would engage love as the practice of freedom (hooks, 2000) for/with those who are younger as the foundation for the reconstruction of our relationships and the agendas that we would establish together. We invite the reader to become part of that *third* space, to struggle, to form solidarities with all of us as we attempt to generate an antioppressive social science (and resultant material actions) for/with those who are younger, and for all of us.

References

Ariès, P. (1962). *Centuries of childhood: A social history of family life*. Translated by Robert Baldick. New York: Vintage Books.

Burman, E. (1995/2008). *Deconstructing developmentally psychology*. New York/London: Routledge.

Cannella, G.S. (1997). *Deconstructing early childhood education: Social justice and revolution*. New York: Peter Lang.

hooks, b. (2000). *Feminist theory: From margin to center*. Cambridge, MA: South End Press.

Kincheloe, J. (2008). Critical pedagogy and the knowledge wars of the twenty-first century. *International Journal of Critical Pedagogy*, 1/(1), 1–22.

Klein, N. (2007). *The shock doctrine: The rise of disaster capitalism*. New York: Metropolitan Books.

Soto, L.D., Cervantes-Soon, C., Villareal, E., Campos, E. (in press). The Xicana sacred space: A communal circle of compromiso for educational researchers. *Harvard Educational Review*.

Walkerdine, V. (1988). *The mastery of reason: Cognitive development and the production of rationality*. London: Routledge.

Section One

Diversity, Multiplicity and Childhoods

CHAPTER ONE

Un/thinking Children in Development

A Contribution from Northern Antidevelopmental Psychology

ERICA BURMAN

Abstract

This chapter outlines a feminist antipsychological approach to analyzing childhoods. Taking up Squire's (1990) characterisation of feminism as antipsychology, this chapter analyses child development as text. Examples drawn from a range of institutional practices, and genres are juxtaposed, to highlight some newly emerging twists of contemporary tropes of northern, normalised childhoods. Unsurprisingly perhaps, recent departures from the rational, autonomous, unitary subject of modern developmental psychology (cf. Henriques et al., 1984; Burman, 1994, 2008a) betray political continuities with older formulations (especially in relation to familialism). Notwithstanding these supposedly flexible times, it will be argued that covert continuities underlying discernable shifts—especially around the configuration of gendered and racialised representations—indicate some key consolidations, albeit now accorded apparently 'democratic' hues. Both in their proliferation and via their juxtaposition, it is suggested, these diverse texts can be installed within a narrative of critique. This political-methodological intervention works, therefore, firstly, to deconstruct the opposition between popular cultural and expert (developmental psychological) knowledge to mediate their mutual elaboration and legitimation. Secondly, this sample of available representations of childhood illustrates a key strategy of (as in Richards's formulation, 1998), putting psychology in its (culturally and historically limited) place. The chapter ends with some more general epistemological and ethical reflections on the alliances and antagonisms of inter- and cross-disciplinary approaches to childhood and their contributions to challenging wider developmental discourses.

A Northern Contribution?

It is fitting for a chapter whose substantive topic concerns the enmeshed psychopolitics of childhood, memory, and representation to start backwards. So, taking the last part of my title first, let me start with the question of contribution.[1] As a British feminist developmental psychologist—the knowledge I have at my disposal, perhaps even my presence, is part of the problem—precisely as someone British, as a developmental psychologist, and in some ways also perhaps as a feminist. I want, at the outset, to topicalise this ambivalence. For, inevitably, I occupy an invidious position: either parochial bystander or global coconspirator. Whether there are other possible positions of transnational and transdisciplinary solidarities and alliances is perhaps the core question at issue at this time, and for this book.

But even as I recognise the privilege, and hopefully anticipate the irrelevance, of my northern position, it is analytically and methodologically important to consider: *which* north? Of course, what space or place or (especially) home is, and whose, is very much at issue—whether in terms of home discipline, home language, home town, familial home, or the originating home cultural contexts from which dominant theory is elaborated.[2] In acknowledgment of the many norths and souths that exist within, as, and alongside, the global geopolitics of north–south relations, it is relevant to the kinds of texts that I analyse below to explain that I live and work in the North of England. Within England (as well as across the UK generally), the discourse of north and south positions northern England (along with Scotland and Wales) as less developed, economically and culturally, than the more affluent south (although we are supposedly more friendly and with a thriving counterculture of music and humor)—in other words, this geographical division is (generally speaking) marked in terms of class.

The British State of Childhood

Before examining some idealised texts of childhood, at this point, methodologically speaking, I should offer some account of the contemporary state of British children. Current social statistics consistently indicate that the gap between rich and poor in Britain—as elsewhere—is widening, and that at least a third of all British children live in poverty. There is also a sense (at least among British childhood and educational researchers) that Britain is a particularly child-hating nation, as reflected perhaps also in the UN report published in October 2007 that suggested that British children are the most unhappy children in Europe, a finding that sits significantly alongside the October 2008 report criticising Britain as having the most punitive approaches to children (in terms of practices of detention of young offenders and the imposition of Anti-social Behaviour Orders), although it has also been questioned for its partiality on other grounds (Morrow and Mayall, in press). Nevertheless, alongside having the least state support for childcare in Europe, it is largely accepted that children are unwelcome in many public spaces because they are deemed to be a nuisance, a risk or at risk—and of course these three aspects often become elided. Corporate notices up in my workplace, for example, exclude children in the name of protecting them from hurt in "buildings not made with children in mind." In fact, these notices contradict precisely what they proclaim by disclaiming (legal) responsibility for any injury to children occurring on the premises. Such notices, of course, enrage and inconvenience our many mature students, many of whom have no alternative but to bring children with them into the university during school holidays. They are an indication of the increasing impact of a culture of litigation, of defensive practice, that in the name of choice transfers the onus of responsibility from the state and organisations onto individuals, and produces a proliferation of bureaucracy around children that fails to meaningfully address or engage with them, or their careers.

Even in the heartlands of the North, therefore, childhood as a state is not only endangered, but children themselves easily acquire the pathologised status of risk (that is, as being 'risky'), by transgressing some normative threshold, portrayed as being in one way or another (metaphorically or even physically) too much. This is all the more paradoxical in the current political context where neoliberal state policies increasingly aim to mold active and flexible children for the creation of autonomous and economically self-sufficient citizens (Fendler, 2001; Lister, 2005, 2006; Ailwood, 2008).

More generally, the British state is regarded as more protectionist and less participatory in relation to children when compared to other European countries. It has particularly segregated services, and appears to be especially ambivalent around questions of children's agency (Moss and Petrie, 2002; Dahlberg and Moss, 2005). Currently, British newspapers are full of reports of rising violence directed to and by children,[3] and the rise in 'knife crime' produces on average around two murders of young men a week. On the other hand, escalating concern about child abuse, and particularly child sexual abuse, increasingly renders work with children a zone of acute anxiety for child professionals, often working also to prohibit the building of emotional connections and relations (Piper and Stronach, 2008).

An Antipsychological Approach

Moving from geographical to disciplinary spaces of belonging, in terms of intellectual history my home discipline is psychology, specifically developmental psychology. This is rarely a popular discipline in childhood and child rights circles—with good reason. Indeed part of why I am here is to work out how feminist critics in psychology can challenge (and even contribute to undoing) the damage done by much developmental psychology to children worldwide.

The widespread developmental anxiety about saving the childhoods of poor children, which is so routinely mobilised within aid imagery, alludes to the overdetermined linkages between child and national development, and the global capitalist agendas played out via the concern for children. The injustices, exclusions, and pathologisation of the discourse of development are writ small in the story of what happens to children and their families while, reciprocally, the story of individual development is writ large in the story of national and international development (Burman, 2008a). But even if we accept those resonances across different units and disciplines of development, psychology is not the only culpable discipline within the instrumentalisation and maximisation of children that is also a key consequence of globalisation. Hence rights discourses are subject to similar problems of universalisation and normalisation (often also because the norms are derived from elsewhere). Nevertheless, while psychology is not the only source for all that is wrong in educational, legal, social support, or health practices around children and families, it certainly has played its role (Walkerdine, 1984; Urwin, 1985).

So far I have been trying to indicate how my own context is disciplinarily but also necessarily nationally and culturally located. My conceptual-methodological approach is precisely to aggravate the tensions and play up the disjunctions between these different forms of development (as Nieuwenhuys (2008) has noted in relation to tensions around child rights). Clearly this is a strategy with limitations: there is little difference between universalisation and cultural relativism if all that this means is that we agree that we are all different. Nevertheless it is useful to draw attention to the partiality and limitations of all available developmental accounts and to attempt to resist accounts of developmental completion. Any general model tends to obscure the complexity of practices and contexts of development and the structurally diverse character of the economic, cultural, and interpersonal relationships that produce these varied developments (Burman, 2008a, 2008b).

Feminist Critique as Antipsychology

Positioning feminism as antipsychology, as in Squire's (1990) early characterisation, pits feminist debate against, rather than in relation to, mainstream/malestream psychology. It plays up their tensions and necessary irreconcilabilities in order to refuse easy compromises or collaborations (see also Burman, 1998). Clearly feminist theory and practice are also under interrogation here, in relation to similar charges of universalist, exclusionary models but also in relation to their (understandable, if also ultimately misplaced) suspicion or overlooking of children's rights work (Thorne, 1987; Burman, 2008c). I suggest that feminist political rhetoric offers a stronger safeguard against assimilation into mainstream models, even as it also poses new challenges. These challenges arise in particular, in relation to the treatment of plural childhoods. For the current focus in feminist theory on intersectionality (e.g., Nash, 2008) intimates the instability, as well as disunity, of any category of analysis when we start to take questions of gender, class, and other encultured meanings of gendered positions seriously in relation to childhood (see Burman, 2006a).

A particular benefit of claiming feminism as antipsychology is that it sidesteps interminable preoccupations of (for example) critical psychologists about whether, how, or how much they are (or their work is) part of psychology. But it also mobilises the wider reaches of feminist inquiry and brings these to bear on more apparently parochial psychological matters. Claiming this does not appropriate feminist debates, in the sense of confining their remit merely to antipsychology (for perhaps they equally are antisociological and are certainly relevant to development, Elson (1995)). Rather, there are particular moments or issues when playing up the antagonism can be useful.

Antipsychology identifies as its topic the refusal to accept psychological claims on their own terms but rather interrogates their concepts and underlying assumptions and evaluates them in terms of their epistemological, methodological, and especially practical effects. This is a particularly relevant approach to the critical evaluation of developmental psychology, owing to the metonymic role developmental psychology plays within psychology in securing psychology's truth claims. By curious circularity, developmental psychology functions both as method (by which to measure psychological change) and as a topic (so becoming the exemplary arena in which psychological models can be tested and warranted) (see Burman, 2008d). Further, developmental psychology also seems to function as a key foundering point for more socoiologically oriented childhood researchers and child rights—in terms of how developmental knowledges are mobilised within discussions of best interests and competence in ways that confirm children as deficient or incomplete and so in fact incapable of exercising their participatory rights.

There are two other factors for an antipsychological agenda: psychologisation and feminisation. These two notions are intertwined via their explicit concern with instrumentalising the domain of the personal (including the home, the domestic, and relational qualities). Epitomised perhaps by the rise of emotional intelligence programmes (Boler, 1999; Burman, 2009), both are central to individualism and the incursion of contemporary practices of individualisation that separate people from each other and prevent wider reflection on the conditions producing such subjectivities. As a correlate of the contraction of public sensibility and engagement under neoliberalism, there has been an expansion of the psychological domain in true voluntarist mode from specialist expertise to self-help, such that we are saturated with incitements to grow, learn, change yourself, make yourself better. In sum, to develop and demonstrate the flexibility and determination to optimise oneself (or what Fendler, 2001, termed *developmentality*). Similarly, although in some ways women's work has never fitted models of patriarchal capitalist production (Staples, 2007; Pearson, 2007), its affective features as well as temporal and cultural capital are currently being colonised into global capitalism (Nieuwenhuys, 2007).

We need to connect critical childhood studies with feminist critiques to make sense of these economic practices. This means reading the current promotion of feminine-style skills against the grain to insist that feminisation is not feminism, and that women have much to worry about in the celebration of supposedly feminine relational and intuitional qualities now entering business and education (Burman, 2006b; 2009).[4] In this chapter, therefore, I highlight how these features are now filtering through into models of childhood, including particular emotionally inflected understandings of memory and activity mobilised through and by the child.

Childhood as Text

Many resources support this kind of antipsychological consideration of childhood as text—in particular from historical and cultural analyses. Treating mainstream psychological theory and practice as text disrupts its scientism and naïve realist claims and facilitates attention to how the knowledge, facts, norms and models are the outcome of specific contextual productions and interactions. At least eight key features about this strategy can be noted:

- It emphasises the cultural-historical situatedness of the emergence of particular forms of knowledge and practice (as a specific challenge to the timelessness of scientist psychology).
- It embeds a particular disciplinary practice within wider contexts and so disrupts its specialist claims.
- It deconstructs the high/low culture binary of expert vs. popular/layperson by highlighting the circularity of underlying conceptual models, cultural assumptions and political preoccupations.
- It undermines the position of psychology as neutral, value-free, detached, etc., including also how
- It challenges the authority of the psychologist (or the other child expert).
- It draws attention to the role of the theorist/storyteller in their theory/story, so
- In doing all this, it renders their account more contestable.

Lest this should imply only the rather distant analysis of already existing, contemporary, or historical texts, there is a further point:

- It incites attention to the production of attributions of knowledge about, or to, children, including destabilising claims to 'give voice' to children (Stainton Rogers and Stainton Rogers, 1998; Alldred and Burman, 2005; Jackson and Mazzei, 2009).

In particular, I have been preoccupied with the affective investment in childhood, in terms of the grip that images of childhood seem to have on the northern cultural imaginary. This forms a further rationale for focusing on analyses of psychologisation and feminisation in terms of how representations of childhood connect with calls to memory, attachment, self-hood, and interiority.

Methodologically speaking, this concern with the practices and tactics of psychologisation also affords a warrant for some latitude in the selection of materials for analysis. The proliferation and saturation of the domain of the psychological bring into focus everyday, widely circulating materials, rather than only specialist policy or technical texts. Unlike other kinds of analysis, the challenge around conceptualisations of childhood is to find ways of making sense and critically engaging with texts that are obvious and overdetermined. While the kind of analytic practice undertaken below is probably anathema to cultural analysts, moving across diverse media that merit particular attention to questions of genre, history, and material conditions of production (which are largely overlooked here), I suggest that these texts in wider circulation are worthy of attention precisely because of their banality. They provide clues about the shaping of assumptions that quickly become normalised into absence, or what might be described as the contours of the contemporary Euro-U.S. cultural unconscious. Like banal nationalism and racism (Billig, 1995), banal developmentalism needs to be identified and analysed rather than overlooked or excused.

There is also something particularly apt about treating childhood as text. In the northern cultural imaginary, from the nineteenth century onwards, the child has come to signify the self, the innermost, precious core of subjectivity, within us all. Carolyn Steedman's (1995) historical analysis traces its emergence at the fateful confluence of the early origins of cell theory, romantic philosophy, and psychoanalysis to configure the child as the quintessential modern subject.

> The idea of the child was the figure that provided the largest number of people living in the recent past of Western societies with the means for thinking about and creating a self: something grasped and understood: a shape, moving in the body…something inside: an interiority. (p. 20)

This self—whether lost or regained—circulates as a significant cultural trope that combines notions of memory and fantasy, while most significantly its ambiguities and varieties are anchored by invocations of childhood. This equation between self and child helps to explain some of the ambiguities and mobility, as well as persistence, of the commitment to a particular notion of childhood, despite these being obviously (and increasingly) inadequate and untenable (Burman, 2002). The child appears as both topic and text: being both what is written and onto which is written a wider societal story. The rest of this chapter therefore analyses various contemporary everyday UK texts about childhood to highlight mutual tensions between these competing representations, and implications for the ways in which children of the south figure and are configured. The theme of hygiene turns out to be an intertextual link across the various images I will be discussing. This is predictable if we bear in mind how social order and disorder have historically connected the bodies of women and children with the body politic of the nation state. More surprising, perhaps, is just how literal are the links between moral and physical hygiene within these contemporary representations. And this seems to extend even to a societal imperative to clean up our memories….So let us turn to the texts.

What's (Not) on TV: 'Embracing the Nemesis'

My first text arrived on my doorstep as a supplement to the 2–9 August 2008 edition of *What's on TV*, the UK's best-selling (and cheapest) weekly television listings magazine. Entitled *What's [Not] on TV*, it publicised the washing powder Persil's current marketing campaign, which runs under the slogan 'Dirt is good!' Here it is important to note that 'Persil' is the multinational company Unilever's premium UK brand. As the first commercially available laundry detergent (invented in 1907), and the first to mount TV advertising campaigns (in the 1950s), it is positioned at the cutting edge of capitalist strategy. Moreover in the UK it is synonymous with middle class (aspirational) status, from its earlier slogan 'washes whiter,' to the current (2006 onwards) poster and television campaign 'Dirt is good!' [5]: D.I.G. in its double meaning (as both acronym and verb) thus emphasises the importance of self-directed, agentic, purposeful activity. The message here is that we should not stop children from engaging in activities on the grounds that they create a mess, or mess up their clothes. Getting dirty, the message goes, is natural. It's good for children.[6]

This is all of a piece of contemporary parenting and childcare advice. While contemporary pedagogies are (as we shall see) contradictory, nevertheless parents, especially mothers, are often as circumscribed as children in the modes of interaction and play prescribed by psychological theory for their children. Child-centred discourses of sensitive mothering and authoritative parenting not only socialise children (in gender-normative ways), they also regulate mothers (Walkerdine and Lucey, 1989). While post–World War II social policies looked to psychological models of antiauthoritarian parenting as the route toward promoting democracy and social harmony (and, significantly, efficiency—and actively promoted by such key figures of developmental psychology as Piaget and Gesell—see Piaget, 1933; Gesell, 1950), the discourse of sensitive mothering remains highly class-coded and culturally encrypted to privilege white, middle-class mothering practices.[7]

'Dirt is good!' addresses the contemporary paradoxes facing parents and families. Beyond the need to keep a tidy, clean house (surely a concern coded as working class) is that of engendering a developmentally creative and supportive environment. As the marketing blurb suggests, the brand made the daring move to "embrace its nemesis to examine the developmental and psychological benefits of getting dirty" http://www.brandrepublic.com/Campaign/News/518811/ (accessed 28 September 2008). There is a key dynamic of negation that maintains what it repudiates. 'Dirt is good!' for children, and in this collaboration with *What's on TV,* so is watching television. Or at least the paradoxes generate attention (which is success enough in marketing). Through the *What's [Not] on TV* supplement, both companies are perhaps offsetting their otherwise presumed role in keeping children passive either on the grounds of staying clean or of being pacified by watching television. Here it is important to note how this initiative coincided with increasing public and political concern, both about childhood obesity and impact of television/media images on (and of) children (notwithstanding the much more nuanced academic and popular accounts; Buckingham, 2007; Messenger Davies, 1989).

In this eight-page free supplement to the magazine, there is an overdetermined focus on free play—mobilising the discourse of freedom and emancipation central to the antiauthoritarian self-image of liberal democracies. Hence a (free) promotion 'not' to watch TV works since it offsets supposed claims that children are being socialised or otherwise culturally pressured to spend their leisure time engaged in un-childlike inactivity. (It also endows the free supplement with a moral rather than monetary surplus value.) Given the presumed class differences, audience and access between the website and *What's on TV,* it is of some minor interest to note that there is a slightly different arrangement (order of 'rights') and simpler language is used in the paper text as opposed to the Persil website, although the main materials are similar. One feature of the supplement is the way it opens by adopting a vernacular narrative style: "Today, experts are worried that our kids' childhoods are being lost, with them spending too much time in front of a screen or with every moment structured or spoken for." This strangely constructed statement betrays the slippage between child and attributed or remembered childhood: for how can kids 'lose' their childhoods?[8] But its looseness of phraseology presumably is intended to convey informality and proximity.[9] It works to soften the way into the much more authoritative and didactic claim that succeeds it, expressed in the timeless, context-free, present tense that conveys factuality or truth: "It stops children learning how to make their own decisions, deal with the unexpected and make friendships on their own terms."

Reiterating current advertising practice, there is even a competition at the end, whose answer, within the well-known genre of such promotions, is contained in the accompanying text. Its question "Free Play focuses on how many areas of development? a) 1, b) 3 or c) 5?" arguably suggests more about the banality and vacuity of developmental psychology, as well as the structure of power relations that surround it (parents as subjects, children as objects, psychologists, and other 'experts' as authorities), than all other critiques of developmentalism put together. As competent readers, we know that we should look through the leaflet and count up the five areas identified, in order to send off for the chance to win a Center Parcs UK holiday (Center Parcs are family-oriented holiday arenas, with lots of facilities for children). The very fact that there are numerous areas of development (more than five) mentioned within the text (one inset box lists nine 'rights': to…be a child, play, explore, use their imagination, express themselves, join in, discover their own world, be spontaneous, experience life for themselves), paradoxically emphasises how arbitrary such apparently incontestable areas in fact are.

(Not) Capitalism: Democracy through Consumption

These marketing interventions seem to rely on a motif of negation that precisely reinstates that which it denies. So, there is little mention of the product, the commercial transaction, of the embodied practices of buying a washing aid, cleaning up mess, or even watching TV. This is of a piece with mobilising consumption as the route for social intervention, of a new, caring capitalism that looks after, rather than exploits, us and is seemingly only incidentally interested in making us part with our money, or with how much money we have (i.e., our class position). The high sentiments invoked distract from the rather mundane business of merely occupying children during school holidays, or going out shopping to buy a washing powder, and elevates these into moral practices of good parenthood that rely upon a double reading between the child depicted as the offspring of the viewer and their earlier, or fantasised earlier, self. Notwithstanding the explicit injunctions to, and visual images of, exteriority (the natural outdoors, exercise, activity, the other), the structure of subjectivity that is installed by such materials is one of self-preoccupation, of interiority. It assumes the desire to get children's development right; indeed it explicitly addresses the reader in this way: It thus reflects a new mode of democracy through consumption, with a self-regulating subject who exercises their freedom through the choice of goods they buy, with the good life of riches now acquiring a moral surplus and mobilising the moral status of work through associating childcare prescriptions with specific products. Here we see the logical conclusion of the commodification of childhood—alongside the injunction to turn parenthood into work—that paradoxically reinstates the adult–child opposition: for you can set your child free to play by doing the correct parent work—so even your family life, that haven in a heartless world, even child's play becomes an arena of production devoid of time away from market pressure (Lafargue, 1883).

Indeed, aside from the pages specifically concerned with cleaning, the only visual reminder on both the website (Persil.com) and in the supplement about Persil as a soap powder is the small but constant image of little bottles (in the sketchy line drawing genre associated with children's books) on the left hand of the page with the header "Try Persil, small and mighty," which is positioned more or less (in a just sufficiently child-like awry style), on the right hand side which asks: "How often does your child play outside?," with four options: Never; 1–3 times a week; 3–5 times a week; 6–7 times a week. The reader is (bizarrely) invited to 'Vote!' on this (rather than respond, or enter their own answer), so shifting from a genre of self-help/magazine pedagogical questionnaire to one of pseudodemocratic audience participation.

Overall, the D.I.G.! campaign is in line with the debates happening in the UK over claims of the emergence of *Toxic Childhood* (Palmer, 2006). This portrays (even as it decries) the presumption of a northern industrialised childhood that is seen as having lost touch with 'nature' and so produces children who are both contaminated and contaminating, illustrating how combining the register of child and environmental concern can shift quickly from being *for* children to *against* them. As indicated above, this also works in turn to marginalise and trivialise adult and children's involvement with sustainable agricultural practices via their association with play. And from here we see the romantic and nostalgic associations of childhood migrate from fictional or real histories onto contemporary disparities in children's lives and livelihoods across the planet.

Intertextual Moment # 1: 'No Job Too Dirty'

Cleans quietly and efficiently

This is the kind of work Farida does 17 hours a day, 7 days a week. It could be worse. In parts of the world, children as young as 6 are being sold into prostitution or hazardous work. All because they are desperately poor and desperately vulnerable.

. . . .

UNICEF is working to end the exploitation of children. With your help we can make sure they get a proper education. We can help their families to earn an income. And we can lobby governments to protect them by law.

. . . .

CHILDREN LIKE FARIDA CAN'T ASK YOU FOR HELP, SO WE ARE. PLEASE, SEND AS MUCH AS YOU CAN TODAY

(UNICEF, advertisement appearing in *Guardian,* 6 February 2003)

Farida brings us more directly to questions of hygiene. Persil (as its earlier slogan put it) 'washes whiter' (admitting its racialised as well as classed partialities),[10] and girls (like women) do washing. UNICEF's advertisement attempts some subversion. The genre of washing machine powder, as a product that can be purchased, is ironically applied to the miraculous labour of Farida. Like the washing machine (that liberates northern, richer women so that they too can enter the waged labor market; Hardyment, 1988), she 'cleans quietly and efficiently.' Her attributes are likened to the marketing qualities of a new brand, because she is not priceless but rather her labor power is sold. She does not complain, because—the reader is told—'it could be worse,' alluding to how we could be faced with a 'worse' image—presumably of child prostitution or other obviously hazardous work. So, in a way, the guilt of the viewer is invited to be attached to a sense of relief that s/he is not seeing something worse, but perhaps exacerbated because of the luxury of their viewing position as not being so 'desperately poor and desperately vulnerable,' as to be in a subjectless position akin to a disposable, dispensable washing agent.

What remains unclear, moreover, is the extent to which the text resists or merely reiterates prevailing representations of childhood. In particular, how discretionary or mandatory the measures being advocated are, the significance of the portrayal of a girlchild as the quintessential (deserving?) victim, and the kind of relationships between donor and recipient(s) elaborated (which I address in more detail elsewhere: Burman, 2008a; Burman and Maclure, 2005). Not least of these concerns the kind of appropriate childhoods, family and state relations that are implied. Moreover, what we see reiterated here are prevailing cultural discourses of work and play (Sutton Smith, 1997; Sutton Smith and Kelly Byrne, 1984), with play seen as the work done by properly developing northern children (so also suppressing the ways in which such children in fact also work, even if this work is generally rather differently structured (Mizen et al., 1999).

While child labor incites controversy, the UNICEF text skillfully sidesteps this by maintaining some ambiguity over whether all working children are exploited. Yet we should note the further work done by representing poverty through this image of domestic labor done by a girlchild. This is an infantilisation of the wider problem of north–south economic inequalities, which is contagious, not only qualifying children but all those who subscribe to and consume such representations. Hutnyk (2004), in his impassioned analysis (which includes explicit discussion of UNICEF's Farida), discusses the commodification of poverty characterising images of children of the south in relation to wider practices of wilful de-politicisation. He links this 'trinketisation,' the selective abstraction and decontextualised engagement that is exemplified by the conventional use of images of children (including aid and development campaigns), with an affective and economic modality that he describes as infantilisation. While this infantilisation is, within dominant imagery, attributed to the south, it in fact characterises the northern subject.

I will return to the links between children and souvenirs in the discussion of memory later. Right now, we might recall Pupavac's (1998, 2002) analyses of the international child rights regime become relevant here in this marketing for the 'nanny state,' with a diminished political subjectivity and (economic and political) activity accorded mothers as much as children. Yet in these days of increasing pressure and political rhetoric associated with women's participation in the waged labor market, the images and text seem curiously anachronistic. Perhaps this is a clue.

Intertextual Moment #2: Fit or Fat?

As already noted, the D.I.G.! campaign coincides with the current British policy concern around rising rates of obesity, linked with poor diet and ill health. Indeed, apparently, crematoria are now building bigger furnaces to accommodate the larger corpses (*The Week*, 22 August 2008). Almost on the very day of Persil's play day (August 8, which despite its hype did not appear to generate much public attention, even on its own website[11]), a British government report was published announcing that schools will be mandated to send letters to parents of overweight children (5 August 2008, p. 4). The image accompanying the news in the liberal/left newspaper *The Guardian* offered a middle-class window onto the perception of *which* children this concerns. An overdetermination of raced and classed assumptions was encapsulated in the image of the toes of the podgy child on scales, encased in white socks striped by the red St. George's cross. Hence the classed nationalism of the St. George's cross—which, by virtue of its links with nationalist tradition, was once seen as fascist but is now associated with the England football team (that is, a relatively benign, but classed, form of nationalism)—is mobilised to designate which children are presumed to have problematic weight, diet, and exercise issues. Via such signifiers, and notwithstanding the overt lack of physical indications of racialised status (since the feet are in fact covered—and so prevent any actual visual cues—of racialised background for example that might generate criticism), the fat children are configured as being white and working class.[12]

Naturally, no such explicit comments were made in the written report, and indeed any claim regarding such implications could specifically be denied as being in the mind of the reader rather than in the text. Rather, press comment focused on the decision that use of the word 'obese' was proscribed. This covert deference to, plus ridicule of, parental rights and sensibilities was widely hailed as an obvious sop to the political correctness brigade, posing the problem in terms of the 'nanny state' duty of intervention vs. individual (parental) privacy rights. But, far from telling parents what to do, Ivan Lewis, the health minister, claimed this as a matter of information for parents: "This important move isn't about pointing the finger and telling parents that their children are overweight. Instead it's about equipping parents with the information they need to help their children to lead healthier lives." Under the psychological complex (Rose, 1985, 1990), where regulation happens through self-regulation, information codes for responsibility (with the implication that if you fail to fulfil your responsibilities then you are no longer deemed suitable to exercise them). Here we see the discretionary character of neoliberalism—you have to make the right choices or else the state will step in and shame/punish you.

Intertextual Moment #3: Indulging the Precocious (Consuming, Technological, Boy) Child

If children are largely only indirectly addressed within the D.I.G.! materials, notwithstanding the incitement to be active and agentic, they are still represented within a very traditional, romantic, European model of childhood innocence, swathed in the golden leaves[13] of nostalgia. It was also particularly ironic to see the sunny gardens, playgrounds, meadows, woodlands, and beaches on which children are depicted as playing, since August 2008 (including the 8 August, the Play Day) turned out to be the wettest and dullest for 100 years (indicative also of the direction of the effect of global warming in Britain), and so real, embodied children were particularly unlikely to have engaged in anything like these activities. But while changing childhoods are not necessarily to be mourned or resisted (for that would be to institute nostalgia for times past that were perhaps just as arduous and unequal), discernible directions of children's development widely attract critical attention; blaming the children for coveting the products they are manipulated to desire, and even attracting some unwilling admiration for their facility and ability with the new forms of (technological) engagement that adults struggle to achieve.

But here too the romance of the child is maintained even as it is updated. In late 2006 an item in the funny slot (at the bottom of the front page) of a British 'quality' newspaper carried the story of a three-year-old Lincolnshire[14] boy who had used his parents' computer password to purchase a vintage car on the Internet shopping site eBay. Significantly, this was presented as an action whose contractual obligations could be discounted precisely because it was entered into by a child. Indeed the child's own intentionality, while clearly documented ("The following morning Jack woke up and told his parents 'I've bought a car'"), is dismissed: "She [his mother] said: 'Jack's a whizz on the PC and just pressed all the right buttons.'" The story is marked as nonserious by virtue of its spatial location in the newspaper, but this also is reinforced by the child status of the protagonist. In accounting for how he did not press for the realisation of the purchase of the 'Barbie-pink' 1.0 litre Nissan Figaro,[15] the 'owner and co-director of Worcester Road Motors, Stourport-on-Severn, Worcestershire' mobilised the following normalising statements about children.

as soon as I heard it was a young boy who had done it by mistake I cancelled the bid…He must have good taste in cars. We've all got children and they do silly things at times, so it was no problem. (c.f. 'Boy aged three buys £9,000 car on Internet, *Guardian*, 26 September 2006)

The predication of indulgence on assumptions of incompetence (but appropriate aspiration) is what marks this story as one originating from the global north. Elsewhere such notions of triviality and irresponsibility might not have been so easily deployed, while the responsibilities typically assumed by the poorer children of the south became part of what stigmatises and pathologises them. Among many other matters, this is a document of the shaping of consumer desires, minimised and naturalised by this story of childlike rehearsal for a future role (which also overlooks or occludes how children now are exerting their own market pressures, via their 'pester power' over their parents). More 'serious,' perhaps, are the moral evaluations attending such consumer desires, including intra-familial divisions produced through efforts to embed the generalised gesture of humanitarian assistance within a specified local context, 'individualising' relationships of care and support through institutions such as child sponsorship (Bornstein, 2001).

Childhood as Memory

The final theme I want to draw attention to concerns the role of recourse to memory in childhood. This is the trope that links the child of the present, with that of the future, but also with the past of the adult who cares for them. The right to be a child collaboration (between *What's [Not] on TV* and Persil) deploys all of these and more, suggesting how memory may be implicated in the too easy shifts made between rights and developmental claims.

First, we have the adult past: "Remember when you were a child? Plenty of scraped knees climbing trees and muddy hands from making mud pies" (*What's [Not] on TV*) that is mobilised to warrant the more serious and abstract voice of the expert in the sentence that follows: "Today experts are worried that our kids' childhoods are being lost…" (ibid.). The wider associations of simplicity, proximity to nature and therefore being more natural, offer not only a contrast but also the warrant of authenticity. The effect is a mutual strengthening of each claim, with such links both conferring and being conferred, greater legitimacy by the expert opinion.

Secondly, there is an address to the adult that the child will become. The desire of the parent/mother is central to this transition between past and present: "We understand mothers want their children to grow up having a variety of stimulating experiences" (ibid.)

As I discuss more elsewhere (Burman, 2008e) Persil invokes, via its conflation of children's rights with developmental statements, a strange hybrid model of childhood as state and childhood as futurity. The key point here is that childhood is, unsurprisingly, presented as both (privileged) state and stepping point: "There's nothing more precious than childhood: it's a time of wonder, discovery and exploration…along with a sense of its proper (natural) temporality that, precisely because of its transience, confers greater poignant value upon it: "children today seem to grow up faster" (Persil.com). But it is this *seem*, this trace of the viewing, desiring adult that perhaps offers a different route to ward off the developmental imperative. Faster than whom?, we should be asking. And the answer, of course, is us, we who remember ourselves *as* children:

> If the child-figure's embodiment is so often utterly material, its materiality is also always the (im)materiality of a sign, with its endless chain of significations. Interest, desire, and knowledge are part of what constitutes—realizes—bodies, and part of what bodies realize in turn. (Castaneda, 2002, p. 81)

Thus we arrive at a further layer in its meanings: childhood as memory. The child becomes the emblem of memory, detached from who is doing the remembering. Even this is complicated, with subtle exchanges and substitutions of identification (Burman, 1997; Burman, 1998, 2008b). The first is, as we have seen, that of the childhood remembered, or wished as remembered, by the parent. But the second focuses on shaping the childhood that you, as your child's parent, would want her to be able to remember: "…helping you give your children a childhood to remember," "to encourage Mums and kids to keep a record of summer play time," "get out there, have fun and make some fantastic memories" (Persil.com and *What's [Not] on TV*). Of course, we might note, this presumes that (unlike most remembered childhoods) these memories are positive, precisely through the equation of childhood and nostalgia.

But Persil.com's installation of desire, the desire for the parent to confirm they are being a good parent through the generation of (good) memories of childhood, is taken a step further. And in so doing it returns to pedagogical/developmental mode. For it proposes that, as an activity with your child you should record such memories in a virtual scrapbook: "To start things off we've made a virtual scrapbook to encourage Mums and kids to keep a record of summer play time, whatever shape or form it takes!" One cannot escape the irony here that the injunction to active, outdoors play is here converted into one of inside, desk-based work, of precisely the (adult-directed) kind that Roboboy (the subject of the promotional video on the Web site) was supposed to be being liberated from. Once again, in the name of helping mums, it addresses them as developmental subjects too, in need of education (to become child-centred parents) with inspiration, ideas, to help secure their own Roboboy's transformation into a 'real' (human) through his own activity and contact with nature.[16]

So we have come full circle, as the childhood memories of adults are tidied up and, albeit perhaps reparatively, pinned onto the anticipation and manipulation of children's remembered childhoods. Such souvenirs, like the travel variety discussed by Hutnyk (2004), function performatively, simultaneously acknowledging, but in that very process fixing, the various instabilities and ambiguities set in play by representations of childhood as a (nondevelopmental) state associated with time past (but whose?) vs. what this childhood is for (developmental) (but whose?). What fills in these gaps to enable such fixing, is rendered (as psychotherapists would say) concrete or material in the scrapbook. This record of fantasy and reality must surely alert us to how the backward reach toward the past is shaped by present demands and how memory and childhood mobilise complex identifications formed of adults' projections and including also, perhaps necessarily, children's identifications with these.

Conclusion

In this chapter, I have outlined some methodological strategies and presuppositions to inform attempts to unthink or deconstruct developmental discourses as they link child development to economic development, and in which, under contemporary neoliberal conditions I suggest, tropes of psychologisation and feminisation centrally feature. Through analysis of a key dominant text, alongside some intertextual materials, I have attempted to indicate how both in their proliferation and via their juxtaposition, prevailing discourses around childhood and child development can be installed within a narrative of critique. It could be argued that such materials do not merit such close scrutiny, as mere marketing, or passing news trivia, nevertheless this paper has attempted to indicate how their focus (on very particular, normalised models of childhood, play, activity) as well as occlusions (gendered, classed and racialised, familial organisation and wider political practices) offer access to significant cultural themes that connect childhood to wider political and affective economies. Given the abstraction with which childhood is often overtly treated, this is important. In particular, the treatment here has attempted to identify and reflect upon two key elements currently inflecting childhood: first, the contemporary discourse of political participation enacted and modeled through consumption; and second, a new mode of moral-affective engagement installed through particular inflections of temporal matrix associated with childhood and memory.

Clearly such interventions involve epistemological and ethical reflections on the alliances and antagonisms of inter- and cross-disciplinary approaches to childhood, and their contributions to challenging wider development discourses. In elaborating these ideas, and drawing on the undisciplined methodological approaches I outlined at the beginning, I hope my intervention achieves at least two things: firstly, to deconstruct the opposition between popular cultural and expert (developmental psychological) knowledges, in order to mediate their mutual elaboration and (de)legitimation; secondly, that this sample of available representations of childhood situates developmental psychology in its (culturally and historically limited) place—indicating not only its hegemony and contiguity with dominant strategies of capital—in determining the variable, intersecting overlap as well as tension between children and women's interests but also some limits to its reach.

Notes

1. Phrasing this issue in this way is particularly resonant to me. Although I was not consciously thinking of this incident when I selected this title, some years ago on perhaps my third visit to (the 'new') South Africa, when relaxing after a day at the university in a café-bar in Johannesburg's chic district of Melville, I recall being challenged on the way out by a young, perhaps rather inebriated black man, demanding of me: "What is your contribution?" We spoke for a while, and I recall coming up with nothing that was very convincing to either of us. This taught me that this question must be asked, even if it cannot be easily answered.

2. Just to complete the set of resonances, I want to acknowledge that thematising home and the necessary risky work to displace conventional epistemological anchors is not to romanticize either the cosy intimacy of 'home' (since much of my work has concerned domestic violences of various kinds), nor homelessness. Anyone who thinks about the position of displaced or homeless people, especially children, must surely worry about the ease with which academics ennoble nomadity, while the 'home' of the mind is very much what the theme of childhood both settles and unsettles.

3. For example, around the time of drafting this chapter, there was a report in the rightwing *Daily Telegraph* that 55,000 violent crimes are committed by school-age offenders in 2007 (1 in 8 of the total), which was up by 27,000 in 2006 (reported in *The Week*, Friday 15 August 2006, p. 16).

4. As a small indication of such reversals in traditional gender categories, this transformation has even entered the supposedly macho arena of war, with the British secret service recruitment promotions now cast in terms of people skills ("There are three strangers in the room that you need on your side, How do you get them to warm to you?," M16 SIS *www.mi60fficers.co.uk*). Now, in the aftermath of the 'nanny state,' it seems that it is big sister who is watching us all, while MI5 have recently (early October 2008) been advertising for recruits for the British Intelligence services on Facebook and other social networking websites.

5. The brand name for the washing powder Persil is derived from combining the names of two of its principal ingredients (perborate and silicone). However the name is not used internationally as it is hard to pronounce in some languages, with local names being 'le Chat,' 'Dixan' and 'Wipp' (*http://en.wikipedia.org/wiki/Persil* (accessed 29 September 2008). Although taken for analysis here because of my need to find some suitable text for this paper, it turns out to be uncannily apposite on at least five grounds: (1) As noted, it is Unilever's premium UK brand (retailing in Canada under the distribution of its German co-manufacturer Henkel at around $40 a box as the recommended detergent for its Miele washing machines, and also available only through speciality importers in the United States) (*http://en/wikipedia.org/wiki/Persil*, accessed 29 September 2008); (2)

Political economy. According to the report produced by Collaborative Research on Corporations (2008) Unilever is the world's second largest food business (after Nestle), even creating its own internet company to enable its leadership in e-commerce. As one of the major multinational corporations, it exerts pressure on World Bank and UNDP (e.g., in relation to its position promoting GM foods) and using bullying tactics to regulate its price: "In the mid 80's, when the Indian tea price started to rise, Unilever and other corporations acted to bring it down by temporarily boycotting Indian tea. When the Indian government tried to set a minimum export price, the multinationals collectively withdrew from the market, forcing the government to retreat, and slash the price" (see *http://www.crocodyl.org/wiki/unilever*, p. 7 of 13, accessed 29 September 2008). (3) Bad employment practices. In India, Unilever and its Indian subsidiary Hindustan Lever Ltd has been documented as perpetrating some major employer abuses including smashing unions by intimidating workers and violating their rights to unionise (in July 2007 in Assam) and attempting to break collective bargaining power by transferring production to arenas where there are bigger tax concessions (in Mumbai in 2007). Similar initiatives to undermine workers' rights have been reported in the Philippines (in July 2008), while the casualisation of recruitment at the Unilever tea factory in the Punjab (Pakistan)—where 97% of the labor is casual—has (as of September 2, 2008) led to the closure of the Lipton factory and complete outsourcing of production (ibid. p. 8); (4) Ecological issues. Unilever has been accused of dumping several tons of toxic mercury in the densely populated area of Kodaikanal, near the nature reserve of Pambar Shola in Tamil Nadu. The mercury was used in a thermometer factory. No protection was offered to workers nor any precautions taken in disposing of the waste despite the known highly harmful effects of exposure to mercury to the nervous system and kidneys; (5) Child labor. Finally in terms of children, in the early years of the twenty-first century, Unilever has been accused of being involved with bonded child labor in cotton seed production in Andhra Pradesh, with very low wages, long hours, no protection from the health hazards of pesticides and insecticides. Venkateswarlu's studies report children as young as 6 years, the majority girls, working in cottonseed production. Though the numbers of child labourers involved in Andhra Pradesh are reported to be declining, this may be attributed to production being moved to other parts of India (*http://www.powerset.com/explore/semhtml/Child_Labour_Issues_of_Unilever_in_India*, accessed September 28, 2008). It should be noted that Unilever is at no point directly involved in these practices, rather they occur through its subsidiary companies and their joint ventures. Nevertheless, "Various studies by Davuluri Venkateswarlu reveal a clear linkage between procurement prices and employment of child labour in cotton seed production. Even though companies obtain a huge profit margin, they do not seem to be making any rational calculation about the cost of cultivation while fixing the procurement prices to be paid to their seed companies. With the procurement prices of companies willing to pay, seed farmers cannot afford to pay better wages to labourers and still make reasonable profits Unless better wages are paid, farmers would not be in a position to attract adult labourers to work in their fields in sufficient numbers." (ibid. p.4 of 5)

6. This shift from whiteness to dirt was considered a significant shift in the marketing world: "Then, after half a century of washing whiter, Persil embarked on a radical new approach: new creative treatments showing the reality of family life—dirt and all—replace the brand's trademark pristine white imagery. This approach goes way beyond traditional soapbox advertising as Persil embraces its nemesis to examine the developmental and psychological benefits of getting dirty. Straplines such as 'It's not mess, it's curiosity' and 'It's not mess, it's imagination' capture the vibrant spirit behind a child's paint splattered T-shirt or grass-stained dungarees. Persil's current campaign takes this thinking a step further. Through inspiring music and thought-provoking imagery, it positions dirt as an essential part of a child's development. From images of a young boy getting covered in marmalade as he makes breakfast for his parents to an old man battling with a fish on a muddy riverbank, the campaign explores the value of dirt and shows how Persil gives families freedom to live life to the full." (Ganczakowski, "ITV 50 Years of Fame: Private View—Persil." *http://www.brandrepublic.com/Campaign/News/518811/* (accessed 28 September 2008).

7. The early 1990s (a period of economic recession in Britain, now being seen as equivalent to the contemporary economic crisis) saw a revival in marketing attention to the working-class fear of being found to be dirty or smelly, a fear that is necessarily class-structured via dominant images. Thus along with the new generation of plug-in de-oderisers for offices and bathrooms, the washing powder Radion appeared, explicitly targeting and

reviving these anxieties.

8. This misattribution of agency here of course betrays the dominant victim-blaming ethos of contemporary voluntaristic approaches that also marks the collusion between child-centred approaches and neoliberalism (Avis, 1991).

9. This device is also echoed by the definition of "free play" offered in the second paragraph of the press release, a formal educational definition followed by the more informal "stuff like…: "By free play we mean play that gets children thinking, exploring and imagining so not video games or organised fun, but more unstructured play, stuff like climbing trees, building dens, playing pretend games/role playing, using their imagination and exploring."

10. The first TV ad in 1955 features a juxtaposition of media. It shows a billboard poster being pasted up as a dapper broadcaster asks the audience to guess the brand. The poster features an aspirational image of two attractive young women in pristine white dresses with the simple slogan: "Persil washes whiter—that means cleaner." It was the start of 50 years of TV heritage with whiteness right at the very core of Persil's personality and success. (Ganczakowski, "ITV 50 Years of Fame: Private View—Persil," *http://www.brandrepublic .com/Campaign/News/518811/* (accessed 28 September 2008).

11. However, the self-identified child-centred blog "netmums" reproduced the claims of the "whitepaper" and discussed them (favorably).

12. Here are two indicative examples. The "England flag," as it is now known, has recently acquired the status of being the informal sign of a roadside mobile snack bar, of the kind typically used by truck drivers (serving cheap, fast food). Further, the British Asian mayor of the (sometimes troubled, racially very diverse) city of Bradford provoked some controversy during the local elections of 2006 by flying the England (St. George's Cross) flag on his car. He claimed this was an expression of his football affiliation, but it could also be interpreted as appropriating a traditionally white and potentially racist symbol to thereby also assert his own Englishness, and corresponding fitness to hold civic position.

13. 'Autumn Leaves' is an iconic image of Victorian childhood—intertextual relation with p. 2 of *What's [Not] on TV*, "Set your kids free"/ "What can parents do to help?"

14. Lincolnshire is a rural county in the east of England, which connotes parochiality.

15. The Barbie-pink designation works to emphasize how young the boy is, and so also his feminised status, since he is portrayed as oblivious to the obvious gender-coding that would typically generate antipathy in older boys.

16. The advertising Web site *http://www.visit4info.com/advert/Persil-Dirt-is-Good-Persil-Range/61597* (accessed 28 September 2008) provides a description of the video as follows: "A small robot in a hall cupboard is splashed with dirt by a dog shaking itself after coming in from the garden, and starts to move slowly outdoors. Walking through the fallen leaves its mechanical feet become human, as do its hands when picking up a worm. Rain falls, and splashing around in a muddy pool the robot evolves into a young boy, as the narrator says that every child has a right to get dirty and the right to be a child—'Dirt is Good' she concludes."

References

Ailwood, J. (2008) Learning or earning in the "Smart State," *Childhood: A Global Journal of Child Research, 15(4):* 535–551.

Alldred, P. and Burman, E. (2005) Hearing and interpreting children's voices: discourse analytic contributions, in S. Greene and D. Hogan (Eds.), *Researching children's experience: Approaches and methods* (pp. 175–198). London: Sage.

Avis, J. (1991) The strange fate of progressive education, in Education Group II, Cultural Studies University of Birmingham, *Education limited: Schooling and training and the new right since 1979*, London: Unwin Hyman.

Billig, M. (1995) *Banal nationalism*, London and Thousand Oaks, CA: Sage.

Boler, M. (1999) *Feeling power: Emotions and education.* New York and London: Routledge.

Bornstein, E. (2001) Child sponsorship, evangelism and belonging in the work of World Vision Zimbabwe, *American Ethnologist, 28(3):* 595–622.

Buckingham, D. (2007) *Beyond technology: Children's learning in the age of digital culture.* Cambridge: Polity.

Burman, E. (2009). Beyond emotional literacy in feminist and educational research. *British Education Research Journal, 35(1):* 137–144.

Burman, E. (2008a) *Developments: Child, image, nation.* London and New York: BrunnerRoutledge.

Burman, E. (2008b) *Deconstructing developmental psychology,* 2nd ed. London and New York; BrunnerRoutledge.

Burman, E. (2008c) Beyond "women vs. children" or "womenandchildren": Engendering childhood and reformulating motherhood, *International Journal of Children's Rights, 16(2):* 177–194.

Burman, E. (2008d) Developmental psychology, in W. Stainton Rogers and C. Willig (Eds.), *Handbook of qualitative psychology.* London and Thousand Oaks, CA; Sage.

Burman, E. (2008e). Unthinking children in development. Keynote for Childhood and Child Rights in India Conference. Centre for the Study of Developing Societies. Delhi.

Burman, E. (2002) Therapy as memorywork: dilemmas of construction and reconstruction, *British Journal of Psychotherapy, 18(4):* 457–469.

Burman, E. (2006a) Engendering development: Some methodological perspectives on child labour, *Forum for Qualitative Social Research, 7(1)* (http://www.qualitative-research/net/fqs -texte/1–06/06–1–1-e.pdf)

Burman, E. (2006b) Emotions, reflexivity and feminised action research, *Educational Action Research, 14(3):* 315–332.

Burman, E. (1998) Pedagogics of post/modernity: the address to the child in Walter Benjamin and Jean-Francois Lyotard, in K. Lesnik-Oberstein (Ed.), *Children in culture: Approaches to childhood* (pp. 55–88). New York/London: Macmillan, also reprinted in *Developments: Child, image, nation.* London and New York: BrunnerRoutledge.

Burman, E. (Ed.) (1998) *Deconstructing feminist psychology.* London: Sage.

Burman, E. (1997) False memories, true hopes: revenge of the postmodern on therapy, *New Formations, 30:* 122–134.

Burman, E. (1995) What is it? Masculinity and femininity and the cultural representation of childhood, in S. Wilkinson and C. Kitzinger (Eds.), *Feminism and Discourse* (pp. 49–67). London: Sage.

Burman, E. and MacLure, M. (2005) Deconstruction as a method of research: Stories from the field, in B. Somekh and C. Lewin (Eds.), *Research methods in the social sciences* (pp. 284–293). London: Sage.

Burman, E. Aitken, G., Alldred, A., Allwood, R., Billington, T., Goldberg, B., Gordo Lopez, A., Heenan, C., Marks, D., and Warner, S. (1996) *Psychology discourse practice: From regulation to resistance.* London: Taylor & Francis.

Burman, E., Alldred, P., Bewley, C., Goldberg, B., Heenan, C., Marks, D., Marshall, J. . Taylor, K., Ullah, R., and Warner, S. (1995) *Challenging women: Psychology's exclusions, feminist possibilities,* Buckingham: Open University Press.

Castaneda, C. (2002) *Figurations: Child, bodies, worlds.* Durham and London: Duke University Press.

Dahlberg, G. and Moss, P. (2005) *Ethics and politics in early childhood education.* London and New York: RoutledgeFalmer.

Elson, D. (Ed.) (1995) *Male bias in the development process,* 2nd ed. Manchester: Manchester University Press.

Fendler, F. (2001) Educating flexible souls: the construction of subjectivity through developmentality and interaction, in K. Hultqvist and G. Dahlberg (Eds.), *Governing the child in the new millennium* (pp. 119–142). New York and London: RoutledgeFalmer.

Gesell, A. (1950) *The first five years of life: A guide to the study of the pre-school child,* London: Methuen.

Hardyment, C. (1988) *From mangle to microwave: The mechanization of household work.* Cambridge: Polity Press.

Henriques, J., Hollway, W., Urwin, C., Venn, C., and Walkerdine, V. (1984) *Changing the subject: Psychology, social regulation and subjectivity,* London: Methuen.

Hutnyk, J. (2004) Photogenic poverty: souvenirs and infantilism, *Journal of Visual Culture, 3(1):* 77–94.

Jackson, A.Y. and Mazzei, L.A.(Eds.) (2009). *Voice in qualitative inquiry: Challenging conventional, interpretive, and critical conceptions in qualitative research.* London and New York: Routledge.

Lafargue, P. (1883) The right to be lazy. See text at http://www.marxists.org/archive/lafargue/1883/lazy/index.htm (accessed August 6. 2006).

Lister, R. (2005) Investing in the citizen workers of the future, in H. Hendrick (Ed.). *Child welfare and social policy* (pp. 449–462). Bristol: The Policy Press.

Lister, R. (2006) Children (but not women) first: New Labour, child welfare and gender, *Critical Social Policy, 26, 2:*

315–335.

Messenger Davies, M. (1989) *Television is good for your kids.* London: Shipman.

Mizen, P., Bolton, A., and Pole, C. (1999) School age workers: the paid employment of children in Britain, *Work, Employment and Society, 13(3):* 423–438.

Morrow, G. and Mayall, B. (in press) A critical review of UNICEF's report: Child Poverty in perspective: an overview of child-wellbeing in rich countries, in A. Morgan, E. Ziglio, M. Davies, and R. Barker (Eds.), *International health and development: Investing in assets of individuals, communities and organisations.* New York: Springer.

Moss, P. and Petrie, P. (2002) *From children's services to children's spaces.* London: RoutledgeFalmer.

Nash, J. (2008) Re-thinking intersectionality, *Feminist Review, 89:* 1–15.

Nieuwenhuys, O. (2008) Editorial: the ethics of children's rights, *Childhood, 15(1):* 4–11.

Nieuwenhuys, O. (2007) Embedding the global womb: Global child labour and the new policy agenda, *Children's Geographies, 5, 1–2:* 149–163.

Palmer, S. (2006) *Toxic childhood: how the modern world is damaging our children and what we can do about it.* London: Orion.

Pearson, R. (2007) Reassessing paid work and women's empowerment: lessons from the global economy, in A. Cornwall, E. Harrison and A. Whitehead (Eds.), *Feminisms in development: Contradictions, contestations and challenges* (pp. 201–213). London: Zed Press.

Piaget, J. (1933) Social evolution and the new education, *Education Tomorrow, 4:* 3–25.

Piper, H. and Stronach, I. (2008) *Don't Touch! The educational story of a panic.* London and New York: Routledge.

Pupavac, V. (1998) Children's rights and the infantilisation of citizenship, *Human Rights Law Review (March):* 3–8.

Pupavac, V. (2002) The international children's rights regime, in D. Chandler (Ed.), *Re-thinking human rights: Critical approaches to international politics* (pp. 57–75). London: Palgrave.

Richards, G. (1998) *Putting psychology in its place.* London: Routledge.

Rose, N. (1985) *The psychological complex: Psychology, politics and society in England 1869–1939.* London: Routledge & Kegan Paul.

Rose, N. (1990) *Governing the soul: the shaping of the private self,* London: Routledge.

Squire, C. (1990) Feminism as antipsychology, in E. Burman (Ed.), *Feminists and psychological practice* (pp. 76–88). London: Sage (available on www.discourseunit.com)

Stainton Rogers, R. and Stainton Rogers, W. (1998) Word children, in K. Lesnik-Oberstein (Ed.), *Children in culture: approaches to childhood* (pp. 178–203). London: Palgrave/Macmillan.

Staples, D. (2007) Women's work and the ambivalent gift of entropy, in P. Ticineto Clough with J. Halley (Eds.), *The affective turn: Theorizing the social* (pp. 119–150). Durham and London: Duke University Press.

Steedman, C. (1995) *Strange dislocations: Childhood and the idea of human interiority 1780–1930.* London: Routledge.

Sutton-Smith, B. (1997) *The ambiguity of play.* London: Harvard University Press.

Sutton Smith, B. and Kelly Byrne, D. (1984) The idealisation of play, in P. Smith (Ed.), *Play in animals and humans* (pp. 305–322). Oxford: Blackwell.

Thorne, B. (1987) Re-visioning women and social change: where are the children? *Gender & Society, 1(1):* 85–109.

Urwin, C. (1985) Constructing motherhood: the persuasion of normal development, in C. Steedman, C. Urwin, and V. Walkerdine (Eds.), *Language, gender and childhood* (pp. 164–203). London: Routledge & Kegan Paul.

Walkerdine, V. (1984) Developmental psychology and the child-centred pedagogy, in J. Henriques, W. Hollway, C. Urwin, C. Venn, and V. Walkerdine (Eds.), *Changing the subject: Psychology, social regulation and subjectivity* (pp. 153–202), London: Methuen.

Walkerdine, V. and Lucey, H. (1989) *Democracy in the kitchen: Regulating mothers and socialising daughters,* London: Virago.

CHAPTER TWO

Transnational Childhoods

Bodies That Challenge Boundaries

CINTHYA M. SAAVEDRA AND STEVEN P. CAMICIA

Abstract

Using a transnational feminist(s) theoretical framework, we situate our transnational identities as a way to find a common interest and form a transnational feminist alliance/space to critique current discourses of childhoods but at the same time offer a different way to envision working with children. We do so by (a) centering the multiple realities of our mestizo/a and immigrant children (Sánchez, 2001) and (b) using antineoliberal metaphors from the Zapatista movement. Our hope is to begin a dialogue that offers *nuevas posibilidades* of/for resistance and agency that radiate from students' transnational experiences/bodies and the anticolonial voices from the Zapatista movement which aims to radicalize and change the story of childhoods.

> Hence childhood becomes a site of multiple emotional as well as political investments: a repository of hope yet a site of instrumentalisation for the future, but with an equal and opposite nostalgia for the past. (Burman, 2008, p. 13)

> As a radical standpoint, perspective, position, "the politics of location" necessarily calls those of us who would participate in the formation of counter-hegemonic cultural practice to identify spaces where we begin the process of revision. (hooks, 1989, p. 15)

Introduction

We come together in this moment to visualize and imagine a different way to work with children—our process of revision. We hope that this chapter inspires a connectionist way to relate to children. As Gloria Anzaldúa wrote, "[w]hen perpetual conflict erodes [such as the Western child/adult dichotomy] a sense of connectedness and wholeness *la nepantlera* calls on the 'connectionist' faculty to show the deep common ground and interwoven kinship among all things and people" (2002, pp. 567–8). As such I, the first author, have asked Steven Camicia, the second author, to "stand by me over and against a third" (Dean, as quoted in Mohanty, 2003, p. 7). This "third" is the social imaginaries that are running rampant, constructing and creating new truths about children. For us, it is the social imaginaries like globalization and neoliberalism that generate new postmodern anxieties about the future of our societies, nation, and world. Left and right discourses are being constructed in an attempt to make sense of uncertainties (Apple, 2000). These discourses create ways to envision the world as ways to feel, ascertain and explain types of control over the uncontrollable. In education, globalization and neoliberalism are creating new ways to regulate the bodies of children and diminish their present beings.

It is within this current context that we ask for careful critique as well as renewed and or invented alliances. We, the authors, situate ourselves among the "we" because it is difficult to escape dominant ideas of children. We are embedded in the discursive struggles that unfortunately dictate how to view, construct, and manage the "child." For example, Cinthya Saavedra, the first author, is an early childhood educator and Steven Camicia, the second author, is an elementary social studies educator. Both of our fields are saturated with ways to teach, define, and control "the child" (Cannella, 1997). Moreover, our fields are also responding to and being shaped by neoliberal claims on our communities that create regimes of truth that function to categorize, regulate, and oppress further any forms of human resistance or emancipation. These narratives, such as neoliberal education, are hard to escape, but we contend that perhaps they can be resisted and transformed (McLaren, 1995), or even changed.

For adults, but in particular those with labeling and naming power—White males—theorizing about the world is always implicated with power and privilege as social constructions about gender, sex, race, class and nationalism, to name a few, are reinscribed and perpetuated in new and different ways. Careful critique is needed of neoliberal discourses that impact early childhood in order to navigate through and among currents of power to excavate and create counter-hegemonic stories and bodies. Chela Sandoval captures such navigation as "a specific methodology to be used as a compass for self-consciously organizing resistance, identity, praxis and coalition building under U.S. late-capitalist conditions" (2000, p. 62).

We begin with a look at the current social imaginaries that center around adult talk and angst: globalization and neoliberalism and their ties to specific early childhood educational discourses of standards and accountability. We then proceed by situating our transnational identities. This served two purposes. First, it allows us to listen to each other's experiences and find/express our politics of location. In remembering our multiple localities, can we transform our present reality? bell hooks contends that in critical theory "there is an effort to remember that is expressive of the need to create spaces where one is able to redeem and reclaim the past, legacies of pain, suffering, and triumph in ways that transform present reality" (1989, p. 17). Second, situating our transnational identities helps us to find a common interest and form a transnational feminist alliance/space (Saavedra, Chakravarthi, & Lower, 2009) to critique but at the same time offer a different way to envision working with children—transforming our present. Camicia's positionality, as an embodiment of dominant discourses, was integral in our attempts to interrupt current dominant discourses of neoliberalism and globalization and their gaze upon children. It helped us to situate current discussions of neoliberalsim and globalization in early childhood and open a space for Saavedra. In this space, she was able to offer, in conjunction with Camicia, her transnational identity and visions as *nuevas posibilidades* for theorizing children in current times. Alongside these, the adult imaginaries and our politics of location, we searched for counterhegemonic discourses emanating from transnational alliances that stem from transnational children. We then hope to illuminate the multiple realities of our mestizo/a and immigrant children (Sánchez, 2001) in order to offer *nuevas posibilidades* of/for resistance and agency that radiate from transnational experiences/bodies, thereby radicalizing the story of childhoods.

Globalization and Neoliberalism: Adult Panic and (Un)certainty

Globalization is much discussed in educational policy and reform (Burbules & Torres, 2000; Apple, 2000). Globalization is many things and not a new phenomenon, as many would have us think. Here are few ways that globalization is being operationalized. Held and McGrew define globalization as "the expanding scale, growing magnitude, speeding up and deepening impact of transcontinental flows and patterns of social interaction" (2002, p. 1). Others conceptualize it as a phenomenon of human civilization that has been taking place for many centuries, and yet others make specific ties to the origins of capitalism (Morrow & Torres, 2000). It is this last, more specific origin in which neoliberal discourse gave rise to new regimes of truth, regimes that inscribed definitions, categorizations, and hierarchies upon children all in the name of efficiency and standardization. Neoliberalism is evident in calls for educational reform and for educators to react to the demands of a global marketplace (Suárez-Orozco & Qin-Hilliard, 2004).

Neoliberal globalization places global governance in the hands of transnational corporations and NGOs with market rationality as the guiding principle (Smith, 2003). Under such a regime, the desire for economic efficiency has increased the power of the discourses of standardization, accountability, privatization, and efficiency. These are discourses that have gained unprecedented dominance in curriculum and educational policy around the globe (Apple, 2000). The escalation in the number of international and dual language emersion schools in the United States illustrates a response to the growing "demand" to teach students how to behave and function in increasingly global (and hyper-capitalistic) communities (Camicia & Saavedra, 2009).

We provide the example of the No Child Left Behind Act of 2001 (NCLB) in the United States as one example of how neoliberal globalization has enfleshed market discourses upon new generations of children. These market discourses are evident in the types of reform that the legislation invokes. Pena (2006) describes the key discourses in the legislation as promoting "accountability, choice, flexibility, and reading" (p. 179). Accountability in the form of quantitative measures serves administrative functions necessary to categorize, name, and manage mass numbers of children, defining standardized/one-size-fits-all outcomes. If children don't measure up to these outcomes, they, as well as schools, are categorized as failing or in need of improvement. Choice, another discourse of neoliberalism, is promoted as a way to force schools that are not able to produce standardized outcomes to improve their performance. Students and parents are given the choice to seek out schools that are not deemed deficient by NCLB. Rather than providing flexibility related to the diverse positionalities of children, Pena, referring to Popkewitz, describes NCLB outcomes as producing children who internalize the norms of standardization and thus are flexible.

Finally, the discourse of reading in NCLB combines elements of accountability and flexibility under the guise of research-based instruction. Not only are learning outcomes standardized, but children's behaviors are standardized and governed (Pedroni, 2004). Profoundly tied to neoliberal globalization discourses, the discourses of NCLB are intended to *train/produce/educate* children in the new millennium to be self-starting entrepreneurs who are flexible "life-long-learners" in a global market-place. Ultimately these discourses serve to eradicate the experiences and identities of children and in particular bodies of color (Cruz, 2001)—a total assault on the brown/black bodies.

Uncertainties Throw Us into Disarray

In education, this disarray produces discourses that function to control and manage the present/past in order to secure a certain vision and outcome for the future. A scientific, psychological, sociological, curricular/pedagogical gaze then is cast upon children. The educational and moral commitment to saving, improving, remedying, and changing the lives of children blinds us (intentionally or not) to the complexity of the multiple realities facing not only children but adults as well. In Western societies, children are seen as the perpetual modern project needing constant guidance, protection, and managing in order to become competent adults who will create a better future (Bloch, 2006). In this linear and progress-oriented adult world, children will always have particular "needs" (curricular, social, psychological, etc.) defined by us (adults) but never in relation to how we live complicated lives *with* children (Cannella, 1998). Because children are positioned as undeveloped and outside of sociopolitical, historical, and economical contexts, we feel compelled to teach them how to live, maneuver and experience such complexities. We thus create discourses that reinscribe dominant ways to "belong" and "become." We forget that the management and constant surveillance of childhood is a modern and Western invention (Ariès, 1962) and perhaps a reflection of adult uncertainties about the future.

Furthermore, our commitments to help children and work with children do not exist in a vacuum but are very much embedded and created from power struggles. That is, struggles over the right to claim, define and ultimately control the lives, experiences and bodies of children and those who are most intimately and (un)problematically connected to them—women (Cannella, 1997; Phelan, 1997; Saavedra, 2006). Experts make these claims in the name of the economic interests, the nation, what is best for *ALL* children and a myriad of other potentially dangerous discourses that mask power and privilege for some over others. These neoliberal discourses are enfleshed on the bodies of our youth without apology. Consequently, those who embody dominance willfully ignore how immigrant children embody transnational identities, bodies, and spaces from which we can cocreate with them conditions for a new world. We now jump into the margins and examine discourses that might help us navigate the geopolitics of bodies, identity, and belonging within the perilous discourses of neoliberal globalization.

Transnational Identities and the Politics of Locations

> That's precisely why this conversation is itself a form of activism; it's our resistance to that idea of separation. We have differences, but our commonalities are just as strong, and they represent hope for resistance and freedom (hooks & Mesa-bains, 2006, p. 3).

In this section, we excavate our experiences as a space for theorizing our identities and how we have come to know. Our histories and experiences are central in our lenses, in who we read, in who has influenced us and in the text that we produce. But it has been our genuine dialogue about our lives, our work, and how we embody different transnationality based on our bodies and experiences that has made us move beyond oppositional identities and enter a realm of transformational pedagogy (Keating, 2007)—a pedagogy of connectivity to resist systems, discourse, and knowledges of oppression. We come together to stand against a third.

> We can no longer camouflage our needs, can no longer let defenses and fences sprout around us. We can no longer withdraw. To rage and look upon you with contempt is to rage and be contemptuous of ourselves. We can no longer blame you, nor disown the white parts, the male parts, the pathological parts, the queer parts, the vulnerable parts. Here we are weaponless with open arms, with only our magic. Let's try it our way, the mestiza way, the Chicana way, the woman way (Anzaldúa, 1987, p. 88).

Chicana Transnationality

I constantly travel across/between borders. Although they are mainly metaphorical, sometimes I think metaphorical borders are the most potent, fluid, and real. I have engendered schizophrenia of some sorts. I was born in Nicaragua and lived there until I was four. Then due to the Sandinista–Contra war we moved to Honduras and I lived there for another four years. When I was eight, we made what seemed the inventible move *al norte*—the move that, to the surprise of most U.S citizens, most people around the world probably dread. Not because people around the world hate the United States and "American values" but because it means something is terribly wrong in one's country for a variety of reasons. These reasons are political, economical, and historical reasons as well as, of course, neoliberal policies being championed around the world without apology. And giving a blind eye to the conditions it later creates in other countries. We landed in Brownsville, Texas.

Thus began my new *vida*—a *vida* full of prejudices about "those Mexicanos" already living here. But as the years passed by in Texas, my prejudices toward "those Mexicans" changed drastically. I began to feel as though I were a bit "Tex-Mex" and I began to code switch seamlessly between Spanish and English. To the point that my father would say "*en español o ingles no mescles los idiomas.*" But it would be after I took my first ethnic and immigration history course in college, I began to feel certain politics awakening inside of me, ones that rejected imposed borders of any kind. As Anzaldúa claims, "[b]efore the Chicano and the undocumented worker and the Mexican from the other side can come together, before the Chicano can have unity with Native Americans and other groups, we need to know the history of their struggle and they need to know ours" (1987, p. 86). I didn't cringe anymore when someone asked me if I was from Mexico. I am embarrassed to even write this down! I feel like it makes it more real, my unquestioned prejudices that I carried with me like a license to distinguish me from other humans of color. I then began to take "othered" histories and I began to incorporate the politics of other historically oppressed groups in the United States. But it wasn't until graduate school that I began my search for decolonizing my very being, my work, and my politics—which is an on-going project and journey. I developed a thirst for different ways to view and embody the world around me. I read the works of feminist of color like Gloria Anzaldúa, Cherrie Moraga, Sandra Cisneros, bell hooks, Patricia Hill Collins, and many of the Third World feminist perspectives.

So why have I engendered a schizophrenic lens? In many ways, it is my alliance to multiple groups and it other ways it is my own feeling of being from so many places with no home to call my own or as Anzaldúa poetically captures of the displaced *mestizas*, "This is her home…this thin edge of…barbwire" (Anzaldúa, 1987, p. 13). But I think it is a good thing. The entrenched notion that we have to identify with a particular geopolitical space only creates a type of nationalistic egoism and jingoism and a divisive sense of belonging. Physically, I can be from any of the light skin variety of

Latina, Italian, Greek, Moroccan, etc. In many ways, I embody multiple notions of transnationality—through the body and the geopolitical border crossings of my move *al norte*. My body has taught me powerful lessons about being in and embodying the world. It is from this bodily endeavor and recognition and reconciliation with the mind that I engage in a transnational Chicana feminist analysis (Sánchez, 2001) to offer new possibilities, language and images for creating new stories for childhoods.

Privileged Transnational

I, Steve, also embody transnationality, but my embodiment of transnationality is inscribed by discourses of privilege. I am a White upper-middle-class male, and my metaphorical transnationality is inscribed through historical and contemporary discourses of empire, colonization, categorization, progress, oppression, and privilege. As a youth in the San Francisco Bay Area, these discourses were prevalent in mass media, the social studies curriculum in my school, and the artifacts and stories that my father brought back from his transnational business trips. The discourses evident in these sources were clear; the globe is saturated with socially constructed hierarchies that privileged each of my identities. Transnationality, metaphorical and physical, was and is constructed through historical and contemporary forms of colonization.

As a teenager, the metaphorical was replaced by the physical when my father chose to transfer from a position in the Bay Area to a position in Hong Kong. Choice became another inscription of privilege. Similar to Aiwa Ong's (1999) description of flexible citizens who embody privilege through effortless movement across geopolitical borders, my new life in Hong Kong was one of choice. During vacations, members of my family often scattered to separate areas of the globe for play. In addition to the privilege inscribed through my identity as a White male, I attained the privilege of shedding concerns related to nationality. I had become a flexible citizen of the world. In sum, from an early age, my embodiment of multiple identities reflected a transnational experience of privilege.

Now, I struggle to deconstruct the historical and contemporary discourses that benefit me but perpetuate social injustice. I view my collaboration with Cinthya as an important step in this deconstruction process. We represent different embodiments of transnationality but propose an alliance formed upon our wish to create a transnational site of resistance against neoliberal forms of oppression.

Generating Transnational Feminist(s) Spaces

Transnational feminist identities are not loyal to one "nation." In fact, we belong and don't belong. Transnational feminist projects are equally unloyal to particular topics and issues and are always local, partial and contextual (Grewal & Kaplan, 1994). The term "woman" is problematized and a totalizing notion of feminist issues is eschewed. As such transnational feminist projects can produce a space of common interests without necessarily having a common cause (Mohanty, 2003; Kaplan, 1994).

For example, Saavedra in a previous collaborative research project (Saavedra, Chakravarthi & Lower, in press), co-constructed a theoretical framework for early childhood education that would generate transnational feminist spaces of resistance, praxis, and solidarity among the researchers. Merging together their different and multiple localities transformed their study into a critical transnational feminist project of possibility (Chabram-Dernersesian, 1999; Kaplan, Alarcón &

Moallen, 1999; Sandoval, 2000). Following Aihwa Ong (1999), Sánchez (2001) contends that transnationalism "offers 'flexibility' and movement" (p. 378). We contend that it is this very flexibility in thinking that is necessary in transnational global projects, research, and theory. These critical exchanges of particular localities and strategic standpoints are examples of the "flexibility" found in feminist(s) transnational projects (Ong, 1999). Along the critical exchanges between Saavedra, Chakravarthi, and Lower's was their reaction to the transnational bodies of young children that made them (re)consider their positionalities as researchers and allowed the research to turn back onto them for critical reflexivity (Pillow, 2003). As Saavedra, Chakravarthi, and Lower (2009) describe it,

> ...although our research focused on our transnational space, we wonder and urge further inquiry about the transnational spaces that children embodied and how perhaps it was their transnational bodies that allowed us to reflect on our own. After all, much of our "turning research back on us" was from observations that stemmed from their "unruly" multilingual bodies in the classrooms vis-'a-vis their body as resisting English and silent knowers (Cannella, 1997, pp. 14–15).

Since then, Saavedra has been collaborating with the Camicia in ways to create these transnational spaces of resistance and possibility (Camicia & Saavedra, 2009; Saavedra & Camicia, 2009; hooks, 1989). These stories of resistance have always existed; we are excavating these examples with renewed and reinvented lenses. Furthermore, we propose to rethink working *for (or in the name of)* children and instead invoke in our practices a "reflective solidarity" (Dean, 1996). In that way we can co-create with children and move toward "the practice of solidarity [that] foregrounds communities of people who have chosen to work and fight together" (Mohanty, 2003, p. 7). Could we fight together with children?

We contend that this same critical reflexivity needs to happen when theorizing globalization in the name of the child. As such, we center the prospect of allowing the transnational bodies of students to speak to our understanding of the complexity of the world and our participation in it as a navigational tool. We offer here a different story, perhaps a radical story of childhoods that helps us examine our bodies, subjectivities, and identities in relation to and not in opposition to young children's bodies, subjectivities, and identities. This means our questions and even perhaps our concerns would change (Cannella & Viruru, 2004). And after all, "[i]f the process of sexism, heterosexism and misogyny are central to the social fabric of the world we live in; if indeed these processes are interwoven with racial, national and capitalistic domination and exploitation [and neoliberal agendas] such as the lives of women, men, girls and boys, are profoundly affected, then decolonization at all levels (as described by Fanon) become fundamental to a radical feminist transformative project" (Mohanty, 2003, p. 8). As such, we decenter adults while centering in our transnational feminist projects the subjectivities, identities, and bodies of children in such decolonizing projects.

Transnational Bodies: Navigating the Geopolitics of Childhoods

In divulging our politics of location, we recognize not only what made us, the authors, different but also how similar interests have brought us together to create spaces of resistance and possibilities. We both decided that instead of prescribing ways to resist "for" children, that perhaps we needed to do what we did for each other, that is, sit and listen to our stories to create a new one. Why would it be so hard to enter in dialogue *with* children? In many ways, it is the taken-for-granted assumptions that children cannot relate to anything outside of their immediate surroundings and that children have not developed an identity much less discuss how experiences shape identities, create hierarchies, and perpetuate oppression (Camicia & Saavedra, 2009; Cannella, 1997).

But those positioned in dominance forget that Chicanos/as, immigrant children, as well as other children of color, are beings who embody multiple and shifting identities. That is, they carry with them complex identities that of course we attempt to simplify by labeling them "children." We position children as having cultural, historical, and geopolitical bodies. Soto and Lasta (2005) assert, "...children's ideological becoming is affected by multiple contexts..." (p. 163). Adults attempt to erase these complicated contexts. Realizing the predicament that adults have created in constructing the child as the ultimate "Other" (Cannella, 1998), how can research/pedagogy be not only sensitive but also transformative? How can our work *with* children be spaces of possibility and decolonial imaginary (Pérez, 1999)?

For many people (children included) of color, the nomads, and the marginal beings, living in the 'phrenias is a survival strategy. Because many find themselves to be "unlocated and perhaps schizophrenic...more than one process, more than one location..." (Wallace, 1989, p. 49) and thus "world-travelers" (Lugones, 1990), it is hard to have a cemented allegiance to nationalistic and geopolitical belonging. Many children come to our classrooms with an understanding of who they are and embody. As one example, we offer the type of transnationality that is birthed between the metaphorical and political borderlands of the U.S. and Mexico. Anzaldúa reminds us that belonging is spiritual, "[d]eep in our hearts we believe that being Mexican has nothing to with which country one lives in...it is a state of soul—not one of mind, not one of citizenship" (1987, p. 62). Belonging is a personal, cultural, historical, and political understanding about ourselves that goes unnoticed, undetected, and eventually erased in our bodies. Sánchez (2001), in theorizing her transnational Chicana feminist politics, (re)members her transnational childhood as a counterhegemonic strategy to reenvision ways we can approach teaching and research with children.

> As a child, I specifically remember hiding the regular trips we made to southern Chihuahua. In the US, the only persons who knew that my family and I were traveling to Mexico were other relatives....Not once did I tell a schoolteacher that my family and I were traveling to Delicias for the holidays. My in-class essays each September were full of the American trope of summer vacation essays—I lied and said I had traveled to Disneyland and attended an outdoor camp. (p. 376)

It is obvious, that at a very young age, Sánchez was aware of her transnational identity. When she was a young child, she and her family were border crossers or transnationals going back and forth, straddling and living in multiple worlds (Anzaldúa, 1987). The very worlds we deny and eradicate in children because we, adults, cannot conceive of children as knowing anything outside of the "concrete" immediate world (LeRiche, 1987). But if experiences are not concrete, then we ask what is?

Examining transnational bodies allows us to recognize children (as well as adults) in the moment, their identities in the now instead of always seeing them as future beings. We have the nasty and nagging habit of seeing children as potential but never recognizing them for who they are in the moment. Anzaldúa illustrates this in *Borderlands/La Frontera*, "At a very early age I had a strong sense of who I was and what I was about and what was fair. I had a stubborn will" (1987, p. 16). Could we not have and show respect for the identity and experiences of children in the present moment?

Furthermore, how can we allow our transnational Chicano/a children the opportunity to explore their differences and similarities with other children as well as see themselves as producers of knowledge and culture (for examination of *testimonios* with young children, see Flores Carmona, 2009)?

In *Growing up Chicana/o*, Tiffany Ana López edits an anthology of Chicano/a childhoods in order to engage in the "struggle of memory against forgetting" (hooks, 1989, p. 17) the childhoods that reflect her identity and experiences. López remembers,

> [l]ike every child, when I was growing up I felt different. Yet there where definitely things about my life as a Chicana that I didn't dare share. Something as simple as taking a piece of meat wrapped up in a tortilla to school set me apart. I read of children taking their sandwiches to school, yet never in my childhood reading experiences did I read about a child taking a tortilla. (1993, p. 18).

This experience reminds Saavedra of the many times she was mortified when her dad use to tell her to take for lunch a *bolillo* (white bread roll) stuffed with beans to school. She would think to herself: "how would I explain this to everyone taking his or her nice sandwiches or Chef Boy R Dee ravioli cans?" These experiences not only reflect cultural differences in lunch styles but also class differences that are reflected in our brown/black bodies and too often erased in the schooling practice.

Sánchez explains how she had to hide her summer trips across the border because she felt that her trips did not reflect the "American trope of summer vacation essays" (2001, p. 376). Vacation for the White middle-class is about exploring "exotic places" and showing status in the name of family time. In contrast, in the transnational experience depicted by Sanchez, vacation was not a vacation at all; it was becoming another member of the familia, a contributing member with chores, duties, and responsibilities.

Schools are indeed a public space, but as Sánchez (2001) asserts they do "not give my (or other transnationals') lived experiences a public face" (p. 377). What schools seem to achieve is the erasure of bodies and experiences in order to instill a new one, that of the entrepreneurial and enterprising individual, the neoliberal body that is carefully coiffed and managed and eventually dichotomized, zigzagged, and broken. Do we ever get to acknowledge and validate children like Sandra Cisneros's *cuento* of *Salvador Early or Late*, the boy with a body full of "geography of scars, his history of hurt…the body too small to contain the hundred balloons of happiness…" (Cisneros, 1991, pp. 10–11)?

Radicalizing the *Cuento* of Childhoods: Lessons from Durito

We now end, in this moment, with lessons from Durito. Durito—whose full name is Don Durito of the Lacandon Jungle—is a political cartoon created by Subcomandante Marcos. Durito is a knight-errant beetle from Southern Mexican State of Chiapias and is a well-read intellectual who studies neoliberalism and its technologies of domination in Latin America (Acción Zapatista Editorial Collectiva, 2005). We contend that Durito is an excellent metaphor for (re)envisioning and relating to children. We offer this as a way to radicalize or perhaps read a completely new story of childhoods.

Subcomandante Marcos first encounters Durito in a jungle where Subcomandante Marcos asks Durito what he is reading. Durito tells Subcomandante Marcos that he is reading about neoliberalism and its technologies of domination in Latin America. Subcomandante Marcos is surprised to learn that a beetle would be interested in such things. Subcomandante Marcos asks, "And what good is that to a beetle?" Very annoyed Durito replies, "What *good* is it?!…a beetle should care enough to study the situation of the world in which it lives, don't you think, Captain?" (Subcomandante Marcos, 2005, p. 42).

We read this story and immediately linked it with children's participation in our world. Durito is reminding us that all who share the earth have a stake and part in the struggles. We contend that children do as well. They live in this moment in the world with us and not apart from us or in some distant future. The predicament and chasm we have created between children and adults can have a simple solution, that is, if we can imagine new and unthought of possibilities and stories. Research and pedagogy with young children are intimately tied to the sociopolitical anxieties of the time. These adult-created anxieties need to be challenged as they construct children as "ideological puppets" (Smith, 2003, p. 45). Research that excavates such dangerous power relationships is needed. We hope that those engaging in research with young transnational children will co-construct with them critical compasses that help all of us to navigate and maneuver through the technologies and imaginaries of neoliberal globalization. Important to note is that transnational feminist modes of inquiry provide specific and local perspectives and constructions not to be confused with "truth," answers, or conclusion-seeking. After all "…when research is turned upside down and reconceptualized, the reasons and purposes for specific investigations would be changed" (Cannella & Viruru, 2004, p. 149).

We leave the reader with another story to contemplate from Durito—"The Story of The Bay Horse." The story of the Bay Horse can be a metaphor for those who want a different *cuento* for research, theory, and practice in childhood studies. According to Durito, there were these *campesinos* who needed to start eating their animals one by one to survive, the chicken, the pig, etc., in the name of survival—a neoliberal strategy or rationale of domination. But, when it was the "Bay Horse's turn he did not wait for this story to end; and he fled and left to another story" (Subcomandante Marcos, 2005, p. 157). As such we request, let's not wait for neoliberal agendas to usurp our bodies and resist in the name of "economic survival" and let's learn from Bay Horse and jump to another story! If we can imagine a different radical story, then we can act in different radical ways. "Nothing happens in the 'real' world unless it first happens in the images in our heads" (Anzaldúa, 1987, p. 87).

References

Acción Zapatista Editorial Collectiva (2005). *Conversations with Durito: Stories of the Zapatistas and neoliberalism by Subcomandante Marcos*. Brooklyn, NY: Autonomedia.

Anzaldúa, G. E. (1987). *Borderlands/la frontera: The new mestiza*. San Francisco: Aunt Lute.

Anzaldúa, G. E. (2002). Now let us shift…the path of conocimiento…inner, public acts. In G. E. Anzaldúa, & A. L. Keating (eds.) *This bridge we call home: Radical visions for transformation* (pp. 540–579). New York: Routledge.

Apple, M. W. (2000). Between neoliberalism and neoconservatism: Education and conservativism in a global context. In N. C. Burbules & C. A. Torres (Eds.), *Globalization and education: Critical perspectives* (pp. 57–77). New York: Routledge.

Ariès, P. (1962). *Centuries of childhood—a social history of family life*. New York: Knopf.

Bloch, M. N. (2006). Educational theories and pedagogies as technologies of power/knowledge: Educating the young child as a citizen of an imagined nation and world. In M. N. Bloch, D. Kennedy, Lightfoot, T. & D. Weyenberg (Eds.), *The child in the world/the world in the child: Education and the configuration of a universal, modern, and globalized childhood* (pp. 21–42). New York: Palgrave.

Burbules, N. C. & Torres, C. A. (Eds). (2000). *Globalization and education: Critical perspectives*. New York: Routledge.

Burman, E. (2008). *Developments: Child, image, nation*. London: Routledge.

Camicia, S. P., & Saavedra, C. (2009). A new childhood social studies curriculum for a new generation of citizenship. *The International Journal of Children's Rights*. 17(3), 501–517.

Cannella, G. S. (1997). *Deconstructing early childhood education: Social justice and revolution*. New York: Peter Lang.

Cannella, G. S. (1998) Early childhood education: A call for the construction of revolutionary images. In W. F. Pinar (Ed.), *Curriculum: Toward new identities* (pp. 157–184). New York: Garland Publishing.

Cannella, G. S & Viruru, R. (2004). *Childhood and postcolonization: Power, education, and contemporary practice*. New

York: RoutledgeFalmer.

Chabram-Dernersesian, A. (1999). Introduction. *Cultural Studies, 13*(2), 173–194.

Cisneros, S. (1991). *Women Hollering Creek and other stories.* New York: Vintage Books.

Cruz, C. (2001). Towards an epistemology of the brown body. *Qualitative Studies in Education, 14*(5), 657–669.

Dean, J. (1996). *Solidarity of strangers: Feminism after identity politics.* Berkeley, CA: University of California Press.

Grewal, I. & Kaplan, C. (Eds). (1994). *Scattered hegemonies: Postmodernity and transnational feminist practices.* Minneapolis, MN: University of Minnesota Press.

Held, D., & McGrew, A. (2002). *Globalization/anti-globalization.* Malden, MA: Polity Press.

hooks, b. (1989). Choosing the margin as a space of radical openness. *Framework, 36,* 15–23.

hooks, b. & Mesa-bains, A. (2006). *Homegrown: engaged cultural criticism.* Cambridge, MA: South End Press.

Kaplan, C. (1994). The politics of location as transnational feminist critical practice. In I. Grewal, & C. Kaplan (Eds). *Scattered hegemonies: Postmodernity and transnational feminist practices* (pp. 137–152). Minneapolis, MN: University of Minnesota Press.

Kaplan, C., Alarcón, N. & Moallen, N. (Eds.) (1999). *Between woman and nation: Nationalisms, transnational feminisms, and the state* (pp. 63–71). Durham, NC: Duke University Press.

Keating, A. L. (2007). Teaching transformation: Transcultural classroom dialogues. NY: Palgrave MacMillan.

LeRiche, L. W. (1987). The expanding environments sequence in elementary social studies. *Theory and Research in Social Education,15*(3), 137–154.

López, T. A. (1993). *Growing up Chicana/o.* New York: Perennia.

Lugones, M. (1990). Playfulness, "world"-traveling, and loving perception. In G. Anzaldúa, (Ed) *Making face, making soul, haciendo caras: Creative and critical perspectives by women of color* (pp. 390–402). San Francisco, CA: Aunt Lute

McLaren, P. (1995). *Critical pedagogy and predatory culture: Oppositional politics in a postmodern era.* New York: Routledge.

Mohanty, C. T. (2003). *Feminism without borders: Decolonizing theory, practicing solidarity.* Durham, NC: Duke University Press.

Morro, R, A. & Torres, C. A. (2000). The state, globalization and educational policy. In N. C. Burbules & C. A. Torres (Eds.). *Globalization and education* (pp. 27–56). New York: Routledge.

Ong, A. (1999). *Flexible citizenship: The cultural logics of transnationality.* Durham, NC: Duke University Press.

Pedroni, T. (2004). State theory and urban school reform II: A reconsideration from Milwaukee. In Gabbard, D. & Ross, W. (Eds.) Defending public schools, (pp. 132–140) Westport, CT: Praiger Publications.

Pena, K. S. (2006). No child left behind? The specters of almsgiving and atonement: A short genealogy of the saving grace of U.S. education. In M. N. Bloch, D. Kennedy, T. Lightfoot & D. Weyenberg (Eds.), *The child in the world/the world in the child* (pp. 177–194). New York: Palgrave Macmillan.

Pérez, E. (1999). *The decolonial imaginary: Writing Chicanas into history.* Bloomington: IN: Indiana University Press.

Phelan, A. (1997). Classroom management and the erasure of teacher desire. In J. Tobin (Ed.), *Making a place for pleasure in early childhood education* (pp. 76–100). New Haven, CT: Yale University Press.

Pillow, W. (2003). Confession, catharsis, or cure? Rethinking the uses of reflexivity as methodological power in qualitative research. *Qualitative Studies in Education, 16*(2), 175–196.

Saavedra, C. M. (2006). *The teacher's body: Discourse, power and discipline in the history of the feminization of teaching.* Unpublished dissertation. Texas A&M University, College Station.

Saavedra, C. M. & Camicia, S. P. (2009, April). Civic education and immigrant children: Generating transnational feminist research possibilities. Paper presented at the AERA annual meeting. San Diego, CA.

Saavedra, C. M. , Chakravarthi, S. & Lower, J. K. (2009). Weaving transnational feminist(s) methodologies: (re)Examining early childhood linguistic diversity teacher training and research. *Journal of Early Childhood Research,* 7(3), 1–17.

Sánchez, P. (2001). Adopting transnationalism theory and discourse: Making space for a transnational Chicana. *Discourse: Studies in the Cultural Politics of Education,* 22 (3), 375–381.

Sandoval, C. (2000). *Methodology of the oppressed.* Minneapolis, MN: University of Minnesota Press.

Smith, D. G. (2003). Curriculum and teaching face globalization. In W. F. Pinar (Ed.), *International handbook of cur-*

riculum research (pp. 35–51). Mahwah, NJ: Lawrence Erlbaum Associates, Inc.

Soto, L. D. & Lasta, J. (2005). Bilingual border-crossing: Children's ideological becoming. In L. D. Soto & B. B. Swadener (Eds.) *Power and voice in research with children* (pp. 153–164). New York: Peter Lang.

Suárez-Orozco, M. M. & Qin-Hilliard, D. B. (Eds.). (2004). *Globalization: Culture and education in the new millennium.* Berkeley, CA: University of California Press.

Subcomandante Marcos (2005). *Conversations with Durito: Stories of the Zapatistas and neoliberalism.* In Acción Zapatista Editorial Collectiva. Brooklyn, NY: Autonomedia.

Wallace, M. (1989). The politics of location: Cinema, theory, literature, ethnicity, sexuality, me. *Framework 36,* 42–55.

CHAPTER THREE

Childhoods within Africa's Triple Heritage

A. BAME NSAMENANG

Abstract

Science reveals Africa as home to the earliest humans, thus as having the longest experience of childhoods. Over centuries Africans successfully evolved traditions of early childhood care and education (ECCE) within families. Yet, developmentalists and childhood activists are "forcing" the universalism of institutional ECCE from Euro-Western imperialistic enlightenment, which subverts Africa's centuries-old ECCE, thereby unconscionably endangering children and families they believe to be civilizing. The chapter problematizes current ECCE efforts from a historical lens, with the UN Convention of the Rights of the Child provisions on children's rights to own cultural identity and participate in the cultural and productive life of their families and communities. It exposes how hegemonic, Eurocentric narratives trivialize timeless African ECCE traditions to bestow mystifying mélanges of indigenous, Arabic-Islamic, and Western Christian ECCE legacies on Africa. In spite of colonial and postcolonial abrasive policies and programs to expunge Africa's reproductive ideologies and educational praxes, the chapter envisions reconstructing Africa-centric ECCE from the receding but resilient remnants of Africanity, not in isolation but from the position that "all cultures can contribute scientific knowledge of universal value" (UNESCO, 1999).

Introduction

Historically, early childhood development (ECD) care and education have evolved from women's familial duty to professional services in need of more status and funding that accrue from institutional universalism (Nsamenang, in press). The "work" stands to lose the status and control that interest groups located "within the enlightenment spirit" of imperialism (Smith, 1999, p. 23) feel is their right, which is often exercised at the unvoiced detriment of the children and families the groups and professionals believe themselves to be uplifting.

ECD professionalism "involves an encounter between the cultural world of the family, and that of any other representative of society engaged in caring for children" (Bram, 1998, p. 23). The gulf is exacerbated by the fact that every culture has "a framework for understanding the ways that parents think about their children, their families and themselves, and the mostly implicit choices that parents make about how to rear the next generation" (Harkness et al., 2001, p. 12). In addition, in professional ECD work, the cultural background of the family, which the *United Nations Convention of the Rights of the Child* (CRC) (United Nations, 1999) enshrines as the right of every child, tends to diverge from that of the practitioners who serve or support the children, above all in postcolonial Africa, where Western models and international policy standards "have devalued indigenous cultures and traditions" of childcare and projected them as "anti-progressive" (Callaghan, 1998, p. 30). In South Africa, for example, "people with the best intentions, whose frame of reference is different to the indigenous one, and who head up educare organizations, seem to perceive things differently from the people in the community, whom the work or support is meant to serve" (Callaghan, 1998, p. 31).

Colonial and postcolonial interventions to understand and improve the life circumstances of Africa's children have been and continue to be driven by the idea of a "simple society" in the context of four coexisting images of childhood in most African families and communities. This chapter takes a historical perspective to expose the mélange of childhood images present in Africa today from three significant cultures. A basic research and service challenge, in the face of what the convolution engenders, is "how can we construct a bridge across cultural difference, adapt our work to the family's culture, and fully utilize the resources of the home and of organizations and personnel engaged in pre-school work?" (Bram, 1998, p. 23)

Colonialism and its aftermath—postcolonialism—are pervasive themes in this chapter as well as in this handbook. It is not just the physical colonization perpetuated by empires I am referring to, but also the colonization of the idea of childhood by academia and associated professional disciplines and organizations (Cannella, 1997; Cannella and Viruru, 2004; Soto and Swadener, 2002). Although the postcolonial images are limited and normalizing, they are colonizing forces active in the processes of globalization, as it is crafted to drive institutional group care and education of children in continual disregard and contempt for the countervailing local forces underlying the construction of a positive cultural identity, which "is fundamental to realizing every child's rights" (Brooker and Woodhead, 2008, ix). Implicit in the chapter is a call to acknowledge and respect Africa's cultural history and the need to understand Africa as a continent whose current ECD landscape is a restive mixture of three major heritages. The sources of Africa's triple-strand ECD inheritance are indigenous African cultures and traditions or "Africanity" (Maquet, 1972); Islamic–Arabic legacies; and bits and pieces of Western Christian knowledges and practices (Mazrui, 1986), on to which is superimposing a postcolonial global child image that is increasingly homogeneous and Western derived (Pence and Hix-Small, 2007).

Historical Lens on the Triple Heritage of African Childhoods

The best anatomical, archaeological, and genetic evidence upholds Africa as the origin of modern humans (http://www.actionbioscience.org/evolution/johanson.html, 2008). However, Africa's antiquated traditions of childcare and education have been bashed by waves of colonialism, postcolonialism, and globalization, which seemed resolute, albeit stealthily, to force them into insignificance and extinction. First, an Islamic-Arabic heritage image of early childhood care arrived in Africa from the Arabian Peninsula long before the arrival of Euro-Western colonial images of childhood. Second, Western Christian colonialism introduced a "missionary" ethos to "civilize" and dislodge the two pre-existing heritages. The third heritage is indeed postcolonial; it is a rights-based global child image (Pence and Hix-Small, 2007) crafted into the CRC that was conceived mostly within Western psychology in general and U.S. early childhood development (ECD) research in particular. It is crucial to observe that "the majority of the world's population lives in conditions vastly different from the conditions of Americans, underlying doubts of how well American psychological research can be said to represent humanity" (Arnett, 2008, p. 602). Thus, the difficulties faced in Africa in interpreting and implementing the cultural issues enshrined in the CRC are due to its benchmarking on the developmentally appropriate practices of, and child development research in, the United States, a country that has not yet ratified that international instrument.

Waves of Colonizing Influences on African Childhoods

The first wave of foreign early childhood care and education on Africa's childcare traditions arrived in North Africa in A.D. 647 (Hunter, 1977) with Islam from the Arabian Peninsula. By the tenth century, communities of Muslim merchants and scholars who interacted and exchanged knowledge and commodities between Africa, the Arab World and Mediterranean Europe had been established as far south as beyond the Sahel. In fact, between the eleventh and twelfth centuries, the rulers of the kingdoms of Takur, Ancient Ghana, and Gao had converted to Islam and had appointed literate Arabic Muslims as advisers. They also established long distance trade routes between West Africa, the Middle East, and Europe (Winters, 1987).

When imperial Europeans arrived on the West African coast, they permanently reversed the geographical focus of Africa's interests, as they initiated the Trans-Atlantic Slave Trade and the triangular commercial exchanges among Africa, Europe, and the Americas (World Bank, 1999). Incidentally, Africa's intellectual exchanges with the East severed and remain tangential today, as colonizing missionary and cross-cultural research paradigms were crafted as the more acceptable Eurocentric norm failed to blend its scholarly practices and commercial motives with the preexisting intellectual and commodity exchange patterns. European colonialism accentuated out-migratory flows into and permanent settlement in Africa; this reinforced and consolidated a second alien heritage of early childhood care in Africa, the group care of children. Thus, indigenous and Islamic ECD has a longer history in Africa than the advocated institutionalization of early childhood group care and education programs that moved out from Europe as a colonizing force, beginning with the 1820s Infant Schools (Pence, 1980; Prochner and Kabiru, 2008). In the course of history, the period 1989/1990 when CRC was adopted was marked by significant changes for children and for ECD internationally, in that early childhood care and education have increasingly become rights-based issues.

Pence and Nsamenang (2008) saw the period of Africa's independence as representing a transition for most African states from a colonizer-centric focus to a broader international focus and immersion in the geopolitical dynamics of the Cold War. In the 1960s and 1970s, newly established heads of government were courted by international powers in ways not conceivable as a colony. International immersion brought with it the shifting waves of structural adjustments and international policy standards of the Bretton Woods institutions, in particular those of the World Bank and International Monetary Fund (IMF), as well as those of a wide range of United Nations' Organizations and International Non-Governmental Organizations (INGOs). The postindependence era thus represented a very different social, economic, political, and development dynamic from what had before; however, the basic dynamics of a disregard for African practices in children's care and education persisted throughout the new era. Africa was and continues to be under considerable pressure to understand child development and the world as defined by Western civilization (Nsamenang and Dawes, 1998). Interveners ought to be alerted; if stripped of their heritage culture, people become "danglers'" at the fringes of heritage and dominant cultures. Heritage culture matters and is a familiar and secure anchor for personal and collective identity. "In a globalized world, local culture must be the anchor of identity" (Nsamenang, 2008a, p. 13).

The Melange of ECD Traditions in Contemporary Africa

The history of ECD efforts in sub-Saharan African (SSA) countries tends to sideline "childrearing within the framework of an African culture for centuries" (Callaghan, 1998, p. 31) and to cite the early childhood programs modeled on the European system as the first ECD programs in the country (ECDVU SSA1 Initial Country Reports, http://www.ecdvu.org 2004). Analysis of the current ECD dynamic reveals how Euro-Western childcare and development models are promoted in a manner that suggests both an ignorance of the other heritages and also a belief that "others" are incapable of producing a healthy adulthood (Pence and Nsamenang, 2008). ECD programs are part of Eurocentric adjustment agendas to consolidate institutional public schooling (Serpell and Hatano, 1997) in SSA to the detriment of the indigenous African and Islamic–Arabic patterns of early childhood care and education that existed prior to their arrival.

In the rest of this section, I sketch the main features of ECD traditions in each of Africa's three heritages to highlight the current ECD braid in SSA. African communities today are "contexts in which interactions between cultures are highlighting differences, revealing needs, uncovering problems, throwing up concerns, offering alternatives, and signaling the need for changes in attitudes, approaches, methodologies and service provisions" (Smale, 1998, p. 3).

Childhoods within Africa's Indigenous Theory of the Universe

"Every cultural community possesses a worldview or theory of the universe that includes an image of the child and his or her preparation for adult life" (Nsamenang et al., 2008, p. 51). As a fused concept that encapsulates various facets of visualizing, relating to, and dealing with the universe, worldview can be interpreted as "a theorist's view of development [that] is closely tied to his or her view of human nature, a view intimately tied to his or her conception of how the universe works" (Nsamenang, 1992a, p. 210). The holism of Africa's non-Cartesian theory interconnects the sacred and the secular and visualizes the environment, cosmology, and the human condition as conceptually inseparable (Bongmba, 2001). Theories of the universe position the child as a cultural agent to whom cultures teach their cultural curricula at various stages of ontogeny.

In its holistic, pronatalist, and theocentric outlook, an African worldview imputes a sacred value to childbearing and childrearing. Religious ideas such as the theocentric origin of children (Nsamenang, 1992a) are explicit or implicit in and central to every aspect of childbearing, childcare, and education in African family traditions. Indeed, "kinship is the nucleus from which social networks ramify, moral behavior is initiated and prosocial values, productive skills and the mother tongue are learned" (Nsamenang et al., 2008, pp. 55–56). The family is central to all this, because it is the acceptable institution for "the supply" of new members and their care, such that childcare is a collective enterprise rather than a parental prerogative (Nsamenang, 1992b). Zimba (2002, p. 94), for example, reviewed evidence for the southern Africa region that revealed an "indigenous network of support" reserved for newborns and their mothers. Similarly, in both West and East Africa, newborns are "precious treasure[s]…nurtured, and enjoyed by the whole family" (Harkness and Super, 1992) in a "deep and comforting sense of tradition and community" that receives and sustains newborns, at least in the West Africa region (Nsamenang, 1992b, p. 427).

The dominant early childhood development literature places the prime responsibility for children's security and care with mothers. But an analysis of traditional, precolonial childcare in Africa, at least in West Africa, would reveal a landscape in which mothers maintained a delicate balance between caregiving, self-subsistent production, and homemaking, while the bulk of the day care and security of children after they have been weaned reverted to older siblings in neighborhood peer groups (Nsamenang, 2008b). A comparative explanation for this childcare setting is that Euro-Western cultures privilege adults with childcare, while African cultures separate childcare skills from the life period of parenthood and position childcare training as a familial commitment for children to learn (Nsamenang, 2008b) as part of a "shared management, caretaking and socially distributed support" (Weisner, 1997, p. 23) of the family. In this way, "the sharing and exchange norms" bind siblings and the entire social system together (Jahoda, 1982, p. 131). Accordingly, the "typical childcare scenario was one in which mothers were only partially available; the bulk of the daycare of children who were weaned was provided by someone other than the mother—most often older siblings or peers" within in the peer culture (Nsamenang, 1992b, p. 422).

Childcare was a social enterprise in which parents and kin, including sibs, were active participants. Most SSA mothers exclusively breastfed 0- to 6-month-old babies, while permanent live-in relatives or babysitters, most of them girls between 11 and 15 years of age, provided the daycare of infants aged 6–24 months. The usual practice was for a prepubescent female or male relative or a family friend to start hands-on training in home keeping and child tending related chores pending childbirth (Nsamenang, 1992b). From an early age, children observed and participated in family tasks as well as in caregiving to younger siblings with little or no instruction, but with the guidance and encouragement of parents and peer mentors (Nsamenang and Lamb, 1995). This pattern of early learning through caregiving is rooted in African perceptions of children as social agents in their own "becoming" (Erny, 1968) in participatory processes "as participants in cultural communities" (Rogoff, 2003, p. 3) without the usual sense of classrooms and schools (Bruner, 1996). SSA communities socialize children into "sociological gardens" of multiaged others who are better together in mutual helpfulness and developmental sociability. In so doing, children learn or teach themselves through active involvement in the life of families, communities, and the peer group. "An African worldview visualizes phases of human cyclical ontogenesis of systemic socialization of responsible intelligence in participatory curricula that assign stage-appropriate developmental tasks" (Nsamenang, 2006, p. 293).

During the precolonial era, when African mothers left home to go to the farm or to social events outside the home, extended family members or older siblings, especially older female children, were readily available to care for infants and toddlers. In addition, indigenous Africa had its own systems of "public training" to transfer norms, knowledge and skills to youth to ease their transition into adulthood. Examples of such systems include the *poro* (for boys) and the *sande* (for girls) in Liberia (Gormuyor, 1992, p. 337); the *bogwera* (for boys) and *bojale* (for girls) in Botswana (Shumba and Seeco, 2007, p. 87); and seclusion rites in Cameroon (Tchombe, 2007), Kenya (Harkness and Super,

1992), and the southern Africa region (Zimba, 2002). In the postcolonial era, relative and sibling care-givers are no longer readily available though adolescent babysitters are still useful in more intricate childcare arrangements. "The Nigerian urban working mother," for instance, "is able to play the dual roles of being a mother and an employee successfully due to the availability of childcare services such as homemaids, nannies, day care centres, nursery schools and kindergarten" (Ogbimi and Alao, 1998, p. 48).

In reality, schisms and challenges in the childcare landscape now emerge from the scarcity of the traditional support of childcare, especially sibling caregiving, which has become inadequate since most children now attend school. Schooling has not eliminated peer group activities, however, but mod-ified them somehow (Nsamenang, 1992b), as pupils and students of all ages and at different levels of education can be observed functioning in the reciprocal sociability of peer networks for various purposes in educational institutions and non-school settings. The postcolonial African peer culture landscape needs to be charted for beneficial input into ECD policies and program development. If institutional public early childhood development [ECD] programs and services are appropriately advocated as "a good start" for children 0–8 years, they should incorporate the participative spirit, child-to-child sociability, and self-generation of the peer culture, which is an ubiquitous learning space in Africa, even within the context of the school.

Islamic–Arabic Education: The Madrassa System

Islamic education in its varied forms constitutes a longstanding system of education throughout the African continent. It spread to sub-Saharan Africa from North Africa by Ibaadi clerics and from the Horn of Africa by the disciples of Mohammed who fled persecution in Mecca in the early history of Islam (Hunter, 1977; Winters, 1987). The Islamic education system appears to have been mod-eled on the pedagogical principles of the Byzantine primary school system (Bouzoubaa, 1998), although it did somehow incorporate an African content. But since basic Islamic education is reli-gious in nature, the *madrassa* (Islamic basic learning school) was often connected to a mosque. The classic *madrassa* curriculum was the learning of the Koran, Islam's holy book. Although it was an unequal brew of African and Arabic educational inspiration, Islamic education was and is conduct-ed in Arabic, regardless of the African pupil's mother tongue.

The *madrassa* is a system of early Koranic learning for Muslim young people, aged 4–10 or older, who sit with wooden tablets under the guidance of a cleric, reciting Koranic verses, hour after hour, day after day, until they know it by rote learning. The *madrassas* may enroll female students; howev-er, women or girls study separately from the men or boys. Within the *madrassa* system, a group of students study in a classroom setting in an institution or in any available space in poor communities. Islamic education is more rigidly structured than its indigenous host but less so than the Western sys-tem that arrived in Africa much later than Koranic education. In Somalia, as in other Muslim com-munities across Africa, Muslim parents and communities support "Koranic schools [as] part of the basic moral education of the child" (UNDOS, 1995, p. 1). Islamic education gives meaning to life, enriches it, instills discipline, and preserves human values, as well as strengthens and advances human societies (Bugaje, 1993). But in Somalia and Mali, as in much of SSA, Islamic education, like its indigenous counterpart, is not integrated into national education systems. Baxter (2003) record-ed about 3,000 neighborhood Koranic schools in Mali's capital, Bamako, but they were not part of the national school system. The Euro-Western school model is the formal system, despite its incompatibility with "the children's sociological, psychological, and cognitive development" in context (UNDOS, 1995, p. 1).

With its clearly defined goals and methods, the *madrassa* system offered a general basic education framework for the heterogeneous ethnic and racial groups that embody the Muslim world. "The goal was no less than the shaping of the Muslim personality" (Bouzoubaa, 1998, p. 3). Thus, the *madrassa* system was, and remains, an important agent of socializing different Muslim ethnic and racial groups into the Islamic faith and the Muslim way of life. The *madrassa* system (as recorded for Somalia) possesses three essential dimensions of practical application and impact (UNDOS, 1995, p. 1): (1) It constitutes an introduction to the technology of writing, and to a lesser extent numeracy, for the majority of the population, both men and women, many of who would otherwise have little or no schooling. (2) It provides literacy training as well as local leadership, since Islamic instruction is generally accepted to be an indicator of morality, honesty, and discipline, and therefore a primary qualification for assuming community responsibilities. (3) It has equally been—and given the growing disaffection with formal schooling has increasingly become—an avenue for social and economic advancement because of the close relationship between Islamic networks and traditional commercial routes in Africa.

The Western Christian System

When Europe set out on a mission to "civilize" backward Africa, it envisioned education as the most propitious means by which to "save" the continent and its peoples. The first wave of early childhood group care of children and education programs moved out from Europe as a colonizing force of Infant Schools of the 1820s (Pence, 1980; Prochner and Kabiru, 2008). Its various forms—nurseries, crèches, preschools, and childcare and development centers—were exported to SAA on a variety of Euro-Western pedagogies from Froebel through Montessori and could be found in virtually all preindependent African countries. Each newly independent African state had its own particular history and dynamics, but each also had a firm foundation of indigenous values and perspectives overlaid by various external, colonizing initiatives. The process of implantation of Euro-Western education in SSA was a more eventful and subverting factor than its content, whose impact is subtler, albeit imperceptibly and remarkably upsetting. This section adopts a discursive comparative approach to highlight the core features of the Western early childhood group services.

Given that the colonial governments lacked not only the means but also the goodwill to initiate universal basic education in the African colonies (Pence and Nsamenang, 2008), they enlisted Christian missionaries to soften the harshness of imperialism (Mudimbe, 1985) and to establish schools. However, most mission societies were poor and could not support the number of schools to educate the greatest number of Africans, unlike the community-supported Islamic education in Muslim communities. As a result, the colonial schooling services were unevenly developed and produced mixed results and remarkable disparities across countries and regions of the same country. The institutions of early childhood group care and education in the colonial era were unevenly distributed; they largely served the settler population and faith-based enclaves of Christians. In the postcolony, they have reached primarily urban populations and still bypass the insights and benefits of indigenous and Koranic systems of early care and learning. In brief, the "civilizing" and education "missions" were geared more toward resources extraction and dislodgement of Africans from their purported "backwardness" but less for educating Africans into the insights of their circumstances and acquisition of the competencies to harness their resources and improve their awful living conditions. The orientation of SSA's education systems remains basically similar today, hence a recent continental initiative by the Human Development Resource Centre to start off and coordinate a transformative teacher education textbook development project for SSA (HDRC, 2008).

When Islamic education encountered resistance from African ethnic kingdoms as an intruding cultural variant, it acquiesced and its curriculum incorporated local content, but Western education is still timidly embracing the local content. Western education was instead a disruptive process set out to "remake" African societies to render them more amendable "objects" for the European Social Darwinian Project (Nsamenang, 2004). The social engineering of Africa peaked with the 1884 Berlin partition of Africa into 53 tiny spheres (countries) of imperial Europe (Asiwaju, 1984). Consequently, various European languages and schooling traditions were entrenched in those African "spheres", the same patterns persist today, alongside a wide variety of shifting neocolonial structural adjustments and intrigues.

Western patterns of childcare and education at home or in school follow mostly didactic processes and pedagogies of certainty and predetermined benchmarks and outcomes (Urban, 2006) in the face of an uncertain future and an Africa into which the international interest groups continuously inject shifting conditions. Western models claim foreknowledge of "the adult we want the child to become; we know the world in which the adult must live and work. The challenge is to produce the adult to fit into that world, in the most cost-effective way—and with the help of scientific knowledge-as-regulation the challenge can be met" (Dahlberg and Moss, 2005, p. 6). The raging crisis in Western financial markets, with obvious snowball effect on Africa, is not unrelated to such frames of reference. African pedagogies, by contrast, are premised on the changing fortunes of life to handle children in their "becoming" (Erny, 1968), "not as a set of organisms to be molded into a pattern of behavior specified in advance as educational outcomes, but as newcomers to a community of practice, for whom the desirable outcome of a period of apprenticeship is that they would appropriate the system of meanings that informs the community's practices" (Serpell, 2008, p. 74).

Furthermore, for African parents, children are "better together" in the "school of life" (Moumouni, 1968, p. 29), an environment imbued with invisible cultural scripts that foster the individuation of relational interconnectedness, such that "a person is only a person with other people" (Zimba, 2002, p. 98). Euro-Western cultures, by comparison, socialize children to individuate by relying on their own internal repertoires of thoughts, feelings, and actions to construct a sovereign self, beginning at birth. African sociogenic orientations bind and mutually oblige individuals to promote a sense of relatedness as well as to inspire a life path that differs "in theoretical focus from the more individualistic accounts (of ontogeny) proposed by Freud, Piaget, and Erikson" (Serpell, 1994, p. 18). In spite of this, the early childhood development science that is taking roots in Africa seems, like the world order, decisively blind to all other ontogenetic paths except the Anglo-American.

A Discursive Look at Postcolonial ECD Efforts in Africa

Africa's indigenous reproductive ideologies and childcare practices remain mostly positive today, although colonial and postcolonial abrasive policies and programs have eroded them considerably. But "nowhere has this led to the total social disintegration of indigenous structures" (Nsamenang, 1987, p. 276). For example, the African practice of breastfeeding until children were weaned at 2–3 years was interrupted by commercial formula feeds, but did not cease, and early childhood development nutrition science is embracing it today as state-of-the-art practice for the first 6 months of life. "By placing excessive emphasis on externally provided, stand alone" interventions and efforts such as psychosocial support "we stand the danger of discounting the importance of everyday love, support and reassurance that children receive from families and communities" (Richter et al., 2006, p. 9).

"Africa's systems possess their own coherence and purposeful consistency, which deserve attention and discovery" (Nsamenang, 2005, p. 276). But "European colonialism more than perhaps any other epoch in Africa's history had the immediate and long-term effect of altering this situation" (Kashoki, 1982, p. 37). In fact, imperialism continues to be played out in economic structures, societal institutions, and the ways the people view themselves (Cannella and Viruru, 2004), as prompted by various emissaries of Easternization (influences from the Islamic–Arabic East) and Westernization (Western Christian legacies) of Africa.

Most of the initiatives in Islamic communities in Africa to mobilize support for early childhood education by INGOs such as the Bernard van Leer Foundation and the Aga Khan Foundation (AKF) have been in the East African region. The AKF agenda is coordinated from the Mombasa *Madrassa* Resource Centre (MRC), (Oluoch, 2007) and is an initiative that has gone beyond traditional Koranic learning to integrate early childhood development, teacher empowerment, and community participation. In East Africa, the *madrassa* system has evolved from "a paternal institution once exclusively managed by men" (Bouzoubaa, 1998, p. 7) to 49 percent of its school management committees as recorded at the MRC being women (Oluoch, 2007), which is a commendable feat. In spite of their ubiquity in SSA, indigenous African and Islamic–Arabic patterns of care and education are a "submerged system" in that, despite their successful operation from antiquity, they remain relatively unknown to development planners and therefore are seldom taken into explicit account in their Eurocentric policy development and programmatic models (World Bank, 1999, p. 1). The "remaking" of Africa thus continues and stands against evidence that "people entirely dislodged from their cultural roots" can never "make progress with development" (Nsamenang, 2005, p. 276).

The contemporary condition represents a very different educational, social, economic, political, and development dynamic from what had come before, in that the period of independence represented a transition for most African states from a colonizer-centric focus to a broader international focus and accentuating immersion in the geopolitical dynamics of the post–Cold War era (Pence and Nsamenang, 2008). The international immersion progressively brought with it the adjustment programs of the Bretton Woods Institutions, in particular the World Bank and International Monetary Fund (IMF), as well as those of multiple United Nations' organizations and INGOs. The basic disregard for local practices in children's care and education persists throughout the new era, however. Overall, the Western institutional group care of children being advocated for Africa decontextualizes and universalizes the child in the image of the Western child, thereby instinctively pathologizing Africa's children immersed in or hybridized by indigenous and Islamic–Arabic childcare traditions. Whereas "many Africans accepted, seemed to accept, the new universalism, seeking to learn its secrets, seeking to tame this god, seeking to gain its favor," others, "(often the same ones) rebelled against it....The situation is such that we can speak of a double bind, in which there is no reaction that could remove the [African] pressure and oppression" (Wallerstein, 1988, p. 332).

The postcolonial dynamic in Africa is one in which imperialism is discernible not only in colonized "places, spaces, bodies, and minds" but also in ECD "understandings, forms of assistance and constructions of appropriate actions" for childcare and education that have become "decidedly

European and American" (Cannella and Viruru, 2004, p. 16). Thus, Kashoki (1982, p. 37) claimed, "The single most significant accomplishment by Western man [sic] on a global scale has been the creation [or more accurately the re-creation] of non-Western man in the image of Western man." This applies much more to Africans south of the Sahara than to any other colonized racial group in that SSA is the only world region whose tremendous resources continue to be brazenly exploited by and for the interests of the West while its peoples suffer in abject poverty (Nsamenang, 2007a). And there is no evidence of any coherent discourse, even by rights advocates and munificent donors, about the destination of Africa's rich resources or why the continent cannot garner the means to research into and set relevant viable ECD programs and services for its next generations in the face of such riches.

It is regrettable that even imminent African scholars, international civil servants, and the political classes in Africa remain mute on Africa's considerable resources having significantly served and continuing to serve Western interests instead of alleviating Africa's poverty. Mineral extraction from many African countries, for instance, continues ineluctably, as the international community classifies them at the lowest rungs of the poverty index and deploys ostensibly high visibility efforts to "save" the continent from abject misery. Africa is the only continent where high-profile rhetoric and policy standards to uplift its children fail to take into account the children's daily routines, ontogenetic trajectories, and the livelihoods of their families, with the complicity of some Africans with impressive credentials. The *Human Development Report 1994* brings to the fore the ineffectiveness of foreign aid, as the United Nations Development Programme (UNDP) pointed out unmistakably that technical assistance does not come cheap; no donor lunch is free. "In practice, the record of technical assistance has often been unsatisfactory....Perhaps the most disturbing is that after 40 years, 90% of the $12 billion a year in technical assistance is still spent on foreign expertise—despite the fact that many national experts are now available in many fields" (UNDP, 1994, p. 96). The most pernicious cost of postcolonialism for Africa is and has been in mental or intellectual colonization, which has disposed the African to eternally seek the West for moral, spiritual, technical, and intellectual guidance and, more demeaning, to resort to readymade Western solutions and leadership for Africa's security (Kashoki, 1982).

Of course, grim statistics and other unvoiced factors aptly expose the appalling situation of Africa's children, but it is hard to come to terms with why the powerful representatives of an allegedly "generous" and "well-intentioned" donor community have so hardheartedly resisted fair trade policies to reverse the unfair power balance in world trade that could beat Africa's poverty and misery? "If Africa could be granted an additional 1% share in global trade, she would earn for herself much more than she is currently being given in foreign aid" (Barsby, 2007, p. 54). Gröhn (2008) charges the UN Millennium Development Goals (MDGs) are arbitrary and unfair to the region of SSA; they merely scratch the surface of Africa's development crisis and give little room for opportunities to achieve the targets.

The colonial and postcolonial assault on Africa has not only been limited to one of undermining Africa's sociocultural structures, institutions, and knowledge systems; its most malicious impact has been to wittingly and unwittingly undercut the acceptance, tolerance, and investigation of Africa's un-Western systems in the light of growing global age openness to how "all cultures can contribute scientific knowledge of universal value" (UNESCO, 1999, p. 1). Another muted mugging of Africa is postcolonial actions and discourses that detach North Africa from the continent, a single geographical entity that the United Nations organs and many international nongovernmental organizations regionalize with part of the Asian continent—the Islamic-Arabic Middle East. This subverts continental unity and the efforts of the African Union, as it exacerbates the value orientations and affiliative chasm between Maghreb Africans and Africans south of the Sahara. In sum, the often-posited extreme poverty evident in SSA is not the major obstacle to developing appropriate policies and mounting cost-effective ECD programs but the exclusion of Africa's centuries-old traditions of childrearing, especially the failure to recognize and mesh the positive elements of the three significant co-existing ECD heritages in Africa today into culturally meaningful and contextually viable service systems (Pence and Nsamenang, 2008). "In fact, the failure to 'modernize' Africa as rapidly as the 'civilizing mission' anticipated stems largely from the neglect, if not refusal, to blend Africa's indigenous systems with those imported to 'civilize' the continent" (Nsamenang, 2008c, p. 144).

Another disturbing concern is Africa's marginal voice within a relentless international narrative that denigrated Africa's child development beliefs and practices from precolonial times, although they have great potential to enrich and extend the frontiers of the discipline's knowledge, theories, and methods (Nsamenang, 2007b). A key reason for Africa's inability to do so is absence of original scholarship; African research tends to be "essentially imitative of, or largely patterned after, contributions by Western scholars" (Kashoki, 1982). The prime factor underlying this state of the field is the education dispensed in Africa, which "diffuses mainly disparate chunks of Western knowledges and skills repertoires" (Nsamenang, 2005, p. 279), losing "sight of the soil out of which the existing African society has grown and the human values it has produced" (Kishani, 2001, p. 37). A related reason is that most African psychologists were inducted into scientific research through a colonizing cross-cultural research paradigm that sought to determine, not how African children acquired the "cognitive skills or patterns of intelligence that exist already in their culture because their culture requires it; it is functional in the culture" (Ogbu, 1994, p. 366), but to understand how the developmental patterns and intellectual profiles of African children failed to measure up to those of Western children. A third reason is a degrading attitude of African "experts" and scholars, who desire to secure or sustain lucrative jobs with INGOs, such as the World Bank, who ignore the role of Western governments and international agencies in the corruption of the African state but instead reinforce the blame of African traditions for failing to embrace modernization (Diawara, 1998, p. 123).

Conclusion

I see a befitting conclusion to this chapter as necessarily discursive, as it zooms into the broad strokes of my vision of a transformative Africentric ECD project.

Africa deserves a niche in the international narratives on ECD science in which to hear its own narrative and from which to share its realities and perspectives. The "niche" should also serve as a platform on which to mount self-generating ECD programs that should be followed up to tertiary education. The platform should draw strength from the wisdom and pragmatism of the African peer culture and reduce the extensive reliance on the transient respites of donor initiatives that to a large extent are incongruous with the life journeys of African children (Serpell, 1993) and that indiscernibly disrespect the cultural identity of African children. This need compels a transformative ECD project that should not focus on the haste of momentous achievements but that seeks to put in place a systematic, sustainable process to cumulate a mass of talented emergent young ECD leaders who are global visionaries and local "experts." The competitive competencies required of them are ingenious productive mindsets, perceptive understanding of the realities and challenges of global geopolitics vis-à-vis local contexts, an entrepreneurial spirit in global discourses, and the brokering of power blocs to outsource the means and the opportunities for relevant research, practice, and productivity to output a respectable and influential African voice. These competencies are not tuned primarily to global marketplaces but to their local African communities and the sorry fate of the continent in general. The required transformative research leaders, for example, are those who will be able to deal successfully with the global geopolitical and technological challenges of the coming decades (Saasa, 2008). Transformative capacities and proficiencies appropriately sprout at and begin lifelong flourishing from ECD programs, such that over the long haul, Africans would cease to engage in imitative research patterned after Western scholars to undertake creative, original context-relevant research that inputs into disciplinary trends.

Such a transformative project would be impossible without a full understanding of the convoluted nature of the childhoods Africa's triple heritage engenders. If "comparative and cross-cultural analysis reveals a variety of childhoods rather than a single and universal phenomenon" (Prout and James, 1990, p. 8), then efforts at ECD policy development and programming for hybridized African children should be designed within their "longstanding heritages, as well as on 'modern' perspectives" (Pence & Nsamenang, 2008, p. 21). The project should pivot on merging the positive elements of Islamic-Arabic and Western Christian legacies with those of Africa's timeless traditions of early childhood care and education to ensure that the continent does not lose but gains from the benefits of each of its three distinct heritages. Therefore, policy planning and programming should not proceed from the "construction of *a* knowledge which is exclusive of many other knowledges" (Urban, 2006, p. 1) but with the objective of producing appropriate programs and services (Pence and Nsamenang, 2008) "that would reach the children in their cultural context and in which the community would fully participate" (Lanyasunya and Lesolayia, 2001, p. 7). Honoring Africa's cultural-historical realities would provide African children with a more secure base from which to face the world. Therefore, current and future ECD efforts in Africa must heed Sharp's (1970) warning "against destroying too abruptly the traditional background of the African" child, which is still "the best guarantee of the child's welfare and education" (p. 20).

The accentuating evidence of interest in ECD in Africa is accompanied by "increasing restlessness in many parts of Africa to identify what can be considered 'indigenous' in current actions and future activities" (Pence and Marfo, 2008, p. 79). The critical concern, however, is the "image" in which ECD theories and programs would take shape, whether they will emerge from within or from outside Africa (Nsamenang, 2008b). The first step in building a truly African ECD landscape would be to "tune" mindsets, theoretical frameworks, and policy thinking into transcending the current discourse of vulnerability in order to reunite faith in Africa's massive child population as hope and key to the continent's future, a potential productive force, for the continent's uncertain future. This first step obliges "identifying Africentric possibilities" (Pence & Nsamenang, 2008) from the imperatives of Africa's hybridism. The possibilities should not be considered in isolation from trends in the state of the field but should form part of a respectful, generative process that opens new channels for discussion, dialogue and more fruitful cross-cultural interstimulation. The critical issue is how ECD stakeholders in Africa can pull together the positive and useful elements of the continent's triple-strand heritage into viable ECD policies, programs, practices, and pedagogy.

The second step is to come to be proactive in determining whether Africa's inability to provide for its children and wrest a decent standard of living from its enormous resources is a spin-off of the legacy of colonization and unfair trade or whether Africa indeed is "unfit" and therefore must be dominated by the "fittest," as envisioned by social Darwinism. The third step should involve mapping out a policy platform on which to design and mount Africa's transformative ECD systems. In so doing, it would be instructive to be sensitive to African worldviews, which exist mainly in invisible cultural precepts and norms that diverge from the ideologies and ethos, which inform Euro-Western ECD science that so far provides the global standards of ECD for the rest of the world. This would entail charting Africentric theoretical frames and innovative practice models with which to explore, understand, and intervene the intricate but dreadful circumstances of Africa's children. If we could "listen to, and learn from, the African worldview, seeing a holistic and integrated way of looking at the family and the universe, we might see things in a new way" (Callaghan, 1998, p. 32).

There is much the Western world can do to support Africa in its quest for ECD systems that contextually address children's well-becoming (Dawes, 2006) because it controls the world's resources and knowledge bases. In the social sciences the United States, for instance, "has knowledge and power out of proportion to its size and population" (Ojiaku, 1974, p. 204). "Those powers should not be used to 'show the way,' but to support Africa's efforts to hear its own voices, among others, and to seek its own way forward. It will find that way through children who understand and appreciate multiple worlds, through young scholars that frame their own contextually sensitive research questions, and through leaders that appreciate the riches of the past, as much as the possibilities of the future" (Pence and Nsamenang, 2008, p. 43). The designers of Africa's ECD programs in a global age should draw strength from the community-based participative learning mode of the African peer culture, inspiration from the context-focused nature of the ECD field in New Zealand, and the "hope mission" of the First Nation of Canada for children and young citizens, which is as follows:

> "It will be children who inherit the struggle to retain and enhance the people's culture, language and history, who continue the quest for economic progress for a better quality of life, and who move forward with a strengthened resolve to plan their own destiny" in the imperatives of the shrinking global village (Meadow Lake Tribal Council, 1989).

Young citizens "hold the key to society's future. Their ambitions, goals and aspirations for peace, security, development and human rights are often in accord with those of society as a whole" (Ocampo, 2005, p. iv).

To summarize, granted that "science" is much more about the disciplined application of systematic procedures than about reliance on a specified "body of knowledge," the handiest tool in the process of "creating" an African ECD space is the "scientific method," which must be applied at every step of the "transformation." Difficulty or failure to apply the "scientific method" to Africa's ECD knowledge bases should be blamed, not on the nature of Africa's ECD "knowledges" that await scientific exploration but on the shortcomings of the "science," if not the myopia of its scientists.

References

Arnett, J.J. (2008). The neglected 95%: Why American psychology needs to become less American. *American Psychologist, 63 (7)*, 602–614.

Asiwaju, A.I. (1984) *Partitioned Africa: Ethnic relations across Africa's international borders, 1884–1984*. Lagos, Nigeria: University of Lagos Press.

Barsby, J. (2006). Fair trade: What cost a cup of coffee? *The Traveler Msafiri, 57*, 50–54.

Baxter, J. (2003) *Mali's Koranic schools of hard knocks*. Retrieved on 11/09/07, from http://news.bbc.co.uk/1/hi/world/africa/2838201.stm

Bongmba, E.K. (2001). *African witchcraft and otherness: A philosophical and theological critique of intersubjective relations.* New York: New York University Press.

Bouzoubaa, K. (1998) *An innovation in Morocco's Koranic preschools.* The Hague, The Netherlands: Bernard van Leer Foundation.

Bram, C. (1998). A culturally oriented approach for early childhood development. *Early Childhood Matters 89*, 23–29.

Brooker, L. and Woodhead, M. (2008). Preface. In L. Brooker and M. Woodhead (Eds.), *Developing positive identities: Early Child in Focus 3—Diversity and young children.* Milton Keynes, U.K.: The Open University.

Bruner, J. (1996). *The culture of education.* Cambridge, MA: Harvard University Press.

Bugaje, U. (1993) Some observations on Islamic education in Katsina State, Nigeria. Retrieved on 11/09/07, from http://www.webstar.co.uk/~ubugaje/kteduc.html

Callaghan, L. (1998). Building on an African worldview. *Early Childhood Matters, 89*, 30–33.

Campo, J.A. (2005). *World Youth Report 2005: Young people today, and in 2015.* New York: United Nations.

Cannella, G.S. (1997) *Deconstructing early childhood education: Social justice and revolution.* New York: Peter Lang.

Cannella, G.S. and Viruru, R. (2004) *Childhood and postcolonization.* New York: RoutledgeFalmer.

Dahlberg, G. and Moss, P. (2005) *Ethics and politics in early childhood education.* London: Routledge Falmer.

Dawes, A. (2006). *Doing child development research that aims to make a difference: South African reflections.* Invited Address presented to the 19th Biennial Meetings of the ISSBD (International Society for the Study of Behavioral Development), Melbourne, Australia, July 2–6.

Diawara, M. (1998). Toward a regional imagery in Africa (pp. 103–124). In F. Jameson and M. Miyoshi (Eds.), *The cultures of globalization.* Durham, NC: Duke University Press.

ECDVU (2004). ECDVU SSA1 Initial Country Reports. Retrieved on 12/12/2008, from http://www.ecdvu.org

Erny, P. (1968). *L'Enfant dans la pensee traditionnelle d'Afrique Noire [The child in traditional African social thought].* Paris: Le Livre africain.

Gormuyor, J.N. (1992) Early childhood education in Liberia (pp. 337–341). In Woodwill, G.A., Bernhard, J., and Prochner, L. (Eds.), *International handbook of childhood education.* New York: Garland.

Gröhn, K. (2008, March 7). UN Millennium Development Goals merely scratch the surface of Africa's development crisis. International Institute for Justice and Development, pp. 6–11.

Harkness, S. and Super, C.M. (1992) Shared childcare in East Africa: Socio-cultural origins and developmental consequences (pp. 441–459). In Lamb, M.E., Sternberg, K.J., Hwang, C.P. . and Broberg, A.G. (Eds) *Child Care in Context: Socio-cultural perspectives.* Hillsdale, NJ: Lawrence Erlbaum.

Harkness, S., Super, C.M., Axia, V., Eliasz, A., Palacios, J., and Welles-Nystrom, B. (2001). Cultural pathways to successful parenting. *ISSBD News Letter 1 (38)*, 9–13.

http://www.actionbioscience.org/evolution/johanson.html. The Out-of-Africa-Theory Origin of *Homo sapiens.* Retrieved on 24/10/2008, from http://www.actionbioscience.org/evolution/johanson.html

Hunter, T.C. (1977) *The development of an Islamic tradition of learning among the Jakhanke of West Africa.* PhD dissertation, University of Chicago, Chicago, IL.

Jahoda, G. (1982) *Psychology and anthropology.* London: Academic Press.

Kashoki, M.E. (1982) Indigenous scholarship in African universities: The human factor (pp. 35–51). In Fahim, H. (Ed.), *Indigenous anthropology in non-Western countries.* Durham, NC: Carolina Academic Press.

Kishani, B.T. (2001) On the interface of philosophy and language: Some practical and theoretical considerations. *African Studies Review 44*(3): 27–45.

Lanyasunya, A.R. and Lesolayia, M.S. (2001) El-barta child and family project. Working Papers in Early Childhood Development, No. 28. The Hague, The Netherlands: Bernard van Leer Foundation.

Maquet, J. (1972). *Africanity.* New York: Oxford University Press.

Mazrui, A.A. (1986) *The Africans.* New York: Praeger.

Meadow Lake Tribal Council (1989). Vision statement. Unpublished report. Meadow Lake Tribal Council, Meadow Lake, Saskatchewan.

Moumouni, A. (1968). *Education in Africa.* New York: Praeger.

Mudimbe, V.Y. (1985). *African gnosis: Philosophy and the order of knowledge: An introduction.* New York: Garland.

Nsamenang, A.B. (1987). A West African perspective (pp. 273–293). In M.E. Lamb (Ed.), *The father's role: Cross-*

cultural perspectives. Hillsdale, NJ: Erlbaum.

Nsamenang, A.B. (1992a). *Human development in cultural context: A third world perspective*. Newbury Park, CA: Sage.

Nsamenang, A.B. (1992b). Early childhood care and education in Cameroon. In M.E. Lamb et al. (Eds.), *Day care in context: Socio-cultural perspectives* (pp. 419–439). Hillsdale, NJ: Erlbaum.

Nsamenang, A.B. (2004). *Cultures of human development and education: Challenge to growing up African*. New York: Nova.

Nsamenang, A.B. (2005). Educational development and knowledge flow: Local and global forces in human development in Africa. *Higher Education Policy, 18*, 275–288.

Nsamenang, A.B. (2006). Human ontogenesis: An indigenous African view on development and intelligence. *International Journal of Psychology, 41* (4), 293–297.

Nsamenang, A.B. (2007a). A critical peek at early childhood care and education in Africa. *Child Health and Education, 1* (1), 14–26.

Nsamenang, A. B. (2007b). Origins and development of scientific psychology in *Afrique Noire*. In M. J. Stevens and D. Wedding (Eds.), *Psychology: IUPsyS global resource*. London: Psychology Press.

Nsamenang, A.B. (2008a). In a globalized world, local culture must be the anchor of identity. Interview with A. Bame Nsamenang. *Early Childhood Matters, 111*, 13–17.

Nsamenang, A.B. (2008b). Agency in early childhood learning and development in Cameroon. *International Journal of Educational Policy, Research, and Practice* [Special Issue].

Nsamenang, A.B. (2008c). (Mis)understanding early childhood development in Africa: The force of local and global motives (pp. 135–148). In M. Garcia, A. Pence, and J.L. Evans (Eds.), *Africa's future—Africa's challenge*. Washington, DC: The World Bank.

Nsamenang, A.B. and Dawes, A. (1998). Developmental psychology as political psychology in sub-Saharan Africa: The challenge of Africanisation. *Applied Psychology: An International Review*, 47 (1), 73–87.

Nsamenang, A.B., Fai, P.J., Ngoran, G.N., Ngeh, M.M.Y., Forsuh, F.W., Adzemye, E.W., and Lum, G.N. (2008). Ethnotheories of developmental learning in the Western grassfields of Cameroon. In P.R. Dasen and A. Akkari (Eds.), *Educational theories and practices from the majority world* (pp. 49–70). New Delhi, India: Sage.

Nsamenang, A.B. and Lamb, M.E. (1995). The force of beliefs: How the parental values of the Nso of northwest Cameroon shape children's progress towards adult models. *Journal of Applied Developmental Psychology*, 16 (4), 613–627.

Ocampo, J. A. (2005). Unpacking the human potential for public sector performance: World public sector report(2005). United Nations Publications.

Ogbimi, G.E. and Alao, J.A. (1998) Developing sustainable day care services in rural communities of Nigeria. *Early Child Development and Care* 145: 47–58.

Ogbu, J. U. (1994) From cultural differences to differences in cultural frames of reference (pp. 365–391). In Greenfield, P.M. and Cocking, R.R. (Eds) *Cross-cultural roots of minority child development*. Hillsdale, NJ: Erlbaum.

Ojiaku, M. O. (1974). Traditional African social thought and Western scholarship. *Presence Africaine, 90*, 2nd Quarterly.

Oluoch, F. (2007) *East Africa: Madrassa to the Rescue*. Retrieved on 12/10.2007, from http://allafrica.com/stories/200709110669.html

Pence, A.R. (1980) *Preschool programs in the 19th century*. Unpublished dissertation. University of Oregon.

Pence, A.R. and Hix-Small, H. (2007) Global children in the shadow of the global child. *International Journal of Educational Policy, Research and Practice* 8(1): 83–100.

Pence, A.R. and Marfo, K. (2008). Early childhood development in Africa: Interrogating constraints of prevailing knowledge bases. *International Journal of Psychology, 43* (2), 78–87.

Pence, A.R. and Nsamenang, A.B. (2008). *A case for early child development in sub-Saharan Africa*. The Hague, The Netherlands: BvLF.

Prochner, L. and Kabiru, M. (2008) ECD in Africa: A historical perspective. In Garcia, M., Pence, A.R. and Evans, J.L. (Eds) *Africa's Future, Africa's challenge: Early childhood care and development in sub-Saharan Africa*. Washington DC: World Bank.

Prout, A. and James, A. (1990). A new paradigm for the sociology of childhood? Provenance, promise and problem. In A. James and A. Prout (Eds.), *Constructing and reconstructing childhood: Contemporary issues in the sociological study of childhood* (pp. 7–34). London: The Falmer Press.

Richter, L., Foster, G. and Sherr, L. (2006). *Where the heart is: Meeting the psychosocial needs of young children in the context of HIV/AIDS.* The Hague, The Netherlands: Bernard van Leer Foundation.

Rogoff, B. (2003) *The cultural nature of human development.* Oxford, UK: Oxford University Press.

Saasa, O.S. (2008). *Enhancing institutional and human resource capacity for improved performance.* Building the capabale state in Africa. 7th African Governance Forum. From http://www.undp.org/africa/agf/documents/en/background_info/papers/Paper7-enhancinginstitutionalandhumancapacity.pdf. Retrieved 2/15/2010.

Segall, M.H., Dasen, P.R., Berry, J.W., and Poortinga, Y. H. (1999) *Human behavior in global perspective.* Boston, MA: Allyn and Bacon.

Serpell, R. (1993) *The significance of schooling: Life-journeys into an African society.* Cambridge: Cambridge University Press.

Serpell, R. (1994). An African social ontogeny: Review of A. Bame Nsamenang (1992): *Human development in cultural context. Cross-Cultural Psychology Bulletin, 28* (1), 17–21.

Serpell, R. (2008). Participatory appropriation and the cultivation of nurturance: A case study of African primary school health science curriculum development (pp. 71–97). In P.R. Dasen and A. Akkari (Eds.), *Educational theories and practices from the majority world.* New Delhi, India: Sage.

Serpell, R. and Hatano, G. (1997) Education, literacy and schooling in cross-cultural perspectives (pp. 345–382). In Berry, J.W. Dasen, P.R., and Saraswathi, T.M. (Eds.), *Handbook of cross-cultural psychology* (2nd Ed., Vol. 2) Boston, MA: Allyn and Bacon.

Sharp, E. (1970) *The African child.* Westport, CT: Negro University Press.

Shumba, A. and Seeco, E.G. (2007) Botswana (pp.87–99). In Arnett, J.J. (Ed.), *International encyclopedia of adolescence.* New York: Routledge.

Smale, J. (1998) Culturally or contextually appropriate? *Early Childhood Matters* 90: 3–5.

Smith, L.T. (1999). *Decolonizing methodologies: Research and indigenous peoples.* London, UK: Zed Books.

Soto, L.D. and Swadener, B.B. (2002) Toward liberatory early childhood theory, research and praxis: Decolonizing a field. *Contemporary Issues in Early Childhood* 3(1): 38–66.

Tchombe, T.M. (2007) Cameroon (pp.127–139). In Arnett, J.J. (Ed) *International Encyclopedia of Adolescence.* New York: Routledge.

UNDOS (United Nations Development Organization for Somalia). (1995) *Koranic School Project North West Zone, Somalia.* Save the Children Fund (SCF)-United Nations Children's Fund (UNICEF) Documentation Unit, Mogadishu, Somalia. Retrieved on 24/11/2007, from www.pitt.edu/-ginie/somalia/pdfkoran.pdf

UNDP (1994). *Human development report 1994.* New York: Oxford University Press.

UNESCO (1999). UNESCO World Conference on Science Declaration on Science and the Use of Scientific Knowledge. Retrieved on 4/24/2003, from http://www.unesco.org

United Nations (1999). Convention on the Rights of the Child. Retrieved on 8/1/2008, from http://www.un.org/documents/ga/res/44/a44r025.htm

Urban, M. (2006) Strategies for change: Reflections from a systematic, comparative research project. Unpublished manuscript presented to the early childhood care and education policy seminar on "A Decade of Reflection from the Introduction of the Childcare Regulations 1996 through to Today," CSER, Dublin, November 3, 2006.

Wallerstein, I. (1988). A comment on epistemology: What is Africa? *Canadian Journal of African Studies,* 22(20), 331–334.

Weisner, T.S. (1997) Support for children and the African family crisis (pp. 20–44). In Weisner, T.S., Bradley, C., and Kilbride, C.P. (Eds.), *African families and the crisis of social change.* Westport, CT: Bergin and Garvey.

Winters, C.A. (1987) Koranic education and militant Islam in Nigeria. *International Review of Education* 33: 171–185.

World Bank (1999) Education and Koranic literacy in West Africa. *IK Notes* 11: 1–4. www.jacobsfoundation.org/ Jacobs Foundation: Mission Statement.

Zimba, R.F. (2002) Indigenous conceptions of childhood development and social realities in southern Africa (pp. 89–115). In Keller, H., Poortinga, Y.P., and Scholmerish, A. (Eds.), *Between cultures and biology: Perspectives on ontogenetic development.* Cambridge: Cambridge University Press.

CHAPTER FOUR

Negotiating Sameness and Difference

American[1] Jewish Childhood

DEVORAH KENNEDY AND MARIANNE BLOCH

Abstract

This chapter focuses on the concept of childhood within a post-modern perspective in which cultural and historical contingencies are critical to the construction of how childhood is mobilized as a cultural construct that marks boundaries of sameness (inclusion) and difference (varieties of exclusion). The example of "Jewish" childhood in the USA is taken as one example of how the concept of childhood has been mobilized to assert sameness but also to maintain an acceptable difference within the parameters of that sameness. We examine the mobilization of the discourse of childhood and the power effects of such mobilizations within Jewish educational literature to critically analyze how difference, sameness, and the language of culture and history play an important role in our notions of universal childhood—a construct that relies on difference and exclusion, while appearing to include everyone.

> Childhood is the most intensely governed sector of personal existence. (Rose, 1990, p. 121)

> This unnameable is the play which makes possible nominal effects, the relatively unitary and atomic structures that are called names, the chains of substitutions of names in which, for example, the nominal effect différance is itself enmeshed, carried off, reinscribed, just as a false entry or a false exit is still part of the game, a function of the system. (Derrida, 1982, pp. 26–27)

In this chapter, we examine the play of power relations that circulate in conjunction with universalized concepts of childhood. We employ a historical analysis to examine complex interactions of shifting configurations of childhood with shifting reasoning of how we understand differences between types of people. Focusing attention on the particular case of American Jewish childhood, we explore the delicate interplay of discourses of sameness and difference as they interact with discourses of childhood. We ask: How has the American Jewish childhood been constituted in relationship to parameters of American childhood? How have American Jewish educational thinkers mobilized such discourse to constitute an American Jewish childhood that is both the same (an American child) and acceptably different (Jewish)? What governing and differentiating power effects have the uptake and mobilization of discourses of childhood within Jewish educational literature had upon American Jewish life? In short, we explore the delicate negotiation of maintaining difference while also asserting normalness, and we examine the effects of such negotiation within Jewish educational discourse. We view this analysis of American Jewish childhood within the broader context of negotiating inclusion of cultural difference within constraints of shifting rules and standards of systems of reasoning.

Frameworks for Analysis of the Negotiation of Sameness and Difference

Following Popkewitz's conceptualization of a social epistemology, our analysis draws upon a "broad band of conversations...collectively call[ed] postmodern social and political theory" in order to highlight the political and social implications of educational research and knowledge (1997a, p. 18; also see 1997b). The primary "conversations" upon which we draw for this analysis are Foucault's historical studies of knowledge, his theorizations of the power/knowledge relationship, and Derrida's (1982) conceptualization of *différance*. Briefly, Foucault's (1969/1972, 1966/1973) historical analyses of the history of western knowledge assert that modern, secular knowledge is not simply the result—nor is it evidence—of the steady and linear progress of western man.[2] Rather, his body of work indicates that modern scientific reasoning marks a break (or rupture) with previous rules about what might be considered truthful or factual knowledge. These breaks or ruptures were neither inevitable nor did they simply appear. Rather, they emerged from a grid of "conditions of possibility"—shifts in reasoning and conditions that opened a variety of possibilities for new thought and action.

A primary rupture of concern in this analysis is that which occurred in the decades on either side of the turn of the twentieth century—the rupture between modern, scientific knowledge and theological thought. Among the many conditions of possibility for this rupture were encounters with new and different populations, changing economic conditions, and demographic patterns of migration, which were accompanied by shifts in reasoning about nations and nationality, economy, family, race, and religion (see, for example, Foucault 1978/1991, 1997/2003). The conditions of possibility for the emergence of the rules of our modern system of reasoning are often traced back to shifts in reasoning associated with the Enlightenment. Cannella has summarized these shifts clearly and concisely stating, "Human nature was thought to be considered natural and constant, understood and controllable through universal principles, and discoverable through reason and the newly emerging scientific tools" (1997, p. 23). While these new tools were attributed to the advancement of western civilization "scientific" reasoning was not yet secular—truth and knowledge remained within what we today would consider the theological sphere (Baker, 2001).

In his discussions of modern scientific reasoning, Foucault (1980) articulated a circular relationship between power and knowledge; knowledge produces effects of power, and these effects of power are re-inscribed in emerging new knowledges. This conceptualization of the power–knowledge relationship draws into question assumptions that knowledge "discovered" through scientific methodologies is neutral and objective. Rather, we note that scientific method becomes the gatekeeper—it constrains and limits what may be considered "real," or truthful, knowledge. Further, as Foucault (1980) has noted, both discourse and counterdiscourse are constrained within the limits of the rules of reasoning. Thus, the point of power is also the point of resistance to power—all inter-actions are interactions in which relations of power come into play.

Acceptance of the idea that power circulates through knowledge and is always reinscribed with-in new and emerging knowledges suggests that assertions about universal characteristics or general-izable traits of childhood have effects of power. The "scientific" discovery of the universality or normalcy of some traits, actions, behaviors, and desires has effects of producing hierarchical ranking and ordering of "other" traits, actions, behaviors, and desires. Difference, or deviation from the norm, has effects upon real lives. Hence, the norms, and our knowledge of how best to attain or sur-pass the norms, come to govern the conduct and desires of those who interact with children—fam-ilies and educators. We might say that our knowledge of normal and appropriate conduct and traits produces who we are and who we are not, who we may become and who we may not become. It pro-duces our knowledge of appropriate and inappropriate interactions between different types of peo-ple—mothers and children, fathers and children, teachers and different types of children, teachers and different types of parents.

If knowledge produces how we "know" ourselves and others as particular types of people, and has effects of governing interactions between different types of people, then we can no longer assume that childhood is a naturally and universally occurring stage of life. This does not mean that no differ-ence exists. In order to reconceptualize difference we draw upon Derrida's concept of *différance*. This concept suggests that while there are differences between types of people—this difference is neither essential nor foundational. Rather, differences are consistently reinterpreted through the emergence of new categories for comprehending and understanding differences. That is, difference is "know-able" only through the discourses of a particular time and space. [3]

Taken together, these "conversations" lead us to approach the child as a discursive formation; a subject given form as multiple discourses—discourses of what the child is and what it is not—inter-act in determining the parameters of normal and not normal childhoods. Further, using the illustra-tive examples of this chapter, both "Americanness" and "Jewishness" are approached as discursive formations that, given the multiplicity of discourses making up the grids from which they emerge, are interrelated with each other and with childhood. Thus, we approach childhood, Americanness, and Jewishness as three interrelated discursive formations—each informed by, and informing, the oth-ers, and others as well (e.g., non-Jewishness, non-Americanness, Jewish families/non-Jewish fami-lies). For example, we do not conceptualize the Jewish childhood constituted within Jewish educational literature simply as a hybrid formation emerging from the uptake of new reasoning about childhood and Americanness. Rather, in this example, we argue that it is a configuration that emerges as par-ticular discourses are taken up in response to configurations of Jewish difference that, at the same moments, come into play within discourses of Americanness and childhood. We focus particularly upon the interplay of sameness and difference as discourses of childhood, Americanness and Jewishness interact as American Jewish childhood is reconfigured as both the same (American, child), but also acceptably different (Jewish).

Methods and Data

Uses of Foucault in educational research have focused largely upon the governing and differentiat-ing effects of discourses of normal childhood. Yet, in the case of Jewish education, we find the relationship very complex. Educational discourse operates as a governing discourse that constitutes the parameters of inclusion and exclusion as a "universal" child, or as a potential member of cultural or national collectives. Thus, despite claims to objectivity or universality, "universal" childhood remains connected to the transmission of particular cultural values (same and different), although connections to cultural identities, alliances, etc. are, admittedly, hidden within the discourses which assign names (for more in-depth analysis of making up people, see Hacking, 2002).

One Analysis of Sameness and Difference

"American Jewish childhood"

In Jewish educational discourse childhood operates to both govern the parameters of culture while also resisting the loss of culture. This is not "new" to modern educational reasoning. For example, the codification of Jewish oral law, and the emergence of requirements for Jewish universal education emerged during the Babylonian exile and the Roman occupations, respectively. Jewish education, then, operated to govern Jewish life while also resisting the ways of dominant populations. Jewish educational discourse continues to operate in this manner. While the discourse of any time and space remains constrained within the limits of rules of systems of reasoning, it both takes up shifting rules of reasoning while resisting some interpretations of Jewish difference. In reviewing Jewish educational literature we did not find any one dominant model for the uptake of discourses of childhood, nor did we find any one response to dominant configurations of Jewish difference. Thus, the texts (Dushkin, 1918; Gamoran, 1924/1975) chosen for more intense analysis were those in which both the sameness and the difference of the American Jewish child were of primary concern—resisting complete assimilation (or fusion) into American mainstream while, at the same time, focusing upon inclusion within American society.

Our analysis[4] of Jewish educational literature was informed by our reading of educational and Jewish history in addition to analyses of educational discourse, early childhood education and child development. Our approach was to explore the interrelated discourses through which American Jewish childhood is constituted and govern American Jewish life. Hence, rather than provide a deep analysis of shifting configurations of racial difference, gender difference, or economic difference, we have pulled these trajectories of reasoning about difference together to create a broad view which deserves deeper analysis in the future.

Jewish education and the configuration of an acceptably different Jewish childhood

In his 1918 survey of Jewish education in New York, Alexander Dushkin declared that Jewish educational reform must be undertaken "in the light of the two universal tendencies that have affected all our modern life, namely, Science as method, and Democracy as an aim" (1918, p. 140). The declaration operates to situate American Jewishness within the parameters of modern and progressive society—scientific methods are the rules through which truth can be known and democracy is the by-product of an advanced and civil society. The statement also reflects the rupture in rules of reasoning that had occurred in the nineteenth and early twentieth century. Through science, reason and truth were explicitly uncoupled from God and religion, while democracy marked a distinctive shift in concepts of the nation and the responsibilities of government. By the late nineteenth and early twentieth centuries, childhood was reconstituted within the constraints of reasoning in which truth was known through a scientific method of inquiry (see Bloch, 1987, for one discussion of the growth of the importance of "science" in American early childhood.) Education, based upon expert (scientific) study of the child, was a crucial governing technology that was linked to what was perceived as the continuing progress of American democratic society.

Scientific knowledge of childhood reframed the role of the teacher, the child and family through new, psychological, discourses. Rose (1990) has described this emphasis upon scientific knowledge as a shift from moralization to normalization in discourses of childhood that occurred during the late nineteenth century. Popkewitz (1998) describes this shift through which the psychological categories that emerged from scientific knowledge operated to constitute the child/subject quite differently than had earlier discourses of morality.

> The psychological categories of learner and development [within constraints of scientific inquiry as truth] …produced particular practices that replaced the early nineteenth century construction of teaching which saw children as part of the prophetic task of professing Christian faith. The child was good or bad, pious or nonpious. Development and learning theories, in contrast, opened the child's behaviors, attitudes, and beliefs to scrutiny, such that they could be acted on to effect change in cognition and affect. (Popkewitz, 1998, p. 545)

Of course, reasoning did not suddenly become scientific and secular. The shift from moralization to normalization, the shifting rules and standards of reasoning through which the child was reconstituted as a psychological subject, occurred in conjunction with shifting reasoning about nation, family, race, culture, and religion.[5] These shifts in reasoning operated in conjunction with the emergence of new reasoning associated with social problems related to the movement of populations (rural to urban migration), governmental concerns for the health and well-being of the population, changing economic systems, and the unlinking of church and state (Foucault, 1978/1991, 1997/2003). Nor can these new social problems be divorced from the increasingly important role of education as a technology for the maintenance of a self-disciplined citizenry (Foucault, 1978/1991).

In the American context, these emerging social concerns were also linked with a populist broadening of the concept of democracy (Wood, 1991), increasing immigration from abroad, the emancipation of the slave population, and, as Gomez (2007) notes, with the acquisition of large territory in the war with Mexico, an increased native population and a large Mexican population. Social anxiety and fear of otherness accompanied the variety of differences that were to be brought together under a broadening interpretation of democracy; these were inscribed within educational discourses concerned with the morality and virtue of children and their families—a morality which remained linked with particular types of religious practice and belief.

Not surprisingly, discourses circulating in conjunction with the emergence of the Jewish Sunday School movement were similar educational discourses that circulated surrounding those of the common school and American Sunday school movements. A concern for morality and virtue tied to the future of the nation was clearly evident in Jewish educational discourse. For example, in 1844 Gutheim declared:

> We must have in view not the past but the present and more truly the future; …we have to see in the child the future man, our aim is to make him master not of his faculties only but of his passions; to give him knowledge and knowledge virtue, so that in his future capacity of husband, parent, "citizen,"…education may render the individual good and happy and society prosperous and permanent. (1844, 13, quotation marks added)

The centrality of virtue and morality within Jewish educational discourse operated as a double movement—as an uptake of dominant discourse that marked the sameness of the American Jewish child, and as resistance to linkages to morality and Christianity inscribed within this discourse. [6] While a variety of discursive trajectories come into play in the constitution of American childhood here we also briefly note the interplay between moral childhood and the governing formations of religious practice, poverty and gender.

First, the ranking and ordering of morality within American educational discourse cannot be separated from a ranking and ordering of religious beliefs and practices descending from rational protestantisms at the apex to heathen beliefs at the base. Jewishness was constructed in different texts as being situated in the middle of this ranking—it was a revealed religion that had a moral foundation (the Old Testament), but the failure to accept Jesus as savior (ascribed to all Jewish people) led to a decline into superstition and empty legalisms. The uptake of discourse of moral and virtuous childhood within Jewish educational discourse had effects of constituting the American Jewish child as the same—an American childhood with the same capacities to become moral and virtuous. At the same time, the uptake of these discourses was a response to Christian beliefs and practices related to the conversion of Jews (see, Leesor, 1843, for expression of these concerns)—it reiterated a desire to maintain Jewish difference. Re-framed within discourses of moral and virtuous childhood, Jewish beliefs and practices had similar goals (and interpretations) of morality—yet they remained different.

Second, morality operated as a governing discourse by differentiating between the conducts of the moral and immoral poor (See, Proccaci, 1978/1991). Focusing upon conduct moral childhood had effects of ranking and ordering behaviors of both the poor and the wealthy, including differentiating between peoples based upon how wealth was obtained and maintained. The future morality of all children, particular to "the poor," was central in Jewish educational discourse but, in addition, the uses of wealth—communal as well as familial responsibility for the moral education of all children was important. Concern for the future well-being of the nation through the moral education of children AND evidenced through philanthropic activities of the affluent in providing that education had effects of constituting Jewishness itself within parameters of moral Americanness and moral childhood.[7] It also had effects of maintaining Jewish difference, albeit the parameters of that difference were reconfigured within bounds of acceptability.

Finally, the twin educational goals of morality and virtue were intertwined with shifting configurations of gender roles within the family and society and had effects of governing the lives of Jewish American women. As Foucault (1975/1979) has noted by the nineteenth century "family" had become a governing discourse that made possible our concepts of democratic freedom. In the nineteenth century morality and virtue, once constituted within the domain of masculine reason that was linked with the advancement of civilization, were increasingly situated within the feminine domain as the natural and emotional capacities of women (See Wood, 1991). Thus, the uptake of discourses through which women became the models and gatekeepers of virtue and morality, reconfigured Jewish childhood within parameters of acceptable American family life. The role of women (as administrators and teachers—but not necessarily board members) in the Jewish Sunday School movement, and the praise heaped upon them by Jewish community leaders, are evidence of the uptake of virtuous motherhood/womanhood inscribed within Jewish educational reasoning (for shift to female responsibility for Jewish religious life see Baum, Hyman, & Michel, 1976). Their involvement in Jewish education showcased the civic and moral virtue of Jewish womanhood—the virtue and morality of the Jewish mother had effects of constituting the virtue and morality of the entire Jewish community—rich and poor, male and female.

The uptake of educational reasoning about moral and virtuous childhood had effects of recon-figuring Jewish difference—in addition to Jewish childhood, family life and religious belief and prac-tice—within parameters of moral Americanness. It also had effects of governing American Jewish family, social, and religious life. Another effect of the uptake of these discourses was the reinterpre-tation of differences between different types of Jewishnesses—morality and virtue were interwoven with conducts related to economic status, gender, and Jewish knowledge to constitute a ranking and ordering of moral Jewishnesses.

Morality as a concept through which to differentiate between, and govern the conduct of, types of peoples did not disappear—nor was it replaced—within the constraints of modern scientific rules of reasoning of the early twentieth century. Overt linkages between education, moral conduct and the future of American democracy gave way to overt linkages between scientific knowledge of child-hood, normal conduct, and the future of American democracy; hierarchical rankings and orderings were re-inscribed within the educational reasoning. Even as G. S. Hall scientifically ordered racial groups (still often described as nationalities) according to capabilities and potential to learn he placed the Anglo-Saxon race at the apex and described Anglo-Saxons as practicing the "highest form of revealed Christianity" (Hall, 1882).

Increasingly, differences between types of people were constituted as racial characteristics that determined individuals' (and groups) capability of achievement within, and contribution to, American life. As Foucault (1997/2003) has noted, the term race was not new however, by the end of the nine-teenth century it was reinterpreted as a biological determinism and the relative advancement of dif-ferent groups of peoples was attributed to biology. If the advancement of European civilization had previously been explained as the result of the education, reason, and consciousness (hallmarks of enlightened Christianity), the shift to a biologically deterministic racial reasoning reinterpreted social progress as determined by the capabilities of particular racial types (for education, see Baker 1998). Levels of intelligence, poverty or wealth, and family practices and conduct were interrelated effects of the racial traits attributed to various groups.

Markers of such difference from the American (Anglo-Saxon) norm—primitive practices, inap-propriate conduct, and poverty—were evident in the American Jewish population (a large propor-tion of whom were immigrants). Yet, the academic success of individuals from this group also suggested that Jews were not an unintelligent race. However, Jewish intelligence was not considered "normal" intelligence, as there was believed to be a wide range of variability between individuals with-in the race. Jewish intelligence was marred by a variety of psychological pathologies and character deficits (See Heinze, 2004[8]).

With the normal child (rather than the moral child) as the center of American Jewish educa-tional discourse, abnormal Jewish differences were not denied. Dushkin advocated Jewish education-al reform in order to combat the "mental conflicts and psychic repressions…[that] tend to express themselves in increased nervosity and even in cases of unbalanced mentality" (1918, p. 23). Taking up discourses of progressive and scientific education Jewish educational reform focused upon the cur-riculum, the pedagogy, and the institutions of Jewish education. Advocacy of Jewish educational reform addressed the markers through which Jewishness was constituted as less than normal with-in American educational discourse. First, both Dushkin and Gamoran took up discourses of envi-ronmental causality rather than biological determinism to explain racial differences. Second, they mobilized the discourse of advanced democracy to challenge narrow configurations of Americanness.

The mobilization of a discourse of "too rapid denationalization" operated both to explain difference and to challenge exclusion based upon difference. This discourse made possible the assertion that although immigrants appeared to have lower rates of intelligence, more social pathologies, and higher rates of illegal activities and immoral conducts, these deficiencies were not necessarily biologically determined. Rather, they were the effects of children rejecting their parents' national knowledge and practices in favor of an Americanness they did not yet fully understand. The theory offered the opportunity to explain rejection of parental beliefs and practices—explanations of poverty, seemingly primitive religious practices, and improper family conduct—and at the same time opened possibilities for criticizing parameters of an Americanness that was not easily understood—one that was the same (American/family/childhood) while also, at the same time, different (Jewish/poor/immigrant).

A full understanding of Americanness was not possible without a rich concept of democracy—one which, perhaps, not all Americans understood. Challenging narrow configurations of Americanness and the hierarchical ordering of difference that served as a basis for political and social exclusion Gamoran stated:

> [the immigrant] is entitled to live his own life and not be compelled to give up his individuality or merely accept conditions for the creation of which he is not responsible. Nor is it true to fact to assume the existence of an American type which the immigrant must strive to approach…."Shall the Anglo-Saxon type then be the sole American character?" (Gamoran, 1924/1975, II, p. 44, quotation marks added)

Discourses focusing upon such conceptualizations of advanced democracy in effect reinscribed Jewish difference but also asserted that the parameters of normalness should be extended to provide for the maintenance of cultural difference. It suggested that less modern populations would become modernized in their own ways within these extended parameters, and that this modernization would not occur through education in the absence of political and social inclusion, but rather that political and social inclusion would improve education. Thus, this type of bold challenge to Anglo-Saxon Americanness is balanced in Jewish educational discourse by assertions that inclusion in democratic society leads to the development of democratic conduct, sensibilities, and character/morality. As such, while challenging the parameters of Americanness, Jewish educational discourse focused upon explaining and addressing non-normal Jewish differences—primitiveness and poverty. These differences could be constituted, through discourses of environmental causality such as denationalization, as problems of the Jewish immigrant rather than problems of the Jewish race.

First, the primitive religious practices of the immigrant population certainly marked them as unintelligent and superstitious, lacking both reason and morality. These practices were explained as the result of tyrannical and exclusionary governmental practices in the nations of origin of immigrants—having been denied modern secular education, or when given educational opportunities, the possibility of participation in society, Jews were denied the possibility of modernizing religious practices. The modernization of Jewish religious practice would be addressed as the curriculum was constructed in accordance with knowledge of how normal children learn—as the curriculum was more meaningful and interesting to children, new topics would be added (like American Jewish history) and others (such as dietary laws) would be given less emphasis.

Second, and related to religious practices, were inappropriate family practices—related to high rates of delinquency, failure to properly educate female children, and the "traditional hierarchy of learning" that had meant some groups of Jewish men were not necessarily accustomed to supporting their families. The strength of the Jewish family prior to immigration was mobilized to illustrate the potential normalness of the immigrant child. If the problem of denationalization and too rapid Americanization was addressed the American Jewish family would again become a strong unit. The poverty of immigrant families and the loss of common language with children who more rapidly learned English were environmentally caused, according to texts, rather than racial causes for the breakdown of Jewish family-life. Further, parental adjustment was inhibited by traditional religious practices (particularly, in the late 19th and early 20th century, these discourses related to recent Eastern European Jewish immigration thus creating differentiation within "Jewish childhoods" as well as American childhoods). While discourses of the value placed upon education in traditional Jewish life were mobilized as evidence of Jewish intelligence, the failure to educate women was noted as a barrier to normal family life. Undereducated Jewish women could not meet their communal responsibilities. At a time when women were a rapidly increasing proportion of the teaching profession, Dushkin declared that the lack of female teachers in the field of Jewish education was "wholly explicable in the light of traditional neglect of formal education for Jewish girls" (1918, p. 277).[9] The female educator was a marker of an educated society. Worse, the undereducated immigrant mother could not control her American-educated children—lack of common language and common values contributed to the breakdown of the Jewish home. In addition, traditional Jewish education had not prepared immigrant men for the types of labor they faced in the American context. Gamoran asserted that there was an "undue weight given to financial success" in American society that conflicted with more communal Jewish [read in any population struggling for acceptance within Americanness] values and culture (Gamoran, 1924/1975, II, p. 11). This conflict was believed to undermine parental authority as immigrant youth came to value material goods as markers of success.

Clearly, the poverty of the immigrant was central in Jewish educational discourse, and addressing this issue was crucial to reconfiguring Jewish difference acceptably within parameters of Americanness. A primary concern, as in the nineteenth century, was communal responsibility for the Jewish poor. However, the goal was for immigrants to develop individual responsibility (as it was assumed to be for immigrants and other Americans at the same time). The goal was to assist immigrants in moving from dependence upon philanthropy to self-regulation. Dushkin suggested the development of Jewish educational institutions that served as community centers in which community members would be active decision-makers. Self-government, rather than dependence, was an important goal of including immigrant community members in center management decisions. Of course, while decision-making was to be in the hands of community members the administration of these centers was to be guided by educated experts (there were similar patterns in settlement houses at the turn of the century).

Similar to the uptake of discourse in which morality explained differences between groups of people, the uptake of normal childhood performed a double movement. It asserted the sameness (or potential sameness) of the American Jewish child while making a case for the maintenance of Jewish difference within parameters of normal American childhood. Jewish education based upon normal childhood would have effects of governing not only normal Jewish childhood but also Jewish family and community life. Second, in asserting the educability of the Jewish child—and the Jewish family—discourses of normal childhood, in conjunction with discourses of advanced and progressive democracy, operated to challenge narrow configurations of Americanness.

The problem for proponents of Jewish educational reform was to reconstitute Jewish difference in response to, and within the rules of, scientific reasoning in such a way as to also constitute Jewishness within the parameters of Americanness.

The Price of Acceptability and the Struggle to Maintain Jewish Difference

The privileging of normal childhood within Jewish educational discourse also had effects of differentiating between types of Jewishnesses. First, markers of Jewish non-normal difference were predominantly situated within the immigrant population. As suggested earlier (see, for example, endnote 9), the American-born Jewish child was constituted as already normal. This, in conjunction with the mobilization of discourses of environmental causality, strengthened the configuration of the immigrant child as potentially normal.

From a progress-oriented perspective one might assume that Jewish Americans have "now" become normal. Within current American Jewish educational discourse there is little evidence that the Jewish child and family are situated outside the parameters of American childhood. There has been an apparent acceptance of Jewish difference as a "religious" difference which most of the Jewish population practice in appropriate ways. The acceptance of American Jewish difference, has often been discussed within the discourses of race and class—becoming white and middle class (see Brodkin, 1999). Yet, there has been a price for acceptance within Americanness. Brettschneider (2006) has noted that the normal middle-classness of Jewish Americans has come at a price, one of these being a silencing of Jewish women. While mobilizations of normal childhood and environmental causality at the turn of the twentieth century strengthened possibilities for Jewish inclusion, the interplay of these discourses is more complex. It is worthwhile to reexamine the effects of this discourse in governing American Jewishness and upon differentiating between types of Jewish families.[10]

Nineteenth-century shifts in reasoning reconstituted morality from a characteristic of enlightened reasonable masculinity to a natural affective quality of women. It was not simply women who were judged based upon their virtue and morality. The treatment of and conduct of women of different population groups were standards for comparison between populations.[11] However, the appropriate treatment of women was (and remains) a discourse that privileges particular cultural ways of living in the world. Turn-of-the-twentieth-century Jewish educational discourses concerned with the conduct and education of women were always comparative as Jewish practices and ways of living were compared to modern "American" ways of being and living in the world.

Concern about, and explanation of the lack of, formal education of Jewish women, had effects of reiterating stereotypes of Jewishness as a primitive religious tradition. Interestingly, more recent scholarship has noted that the prohibition against women studying the Jewish texts was debated within early Rabbinic literature. It had also been interpreted as an exemption from study (although related to the extent of women's other responsibilities) rather than a prohibition (Boyarin, 1991; Baumgarten, 2004). Additionally, as Brettschneider has noted, the basic education of Eastern European Jewish women was generally better than the educations of non-Jewish women in the societies from which they immigrated. Finally, the ranking and ordering of cultural populations based upon the treatment of women was relatively recent and focused upon a particular configuration of women's roles and abilities as well as the conception of "educated women" used. The possibilities for higher education that were available from the late nineteenth century were focused upon education for the role of motherhood, or professions considered as extensions of women's natural capabilities, e.g., teaching and social work. Of course, the argument remained somewhat circular: if the failure to educate women was a marker of the primitive and superstitious aspects of Eastern European Jewishness, the provision of a traditional Jewish education to women might have had the effect of increasing their adherence to primitive and superstitious religious practices.

The focus upon treatment of women extended only to those issues constituted within the rules of the system of reasoning as natural to the gender. Thus, participation in economic and commercial life was a marker of non-normal motherhood and inappropriate womanly conduct. The participation of the immigrant mother in paid labor was described as a temporary situation that would pass as the immigrant family adjusted to, and succeeded in, modern America, in which the ideal seemed to be that fathers were economic breadwinners, and mothers stayed at home. This explanation ignores the extent to which women had participated in economic life in Eastern Europe. While women's roles were circumscribed within traditional Jewish belief, women had participated in economic life. One price of becoming a normal Jewish American woman and mother—with a special feminine nature and appropriate conduct and behavior—was to constrict the spheres of activity of Jewish women, if they were to fit the then current ideals or desired behaviors of other American women, even other Jewish American women.

The discourse of childhood, the particular emphasis upon normal motherhood and womanly conduct, cannot in the case of the Jewish community be divorced from configurations of Jewish difference focused upon masculinity. In a sense, the conduct of Jewish women was also crucial for reconstituting the Jewish male within parameters of normal masculinity. Within western reasoning interpretations of Jewish male difference there was a reinscription of iterations of this difference as a privileging of the study of empty legal codes over traditional manly pursuits. Turn of the twentieth century iterations of this difference (which American Jewish educational discourse both challenged and reiterated) were accusations of laziness and dependence upon women and children in sharing economic responsibilities. Scientific identification of Jewish racial attributes—nervousness, overemotionality, and sexual degeneracy—was focused upon the mind and body of the Jewish male.

There is little challenge to the normalness of Jewish Americans, children, males and females within current Jewish educational literature. As Jewishness has increasingly been accepted within parameters of Americanness the child has remained at the center of the Jewish educational curriculum. Yet, normal childhood continues to operate as a discourse that governs the family. As Jewishness has been increasingly constituted within parameters of normal Americanness some recent texts on Jewish education suggest there is an apparent increase in concerns for maintaining Jewish difference. Thus Jewish education of the child is to re-enculturate the Jewish child. As discourses of culture (e.g., multiculturalism, authentic cultural experience) have been increasingly privileged within educational discourse, Jewish educational literature reflects an increasing concern for Jewish cultural practice. Knowledge of traditional practices and ways of living is more and more often emphasized within the Jewish educational literature. Of course, as resistance emerges at the point of power and within the constraints of the system of reasoning, the maintenance of Jewish difference—constituting an acceptable Jewish difference—necessitates the uptake of counter-discourse as well as discourses of universal or generalizable characteristics in order to produce a self-governing American Jewish child and family.

However, in the early 21st century, curricular decision-making must meet the needs of normal Americans, and the Jewish parent is an autonomous decision-maker who makes choices based upon personal priorities and personal interpretations of Jewishness. There is little emphasis upon community center schools that will attract children from the neighborhood. As private individuals Jewish parents decide upon their investments in education (both Jewish and secular). There is an acknowledgment that individuals have multiple priorities, and Jewish education may, or may not, be highly ranked within their personal value systems (descriptions of which mimic those related to normal middle-class parenting).

What is absent in the educational literature is the non-normal Jewish child, mother, and family.[12] While Brettschneider (2006) has noted the price women have paid for becoming normal, Yeskel (1996) has noted the near absence of the non-middle class within current Jewish social discourse. While Yeskel's discussion focuses primarily upon the economic questions surrounding participation in Jewish life it is useful to go beyond this discussion. Future projects must begin to examine the price of becoming normal. While concerns about the loss of Jewish knowledge as American Jewishness has been included within parameters of normal Americanness, it is important to examine the extent to which normal Jewish American childhood, operates to exclude, while including. Has the price of normalness been attrition from the community of those who have not become normal? Or, alternatively, we must continue to see the perpetuation of new governing systems that are historically and culturally contingent in their moment and also continue to have varying samenesses and differences.

In Closing

These conclusions, using the example of American Jewish childhood—moving quickly from the 19th into the 21st centuries—were used to provide detailed illustrations of the importance of understanding the multiplicities of childhoods within particular time/spaces, the ways in which normality and universality hide or play with abnormality and difference, at the same time. The use of Foucault and a cultural historicist analysis of American Jewish childhood(s) is to point to the pathways for further research, the continuing need for understanding sameness/difference as a couplet, not a binary, and to reinforce different ways of understanding (or exposing our simplistic understanding) of notions of childhood.

Notes

1. We acknowledge that the term American is indeed problematic. When used to describe the United States, it has effects of excluding the populations of two continents. However, Americanness is also a central concept of one national imaginary of the United States "of America." (We might more appropriately think of the term as "America/n," with recognition of the inclusions/exclusions so often attached to this construction of geographical/territorial/populational/conceptual space.) As it is a crucial component of a national imaginary, it is a critical concept for understanding sameness and difference within (and beyond) the context of the United States. We will continue to deploy this term but with humility.

2. Obviously, the poststructural argument could lead to deconstruction of many concepts used here, including "western," and "man." While we focus on a limited analysis here, we hope our discussion of "American Jewish Childhood" illuminates broader points and conversations and we acknowledge others' work on similar issues and critical discourse analyses that are made elsewhere.

3. For example, initial encounters with native inhabitants of the Americas suggested they were of the ten lost tribes of Israel (See Eilberg-Schwartz, 1990).

4. "Our analysis" largely stems from joint work but primarily from an unpublished dissertation by the first author of this chapter. The particular examples of "American" "Jewish" "Childhood" come from the much larger study by Devorah Kennedy, while the theoretical perspectives and many other ideas are from our shared discussions, joint work (e.g., Bloch, Kennedy, Lightfoot, & Weyenberg, 2006), and ideas of many others, some acknowledged in many of the above citations.

5. Shifts occurring within western systems of reasoning throughout the nineteenth and twentieth centuries are quite evident in the Jewish educational literature. Changing conceptions of nation, race, culture, and religion

become obvious as authors struggled (and continue to struggle) with situating Jewishness within any one of these categories.

6. The linkage between Jewish virtue and citizenship is important. While most states had expanded to the franchise to Jewish men this was not yet the case in all states.

7. While most states had enfranchised Jewish males by the 1860s social acceptance remained difficult to achieve. Affluent Jewish Americans were often merchants, a category that remained suspect and, according to Wood (1991) outside of the American elite.

8. As in many other cases, please note that textual evidence can be found in the cited texts but are also illustrated specifically as part of a discursive analysis in the first author's dissertation (Kennedy, 2008)

9. Again, Dushkin (who had immigrated from Central Europe as a child), was speaking of the cultural primitiveness, the lack of education for women among Eastern European Jewish immigrants, but also in relation to what were perceived as normal, good practices in education for "American girls and women" in the late 19th century and beyond. In these ways, we show the historical and cultural complexity and contingency of discourses of childhood, sameness/difference, normality/abnormality as these shifted or ruptured across different times/spaces.

10. Of course, the discourse of environmental causality as focused particularly upon the immigrant population, immediately differentiated between the modern American-born population and immigrants. Further, descriptions in both texts of the different interpretations of Jewishness evident within the immigrant community suggested the inscription of a hierarchy of religious practice (from superstitious to secular/cultural/national) that differentiated between immigrant Jewish populations—none of these interpretations was equivalent to modern American interpretations. Finally, the constitution of racial difference according to country of origin is also inscribed with the reasoning of normal childhood and family life that was central within turn-of-the-twentieth-century Jewish educational literature.

11. This discourse has not disappeared. It is currently mobilized within discourses concerned with Islamic traditions.

12. Non-normal here is a difficult terminology. As Yeskel has noted Jewish communities have acknowledged and "included" multiple interpretations of women's roles, family configuration (single, or gay for example), and differing learning abilities.

References

Baker, B. (1998). 'Childhood' in the emergence and spread of U.S. public schools. In T. S. Popkewitz & M. Brennan (Eds.). *Foucault's challenge: Discourse, knowledge and power in education.* (pp. 117–143). New York: Teachers College Press.

Baker, B. (2001). *In perpetual motion: Theories of power, educational history, and the child.* New York: Peter Lang.

Baum, C., Hyman, P., & Michel, S. (1976). *The Jewish woman in America.* New York: Dial Press.

Baumgarten, E. (2004). *Mothers and children: Jewish family life in medieval Europe.* Princeton, NJ: Princeton University Press.

Bloch, M. N. (1987). Becoming scientific and professional: Critical perspectives on the history of early childhood education. In Popkewitz, T.S. (Ed.). *The formation of school subjects: The struggle for creating an American institution.* New York: Falmer Press.

Bloch, M. N., Kennedy, D., Lightfoot, D., and Weyenberg, D. (2006). (Eds.) *The child in the world/the world in the child.* New York: Palgrave Press.

Boyarin, D. (1991). Reading androcentrism against the grain: Women, sex, and Torah-study. *Poetics Today, 12*(1), 29–53.

Brettschneider, M. (2006). *The family flamboyant: Race politics, queer families, Jewish lives.* New York: State University of New York Press.

Brodkin, K. (1999). *How Jews became white folks and what that says about race in America.* New Brunswick, NJ: Rutgers University Press.

Cannella, G. S. (1997). *Deconstructing early childhood education: Social justice and revolution.* New York: Peter Lang.

Derrida, J. (1982). *Margins of philosophy*. (A. Bass, trans.). Chicago: The University of Chicago Press. Original work published 1968.

Dushkin, A. M. (1918). *Jewish education in New York City*. New York: The Bureau of Jewish Education.

Eilberg-Schwartz, H. (1990). *The savage in Judaism: An anthropology of Israelite religion and ancient Judaism*. Bloomington, IN: Indiana University Press.

Foucault, M. (1972). *The archaeology of knowledge & The discourse on language*. (A. M. Sheridan Smith, trans.). New York: Pantheon. (Original works published 1969 and 1971)

Foucault, M. (1973). *The order of things: An archaeology of the human sciences*. New York: Vintage. (Original work published 1966)

Foucault, M. (1979). *Discipline and punish: The birth of the prison*. (A. Sheridan, trans.). New York: Vintage. (Original work published 1975)

Foucault, M. (1980). *Power/knowledge: Selected interviews and other writings 1972–1977*. (C. Gordon, trans.). New York: Pantheon

Foucault, M. (1991). Governmentality. In G. Burchell, C. Gordon, & P. Miller (Eds.), *The Foucault effect: Studies in governmentality* (pp. 87–104). Chicago: University of Chicago Press. (Original work published 1978)

Foucault, M. (2003). *Society must be defended: Lectures at the College de France 1975–1976*. (D. Macey, trans.). New York: Picador. (Original work published 1997)

Gamoran, E. (1975). *Changing conceptions of Jewish education*. New York: Arno Press. (Original work published 1924)

Gomez, L. E. (2007). *Manifest destinies: The making of the Mexican American Race*. New York: New York University Press.

Gutheim, J. K. (1844). Objects and means of religious education: How are we to secure to your youth the benefits of a religious education? *The Occident and American Jewish Advocate, 2*(4). Retrieved April, 10, 2005 from http:www.jewish-history.com/Occident/volume2/jlu1844/objects.html

Hacking, I. (2002). *Historical ontology*. Cambridge, MA: Harvard University Press.

Hall, G. S. (1882). The moral and religious training of children. *Princeton Review* APS Online.

Heinze, A. R. (2004). *Jews and the American soul: Human nature in the twentieth century*. Princeton, NJ: Princeton University Press.

Kennedy, D. (2008). *Constituting American Jewish childhood: Parameters of acceptable difference*. Unpublished dissertation, University of Wisconsin-Madison.

Leesor, I. (1843). Jewish children under Gentile teachers. *The Occident and American Jewish Advocate*. 1(9). Retrieved April, 15, 2005 from http:www.jewish-history.com/Occident/volume1/dec1843/children.html

Popkewitz, T. S. (1997a). A changing terrain of knowledge and power: A social epistemology of educational research. *Educational Research 26*(9), 18–29.

Popkewitz, T. S. (1997b). The production of reason and power: Curriculum history and intellectual traditions. *Journal of Curriculum Studies. 29*(2), 131–164.

Popkewitz, T.S. (1998). The culture of redemption and administration of freedom as research. *Review of educational research, 68*(1), 1–34.

Procacci, G. (1991). Social economy and the government of poverty. In G. Burchell, C. Gordon, & P. Miller (Eds.), *The Foucault effect: Studies in governmentality*. (pp. 151–168). Chicago: University of Chicago Press. (Original work published 1978.)

Rose, N. (1990). *Governing the soul: The shaping of the private self*. London: Routledge.

Wood, G. S. (1991). *The radicalism of the American Revolution*. New York: Vintage Books.

Yeskel, F. (1996). Beyond the taboo: Talking about class. In M. Brettschneider (Ed.), *The narrow bridge: Jewish views on multiculturalism*. (pp. 42–57). New Brunswick, NJ: Rutgers University Press.

CHAPTER FIVE

African American Children

Early Childhood Education Recollections and Life Stories

DONALD R. COLLINS

Abstract

This chapter looks at the experiences of African American children as unique in society in general and in the educational milieu of public schools in particular. The chapter explores constructions of the African American experience in specific periods of time in history. While these periods are artificial in nature, and would most likely not be articulated by cultural insiders or outsiders, they provide a structure or framework for the deconstruction of dominant perceptions. Further, this historical deconstruction unveils the multiple hierarchical relationships through which children have been silenced and stereotyped.

Introduction

The American classroom is a microcosm reflecting the social structure of the larger American sociological system (Lamb, Land, Meadows, & Traylor, 2005; Tyack, 1974). Institutional structures like tracking, educational labeling, and intelligence testing have led to the separation of particular groups within educational environments. Skrtic (1995) suggests that this is maintained through a form of "professionalism" in which "professionals set their own standards, regulate entry into their ranks, discipline their members...(p. 6), thereby placing "the client in a potentially vulnerable position" (Schein, 1972; Skrtic, 1995). These structures have, unfortunately, led to problematic educational outcomes for children of color (West, 1993). Illuminating these concerns requires the revealing of multiple perspectives and the continued use of deconstruction applied to dominant paradigms (Caputo, 1997; Derrida, 1976, 1979). Historically, the educational community has attempted to address institutionalized shortcoming using paradigms that are inherently flawed, assuming universality and a monocultural perspective (Skrtic, 1995). These flaws are especially evident as related to educational experiences and opportunities for African American children.

This chapter identifies educational issues faced by different generations of African American children, specifically those who were called or have called themselves Negro, Colored, Black, and African American (NCBAA). Grounded theory allows the researchers to explore how different generations of African American children have been described in the context of their lives and educational experiences (Lincoln & Guba, 1985). In addition to this major issue, other issues include the social and political context that is woven into the interpretation of life and education experiences. Given the social, political, and educational climate experienced by each generation, the beliefs, assumptions, and intentions underlying the education of the NCBAA are important factors. The author believes that the purpose of this chapter is naturalistic and qualitative in nature, designed to reveal experiences and constructions held by African Americans about their childhood education. However, the goal is also deconstruction of dominant perceptions that have limited African American children in their educational settings by exposing the multiple hierarchical relationships through which they (we) have been silenced and stereotyped.

Comparative Historical Periods in Racial Contexts

Social and developmental psychology researchers (Barbarin, McCandies, Coleman, & Hill, 2005; Billingsley, 1992; Coard & Sellers, 2005; Du Bois, 1909; Hill, 1993; Hughes et al., 2006; Marks, Settles, Cooke, Morgan, & Sellers, 2004; Quintana, 2007) focusing on the African American child and family have debated the relevance of race, ethnicity, and culture. Four comparative periods are presented in a constructed historical context. The intent of the historical context description is to provide an understanding of the experiences of African American childhoods. I believe that historical childhood experiences cast light or understanding on contemporary childhoods. Without this historical understanding or connection, societal, and cultural experiences exist in a vacuum (Billingsley, 1992). Further, a critical lens of continuous oppressive experiences is described in a variety of ways by distinct groups of African Americans about their childhood experiences. The periods represent complex frames of reference that include race, ethnicity, and culture placed within in the context of social, developmental, and educational psychology. These periods can be described as the Negro American Period (Slavery, 1930), the Colored American Period (1930–1950), the Black American Period (1950–1980), and the African American Period (1980 to present).

The Negro American period refers to the physical slavery in the United States. It also refers to the "psychologically enslaved Negro identity (Marks et al., 2004, p. 384). Pronounced during this period were phenotypic characteristics. The term "Negro" identifies a consciousness to slavery that in some respects may overlap all periods that are presented here. In terms of the presented framework, however, the period refers to a distinct educational period in which African Americans were legally denied access to education and the beginning of the national movement to educate them. For the people who lived during this period and provide recollections, only respect is intended for their contributions to the success of African Americans throughout history.

The Colored American period reflects a distance from slavery. While the period overlaps the Negro American period, the term "" American denotes a postslavery time when African Americans sought an education for themselves and their children. The period also saw an increased number of African Americans in the areas of politics and society. It is during this time that the doll studies (Clark

& Clark, 1939, 1940; Horowitz & Murphy, 1938) became a major factor as used to understand and shape the racial identity of African American children. These studies played a major role in the outcome of the *Brown* decision (*Brown v. Board of Education of Topeka*, 1954). Despite concerns about the self-esteem of African American children, significant to this period was a burgeoning pride and racial identity.

The Black American period represented a sense of racial, ethnic, and cultural pride for African Americans (Cross, 1991; Phinney, 1992). As African American scholars earned advanced degrees, these new scholars reconceptualized biased and derogatory perceptions of their ancestry (Marks et al., 2004). With this reconceptualization, came as sense of "cultural autonomy and power" (p. 384). Reconceptualized was the new research regarding the doll studies. The research of new African American scholars found that African American children experience high levels of self-esteem where previously they were found to experience low self-esteem (Quintana, 2007). Additionally, educational highlights of this period include access to an education system and its recourses that had eluded African Americans in previous periods.

While significant overlaps exist across periods, they highlight the human experience of children to allow a comparative effect. Although these periods are artificial in nature and would most likely not be articulated by children, cultural insiders, or outsiders, they provide a structure or framework to analyze experiences from past historical perspectives.

Historical Views of Children

The Traditional View of the Progression of the Child

Education is closely tied to the concept of childhood. Until the Enlightenment period, however, in Europe (400–500 years ago) young human beings were not considered different (as distinct groups) from those who were older. The childhood philosopher John Locke (1632–1704), as an example, conceived the child as a blank slate needing to be filled with knowledge. The construction of medicine and psychology was aligned with the construction of the privileged "man's" (wealthy White European man) attempt to understand "himself." Ultimately, alignments have led to the construction of dichotomies like adult and child. Childhood was, however, constructed as different for poor children and females than for wealthier male children. Poor children went to work at an early age. Female children as young as six years of age were hired out as maids. Schools were created to protect the wealthy male child or to control the poor; those schools did not overlap. Further, the concept of childhood was advanced in the notion of individualism through disciples like psychology. Individualism was and still is used as a way of knowing, as a concept of childhood that has been valued in society, politics, power, and also in the issues of schooling. The historical focus on individualism creates a dichotomy with the interests of the group at its opposite pole. Individualism often is identified as the standard to be sought after, thereby subjugating group values (Azibo, 1992). Ultimately, by focusing on the individual, group or societal issues, such as race, are marked as devalued. Consequently, an individual issue, such as socioeconomic status, can emerge as a factor under the control of the person. This results in the creation of power for some groups and disqualification for others (Cannella, 1997).

Science was believed to reveal all truths about how "children" (especially individuals) function in the world. The universal truths of childhood were believed to be applicable to all human beings, therefore constructing power for the "knower of truths" about childhood over younger human beings and any group of adults who do not accept the European universal truth for their children (Cannella, 1997).

An African View of the Progression of the Child in a Culture

While the above accounts for the genealogy (Cannella, 1997) of mostly privileged European children that has dominated western thought, the children and descendants of enslaved African children are not represented, nor does it purport the significance of the culture from which they were removed. This archeology was a culture in which African children existed "…in and for the community" (Atado, 1988).

Parenthood (Nsamenang, 1992) was derived from a symbiotic relationship one had with biological relatives and the greater nonbiological community. One's "personhood" (p. 77) was a trait sought to develop over time. One's personhood was judged to be "competent or better, to fail, or to be ineffective" (Menkiti, 1984; Nsamenang, 1992). For some, African personhood begins with the concept of the "unfinished child" (D'Alessio, 1990) along a continuum of "personalities" (Nsamenang, 1992); that is, becoming a fully competent human as he or she matures. This continuum was composed of three "dimensions" (p. 144). Nsamenang (1992) reports that these dimensions include:

> First, there is a spiritual self-hood beginning at conception and ending with naming. Second, the social self-hood extends from naming until death (in old age). Third, the ancestral self-hood follows biological death (and extends…to the ritual initiation of ancestral spirit into a higher spiritual realm (pp. 144–145).

Nsamenang (1992) explains that, "An unmarried, childless person is never accorded full adult status, and marriage alone confers only proto-adult status" (p. 84). He further explains that adolescents as young as 14 or 15 years could achieve the status of adulthood by marrying and becoming a parent. A married 24-year-old, for example, without at least one child was viewed as "socially immature" (pp. 84–85).

Married brothers and sisters with children made-up and become part of what western culture describes as "extended family" (Nsamenang, 1992). In contrast, this extended family had a distinct close, but complex function or "network" (p. 86). Nsamenang explains that the reference to "brother" (p. 86) referred to all "male members of the group in the same age cohort" (Nsamenang, 1992, p. 86). This distinction applied equally in referring to a female as "sister." The same reference applied to age cohorts for the mother or father's generation. Adults in the family were referred to as more than just a child's parents. Interestingly, Nasamenang (1992) stresses that while fathers were not involved in children, motherhood was not synonymous with "mothering" (Cannella, 1997, pp. 71–75). More appropriate to the African culture was that of "peer care." Jahoda (1982) explains, "some of the fundamental social norms of the culture begin to be systematically and, in the main, painlessly instilled into the children also most immediately after weaning…the powerful role of the sibling group in this process…" (Jahoda, 1982, p. 131; Nsamenang, 1992, p. 151).

Nsamenang (1992) describes individualization and "competitiveness" as faults, while getting along was encouraged using "[the] custom of ritualizing" (p. 86) to foster human development. Specific developmental stages for African children included: "spiritual self-hood; period of newborn; social priming; social apprenticing; social entrée; social induction/internment; adulthood; old age/death; ancestral self-hood" (pp. 147–176). Historically, African children gained knowledge of their "ethnic history and folklore" (Nsamenang, 1992).

While Nsamenang (1972) describes a different view of the life and development of African children, African American children have had their own unique family and world experiences in the United States. Pronounced are the educational experiences of the African American child. Specifically, ignorance of outsiders (Banks, 2001) looking into the emerging and enslaved African American culture at large and the child in particular predominated to the 1930s. From the 1930s through the 1950s, the lack of knowledge and neglect by researchers of the African American child shaped their education. Assimilation, through the 1960s, of the African American child into the established culture constructed "pathologies" or problems to be redressed through the assimilation process. Integration or desegregation, through the late 1970s, of the African American child emphasized tolerance of the new diversity by the established culture. Though the late 1980s, cultural pluralism and multiculturalism began an acknowledgement of differences and the "inequality of opportunity" (Banks, 2001, p. 15), particularly for the African American child. The late 1980s to the present have been marked by an attempt at a "color blind society" that focuses on individualism (Gillborn, 2001).

Educational Experiences of African American Children from Slavery to the Present

Not everyone is privileged with voice in a literate society. Those who have power have voice. Having voice required that franchised people master the codes of the dominant culture (deCastell & Luke, 1983), codes that have been embedded in definitions of educational access. The process of access, however, has unique meaning for African American children.

Accepting the limitations of education is very difficult for African Americans who have placed, except for prayer (Washington, 1994), almost total dependence on it as a liberating factor to combat racism, intolerance, and ignorance. This education primarily meant learning to read and write. It meant becoming "literate." The meaning of literacy as it related to knowing presents complex issues and questions: What does literacy mean for African American children? How does the construct of literacy privilege some children more and others to a lesser degree?

Becoming educated and literate for the children of descendents of African slaves is grounded in the loss of spoken language (language of origin) requiring the creation of a method of communication (to communicate with other slaves) that was inconsistent with ancestral culture and traditional values. It is further grounded in the lack of access and denial of literacy during slavery and to the limited access during the ante-bellum period through the 1900s, to unequal schools through the 1960s, to the current consequences of political desegregation through programs like special education and tracking. Nonetheless, while education has been a liberator, it has not slain the dragons of racism, bigotry, and oppression for African American children.

First Comparative Era : The Slave to the Negro Period (Slavery to the 1930s)

Literacy in the lives of slaves meant something closer to survival than interacting with the printed word. Isolated attempts were made to educate free slaves in ways of being American in such locations as the Goose Creek Parish in South Carolina (Gordon, 1971). Educating African slaves grew out of the clergy's desire to civilize the "heathens of the world" (Woodson, 1919, p. 29). In fact, abolitionists and other supporters like the Society for the Propagation of the Gospel of Foreign Parts produced Africans who could read and write. In Charleston, around 1750, schools recorded the attendance of as many as 60 students. In this spirit, Woodson (1919) provides an account of a school, with legal sanction, for the "bastard or pauper children, Black or White" (p. 29). The masters and/or caregivers of these children were required to teach them to "read and write and calculate as well as follow some profitable form of labor" (p. 29).

Opposition to the education of the Negro took the form of arguments against their education because of a reasoning that these people were "stubborn…and saucier than pious….so far gone in their wickedness, so confirmed in their habit of evil ways that it was vain to undertake to teach them" (Woodson, 1919, p. 30). When this reasoning failed, opponent slaveholders argued that they themselves were too backward to teach the Negro. Despite these pleas, religious leaders in the colonies as far as London, England, admonished masters and mistresses to instruct their Negroes in the Christian faith, regardless of the expense cited by slaveholders. Religious indoctrination of the Negro was the real purpose of education at this time.

With education came a certain knowing that was characterized as militancy (Woodson, 1919). This militancy necessitated the need to shape the Negro's mental development. In fact, it was argued that "neither" literacy nor religious education prepared the Negroes for a life of "usefulness." To this end, in 1787, organizations such as the Presbyterian Synod of New York and Pennsylvania encouraged its members to provide to their slaves "such good education as to prepare them for a better enjoyment of freedom" (Woodson, 1919, p. 74). The purpose of this instruction was to transform the Negro into "good neighbors, good mothers and fathers, good husband and wives, teaching them the duties of citizenship, teaching them to be defenders of their liberty and country and of the good order of society, and whatsoever might make them useful and happy" (Woodson, 1919, p. 80). In the 1790s, the Methodist Conference recommended the establishment of Sunday Schools to teach poor Black and White children to read and how to learn. New Jersey passed an act that made teaching slaves to read compulsory, with a punishment of five pounds for failing to do so. States with strong abolition movements, such as Maryland, Philadelphia, and New York, pushed for the mental shaping and education of Negroes. Woodson (1919) elucidates that in 1810, in preparation for emancipation, New York legally required masters to educate their slaves to read the scriptures.

The Retreat from the Education of the Slave and Freedman

As Whites in the North and Middle States made great advances in literacy, questions arose about the amount and quality of education appropriate for slaves. In spite of the attention given to the education of slaves, their children were not welcome to attend schools in even progressive communities (Woodson, 1919). Once again opposing slaveholders reasoned that the Negro experiences were significantly different than the White race and that "their training should be in keeping with their situation" (Woodson, 1919, p. 94). Therefore, many communities established "special, individual or unclassified" schools. A few communities with a small population of Negro children included them in the classroom with White children, but with the understanding that their special needs would not be met (Woodson, 1919).

Despite attempts through religion to educate the free Negro and slave, the majority of slaveholders did not support this view. Georgia and South Carolina were states that resisted the education of the Negro (Woodson, 1919). A primary reason for the resistance was economic. Not only did slaveholders fear that educated Negroes would threaten the slave economy, they feared that education would elevate the Negro to the status of American citizen. To prevent this from happening, in 1840, South Carolina made it unlawful to educate or use a slave as a scribe (Woodson, 1919). Georgia, in 1870, following South Carolina's lead, made it unlawful to teach or use slaves in an educated fashion. As in Georgia and South Carolina, areas with few slaves experienced great opposition to their education. To further prevent the education of slaves, North Carolina, Delaware, and Maryland restricted slaves from assembling.

Advances in the education of slaves in the eighteenth century were viewed in the nineteenth century as "more dangerous than useful" (Woodson, 1919, p. 153). As slave trade became profitable, particularly with the invention of the spinning jenny, the steam engine, the power loom, the wood-combing machine and the cotton gin, the educated slave population became a liability. Abolitionist literature painted a sharp contrast between the existences of the Negro to that of White people. White men quickly connected any slave uprising with the education of the Negro. Further, Woodson (1919) states that slaveholders told their slaves about the leaders of the French Revolution and their valiant demands for the rights of man, even citing courageous efforts by revolutionists. However, these same slaveholders prohibited such actions by their slaves. To abate such insurrections, many states and territories further restricted the congregation of Negroes for educational purposes and required the presence of a White minister for religious purposes. In 1814, states began to regulate the movement of free persons of color and to prohibit the education of slaves believing this would result in the creation of more activists and make slaves more discontented. Prohibition legislation was enacted with the intent to circumvent communication and reading of any abolitionist literature by slaves and any sympathizers. Thus, slaves were prohibited from communicating with each other, with free persons of color, and liberal Whites. Schools that had been open to them were closed.

With the enactment of these laws, literacy and slavery were incompatible. Masters argued that their safety depended on the illiteracy of the Negro. Educating Negroes in the South became clandestine, then rare, and finally disappeared in some locations altogether (W. E. B. DuBois, 1935). The North grew increasingly intolerant of Negroes because of the large number occupying free states near the border. Fearing an influx of free Negroes, many communities in the North restricted not only the settling of free and fugitive slaves, but also their education.

Du Bois (1935) explains that during the bellum period of the South, education was a low priority for poor Whites. In Southern states, no public education system existed for the children of White laborers. In populated areas, children of White laborers attended free grade schools. However, attendance was more of an exception than a rule. Poor White laborers reasoned that an education could only be attained through hard work. Not only did plantation owners not see the need to educate poor Whites, poor Whites did not seek an education. Education was regarded as a means of becoming a plantation owner and as an extravagance. Poor Whites accepted their position in Southern society. In contrast, because of the dependent nature of the conditions of slaves, many freed slaves saw education as the only means of acquiring wealth and respect. Dubois (1935) indicates that in their vision of gaining wealth, lack of education was "crippling" . It was this vision that contributed to the eventual establishment of public schooling in the South (Anderson, 1988).

Following the Civil War, corporal law was maintained by the military in many Southern states. With the assistance of the Freedmen's Bureau and private philanthropies, schools for emancipated slaves opened in significant numbers. Negroes were instrumental in creating many of these schools. Booker T. Washington stated of the Negro's thirst for knowledge:

It was a whole race trying to go to school. Few were too young, and none too old, to make them attempt to learn. As fast as any kind of teachers could be secured, not only were day-schools filled, but night-schools as well. The great ambition of the older people was to try to learn to read the Bible before they died. (DuBois, 1935)

With the absence of public education in the South, many of the laboring Negroes funded not only their children's education, but their own as well. Du Bois (1935) indicated that this was the beginning of public schools in the South. He further documented that Sunday Schools were created soon after freedom for the purpose of teaching the reading of the Bible and other skills of primary literacy. This was the second major move to educate the Negro in Southern states. The idea of public schooling for the White laboring class also took form and was exemplified in the opening of a public school in Charleston, South Carolina. Children of slaves, the Irish, and Germans attended these schools. While these children played together on the playgrounds, with some exceptions, race played a separating factor as they were taught in dividing classes. The point here is that not only were freed slaves assessing literacy with a fervor, but so were more White laborers (Anderson, 1988; Bullock, 1967; Leloudis, 1996).

The army played a major role in the establishment and maintenance of the public school system in Southern states such as Virginia, South Carolina, Louisiana, Georgia, and Florida. As the Union army withdrew and Confederate rule resumed, the public school system in the Southern states was significantly curtailed. Teachers of Negro students were released from service. Many teachers were threatened, run off, and some were murdered. Schools were vandalized and burned. In 1868, separate school for Negro and White children gained prominence and was exemplified in states like North Carolina (Wood, 1968).

A problem in public schooling was funding. Separate schooling implied separate funding. However, the funding of Negro education was obtained by taxing Negro people. The revenues, however, generated from these taxes were often diverted to noneducational purposes or were lost to waste and theft (Anderson, 1988). While states legislated a variety of funding systems, they provided little educational benefit or economic relief to Negro children. It was Northern philanthropy that sustained the education of the Negro following the Civil War well into the twentieth century. Despite politics, attitudes, and laws to enforce illiteracy (Anderson, 1988), the desire for literacy and its promises was a driving force in the Negro's struggle for intellectual freedom. Consequently, by the turn of the century, more than half of the Negro population in the South claimed to be literate (Anderson, 1988).

By this time many educational reform issues required attention. Previously, schooling focused mainly on the child. With grater immigration, reform included a call for schooling adolescents who were idle. Additionally, the familiar view was that poor parents were incapable of adequately raising their children. This was fueled by laws that restricted immigration between 1921 and 1924. These laws were predicated on immigrants from Mediterranean and Slavic groups. Explicitly, these laws imposed a subordinate status and quotas as late as 1965 (Pratte, 1973). The level of xenophobia grew and was fueled by nativism held by established Americans. In Britain, the issue was class. In the United States, it had become race (Smedley, 1993).

Educating and Schooling the Negro American

Mwalimu J. Shujaa (1995) explores how education and schooling can be mutually exclusive of each other. Shujaa comments that "going to school" does not translate into "getting an education" (p. 14). While Shujaa explains that commonly both "education" and "schooling" serve to transmit, maintain and develop and develop an African-centered cultural orientation and identity, notions of schooling seem to dominate constructions of education (Shujaa, 1995).

More specifically, Shujaa (1995) defines schooling as "a process *intended* to perpetuate and maintain the society's existing power relations and the institutional structures that support those arrangements" (p. 15). Examples of schooling are factors that control and dictate achievement such as policies of tracking, testing, and ranking. Reward systems include grading practices, the granting of achievement credentials, and placement practices. Finally, schooling includes "patterns of human interaction" (p. 17) that dictate the social inclusion and exclusion of people to ultimately "reinforce society's structural conditions" (p. 17). In contrast, education is "the process of transmitting from one generation to the next knowledge of the values, aesthetics, spiritual benefits, and all things that give a particular cultural orientation its uniqueness" (p. 15).

In 1896, the United States' Supreme Court upheld the doctrine of "separate but equal" in the *Plessy vs. Ferguson* decision. This decision institutionalized Southern vestiges of the culture of slavery in schools (V. J. Harris, 1995). Important to remember in this decision is the part of the nation where the decision had the greatest impact. Henry Bullock (1967) explains that between 1860 and 1910, the majority of Negroes lived in the South. Specifically, "of the 9,827,763 Negroes in the entire nation…90 percent lived in the South" (p. 149). States like Georgia, Mississippi, Alabama, North and South Carolina, and Louisiana were the homes of 60 percent of the Negroes at the time of the 1910 census.

Negro parents in the South began to send their children to school in greater numbers by 1870 and represented an increase from less than 10 percent to almost one-third of the 3,228,237 school-age children. By 1910, the number of Negro school-age children increased in this region to 3,403,237 (Bullock, 1967).

The *Plessy vs. Ferguson* doctrine of "separate but equal" bound the development of the education of the Negro child "within this context of political and economic oppression" (Harris, 1995, p. 144). This binding was most obvious in the mainstream teaching material prepared for the Negro child. Harris (1995) cites a book entitled, *The Coon Alphabet*. To cover the letter "A," the following is provided:

A is fo Amos
what rides an ole mule
so he can be early
each monin ter school (Harris, 1995, p. 145)

The author provides pictures of "gross caricatures" that insulted the physical appearance of the Negro child. Harris (1995) explains, "*The Coon Alphabet* was not written for African-Americans. Its racial hatred…[was] intended to amuse non-African Americans and help legitimate racist ideology" (p. 145).

To combat the derogatory nature of the material above, parents and teachers turned to self-made teaching materials. Negro educators such as Alice Howard developed teaching materials that sought to instill "value and goals including the characterization of education as a form of liberation…. race pride, racial solidarity, knowledge of African-American history and culture, and commitment to achieving social equality" (p. 145). Alice Howard "portrayed African Americans as responsible, intelligent and assertive individuals…(p. 145) in teaching materials that included:

> A Stands for Afro American,
> The Race that proved its worth;
> One more true, more noble
> Cannot be found on earth (p. 145)

While a limited number of Negro children had access to Howard's material, it represented the status Negro teachers sought to provide for their students. Other developers included Carter G. Woodson, W.E.B. DuBois, and Silas X. Floyd. Book titles included *Floyd's Flowers* and *Duty and Beauty for Colored Children,* to name a few. This type of material was considered "underground curriculum" (p. 147) in nature because it represented teaching contrary to what was provided to Negro schools and students, presenting Negro children in a positive light. The material "…unabashedly attempted to inculcate [Negro] children with specific ideologies…" (p. 147) and to gain control of the education "beyond rhetorical dichotomies of industrial or classical education" (pp. 147–148).

Because of the limitations of the "separate but equal" doctrine, Negro teachers in the South were legally bound to teach "only in segregated school" (M. Foster, 1997). Negro teachers espoused a curriculum outlined by educators such as W.E.B. DuBois that stressed that "during the first four years of life" Negro children "mastered reading, writing, and counting" (V. J. Harris, 1995, p. 150; Moon, 1972). Primary and later schooling served to "refine and enhance" skills that lifted the student's ability to "read for information as well as exercise, to write for self-expression as well as for mere communication, and to reason more clearly with mathematics correctness" (Harris, 1995, pp. 150–151; Moon, 1972). DuBois further recommended that Negro children study "geography, languages and history" (Harris, 1995, p. 151).

Education Stories from the Negro American Period

Insight is provided in the stores of people who lived in south Texas and were born during this period. The names of the individual story tellers have been changed to protect their identities.

Mrs. Etta Cook (1910–)

Mrs. Etta Cook described her parents as going to the third and fourth grades. She says "…in those days, they would go to school maybe to third and fourth grade…and then they…would work on the farms and things." Ms. Cook revealed that both her parents could read and write. At first, they did not own any property, "…but, they bought some property but somehow they got beated out of it."

Mrs. Etta Cook was born in 1910. She stated that her parents raised her until she was seven or eight years of age. She explained that after her mother's death that a cousin raised her and her brother and sister. Her new parents were unable to have children and gave them their name. She described her parents as, "…they were very interested in school." She restated with more emphasis, "They believed in it [education]."

Mrs. Etta Cook explained that she went to school "out in the country." She started school when she was seven years old. She states that she walked two-and-half miles to school. Her recollection of school was:

> …You had to obey orders. We had morning prayer, morning devotion, and then we would have classes; and we'd
> have recess…the school would close at four o'clock; it would start at eight o'clock in the morning…And you had to

get your lesson and you had to be obedient, and…if you didn't, she [the teacher] had switches tha'd whip you and make you behave. And we would play and have a nice time; the boys would be on one side of the schoolyard, and girls on the other—the boys and girls couldn't play together.

Mrs. Cook recalled her first book as the *Playmate Primer*. She recounts, "They taught math, reading, history, geography, health, [and] spelling." She explained that school usually went for seven or eight months. She recalls,

…But I remember one year they come and closed us out before the time for school to run out. They said all the money had run out for the school, you know, and they come and closed the school out…

Mr. Bigsby (1924–)

Mr. Bigsby is the patriarch of his family. He is college educated and a retired teacher and coach. He and his wife raised six children, three girls and three boys. Mr. Bigsby was born in 1924. He described his parents' education:

I had my grandmother and my great uncle…They were slaves. They were young slaves. They were what they called "house niggers." We were taught all about slavery through them.…They would tell us about how they came up during slave times. Grandmother used to tell us, "Boy, this is an advantage that we had growing up that other children probably didn't have—not necessarily through our parents, but through my grandmother—my grandmother could read, write…she could print, she couldn't write. And she could work algebra, geometry—anything you had— either one of them could work—you know why? The children they were attending…was about the same age as them…and what they would do…they would go and pick them up, go pick the children up in the buggy—bring them home or carry them to school—their children would show them—that's how they got—she [my grandmother] never went to school a day in her life. And she could print—and it was something—she could beat me printing. And she knew all of that stuff. Even thought it came from the slavery days—what she picked up we had a background. It helped me a whole lot.…if they picked up what was going on in their education, then culturally, they picked up the same thing—because those [slave owners] were the only people they had association with. Their speech— and everything else.…They saw life just about as they did.…You could say they treated them as equal, but they wanted them to know certain…things in order that those people had a sense enough to know that what these two Black and White kids were doing and they being the masters—they wanted to make sure they were speaking the right language. And so they [grandmother and great uncle] spent a lot of time trying to speak the right way and they were still doing the same thing as we do today—trying to talk like White folk.

He further recounted his early education (during the Negro American period):

We had to walk a tremendous distance to school. We had to walk 4 to 5 miles to school. School took in at about 8:00 and we had made the five miles and was in school on time.…The first ones there had to kindle the fire. We didn't have any janitors or anything of that nature. And if it was my week and another student's week to start the fire, we had to be there early—So that the building would be warm. And I think it brought a…discipline…in my life.… I went to a two room wood building. We had to use wood for heat. We had to carry water.…We had two teachers. They taught all the seven subjects we were taking. At [this] time…was completely segregated. Everything about that school, teachers and whatnot—students and all was all Black in the school I attended…And basically we had some types of sports consisting of regular games at recess. We didn't have organized sports, we just played baseball and we didn't have too much and we played with rag balls a lot of the times. The rag balls were made when you sew a rock inside a bunch of twine, wrap it up and play with that. We had moved up because we use to use [a] condensed milk can and played with a stick or bat we had cured out ourselves. And we played baseball and we would play "catching the can" and throw it around and whatnot and our hands would bleed sometimes.…But we had a lot of disciple at the time. That's the thing that counted and we just got our lesson; that was number one, lesson was number one.

...There was not everybody mixing up. Boys sat on one side, and girls on the other side....And girls didn't play with boys. We played separate....There was as many as 60 or 70 students attending school....In these buildings there were cloak rooms....One on this side and one where you put your hat and books and whatnots. It was just one big opening so far as when it was time for mathematics, you know, everybody could hear you. And maybe one teacher would be teaching math on this side and another teacher would be teaching English on the other side. There was so much discipline that you could actually understand what was being said or being taught in the same room. It was [in] pretty good condition. It was clean. [It was] kind of wide...at least 24 to 30 feet wide and maybe about 50 rectangle shape inside. [It was a] white wood building. And [it had a] very steep top. We didn't have what they call junior high and all that....Junior high was there, but they just had one school. When you went to school you didn't go to the 11th....they didn't have the 12th grade.

Second Comparative Era: The Colored American Period (1930s-1950s)

During the early 1900s, racist ideology as a basis for social stratification was a contemporary view that took definable shape in North America. Prior to the sixteenth century, human action and interaction did not take race into account (Smedley, 1993). Race classification of human beings appeared in the writings of the Spanish, Portuguese, Italians, French, Germans, Dutch, and English during the colonial period in America and Asia (Smedley, 1993). While people being colonized did not cause this classification, they were instrumental in accepting it and bowing to this new social structure or order. The South did not have tax-supported public school systems (Middlekauff, 1961). Children receiving any education received support through private means. Education became a regional access issue. While working class White children in the North attended "ungraded" (Semmel, Gerber, & Millian, 1994) classes, White children in the South did not attend school. Even in the North, attendance was only for three months a year. As other states ratified compulsory attendance laws, children from different backgrounds became part of the public school picture.

These laws compelled parents to juxtapose or situate their children who were previously excluded from an education next to children who were culturally different. Children from the working class and those labeled as coming from "broke, inadequate homes and low status ethnic groups" (Dunn, 1968, p. 5) were given access to the same educational system. Working class parents viciously resisted the mingling of the masses. To manage the differences in student populations, however, "self-contained and special schools" were created to remove students who were different from "established" children in regular classrooms (Dunn, 1968).

Education Stories from the Colored American Period

Mrs. Etta Cook completed the seventh grade, which was the norm during her time. She married her husband in 1928, which she stressed was the norm during her time. She and her husband had 14 children. Mr. and Mrs. Cook raised 11 children, 4 boys and 7 girls. Mrs. Margaret Cook-Nolin, Mrs. Cook's third child, provided a recollection of the birth order of her children:

I was the third, no I was the fourth of three, I was the fourth child of my parents, but grew up being the third because the first child died in birth. So, I grew up with a brother, who was older, a sister next, and I was the third child. And later, I had a sister two years under me. There was a brother two years after that sister. There was a sister two years after that brother. There was a sister two years after that sister. There were twins in our family; they died when they were babie...and after the twins died, there was another boy. And then the latter two children were two girls. But at home as I was growing up, I can mostly remember, we usually said our family was in groups of threes, because the first, I guess, the first five of us mostly grew up at home together; [and then] we went to school. And the next two were much younger than me and then the very last four probably started school after I went into college....

Mrs. Margaret Cook-Nolin (1935–)

Mrs. Margaret Cook-Nolin graduated from college in 1957. She became a teacher. Reflecting on social issues, she stated:

> *...And it started for me. I noticed it started right after I got out of college. I got out of college in 1957 and it pretty much started during that....To cite a little example....My girlfriend was driving her car and I guessed and I assumed that Blacks had to be careful even the way they drove, you know like they couldn't turn in front of White folk; I guess, I don't know. But from what I heard the principal's wife say, my girlfriend was making this turn, you know when the light is coming on and she continued to make that right, the left turn, and the principal's wife (also riding in the car) said, "Ooowee, you girls are really brave," sort of like the turn, she didn't use that word, I don't know what she used. She said, "Oh, [you] turned right in front of that White person." See, well to us, we hadn't been exposed to that kind of stuff, so we didn't know exactly what she meant other than you can't get in front of White folk. Well, see, we didn't know that. And I guess she, being much older than us, she was along with our parents— so she knew more about that kind of stuff. But those were the issues that were beginning to arise with Black people.*

Regina Bigsby (1946–)

Regina Bigsby is the oldest of Mr. Bigsby's children. She teaches in one of the larger districts in the county. She recalled her school years:

> *I went to a...Black school, you know elementary, junior high, high school, college....I started school when I was five instead of six, because at that time we weren't allowed to start school until we were six years old but since my dad was teaching and I was going to school with him anyway, the principal went ahead and allowed me to start grade school. And I can remember, some of my teachers, second grade especially...[and my] first grade....I enjoyed school....when I was going to school with my dad, we didn't have a cafeteria at the school, we had sort of like a, I guess it was a room, I don't even remember what it was, but you go there and had hotdogs and the hotdogs were nothing but a wiener on a piece of bread and you could get mustard. But I enjoyed that because the older children would take me, you know, teacher's daughter, take me and buy me a hotdog. So anyway, uh, my first grade, I enjoyed, I had a real sweet teacher; second grade school, had a good teacher, but she was so strict....I had a lot of stomachaches in second grade because I just didn't want to go to school because I was afraid of the teacher...I can remember also in elementary we had a May Day, and that, this was all exciting to everybody; everybody looked forward to that. M y junior high years, I enjoyed school period, because...I had teachers who I felt were very caring and loving.*

Third Comparative Era: The Black American Period (1950s to 1980s)

The Black American Period from 1950 to 1980 may also be characterized as The *Brown* Era. For the Black American student, the highlights of this period were marked by the end of legal segregation and the advent of social change. Specifically, the *Brown vs. Topeka Board of Education* (1954) attempted to allow Black students to sit next to White students in public classrooms across the United States. The *Brown* decision reflected the belief by the U.S. Supreme Court that the learning of Black students was inferior when educated in an all Black system. The decision further reflected the belief by the Supreme Court that Black students benefited from a superior schooling when sitting next to or being the classroom with White students (Brown, et al., 1988; Turnbull, 1990).

National views of Black Americans had been constructed by others prior to this period. These held views were perpetuated during the Black American Period. The culture of the Black American at large and the student in general were not valued (Glazer & Moynihan, 1963, p. 53). The view that Black American children existed in a "culture of poverty" (Lewis, 1970) characterized the treatment many received in the schools and justified maintaining the status quo for Black American school children.

The Black American family dynamics was viewed as problematic by officials (Moynihan, 1965). Specifically, Black American mothers were viewed as deficient in their mothering practices and that this resulted in their children's intellectual deficits (Klaus & Gray, 1968). Racist ideology (Jensen, 1969) provided a powerful belief system for educators of this period.

With a view of intellectual deficiency of Black American children, special education was considered a convenient structure to correct deficient mothering practices and problematic family dynamics. As a result of this view, large percentages of Black American students were placed in special education (Dunn, 1968). Initially, the structure of special education was successful in convincing the parents of Black American children "...to accept the judgment that their child is "not normal" (Tomlinson, 1995). Consistent with the national view of Black American students was the constructed mental retardation category these students were placed in. Consequently, a large number of Black American students were resegregated from established or White Americans (Sarason & Doris, 1979). Perceived normal students could be separated from abnormal students (Tomlinson, 1995) who were also viewed as having "low status" in the educational environment (Dunn, 1968).

Throughout this period, researchers and educators began to challenge the outcomes and pejorative school experiences of Black American students. The *Larry P. v. Riles* (1972, 1974, 1979, 1984, 1986) case highlighted the culmination of negative educational experiences of Black Americans. Table 5.1 represents a partial list of these experiences.

The experiences in Table 5.1 were largely predicated on bias assessment (Almanza & Mosely, 1980; Duffey, Salvia, Tucker, & Ysseldyke, 1981). Ironically, these assessments revealed a chasm that existed in the not only the instruction Black American children received, but in the attitudes and perceptions held specifically by teachers and school personnel and society at large. The inability of society and school and their instructional agents to overcome biased attitudes and perceptions was powerful in denying students access to the academic curriculum during this period. Bias, however, was the facilitating agent that implemented the hidden curriculum that resulted in the high numbers of Black American students relegated to special education during this period. Contributing to unchecked bias during this period was the loss of many Black teachers from the segregated era. Many of these teachers were simply laid off from their respective teaching jobs. This pool of teachers represented a loss of understanding and skill in teaching Black students. It also represented what one described as a loss of "love" (Collins, 2003, p. 103) by teachers who knew them. Researchers have documented this bias as differential teacher treatment (Becker, 1952; Chaikin, Sigler, & Derlega, 1974; Dotts, 1978; Harvey, 1980; Oaks, 1982; Rist, 1970; Rosenthal & Jacobson, 1968).

But the questions during this period were, "What were these test measuring?' or "What content were these students deficient in?" The answer to these questions was simply "acculturation" or even the stress of acculturation (Collier, 1998). Acculturation stress occurs when students are overwhelmed by a new cultural environment. The stress of fitting in or even not fitting in may cause psychosomatic complaints such as headaches, stomachaches, free floating anxiety, or other ailments. Acculturation stress may interfere with not only with a student's learning, but also their demonstration of knowledge (Collier, 1998).

Measuring acculturation included measuring class or socioeconomic status. Put another way, separating classes of students allowed for social stratification (Bowels & Gintis, 1976). It was no accident that classes such as algebra served as a gate-keeping mechanism that for many students was insurmountable. Not insurmountable because of inability, but because when a student is tracked to classes such as "basket weaving" (Collins, 2003) but tested on algebra, failure is assured (Sizemore, 1978; Walberg & Rasher, 1979). This furthermore perpetuates the hierarchical socioeconomic class structure of society at large (Taylor, 1976).

Education Stories from the Black American Period

Mr. Anthony Bigsby (1954–)

Anthony Bigsby is Mr. Bigsby's middle child and son. He and his wife built their home next to Mr. Bigsby, and Antony maintains a strong daily contact with his parents. Anthony would always wave at me when I went to his father's house. He recounted social and educational experiences:

> Well, for me, I remember when we integrated. We had to totally integrate in '69—that was my freshman year. But I remember that Daddy was a coach—for football, baseball, track; he also taught [history]. And I remember a youngster coming up, before I was even old enough to participate in sports, I remember that he would always get the uniforms from the White school, and he would stay up there hours, sometimes late at night, mending these shoulder pads and all this stuff, making them complete uniforms for the players. And he'd have to go out there and make, you know, chalk the football field, basketball field. He had to do it all. And I remember him, you know, doing these things for the school, for those- the- kids coming up. And I, you know that we don't have teachers—some of them are still there—but I'm saying like he did a lot, gave a lot of himself for those kids just to be able to participate. And, as for me, when we integrated in '69 it was sort of like ah, well, it was a culture shock. Because even though we lived here in the community and White people, I guess, you see how it is now, it's sort of segregated—Blacks on this side and Whites on that—side and, we first went there…Daddy always taught us to respect people, he didn't tell us about colors or anything like that. So, and when we went over there well, there were people who hadn't been taught that way so I had sort of a hard time coping, because you had to stand up for yourself over there. And sometimes the teachers, administrators, or whoever, if you were a young Black male and you felt like you was, were supposed to be treated equal as other students sometimes you ran into a lot of problems. I had a lot of problems coming up in school.

Mrs. Reba Morton-Johnson (1966–)

Mrs. Reba Morton-Johnson is the granddaughter of Mrs. Etta Cook (see the Negro American Period) and the maternal niece of Mrs. Margaret Cook-Nolin. She is a nurse. Regarding the social and educational issues while she was growing up, she commented:

> The only thing that really sticks in my mind was being the only Black in a private [church] school and I was called "nigger" by a kindergartener, a White kindergartener, and we ended up becoming best friends at the school.

Fourth Comparative Era: The African American Period (1980 to Present)

In his book, *Why Black People Tend to Shout*, Ralph Wiley (1992), describes how African American children function under pressure. He especially points out the treatment African American children face in American society in a story he tells. In his story, Wiley describes two young girls walking along the American–Canadian border. One girl was Black and the other was White. Both girls fall into the freezing water. Several men working in the area immediately rescue the White girl. After ensuring that she is on safe ground, they turn their attention to the Black girl. Wiley further describes that the men took personal precautions that they previously did not take as they saved the other girl. They engaged in a discussion about how to best accomplish extracting the young girl. All the while, the young girl was slowly succumbing to the elements. As the men decided on a course of action, they stretched out in the "classic ice-saving technique" (p. 6) and one of them extended a tree limb. When the little Black girl did not grab the tree limb, the man began to yell obscenities at her and blaming her for her predicament. The Black girl pulled herself out of the freezing water and to safety (Wiley, 1992).

Wiley points out that while one girl has been rescued, the other had survived. The men took credit for saving both children. The truth was something the children would not discuss, as each had a different reality. While the main character in the story is a little Black girl, her survival is analogous to that of African American boys. Wiley's story highlights a reality faced by many African American boys in the American classroom today. Too often, individuals positioned as heroes are antagonisst in the education of African American boys. Whether they are aware of the trauma (Norris, Fielding, Kemp, & Fielding, 1992) that befalls their students before they reach the schoolhouse is unclear. What is clear is the trauma they inflict in isolated classrooms on students (Ross & Jackson, 1991). Also clear is the fact that these students know that their teachers do not value their intellectual gifts (Marcus, Gross, & Seefeldt, 1991). Researchers have documented the driving force of low expectations (Grant, 1985; Holliday, 1985; Rosenthal & Jacobson, 1968; Ross & Jackson, 1991). Interestingly, many of these teachers refuse to individualize instruction but spend countless hours of instruction time constructing and perfecting an individualized "self-fulfilling prophecy" for specific students and then characterizing these students as "pathological" (Palakow, 1993; Swadener & Lubeck, 1995).

Overview of Factors Encountered by African Children

Although prominent researchers acknowledge the success of African American children and their families (Slaughter-DeFoe, Nakagawa, Takanishi, & Johnson, 1990; Swadener & Lubeck, 1995) historically, deficit model proponents (e.g.,Moynihan, 1965) have also construct pathologies to explain the experiences or "problems" experienced by African American children. Problems that are experienced by all children seem to be highlighted as if specific to African American children.

Before examining the construction of these pathologies, it is necessary to gain a better understanding of the ecological experiences of African American children. Despite progress in medicine, education, and social standing, African American children face a greater risk of poverty and other related stressful challenges like mental illness (Parker, Greer, & Zuckerman, 1988), low birth rate, infant mortality, neurodevelopmental disorders, and other developmental disabilities (Institute of Medicine, 1985). Children who experience these problems may also face the risk of demonstrating behavioral problems as adolescents (Dryfoos, 1990). Researchers suggest that African American children are more at risk for being raised in poor, single-parent households than children of other races and ethnic groups (Johnson, Miranda, Sherman, & Weil, 1991). In 1991, 45.9 % of African American children were poor compared to 16.1% of White children (U.S. Bureau of Census, 1992). In this same year, researchers reported that single mothers were raising 54% of African American children, while White single mothers were raising 16.5% of White children. The impact of domestic violence, abuse, substance abuse, and neglect contribute to the deleterious development of youth (Resnick, Burt,

Newmark, & Reilly, 1992). These realities are universal in nature for all children, particularly for those marginalized by society. Unfortunately, the realities of marginalized people create a stereotype that is reinforced through interventions. (See McLoyd, Hill, & Dodge (2005) for a comprehensive review of environmental factors experienced by African American children.)

In the often-reported and stereotypical pathology of African American children, pictures are drawn of the role models for African American boys in poverty as delinquent, sexually promiscuous, substance abusers and sellers, and gang members (Bing, 1991). To make matters worse, these boys usually become involved in criminal activity due to idle time, resulting from a lack of youth activities or employment options (McFate, 1989). Without experience and knowledge that contradicts the previously stated, too many teachers of African American children, accept such dogma, thereby perpetuating a stereotype, resulting in low expectations (Rosenthal & Jacobson, 1968). These carefully constructed pathologies have been cited as early as kindergarten (Slaughter-Defoe & Richards, 1995). Specifically, Slaughter-DeFoe and Richards (1995) express concern about the treatment of boys without regard to their emotional needs in "unreceptive schools" (p. 137). Gay (2000) speaks about the negative impact of the treatment of African American children in unresponsive schools. Specifically, acceptable behavior and learning preferences encouraged in the home culture are not tolerated and acknowledged in the school culture. While White boys are treated as "people," Black boys are treated as objects. This is reminiscent of the little Black girl's experience in Wiley's story.

The emotional, social, and academic experiences of the African American child during the early years are manifest in adolescence and adulthood. A body of research describes the stress reaction to many of the negative experiences as "differential negative feedback" throughout school in which students "disidentify" with academic success. In its place, adolescents place value in peer identity (Entwisle, Alexander, & Cadigan, 1987; Fordham & Ogbu, 1986; Hare & Castenell, 1985). These researchers further suggest that self-esteem is unrelated to academic success but to social networks where individual worth is linked to the worth of the social group. This network is also the place where many boys find role models, often adolescents. An important question at this point might be, "Is the disidentification with academic success a manifestation of marginalization?"

The education system, particularly classroom instruction, has a profound influence on African American children's experience. As early as 1968, educational researchers (Rosenthal & Jacobson, 1968) reported the effects of low teacher expectations and support on classroom learning. This success variable is further weakened by the incompatibilities between school and home. The disconnect between acceptable behaviors at home and school cultures presents a problem. Hale-Benson (1986), in her study of variables that contribute to the success of African American students, focused on learning styles, emotional expressions orientation toward people rather than objects, interpersonal relationships, and language (which is mostly nonverbal) to the compartmentalized teaching styles and behavior expectations of the school culture. The results of this study served to highlight the great dissonance between the goals of the home and those of school. Failure to consider this dissonance contributes to the misconceptions and misperceptions that teachers and society construct about the African American child. Furthermore, the misalignment of cognitive, affective, and behavioral dimensions in the school setting exacerbates negative academic achievement and further success for African American children.

The classroom is a formidable barrier to the success of African American boys. The amount of exposure teachers have to people of different cultures has an impact on their level of tolerance (Delpit, 1995; Howell, 1998). An important factor in understanding students of different cultures is the interaction a teacher engages in with students (H. Foster, 1986). Teachers are intolerant of "those loud Black girls," students playing the age-old dozens, and the "cool pose" of urban Black boys (Majors & Billson, 1992). African American boys may be at greater risk because of misperceptions and/or lower expectations. These students are often judged as less competent than their counterparts (Chinn & Hughes, 1987). Teachers's frames of reference different from those whom they are charged to teach. Wilson (1987) predicted that one-third to one-half of public school students are expected to be comprised of people of color, the majority group (Wilson, 1987). The make-up in special education is projected to reflect an alarming 60% to 80% of students of color (Almanza & Mosely, 1980). More recent data report 74% of elementary and secondary school teachers are female and 87% are White (American Association of Colleges of Teachers Education, 1999). Snyder (1999) suggested that the percentage of White teachers was as high as 90 percent in 1999. While 17 percent of K-12 students were identified as African American, only 4 percent of these students' teachers were African American (Freeman, Alfeld, & Vo, 2001). The question at this juncture is: How successful are the teachers of African American students? One method of analysis is the national achievement data and state data.

Academic Grade Achievement and African American Students

Nationally, African American students are underrepresented in advanced placement classes and overrepresented in special education classes. At the K-12 levels, African American students represent 17 percent of the 48,344,926 public school enrollees (The Education Trust, Fall 2006).

The hallmark in learning for all students is the extent to which they learn to read and ultimately learn information from reading. The National Assessment of Educational Progress (NAEP) provides national achievement data at grades four to eight. The NAEP reports the national reading performance of 4th grade students in 2005 at 30 percent for proficient and above. Sixty-two percent performed at the basic or above level. Two percent of African American 4th grade students performed at the advanced and 11 percent performed at the proficient levels, respectively. Fifty-nine percent performed at the basic level. In contrast, 10 percent of White students performed at the advanced and 30 percent performed at the proficient levels. At the basic and below-basic levels, White students performed at the 35 and 25 percent levels, respectively.

Placement data is crucial to understanding the educational opportunities experienced by African American children. While representing 17 percent of K-12 enrollment in 2002, African American students only represented 8 percent of students taught in gifted and talented classes. However, in 2002, they represented 23 percent of students taught in special education. African American children represented 36 percent of students suspended from public schools.

Comparatively, White students represented 59 percent of K-12 enrollment in 2002. Enrollment in gifted and talented classes for White students was 73 percent. Special education enrollment for white students was 58 percent. White students were suspended at 44 percent.

Education Stories from the African American Period

The participants who informed this story were comprised of two generations, reflecting the experiences of the Black students of the 1954 era and contemporary African American students. Specifically, the participants were Rita and Anthony and their son Jamal and daughter Rachel. The participants' date of birth and years of schooling defined their respective generations. Generational experiences provided an understanding of the issues faced by individual participants as well as revealing cohort information related to gender constructed across generations.

Four participants informed this story. Two participants were the biological parents of the other two participants. Both of the parents were born in 1958 in what Collins (2003) describes as the Black American period. Rachel was born in 1990 and Jamal was born in 1992. Both participants were born during what Collins (2003) describes as the African American period.

Both parent participants grew up in a large metropolitan area in the state of Texas and attended urban schools. Anthony attended segregated schools through 6th grade and integrated schools from 7th through high-school graduation. Rita attended segregated schools through 4th grade and integrated schools from 5th grade through high-school graduation. As the mothers of both participant parents were teachers who were transferred to White schools at integration, both of the parent participants accompanied his and her mother to the integrated school. Subsequently, both parent participants were bussed to an integrated high school. Each parent grew up in different Black neighborhoods. Both parent participants were college graduates.

As both parents worked full-time, both of the student participants attended day care facilities from ages three months to ages nine and seven. At ages five and three, the respective student participants moved from an apartment to a suburban home. The female student participant attended day care facilities owned and operated by African American females through age five. At age five, the female student attended an after school program, while her brother attended an all day care program. When the male student participant began public school at the age of five, he joined his sister in attending an after school programs. She attended integrated after-school day-care facilities through age nine. She then attended an after-school program provided at a predominantly African American church she attended until age 11.

Autoethnographic Story: Family Telling

Parents want the best for their children. We were no different. Expecting our first child set in motion a lifestyle change we anticipated for seven years. A miscarriage a few years earlier made this pregnancy even more valuable. Because we would be new parents, we read from cover to cover the books our doctor's office gave us on expecting a newborn. My wife painstakingly monitored her diet by regularly eating just the right amounts of squash, broccoli, cauliflower, green beans and other vegetables she rarely ate prior to this pregnancy. She ate more fish, less meat and as prescribed by her physician, kept crackers beside our bed for an upset stomach.

We based our home purchase on location. Essentially, we moved to a home that was approximately 15 minutes from both of our jobs. Our planned community home was in an urban suburban school district that achieved top local and state achievement ranking. We knew when we moved into this community that approximately 10% or less of the district's population was African American. Optimistically, we believed our roots in family, church and our ties to our communities of origin could fill any gaps in our school district. We also felt that our family's background as educators would help make our children successful. Family friends also gave us a confidence of capital to be successful in our district.

First Impressions. *With our optimism, we took our 5-year-old daughter to enroll her in half-day kindergarten at our community school. A major image we encountered was an all White office, faculty, and staff. This was contrasted by the all Black custodial and mostly Black cafeteria staff. Thinking on our feet, we began introducing our daughter to the custodial and cafeteria staff. I knew that these people would be important to our daughter and if she needed protection, they would protect her. I observed my mother interact with all people when I was in elementary school. She car-pooled with a custodian,* *who she socialized with after work and depended on and was depended on to do things friends do such as take care of each other's children, share recipes, lunches, and even borrow and lend lunch money. This friend and others who held different positions (cafeteria staff, school secretary, grounds persons, counselor, principal, teachers) was my mother's support group. As her support group, she did not worry about the treatment her children received when they attended school. I knew, as did my siblings, that these people were my parents in my parents' absence.*

Unlike the disinterested responses we received from the principal, assistant principal and office staff, the custodians, and cafeteria workers warmly greeted us. Interesting, as we conversed with the custodial and cafeteria staff, the principal or other White personnel redirected any custodian or cafeteria worker to another task, thereby preempting our brief conversations.

We met our daughter's kindergarten teacher. She was the school's assistant principal for our daughter's grade. As she explained her classroom rules to us, I could not help but wonder how she would manage her two jobs. When asked, she explained that because of the growth of the school, particularly kindergarten students, it was necessary to add another class. However, the school was unsuccessful in hiring a teacher on short notice. While our optimism began to fade, we decided to remain positive.

In the fall, our daughter entered kindergarten. She made many friends. She loved her teacher. She was always in high spirits and seemed to enjoy school. However, reports received from school indicated she had trouble "following" directions. After talking with her teacher on several occasions, I scheduled an appointment with the teacher. After signing-in at the front office, I went to the classroom where the teacher was waiting for me.

I met with the teacher in the afternoon, right after morning class, as this is when she functioned as assistant principal. Upon entering the classroom after the morning class, the neatness of the classroom made me wonder if children were ever here. Everything seemed to be in its place. Commercial material filled the bulletin boards. Blocks and toys were all neatly in their place. Student desks were neat and in straight rows and columns. Nothing in this classroom was out of place and the teacher was dressed immaculately.

Immediately, she told me that our daughter was too sociable and that this prevented her from remaining on task. As she talked, she explained to me that other children had this same problem. When talking about other children, she described them as "those day-care kids" who require more structure than kids who are not in day care. By now, my wife had joined the meeting. The teacher went on to tell us all the things our daughter could not do, but nothing she could do. One problem this teacher identified was behavior. We asked her to explain what she meant. An example she gave was when our daughter went to the restroom. She explained that our daughter made loud noises when she went to the restroom. I asked her to be more specific. She continued to be vague. Initially, I thought she meant she made noises when she had a bowel movement. Instead, and after being pressed, the teacher stated she sang loudly when in the restroom. When asked if she told our daughter not to sing in the restroom, she stated she had not. The teacher provided no explanation for not telling her student not to sing loudly in the bathroom. The teacher stated that students should know the appropriateness of certain behaviors. As in many future conversations with school personnel, we asked this teacher to explain how our daughter would know the appropriateness and the expectations of behaviors unless she was informed.

By Thanksgiving, we knew we had to move our daughter out of this teacher/principal's classroom. At a meeting with multiple district personnel, I struck up a conversation with a Black principal in my district, but at another school. I had accompanied a coworker to this principal's school on designated multicultural days. I got the impression that she expected her teachers to be culturally responsive to the needs of children. After telling this principal who my daughter's teacher was and about her attitude and perception of our daughter, she told us to transfer her to her school.

After the Christmas break, we transferred our daughter to another school in our district. Unfortunately, our hopes were crushed and the imagined promises of a more culturally responsive environment, even with a Black principal, never materialized. We went from a teacher/principal who stereotyped children to a teacher who was ineffective and maybe even incompetent. Because of the concern about the new teacher's poor teaching skills, on weekends we enrolled our daughter in a commercial skill-building program.

Our daughter loved her new teacher. However, when we met with our daughter's new teacher, she told us things like, "...[your daughter] invades the other children's space...she doesn't know how to remain in her own space." When I observed our daughter, it was true, she did invade the space of others—but so did most of the other children. One or two children, who sat very still, remained in their tiny imaginary box the teacher explained as their space. Another observation I made was that our daughter was ignored in this classroom. When the teacher asked a question, she consistently called on the same students who sat near her. When asked about this practice, the teacher responded that our daughter usually did not have the correct answer. In spite of her teacher's behavior, our daughter still adored her teacher.

As on this occasion and after subsequent observations, we met with the principal. She grew increasingly annoyed with us, stating to us that we should have known what we were moving into—. On one of the last occasions, she told us that she had worked hard to build the "self-concept and esteem" of our daughter's teacher and that we were tearing it down. Near the end of the semester, our daughter reported to my wife that the principal called her into her office and screamed and yelled at her that she had better behave in class. The next day my wife confronted the principal, who denied the incident. Our transfer for the next year was denied.

Warnings came from veteran administrators as well as family members. They warned that we should not confront the teacher or the school because we "are not with [our daughter] when she is at school" and this could cause her harm. Of course, we did not want any harm to come to our daughter. However, we began to weigh the harm that we were observing and the projected harm predicted by others. During this time, we observed a confidence in our daughter about herself that did not generalize into her confidence about her schoolwork. Specifically, when asked to demonstrate to us an academic skill, she resisted. The confidence she began school with had dwindled. After multiple meetings and observations of our daughter in her classroom and the relationships with various teachers, I decided that not intervening would be more harmful than intervening in our daughter's schooling.

Over the years, intervening in the form of advocating and in some instances activist activities has been more beneficial than not intervening. On all occasions, I felt it important to know the schools' policies and procedures regarding entering a school building and going to a classroom. I have also made it a point to insist that my children respect their teachers and administrators in spite of their behavior. We have taught our children not to talk back or to talk in an inappropriate way to any teacher. However, I also encourage them to bring to us any problem, with the understanding that we will deal with it. They rarely bring problems to us.

On multiple occasions, I have observed both of our children in their classrooms. When our daughter was in an early grade, one of her teachers suggested in a parent teacher conference that I not inform my daughter beforehand that I would be observing her. The teacher suggested that our daughter's behavior would change. During the conference, I informed the teacher and the administrators at the table that when I schedule to observe my daughter, not only is the teacher notified, but also my daughter. I informed them that just as the teacher is aware of the reason for my observation, I also feel it necessary to inform my daughter. This serves multiple purposes. First, the visit alerts my daughter that there is a problem and it allows her to discuss this problem in detail with her parents. I have been amazed that in most instances, that the teacher had not discussed with our daughter that there was a problem, but sent notification to us about a problem. Second, notification allowed our daughter the opportunity to change her *behavior to that desired by her teacher and for me to observe this behavior. Finally, the notification allowed me to compare our daughter's behavior to that of her classmates. This has been the most informative aspect of all observations that my wife and I have made over the years. Without fail, when we have observed our daughter, as well as our son, we have observed numerous other students in the same classroom behaving in the same manner. When asked why these students' behavior was not problematic, most teachers chose not to respond and the issue was always dropped. One thing I always try to do after an observation is to sit down with the teacher and an administrator and discuss what I observed. Nevertheless, we observed differential discipline practices by our daughter's teachers and by administrators as well.*

We have also addressed the differential instructional behaviors of our daughter's teachers. In the third grade, our daughter's language arts teacher told us that a first writing draft was evidence that our daughter required special education services. She suggested that the school be given permission to test our daughter. What this woman did not know was that my wife had a bachelor's degree in journalism and minored in English. She did not know that she had a master's degree in technical writing. She did not know that she currently teaching writing to college students. She did not know that I had a bachelor's degree in English and had taught high school English for five years. After we reviewed the draft, we asked this teacher to explain the problem with this first draft. She explained that the one-paragraph paper had sentence structure problems, but did not elaborate. I explained to the teacher that for a first draft it was not uncommon and that these problems are usually worked out during the second draft revision. My wife further identified the development of the topic sentence and detail sentences.

A loud voice yelled to us, "You need to do what you are told and let us…." This voice came from our daughter's math teacher. Just as loudly, I asked the teacher to explain what she meant by this statement. The principal silenced the teacher and we continued the meeting. The principal dismissed the language arts and the math teachers. We informed the principal and the remaining teachers that we did not appreciate our daughter not being taught and her teachers trying to convince us that she was the problem. We explained to the principal that we were going to thank neither her staff nor her for not teaching our daughter. Realizing that she had a situation on her hands, the principal quickly apologized for everything that had happened and of course assured us that she and her staff would do the best for our daughter.

Stories' Significance

On the surface, the reader may be inclined to view the story as commonplace. The reader may believe that most or all children have experiences similar to that described. Even if this were true, the impact of the similar treatment on African American children has a distinct outcome. Clearly, "policies, procedures, or practices that are neutral as written but have a disparate impact, in that they disproportionately deny opportunities to students from racial and ethnic minority groups, may have the effect of discrimination" (Markowitz, Garcia, & Eichelberger, 1997). This is evident, for example, in the way feedback, or the lack of, was given by teachers of our daughters. Rather, she was penalized for not knowing the hidden curriculum. This alone creates achievement gaps in African American children.

As a researcher, that is, someone who has taught and worked in public school systems and is familiar with school policies and procedures, I also know that securing an appropriate education is labor-intensive. As parent/educators, we believe that to get teachers to teach our children, we have to fight for or wrangle appropriate instruction out of teachers. We cannot imagine the confusion and disconnect experienced by parents who do not have insider status or knowledge of the workings of schools. The required persistence alone is demanding. As the math teacher suggested in the story, our involvement is different than what she desired. Our children's schools wanted parent involvement. Initially, we thought that meant engaging in a partnership with the schools. However, what we found was that meant coming into a school and being told what to do. It did not mean providing information about our children's learning. It did not mean collaborating with the school to make our children successful. On too many occasions, parent involvement meant participating in or sitting through "dog and pony" shows. These shows did not allow parents to provide input about the issues facing their children. An example of this occurred when a little White boy (who was also our daughter's friend) told our daughter that she could not do something because she was Black. In response, our daughter kicked the little boy and told him that she could do anything she wanted to do. After this altercation between the children, we received a call that evening from the principal. She nervously explained what our daughter had already explained to us. She wanted to assure us that this kind of thing does not happen at her elementary school. When I asked her what she planned to do to deal with the attitudes stated by the little boy, she responded by restating that that kind of thing does not happen at her school. She could not explain how it happened that time, however. I suggested to this principal that she provide diversity training to her staff. I further suggested to the principal that diversity understanding occur with her staff and the students. I explained to her that I was not surprised that the little boy stated this to our daughter. I explained that he was making public the attitude perpetuated by the varied actions of school personnel. He probably did not intend to hurt our daughter and upon reflection was probably saddened at what he had said. Nevertheless, I explained to the principal that what the little boy said to our daughter was an assault. Unfortunately, I believe the principal did not want the situation to escalate. Her goal, as has occurred with other principals, teachers, and staff, was to handle us. I gave similar suggestions to school personnel years later when our daughter and her friends told us that a student had been called a "nigger." The principal's response was that the situation had been contained.

So What Has Changed?

Change can only occur in the presence of stagnation. Stagnation may occur to perpetuate the status quo. It may occur because society is unsure of the direction to take. Stagnation may be symptomatic of the storm about to erupt or even the evidence that the storm has passed. To some, stagnation may represent a calm that is comfortable. The call for change often occurs when society demands something different or when those in power desire change.

The social, political, and educational climate experience of African American children during 1954 was one of change. African Americans without doubt had experienced change from previous periods. They emerged from slavery when education was legally denied. Any slave who received an education did so under great threat. Despite this threat, slaves secretly found ways to educate themselves or to be educated. However, the dominant view of society about freed slaves during this period was extremely negative and rejecting, thereby not deserving of an education. A major focus of this rejection centered on the physical being (e.g., body size and facial characteristics) of the African American.

African American children continued to experience change as they were granted access to a separate but equal education. The hallmarks of this period were disparate resources between Black and White students. The negative attitudes about African American children evolved into what scholars describe as the constructed deficits model or the "cultural deprivation paradigm" (Banks, 2004, p. 18).

No doubt the most significant change for the education of African Americans occurred after 1954. This period ushered in an atmosphere of unprecedented social change. In education, this change resulted in the legal dismantling of segregated education for African American children.

As African American children integrated the schools in the United States, they came to school with the stigma of slavery and the negative attitudes held by the agents of the educational institution. They integrated schools with great courage, but were perceived as disadvantaged because of their parentage, language, community, and lifestyles.

Attitudes and held perceptions were the catalyst for constructions such as biased assessment and the retardation paradigm. From these constructions emerged practices in special education that held large numbers of African American students captive in not only the educational milieu, but also limited their work potential.

Conclusion

In the American social and educational purview, there is in place social stratification systems that are reproduced for the purpose of perpetuating and legitimating the systems (McCarthy, 1993; Weber, 1946). These social stratification systems encompass smaller more microsystems that, in circular fashion, help to support the larger structure. Social scientists that provide discourse in this type of historical foundations include Georg Simmels, Karl Marx, Max Weber, and Emile Durkheim. Issues of cultural power that emerge as a means to stratify or re-legitimate systems are provided in the discourse of Michel Foucault (Foucault, 1980).

Philosophers who describe the stratification experiences of African Americans include Woodson (Du Bois, 1935; Woodson, 1919; Woodson, 1933), Du Bois (1935), and Washington (Harris, 1993). Contemporary philosophers include bell hooks and Cornell West (to name only two of many). Ideologies from all of these contributors imply the direct connection between the social context and educational practices. Hegemonic themes specifically connect the social context to origins in educational practices. These themes have transcended multiple generations and serve to reproduce and re-legitimize social status in the school setting.

References

Almanza, H. P. & Mosely, W. J. (1980). Curriculum adaptations and modifications for culturally diverse handicapped children. *Exceptional Children, 46*, 608–614.

American Association of Colleges for Teacher Education. (1999). *Teacher education pipeline IV: Schools, colleges, and departments of education*. Washington, DC: AACTE.

Anderson, J. D. (1988). *The education of Blacks in the south, 1860–1915*. Chapel Hill: The University of North Carolina Press.

Atado, F. J. C. (1988). *African marriage customs and church law*. Kano, Nigeria: Modern Printers.

Azibo, D. A. Y. (1992). Understanding the proper and improper usage of the comparative research framework. In A. K. H. Burlew, W. C. Banks, H. P. McAdoo & D. A. y. Azibo (Eds.), *African American psychology: Theory, research, and practice* (pp. 18–27). Newbury Park, CA: Sage Publications.

Banks, J. A. (2001). *Cultural diversity and education: Foundations, curriculum, and teaching*. Boston, MA: Allyn and Bacon.

Banks, J. A. (2004). Multicultural education: Historical development, dimensions, and practice. In J. A. Banks & C. A. M. Banks (Eds.), *Handbook of research on multicultural education* (2nd ed.). San Francisco, CA: Jossey-Bass.

Barbarin, O. A., McCandies, T., Coleman, C., & Hill, N. E. (2005). Family practices and school performance of African American children. In V. C. McLoyd, N. E. Hill & K. A. Dodge (Eds.), *African American family life: Ecological and cultural diversity*. New York: The Guilford Press.

Becker, H. S. (1952). Social class variations in teacher–pupil relationships. *Journal of Educational Sociology, 25*, 451–465.

Billingsley, A. (1992). *Climbing Jacob's ladder*. New York: Simon & Schuster.

Bing, L. (1991). *Do or die*. New York: Harper Collins.

Bowles, S., & Gintis, H. (1976). *Schooling in capitalist America*. New York: Basic Books.

Brown, L. M., Argyris, D., Attanucci, J., Bardige, B., Gilligan, C., Johnson, K., et al. (1988). *A guide to reading narratives of conflict and choice for self and voice*. Cambridge, MA: Harvard University Press.

Bullock, H. A. (1967). *A history of Negro education in the south: from 1619 to the present*. Cambridge, MA: Harvard University Press.

Cannella, G. S. (1997). *Deconstructing early childhood education: Social justice and revolution*. New York: Peter Lang.

Caputo, J. D. (Ed.). (1997). *Deconstruction in a nutshell*. New York: Fordham University Press.

Chaikin, A. L., Sigler, E., & Derlega, V. J. (1974). Nonverbal mediators of teacher expectancy effects. *Journal of Personality and Social Psychology, 30*, 144–149.

Chinn, P. C., & Hughes, S. (1987). Representation of minority students in special education classes. *Remedial and Special Education, 8*(4), 41–46.

Clark, K. B., & Clark, M. P. (1939). Segregation as a factor in the racial identification of Negro preschool children. *Journal of Experimental Education, 8*, 161–163.

Clark, K. B., & Clark, M. P. (1940). Skin color as a factor in racial identification and preferences in Negro children. *Journal of Negro Education, 19*, 341–350.

Coard, S. I., & Sellers, R. M. (2005). African American families as a context for racial socialization. In V. C. McLoyd, N. E. Hill & K. A. Dodge (Eds.), *African American family life: Ecological and cultural diversity*. New York: The Guilford Press.

Collier, C. (1998). *Acculturation: Implications for assessment, instruction, and intervention*. Ferndale, WA: CrossCultural Developmental Education Services.

Collins, D. R. (2003). *A multi-generational study of constructed perceptions of African Americans about their education*. Ann Arbor, MI: ProQuest: A published dissertation.

Cross, W. E. (1991). *Shades of Black: Diversity in African-American identity*. Philadelphia, PA: Temple University Press.

D'Alessio, M. (1990). Social representations of childhood: An implicit theory of development. In G. Duveen & B. Lloyd (Eds.), *Social representations and the development of knowledge* (pp. 70–90). Cambridge, UK: Cambridge University Press.

deCastell, S., & Luke, A. (1983). Defining literacy in North American schools: Social and historical conditions and consequences. *Journal of Curriculum Studies, 15*, 373–389.

Delpit, L. (1995). *Other people's children: Cultural conflict in the classroom*. New York: The New Press.

Derrida, J. (1976). *Of grammatology*. Baltimore, MD: John Hopkins University Press.

Derrida, J. (1979). *Positions*. Chicago, IL: University of Chicago Press.

Dotts, W. (1978). Black and white teacher attitude toward disadvantage and poverty. *Education, 99*, 48–54.

Dryfoos, J. (1990). *Adolescents at risk: Prevalence and prevention*. New York: Oxford University Press.

Du Bois, W. E. B. (1909). *The Negro American family*. Atlanta, GA: Atlanta University.

Du Bois, W. E. B. (1935). *Black reconstruction in America*. New York: Atheneum.

Duffey, J. B., Salvia, J., Tucker, J., & Ysseldyke, J. (1981). Nonbiased assessment: A need for operationalism. *Exceptional

Children, 47, 427–434.

Dunn, L. M. (1968). Special education for the mildly retarded: Is much of it justifiable? *Exceptional Children, 23,* 5–21.

Entwisle, D. R., Alexander, K. L., & Cadigan, D. (1987). The emergent academic self-image of first graders: Its response to social structure. *Child Development, 58*(5), 1190–1206.

Fordham, S., & Ogbu, J. U. (1986). Black students' school success: Coping with the burden of "acting White." *Urban Review, 18*(3), 176–206.

Foster, H. (1986). *Ribbin,' jivin,' and playin' the dozens.* Cambridge: Ballinger Publishing Company.

Foster, M. (1997). *Black teachers on teaching.* New York: The New Press.

Foucault, M. (1980). Truth and power. In C. Gordon (Ed.), *Power and knowledge: Selected interviews and other writings 1972–1977* (pp. 109–133). New York: Pantheon Books.

Freeman, K. E., Alfeld, C., & Vo, Q. (2001). *African American teachers: Just the facts.* Fairfax, VA: Frederick D. Patterson Research Institute.

Gay, G. (2000). *Culturally responsive teaching: Theory, research, & practice.* New York: Teachers College Press.

Gillborn, D. (2001). Racism, policy and the (mis) education of Black children in R. Majors *Educating our Black children: New directions and radical approaches* (pp. 13–27). New York: RoutledgeFalmer.

Glazer, N. & Moynihan, D. (1963). *Beyond the melting pot: The Negroes, Puerto Ricans, Jews, Italians, and Irish in New York City.* Cambridge, MA: MIT Press.

Gordon, A. H. (1971). *Sketches of Negro life and history in South Carolina* (2nd ed.). Columbia, SC: University of South Carolina Press.

Grant, L. (1985). Race-gender, classroom interaction, and children's socialization in elementary school. In L. Wilkinson & C. Marrett (Eds.), *Gender influences in classroom interaction* (pp. 57–78). Orlando: Academic Press.

Hale-Benson, J. E. (1986). *Black children: Their roots, culture, and learning styles.* Baltimore, MD: The Johns Hopkins University Press.

Hare, B. R. & Castenell, L. A. (1985). No place to run, no place to hide: Comparative status and future prospects of Black boys. In M. B. Spencer, B. K. Brookins & W. R. Allen (Eds.), *Beginnings: The social and affective development of Black children* (pp. 201–214). Hillsdale, NJ: Erlbaum.

Harris, T. E. (1993). *Analysis of the clash over the issues between Booker T. Washington and W.E. B. Du Bois.* New York: Garland Publishing.

Harris, V. J. (1995). Historic readers for African-American children (1868–1944): Uncovering and reclaiming a tradition of opposition. In M. J. Shujaa (Ed.), *Too much schooling, too little education: A paradox of Black life in White societies* (pp. 143–175). Trenton, NJ: Africa World Press, Inc.

Harvey, M. R. (1980). Public school treatment of low-income children. *Urban Education, 15,* 279–323.

Hill, R. (1993). *Research on the African-American family: A holistic perspective.* Westport, CT: Auburn House.

Holliday, B. G. (1985). Towards a model of teacher-child transactional processes affecting Black children's academic achievement. In M. B. Spencer, B. K. Brookings & W. R. Allen (Eds.), *Beginnings: The social and affective development of Black children* (pp. 117–130). Hillsdale, NJ: Erlbaum.

Horowitz, R., & Murphy, L. B. (1938). Projective methods in the psychological study of children. *Journal of Experimental Education, 7,* 133–140.

Howell, D. W. (1998). *I was a slave: The lives of slave children.* Washington, DC: American Legacy.

Hughes, D., Rodriguez, J., Smith, E. P., Johnson, D. J., Stevenson, H. C., & Spicer, P. (2006). Parents' ethnic-racial socialization practices: A review of research and directions for future study. *Developmental Psychology, 42*(5), 747–770.

Institute of Medicine. (1985). *Preventing low birthweight.* Washington, DC: Committee to Study the Prevention of Low Birthweight, National Academy Press.

Jahoda, G. (1982). *Psychology and anthropology.* London: Academic Press.

Jensen, A. R. (1969). How much can we boost IQ and scholastic achievement? *Harvard Educational Review, 39,* 1–123.

Johnson, C., Miranda, L., Sherman, A., & Weil, J. (1991). *Child poverty in America.* Washington, DC: Children's

Defense Fund.

Klaus, R., & Gray, S. (1968). *The early training project for disadvantaged children: A report after five years* (No. 4, Serial No. 120): Monographs of the Society for Research in Child Development.

Lamb, V. L., Land, K. C., Meadows, S. O., & Traylor, F. (2005). Trends in African American child well-being, 1985–2001. In V. C. McLoyd, N. E. Hill & K. A. Dodge (Eds.), *African American family life: Ecological and cultural diversity.* New York: The Guilford Press.

Leloudis, J. L. (1996). *Schools in the new south: Pedagogy, self, and society in North Carolina, 1880–1920.* Chapel Hill, NC: The University of North Carolina Press.

Lewis, O. (1970). *Anthropological essays.* New York: Random House.

Lincoln, Y. S., & Guba, E. G. (1985). *Naturalistic inquiry.* Newbury Park, CA: Sage.

Majors, R., & Billson, J. M. (1992). *Cool pose: The dilemmas of Black manhood in America.* New York: Lexington Books.

Marcus, G., Gross, S., & Seefeldt, C. (1991). Black and White students' perceptions of teacher treatment. *Journal of Educational Research, 84*(6), 363–367.

Markowitz, J., Garcia, S. B., & Eichelberger, J. (1997). Appendix B: Application of Title XI of the Civil Rights Act of 1964 and Section 504 of the Rehabilitation Act of 1973. In O. Markowitz, S. B. Garcia & J. Eichelberger (Eds.), *Addressing the disproportionate representation of students from racial and ethnic minority groups in special education: A resource document* (p. 55). Alexandria, VA: Office of Special Education Programs, U.S. Department of Education.

Marks, B., Settles, I. H., Cooke, D. Y., Morgan, L., & Sellers, R. M. (2004). African American racial identity: A review of contemporary models and measures. In R. L. Jones (Ed.), *Black psychology* (4th ed., pp. 383–404). Hampton, VA: Cobb & Henry.

McCarthy, C. (1993). Beyond the poverty and theory in race relations: Nonsynchrony and social difference in education. In L. Weis & M. Fine (Eds.), *Beyond silenced voices: Class, race, and gender in United States schools* (pp. 325–345). Albany: State University of New York Press.

McFate, K. (1989). Crime, drugs and the urban poor. *Joint Center for Political and Economic Studies, Urban Poverty Roundtable No. 5* (November).

McLoyd, V. C., Hill, N. E., & Dodge, K. A. (2005). Ecological and cultural diversity in African American family life. In V. C. McLoyd, N. E. Hill & K. A. Dodge (Eds.), *African American Family Life* (pp. 3–20). New York: The Guilford Press.

Menkiti, I. A. (1984). Person and community in African traditional thought. In R. A. Wright (Ed.), *African philosophy.* Lanham, MD: University Press of America.

Middlekauff, R. (1961). Education in Colonial America. *Current History, 41*(July), 5–8.

Moon, H. (1972). *The emerging thought of W.E.B Du Bois.* New York: Simon and Schuster.

Moynihan, D. P. (1965). *The Negro family: A case for national action.* Washington, DC: U. S. Government Printing Office.

Norris, C., Fielding, N., Kemp, C., & Fielding, J. (1992). Black and blue: An analysis of the influence of race on being stopped by the police. *British Journal of Sociology, 43*(2), 207–224.

Nsamenang, A. B. (1992). *Human development in cultural context: A third world perspective.* New York: Sage.

Oaks, J. (1982). Classroom social relationships: Exploring the Bowles and Gintis hypothesis. *Sociology of Education, 55,* 197–212.

Palakow, V. (1993). *Lives on the edge: Single mothers and their children in the other America.* Chicago, IL: University of Chicago Press.

Parker, S., Greer, S., & Zuckerman, B. (1988). Double jeopardy: The impact of poverty on early child development. *Pediatric Clinics of North America, 35*(6), 1–4.

Phinney, J. S. (1992). The multi-group ethnic identity measure: A new scale for use with diverse groups. *Journal of Adolescent Research, 7*(2), 156–176.

Pratte, R. (1973). *The public school movement: A critical study.* New York: David McKay.

Quintana, S. M. (2007). Racial and ethnic identity: Developmental perspectives and research. *Journal of Counseling*

Psychology, 54(3), 259–270.

Resnick, G., Burt, M. R., Newmark, L., & Reilly, L. (1992). *Youth at risk: Definitions, prevalence and approaches to service delivery.* Washington, D.C.: The Urban Institute.

Rist, R. C. (1970). Student social class and teacher expectations: The self-fulfilling prophecy in ghetto education. *Harvard Educational Review, 40,* 411–449.

Rosenthal, R., & Jacobson, L. (1968). *Pygmalion in the classroom: Teacher expectations and pupils' intellectual development.* New York: Holt, Rinehart & Winston.

Ross, S. I., & Jackson, J. M. (1991). Teachers' expectations for Black males' and Black females academic achievement. *Personality and Social Psychology Bulletin, 17*(1), 78–82.

Sarason, S., & Doris, J. (1979). *Educational handicap, public policy, and social history: A broadened perspective on mental retardation.* New York: Free Press.

Schein, E. H. (1972). *Professional education.* New York: McGraw-Hill.

Shujaa, M. J. (1995). Education and schooling: You can have one without the other. In M. J. Shujaa (Ed.), *Too much schooling, too little education: A paradox of Black life in White societies* (pp. 13–36). Trenton, NJ: Africa World Press, Inc.

Sizemore, B. (1978). Education: Integration, welfare, and achievement. In F. Aquila (Ed.), *School desegregation: A model at work* (pp. 13–23). Bloomington: School of Education.

Skrtic, T. M. (1995). Power/Knowledge and pragmatism: A postmodern view of the professions. In T. M. Skrtic (Ed.), *Disability and democracy: Reconstructing (special) education for postmodernity* (pp. 25–62). New York: Teachers College Press.

Slaughter-DeFoe, D. T., Nakagawa, K., Takanishi, R., & Johnson, D. J. (1990). Toward cultural/ecological perspectives on schooling and achievement in African- and Asian-American children. *Child Development, 61,* 363–383.

Slaughter-Defoe, D. T., & Richards, H. (1995). Literacy for empowerment: The case of Black males. In V. L. Gadsden & D. A. Wagner (Eds.), *Literacy among African-American youth: Issues in learning, teaching, and schooling* (pp. 125–147). Cresskill, NJ: Hampton Press, Inc.

Smedley, A. (1993). *Race in North America: Origin and evolution of a worldview.* San Francisco, CA: Westview Press.

Snyder, T. (1999). *Digest of education statistics 1998.* Washington, DC: National Center for Education Statistics, U.S. Department of Education.

Swadener, B. B., & Lubeck, S. (1995). The social construction of children and families "at risk": An introduction. In B. B. Swadener & S. Lubeck (Eds.), *Children and families "at promise": Deconstructing the discourse of risk* (pp. 1–14). New York: State University of New York Press.

Swadener, B. B., & Lubeck, S. (Eds.). (1995). *Children and families "at promise."* New York: State University of New York Press.

Taylor, C. P. (1976). *Transforming schools: A social perspective.* New York: St. Martin's Press.

The Education Trust. (Fall 2006). *Education watch: The nation, key education facts and figues:* The Education Trust.

Tomlinson, S. (1995). The radical structuralist view of special education and disability: Unpopular perspectives on their origins and development. In T. M. Skrtic (Ed.), *Disability and democracy: Reconstructing (special) education for postmodernity* (pp. 122–149). New York: Teachers College Press.

Turnbull, H. R. (1990). *Free appropriate public education: The law and children with disabilities.* Denver, CO: Love Publishing.

Tyack, J. B. (1974). *The one best system.* Cambridge, MA: Harvard University Press.

U.S. Bureau of Census. (1992). Poverty in the United States. *Current Population Reports* (Vol. Series P-60). Washington, DC: U.S. Government Printing Office.

Walberg, H. J., & Rasher, S. P. (1979). Achievement in fifty states. In H. J. Walberg (Ed.), *Educational environments and effects* (pp. 353–369). Berkeley, CA: McCutchan.

Washington, J. M. (1994). *Conversations with God.* New York: Harper Perennial.

Weber, M. (1946). Bureaucracy (H. H. Gerth & C. W. Mills, Trans.). In H. H. Gerth & C. W. Mills (Eds.), *From*

Max Weber: Essays in sociology (pp. 196–244). New York: Oxford University Press.

West, C. (1993). *Keeping faith: Philosophy and race in America.* New York: Routledge.

Wiley, R. (1992). *Why Black people tend to shout.* New York: Penguin Books.

Wilson, W. (1987). *The truly disadvantaged: The inner city, the underclass, and public policy.* Chicago, IL: University of Chicago Press.

Woodson, C. G. (1919). *The education of the Negro prior to 1861.* Brooklyn, NY: A&B Books Publishers.

Woodson, C. G. (1933). *The mis-education of the Negro.* Washington, DC: The Associated Publishers.

CHAPTER SIX

Critical Literacy and Young Children

A Case Study of Literacy Experiences of Six African American Children

M ELINDA M ILLER

Abstract

The educational system in the United States today is designed in such a way that the White, middle-class culture will be perpetuated. Middle-class children, in particular, White, middle-class children come to school equipped with the tools necessary to participate in the school culture, because they are already a part of the dominant culture (Delpit, 1988, 1995, in Power & Hubbard, 2002). Delpit contends that minority children need to be explicitly taught the codes and rules of the culture of power, in order to participate in the culture of power. Goodman (1965, 1973) has emphasized the need for acceptance of dialects that differ from school English in the classroom. Children need to become fluent readers in their own dialect before they can begin to learn school English. This study investigated the literacy experiences of six African American children in school, in the classroom, with special teachers, with mentors from the community, and at home. The author describes the ways in which these children make sense of their literacy experiences, the ways in which they experience literacy in the home, the ways in which they are allowed to acquire the culture of power, the handling of dialect in regard to these children, the ways in which learning is made relevant to the culture of these children, and the ways in which these children's culture is recognized and celebrated.

In *White Teacher*, Paley (1979) reflects on being a Jewish child in a Gentile school and feeling that her teachers denied her Jewishness by not acknowledging it. Paley relates her experience to the experiences of African American students, whose White teachers say, "There is no color difference in my classroom." All my children look alike to me." She quotes an African American mother as saying, "My children are black. They don't look like your children. They know they're black, and we want it recognized. It's a positive difference, an interesting difference, and a comfortable difference" (Paley, 1979, p. 12). To address the recognition of children's cultures, Banks recommends content integration, as one of the dimensions of multicultural education that should be included in the classroom. Content integration "deals with the extent to which teachers use examples and content from a variety of cultures and groups to illustrate key concepts, principles, generalizations, and theories in their subject area or discipline," according to Banks and Banks (1993, p. 21). Through the literature teachers choose to include in the classroom, "we have daily opportunities to affirm that our students lives and language are important and unique," according to Christensen (in Power & Hubbard, 2002, p.174).

Delpit (1988, 1995, in Power & Hubbard, 2002) points out that White, middle-class children come to school already equipped with the tools that they will need to communicate through oral and printed word in ways that ensure their success in the mainstream culture of the school. Christensen (in Power & Hubbard, 2002) describes how her blue-collar dialect was viewed as inferior, while her friend, whose ancestors arrived on the *Mayflower* spoke flawless English and even corrected Christensen's English. Though her friend had never been formally taught to speak the form of English accepted by school culture, she lived in a home where formal English was spoken. Because African American children and other minority children do not belong to the mainstream culture—the culture of the school—Delpit contends that they need to be explicitly taught the rules and conventions of the mainstream culture in order to survive in school. Ken Goodman (1965, 1973) stresses that an African American child's dialect should be accepted and respected by the school while that child is learning the rules of school English. Christensen states that when teachers focus on the correctness of grammar rather than the child's message, "students words and thoughts become devalued" (p. 174), and they learn silence. According to Wolfram (in Power & Hubbard, 2002), "variation in speech is at the core of social and historical identity, interwoven into the fabric of cultural differences" (p. 256). He emphasizes the importance of a teacher's acceptance of a child's dialect. He recommends open and frank discussions about dialects in the classroom.

As African American children develop literacy, there are many factors that affect the ease with which they learn dominant classroom knowledge. At the same time that they are learning to read and write, they are also having to learn a new culture and a new language as well as learning how to act and what to do in a school from a different culture.

Critically Exploring the Issues

The educational system in the United States today is designed in such a way that the White, middle-class culture will be perpetuated. Middle-class children, in particular, White, middle-class children come to school equipped with the tools necessary to participate in the school culture, because they are already a part of the dominant culture (Delpit, 1988, 1995, in Power & Hubbard, 2002). Delpit concludes that members of a culture transmit cultural rules and codes to co-members implicitly. She states that "when implicit codes are attempted across cultures, communication frequently breaks down" (p. 123). Thus, Delpit contends, minority children need to be explicitly taught the codes and rules of the culture of power in order to participate in the culture of power. Teachers must make an effort to learn how to teach reading and writing to students whose culture and language differ from that of the school according to Delpit (in Power & Hubbard, 2002, p. 124.)

Goodman (1965, 1973) has emphasized the need for acceptance of dialects that differ from school English in the classroom. Children need to become fluent readers in their own dialect before they can begin to learn school English. Goodman further states that a teacher should attend to a child's meaning instead of making corrections for dialect. Derman-Sparks & the ABC Task Force(1989), Paley (1979, 1995), Ladson-Billings (1994), Hale (1982), and Christensen (in Power & Hubbard, 2002) discuss the need for making learning relevant for all cultures represented in the classroom rather than teaching to the dominant culture. They stress that each culture should be recognized, celebrated, and valued.

This study investigated the literacy experiences of six African American children in school, in the classroom, with special teachers, with mentors from the community, and at home. I looked at the ways in which children make sense of their literacy experiences, the ways in which they experience literacy at home, the ways in which they are allowed to acquire the culture of power, the handling of dialect, the ways in which learning is made relevant to culture by teachers, and the ways in which the children's multiple cultural experiences are recognized and celebrated.

Philosophical Perspectives of the Research—The Naturalistic Paradigm

Lincoln and Guba (1985) define "paradigm" as a "system of ideas" and a "systematic set of beliefs" (p. 15). I have approached my study from the naturalistic paradigm. Lincoln and Guba (1985) describe the naturalistic paradigm as involving the nature of reality, or ontology. In the naturalistic paradigm, there are "multiple realities that can be studied only holistically" (p. 37). As each question within the study is raised, the study continues to emerge. Also, in the naturalistic paradigm, the knower and the known cannot be separated; and the research applies only to a particular case and cannot be generalized to other situations. The reader of the research makes the generalizations. "Causal links" are not established in the naturalistic paradigm, according to Lincoln and Guba" (p. 38). The authors go on to describe naturalistic research as being, "value bound" (p. 38), and they stress the importance of doing the research in the natural setting of the participant, so as to get a more holistic understanding of the meaning of the situation.

Research Questions

The purpose of this study was, therefore, to attempt to understand the naturalistic literacy experiences of these six African American children to explore the multiple realities that constitute their literacy lives. The following questions served as guides for the initiation of the study:

1. What are the literacy experiences of selected African American children (a) in the classroom? (b) in the special education classroom? and (c) with a mentor?
2. From the parents' perspective, what are the child's literacy experiences (a) at home? and (b) as a reader and writer?
3. How does the child see himself or herself as a reader and writer?

Significance

According to Delpit (1988, 1995, in Power & Hubbard, 2002), African American children, along with other minority children, need to be explicitly taught the skills and conventions of writing that will enable them to participate in the dominant culture. As I studied these six children, I looked for ways in which their literacy experiences contribute to their acquisition of the culture of power. Hale

(1982), Ladson-Billings (1994), Derman-Sparks (1989), and Christensen (in Power & Hubbard, 2002) contend that a teacher should strive to teach to the cultures of all of the children in the classroom to insure that the learning is made meaningful for them and to insure that each child feels that his or her culture is recognized and valued. It was my intent to observe ways in which these African American children's culture is addressed and ways in which learning is made relevant for them.

Hale (1982) states that African American children tend to have different learning experiences from mainstream children, because of the cultural differences in the African American homes. For instance, African American children who are allowed complete freedom of movement at home are labeled "hyperactive" or "ADHD" at school. According to Ladson-Billings (1994), African American children bring many cultural strengths with them to the classroom that are "rarely capitalized on by teachers" (p. 17). Ladson-Billings gives the example of African American children's rich language, which is "useful in both community and work settings" (p. 17), to which the school assigns little value, labeling it as "non-standard English." Ladson-Billings goes on to describe how teachers' racist attitudes can cause them to have low expectations of African American students. Such low expectations are often brought about, states Ladson-Billings, by the "mainstream society's invalidation of African American culture" (p. 22). Goodman (1965, 1973) stresses the importance of a teacher valuing a child's language and responding to the child's meaning, rather than correcting language that deviates from school English. As a part of the study, I have made observations of teachers' and other adults' reactions and responses to the children's dialects.

Methodology

The research was conducted using qualitative methodology. Qualitative methods are usually preferred over quantitative methods by proponents of the naturalistic paradigm because "they are more adaptable to dealing with multiple (and less aggregatable) realities" (Lincoln & Guba, 1985, p. 40). According to Denzin and Lincoln (2000), "qualitative researchers stress the socially constructed nature of reality, the intimate relationship between the researcher and what is studied, and the situational constraints that shape inquiry" (p. 8). In qualitative inquiry, the researcher strives to understand the meaning that the participants assign to their experiences.

Participants

I chose eight African American children, who had previously been in the Reading Recovery program in a southwestern small town community. Six of the children went to the same school—an elementary school where most of the minority children of the relatively small Texas (United States) town attended school. One of the other children went to the intermediate school next door, where all of the fifth and sixth graders from the town went to school. The eighth child had just moved from the elementary school where all the others went, to an elementary school across town that was predominately White.

From the original eight, two dropped out because their parents never gave permission. I wondered if the two mothers became anxious about the study when faced with signing an official document. Or perhaps they had a problem with a White woman studying African American children, or maybe they did not trust me.

The six children in the study were David, a first grade (6-year-old) boy; Jannell, a second grade (7-year-old) girl; Marvin, a second grade boy; Rene, a second grade girl; Devonshire, a third grade (8-year-old) boy; and Jacolby, a fifth grade (10-year-old) boy, who is also Marvin's brother. Jacolby's and Marvin's mother is named Kim; Ellen is Jannell's mother; Jenny is David's mother, and Carrie is Rene's mother. Devonshire is being raised by his grandmother, Francine. David, Jannell, and Devonshire were my Reading Recovery students. Rene, Jacolby, and Marvin were Reading Recovery students of my colleague in the next classroom. In my role as Reading Specialist, I also held special reading classes for small groups of children. Rene and Marvin came to my reading class in second grade, and Jacolby came to my class in the third grade.

I observed the six children in various natural settings, including the classroom, special classrooms, the lunchroom, the home, and the playground. Two of the children came to my classroom for about 30 minutes each day. During the time that they were in my classroom, I did participant observation. I observed them in their regular classrooms several times for about three hours each time. I observed the four students who did not come to my classroom several times in their own classrooms for three to five hours each time. I also interviewed the children, the children's teachers and special teachers, the children's mentors, and the parents. I gathered documents relevant to their literacy experiences, such as anecdotal records taken by the teacher, checklists of skills kept by the teacher, writing pieces, audio tapes, running records taken during reading, and any other records used by the teachers.

Collecting Information

Observations

I went to each child's classroom on the average of five times to make observations of their classroom literacy experiences. I usually stayed for three hours per visit. I sat and watched the activities, or I walked around and looked closely at the work the participants and other children were doing. When the participants went to special classes, I followed them, talking with them on the way. I followed all of the elementary participants to the playground to watch their interaction with their classmates in play situations. Jacolby did not have a playground period on any of the days that I visited his school. As I visited the participants' homes for interviews, I also made observations of their environment, as well as their interactions with siblings and parents. On one occasion, Jacolby gave me a guided tour of his family's new house while I was there to interview him and his mother. I made detailed field notes of all of my observations, writing constantly during the classroom visits. When I ate lunch with the children, watched them on the playground, or observed them in their homes, I made my field notes afterwards. As soon after taking the notes as possible, I transcribed them, so that they would be easier to read, more organized, and easier to analyze.

My observations were completed within a six-month time frame. Lincoln and Guba (1985) state that "a major advantage of direct observation…is that it provides here-and-now experiences in depth" (p. 273). The authors also state, "The basic methodological arguments for observation, then, may be summarized as these: observation…maximizes the inquirer's ability to grasp motives, beliefs, concerns, interests, unconscious behaviors, customs, and the like; observation…allows the inquirer to see the world as his subjects see it, to live in their time frames, to capture the phenomenon in and on its own terms, and to grasp the culture in its own natural, ongoing environment; observation… provides the inquirer with access to the emotional reactions of the group introspectively—that is, in a real sense it permits the observer to build on tacit knowledge, both his own and that of members of the group" (Guba & Lincoln, 1985, p. 193).

Participant Observation

Lincoln and Guba describe the role of the participant observer: "…the observer may act in either a participant or a nonparticipant mode; in the former instance, the observer has but one role to play, that of observer, but in the latter, he or she must play two roles simultaneously, that of observer *and* that of a legitimate and committed member of the group" (1985, p. 274). I acted as a participant observer in the observations that occurred in my own classroom. This was natural to me, as I was accustomed to taking detailed notes on literacy behaviors exhibited by the children during guided reading lessons, Reading Recovery lessons, and Herman Method lessons. Though I had notes on all of my students, I took more detailed notes on the participants, also noting conversation that they might occasionally have in the classroom.

All of my observations took place in natural settings. The natural setting, according to Lincoln and Guba, is "preferred to the contrived for the same reasons that the unstructured interview is preferred to the structured. In most instances, the inquirer is not sufficiently sure about what it is that he or she does not know to manipulate a setting to advantage" (1985, p. 274). To contrive a setting, they go on to say, is to change the outcome for participants who "take their meanings from their contexts" (1985, p. 274). Further, observations taken in a contrived setting are artificial and alter "the phenomenon being studied in fundamental ways" (1985, p. 274).

Interviews

I also conducted interviews with each of the six students, their parents, and their regular classroom teachers, and in some cases, their teachers from years past. Jacolby had a mentor from the community who came once a week for two years to work with him on reading and math. I interviewed his mentor as well.

I gave the parents, the children, the mentor, and the teachers a choice of where their interviews would take place. Some of the interviews took place in my classroom or other teachers' classrooms, and some of the interviews took place in the participants' homes.

I used the unstructured format with my interviews. I asked the participants open-ended questions, starting out with, for instance, "What can you tell me about your child's reading?" I then varied my questions according to their response. I tape recorded the interviews, unless the participants objected, and I took notes, as well. After the interviews, I transcribed the tapes, so that I could have them on paper for analysis.

Lincoln and Guba (1985) state that "the purposes for doing an interview include, among others, obtaining *here-and-now constructions* of persons, events, activities, organizations, feelings, motivations, claims, concerns, and other entities; *reconstructions* of such entities as experienced in the past; *projections* of such entities as they are expected to be experienced in the future; verification, emendation, and extension of information (constructions, reconstructions, or projections) obtained from other sources, human and nonhuman (*triangulation*); and verification, emendation, and extension of constructions developed by the inquirer (*member checking*)" (p. 268).

Lincoln and Guba go on to describe an unstructured interview. "In an unstructured interview," they state, "the format is non-standardized, and the interviewer does not seek normative responses. Rather, the problem of interest is expected to arise from the respondent's reaction to the broad issue raised by the inquirer" (1981, p. 155). In the unstructured interview, the respondent's perspective of the situation, as well as his or her construction of the meaning of the situation is stressed, state Lincoln and Guba. The respondent is allowed to include aspects of the situation that he or she believes to be important and relevant to the situation. Lincoln and Guba go on to state that in an unstructured interview, both the questions and the answers are provided by the interviewee.

Documents

I collected documents that relate to the literacy of the six children, such as running records taken by me and other teachers, report cards, anecdotal records of reading conferences, writing pieces, drawings with titles or labels, photographs, and audio tapes. I asked the teachers for writing samples and other work samples, and in most cases, they gave me the child's cumulative folder and allowed me to make copies of the contents.

At Rene's house, her mother brought out a big box of papers and allowed me to take it and make copies. Several of the teachers brought me copies of things as the children did in class. For the children who were in my classes, I made copies of everything that they did in my class. Rene's Herman Method group made audio tapes of themselves telling stories and reading stories. I made a transcription of Rene's tape before she took it home.

I also took several photographs of the children working, and some of them gave me one of their school pictures. A couple of the teachers gave me photographs that they had taken of the children working.

On several different occasions, the children would write me letters or give me Christmas cards, Valentine cards, or end-of-the-year cards. I kept all of these as documents. I gathered documents throughout the entire six-month duration of my study.

Lincoln and Guba (1985) discuss the value of document collection: Documents are "almost always *available*, on a low-cost (mostly investigator time) or free basis. Second, they are a *stable* source of information, both in the sense that they may accurately reflect situations that occurred at some time in the past and that they can be analyzed and reanalyzed without undergoing changes in the interim. Their richness includes the fact that they appear in the natural language of that setting" (pp. 276–277). The authors go on to state that documents are a good, authoritative source of information, and that they are "nonreactive" (p. 277), although the review of documents does involve interpretation on the part of the investigator.

Interpreting Possibilities

I combined the constant comparative method of analysis, and narrative analysis to determine the themes that emerged from the data and to determine the direction in which my study needed to go next, as the stories of Marvin, Jacolby, Jannell, Devonshire, David, and Rene began to unfold. I attempted to uncover the meanings that the six African American children, their families, and their teachers and mentors made of their literacy experiences. Through the constant comparative method, I looked at my data as it was gathered, looking for trends and categories. Parts of the interviews with the parents became stories they were telling about their children. Narrative analysis seemed to me to be the best method of uncovering the meanings of the stories.

Comparative Method

Merriam (1998) asserts that "data collection and analysis is a *simultaneous* activity in qualitative research" (p. 151). Analysis occurs after each observation, each interview, and after the collection of each document. Because qualitative research is emergent, analysis that is done after collecting each piece of data determines the direction in which the study will proceed. Merriam states, "Emerging insights, hunches, and tentative hypotheses direct the next phase of data collection, which in turn leads to the refinement or reformulation of questions, and so on" (1998, p. 151). I used the constant comparative method of data analysis, in which the researcher constantly compares different incidents in the same set of data in an attempt to see connections from which categories can evolve.

Lincoln and Guba (1985) describe the constant comparative method as a "'continuously developing process' in which each stage provides guidance for the next throughout the inquiry" (p. 340). In describing the process, the authors state that much "effort, ingenuity, and creativity" go into the selection of categories in which to put the data, as the data emerges. Lincoln and Guba point out that Spradley (1979, p. 111) has a systematic method for placing data into categories, which includes various relationships that can be seen between pieces of data, for example, "strict inclusion—X is a kind of Y; spatial—X is a place in Y, X is a part of Y; and cause–effect—X is a result of Y, etc." Lincoln and Guba state that they prefer to replace "cause–effect" with "mutual shaping" (p. 340). As data are put into categories, they are coded. While the researcher is coding the phenomenon, it should be compared with "the previous incidents in the same and different groups coded in the same category," according to Glaser and Strauss (1967, p. 106).

As Bogdan and Biklen (1998) state, "The constant comparative method is a research design for multi-data sources which is like analytic induction in that the formal analysis begins early in the study and is nearly completed by the end of data collection" (p. 66).

As I transcribed my interviews and field notes and collected my documents, I compared them, so as to put them into categories. As categories emerged, I wrote pieces of interviews and field notes on note cards and color coded the note cards, according to category. Each category became a theme. I compared themes that were common among the data about the different children, but I kept the note cards for each child separate within each theme or category, which made it easier to write about each specific child. When I began to write-up my study, I took the information directly from the cards.

Narrative Analysis

As I transcribed the interviews of the parents and grandparents in the study, a strikingly similar thread jumped out at me from the interviews. Each of the parents and grandparents that I interviewed painted a picture for me of their love for their children through stories. The parents' and grandparents' own words are a very powerful means, I think, for portraying the emotions that emerge, as they talk about their children. I, therefore, decided that narrative analysis would be a powerful way to expound upon the theme of parents and grandparents and the impact that they have on the children's lives. I feel that through narrative analysis, I have portrayed the strong feelings that these parents and grandparents expressed to me about their children during our interviews. According to Riessman (1993), narrative analysis investigates "the story itself" (p. 1). She states, "the purpose is to see how respondents in interviews impose order on the flow of experience to make sense of events and actions in their lives" (p. 2). Narrative analysis looks not only at the content of the story, but at how the story is told, why the story is told that way, and the "linguistic and cultural resources it draws on" (p. 2), according to Riessman.

Lieblich, Tuval-Mashiach, and Zilber (1998) state "one of the clearest channels for learning about the inner world is through verbal accounts and stories presented by individual narrators about their lives and their experienced reality" (p. 7). They go on to state that narrative analysis gives the researcher "access to people's identity and personality" (p. 7). I have used Gee's poetic structural analysis (1985) and Labov's categorical structural analysis (1972).

In Labov's narrative analysis, the transcript of the narrative is shortened to a core narrative by deleting the descriptions and interjections by the interviewer, etc. The transcript is then arranged under the headings of abstract, orientation, complicating action, evaluation, and resolution/coda. The abstract gives the subject for the narrative, the orientation typically gives the characters and the setting for the narrative, the complicating action gives the problem or plot twist in the narrative, the evaluation assigns a meaning to the plot, the resolution tells the solution of the problem or the ending, and the coda brings us back to the present. All of the parts may or may not be present in a particular narrative.

In Gee's narrative analysis, the transcript of the narrative is put into stanza form to illustrate the poetic nature of language. Each stanza is labeled by content. The introduction includes the setting and the catalyst, the crisis section includes complicating actions, and the final part, the resolution, includes concluding episodes and a coda. As in Labov's analysis, some or all of the parts may be present in a given narrative. Gee states, "…all human beings are masters of making sense of experience and the world through narrative" (1985, p. 27). He describes the narrative style of a young African American girl in his study: "L. uses language full tilt, with prosody, parallelism, rhetoric, and audience participation all contributing, together with lexical choice and syntax, to the communication of message, emotion, and entertainment" (p. 25).

I have used narrative analysis on one narrative for each parent (two for Marvin and Jacolby's mother), in which they are talking about their children and displaying with emotion the love and concern that they feel for their children. Each of these narratives struck me as being an excellent illustration of the love and support that each of these children has at home. When it came to expressing their deep feelings for their children, they all seemed to find storytelling to be the best way to convey their emotions.

As I began to analyze these narratives, some seemed to fit Labov's structure of narrative analysis: abstract, orientation, complicating action, evaluation, and resolution/coda. Others were more suited to Gee's poetic structure, and I put them into stanza form. For both types, I took out all but the core narrative, and it seemed as if the narratives just flowed into the structure. After putting the narratives into the structure, the thoughts and feelings of the parents became visible and began to emerge into themes. As the researchers stated, telling a story is the most natural way for someone to make sense of his or her experiences. I feel that I was able to get a clear picture of the parents' emotions as they talked about their children, their struggles, and their concerns in these stories.

The following are selected narratives from the interviews with the parents and grandparents that are important insights into the theme of support that emerged from the study.

Carrie (Rene's mother)

1. It's happier now that my husband's gone.

2. We are going through a divorce
3. it's all comin' together
4. Rene needs glasses
5. I got insurance with the CHIPS plan
6. I couldn't qualify for Medicaid with workin' overtime,
7. but I can't quit overtime,
8. 'cause I need the money
9. and then, the CHIPS plan
10. there is a God!
11. I'm sittin' here listening to myself,
12. and it sound like such a sad story!
13. But it's all comin' together now.

I have bolded the "I" to illustrate Carrie's emphasis on the word "I." She begins by saying, "We are going through a divorce." Her repetition of the word "I" illustrates that she has gone from "we" to "I" with the divorce. She feels that all of the responsibility is on her shoulders. She is the one that determines whether or not her children will get what they need in lines 5–8: "I got insurance…I couldn't qualify for Medicaid…I can't quit overtime…'cause I need the money."

Line 9 represents the transition. She does not use the word "I" in this line: "And then, the CHIPS plan," illustrating that some other force has taken over. She is no longer the one in control of the situation. In line 10, she states, "There is a God!" again illustrating that some other force is acting, and that she is no longer acting alone.

This narrative illustrates Carrie's strong desire to provide for her children. She feels overwhelmed at first, feeling that she has a great amount of responsibility on her shoulders. Then she realizes that there is help out there and that other forces also sometimes determine outcomes.

Kim (Marvin and Jacolby's mother)

Abstract

1. Yesterday, I found out that Little Marvin is Dyslexic.
2. Some people from the state came.

Orientation

3. He's Dyslexic…
4. that's the problem…

Complicating Action

5. he's been on grade level,
6. or…they are just about ready to put him on grade level…
7. the parent conference went well…
8. I'm shocked to find out that he's Dyslexic…
9. I had been suspecting that there was something not quite right…
10. I would ask him to do something,
11. and he'd say, "Mamma, what did you tell me to do?"
12. I wrote the School Board a letter…
13. that's how this all came about…
14. now Special Ed isn't like it was when I was in school…
15. but they are not gonna put him in Special Ed.

Resolution/Coda

16. He does so much better in small classes…
17. it's the big classes that he has trouble with…
18. thank God for small classes.
19. They're not gonna put him in Special Ed.
20. He's too smart for Special Ed.

In the orientation, Kim states, "It's Dyslexia…that's the problem," as if this was the answer she had been searching for. She shows that she has been concerned about Marvin and now, she is relieved to have an answer. In the complicating action, however, she states: "He's been on grade level, or they are just about to put him on grade level, the parent conference went well," hinting that she was not really aware that Marvin's problem would be so severe. Then she states, "I'm shocked to find out that he's Dyslexic."

Kim then talks about how she knew he had a problem, and she even wrote a letter to the school board about it. In line 15, it appears that Kim is trying to convince herself that Special Ed is a good thing—that it does not have the stigma that it did when she was in school. Then in line 16, she states that the school is not going to put Marvin in Special Ed. She appears to be a little confused as to what exactly the school is going to do for Marvin.

Kim then states, "He does much better in small classes…it's the big classes he has trouble with …thank God for small classes." She seems to be drawing a conclusion, trying to convince herself that putting Marvin into a small class is the answer to the problem, though she still seems confused as to what is actually going to come about.

Kim is obviously very concerned about Marvin. She knew that he had some kind of problem, but she was not expecting it to be dyslexia—something with a label. She seems to be trying to convince herself that it is OK to be dyslexic, that it doesn't have anything to do with intelligence. She stated again, "They're not gonna put him in Special Ed." And then, "He's too smart for Special Ed." She wants what is best for Marvin, but she is not sure what that is. She wants to be involved in the decisions made about Marvin's education.

Results/Themes

As I studied the data I had collected, the following themes emerged: Many diverse forms of literacy exist in the lives of the children in the study; the children were all in classrooms where their teachers used a combination of direct teaching of language skills and the whole language approach; most of the children in the study had teachers that address the issue of school English; and all of the children in the study had a parent or grandparent who believed that it is important for them to read to their children at home, that it is important for them to be active in their children's school, and that it is important for their children to succeed in school.

Different Forms of Literacy

I saw many different forms of literacy in the experiences of the children in the study, including, but not limited to singing, storytelling, chanting, cheering, making art projects, copying stories from books, writing letters, writing messages, dictating stories, narrating stories while drawing pictures, and presenting plays. While some of these literacies were learned in the school setting, the children brought many of these literacies with them from home.

The children in the study were given many opportunities to express their literacy in different ways. For example, Marvin and Rene felt more comfortable copying stories from books than they did composing original pieces. They were both allowed to copy from books in the classroom. David was most comfortable drawing a picture and narrating a story to go along with it. He was allowed to write in that way, and, in fact, this is what David referred to as "writing." He would say, "I want to write something," and he would begin his drawing and narrating.

The children in the study were given the freedom to express themselves through different forms of literacy. The teachers were required, however, to compare their students to certain standards, and they were not allowed to send them on to the next grade until they were able to read and write in conventional ways at the appropriate level.

Balanced Curriculum

Each of the children in the study had been in a classroom during the past year, in which the teacher implemented a balanced literacy program (Delpit, 1988, 1995; Cooper & Kiger, 2008; Tompkins, 2010)—a combination of the whole language approach to language instruction and the skills-based approach.

The children were given multiple opportunities to read and write during the day. They had individualized reading, guided reading, and content area reading; and their teachers read to them. In addition, most wrote in journals or draft books, they wrote stories, books, and letters; and they had writing conferences to discuss revising and editing. They had spelling assignments and explicit skills instruction, as well as reading and writing conferences, during which skills were directly taught. The children studied parts of speech, subject–verb agreement, capitalization, punctuation, sentence structure, story structure, etc. through direct teaching, through writing conferences, and through written practice, such as Daily Oral Language and TAAS objective writing practice. They were given an opportunity to use and practice what they had learned through components of the whole language approach. As they took writing pieces through the writing process, they had the opportunity to fine-tune their writing with the writing mechanics they learned from skills instruction.

Parents and Grandparents

The children in the study all had a parent or grandparent who believed that it is important for them to read to their children at home, that it is important for them to be active in their children's school, and that it is important for their children to succeed in school. The parents all described things that they did for their children in terms of literacy that they felt were important to their child's literacy development. In Carrie's case, she identified things that she thought to be important—reading to her children and buying her children books. She described her desire to do those things for her children, but she stated that she was not doing those things for her children, obviously feeling a tremendous amount of guilt. Ellen realized that Jannell was having trouble with comprehension and hired a tutor to help her.

Kim enlisted the help of her daughter for tutoring the boys in areas in which they needed extra help. She also realized that Marvin was having trouble with reading, and because she wasn't satisfied with the help that the school gave him, she wrote a letter to the school board requesting for him to be tested. Jenny realized that David was having trouble concentrating on his homework, so she asked him to go in his room and close the door, so that nothing would distract him.

School English

Most of the children in the study were in a class in which the teacher addressed the need for the children to learn school English. The children were instructed in school English through Daily Oral Language, through direct teaching, and through writing conferences. Jannell, Devonshire, and Jacolby had acquired school English, according to their teachers. The teachers also recognized the fact that use of home language on the part of the children is appropriate in some situations, such as on the playground, at home, and in casual conversation with the teacher or a classmate. For example, Tammy Corbin, Devonshire's teacher, mentioned that he spoke in dialect when he was telling her a story. Corbin recognized that this was the natural language for him to use in telling a story, illustrating her acceptance of Devonshire's home language.

The issue of the treatment of African American children's dialect is closely related to the issue of the acquisition of the culture of power on the part of the African American child. In teaching the children school English, the teachers were helping the children to acquire the culture of power.

The Recognition of African American Children's Race

Paley (1979) expressed her desire for the recognition of her Jewishness, and she described the African American mother's desire for her children's race to be recognized: "My children are black. They don't look like your children. They know they're black, and we want it recognized. It's a positive difference, an interesting difference, and a comfortable difference" (Paley, 1979, p. 12). In Connie Bailey's classroom, I witnessed an open and frank discussion about African American children's race, during the lesson on Martin Luther King, Jr., Bailey addressed the fact that the African American children are Black, and she pointed out situations in the past that had been unfair toward African Americans.

In my classroom, we always had an open forum for the discussion of race, color, culture, etc. I believe that providing the art supplies with different skin colors set the stage for the discussions that occurred throughout the year. I also believe that the literature on diverse customs and beliefs made the discussions about differences between different races, cultures, and families natural. When students brought and shared family photographs and talked about their lives in their own families, more natural discussions concerning family, racial, and cultural differences were encouraged.

The acceptance of diverse forms of literacy is illustrated in the following examples: David was allowed the freedom to "draw" his stories, and Marvin and Rene were allowed to copy from books. They were allowed to express themselves through the type of literacy that was most meaningful to them. In addition, the school-wide study of tolerance is an example of recognition and acceptance of differences between people of different races and cultures. Though only one month each year is dedicated to the study of tolerance, the students and teachers are expected to practice tolerance all of the time. Role-playing of different situations relating to tolerance as well as class discussions that arose in each class about the theme of tolerance were used to help the children and teachers to practice tolerance toward people of all different races and cultures.

Discussion

Goodman (1965) advocates the acceptance of an African American child's dialect and simultaneous instruction in school English. I saw several examples in the schools in the study of the acceptance of the children's dialect and instruction in school English. Especially in the younger grades, the teachers in the study responded to the meaning of the children's speech, rather than correcting their speech, when dialect was used. On a few instances, I witnessed other school personnel correcting students who spoke in their home language. As I discussed in the last section, the teachers did, for the most part, address the children's dialect, recognizing the need to accept the child's dialect, while teaching the child school English. Also, I saw some recognition of the African American children's race in Connie Bailey's classroom and in my own classroom. The issue was touched on by the school-wide study of tolerance, and the acceptance of diverse forms of literacy on the teachers' part. Although I have seen some examples in these schools of the recognition of the race of African American children, I did not see as much as I thought I would. I would suggest more education about anti-bias curriculum (Derman-Sparks & the ABC Task Force, 1989; Banks & Banks, 1993) and culturally relevant teaching (Ladson-Billings, 1994) by all school staff, and the making of a plan of action for implementation of anti-bias curriculum is needed in order to truly recognize and accept all of the races and cultures represented in the school. All school personnel must be educated on anti-bias curriculum, and all school personnel must buy in to the ideas and make a commitment to make the positive changes in the school that anti-bias curriculum would bring about. Anti-bias curriculum can be integrated nicely into a balanced literacy program. By providing a wide range of books on different cultures, a teacher can set the stage for discussions and writing activities about the different cultures represented in the classroom. The teacher can also provide pictures and posters that depict people from diverse cultures, as well providing art supplies that represent different skin colors.

Finally, I believe that the issue of the recognition of African American children's race goes hand in hand with the relevance of the school life to the lives and experiences of African American children. The school culture is the dominant culture—the White middle-class culture. I did not see much evidence in these schools that anything special was done to insure that the school experience would be relevant to the African American children. As far as I can see, the African American children had the same school experiences as the White children. A reason for this is, perhaps, that there were only a few African American teachers in the schools, and the rest were White. According to Ladson-Billings (1994), negative effects are brought about "by not seeing one's history, culture, or background represented in a textbook or curriculum or by seeing that history, culture or background distorted" (p. 17). Additionally, Ladson-Billings identifies "staffing patterns" in the schools as potential problems "when all of the teachers and principal are white and only the janitors and cafeteria workers are African American, for example" (p. 17). The White teachers need to be educated as to how they can make school life relevant to the lives of African American children.

At this point, I would like to point out that all of these African American children have some very positive experiences in their lives. They have rich literacy experiences at home and at school. They have a very loving, supportive parent or grandparent at home, they are being taught the skills that they need in order to succeed in the culture of power, and they are learning (or have already mastered) school English. Some of them are excelling in school, others are successful, but some of them are not succeeding. I feel that they will eventually do well, but I wonder why, when they have all of these strengths on their side, they have not been what the school calls "successful" thus far.

I also raise two more questions regarding the African American children's school experiences: Why I am not seeing more recognition of the African American children's race in the school? And why is there not more relevance in the schools to the African American children's lives? Possibly, there is a mismatch between the school culture and the children's real-life experiences. It could be that the school culture continues to fit only the White middle-class culture. Perhaps part of the reason is the predominance of White teachers in that school specifically and in schools generally.

Delpit states that "Progressive white teachers seem to say to their black students, 'Let me help you find your voice. I promise not to criticize one note as you search for your own song.' But black teachers say, 'I've heard your song loud and clear. Now, I want to teach you to harmonize with the rest of the world'" (1986, p. 384). Delpit recognizes the White teachers as meaning well but just not really knowing what it is that the African American children need. I think that the same scenario is true in the schools in my study. The White teachers are doing what they think is best for the African American children, but they are just not really aware of several issues involved in the education of African American children. For example, although they are very accepting of the children's home language and recognize the need for them to learn school English, they do not seem to understand that by calling school English "Standard English" or "proper English," they are implying that the children's home language is wrong or incorrect.

Also, the White teachers in the study do not seem to be aware of the importance of learning about the African American children's culture and including it as a part of everyday life, along with the cultures of the other children. The schools seem to reflect only the culture of the White middle class. Again, the teachers mean well by including a study of tolerance and by studying Martin Luther King, Jr., but they need, in my opinion, to go a few steps further and make the African American children's culture a part of everyday life by including literature depicting African Americans, by including African American traditions, music, folklore, history, and dance, and by including African folktales and folksongs. Additionally, I think that they should use people crayons and markers and paper of all different skin colors. Not only should all of these things be included for the African American culture, but for the cultures of all of the children in classroom as well. Multiculturalism should permeate the day, rather than having what Derman-Sparks describes as tourist multiculturalism (1989).

It is my belief that this study is significant because it addresses some of the issues that are important in an African American child's acquisition of literacy. I hope my study will help make other educators aware of the cultural issues that exist in schools for African American children. By making teachers and administrators aware of the importance of the school's recognition and acceptance of a child's race, culture, and dialect, I hope to make progress towards changing the ways in which African American children are educated in our society. An important first step, according to Ladson-Billings (1995), is to recognize children's ethnic and cultural differences, rather than to claim to be color-blind. Ladson-Billings states, "given the significance of race and color in American society, it is impossible to believe that a classroom teacher does not notice the race and ethnicity of the children she is teaching. Further, by claiming not to notice, the teacher is saying that she is dismissing one of the most salient features of the child's identity and that she does not account for it in her curricular planning and instruction" (p. 33). Ladson-Billings advocates culturally relevant practices, pointing out that all children have different needs and learn differently. The best way to teach children is to address their individual needs, states Ladson-Billings, rather than pretending that differences—racial, ethnic, language, etc.—do not exist (1994). It is my hope that bringing an awareness of culturally relevant teaching might contribute to changing the attitudes of educators towards African American children; and our schools can become a place where African American children learn school English, as their own language is accepted and valued; where African American children are taught in ways that are culturally relevant to their lives; and where African American children are empowered as they acquire the "culture of power" (Delpit, 1995, p. 24) while holding on to their own cultural values.

Viruru states, "the biggest issue that arose out of this study is whether research, even ethnographic research, is a construction that should be used in diverse contexts (p. 189). As I was conducting the study, I could not help wonder why I had the right to "study" people. I wondered if the participants saw me as a person with power and themselves as persons without power. As I was interviewing the parents, in particular, I was aware of a certain vulnerability that they possessed. They were telling me very personal things about their children, and I couldn't help wonder why I had the right to know these things. Similarly, I wondered what they thought about a White middle class woman studying African American children. I wondered if they felt that I was invading their territory, or that I could not possibly understand the experiences.

I was also aware of a closeness and a kind of bond that I felt with the parents and the children. When the data collection was over, I had the feeling that I was abandoning them.

Despite the questions that have arisen about research itself, I believe that my study has pointed out some interesting and valuable information about the literacy experiences of the six African American children. I am in no way suggesting that all African American children have the same experiences. I do hope, however, that readers can make connections between the children in my study and other children.

The six African American children have so many strengths, so much brilliance, and so much possibility. They come from homes that have given them strong support, and they have understanding teachers who are helping them to acquire the culture of power. In addition to all of these strong points, all of these children have something that will help them to go far in life: they all have the desire to learn and the desire to succeed.

I want to close with a statement that I feel strongly about: A teacher's job is to recognize and accept African American children's culture, race, and dialect; give them school experiences that are relevant to their home lives; and teach them everything that they need to know in order to be successful in the school environment as well as succeeding in the dominant culture. And, as Delpit puts it so nicely, "those who are most skillful at educating black and poor children do not allow themselves to be placed in 'skills' or 'process' boxes. They understand the need for both approaches, the need to help students establish their own voices, and to coach those voices to produce notes that will be heard clearly in the larger society" (Delpit, 1995, p. 46).

References

Banks, J. A. & Banks, C. A. M. (Eds.) (1993). *Multicultural education: Issues and perspectives.* Boston, MA: Allyn and Bacon.

Bogdan, R. C. & Biklen, S. K. (1998). *Qualitative research in education: An introduction to theory and methods.* Boston, MA: Allyn & Bacon.

Cooper, D. & Kiger, N. (2008). *Literacy assessment: Helping teachers plan instruction.* Boston, MA: Houghton Mifflin Company.

Delpit, L. (1995). *Other people's children: Cultural conflict in the classroom.* New York: The New Press.

Delpit, L. (1986). Skills and other dilemmas of a progressive black educator. *Harvard Educational Review, 56*(4), 379–385.

Delpit, L. (1988). The silenced dialogue: Power and pedagogy in educating other people's children. *Harvard Educational Review, 58*(3), 280–298.

Denzin, N. & Lincoln, Y. (2000). *The handbook of qualitative research.* Thousand Oaks, CA: Sage.

Derman-Sparks, L. & the ABC Task Force (1989). *Anti-bias curriculum: Tools for empowering young children.* Washington, D.C.: National Association for the Education of Young Children.

Gee, J. P. (1985). The narrativization of experience in the oral style. *Journal of Education, 167 (1).*

Glaser, B. G. & Strauss, A. L. (1967). The discovery of grounded theory: Startegies for qualitative research. Chicago, IL: Aldine Publishing Company.

Goodman, K. S. (1965). Dialect barriers to reading comprehension. *Elementary English, 42*, 853–860.

Goodman, K. S. (1973). Dialect barriers to reading comprehension revisited. *Reading Teacher, 27 (11)*, 6–12.

Hale, J. E. (1982). *Black children: Their roots, culture, and learning styles.* Provo, UT: Brigham Young University Press.

Ladson-Billings, G. (1994). *The dreamkeepers: Successful teachers of African-American children.* San Francisco, CA: Jossey-Bass Publishers.

Lieblich, A., Tuval-Mashiach, R., & Zilber, T. (1998). *Narrative research: Reading, analysis, and interpretation.* Thousand Oaks, CA: Sage Publications.

Lincoln, Y. S. & Guba, E. G. (1985). *Naturalistic inquiry.* Beverly Hills, CA: Sage.

Labov, W. (1972). The transformation of experience in narrative syntax. In *Language in the inner city.* Philadelphia, PA: University of Pennsylvania Press.

Merriam, S. B. (1998). *Qualitative research and case study applications in education.* San Francisco, CA: Jossey-Bass Publishers.

Paley, V. G. (1995). *Kwanzaa and me: A teacher's story.* Cambridge, MA: Harvard University Press.

Paley, V. G. (1979). *White teacher.* Cambridge, MA: Harvard University Press.

Power, B. & Hubbard, R. (2002). *Language development: A reader for teachers.* Upper Saddle River, NJ: Merrill Prentice Hall.

Riessman, C. K. (1993). *Narrative analysis.* Newbury Park, CA: Sage Publications.

Spradley, J. (1979). *The ethnographic interview.* New York: Holt, Rinehart, and Winston.

Tompkins, G. (2010). *Literacy for the 21st century.* Upper Saddle River, NJ: Merrill Prentice Hall.

Viruru, R. (2001) *Early childhood education: Post colonial perspectives from India.* London: Sage.

Section Two

Corporatized Childhoods, Neoliberalism, and Critical Policy Perspectives

CHAPTER SEVEN

Governing Families in the Social Investment State

MICHEL VANDENBROECK, RUDI ROOSE AND MARIA DE BIE

Abstract

In this chapter we critically analyze the alleged "progressive" evolution from child protection (as a coercive practice) toward child welfare (as a preventative and empowering alternative). We use Michel Foucault's frameworks to critically look at this dichotomy and to analyze the discourse on welfare and its vocabulary on "prevention," "children's rights," "active citizenship," or "the autonomous individual." The evolution from child protection to child welfare and the central role of prevention leads to the idea that there really can exist such a thing as powerless social work; the further away we are from judicial power, the more empowering we would be. The expert on child welfare today resembles more a caring and loving companion, a "pastor," in the early Christian metaphoric sense of the kind shepherd, shaping (and shaped by) an autonomous, entrepreneurial citizen/parent. This evolution is contingent with evolutions of the welfare state in global capitalism or neoliberal societies (sometimes labeled as the politics of the Third Way). The "technologies" that are developed in these new forms of governance may take multiple forms, such as the Anti-Social Behavior Orders in the UK or the prevention of adolescent delinquency at an early age in France, but they invariably lead to the individual responsibilization (and consequent pedagogization) of parents. Remarkably, parents themselves are often excluded from the debates on what "their" problem is supposed to be, reducing them to being spectators of their own life.

Introduction

The evolution of the welfare state, and of social work as an element within this welfare state, is often defined as a move forward toward more social justice and a more emancipatory approach of social problems. With regard to the approach of children and families, it is stated that in many European countries the child protection discourse has developed towards a child welfare discourse (Spratt, 2001). Child protection is seen as controlling and repressive, while child welfare refers to a more supportive and participative approach. Child welfare indicates a view of the relationship between social workers and families as partnerships. This child welfare approach is—among others—translated into a more preventative and empowering approach (Stepney, 2006) for children and parents. The rights of the child are an important framework in this development (Roose & De Bie, 2007).

The idea of progression marks a dichotomy between child protection as coercive practice and child welfare as its liberating alternative. This dichotomy must be critically analyzed. Payne (2005) states that the development of the welfare state and of social work is one of change and continuity. Margolin (1997) even refers to the changing discourse as an instrument for continuity: social work states to do something else, so that it can keep doing the same! The dichotomy between child protection and child welfare is predominantly presented as an opposition between oppression and empowerment, control and emancipation, and therefore issues of power relations and governmentality are at the core of this analysis, if we consider pedagogy as a specific site that relates political rationalities to the capabilities of the individual (Popkewitz, 1996). As Foucault (1975) showed in his genealogical study of the prison, the disappearance of sovereign power relations did not necessarily create liberty, but rather a new form of governmentality, labeled as disciplining power relations. The French philosopher Michel Foucault (1926–1984) devoted much of his professional life to the study of subtle power relations and how individuals are governed both by the state and by themselves. We will therefore use his frameworks to critically look at this dichotomy and to analyze the discourse on welfare and its vocabulary on "prevention," "children's rights," "active citizenship" or "the autonomous individual." It simply cannot be assumed that the transition from protection to welfare may be framed as a liberating practice, bearing in mind this Foucauldian adagio (Foucault, 1983: 1205 [in French]):

> *Je ne cherche pas à dire que tout est mauvais, mais que tout est dangereux—ce qui n'est pas exactement la même chose que ce qui est mauvais. Si tout est dangereux, alors nous avons toujours quelque chose à faire*[1]

From Coercion to Pastoral Power

In Foucault's view, power is not to be analyzed in its essence but rather as an operation, a relationship. The central question is not what power is or where it is located but how it operates (Deleuze, 1985). Power is to be considered as the production of specific forms of truth, in which science (and human and social sciences in particular) plays an important role (Foucault, 1975), as well as the production of specific practices in many fields, including education and social work, determining how problems are constituted, how people are classified and what are considered appropriate ways to shape behavior (Moss, Dillon, & Statham, 2000). The aim of such an analysis is not to produce a new truth, to say what needs to be done, or what is good. Such an ambition would not fundamentally differ from the old prophetic function of scientists or intellectuals (Foucault, 1990). Rather, the aim is to deconstruct what is obvious, taken for granted or presented as "natural," in order to open up for choice, to reinstall a debate about possibilities, to "bring back politics into the nursery" (Moss, 2007), acknowledging that disagreement is a condition for debate and the possibility of choice, and therefore of conflicting opinions, is the essence of democracy (Mouffe, 2005).

It is obvious that the coercive practices of child protection have gradually lost their appeal in social work and that the disciplining power relations between the expert who knows what is good for the child and the lay parent have rightly been criticized. However, the idea that friendly social work is better than repressive social work is not new. Typical for early child protection interventions is the idea of friendly visits: a kind word works better than an obvious use of power to convince the parents that they have to change. This idea was also translated in the development of social casework, in the beginning of the nineteenth century. An idea central to child protection is that social work interventions must be organized as much as possible outside of the judicial system, as this system is clearly linked with the idea of power. Hence, care and control must be separated from each other. Prevention is the key word, not only prevention of social problems, but also of judicial interventions. This idea is reinforced with the development of the welfare state and the rise of all kinds of social institutions, which must make it possible to prevent child protection interventions as a whole. While the idea is that judicial interventions must be avoided, the judge becomes central, by stressing the fact that his interference must be avoided whenever possible (Franssen, Cartuyvels, & De Coninck, 2003).

We notice in the development of child protection that this notion of prevention of power leads to the idea that there really can exist such a thing as powerless social work: the further away we are from judicial power, the more empowering we would be. This idea disregards the notion of pastoral power, as coined by Foucault. Although the idea of friendliness existed, there was still a clear-cut divide between the expert social worker and the client. The expert in child welfare today resembles more a caring and loving companion, a *pastor*, in the early Christian metaphoric sense of the kind shepherd. As Foucault (1990) explained in the "Tanner Lectures on Human Values" in 1979, if the state is the political form of centralizing power, let us call pastorship the individualizing power. Shepherdly kindness is close to "devotedness." Everything the shepherd does is geared to the good of his flock. That is his constant concern. When they sleep, he keeps watch (Foucault, 1990). Pastoral power is based on the individual attention for each member of the flock. She exercises this power not through coercion, but through individual and unlimited kindness. The pastor (i.e. the social worker) is accountable for each sheep, as is obvious in the increasing number of cases where social workers are brought to justice in cases that they have for instance failed to detect child maltreatment. The "sins" of the sheep are considered to be also the pastor's sins. This concept of pastoral power requires a specific knowledge by the shepherd of the soul of each member of the flock. To produce this knowledge, specific technologies are developed, based on the "self examination and the guidance of conscience," a combination of obedience, knowledge of the self, and confession, to ensure redemption and salvation (Foucault, 1993). Today, parents need to scrutinize themselves, to explain themselves, to reveal what one is, in parent support groups, exchange programs, and other social support groups in which the "expert" refuses to say what is "good" but facilitates the self-examination and the (public) confession. There are multiple examples of this to be found both in Europe and the United States such as the flourishing parent sessions, based on the approach of Gordon's *Listening to Children*, or parent advice books that are not written any more by the expert who knows (such as Benjamin Spock) but by the caring parent (such as Bill Cosby). The disciplining power relation, moreover, relies on the fact that the "punishment" for the sin (e.g., a too authoritarian approach to children, rather than "positive parenting") does not follow upon the sin, but will become obvious only in later life (e.g. in adolescence). The literature on what constitutes "good parenting" (e.g., the categorization of parents as laissez-faire; authoritarian and authoritative) connects parenting styles with developmental outcomes many years later, such as academic achievement or delinquency (e.g., Dwairy & Menshar, 2006;

Mandara, 2006; Villar, Luengo, Gomez-Fraguela, & Romero, 2006). This has two major disciplining effects, the first being that one is deprived from his senses in judging what is good, since the effects of parenting are only to be measured many years later. The second, related to this, is a specific and mutual dependency on the expert pastor to advice us on what is good and to assist us in scrutinizing ourselves and in reflecting on our parenting. Foucault labels this as the hermeneutics of the self, the construction of an autonomous self, which is able to rationally analyze what is good, to make the right "choices" for herself and her children, to invest in later life (Foucault, 2001).

This development, that became obvious since the 1980s, is reinforced by important developments in the conception of the welfare state, influenced both by the economic crisis of the 1980s and the collapse of the Soviet empire, with the fall of the Berlin wall in 1989 as emblematic figure, resulting in the hegemony of neoliberal market economies. The welfare system after the Second World War evolved into a social investment state (Giddens, 1998), a welfare state that does not compensate for failure but invests in future success, since the traditional welfare state could no longer efficiently tackle the new social questions such as re-emerging poverty and unemployment. Rosanvallon (1995) argued that the end of the twentieth century was marked by a triple crisis. The first crisis is a financial crisis: states were faced with increasing spending in social security issues such as unemployment benefits, while facing reduced income. The second is a bureaucratic crisis: states were increasingly perceived as being ineffective and inefficient by the general population as well as by policy makers and as a consequence, a neoliberal discourse on smaller states emerged. Finally, a philosophical crisis coincided, raising questions about the very concept of social welfare and social security. As a means of dealing with these new social fractures, Rosanvallon pleaded for more individual attention by the state, one that valued social inclusion. However, especially in English language countries, social inclusion has increasingly been defined in terms of employability and markets. This dominant construction of the welfare state in capitalist hegemony entails a growing focus on risk management, individual responsibility and a discourse of "no rights without duties" in which allowances are no longer taken for granted entitlements. These manifestations have been described as "the enabling state" (Gilbert & Gilbert, 1989): the "employment first welfare state" (Finn, 2003) or the "contractual state" (Crawford, 2003). They have affected the relationships between parents and the state since the focus shifts again towards a radicalization of parental responsibility, where parents are seen as responsible for the future success of their children (Featherstone, 2006; Parton, 2006). This legitimated the renewal of coercive practices. It concerns new coercive practices—such as parental orders—which may relate to a "pastoral" nature, yet at the same time, we also witness the re-emergence of "older" forms of disciplining power technologies, such as the (threat of) prison. Wacquant (2002) has argued how in the case of the United States and France, a transition occurred from investing in the welfare system to investing in the penal system, showing for instance how budget cuts in parent allowance systems have been contingent with investments in the penal system. In continental Europe, this development has a less brutal face than in the United States, as we see a form of social panopticism: social service bureaucracies are called on to take an active part in the pacification of social problems, "since they possess the informational and human means to exercise a close surveillance of 'problem populations'" (Wacquant, 2001: 407). Bradt and Bouverne-De Bie (2007) have documented how the two domains of welfare and justice are not separate, but that a penalization occurs *inside* the welfare system in the case of the United Kingdom and Belgium, and especially, how these changes are also enacted by social workers and educators and in particular by their silence in the debates on these issues. This silence is, according to their study, not a result of being silenced, but rather a self-chosen isolation, in order not to be involved in the penal system.

The transition to the welfare system of the "Third Way" calls for active individuals, taking the responsibility of their own life, acting as the entrepreneurs of their life history, and investing in the future success of their children. The increasing use of a language of "choice" implies equality of access to the market and denies actual structural positions of disadvantage (Burman, 1994).

Technologies

Let us now look at some specific examples of changing practices that may be considered as technologies of these forms of governing families and children in the social investment states.

In the case of France, the riots in the suburbs in the autumn of 2005 have, in dominant discourse, been framed as "juvenile delinquency" rather than as protests against social inequalities. Consequently, they are considered to be an individual and educational (or cultural) issue, rather than a political and social problem of racism and inequity (Schneider, 2007), which seemed almost inevitable, considering the living conditions in these suburbs that Bourdieu and colleagues (1993) recorded more than a decade earlier. The riots drew new attention to a report by the Institut National de la Santé et de la Recherche Médicale (2005), which analyzed the causes of juvenile delinquency through a developmental lens, and adopted a stepping stone approach, which identified the risk factors for juvenile delinquency in early childhood. This report formed the core of a political discussion in the French Senate that led to a report proposing several legislative initiatives to prevent the risk of juvenile delinquency (Bénisti, 2005). Notwithstanding broad public protests (i.e., a petition with 200,000 signatures of professionals in early childhood), several of these proposals have been legislated, including changes in the legal protection of the professional secrecy of social workers, the possibility of forcing parents of young children "at risk" to accept the custody of an educator and the forced placement of children in internship, in cases where their parents refuse the aid offered to them in parent support programs (Collectif, 2006; Neyrand, 2006).

The English Antisocial Behaviour Orders (ASBO) and Parental Orders likewise frame "deviant" behavior that is not strictly "illegal" (such as nuisance) and argue for a coercive use of parent support programs. In Belgium, the new youth protection law inscribed the possibility to forcing parents— by the threat of a fine or prison sentence—who are seen as indifferent toward the delinquent behavior of their children to attend a parental support program. The experience was that these parents could not be found, unless we interpreted indifference in an extremely broad way (for instance not being able to find help on your own). In the case of Flanders (Belgium), poor PISA (testing) results (providing comparative data on schooling outcomes) show that there is a substantial educational gap at age 14–16 years and that school results are significantly linked with the socioeconomic and ethnic backgrounds of the pupils. This problem of inequality is, again, framed as an educational problem and—at least in part—a matter of parental responsibility, since the Minister of Education invests in home visits to families from ethnic minorities to convince them to send their children to kindergarten earlier (Vandenbroucke, 2006). In addition, discussions to lower compulsory school age have begun, even when—in the case of Flanders—over 98% of three-year-olds attend kindergarten (Organisation for Economic Co-operation and Development, 2006).

Some common threads can be observed in these manifestations. As in the beginning of the twentieth century and the child protection approach, there is again an ongoing focus on parental responsibilities and the "pedagogicalization" of parents (Popkewitz, 2003). This development is also strengthened through a specific interpretation of the rights of the child as a frame of reference for pedagogical action (Roose & De Bie, 2007; 2008), where the child is viewed as competent and vulnerable, and the parent as to be educated (Moqvist, 2003). Social problems are—in the name of realizing the rights of the child—translated into problems of parental behavior, and parents are seen as responsible for the problems of their children. We notice for instance that in the strategies for tackling poverty, parents can be seen as responsible for the poverty of their children (as we notice in the United Kingdom, e.g., Hamilton & Roberts, 2000) or they are not held responsible, but—as is the case in Flanders—the main strategy for tackling poverty is seen in the increase of parents support programs.

There is a significant change in the management of what is constructed as "illegal." Legislation is, according to Foucault (1975) and Deleuze (1985), a matter of managing illegalisms: some are permitted, made possible or invented as a privilege of the dominating classes, some others are tolerated as a compensation for the dominated classes, and some are prohibited, isolated, and taken as an object of intervention as well as of domination. Finally, there is a focus on the provision of parent support as risk management, to prevent later costs to society, in the context of the social investment state. As we indicated earlier, the concept of prevention has always been, and continues to be, a core aspect of the governing of families. Prevention can be approached in different ways (Stepney, 2006). One approach stresses the need for targeted intervention with high-risk clients; another approach is concerned with establishing wider support in the community to tackle problems of poverty and disadvantage.

Currently, prevention is again mainly understood as the prevention of risks provoked by the individual (the self), rather than as societal prevention of exclusion. Today, this discourse of prevention is backed by a scientific regime of truth about risk factors, based on population studies (e.g., Sanders, Markie-Dadds, & Turner, 2003). Yet, much of this empirical research is criticized for its lack of rigor, while its academic appearance and its use of quantitative measurements turn its discourse into supposedly objective and unquestionable truths. As critical scholars argue, cross-sectional research cannot allow interpretations of correlations as causal relations, such as between maternal depression and later adolescent misbehavior. Fendler (2006) explains that correlational statistics are probability studies with limited generalizability. Notwithstanding the caution to consider when analyzing population data, these are often interpreted as if each member of the identified group (e.g., black children) represents the characteristics of the group (e.g., underachieving in education). This ecological fallacy (Connolly, 2006) would mean a false generalization, as if for instance each child of an ethnic minority would accumulate risk factors, or each child accumulating risk factors would develop some form of delinquency. In the French case, correlations between problematic language development and externalizing behavior in young children, reported in academic literature, are interpreted in the INSERM report for the government as if speaking a minority language may be a risk factor for juvenile delinquency (INSERM, 2005). The statistical basis of the prevention programs may show that an accumulation of four or more risk factors does correlate with a significantly higher prevalence of contacts with justice, or child abuse services but does not explain how these links occur and more importantly, does not account for the agency of the majority of children and families that, while accumulating risk factors, do not end up in trouble. Research may show for instance that the accumulation of four or more risk factors is associated with a significant increase of child maltreatment (e.g. Brown, Cohen, Johnson, & Salzinger, 1998). Yet, even when accumulating four or more risk factors, more than 65 percent of the children do not encounter any maltreatment. As Burman (1995) states, we simply lack information about normal interaction patterns in unconventional families and problems in conventional families, to have a good basis for assessing the relative advantages and disadvantages of different family conditions.

Another concern is that prevention programs intervene *before* a problem occurs. Therefore, they legitimize coercive intrusions in populations that do not (yet) present any problems, and they may confirm existing stereotypes about specific families (e.g,. living in poverty, having particular ethnic or cultural roots, and single-parent families).

Finally, the regimes of truth in which these programs are embedded exclude parents from defining the problems that need to be tackled, the debate about these definitions being reserved to experts. It is far from being obvious that the societal targets of prevention always coincide with the enhancement of well-being or dignity, as perceived by the families. For instance, framing externalizing behavior of young children as possible future delinquency is considered by parents as quite intrusive and may be a reason for parents for not seeing their demands met (De Mey, Coussée, Vandenbroeck, & Bouverne-De Bie, 2009). This is also Biesta's (2007) concern about the tension between scientific and democratic control, or, as he puts it, the democratic deficit of evidence-based education. Prevention programs, such as the Positive Parenting Programs or Parent–Child Interaction Therapy, are based on the assumptions that parents should be "taught" what positive parenting is; that parents do not know how to perform positive parenting, while the expert does; and that parents can "progress" when looking critically at themselves and confessing to the professional. In many cases, however, parents may be very aware that things are not going well but are caught in difficult circumstances that do not allow them to act as they would wish, such as poverty or bad housing conditions. This may in part explain why the populations in Triple P studies are predominantly middle or higher socio-economic status (SES) and why, as Thomas and Zimmer-Gembeck (2007) conclude, it is not certain that findings can be generalized to low-income groups. In short, the focus on prevention entails the risk of individualizing social problems in the social investment state. This may mean that the family is instrumentalized as the place where early socialization needs to be shaped without acknowledging children's and parents' voices on these socialization processes.

Discussion

In this final part of the chapter we come back to some common threats in the different examples such as decontextualization and inclusion/exclusion (or silencing specific families). Decontextualization means that moral standards are put forward, disregarding the specific contexts in which education takes place. At the end of the nineteenth century, one of the major concerns regarding education was child mortality. In many European cities up to 20 percent of the children did not live until their first birthday. This *social problem* may be analyzed in the context of dramatic living conditions of the working poor: extremely low wages, abominable housing conditions without sanitation, and the complete absence of any social legislation (maternity leave, paid sickness leave, etc.). However, in official discourse, the child mortality was not analyzed in these terms, but rather as the result of incompetent and negligent mothers. The interventions, set up by the bourgeoisie, framed labor class mothers that needed to be educated and civilized in order to raise their awareness of their maternal duties (Vandenbroeck, 2003). In turn, these individualizing interventions reinforced the dominant idea that these mothers were indeed responsible for the health of their children. Similarly, many of the present-day parent support programs analyze "positive parenting" as a matter of individual competencies, disregarding the contexts in which families live. School failure, for instance, is dominantly framed as a deficiency of families (not adapting to the school culture), rather than of schools (not adapting to the family cultures and contexts). Parent support programs are designed to tackle this problem with friendly visits that in turn reinforce the dominant construction of the parental responsibility. As a result, many parents, living on the margins of society (e.g., immigrant parents) are convinced that the future of their child (or the lack of future) is in their hands, a very salient and actual form of what Paulo Freire (1970) labeled as *internalized* oppression. The idea that parent support programs—and educational programs in general—are a modern way to tackle problems of poverty denies the fact that these approaches rather refer to a continuity in history and in social work, where the blatant (and growing) social inequality is disregarded, which makes it even virtually impossible to think of poverty in a different vocabulary than the vocabulary of individual choice. In this sense, education may be viewed as a powerful technique to individualize social problems by decontextualizing them.

Today, this individualization of social problems is embedded in emerging discourses on freedom of choice. The discourse of choice assumes two things that may be critically discussed: that choice exists and that choice is desirable. Many scholars, both in Europe and in the United States have documented that in early childhood education for instance, there is no such thing as choice. Children from poor families and from immigrant families are predominantly to be found in early childhood education of poor quality and this cannot be understood as a result of parental choice (e.g., Himmelweit & Sigala, 2004; M. Vandenbroeck, De Visscher, Van Nuffel, & Ferla, 2008; Wall & Jose, 2004). As a matter of fact, the language of choice masks effects of social inequality, i.e. the mere fact that some parents have more choice than others. The ideology of choice, however, presupposes that choice exists for all parents and as a consequence, it looks at parental behavior (e.g., the choice for low quality early childhood education) as the result of bad choices (e.g., Peyton, Jacobs, O'Brien, & Roy, 2001). Moreover, examples of democratic experimentalism, to use the words of Peter Moss, show that excellent early childhood education can exist without choice. Practices such as in Reggio Emilia, in some children's centers in the United Kingdom (e.g., Sheffield), or in the French parental crèches, where curricula are developed with the local communities in a critical and collaborative way, show that parents can have a voice that is listened to. Their curricula take into account the social contexts but do not speak the neoliberal language of choice that is omnipresent in neoliberal market ideologies (for a more elaborated documentation on these practices, see Blanc & Bonnabesse, 2008; Moss, 2008).

The emerging discourses on freedom of choice are supported by specific constructions of childhood and parenthood. The current emphasis on the rights of the child arose within a climate of sentimentalization and a growing focus on the symbolic value of the child (King, 1997; Pupavac, 2001). Beck states that this relates to the development of a risk society in which "the child is the source of the last remaining irrevocable unexchangeable primary relationship. Partners come and go. The child stays. Everything that is desired, but not realisable in the relationship is directed to the child" (Beck, 1997a, p. 118). This sentimentalization refers to the "priceless child" (Zelizer, 1994), the child as Emperor, or the Holy Child. It is the child that is agentic, to be listened to, able to make choices (and willing to do so), the child with rights, among which the right to the best possible parents (those who make the right choices). It is an autonomous child, autonomy, serving as a proxy for the active consumer, self-sufficient, and detached from maternal constraints, the perfect future entrepreneur and—in this sense—the future capital of the nation.

The view of the child as "priceless" may have negative consequences (Roose & De Bie, 2007). For instance, it might lead to a "misanthropic view of adulthood" in which "the very idea of parental authority has been compromised as abusive in itself" (Pupavac, 2001, p. 106). From this view on the child the rights of the child are prioritized. The emphasis on individual autonomy of the child and on the prioritization of the rights of the child creates a dichotomy between the rights of children and the rights of parents. At the extreme, in the light of this concept educational practices are considered as a type of legal protection of the child in which parents only have rights as long as they act in the child's best interests (Westman, 1999; Howe, 2001).

Constructions of childhood cannot exist without parallel constructions of parenthood. These constructions of childhood frame parents as their mirrors: the entrepreneurial self (Masschelein & Quaghebeur, 2005), capable of *managing* his life, taking the best possible decisions to invest in the future of his child, and willing to do so. It is the parent who is informed, who is aware of the importance of an early "head" start in life, who subscribes to the meritocratic ideology that anyone can achieve anything in life, provided one does his best. Vis-à-vis the state, the parent becomes a parent who has to be educated and a parent who must learn to act in the child's best interests (Moqvist, 2003). The construction of the autonomous entrepreneurial self evidently leaves little room for concepts such as interdependency and the ethics of care, just as it makes it difficult to speak a language of solidarity and community learning. It is at its culminating point in the language on leadership that is so present today. Yet, as Freire (1970, 138) already stated: "These courses [leadership training courses] are based on the naïve assumption that one can promote the community by training its leaders—as if it were the parts that promote the whole and not the whole which, in being promoted, promotes the parts." Obviously, the entrepreneurial ideology, also constructs its own downside: the parent not negotiating the right choices and therefore responsible for jeopardizing his child's future in the pursuit of happiness in the global market. It is an individualizing construction that may exclude precisely those who have always been on the margins.

Note

1. I do not wish to say that everything is bad, but that everything is dangerous, which is not the same as what is bad. If everything is dangerous, we will always have work to do (tentative translation by us).

References

Beck, U. (1997a). Democratization of the family. *Childhood, 4*(2), 151–168.

Bénisti, J. A. (2005). *Rapport de la commission prévention du groupe d'étude parlementaire sur la sécurité intérieure.* Paris: Assemblée Nationale.

Biesta, G. (2007). Why "what works" won't work: evidence-based practice and the democratic deficit in educational research. *Educational Theory, 57*(1), 1–22.

Blanc, M. C., & Bonnabesse, M. L. (2008). *Parents et professionnels dans les structures d'accueil de jeunes enfants.* Rueil-Malmaison: ASH.

Bourdieu, P. (1993). *La misère du monde.* Paris: Seuil.

Bradt, L., & Bouverne-De Bie, M. (2007). Social work and the shift from welfare to justice. *British Journal of Social Work, DOI* 10.1093/bjsw/bcm072.

Brown, J., Cohen, P., Johnson, J G. & Salzinger, S. (1998). A longitudinal analysis of risk factors for child maltreatment. Child Abuse Neglect, Nov. 22. Vol. II, 1065-78.

Burman, E. (1994). *Deconstructing developmental psychology*. London: Routledge.

Collectif, L. (2006). *Pas de 0 de conduite pour les enfants de 3 ans*. Ramonville Saint-Agne: Erès.

Connolly, P. (2006). Summary statistics, educational achievement gaps and the ecological fallacy. *Oxford Review of Education, 32*(2), 235–252.

Crawford, A. (2003). Contractual governance of deviant behaviour. *Journal of Law and Society, 30*(4), 479–505.

De Mey, W., Coussée, F., Vandenbroeck, M., & Bouverne-De Bie, M. (2009). Social work and parent support in reaction to children's antisocial behaviour: Constructions and effects. *International Journal of Social Welfare, 18*, 299–306.

Deleuze, G. (1985). *Foucault*. Paris: Les Editions de Minuit.

Dwairy, M., & Menshar, K. E. (2006). Parenting style, individuation, and mental health of Egyptian adolescents. *Journal of Adolescence, 26*(1), 103–117.

Featherstone, B. (2006). Rethinking family support in the current policy context. *British Journal of Social Work, 36*, 5–19.

Fendler, L. (2006). Why generalisability is not generalisable. *Journal of Philosophy of Education, 40*(4), 437–449.

Finn, D. (2003). The employment first welfare state. Lessons from the New Deal for young people. *Social Policy and Administration, 37*(7), 709–724.

Foucault, M. (1975). *Surveiller et punir*. Paris: Gallimard.

Foucault, M. (1983). A propos de la généalogie de l'éthique : un aperçu du travail en cours. In M. Foucault (Ed.), *Dits et écrits II, 1976–1988* (pp. 1202–1230). Paris Gallimard.

Foucault, M. (1990). *Politics, philosophy, culture. Interviews and other writings 1977–1984* Routledge: London.

Foucault, M. (1993). About the beginnings of the hermeneutics of the self. *Political Theory, 21*(2), 198–227.

Foucault, M. (2001). *L'Herméneutique du sujet. Cours au Collège de France 1981–1982*. Paris: Seuil / Gallimard.

Franssen, A.,, Cartuyvels, Y., & De Coninck, F. (2003). *Dix ans de décret de l'aide à la jeunesse: des principes aux pratiques. L'aide à la jeunesse à l'épreuve de la (dé)judiciarisation*. Liège: Editions Jeunesse et Droit.

Freire, P. (1970). *Pedagogy of the oppressed*. New York: Herder and Herder.

Giddens, A. (1998). *The Third Way: The renewal of social democracy*. Cambridge: Polity Press.

Gilbert, N. & Gilbert, B. (1989). *The enabling state: Modern welfare capitalism in America*. Oxford: Oxford University Press.

Hamilton, C. & Roberts, M. (2000). State responsibility and parental responsibility: New Labour and the implementation of the United Nations Convention on the Rights of the Child in the United Kingdom. In D. Fottrell (ed.), *Revisiting Children's Rights. 10*

Himmelweit, S., & Sigala, M. (2004). Choice and the relation between identities and behaviour for mothers with preschool children: some implications for policy from a UK study. *Journal of Social Policy, 33*(3), 455–478.

Howe, R.B. (2001). Do parents have fundamental rights? *Journal of Canadian Studies, 36*(3), 61–78.

Institut National de la Santé et de la Recherche Médicale. (2005). *Troubles de conduite chez l'enfant et l'adolescent*. Paris: INSERM.

King, M. (1997). *A better world for children. Explorations in morality and authority*. London/New York: Routlegde.

Mandara, J. (2006). The impact of family functioning on African American males' academic achievement: a review and clarification of the empirical literature. *Teachers College Record, 108*(2), 206–223.

Margolin, L. (1997). *Under the cover of kindness. The invention of social work*. Charlottesville, VA: University Press of Virginia.

Masschelein, J., & Quaghebeur, K. (2005). Participation for better or for worse? *Journal of Philosophy of Education, 39*(1), 51–65.

Moqvist, I. (2003). Constructing a parent. In M. Bloch, T. Holmlund, I. Moqvist & T.S. Popkewitz (eds), *Governing children, families and education. Restructuring the welfare state* (pp. 117–132). New York: Palgrave Macmillan.

Moss, P. (2007). Bringing politics into the nursery: early childhood education as a democratic practice *European Early Childhood Education Research Journal, 15*(1), 5–20.

Moss, P. (2008). *Markets and democratic experimentalism. Two models for early childhood education and care*. Working Paper No. 53. The Hague, The Netherlands: Bernard van Leer Foundation and Bertelsmann Stiftung.

Moss, P., Dillon, J., & Statham, J. (2000). The "child in need" and the "rich child": discourses, constructions and practice. *Critical Social Policy, 63*(2), 233–254.

Mouffe, C. (2005). *On the political*. London: Routledge.

Neyrand, G. (2006). *Faut-il avoir peur de nos enfants? Politiques sécuritaires et enfance*. Paris: La Découverte.

Organisation for Economic Co-operation and Development. (2006). *Starting strong II. Early childhood education and care*. Paris: O.E.C.D.

Parton, N. (2006). Every child matters: the shift to prevention whilst strengthening protection in children's services in England. *Children and Youth Services Review, 28*(8), 796–992.

Payne, M. (2005). *The origins of social work: Continuity and change*. Basingstoke: Palgrave Macmillan.

Peyton, V., Jacobs, A., O'Brien, M., & Roy, C. (2001). Reasons for choosing child care: associations with family factors, quality, and satisfaction. *Early Childhood Research Quarterly, 16*, 191–208.

Popkewitz, T. (1996). Rethinking decentralization and the state/civil society distinctions: The state as problematic governing. *Journal of Educational Policy, 11*(1), 27–51.

Popkewitz, T. (2003). Governing the child and pedagogicalization of the parent: A historical excursus into the present. In M. Bloch, K. Holmlund, L. Moqvist & T. Popkewitz (Eds.), *Governing children, families and education. Restructuring the welfare state* (pp. 35–62). New York: Palgrave.

Pupavac, V. (2001). Misanthropy without borders: The international children's rights regime. *Disasters, 25*(2), 95–112.

Roose, R. & De Bie, M. (2007). Children's rights; a challenge for social work. *International social work, 51*(1), 37–46.

Roose, R. & De Bie, M. (2008). Do children have rights or do their rights have to be realised? The United Nations convention on the rights of the child as a frame of reference for pedagogical action. *Journal of Philosophy of Education, 41*(3), 431–443.

Rosanvallon, P. (1995). *La nouvelle question sociale: repenser l'Etat-providence*. Paris: Seuil.

Sanders, M., Markie-Dadds, C., & Turner, K. (2003). *Theoretical, scientific and clinical foundations of the Triple P—Positive Parenting Program: A population approach to promotion of parenting competence*. (Vol. 1). Queensland: The University of Queensland.

Schneider, C. (2007). Police power and race riots in Paris. *Politics & Society, 35*(4), 523–549.

Spratt, T. (2001). The influence of child protection orientation on child welfare practice. *British Journal of Social Work, 31*(6), 933–954.

Stepney, P. (2006). Mission impossible? Critical practice in social work. *British Journal of Social Work, 36*(8), 1289–1307.

Thomas, R., & Zimmer-Gembeck, M. J. (2007). Behavioral outcomes of Parent–Child Interaction Therapy and Triple P—Positive Parenting Program: A review and meta-analysis. *Journal of Abnormal Child Psychology, 35*, 475–495.

Vandenbroeck, M. (2003). From crèches to childcare: constructions of motherhood and inclusion/exclusion in the history of Belgian infant care. *Contemporary Issues in Early Childhood, 4*(3), 137–148.

Vandenbroeck, M., De Visscher, S., Van Nuffel, K., & Ferla, J. (2008). Mothers" search for infant child care: the dynamic relationship between availability and desirability in a continental European welfare state. *Early Childhood Research Quarterly, 23*(2), 245–258.

Vandenbroucke, F. (2006). *Maatregelen ter stimulering van de participatie aan het kleuteronderwijs. Non Paper*. Brussel: Ministerie van Werk, Onderwijs en Vorming.

Villar, P., Luengo, M. A., Gomez-Fraguela, J. A., & Romero, E. (2006). Assessment of the Validity of Parenting Constructs Using the Multitrait-Multimethod Model. *European Journal of Psychological Assessment, 22*, 59–68.

Wacquant, L. (2002). *Punir les pauvres. Le nouveau gouvernement de l'insécurité sociale*. Marseille: Agone.

Wall, K., & Jose, J. S. (2004). Managing work and care: a difficult challenge for immigrant families. *Social Policy and Administration, 38*(6), 591–621.

Westman, J.C. (1999). Children's rights, parents' prerogatives, and society's obligations. *Child Psychiatry and Human Development, 29*(4), 315–328.

Zelizer, V.A. (1994). *Pricing the priceless child. The changing social value of children*. Princeton, NJ: Princeton University Press.

CHAPTER EIGHT

Global and Local Trends for Governance and Planning in Early Childhood Education and Care

Effects of Preschool Vouchers

I-FANG LEE

Abstract

For governments around the world, conceptualizing early childhood education and care as a site for an early start on educational, social, and economic investment has become a dominant trend of educational planning. Contemporary educational policies, such as preschool vouchers, reflect the effects of a neoliberal political economic reasoning system both locally and globally. The concept of the educational voucher is a typical example of how neoliberal notions of freedom, equality, and choice could become a problematic interpretation of democracy to achieve the goal of education for all. Therefore, in this chapter, I highlight two different preschool voucher schemes in Taiwan and Hong Kong to discuss how educational reform discourses can rework and reconstruct the ways in which we come to construct and desire equality and social justice in education for young children. In addition, an overarching theme of this chapter seeks to unpack the systems of reasoning that organize and order our common sense of educational knowledge at the present historical moment to understand how educational reform discourses and policies, such as vouchers, produce certain new but dangerous mentalities as contemporary desirable normative knowledge and truth(s) to shape and discipline the ways in which we come to construct and imagine equality and social justice in early education and care.

Introduction

The field of early childhood education and care has been constructed and conceptualized as a site for educational, social, and cultural interventions as well as political-economic investment in multiple geopolitical spaces. This particular conception of early childhood education and care as a form of investment, whether we like it or not, has been widely circulated to reflect a neoliberal political economic reasoning system (Dahlberg, 2000; Dahlberg & Moss, 2005; Keeley, 2007; Lee, 2008, 2009) as a dominant contemporary reform logic in planning for a better early childhood education and care system at the global and local levels. In that, despite political, theoretical, and philosophical differences among different stakeholders, a common hope to create or (re)develop a better early childhood education and care system for all children seems to be a universal goal and shared desire.

Thus, issues concerning educational accountability, accessibility, and affordability in the field of early childhood education and care have been frequently discussed and often debated when developing contemporary educational reform plans. Within the spectrum of different theoretical frameworks and philosophical beliefs, different stakeholders such as researchers, parents, teachers, policymakers, etc. often draw on different frames of reference when defining *what constitutes quality early childhood education and care* as well as *what we should be doing to plan better ways of governing the field of early childhood education and care*. In addition, the issues regarding educational equity and equality have also been up for debate and discussion on multiple grounds. While there are different ways to analyze and discuss these issues of educational accountability, fairness in accessibility of early childhood education and care, and affordability of quality programs among different families, it is important to note that a particular intelligibility of these issues is shaped by the emergence of a dominating voice from various coalitions of "the right" (Apple, 2001) to (re)configure a new universal truth for all. Therefore, in this chapter, in order to rethink and critically understand global circulations and local (re)interpretations of a particular dominating voice from the right, I highlight preschool vouchers as an example to discuss the ways in which contemporary educational reform discourses and policies can (re)work and (re)constitute a dominant and popular construction of social justice in education for young children.

In the first section of this chapter, through questioning vouchers as a universal solution for all, two examples of preschool vouchers from Asian localities—Taiwan and Hong Kong—are highlighted. In addition, while noting the different contextual factors for the birth of preschool vouchers in Taiwan and Hong Kong, I seek to underscore how a similar and almost identical logic of governance in the field of early childhood education and care is at work as a *glocal* educational planning and governing strategy. In the second section, critical and poststructural theories are used as analytical tools to unpack how preschool vouchers are problematic while appearing to promise a solution to problems of educational accountability, fairness in accessibility of early childhood education and care, and affordability of quality programs among different families. Following the discussion of preschool vouchers as a problematic glocal educational reform policy, in the third section, I call for the need to reconceptualize current and popular constructions of the roles and functions of early childhood education and care. Coming from a poststructural theoretical perspective, I argue against the current trend of ignoring multiplicities while constructing a label of "homogenous others" through the mobilization of vouchers as the magical reform policy.

Vouchers: A Universal Solution?

Among multiple contemporary educational changes, the formation and deployment of preschool vouchers can be "seen" as an example in which notions of decentralization and deregulation, and issues of empowerment through freedom to choose have been strategically mobilized to depict progress and development. Since Friedman's (1955, 1982) articulation and proposal of a voucher plan within the United States, it has become a controversial educational reform policy that has appeared in local and global political debates. While Friedman's contextual idea of an educational voucher plan is rooted within the context of the United States, thoughts on vouchers have never been confined within the U.S. borders but have become widely circulated and constructed as an example of emancipatory and democratic educational reform practice for all to gain greater freedom and to ensure equity in the field of education.

Obviously, nested within Friedman's idea of the educational voucher is a notion of "freedom to choose." Currently, a popular and worldwide common belief about Friedman's concept of educational vouchers is the promise of greater freedom in which all families are empowered through a notion of choice. Therefore, the concept and traces of vouchers can be found and identified across multiple geopolitical regions. For example, a Chilean voucher plan allows parents to choose a school for their children, whether public, private, or religious schools. Under a national voucher plan, parents are empowered to make educational/school choice as public funding follows to whatever school their parents deem "appropriate" and choose for them (for an example of Chile's national voucher plan, see Carnoy & McEwan, 2003).

Another example is England's nursery voucher scheme (1996–1997). Within the scheme of this voucher plan, parents were able to "buy" early childhood education or care provisions/services of their choice with public funding for their four-year-old children. This educational reform was first deployed by the Conservative Party to promote educational equity for all children. However, this nursery voucher scheme came to an end after the Conservative Party lost the election in 1997 to the Labour Party.

Still another notable example is the various current voucher and school choice programs in selected U.S. cities, such as the one in Milwaukee, Wisconsin—known as the Milwaukee Parental Choice Program (for an example of the Milwaukee voucher plan, see Witte, 2000). These voucher plans, across different U.S. cities, have been recognized and acknowledged by some minority groups and conservative politicians as providing a partial but instant solution for families who are otherwise not able to "afford" educational "choice." The words, "afford" and "choice" have become major parts of the educational reform language that is taken as natural, is no longer questioned, is accepted as "good," and that often is taken as simply a part of the United States' cultural imaginary—a capitalist society that offers choices to those who can afford them. In the case of voucher policies, however, the targeted groups are often lower income and minority families, although the "good intention" of vouchers is directed towards everyone—where affordability and choice become desirable, natural, and unquestioned parts of the reform language. In the U.S. voucher plans, there also seems to be a sense of greater freedom for educational choice that is combined, rhetorically/discursively, with an offer of a degree of "social justice."

These above examples of vouchers from Chile, England and the United States, while each has a different sociopolitical and cultural background, together they share a similar vision, which is a market approach to early childhood education and care. In that, it is assumed that a market approach to education will not only empower the parents and students as "free choosers" but will also improve the quality and equality of education and care for all children. Such assumptions of a market approach in the field of education reflect the core elements of a neoliberal political economic reasoning system that has been widely circulated at the global level to facilitate a universal intelligibility of educational vouchers.

Therefore, traveling into the geopolitical spaces of Taiwan and Hong Kong, the concept of "voucher," similar to those cases in the United States, England, and elsewhere in the international community, has become a signifier in contemporary reforms. In the following sections, I draw on the preschool vouchers in Taiwan and Hong Kong as two cases to illustrate how reform discourses, such as vouchers, can rework and reconstruct the ways in which we come to construct and desire equality and social justice in education.

Taiwanese Preschool Vouchers: Illusions of Freedom, Equality and Democracy

The first voucher program was deployed in Taipei, Taiwan in 1998, for five-year-old children who attend private licensed and registered kindergartens or childcare institutions. By the 2000–01 school year, such preschool vouchers were available throughout Taiwan. The face value of the vouchers is NT$10,000 (US$312) per year as a tuition reimbursement to parents. However, using public funds to reimburse parents with children in licensed private preschool programs only exacerbates the problems and ambiguities that are embedded with the Taiwanese version of preschool vouchers.

For example, embedded within the concept of the voucher is the desire for decentralization and deregulation. In other words, with a voucher scheme, it is anticipated that education/schools shall no longer be regulated by the government as a centralized monopoly system (Friedman, 1955). However, in the ways in which the Taiwanese version of preschool vouchers work, the government has "reversed its previous hands-off approach to private preschool education" (Ho, 2006). Moreover, with the "rules" of early childhood educational vouchers in mind and noting tuition differences between public and private programs in Taiwan, for a family to be able to afford private early childhood education and care services, economic capital is an imperative material condition and reality.[1] Therefore, the Taiwanese preschool voucher scheme is filled with ambiguities and controversies when it comes to issues of accessibility and affordability.

Issues of Accessibility and Affordability for Taiwanese Early Childhood Education and Care Programs

There are both public and private kindergartens and childcare programs in Taiwan. Currently, the enrollment method for public early childhood education and care programs is organized through a lottery system, which operates on a district by district basis. Such an enrollment method requires parents who desire to enroll their children in public programs (both kindergartens and childcare institutions) to learn and know how to maneuver the rules of a lottery game.[2] If parents cannot win spots in public programs for their children through a lottery system, they have no choice but to forgo the choice of early childhood education and care unless they can afford to look into private programs as options.

Furthermore, according to the government's public statistical records from the Ministry of Education and Children's Bureau for the 2007–08 school year, there were 138,287 children attending public kindergartens and childcare programs whereas there were 295,474 children in private provisions. Among the total population for 3–5 years old for the 2007–08 school year, 37.33% of the children 3–5 years old did not attend any public or private kindergartens/childcare programs. Taking such official records as an example for discussion, this simple statistical calculation elucidates that accessibility to public programs (whether kindergarten or childcare programs) for young children is relatively limited and the affordability of private programs may be an expensive option for numerous families with young children in Taiwan. This issue of affordability is represented by the alarmingly high percentage of children not attending any program. For that, while being careful not to make an overgeneralized conclusion about the 37.33% of young children who are not enrolled in any type of public or private programs, given the common parental belief in early childhood education in Taiwan, it is possible to interpret that a significant number of children in the 37.33% may come from disadvantaged families whose parents may not be able to afford private early education and care services.

Therefore, the Taiwanese version of the preschool voucher scheme further amplifies socioeconomic differences and sustains or even further perpetuates the existing status quo for children and their families in Taiwan (Lee, 2006). Through preschool vouchers, discussions on educational equality and social justice have been embraced by particular groups of educators and parents, such as middle-class families, private preschool owners and administrators, and the so-called neoliberal and/or conservative politicians, to "protect" or "preserve" the particular social and cultural dispositions for their own children and families. Taiwanese preschool voucher policies have not only transformed the field of early childhood education through a notion of "democratic governance" but have also produced an idea of the "market" as the new "normative" way of reasoning and being. Thus, the Taiwanese version of preschool vouchers presents a dangerous emergence of a problematic combination of sociopolitical democratization and education marketization (Ho, 2006). As Ho (2006) notes: "democratization and educational marketization emerged jointly in Taiwan" (p. 71).

Associating sociopolitical democracy with educational marketization is problematic as it dangerously re-constitutes a new notion of democracy and freedom that works to exclude particular disadvantaged groups of families. In that, such an ambiguous combination of sociopolitical democracy with marketization certainly reflects the core logic of neoliberalism (Apple, 2001) and, whether we like it or not, mobilizing the concept of choice as a representation of democracy and freedom through vouchers to improve problems of social justice and equality in education has become a dominant glocal educational reform practice.

Preschool Voucher Schemes in Hong Kong: A New Milestone for What?

Along the similar trend of neoliberal influences of planning and governing in the field of early childhood education, the Government of the Hong Kong Special Administrative Region of the People's Republic of China introduced a *Pre-primary Education Voucher Scheme* in 2006. As projected by the local government, this voucher scheme can be beneficial to multiple members in the field of early childhood education and care in Hong Kong. For example, such a voucher scheme shall reduce parents' financial burden of preschool tuition costs, provide professional development for all teachers, improve the quality of preschool education by raising the minimum requirements of the teacher's qualifications, and benefit at least 90% of the children 3–6 years old in Hong Kong. Packaging it as a miracle solution/reform policy to fix problems, the local government plans a five-year timeline for the preschool voucher scheme to steer the development of early childhood education and care in Hong Kong. Therefore, as much as this preschool voucher scheme functions as a short cut to fix problems in the field of early childhood education and care in Hong Kong, it paradoxically creates new problems on issues of accessibility, affordability, and accountability.

Issues of Accessibility, Affordability, and Accountability in Hong Kong's Preschool Education and Care

Although the current preschool voucher scheme is constructed as a "new milestone" by the government for the field of early childhood education and care, it has stoked many heated discussions among different groups of stakeholders, such as parents, teachers, policy-makers, etc. (Yuan, 2007). For example, although this voucher scheme aims to increase the accessibility of early childhood education as well as to make preschool education and care more affordable for all families by providing vouchers as tuition reimbursements to relieve the financial burdens of parents, the rules of such a policy ironically work to further marginalize many families that have already been disadvantaged. A critical read into the voucher policy could reveal how children of lower income families may be the ultimate others to be excluded through this scheme.

Among the different restrictions of this voucher scheme, it is important to note that all children of legal residents in Hong Kong are eligible to apply for vouchers; however, children of lower income families shall not combine vouchers with other forms of subsidies from the Welfare Department. For example, when comparing the face value of preschool vouchers with multiple forms of subsidies from the Welfare Department, preschool vouchers do not provide sufficient financial support for families of lower income groups. However, since the deployment of this preschool voucher scheme, many previously existing social subsidies for young children from the Welfare Department are gradually subsiding. From this perspective, the current preschool voucher scheme in Hong Kong does not seem to address the problems of accessibility and affordability for children from disadvantaged families.

In addition, vouchers can only be redeemed at nonprofit-making private schools offering a local curriculum and that charge a tuition fee lower than HKD$24,000 (US$3,077) per year for half-day programs (or HKD$48,000 for full-day programs).[3] Given that the face value of the voucher remains the same regardless of the length of the programs (i.e., half-day or full-day programs, what is at issue here is the lack of attention to families with the need for full-day childcare programs. It is important to note that families in need of full-day early childhood education and care programs in Hong Kong are most likely to be families of lower income groups.[4] Therefore, in spite of the fact that the current voucher scheme aims to fix the problems of affordability, preschool education and care services have become more unaffordable than ever for families.

Moreover, coupled with the deployment of this voucher scheme is a problematic and ambiguous official construction of teacher professionalization and accountability that is associated with the issue of education quality.[5] Among the multiple regulations that are associated with the voucher scheme, it is important to highlight the changes in teacher qualification and the new system of a quality assurance scheme. Under this voucher scheme, all in-service teachers are required to come back to school for teacher education programs in order to obtain a higher level certificate in early childhood education.[6] However, on the one hand, while this voucher scheme requests a higher professional standard by obligating all in-service preschool teachers to obtain a higher level certificate in early childhood education, on the other hand, it excludes all preschool teachers from a government salary scale to ensure minimum salary security by canceling a salary scale.[7] This practice of raising the standard but leaving teachers' salaries up to a floating market system has created a growing turnover rate in the field of early childhood education. In that, it is important to question how can the quality of education be improved when teachers' turnover rate is growing to reflect the uncertainties and insecurities in the field (Lee, 2008)? Moreover, accompanying this current voucher scheme is a shift of responsibility. Instead of holding the government accountable for quality preschool education, through mobilizing the concept of parental choice in the voucher scheme, parents are now held accountable for making the right choices for their children's education while the schools are held accountable for providing quality education through a mechanism of self-evaluation and a centralized quality assurance scheme. All nonprofit-making private schools that are now receiving public and government funding through vouchers shall be held accountable to respond to a centralized quality assurance scheme that is run by the Education Bureau.

In sum, what's problematic about the voucher scheme in Hong Kong is its incapability to address issues of accessibility, affordability, and accountability. While recognizing the government's effort in planning the development of preschool education, some local critics and politicians have argued that instead of spending public funds to further marginalize the already disadvantaged, universal and free preschool education and care services would be better than the current voucher scheme (Lee, 2008, 2009).

Lessons from Taiwan and Hong Kong: Preschool Vouchers as Glocal Reform Policy

Examples of educational vouchers can be found around the world as the new hope for many educators and parents, mobilizing them to imagine different ways of changing the field of education for the better. Such imagination about betterment is fabricated though utilizing vouchers to mobilize choice discourse as the perfect means to fix problems for the sake of creating improvement and progress. Therefore, vouchers can be conceptualized as a glocal discourse. That is, while the idea of the educational voucher is a global concept, it has been interpreted and translated differently to fit local contexts as well as local cultural mentalities or reasoning systems.

As shown by the example from Taiwan, the mobilization of vouchers has strategically transformed parents into consumers to stress that parental freedom to choose through the voucher scheme is an embodiment of sociopolitical democracy. However, what are left without critical reconceptualization are the illusions of freedom, equality, and democracy under the slogan of parental choice in vouchers. In addition, learning from the preschool voucher scheme in Hong Kong, while the government may perceive the voucher scheme as a perfect plan to address issues of accountability, accessibility, and affordability, it is important to note that good intentions of providing financial relief to parents with preschoolers may fall short of their promises.

Therefore, as a glocal reform policy, in the case of educational vouchers, whether one advocates or opposes their deployment, it seems to return to the universal educational arguments on issues of accountability, accessibility, and affordability as well as political concerns on issues of freedom, democracy, equity, and social justice. To better understand the multiple layers and complexities of vouchers as a glocal reform practice, in the following section of this chapter, I draw on critical and poststructural theories as analytical tools to reconceptualize the effects of vouchers.

Rethinking the Effects of Preschool Vouchers: Preschool Vouchers as a New Sociocultural Administration

Coming from a poststructural theoretical perspective, preschool vouchers can be conceptualized as social and cultural administration in which new "norms" and "truths" are produced to (re)define the normative ways of thinking, acting, and being. That is, the systems of reasoning that underpin the intelligibility of preschool voucher policies produce sociocultural disciplinary guidelines to shape a particular normative understanding of what a *good and appropriate* early childhood educational program means for children and parents to shape the development of the field. Moreover, embedded within the texts of preschool vouchers, take the Taiwanese preschool vouchers as an example, the "good and appropriate" preschool programs are the ones that are licensed by the government to meet the standards of "high" quality. In addition, the notion of "good" parents is also inscribed through preschool vouchers as those who know how to choose or "shop" within the "market" of preschool education. The *normal* parents are those who are active, flexible, and responsible participants/players with an entrepreneurial spirit in the voucher "game" and who know how to exercise their "parental choice" in an appropriate manner to choose quality preschool programs for their children. In addition, the different social and cultural dispositions among parents cannot be ignored. The differences in social and cultural dispositions among groups of parents and families have been noted by Bourdieu (1984) as "habitus"—a theoretical analytical notion through which social actors (such as parents) can be mapped and positioned in different social spaces of a fluid and shifting social field.

In other words, from a critical class perspective and analysis, Bourdieu's notion of the *habitus* illuminates that parents of certain social dispositions understand and embody specific cultural codes or a particular set of tastes to exercise their "choices" when using vouchers. That is, when parents are searching for and choosing schools—cultural and economic institutions—their eyes look through a particular cultural lens that filters out and yet focuses on specific qualities among the various types of schools. What is considered a "good" program/school for their children has to do with the parents' notion/perception of what types of cultural and economic institutions are suitable for shaping and cultivating their children's identities.

Therefore, Bourdieu's (1984) concept of *habitus* not only situates the idea of choice within webs of class and cultural differences but also associates the consequence of choice within the classed social dispositions. To understand the complex relations between notions of *habitus*, *taste*, and *choice*, Bourdieu further explained:

> The habitus is both the generative principle of objectively classifiable judgments and the system of classification (principium divisions) of these practices. It is in the relationship between the two capacities which define the habitus, the capacity to produce classifiable practices and works, and the capacity to differentiate and appreciate these practices and products (taste), that the represented social world, i.e., the space of life-styles, is constituted (1984, p. 170).

In this sense, parents' educational choice not only echoes their taste in cultural and economic institutions but also serves as a vehicle to further distinguish their children by choosing a particular type of school. Thus, choice in education not only is shaped by class and cultural differences but is also a product of such different dispositions. Within the particular rules of educational vouchers in Taiwan for early childhood education, to understand the effects of reform discourses, the way that class and cultural differences play a big part in helping or hindering the parents' understanding of preschool vouchers should not be dismissed. [8]

To unpack the construction of "good" parents, it is imperative to problematize the construction of the "modern entrepreneurial" subjectivity through which individual autonomy and freedom have been emphasized within a "Western" notion of advanced liberalism's political rhetoric (Rose, 1996, 1999). In other words, while promoting "freedom to choose," Taiwanese preschool vouchers produce rules and norms regarding how to choose, and a new definition of the "modern entrepreneurial self" is at work through voucher policies. Through the circulation of preschool vouchers as a form of educational reform, not only are the parents disciplined by the rules of voucher policies but also the field of early childhood education and care is regulated through the licensing-granting process. Through voucher policies, parents are simultaneously governed and self-governed as their choices are shaped by the rules of voucher policies to think of licensed programs as *appropriate* high-quality or *normal* early educational and childcare institutions (Dahlberg, 2000; or see Dahlberg et al., 1999).

In addition, conceptualizing preschool vouchers as a sociocultural governing technology that regulates, normalizes, and administers the parents, as well as the field of early childhood education, also leads to a re-conceptualization of the concept of social inclusion/exclusion (Popkewitz, 2000). As a social and cultural governing technology, educational voucher policies (re)-define the norms of "good" and "appropriate" or "voucher-worthy" kindergarten and childcare programs through government licensure and voucher granting processes. Kindergarten and childcare programs without licenses are constructed as underground, "abnormal," or "inappropriate" cultural institutions for young children. Parents who enroll their children in nonlicensed programs are not only excluded from being rewarded with educational vouchers as partial tuition refund/credits for their children, but they are also included and/or perceived as being within the category of "abnormal/bad" parents. As much as the political rhetoric of vouchers initially publicizes notions of liberal democracy to promote greater social inclusion by framing vouchers as beneficial for *all* five-year-old children, ironically, social exclusion occurs simultaneously.

As governance through educational policies is not through brute force in which the parents, children, teachers, and preschool programs are oppressively controlled, organized, and ranked, governance through educational policies shall focus on the productive effects of power in which new mentalities, systems of reasoning, and rationalities are made intelligible and logical. Governance through such constructions of mentalities becomes implicit and indirect and requires the formation of new subjectivities to produce a new classification logic. At this point, Foucault's (1991) concept of governmentality (governmental rationality) helps to shed light on how educational reforms and policies such as preschool vouchers can be thought of as ruptures that interject different ways of reasoning and thinking and fabricate new forms of knowledge about changes as the "truths" in the field of education. The constructions of the new "norms," which have become a new "regime of truth" are constituted within a complex web of power/knowledge relations where power is omnipresent.

With this notion of power-as-governmentality, it becomes possible to understand how power is not just repressive but also produces desirable norms in which we gradually become self-disciplined to fit into the descriptions of the new norms. As Popkewitz (1991) clarifies, such a notion of power:

> …is intricately bound to the rules, standards, and styles of reasoning by which individuals speak, think, and act, in producing their everyday world. Power is relational and regional (p. 223)

Through this notion of power, it helps to explain how vouchers work as an effective glocal reform discourse to inscribe new norms and codes of conduct while being accepted as democratic reform policies and a desirable global trend in planning the development of early childhood education and care.

To summarize at this point, preschool vouchers function as a social and cultural administration to (re)inscribe a new subjectivity and rationality in which we are tamed as we become self-disciplined to accept such mentalities as normative ways of being, acting, and thinking. This is the transformativity of educational reform discourses, such as preschool vouchers, through which our "common sense" can be dangerously transformed to redefine progressive political notions of freedom, social equality, and a neoliberal image and practice of "democracy" that includes selected groups of parents, families, and politicians, while at the same time it is a discourse and reasoning system that excludes others from being good, or normal.

Constructing "What" Through Preschool Vouchers?

Preschool vouchers have helped to construct hopes of progress and outline visions of a better field of early childhood education and care in many different localities. When traveling into Taiwan at the present time and space, vouchers seem to promote choice, generate positive competition among preschool programs, and increase the affordability and accessibility of early childhood education and care for all children, at a time when funding is still low. As for the development of preschool education, vouchers seem to function as an alternative form of government subsidy for all children to attend at least half-day programs as well as an initiative to improve the quality of education. Therefore, at first glance, preschool vouchers appear to be a "magical" and modern progressive reform practice through which many perceived problems can be fixed, and children and their families can be helped, or saved. However, as I have argued throughout the previous sections of this chapter, vouchers can be dangerous.

The systems of reasoning embedded within vouchers have inscribed new norms and truths. For example, through the circulations of Taiwanese and Hong Kong versions of preschool vouchers, new categories of "appropriate and good" preschool programs and classifications of "good and normal" parents are constructed. Despite the notion of "freedom to choose" as a problematic construction within the Taiwanese preschool voucher system, the notion of "choice" has been dangerously mobilized as a taken-for-granted modern and democratic educational practice. The Taiwanese and Hong Kong versions of "truth" about "choice" is mobilized, in part, by the U.S. Chicago School's neoliberalism through which the economic analytical perspectives and analyses are expanded to become the universal reasoning system for all. Thus, within the framework of Chicago School neoliberalism, through which the concept of the voucher is mobilized, all spheres or fields are redefined as an extension or a form of the economic domain (Lemke, 2001), while also nested within political, cultural, and other discourses that, together, make "sense."

In attempting to address and solve the problems of the affordability, accessibility, and accountability of early childhood education and care, the deployment of preschool voucher discourses has transformed educational problems into economic rationalities. Thus, it becomes "normal" to transform the field of early childhood education and care into a preschool *market* in which the parents are deemed consumers while the children are thought of as *human capital*. Rationalizing educational issues through economic logic has become a norm in contemporary educational reform discourses through which education is thought of as a form of investment at both the local and global levels. For example, in Taiwan, it is believed that in order to achieve a better future that is filled with prosperity, adequate and smart investment at the present in education is necessary. Constructing today's children as tomorrow's citizens-to-be, proper educational planning and an appropriate early head start in early childhood education become indispensable modern normative educational practices. As noted: "investing in education is investing in our future" (CER, 1996).

Parents who know how to invest in their children through choosing appropriate and good preschool programs are tamed normal modern subjects with entrepreneurial spirits. This construction of normality is dangerous as it silently shapes the reasonable subject by reconfiguring the desirable subjectivity. In constructing a particular notion of hope, preschool vouchers have inscribed an economic logic as the normative narrative to depict how the field of early childhood education and care should be organized and how parents should embody and exercise "choice" while children are redefined as "human capital." Such a normative narrative not only disciplines the field of early childhood education but also governs the parents. Thus, it is important to be critically wary of the effects of educational reform discourses in which transformations are at work.

While vouchers have been analytically associated with neoliberal discourses and classified as governing policies of the "Right" (i.e., see the work of Apple, 2001) that are either good or evil, if we are "trapped" by such binaries in our reasoning, we risk ignoring the complexities and multiple dimensions of educational reform discourses that we need to scrutinize (Lindblad & Popkewitz, 2004; Popkewitz, 2006). It is from such a standpoint that I call for a shift toward a poststructural dimension of analysis related to the intelligibility of preschool vouchers as a case of educational reform discourses through which a particular vision of the future for all is crafted.

The ambiguities and tensions of Taiwanese and Hong Kong versions of preschool vouchers, as discussed in this chapter, serve as examples of how contemporary educational reform discourses produce illusions. Despite the "good" intentions of preschool vouchers to re-plan the field of early childhood education and care in the name of freedom, democracy, and equity/fairness on issues of affordability, accessibility, and accountability, such reform practice ironically perpetuates differences by privileging certain families over others. In a way, preschool vouchers paradoxically function as an "othering" practice to sustain distinctions as well as a governing practice to shape who we are and who we should be. From this perspective, educational reforms dangerously prescribe who we are through the deployment of policies to govern the subject while molding desirable subjectivity as the norm. Reforms thus are technologies of the self through which the governing of others and the governing of the self are interlaced together by reform discourses to prescribe how one should act or think or be. Reforms, understood within such analytical modes, are less about emancipation and more about specifying the conduct of conduct (for example, see Lather, 2004; Popkewitz, 2006).

Within the framework of such theoretical and analytical perspectives, educational reform policies, such as preschool vouchers, become a tactic to regulate as well as to care for both the field of early childhood education and care and the families' "choices" in their children's preschool education. This is thought to be a form of "reasonable" modern state intervention in governing and cultivating the subjects'-as-citizens' lives in a "democratic" approach toward normalization. That is, "governance" or "regulation" is no longer done through brute force but through laws and policies which are thought to be formed in a democratic manner rather than under a dictatorship. The disciplinary tendencies of reform discourses and policies highlight a close link between power/knowledge relations and the making of subjectivities as well as the processes of subjectification. Having pointed to the "biopolitics" (Lather, 2004) of reform policies, my intention is to problematize the contemporary reform discourses as a form of salvation narrative for all in Taiwan.

The concept of "biopolitics" is rooted within Foucault's (1978) notion of "bio-power" through which "diverse techniques for achieving the subjugation of bodies and the control of population" (Foucault, 1978, p. 140) are made. The preschool voucher system makes young children a population category. Through the deployment of vouchers, not only the parents but also the preschools are regulated to fit the "rules/codes" of the voucher system/policy. While the parents are becoming "entrepreneurial" selves through self-governance, how to appropriately practice self-governance is also prescribed. In other words, "docile bodies" are created through the formation and deployment of educational reform discourses and policies. From such a perspective, reform policies can be thought of as "instruments of the state, as *institutions* of power" to ensure the maintenance or the production of relations and orders (Foucault, 1978). To borrow again from Foucault (1978), reform discourses and policies thus should be thought of as "techniques of power present at every level of the social body and utilized by very diverse institutions" (i.e., the family, schools, and the administration of collective bodies) to sustain norms and orders (p. 141). Therefore, to make the taken-for-granted construction of reforms as the problematic is to disturb the habitual ways of reasoning of our time to reconceptualize what is said and not said. This is to rupture the production of "truth" and to re-imagine how the present and future conditions could be otherwise.

A Concluding Note

My efforts throughout this chapter are not to disregard the hopes for a democratic and equitable educational system for all children. Rather, I believe that reform discourses can interject changes to produce new ways of thinking, being, and acting. It is such a production of "change" that makes reform discourses, such as vouchers, dangerous. The examples of vouchers in Taiwan and Hong Kong are helpful for us to rethink how neoliberal political economic discourse at the global and local levels has not only ruptured the field of education but also become a dominating reasoning to (re)constitute educational norms. In the name of freedom, democracy, and equity, the idea of preschool vouchers has been dangerously constructed as the miracle solution to address issues of affordability and accessibility in Taiwan and Hong Kong. While I do not ignore the fact that preschool vouchers do make early childhood education and care more affordable and accessible for some parents and families, I argue we should be critical in reconceptualizing how freedom to choose is constructed. When preschool vouchers in Taiwan and Hong Kong appear to promise freedom, choice, and quality education, shouldn't we question to whom do vouchers promise social justice and equity? Without the problematization and reconceptualization of preschool voucher discourses to critically reflect on what we think we know, we would not be wary of how reforms could promise to create democracy, equity, and freedom for all but produce illusions of inclusionary reasoning while exclusions remain unexamined.

Notes

1. Tuition differences between public and private kindergartens/childcare programs are significant in Taiwan.
2. Children from low-income families or children of disabled parents can be enrolled in public kindergartens or childcare programs without winning a lottery game. That is, minority or disadvantaged families have the first priority to be accepted into public preschool programs.
3. Currently, there are no public early childhood education and care programs in Hong Kong. All preschool institutions are privately owned. The only differences between these schools are whether a school is a profit-making or non-profit-making institution. For those schools that are categorized as profit-making/independent schools, they are not qualified for vouchers.
4. In Hong Kong, most children attend only half-day programs and return to their homes for childcare by parents, grandparents, nannies, or maids from overseas. Therefore, children that need full-day programs are more than likely to come from disadvantaged families.
5. As a means to improve the quality of education, the Hong Kong government has called for raising the stan-

dard of teacher qualification through the implementation of a voucher scheme. In that, schools that are eligible for parents to redeem vouchers need to meet the new regulations from the government

6. This program is known as High Diploma in Early Childhood Education, which is a sub-degree level program for both in-service and pre-service teachers as the minimum qualification.

7. School teachers' salary points are regulated and advised by the government of Hong Kong Special Administrative Region. However, the deployment of this Pre-primary Education Voucher Scheme has worked to de-regulate all preschool teachers from this centralized salary scale through the introduction of a market mechanism. Unlike school teachers in primary and secondary education sectors, preschool teachers' salaries are no longer protected by any fair scale but are shifted to a market mechanism.

8. A fraction of Taiwanese scholars have strategically deployed critical social theories to critique current preschool/early childhood educational vouchers as an "awful policy that deprives the poor" (Liu, 2000). Similarly, critiques of the marketization and privatization of education in Taiwan focus on issues of social inequality while attempting to give "voice" to the marginalized groups.

References

Apple, M. W. (2001). *Educating the "Right" Way: Markets, Standards, God, and Inequality*. New York: Routledge Falmer.

Bourdieu, P. (1984). *Distinction: A Social Critique of the Judgment of Taste*. Cambridge, MA: Harvard University Press.

Carnoy, M. & McEwan, P. J. (2003). Does Privatization Improve Education? The Case of Chile's National Voucher Plan. In D. N. Plank and. G. Sykes (Eds.), *Choosing Choice* (pp. 45–67). New York and London: Teachers College Press.

Commission on Education Reform (1996). *The Executive Report on Educational Reforms*. Taipei, Taiwan: Executive Yuan.

Dahlberg, G. (2000). From the "People's Home"—Folkhemmet—to the Enterprise: Reflections on the Constitution and Reconstitution of the Field of Early Childhood Pedagogy in Sweden. In T. S. Popkewitz (Ed.), *Educational Knowledge: Changing Relationships between the State, Civil Society, and the Educational Community* (pp. 201–220). Albany, NY: State University of New York Press.

Dahlberg, G., & Moss, P. (2005). *Ethics and Politics in Early Childhood Education*. London: RoutledgeFalmer.

Dahlberg, G., Moss, P., & Pence, A. R. (1999). *Beyond Quality in Early Childhood Education and Care: Postmodern Perspectives*. London, Philadelphia, PA: Falmer Press.

Foucault, M. (1978). *The History of Sexuality: An Introduction* (R. Hurley, Trans.). New York: Random House.

Foucault, M. (1991). Governmentality. In C. G. G. Burchell, P. Miller (Ed.), *The Foucault Effect: Studies in Governmentality* (pp. 87–104). Chicago, IL: The University of Chicago Press.

Friedman, M. (1955). *The Role of Government in Education*. New Brunswick, NJ: Rutgers University Press.

Friedman, M., & Friedman, R. D. (1982). *Capitalism and Freedom*. Chicago, IL: University of Chicago Press.

Ho, M.S. (2006). The Politics of Preschool Education Vouchers in Taiwan. *Comparative Education Review*, 50(1), 66–89.

Keeley, B. (2007). *Human Capital: How What You Know Shapes YourLlife*. OECD Publishing

Lather, P. (2004). This IS your Father's Paradigm: Government Intrusion and the Case of Qualitative Research in Education. *Qualitative Inquiry*, 10(1), 15–34.

Lee, I. F. (2006). Illusions of Social Democracy: Early Childhood Educational Voucher Policies in Taiwan. In M. Bloch, D. Kennedy, T. Lightfoot, and D. Weyenberg (Eds.), *The Child in the World/the World in the Child: Education and the Configuration of a Universal, Modern, and Globalized Childhood*. New York: Palgrave Macmillan.

Lee, I. F. (2008). Formations of New Governing Technologies and Productions of New Norms: The Dangers Of Pre-School Voucher Discourse. *Contemporary Issues in Early Childhood*, 9 (1), 80–82.

Lee, I. F. (2008). Universal Preschool Education Is Better Than Preschool Voucher Scheme. (In Chinese), *Hong Kong Economic Times*, A28, September 10.

Lee, I.F. (2009). *Promising What through Preschool Vouchers? Illusions of Freedom, Equality, Democracy*. New York: VDM Verlag Dr. Müller.

Lemke, T. (2001). The Birth of Bio-politics: Michel Foucault's Lecture at the College de France on Neo-Liberal Governmentality. *Economy and Society*, 30(2), 190–207.

Lindblad, S., & Popkewitz, T. S. (2004). *Educational Restructuring: International Perspectives on Traveling Policies*. Greenwich, CT: Information Age Publishers.

Popkewitz, T. S. (1991). *A Political Sociology of Educational Reform: Power/Knowledge in Teaching, Teacher Education, and Research*. New York: Teachers College Press.

Popkewitz, T. S. (2000). Rethinking Decentralization and the State/Civil Society Distinctions: The State as a Problematic of Governing. In T. S. Popkewitz (Ed.), *Educational Knowledge: Changing Relationships between the State, Civil Society, and the Educational Community* (pp. 173–200). Albany, NY: State University of New York Press.

Popkewitz, T. S. (2006). Hopes of Progress and Fears of the Dangerous: Research, Cultural Theses, and Planning Different Human Kinds. In G. Ladson-Billings and W. F. Tate (Ed.), *Education Research in the Public Interest: The Place for Advocacy in the Academy*. New York: Teachers College Press.

Rose, N. S. (1996). *Inventing Our Selves: Psychology, Power, and Personhood*. Cambridge, New York: Cambridge University Press.

Rose, N. S. (1999). *Powers of Freedom: Reframing Political Thought*. Cambridge, United Kingdom; New York: Cambridge University Press.

Witte, J. F. (2000). *The Market Approach to Education: An Analysis of America's First Voucher Program*. Princeton, N.J.: Princeton University Press.

Yuen, G. W. K. (2007). Vouchers in Hong Kong: a New Milestone of Early Childhood Education? *Contemporary Issues in Early Childhood*, 8 (4), 355–357.

CHAPTER NINE

Disaster Capitalism as Neoliberal Instrument for the Construction of Early Childhood Education/Care Policy

Charter Schools in Post-Katrina New Orleans

MICHELLE SALAZAR PEREZ AND GAILE S. CANNELLA

Abstract

This chapter examines the impact of neoliberalism on early childhood education, care, and policy both as a global phenomenon and in the form of disaster capitalism in post-Katrina New Orleans. Neoliberalism is discussed in general terms and then analyzed through a critical, feminist, poststructural, and postcolonial lens in order to reveal the way in which early childhood policy and practices in the United States (such as with NCLB, school choice initiatives, and the charter school movement) have been used as mechanisms to control and privatize services like public education for young children, creating vast inequities and denying access to a free and appropriate education for many. Neoliberal policy is examined by using examples of disaster capitalism occurring in New Orleans, post-Katrina. Often coined as the "great experiment," New Orleans is viewed as a model for privatizing once-public services for young children, both nationally and globally. Therefore, we call for a rethinking of early childhood policy, one that exists outside of current neoliberal, capitalist-driven ideologies, and instead supports the equitable common good of all children in New Orleans, nationally and globally.

In August of 2005, Hurricane Katrina hit the Gulf Coast of the United States. When the levees failed to control the influx of water coming into New Orleans, the city flooded, and the most vulnerable areas, mainly poor neighborhoods and/or communities that were predominantly of color, were devastated. During the hours and days that immediately followed, using disaster relief and recovery as the legitimating discourse, city, state, and national officials rapidly modified public policy rules, regulations, and procedures. Childhood public services such as education and care were dismantled and taken over by the state of Louisiana (rather than by local government entities, which is the public education structure in the United States) or by private agencies that were given corporate contracts to control resources. Further, using the discourse of recovery, new entities were reestablished in what appeared to be an increasingly privatized system. This change was, and is, especially obvious as formerly public schools that served young children were opened and operated by a mixture of for-profit and nonprofit private organizations. This policy and practice continue today as an illustration, however, accelerated and labeled as a "great experiment," of a creeping neoliberal capitalism that is increasingly embedded within childhood policy conceptualizations and practices around the globe as well as in the United States.

The purpose of this chapter is to explain neoliberal capitalism as invading childhood public policy. The public school situation in post-Hurricane Katrina New Orleans in the United States is discussed as an example of the neoliberal public policy that has been accelerated as a result of practices of disaster capitalism. The reader is cautioned that these practices are occurring around the globe and are embedded within discourses of emergency, rescue, and liberation, as well as currently accepted capitalist discourses of competition, accountability, and responsibility.

Neoliberalism

Neoliberalism is grounded in the philosophy of classic liberalism that assumes that the individual should function autonomously, based on self interest, and be free from the intervention of the state (Olssen, 1996; Olssen & Peters, 2005). Further, classic liberalism puts forward concepts like free trade and free markets as conditions that perpetuate capitalism (Martinez & Garcia, 2000). Neoliberalism is the belief that the state's role is to facilitate an economic marketplace "by providing the conditions, laws, and institutions necessary for its operation" (Olssen, 1996, p. 340) and to produce individuals that become "enterprising and competitive entrepreneur[s]" (Olssen, 1996, p. 340). Key aspects of a neoliberal market include (1) privatization, or shifting the control of public services operated by the state to corporate, for-profit groups and (2) a reliance on the "human nature" (Olssen, 1996, p. 340) of individuals to remain socially responsible, self-motivated citizens who actively participate in the market in order to keep the private sector competitive and the economy balanced (Duggan, 2003). From a neoliberal perspective, those individuals who are thought of as lacking self-initiative (for instance, by needing assistance with food, housing, child care or health care from government welfare programs) are seen as irresponsible and an inevitable component of a capitalistic system (viewed as the "best" economic form) where economic privilege will always be skewed.

Olssen (1996) suggests that neoliberalism is "governing without governing" (p. 340) in that although the state claims to refrain from regulating individuals in order to allow them to remain free, autonomous consumers, since there are some who are viewed as lacking the self-initiative to be actively engaged in the economy, government resorts to tactics such as measurement and surveillance to surreptitiously control those who are viewed as unmotivated. This implicit form of control can be illustrated by U.S. national policy like the No Child Left Behind (NCLB) Act, which was created to hold teachers and schools who serve children labeled as "at risk" (often children of color) accountable by measuring students' "achievement" on standardized tests. Children who do not reach assessment "standards" are often mistakenly viewed as lacking the self-initiative or motivation to be successful in school, when in actuality it is the use of culturally biased instruments and narrow constructions of learning and education that create the illusion that particular groups of children do not "achieve" because their teachers and families are not adequate and must be controlled. Therefore, the state intervenes by creating regulations to raise the achievement levels for students "at risk" of failing. Further, without national policy like NCLB to regulate individuals and groups based on neoliberal, modernist assumptions, the testing industry along with the curriculum, tutoring and textbook corporations who support them would no longer be profitable (Meier & Wood, 2004; Saltman, 2007).

Feminist, postcolonial, and poststructural scholars from a range of fields have critiqued neoliberalism as a harmful ideology embedded within modernism, patriarchy, and colonialist assumptions (Bergeron, 2006; Cannella & Viruru, 2004; Gibson-Graham, 2006; Nelson, 2005; Spivak, 1999). Critical issues raised by these philosophies that are typically disregarded by supporters of a free market-based ideology include (1) political uses of modernist universalisms to normalize or completely ignore societal inequities based on racial, socioeconomic, or gender privilege, (2) intensification of economic inequalities between the privileged and the oppressed, and (3) problems with the hegemonic discourse that exists both in the United States and globally asserting that the societies and the services they provide (like education and health care) can only function under a capitalist, market-based system.

Critiques of Neoliberal Rhetoric

Neoliberalism, Structural Inequities, and Privileging the "Responsible, Efficient, Individual"

Neoliberal rhetoric attempts to separate economic policy from cultural identity and societal structural inequities (Duggan, 2003) because of the belief that a privatized market (when allowed to function autonomously without interference from the government) will naturally create an efficient, competitive, and balanced economy (Nelson, 2005). This unquestioned "faith" in the market masks the conceptualization of markets as almost always privileging those who control them and oppress, or at least make invisible, those who do not. Further, by ignoring diversity, policymakers are able to assume that it is the *individual's responsibility* to *choose* whether or not to be "successful" by adopting the values for which the market was developed and accepting that there will always be an imbalance of economic opportunity.

This focus on individual economic responsibility reflects modernist assumptions that (1) science, reason, and rational thought can reveal what we know about "human nature," (2) universal truths exist such as the notion of individualism, which assumes that we are autonomous, rational, and moral beings, and (3) "progress" is desirable, linear, and predetermined, whether in terms of economic wealth, knowledge accumulation, or the way in which humans develop from childhood to adulthood (Burman, 2008; Dahlburg & Moss, 2005; Seidman, 1998; Cannella, 1997; King, 1997; Gray, 1995; Santos, 1995; Bauman, 1993; Tronto, 1993). Modernist assumptions of human nature, individualism, and progress are used as mechanisms in neoliberal politics to ignore diversity and societal-based inequities, and to legitimate the "fairness" of particular groups benefiting from a market-based economy. This perspective is illustrated in the following example.

Those who *choose* to be in a heterosexual marriage with the male as the "breadwinner" while the female participates in unpaid labor (i.e., taking care of children, the household, etc.) (Cameron & Gibson-Graham, 2003) are interpreted as *choosing* to participate successfully in the market. On the other hand, if a woman *chooses* to be single, take a job in a male-dominated workforce, and/or be a part of a same-sex relationship, then she is interpreted as *choosing* to live with the hardships associated with being a single parent, discrimination against same-sex couples, sexism in the workforce, or needing financial assistance from the government. Therefore, those who do not fit the assumed, very narrow, neoliberal model of identity are constructed as making "wrong" market choices and unjustly deemed as unable to benefit from a market-based economy.

Although a market that functions under a neoliberal ideology claims to separate factors of cultural identity from the economy, it clearly relies heavily on modernist assumptions to establish hierarchies of race, class, gender, and sexuality in order to uphold privilege for those in power (most often those who are White, middle class, male, and heterosexual (Duggan, 2003)). However, diverse cultural experience, identity, and privilege for particular groups are certainly not separate from the economy.

The construction and privileged practice of efficiency as necessary for profitability in a neoliberal market further intensifies inequities. As Warren (2000), an ecofeminist scholar, explains, "mechanisms of free-market capitalism alone (e.g., without government interference through social regulation) may produce efficient but socially unjust outcomes: Markets may distribute burdens and benefits efficiently but inequitably" (p. 180). In other words, even though it may be more efficient for markets to function in a way that allows the private business sector to profit, more often than not, this neoliberal approach widens the gap of inequality and produces social injustice. For example, waste management corporations may attempt to run more efficiently by dumping hazardous materials in inexpensive, centrally located communities (often of color and/or living in poverty) that have seldom been granted permission to establish laws to prohibit this act from occurring. These communities that are less privileged in a market-based economy are more likely to be compromised and further marginalized.

Capitalism: A Mantra of Privitization, Competition, and Profits

Capitalism relies heavily on modes of efficiency and is a pillar of neoliberal politics. Encarta defines capitalism as "an economic system based on the private ownership of the means of production and distribution of goods, characterized by a free competitive market and motivation by profit" (Encarta Dictionary, 2007). When profit is upwardly redistributed as a result of diverting funds and support from public services and resources (not limited to money but also resources like the environment), economic disparities are intensified and a social tolerance is developed for inequality to be a "natural" part of our society (Duggan, 2003; Mies & Shiva, 1993). This uneven redistribution of funds and resources occurs globally, allowing capitalist systems to transfer wealth and power from the poorest parts of the world to the West, with the United States being one of the primary nations to profit (Duggan, 2003). In fact, by the 1990s, the United States surpassed Europe as the leader in Western privilege and inequality (Phillips, 2002).

We agree with those who have suggested that capitalism has evolved to a state of hypercapitalism, which can be characterized by "(1) interpretations of the world that are based on capital, resources, and markets, (2) a fear of losing material commodities, [and] (3) a belief that capital (rather than Enlightenment/modernist science) is now the solution to human problems" (Cannella and Viruru, 2004, p.117). A feminist analysis of hypercapitalism reveals an intensified neoliberal shift becoming further embedded in local, national, and global politics. This strengthened hegemony has had a major impact on many (if not all) facets of policy both in the United States and globally.

Neoliberalism and Disaster Capitalism

Social constructivist theories have recently been accepted in disaster inquiry and have led to the study of natural disasters as socially constructed phenomena (Dynes, 2000; Spector & Kitsuse, 1977) and to an openness to notions like "disaster capitalism" (Klein, 2007). Scholars have proposed that the construction of disasters is highly influenced by policy that determines what is even considered to be a disaster (Klinenberg, 2002; Platt, 1999; Stallings, 1995). These policy decisions impact the amount of relief given to particular regions after a catastrophic event, or in some cases, give financial opportunity to large corporations for whom it is essential that an area be considered a nondisaster site in order to build and gain investment interest for development projects (Davis, 1998; Green, 2005).

Some have also argued that even within the social sciences, disasters have been decontextualized from the social (Blaikie et al., 1994; Hewitt, 1983), claiming that "disasters are episodic, foreseeable manifestations of the broader forces that shape society" (Tierney, 2007, p. 509). Kousky and Zeckhauser (2005), and Mileti (1999), suggest that human actions have caused the rise in the construction of disasters through practices that destroy the ecosystem and lead to a less sustainable world. Others have analyzed racism and classism in the construction of disaster including human actions that take place during and following a catastrophic event (Allen, 1996; Barry, 1997; Bolin & Stanford, 1993; Bolton, 1997; Brinkley, 2006; Cooper & Block, 2006; Fradkin, 2005; Henderson, 2005; Hewitt, 1998; Horlick-Jones, 1995; Phillips, 1998; Ryang, 2003; Tierney et al., 2006; Weiner, 1989).

Disaster capitalism is the notion that catastrophic events (such as 9/11 that resulted in the increase of the military industrial complex through the "war on terror" in Iraq) are foreseeable and strategically devised to allow for corporate profiteering at the time of disaster and during the recovery efforts that follow. Naomi Klein (2007), the author of *The Shock Doctrine: The Rise of Disaster Capitalism*, describes this calculated practice as "orchestrated raids on the public sphere in the wake of catastrophic events, combined with the treatment of disasters as exciting market opportunities" (p. 6).

During instances where disaster capitalism is operating, rather than rebuilding what existed previously, those hoping to advance corporate goals use "moments of collective trauma to engage in radical social and economic engineering" (Klein, 2007, p. 8), allowing industries to redevelop devastated areas rapidly with little to no awareness of the impact of their actions by local communities (Klein, 2007). By producing and exploiting disasters, businesses have created a means to profit with no-bid reconstruction projects, resort development, and even public services for children.

As a growing global phenomenon, Saltman (2007) suggests "this movement also needs to be understood in relation to the broader political, ideological, and cultural formations most prevalent at the moment—namely, neoliberalism and neoconservatism" (p. 3) (Apple, 2001; Giroux, 2004). The "fundamentalist form of capitalism has always needed disasters to advance" (Klein, 2007, p. 9).

Neoliberal Hegemony and Public Policy

There has been a shift "from an understanding of the economy as something that can be transformed, or at least managed [by the people or the State]…to something that governs society" (Gibson-Graham, 2006, p. 53). This "culture of thinking" (Gibson-Graham, 2006, p. 3) has made it difficult for policy makers, scholars, and the general public to imagine a world or society that can function outside of a capitalist economy (Cannella & Viruru, 2004; Spivak, 1999).

Neoliberal capitalism reproduces inequalities between the services available for the privileged and those who do not fit the mainstream. An example of this occurs when public funding and support are minimized for "sites of non-market politics—[such as] the arts, education, and social services" (Duggan, 2003, p. 21). Those who are economically privileged by neoliberal politics are often able to privately seek and pay for services like education by using supplemental income if the state lessens or discontinues financial support. Others, however, find it necessary for the government to maintain its role in providing these services because of vast inequalities that exist and that are purposely maintained through hierarchies of gender, class, race, and sexuality. Decreasing national funding for public no-market programs or moving them into the private business sector will only intensify inequalities and strengthen patriarchal, colonialist structures of power that marginalize women, people of color, and others (Collins, 2000) who rarely benefit from a system that functions under neoliberal politics.

While it is important to refrain from limiting our conceptions of the world and the multiple economies that exist within it, since Bergeron (2006) reminds us that "the local penetrates the global and vice versa" (p. 161), it is important to acknowledge that capitalism and neoloberalism impact all societies globally and continue to dramatically skew economic and social privilege around the world. Capitalist hegemony has penetrated the boundaries of publicly funded and regulated social services like education and will continue to gain momentum unless the consequences of privatizing public programs are revealed and a "political imaginary" (Gibson-Graham, 2006, p. xxvi) open to diverse economic ways of being is reconceptualized.

An Illustrative Case of Neoliberal Policy: Early Childhood Education and Disaster Capitalism in Post-Katrina New Orleans

Prior to Hurricane Katrina, public education was a service used by children and families who could not afford to attend one of the many private religious schools or to live in an area available only to the elite that allowed access to the few public schools with resources. Therefore, many of the most economically and socially privileged in New Orleans were not participating in the public school system before the storm (Flaherty, 2008). This is an important factor when considering the way in which public education is being reestablished post-Katrina, since the elite have once again been able to avoid placing their children in struggling public schools by either enrolling them in private institutions or by having the means to reside in a high-cost area that allows attendance to one of the few privileged new schools that are supported by such organizations as the Business Roundtable (Carr, 2008; Saltman, 2007).

Neoliberalism and Public Education

The past two decades of educational reform in the United States have been spearheaded by neoliberal agendas (Giroux, 2004). Apple (2001) suggests that "rather than democracy being a *political* concept, it is transformed into a wholly *economic* concept" (p. 39), allowing an "economic rationality" (p. 38) to be used as a lens to analyze and transform public education policy. Consequently, a neoliberal approach to educating young children attempts to commodify schools by placing them in a "self-regulating" (Apple, 2001, p. 39) market and identifies students as "human capital" (Apple, 2001, p. 38) and parents as consumers. Moreover, this market-based ideology has given momentum to school choice initiatives nationwide and after Hurricane Katrina, has provided a platform for corporate-based schools in the reestablishment of the public school system in New Orleans.

School Choice as Public Policy

The movement to privatize public education in the United States now uses the discourse of "choice." The discourse began with the voucher concept and has more recently used charter schools as the vehicle for decentralization, deregulation, and privatization.

Economist Milton Friedman proposed a neoliberal, market-based model of education in the mid 1950s that would not be controlled directly by the government but rather allow families a "choice" to attend any state-approved school with the use of a state certificate or voucher. Under Friedman's plan, schools receiving vouchers would be required to meet standards set by the government. Quality would be controlled by competition, forcing failing institutions to shut down and average performing schools to raise achievement if they wished to remain in the market (Finn, Manno, & Vanourek, 2000). Although vouchers have been implemented sparingly in a limited number of locations and resisted by public education proponents, Friedman's market-based model of education has paved the way for the emergence of varying forms of school choice (Bracey, 2003; Engel, 2000) on a much grander scale than individual vouchers would ever have facilitated.

There are a range of models that have been generated (all centering on Friedman's neoliberal philosophy) as ways in which to create a market-based education system in the United States. These models advocate less government control and the creation of a competitive market where the individuals (i.e. the parents) become active, self-motivated consumers. Many claim that school choice does not equate to privatization since public funds are used to support the system. However, when choice initiatives (like vouchers) allow parents to use nationally generated tax payer funds to place children in private schools, the funds become a source for corporate profits. This form of "choice" will inevitably take money from public schools, feed the business sector, and create a larger inequitable circumstance for children who are already marginalized by the current system (Apple, 2001; Bracey, 2003; Giroux, 2002).

"Charter Schools" as New Forms of Privitization

Although still used in small numbers, vouchers failed to gain the momentum anticipated by Milton Friedman and his supporters. Charter schools as a concept have been reconceptualized and used as a way to re-establish support for school choice by convincing those who initially opposed vouchers to support the charter school movement. The concept of a charter in education was first developed in the 1970s by Ray Budde, a former teacher, junior high-school principal, and professor at the University of Massachusetts (Kolderie, 2005). Budde based his initial ideas for a charter on Henry Hudson's 1609 charter with the Directors of the East India Company. In the charter, Hudson describes "the purpose and vision of his trip, the risks entailed, what he must do to satisfy accountability requirements, how he will be compensated, and what rewards there might be for high productivity" (Bracey, 2003, p. 77). Budde based his concept of a charter in education on the principles outlined by Hudson while incorporating instructional autonomy suggesting that "teachers could be 'chartered' directly by a school board…[and] no one—not the superintendent or the principal or any central office supervisors—would stand between the school board and the teachers when it came to matters of instruction" (Budde, 1996, p. 72). When there was no response in the 1970s by Budde's colleagues to his initial proposition, he discontinued any efforts to further develop his ideas.

About ten years later, after the publication of *A Nation at Risk* which prompted policy makers and the general public to become more interested in reforming education in the United States (Kolderie, 2005), Budde revisited his charter concept and wrote a book that was published in 1988 by the Northeast Regional Laboratory entitled *Education by Charter: Restructuring School Districts*. In his book, Budde focused primarily on the idea of "chartering" departments or programs within a school (rather than chartering entire schools, which is the current interpretation of a charter). Budde immediately distributed his book nationally to anyone he thought may be interested in reforming public education at the local level and even sent a copy to then President George H.W. Bush (Budde, 1996; Kolderie, 2005).

In July of 1988, Budde's wife discovered a *New York Times* article where Albert Shanker, the president of the American Federation of Teachers, suggested that "local school boards and unions jointly develop a procedure that would enable teams of teachers and others to submit and implement proposals to set up their own autonomous public schools within their school buildings" (Shanker, 1988, p. 7). Albert Shanker spoke of a system that allowed schools "to be created by groups of teachers, or parents with teachers, who wanted to develop a new curriculum or teaching strategies to improve both instruction and student learning" (American Federation of Teachers, 2008, p. 1). Budde admits that he initially had mixed feelings about Shanker changing his original idea of chartering programs to chartering entire schools but eventually embraced new models that emerged from his initial interpretation (even the ones that were later developed in the early 1990s) (Budde, 1996). Members of the American Federation of Teachers (AFT) on the other hand believe Shanker's vision of charter schools has been compromised over the years, stating that his original intent to "free teachers and administrators from bureaucratic red tape and encourage innovation…has been transformed into a rhetoric of reform by choice and competition" (AFT, 2008, p.1). Therefore, the AFT no longer supports charter schools and what they claim to provide as a means for educational reform.

Charter schools have become the most popular and widely accepted form of school choice in the United States for many reasons (Lubienski, 2001). Some argue that unlike vouchers, charter schools allow for a market-based model to be established in public education (by functioning autonomously and providing more options and competition for standard public schools) without privatizing the system. Therefore, positioning charters as a nonprivatized model for school choice has allowed for the charter school movement to gain the support of those who may have originally been skeptical of school choice under the voucher initiative. Some insist that redefining education by supporting charter schools will keep voucher programs from threatening to privatize and dismantle the public school system (Lubienski, 2001). However, this argument manipulates and falsely represents the neoliberal agenda of charter schools and the school choice movement. One point is certain, these schools are being constructed by those without backgrounds in education, are literally taking over public education buildings, and operated to a major extent by corporations like Edison and Knowledge Is Power Program (KIPP) (Saltman, 2005, 2007; Sizer & Wood, 2008)

Childhood Education Policy: Post-Katrina New Orleans and Disaster Capitalism

Following Hurricane Katrina, the Bush administration created national recovery funding for New Orleans schools that privileged the establishment of charter schools, resulting in the most concentrated number of charter schools in a public school system in the United States. There is a mixed response from communities in New Orleans about the reestablishment of public education with charter schools. Those with neoliberal agendas believe that charter schools will ultimately save public education, while critics have spoken out about the harms of creating a market-based system. Many local communities in New Orleans, however, whether advocates or adversaries, do not appear to be aware of the issues that other public school systems in the United States have had when discourses of competition and privatization emerge.

Examples of the situations produced by policy changes after Katrina include (1) the ability to quickly and exuberantly refurbish particular schools serving the wealthy like Lusher charter school in Uptown New Orleans, (2) access interpretations that inhibit free, and continued right of entry to a public school because of "hidden" admissions requirements (e.g., parent participation standards that influence the child's continued acceptance as a student in the school), (3) a decentralized system that results in some children and their parents searching for a school (e.g., 20+ different entities operating 30 schools at one point in time), and (4) the creation of a business model for education that encourages cuts in school expenditures, adversely impacting teachers, students, and communities (for example, by eliminating enrichment programs and services for children with special needs and failing to provide adequate facilities/instructional materials for students and teachers). The number of charter schools is expected to rise as enterprising, for-profit and non-profit organizations seek investment opportunities, including FirstLine Schools, Knowledge Is Power Program (KIPP), New Beginnings School Foundation-Capital One-University of New Orleans Charter Network, and the Einstein Group, Inc.

The specialized circumstances found in a city that has experienced disaster as catastrophically as New Orleans has allowed for charter schools, and various forms of privatization, to emerge in an unprecedented manner. When a dire situation literally results in no schools for young children to attend, everyone becomes desperate for any kind of possibility, producing an environment that influences equity and access to public education. In order to address these concerns and understand the differing perspectives of the seemingly privatized shift in public education in New Orleans post-Katrina, much consideration must be given to the development of research questions and practices along with further, extensive immersion in the culture of the city.

Naomi Klein (2007) describes disaster capitalism as "orchestrated raids on the public sphere in the wake of catastrophic events, combined with the treatment of disasters as exciting market opportunities" (p. 6). This entrepreneurial trend has played a key role in targeting and exploiting all children, people of color, women, the poor, and the colonized in larger society and more recently in New Orleans post-Katrina. Because modernist assumptions have constructed children and the traditionally marginalized as intellectually and physically less advanced (Burman, 2001; Rose, 1990; Cannella, 1997; Lichtman, 1987; Voneche, 1987), dominant ideologies, fueled by disaster capitalism, have allowed leaders at the local, state, and national levels to rebuild public education in New Orleans in a way that appears to create profit for corporations and may leave younger human beings who rely heavily upon open access to a free and appropriate education with the burden of suffering from the consequences of the inequalities that capitalism produces.

The original concept of a charter developed by Ray Budde in the 1970s was an initiative created to give teachers instructional autonomy within already established public schools and had no agenda for allowing nonprofit and/or for-profit management companies to charter and operate entire schools (Kolderie, 2005; Budde, 1996). Now part of the larger, neoliberal school choice movement that initially focused on vouchers as a way to reform and eventually privatize the public school system by using a market-based approach to education, charter schools are another way in which school choice is attempting to corporatize public education (Apple, 2001). Although similar in agenda to voucher initiatives, the charter school movement has been able to mask its privatization efforts and therefore has gained more support politically and from local communities who are not aware of the dangers that charter schools present for a public school system that attempts to educate children justly and equitably.

Global Cautions Regarding Neoliberal Childhood Public Policy

Neoliberalism is embedded in childhood policies around the world, with capitalism and discourses of competition increasingly penetrating childcare services, educational curriculum, and public school systems. Policy makers must discontinue the crafting of legislation that positions children and families as commodities, and a critical disposition must be generated to uncover the injustices produced by a neoliberal, capitalist ideology in order to serve *all* children equitably.

Some have proposed that capitalism does not function as "a single and coherent 'system'" (Duggan, 2003, p. x) and that diverse forms of economic functioning exist, including those that are noncapitalist (Bergeron, 2006). By "repoliticizing"(Gibson-Graham, 2006, p. xxviii) economic politics and examining spaces where others have resisted capitalism, boundaries established by neoliberal, patriarchal discourse may be broken and allow for alternative ways of functioning (outside of capitalism) to become more prevalent (Gibson-Graham, 2006, p. xxiii). Living at a time in which neoliberal capitalism is literally causing economic crashes and increased poverty around the globe, we must be especially attentive to the embeddedness of neoliberal agendas within our conceptualizations and practices of early childhood public policy. Otherwise, we may soon be asking why our supports for an equitable common good have become competition for services, further labeling of individuals (children and teachers), the practice of literally rejecting young children from public education, and increased inequities between young children who are privileged and those who are not. Our policy conceptualizations and practices must not become themselves the creators of lived disaster for young children.

References

Allen, J. M. (1996). The price of identity: The 1923 Kanto earthquake and its aftermath. *Korean Studies*, 20, 64–93.

American Federation of Teachers (2008). *Charter schools* [Online]. Retrieved March 24, 2008 from the World Wide Web: http://www.aft.org/topics/charters/

Apple, M. (2001). *Educating the "right" way: Markets, standards, god, and inequality*. New York: RoutledgeFalmer.

Barry, J. M. (1997). *Rising tide: The Great Mississippi Flood of 1927 and how it changed America*. New York: Simon & Schuster.

Bauman, Z. (1993). *Postmodern ethics*. Oxford: Blackwell.

Bergeron, S. (2006). *Fragments of development: Nation, gender, and the space of modernity*. Ann Arbor, MI: The University of Michigan Press.

Blaikie, P., Cannon, T., Davis, I., & Wisner, B. (1994). *At risk: Natural hazards, people's vulnerability and disasters*. New York: Routledge.

Bolin, R. C., & Stanford, L. M. (1993). Emergency sheltering and housing of earthquake victims: The case of Santa Cruz County. In P. A. Bolton (Ed.), *The Loma Prieta, California, Earthquake of October 17, 1989—public response* (pp. 43–50). Washington, DC: USGPO.

Bolton, M. (1997). *Recovery for whom? Social conflict after the San Francisco earthquake and fire, 1906–1915*. PhD dissertation, University of California, Davis.

Bracey, G. W. (2003). *What you should know about the war against America's public schools*. Boston, MA: Pearson Education.

Brinkley, D. (2006). *The great deluge: Hurricane Katrina, New Orleans, and the Mississippi Gulf Coast*. New York: HarperCollins.

Budde, R. (1996). The evolution of the charter concept. *Phi Delta Kappa*, *78*(1), 72–74.

Burman, E. (2008). *Developments: Child, image, nation*. London: Routledge.

Burman, E. (2001). Beyond the baby and the bathwater: Postdualistic developmental psychologies for diverse childhoods. *European Early Childhood Education Research Journal*, *9*(1), 5–22.

Cameron, J., & Gibson-Graham, J.K. (2003). Feminizing the economy: Metaphors, strategies, politics. *Gender, Place, and Culture*, 10(2), pp. 145–57.

Cannella, G.S. (1997) *Deconstructing early childhood education: Social justice and revolution*. New York: Peter Lang.

Cannella, G.S., & Viruru, R. (2004). *Childhood and postcolonization: Power, education, and contemporary practice*. New York: RoutledgeFalmer.

Carr, S. (2008, May 18). Charters break mold by picking, choosing; Several in N.O. require students to pass tests, show skills to enroll. *Times-Picayune*, p. 1.

Collins, P. H. (2000). *Black feminist thought: Knowledge, consciousness, and the politics of empowerment* (2nd Ed.). New York: Routledge.

Cooper, C., & Block, R. (2006). *Disaster: Hurricane Katrina and the failure of homeland security.* New York: Times Books and Holt.

Dahlburg, G., & Moss, P. (2005). *Ethics and politics in early childhood education.* New York: RoutledgeFalmer.

Davis, M. (1998). *Ecology of fear: Los Angeles and the imagination of disaster.* New York: Metropolitan Books.

Duggan, L. (2003). *The twilight of equality? Neoliberalism, cultural politics, and the attack on democracy.* Boston, MA: Beacon Press.

Dynes, R. R. (2000). The dialogue between Voltaire and Rousseau on the Lisbon earthquake: The emergence of a social science view. *International Journal of Mass Emergencies and Disasters, 18,* 97–115.

Encarta Dictionary (2007). *Microsoft Office Word.* Redmond, WA: Microsoft Corporation.

Engel, M. (2000). *The struggle for control of public education: Market ideology vs. democratic values.* Philadelphia, PA: Temple University Press.

Finn, C. E., Manno, B. V., & Vanourek, G. (2000). *Charter schools in action: Renewing public education.* Princeton, NJ: Princeton University Press.

Flaherty, J. (2008). New Orleans' culture of resistance. In P. Steinberg & R. Shields (Eds.), *What is a city? Rethinking the urban after Hurricane Katrina* (pp. 30–55). Athens, GA: The University of Georgia Press.

Fradkin, P. (2005). *The great earthquake and firestorms of 1906: How San Francisco nearly destroyed itself.* Berkeley, CA: University of California Press.

Gibson-Graham, J.K. (2006). *A postcapitalist politics.* Minneapolis, MN: University of Minnesota Press.

Giroux, H. A. (2002). Schooling for sale: Public education, corporate culture, and the citizen-consumer. In A. Kohn & P. Shannon (Eds.), *Education, Inc.: Turning learning into a business, revised edition* (pp. 105–118). Portsmouth, NH: Heinemann.

Giroux, H. A. (2004). *The terror of neoliberalism: Authoritarianism and the eclipse of democracy.* Boulder, CO: Paradigm Publishers.

Gray, J. (1995). *Enlightenment's wake: Politics and culture at the close of the modern age.* London: Routledge.

Green, P. (2005). Disaster by design: corruption, construction, and catastrophe. *The British Journal of Criminology, 45,* 528–46.

Henderson, A. D. (2005). *Reconstructing home: gender, disaster relief, and social life after the San Francisco earthquake and fire, 1906–1915.* PhD dissertation, Stanford University Press, Stanford, CA.

Hewitt, K. (Ed). (1983). *Interpretations of calamity: From the viewpoint of human ecology.* Boston, MA: Allen & Unwin.

Hewitt, K. (1998). Excluded perspectives in the social construction of disaster. In E. L. Quarantelli (Ed.), *What is a disaster? Perspectives on the question* (pp. 75–91). London: Routledge.

Horlick-Jones, T. (1995). Modern disasters as outrage and betrayal. *International Journal of Mass Emergencies and Disasters, 13,* 305–15.

King, M. (1997). *A better world for children: Exploration in morality and authority.* London: Routledge.

Klein, N. (2007). *The shock doctrine: The rise of disaster capitalism.* New York: Metropolitan Books.

Klinenberg, E. (2002). *Heat wave: A social autopsy of disaster in Chicago.* Chicago, IL: University of Chicago Press.

Kolderie, T. (2005). Ray Buude and the origins of the 'charter concept.' *The Center for Education Reform* [Online]. Retrieved March 24, 2008, from the World Wide Web: www.edreform.com/index.cfm?fuseAction=document&documentID=2093

Kousky, C., & Zeckhauser, R. (2005). JARring actions that fuel the floods. In R. J. Daniels, D. F. Kettl & H. Kunreuther (Eds.), *On Risk and disaster: Lessons from Hurricane Katrina* (pp. 59–73). Philadelphia, PA: University of Pennsylvania Press.

Lichtman, R. (1987). The illusion of maturation in an age of decline. In J.M. Broughton (Ed.), *Critical theories of psychological development* (pp. 127–148). New York: Plenum Press.

Lubienski, C. (2001). Redefining "public" education: Charter schools, common schools, and the rhetoric of reform. *Teachers College Record, 103,* 634–666.

Martinez, E., & Garcia, A. (2000). What is neo-liberalism: A brief definition. *Global Exchange* [Online]. Retrieved March 24, 2008, from the World Wide Web:http://www.globalexchange.org/campaigns/econ101/neoliberalDefined.html

Meier, D., & Wood, G. (Eds.). (2004). *Many children left behind: How the No Child Left Behind act is damaging our children and our schools.* Boston, MA: Beacon Press.

Mies, M., & Shiva, V. (1993). *Ecofeminism.* London: Zed Books.

Mileti, D. S. (1999). *Disasters by design: A reassessment of natural hazards in the United States.* Washington, DC: Joseph Henry.

Nelson, J. (2005). Rethinking development and globalization: Insights from feminist economics. *The Good Society*, 14(3), 58–62.

Olssen, M. (1996). In defense of the welfare state and of publicly provided education: A New Zealand perspective. *Journal of Education Policy*, 11 (3), 337–362.

Olssen, M., & Peters, M.A. (2005). Neoliberalism, higher education, and the knowledge economy: From the free market to knowledge capitalism. *Journal of Education Policy*, 20(3), 313–345.

Phillips, B. (1998). Sheltering and housing of low-income and minority groups in Santa Cruz County after the Loma Prieta earthquake. In J. M. Nigg (Ed.), *The Loma Prieta, California, Earthquake of October 17, 1989: Recovery, mitigation, and reconstruction* (pp. 17–28). Washington, DC: USGPO.

Phillips, K. (2002). *Wealth and democracy: A political history of the American rich.* New York: Broadway Books.

Platt, R. H. (1999). *Disasters and democracy: The politics of extreme natural events.* Washington, DC: Island.

Rose, N. (1990). *Governing the soul: The shaping of the private self.* London: Routledge.

Ryang, S. (2003). The Great Kanto earthquake and the massacre of Koreans in 1923: Notes on Japan's modern national sovereignty. *Anthropology Quarterly*, 76, 731–748.

Saltman, K. J. (2005). *The Edison schools: Corporate schooling and the assault on public education.* New York: Routledge.

Saltman, K. J. (2007). *Capitalizing on disaster: Taking and breaking public schools.* Boulder, CO: Paradigm Publishers.

Santos, B. de S. (1995). *Towards a new common sense: Law, science, and politics in the paradigmatic transition.* London: Routledge.

Seidman, S. (1998). *Contested knowledge* (2nd ed.). Oxford: Blackwell.

Shanker, A. (1988). Convention plots new course: A charter for change. *New York Times*, July 10, sec. 4, p. 7.

Sizer, T., & Wood, G. (2008). Charter schools and the values of public education. In L. Dingerson, B. Miner, B. Peterson & S. Walters (Eds.), *Keeping the promise? The debate over charter schools* (pp. 3–16). Milwaukee, WI: A Rethinking Schools Publication.

Spector, M., & Kitsuse, J. I. (1977). *Constructing social problems.* Menlo Park, CA: Cummings.

Spivak, G.C. (1999). *A critique of postcolonial reason: Toward a history of the vanishing present.* Cambridge, MA: Harvard University Press.

Stallings, R. A. (1995). *Promoting risk: Constructing the earthquake threat.* New York: Aldine De Gruyter.

Tierney, K. J. (2007). From the margins to the mainstream? Disaster research at the crossroads. *The Annual Review of Sociology*, 33, 503–525.

Tierney, K. J, Bevc, C., & Kuligowski, E. (2006). Metaphors matter: Disaster myths, media frames, and their consequences in Hurricane Katrina. *The Annals of the American Academy of Political and Social Science*, 604, 57–81.

Tronto, J. (1993). *Moral boundaries: A political argument for the ethics of care.* London: Routledge.

Voneche, J. J. (1987). The difficulty of being a child in French-speaking countries. In J.M. Broughton (Ed.), *Critical theories of psychological development* (pp. 61–86). New York: Plenum Press.

Warren, K.J. (2000). *Ecofeminist philosophy: A western perspective on what it is and why it matters.* New York: Rowman and Littlefield Publishers, Inc.

Weiner, M. (1989). *The origins of the Korean community in Japan, 1910–1923.* Atlantic Highlands, NJ: Humanities.

CHAPTER TEN

Why and How Poverty Matters in Schooling in the USA

SUE BOOKS

Abstract

Although the United States prides itself on an ideal of providing equal opportunity to all, our social reality betrays this idea. Children growing up in poverty for the most part do not "escape." Rather, as they grow and mature, they find that their lives have been constrained by policies and practices that limit their opportunities. To try to show how this works—that is, to explore "the mechanics of unfairness"—this chapter describes some of the policy- and practice-based obstacles that create and sustain inequalities in opportunity. These obstacles include a childcare crisis that relegates the poorest children to an unregulated patchwork of arrangements ranging in quality from adequate to terrible; school funding laws and policies that leave children in poor districts with significantly less state and federal per-pupil funding than their peers in wealthy districts; schools districting practices that keep poor students, disproportionately of color, away from others; college admission policies that rubber-stamp preparation gaps; and college tuition and financial aid policies and practices that increasingly are squeezing out the poor. The chapter concludes not with a quick-fix solution, but rather with a discussion of how teachers can best respond to the reality of millions of children being forced to struggle against the odds.

Introduction

Children enter the world full of promise matched only by the dreams and aspirations of their parents. They embark on life's journey with relatively equal potential regardless of race, ethnicity, sex, or economic background....Collectively, we are responsible for making sure the road ahead is safe and filled with opportunity. (Duncan Lindsey 2009)

We can't afford to lose a generation of tomorrow's doctors and scientists and teachers to poverty. We can make excuses for it or we can fight about it or we can ignore poverty all together, but as long as it's here it will always be a betrayal of the ideals we hold as Americans. It's not who we are. (Barack Obama 2008)

Poverty matters in schooling, but not in the ways that many commentators and political leaders presume it matters. Poverty does not doom children to school failure. Many young people thrive educationally despite growing up in families chronically stressed by not having enough resources to meet basic needs. Poverty also does not "brand" children educationally. Poor children need good teaching, not a special "pedagogy of poverty" consisting of excessive regimentation, drill of the basics, and harsh discipline (Haberman 1991). At the same time, it is important to recognize that children growing up in poverty, as a group, do bear the brunt of a whole range of social injustices, and that these injustices constrain their educational opportunities sharply and therefore also their social and economic opportunities.

As the U.S. recession entered its second year in 2008, a *New York Times* editorial puzzled over the absence of discussion of how the faltering economy was affecting "the 37 million Americans who are already living at or below the poverty line—and the millions more who will inevitably join their ranks as the downturn worsens" and predicted that "the experience of being poor in American, never easy, will soon become even more difficult for more people" ("Sewing Up" 2008). In 2007, the United Nations ranked the United States top among 24 wealthy nations in child poverty (UNICEF 2007). This ranking was based on a measure of relative poverty, defined as family income of less than half the national median—the standard measure of poverty widely used throughout Europe. Based on the far more conservative U.S. federal poverty line, 18 percent of all children in the United States are now officially poor (Fass & Cauthen 2008). However, this group includes almost half of all white children under five in single-mother households, and almost 60 percent of all black and Latino children under five in single-mother households (U.S. Census Bureau 2006). For the poorest families the trend, sadly, has been downward. Between 2000 and 2005, the poorest 20 percent of all families with children experienced a decline in household income (adjusted for inflation) of almost 11 percent (Dahl 2007).

Many of the injustices poor children suffer, such as the whole array of untreated medical and dental problems they experience in disproportionate numbers (Alstott, 2007; U.S. Department of Health and Human Services 2000), fall outside the educational arena per se. At more than twice the average rate, poor children cope with vision problems that are undetected and uncorrected (Ethan & Basch 2008; Gould & Gould 2003).

"The cost of being poor" also includes disproportionate exposure to lead (Richardson 2005)—a toxin that, at low levels, can cause learning disabilities, behavioral problems, and, at high levels, seizures, coma, and even death (U.S. Department of Health and Human Services 2008). Caused primarily by exposure to lead-based paint and lead-contaminated dust, lead poisoning has been identified for years by the Department of Health and Human Services as the most significant environmental health hazard to children in the United States. Nevertheless, despite "decades of research tout[ing] the deleterious defects of lead exposure" as well as legislation since the mid-1970s "heralding the harm lead can cause children in particular…we continue to miss the mark of ameliorating the unbalanced exposure of low-income, urban children, most of whom are African American" (Richardson 2005, 143). As an outreach worker with an initiative to reduce lead poisoning in Richmond, Virginia, expresses so aptly, with lead poisoning, the harm cannot be undone:

The hard part is to know that a child has gotten a disease that was 100% preventable and know what effects it will have on that child for the rest of their life and a lot of the parent's. A lot of people, not just parents, say once [children] get lead poisoned, can't you change them back the way they were? But you can't. The damage is done. (quoted in Richardson, 2005, p. 150)

A neurological "poison" induced by stress also mars the development of many young brains (Cookson 2008). Children who grow up in poverty experience this "toxic stress" far more often than others (Shonkoff 2005) and not surprisingly therefore are far more likely than others to struggle in school.

Given the preposterousness of trying to close achievement gaps without closing neurological damage gaps, the notion of what counts as an educational issue clearly needs to be expanded (Anyon 2005; Books 2004). At the same time and at the very least, we need to ensure that children disadvantaged from the start (Lee & Burkam 2002) do not experience school as a place of further damage. Sadly, however, "instead of structuring our schools to ameliorate the challenges outside of school, we do the opposite—we take the kids who have the least outside of school, and we give them less inside of school, too" (Ali 2006). This is the problem addressed in the sections that follow: school law and policy structures that shortchange poor children. More specifically, the sections explore the consequences for poor children of our system of funding public schools largely through property taxes linked to geographic districts, of our patchwork system of child care that shapes many children's pre-school years, and of our allocation of access to higher education—a competition that favors those who can pay and those groomed to meet narrow standards of academic qualification. Elsewhere I have described this chain of injustices as the "mechanics of unfairness" (Books 2009).

Public School Funding

As Kozol (1991, 2006) has argued doggedly, school funding is one of the few places where we tell children exactly what we think they are worth. Per-pupil spending figures suggest starkly different evaluations of children in affluent families, disproportionately white, and children in poor families, disproportionately black and Latino. Kozol's observation, really an accusation, is troubling because it suggests not only that poor children suffer from the moral judgments institutionalized in our educational policies and practices but also that adults, even those far removed from poor children's personal lives, contribute to the suffering.

As most readers probably know, public school funding in the United States comes from three primary sources: state revenues, local property taxes, and federal funds. The size of the state and local shares vary considerably from state to state, but on average account for about 45 percent each of the total pie. Disparities exist at every level—among the states, among the 14,000 school districts spread across the nation, and among individual schools within the districts. In 2005–06, the ten highest-spending states spent, on average, $5,660 more per student than the ten lowest-spending states,[1] which are clustered in the South, Southwest, and West and serve a disproportionate share of the nation's poorest children. Per-pupil spending in 2005–06 ranged from a high of $14,884 in New York to a low of $5,437 in Utah (U.S. Census Bureau 2008). Although educational costs differ from state to state, the disparities result largely from differences in state wealth, not costs. For example, whereas public schools in Connecticut spent an average of $12,323 per student in 2005–06, 71 percent more than the $7,221 Mississippi spent, Connecticut's costs were only 32 percent higher than Mississippi's (Carey & Roza 2008).

Interdistrict differences in property wealth compound these state-to-state disparities. In any given state, the local property wealth per capita in the richest district can be 50 times that in the poorest. Property-rich districts consequently can and do raise more in property taxes, and often much more, than their poorer counterparts, even when, as is often the case, the richer districts have lower tax rates. Heavy reliance on local property taxes as a source of school funding means parents who can afford to buy million-dollar homes essentially can afford to buy top-shelf (but publicly subsidized) schooling for their children as well. Although some states use state revenues to ameliorate property-tax-based disparities, large gaps remain. In 2005 low-poverty school districts (the 25 percent nationwide with the least poverty) received *$938 more* in state and local funds than high-poverty districts (the 25 percent with the most poverty) (Arroyo 2008).

Gaps in funding among districts are especially significant between large predominantly minority high-poverty city districts and nearby predominantly white suburban districts. For example, Illinois Board of Education data for 2003 show per-pupil spending of $8,482 in Chicago (87 percent minority), but $17,291 in nearby suburban Highland Park (10 percent minority). This pattern characterizes large metropolitan areas across the nation. As in the Chicago area, so too in the Philadelphia, Detroit, Milwaukee, Boston, and New York City areas (Kozol 2006). Even among buildings within single school districts, one finds "hidden disparities." Nationwide, teachers in high-poverty schools are paid less, and often significantly less, than their colleagues in low-poverty schools (Clotfelter et al. 2006; Roza 2006). These disparities often do not show up in district-wide budget reports, which generally list the distribution of staff positions, not teacher salaries.

Federal funding, the third source for public schools, comes primarily through Title I of the Elementary and Secondary Education Act, reauthorized most recently as the No Child Left Behind (NCLB) Act. Title I funds are supposed to benefit poor children and to supplement state and local revenues. However, because federal regulations direct more money to states that spend relatively generously on education and because these states tend to be low-poverty states, the federal funding actually makes matters worse (Carey & Roza 2008). For example, whereas Arizona, a low-spending state with considerable child poverty, received $881 for each poor child in the state in 2003–04, Wyoming, a high-spending state with much less child poverty, received $2,957 per poor child (Liu 2006). Under NCLB, several streams of Title I funding were redirected from high-poverty small and rural districts to larger and lower-poverty districts (Rural School and Community Trust 2008).

This way of funding public schools results in children in the poorest schools in the poorest districts in the poorest states receiving far, far less than they should, based on any notion either of fundamental fairness or of educational need. "Put simply: money follows money. At every level of government…policymakers give more resources to students who have more resources, and less to those who have less" (Carey & Roza 2008). Even funding for basic infrastructure goes disproportionately to schools in wealthier communities. Despite record-level spending in the decade 1995–2004, the most disadvantaged students received only about half as much per pupil as their wealthier counterparts. The poorer schools had to spend most of the money they got on basic safety provisions, such as roof repairs and asbestos removal, rather than improvements such as science labs and computer rooms, which the wealthier schools bought (Filardo et al. 2006).

Outside the formal structure of funding, private donations from parents, alumni, and corporations add to the disparities. These donations, on the rise in recent years, have funded a wide range of needs and wants for the target schools: equipment, supplies, artists-in-residence, and even "greenhouses and weather stations, climbing walls and film libraries, and in one case, a quilting machine"

(Cowan 2007). Many schools, of course, have no significant donors. Concerned about this unfairness, school administrators in Greenwich, Connecticut, in 1997 tried to cap the amount a single school could receive. However, an analysis in 2005 by the local school board showed "continuing inequities," especially among elementary schools: $17,000 for one school compared to more than $50,000 each for eight others (Cowan 2007).

Although the question of whether "money really matters" continues to arise in school funding lawsuits, decades of litigation in all but a handful of states attest to broad agreement that is does.[2] Significant disparities in funding mean that students in property-rich districts typically attend classes in well-maintained buildings, with well-qualified and adequately compensated teachers and abundant opportunities to participate in art, music, and sports programs. Students in property-poor districts, on the other hand, all too often face years of schooling in buildings in varying states of disrepair, with outdated textbooks that must be shared, with few extracurricular activities, and with teachers lacking credentials (or even full-time positions). With more money at their disposal, wealthier school districts can and do lure the "better teachers," and children in high-poverty districts end up with the newest teachers, teachers with the weakest credentials, and teachers who have been pushed out of other schools (Clotfelter et al. 2006; Kozol 1991, 2006; Peske & Haycock 2003; Roza 2006). As Thurgood Marshall wrote in 1973 in his passionate dissent in the landmark school funding case *San Antonio v. Rodriguez*, "It is an inescapable fact that if one district has more funds available per pupil than another district, the former will have greater choice in educational planning than will the latter."

School Districting

Of course, there is another way to look at funding inequities. If funding is linked to districts, why not redraw the lines to spread the money around more equitably? We have carved the nation into 14,000 separate school districts in ways that, on the surface, seem illogical—no consistency in size or shape and sometimes no correspondence with other natural boundaries. In fact, though, the gerrymandering serves a social purpose: it keeps poor students, disproportionately students of color and children for whom English is a second language, away from others. Intentionally or not, we have divided children on the basis of family income, race, ethnicity, and increasingly native language, then used these divisions to rationalize the disparities cited above.

The separations matter, both because poor children consistently get less—less qualified teachers, a less rigorous curriculum, fewer extracurricular opportunities, and buildings that are often bleak, if not dangerous (Kozol 1991, 2006)—and because concentrated poverty puts so much stress on schools. In their analysis of the federal Chapter 1 program, a precursor to Title I, Kennedy, Jung, and Orland (1986) found that schools with high concentrations of poverty, in themselves, depress student achievement. These researchers found that a typical poor child attending a high-poverty school (where more than half the students were also poor) suffered an achievement decline of approximately 30 percent between grades two and four relative to their middle-class peers in middle-class schools. More recently, Harris (2006) found that almost no high-poverty schools consistently perform at high levels on standardized tests. In an analysis of data from the U.S. Department of Education for the years 1997–2000, Harris (2006) found that only 1.1 percent of high-poverty schools had two years of scores in the top third of a national achievement database in English and math and in two grades. By contrast, 24.2 percent of schools that are majority middle-class met this standard.

As an illustration of the economic segregation rooted in school districting, consider three districts near my home in eastern New York: Roosevelt, Spackenkill, and Port Chester-Rye. The Roosevelt Union Free School District is a municipal jurisdiction on Long Island in Nassau County. This tiny, 1.5 square-mile district exists only as a school district, not as a town or village. Half the 2,682 students enrolled in 2006–2007 were eligible for free or reduced-price lunch. Only two of these students were white; 99 percent were African American or Latino (New York State Education Department 2008). Although Roosevelt's property tax rate is among the highest in New York State, its per-pupil school spending for many years was the lowest in the county because its property values are so low.[3]

Several years ago when the State Commissioner of Education and the New York Board of Regents considered dissolving the Roosevelt district and dispersing its students to surrounding schools, parents in the neighboring districts protested loudly. A flyer campaign in the predominantly white district of East Meadow urged residents to "keep Roosevelt students out" and warned that, if the plan went through, "We will have no choice except to remove our children from the East Meadow school and move away. But who will buy our homes? People with a lot less money, for much lower prices. Our property values will drop dramatically" (cited in Kozol 2006, 158). The campaign seemingly succeeded, as the proposal was dropped shortly thereafter. As Kozol (2006) notes, "If ever there had been an opportunity to end the educational apartheid of a small community of children, this had been it. The tiny population of the Roosevelt schools could, physically at least, have been absorbed with ease into surrounding districts" (159).

Like Roosevelt, the Spackenkill Union Free School District exists only as a school district. Located within the town (but not the city) of Poughkeepsie, the Spackenkill district borders the Poughkeepsie City School District. Throughout the 1960s and early 1970s, the Spackenkill Board of Education battled with the New York State Education Department over the state's plan to merge the six-mile-wide Spackenkill district, which includes an IBM plant, with the Poughkeepsie schools. With help from its friends in the State Legislature and strong community support, the Spackenkill school board defied a state directive, built its own high school, initially without state funding, and thereby created a K-12 district that enabled it to pull the Spackenkill students out of Poughkeepsie High School (Books 2006). Lilli Zimet, a Poughkeepsie resident who lived through the struggle, recalled in 2005:

> The feeling was that [Spackenkill going its own way] was detrimental to the rest. The fear was that it would split off, well, a "well-off" group. Real estate was higher there. The fear was it would deprive the Poughkeepsie district, which would become more imbalanced, financially and in terms of [academic] standards. And, of course, that's what did happen. Poughkeepsie [High] became an inner-city school. (quoted in Books 2006)

Today, 1,801 students attend the Spackenkill schools; 81 percent are white or Asian and 10 percent are eligible for the federally subsidized lunch program. Next door, 4,660 students attend the Poughkeepsie City Schools, where only 18 percent are white or Asian and *81 percent* are eligible for subsidized lunch (New York State Education Department 2008).

Finally, consider public schooling in Westchester, a 433 square-mile county just north of New York City that contains 40 school districts. Although Westchester had the eighth highest per-capita income in the nation in 2004, it also has pockets of poverty. One consequently would expect to find significant economic integration in the schools. State data show instead economic segregation.

For example, at JFK Magnet Elementary in the Port Chester-Rye Union Free School District, 70 percent of the students (only 6 percent of whom are white) are eligible for the subsidized lunch program. *Two miles away* at Midland Elementary in the neighboring Rye City School District, only 2 percent of the students (83 percent of whom are white) are eligible for subsidized lunch. Merging these districts would require neither massive bussing nor loss of a concept of neighborhood schools. It would mean, however, that poor children, largely children of color, would go to school with much wealthier and largely white children and would enjoy access to more resources. Whereas the Port Chester-Rye schools spent $16,102 per pupil in 2006–07, the Rye City schools spent $20,064— almost 28% more (New York State Education Department 2008).

As in these districts in New York, so too in public schools across the nation: de facto segregation along racial lines means segregation along economic lines as well. In 2005–06 about a third of all black and Latino students (32 percent and 34 percent, respectively) attended schools in which three-quarters or more of the students were eligible for subsidized lunch while only 4 percent of white students attended such high-poverty schools (Planty et al. 2008). In their study of public schools in North Carolina, Clotfelter et al. (2006) found the rich–poor gap among schools is actually increasing. High-poverty schools have become poorer over the last decade, both absolutely and relative to low-poverty schools. To gain a fuller perspective of what poverty means for children's educational opportunity, let us consider what happens before and after poor children enter the public school system.

The Child Care Crisis

In 2007, almost three-quarters of all mothers and more than three-quarters of all single mothers with children under 18 years old (71 percent and 76.5 percent, respectively) were in the labor force, as were more than 60 percent of all mothers and more than 63 percent of all single mothers with children younger than 2 (Bureau of Labor Statistics 2008). Because mothers are still children's primary caregivers and because the United States stands alone among all major industrialized countries in failing to provide paid parental leave, child care, and health care for all children, we have a child care crisis (Polakow 2007). Gornick and Meyers' (2003) question still hangs heavy in the air: "If everyone is at the workplace, who will care for the children?" (cited in Polakow 2007, 10).

Because public childcare programs are so underfunded and private care is so expensive ($4,000 to $11,000 a year for a four-year-old and up to $15,000 for an infant), the child-care crisis in the United States hits hardest those children in the poorest families (National Association of Child Care Resource and Referral Agencies 2007). These families often must settle for whatever care they can find and afford, not what they might want. Implementation of the 1996 welfare "reform" legislation, euphemistically titled the Personal Responsibility and Work Opportunity Reconciliation Act, pushed millions of poor single mothers into the low-wage labor market, including those with infants as young as twelve weeks. Between 1996 and 2005, the number of families receiving public assistance plummeted 57 percent (U.S. Department of Health and Human Services 2006). Affordable, quality care has not been provided for the millions of children in these families on anywhere near the scale required.

Low-income mothers spend on average more than 18 percent of their income on child care, and some spend as much as 25 percent, compared to an average of 6 percent by mothers in upper-income households (Boushey & Wright 2004). The federal Head Start program, chronically underfunded, serves only half the four-year-olds nationwide who meet the income guidelines,[4] and most programs do not provide "wraparound care" for working parents (Polakow 2007). Given this squeeze—a seller's market on one hand and a woefully inadequate public safety net on the other—the result is predictable: the nation's poorest children are in unregulated patchwork arrangements that range from adequate to terrible. In Polakow's (2007) words, this "netherworld of informal, unregulated, custodial care" provides "the worst of child care—harsh and dreary landscapes, disrupted attachments, shifting arrangements, unsafe spaces" (2).

Welfare "reform" radically reduced welfare rolls, but did not ameliorate child poverty. On the contrary, "we find…more children in poverty, more children receiving food stamps, more children receiving federally subsidized free lunches" (Lindsey 2009, 7). As the U.S. economy continued unraveling into 2009, the outlook for poor families was worrisome. Whether child-care subsidies aimed at helping poor families survive in the wage-labor market would survive themselves or whether these programs would be cut in state budget retrenchments was an open question (Winerip 2008).

Higher Education

As Patrick Callan, president of the National Center for Public Policy and Higher Education, has noted, the United States is "one of the few countries where 25- to 34-year-olds are less educated than older workers" (quoted in Lewin 2008). Today, more than one in three African American, Latino, and Native American students—three groups that are disproportionately poor—do not graduate from high school (Habash 2008). In urban schools—again, sites of disproportionate poverty—only about 60 percent of the students graduate, compared to almost 75 percent in suburban schools (Swanson 2008). In the nation's largest cities, "graduating from high school…amounts, essentially, to a coin toss" (Swanson 2008, 8). No more than about half the students (52 percent) in the principal school systems of the 50 largest cities graduate with a diploma. In Baltimore, Cleveland, Detroit, Indianapolis, and some other major cities, fewer than 35 percent of the students graduate with a diploma (Swanson 2008).

Poor students who do graduate, despite the inequities shaping the pre-k through 12 educational experience, face daunting odds in continuing their education. Although President Lyndon B. Johnson promised, upon signing the Higher Education Act of 1965, that "a high school senior anywhere in this great land of ours can apply to any college or any university in any of the 50 States and not be turned away because his family is poor," the United States has not kept that promise. In 1986–87 Pell Grants, the primary federal need-based aid program, funded 52 percent of the average cost (tuition, fees, room and board) of a four-year public college. By 2004–05, these grants covered only 32 percent of the cost (Baum & Steele 2007). The Advisory Committee on Student Financial Assistance (2002) estimates that financial barriers—primarily rising tuition and insufficient need-based grant aid—keep 48 percent of college-qualified low-income high school graduates from continuing their education at a four-year college, and keep 22 percent from continuing at any college.

College tuition and fees, adjusted for inflation, increased 439 percent between 1982 and 2007, while median family income rose only 147 percent. In 2007, the net cost of a year at a public university equaled 55 percent of the median income for the poorest 20 percent of families, up from 39 percent in 1999–2000. At community colleges, long regarded as a safety net, the cost was 49 percent of the median income of the poorest 20 percent of families, up from 40 percent in 1999–2000

(National Center for Public Policy and Higher Education 2008).

Although some higher education institutions have continued to increase their spending on financial aid, "in fact they are just compensating for becoming more expensive and are not necessarily providing greater assistance to low-income and middle-income students" (Wilkinson 2005). By the early 2000s, students with family incomes of $160,000 and up were qualifying for need-based grants at some of the most expensive colleges. Currently, students from middle- and upper-income families receive larger grants from colleges and universities than students from low-income families (National Center for Public Policy and Higher Education 2008).

Not surprisingly, in the face of this "deterioration of college affordability," student borrowing over the last decade has more than doubled—because college costs have continued to rise, because family incomes have not kept pace, and because there has been a significant shift towards merit-based aid (Long & Riley 2007). Whereas need-based grant aid almost doubled over the last decade, spending on merit-based grant aid grew by almost 350 percent (National Association of State Student Grant and Aid Programs 2006). Merit-based aid does not favor poorer students who tend neither to attend academically competitive high schools nor to score especially well on the SAT, a test that arguably functions primarily as "a sort of diagnostic assessment of the deficit the children suffer during their earliest years before they enter school" (Lindsey 2009, 24).

Although student borrowing increased sharply over the last decade, many student loan providers, in response to the credit crisis embedded in the economic downturn that started in 2007, stopped making federally guaranteed loans, private loans, or both. Others tightened credit standards and raised interest rates (Glater 2008a, 2008b). Meanwhile, some of the nation's biggest banks appeared to be "breaking the marketplace into tiers," by continuing to lend to students at elite universities but not to students at less-selective four-year institutions and community colleges (Lewin 2008). In a deteriorating economy many universities that had taken pride in their "need-blind" admissions policies started rethinking those policies (Lewin 2008).

Between 1992 and 2004, despite an increase in students' overall academic preparedness, a major shift in enrollment away from four-year colleges occurred among academically qualified high school graduates from low- and moderate-income families (Advisory Committee on Student Financial Assistance 2008). Among low- and moderate-income graduates in the class on 2004 who took at least algebra II (one standard the Advisory Committee on Student Financial Assistance used for "college qualified"), only 40 percent subsequently enrolled in a four-year college, down from 54 percent in 1992. Among these graduates who took at least trigonometry (a higher standard of "college qualified"), only 55 percent enrolled in a four-year college, down from 73 percent in 1992. On this basis, the Advisory Committee on Student Financial Assistance (2008) estimates that 1.7 million to 3.2 million degrees have been "lost" in this decade alone.

In sum, poor children who make it through high school face daunting odds if they try to continue their education. As tuition costs at public colleges and universities continue to rise (in part because state support for public higher education continues to fall) and as the most prestigious schools become ever more selective, those pushed out all too often are the students with the greatest financial need. Unpreparedness is systematically produced in high-poverty schools, then "discovered" in the competition for merit-based college aid. In their analysis of Michigan data Haveman and Wilson (2005) found that only 7 percent of all college graduates came from the 25 percent of families with the least income and greatest financial need, and less than 3 percent came from the 10 percent of families with the least income. Looking at educational outcomes from another angle, Tom Mortenson reported, based on 2003 U.S. Census data, that whereas almost 75 percent of all young people in the top income quartile had earned a bachelor's degree by age 24, less than 9 percent in the bottom income quartile had done so (cited in Bracey 2005). In other words, "Children lucky enough to be born into the highest-income families are now virtually assured of a bachelor's degree by age 24, while those unlucky enough to be born into the bottom quartile of family income have only the very slimmest chance of gaining similar status" (Mortenson, cited in Bracey 2005).

What Can and Should We Do?

A discussion such as this one cries out for something more: a "solution" or way forward. What can we do? What should we do? The numbers are consistent: Poor children are systematically short-changed by our provision of educational opportunity almost from day one. Relegated to the worst child-care situations, then assigned to the worst public schools where they are ill prepared to compete for college aid that increasingly rewards narrowly defined achievement rather than supporting financial need, young people who grow up in poverty, not surprisingly, attend college in distressingly small numbers. This constriction of opportunity is an abdication of collective responsibility and a betrayal of the ideals on which the country was founded.

In one sense, steps in the right direction could be taken fairly easily. We could stop "shackling students to the economic circumstances into which they are born" by tying educational opportunity to local property wealth (Carey & Roza 2008, 13) and instead fund public schools in the way almost all other industrialized nations do: primarily through our national wealth. We also could stop trying to justify this illogical connection through a euphemistic discourse of "neighborhood schools." Neighborhoods are made and can be remade and enlarged. We could choose to draw school district lines in ways that would reduce, if not eliminate, economic as well as racial and ethnic segregation—not because there is anything magic about a black child sitting next to a white child or a poor child next to a wealthy child, but because segregation reflects and invites jockeying for advantage and callousness towards the plight of others.

In Alaska, New Jersey and Maryland, students in the poorest 25 percent of districts now receive considerably more funding per pupil in state and local revenues ($1,000 or more) than students in the wealthiest 25 percent of districts (Arroyo 2008). Other states could follow suit. Recognizing the toll that concentrated poverty takes on school achievement, the LaCrosse district in Wisconsin implemented a school assignment plan fifteen years ago to ensure that poor children of color are not clustered together in a few schools. About 40 other districts have now followed that district's lead and implemented similar plans as a way to increase student achievement district-wide, largely with good results (Rimer 2003). More districts could try this.

The United Nations Human Rights Committee (2006) has expressed concern about the continuing "discrepancies between the racial and ethnic composition of large urban districts and their surrounding suburbs, and the manner in which school districts are created, funded and regulated" in the United States. We could take this embarrassing critique to heart and do as the U.N. commission suggests: "respect and ensure that all persons are guaranteed effective protection against practices that have either the purpose or the effect of discrimination on a racial basis,…conduct in-depth investigations into…de facto segregation…and take remedial steps, in consultation with affected communities" (United Nations Human Rights Committee 2006). NCLB has not been helpful in this regard as its transfer provision depends on the availability of spaces in other schools and has hardly been used (Bazelon 2008).

That said, I believe the fundamental challenge is not primarily one of policy-making but rather of moral sensibility and commitment. Our system of public schooling in too many ways invites a spirit of competitiveness and selfishness that seeks not the best for all, but the best for one's own children. We have lost and need urgently to regain a sense of the common good. Who are we, as Kozol charges, who put price tags on individual children, however indirectly and with whatever rationalizations? By "common good" I mean a feeling that the whole matters, each and every child, and that we cannot take pride in the fruits of our collective labor until we know it is shared by all.

I think of a scene in a beautiful film, *Etre et Avoir* ("To Be and to Have"), about a one-room schoolhouse in rural France. It's pouring rain one afternoon when the school ends, so the teacher takes the children two by two under an umbrella to their bus. One child runs ahead, and the teacher can't cover both, so the other child gets wet—a simple metaphor for a profound truth. In calling for a stronger sense of the common good, I am appealing not to obligation, but rather to a sense of family or community that is incompatible with exclusion, scorn, or leaving behind in a race to be first.

We had opportunities to come together in grief as a people after the 9/11 terrorist attacks in 2001 and especially after the predictable (and predicted) failure of the New Orleans levees after Hurricane Katrina in 2005. Sadly, both opportunities were squandered to a considerable extent. Ground zero workers with a host of respiratory problems after 9/11 are now mired in lawsuits over health insurance claims (Navarro 2008), and victims of the levee breaches have been shortchanged by almost everyone, including and especially apathetic federal officials and insurance companies looking for legal loopholes to let themselves off the hook.

"After more than three years of nomadic uncertainty, many of the children of Hurricane Katrina are behind in school, acting out and suffering from extraordinarily high rates of illness and mental health problems. Their parents, many still anxious or depressed themselves, are struggling to keep the lights on and the refrigerator stocked" (Dewan 2008). Even before the disaster, these were some of the country's neediest children. Now, says Irwin Redlener, president of the Children's Health Fund (CHF) and a professor at the Columbia University Mailman School of Public Health, the children of Katrina who stayed longest in formaldehyde-laden government trailer parks in Baton Rouge are "the sickest [he's] ever seen in the U.S." (quoted in Carmichael 2008). A study in 2008 of 261 displaced children by CHF and Mailman found that the well-being of the poorest children had "declined to an alarming level." Forty-one percent were anemic (twice the rate found in children in New York City's homeless shelters), more than half had mental health problems, and 42 percent had respiratory infections and other disorders (Carmichael 2008). In its third anniversary edition of the New Orleans index the Brookings Institute reported that

> Many recovery trends have slowed or stagnated…as tens of thousands of blighted properties, lack of affordable housing for essential service and construction workers, and thin public services continue[d] to plague the city and region….Basic services—including schools, libraries, public transportation, and child-care—remain at less than half of the original capacity in New Orleans, and only two-thirds of all licensed hospitals are open in the region (Liu & Plyler 2008, 1).

Nevertheless, there were moments after both 9/11 and Hurricane Katrina when it seemed possible as a nation to rise above narrow interests and to reach out to others in a spirit of generosity and compassion. We need to remember those moments and learn from them. The wisdom of the Dalai Lama comes to mind. Education, he once said, "is much more than a matter of imparting the knowledge and skills by which narrow goals are achieved. It is also about opening the child's eyes to the needs and rights of others." Similarly, I would say that educators—those of us who see teaching as part of our responsibility as adults, whether or not we are paid to do this work—need to do much more than help young people figure out how to work the system in their favor. Rather, we need to encourage broad reflection on the needs and rights of others and on the flip side of this coin—namely, our responsibility to foster a sense of the common good as the foundation of a lasting community. As Barack Obama's ascendancy to the presidency suggests, evocation of a sense of community and a call to shared responsibility resonates with many, many people. Knowing that structures that benefit one's own children harm others is not a satisfying way to live.

More specifically, I believe that teacher educators, including myself, need to consider the relevance of a teacher-education curriculum that encourages prospective teachers to learn to "differentiate instruction" but not always to consider the deep injustices and differentiations that take such a harsh toll on children. A better understanding of the educational experience of poor children will not make any one child's life less difficult, but it could provide the foundation for a broad public conversation about the responsibility of the adult generation to provide, at a minimum, a viable path for all young people to a fulfilling life unconstrained by poverty. We could to this and we should, if for no other reason than because we can. Widespread reflection on the needs and rights of poor children could provide an ethical anchor—a way to set priorities, to make decisions, and to remind ourselves that the children who suffer from so many of the social policies and practices we rationalize and sustain are in fact our greatest responsibility.

Notes

1. Author's calculations based on 2008 Census data. See *Public Education Finances*: http://ftp2.census.gov/govs/school/06f33pub.pdf.
2. As of 2008, lawsuits challenging school funding had been brought in 45 states (National Access Network 2008).
3. The Roosevelt Union Free School District was taken over by New York State in 2002. Despite the takeover, the Roosevelt schools continued to struggle academically and financially. In 2008, the state awarded the Roosevelt schools a "fiscal relief package" designed to address the district's $8 million deficit and its chronic underfunding relative to other districts in Nassau County ("Governor Spitzer signs" 2008).
4. This percentage is derived from calculations by the National Women's Law Center based on data from the U.S. Head Start Bureau and the U.S. Census Bureau; cited in Stebbins & Scott (2007).

References

Advisory Committee on Student Financial Assistance (2002, June). *Empty promises: The myth of college access in America.* Washington, DC: Author.

Advisory Committee on Student Financial Assistance (2008, May 1). Shifts in college enrollment increase projected losses in bachelor's degrees. *Policy Bulletin.* Washington, DC: Author.

Ali, R. (2006, April 11). *Testimony of Russlyn Ali, Director, Education Trust-West, before the Commission on No Child Left Behind.* Retrieved from http://www2.edtrust.org. April 30, 3006

Alstoff, A. (2007, May 29). Hidden rations. *Slate.* Retrieved from http://www.slate.com/toolbar.aspx?action=print&id=2167190. May 30, 2007.

Anyon, J. (2005). *Radical possibilities: Public policy, urban education, and a new social movement.* New York: Routledge.

Arroyo, C. (2008). The Funding Gap. The Education Trust. From http://www.closingtheachievementgap.org/cs/ctag/view/resources,75. Retrieved 2/14/2010.

Baum, S., & Steele, P. (2007). *Trends in student aid 2007.* The College Board. Retrieved from www.

collegeboard.com/trends.

Bazelon, E. (2008, July 20). The next kind of integration. *The New York Times.* Retrieved from http://www.nytimes.com July 30, 2008.

Books, S. (2004). *Poverty and schooling in the U.S.: Contexts and consequences.* Mahwah, NJ: Erlbaum.

Books, S. (2006). The politics of school districting: A case study in upstate New York. *Educational Foundations, 20* (3/4), 15–34.

Books, S. (2009). Mechanics of unfairness: How we undercut poor children's educational opportunity. In H. Svi Shapiro (Ed.), *Education and hope in troubled times: Visions of change for our children's world* (pp. 63–75). New York: Routledge.

Boushey, H., & Wright, J. (2004, May 5). Working moms and child care. Data Brief No. 3. Washington, DC: Center for Economic and Policy Research. Retrieved from http://65.181.187.63/documents/publications /child_care_2004.pdf May 30, 2004.

Bracey, G. W. (2005, November). The bachelor's degree: a hereditary privilege? *Phi Delta Kappan, 87* (3) 253.

Carey, K., & Roza, M. (2008, May). *School funding's tragic flaw.* Seattle, WA: Center on Reinventing Public Education, University of Washington. Retrieved from http://www.educationsector.org/usr_doc/Tragic_Flaw_may14 _combo.pdf.

Carmichael, M. (2008, Dec. 1). Katrina kids: Sickest ever. *Newsweek.* Retrieved from http://www.newsweek .com/od/170370/output/print December 31, 2008

Clotfelter, C., Ladd, H., Vigdor, J., & Wheeler, J. (2006, December 7). *High poverty schools and the distribution of teachers and principals.* National Center for the Analysis of Longitudinal Data in Education Research (CALDER) working paper. Retrieved from http://www.caldercenter.org/PDF/1001057_High_Poverty.pdf December 31, 2006.

Cookson, C. (2008, February 16). Poverty mars formation of infant brains. *Financial Times.* Retrieved from http://www.ft.com February 28, 2008.

Cowan, A. (2007, June 3). Schools' deep-pocketed partners. *The New York Times.* Retrieved from www.nytimes.com June 30, 2007.

Dahl, M. (2007, May). *Changes in the economic resources of low-income households with children.* A CBO paper. Washington, DC: Congressional Budget Office.

Dewan, S. (2008, December 5). Many children lack stability long after storm. *The New York Times.* Retrieved from http://www.nytimes.com December 31, 2008.

Ethan, D., & Basch, C. E. (2008, August). Promoting healthy vision in students: Progress and challenges in policy, programs, and research. *Journal of School Health, 78* (8), 411–416.

Fass, S., & Cauthen, N. K. (2008, October). Who are America's poor children? The official story. National Center for Children in Poverty, Mailman School of Public Health, Columbia University. Retrieved from http://www.nccp.org/publications/pub_843.html October 31, 2008.

Filardo, M. W., Vincent, J. M., Sung, P., & Stein, T. (2006). *Growth and disparity: A decade of U.S. public school construction 1995–2004.* Washington, DC: BEST (Building Educational Success Together).

Glater, J. D. (2008a, June 2). Student loans start to bypass 2-year colleges. *The New York Times.* Retrieved from http://www.nytimes.com June 30, 2008.

Glater, J. D. (2008b, October 17). In downturn, families strain to pay tuition. *The New York Times.* Retrieved from http://www.nytimes.com October 30, 2008

Gould, M. C., & Gould, H. (2003). A clear vision for equity and opportunity. *Phi Delta Kappan, 85* (4), 324–328.

Gornick, J., and Meyers, M. (2003). *Families that work.* New York: Russell Sage.

Governor Spitzer signs bill to restore fiscal stability to Roosevelt Union Free School District (2008, January 29). Press release. New York State Executive Chamber. Retrieved from http://www.state.ny.us/governor/press/0129083.html January 31, 2008

Habash, A. (2008). *Counting on graduation: an agenda for state leadership.* Washington, DC: The Education Trust.

Haberman, M. (1991). Pedagogy of poverty v. good teaching. *Phi Delta Kappan*, 73, 290–294.

Harris, D. N. (2006). *Ending the blame game on educational inequity: A study of "high flying" schools and NCLB.* Tempe, AZ: Education Policy Research Unit, Arizona State University.

Haveman, R., & Wilson, K. (2005). *Economic inequality in college attendance, matriculation, and graduation.* Working Paper No. 2005–032. LaFollette School of Public Affairs, University of Wisconsin-Madison. Retrieved from www.lafollette.wisc.edu/publications/workingpapers/haveman2005–032.pdf.

Kennedy, M.M., Jung, R.K., & Orland, M.E. (1986, January). *Poverty, achievement and the distribution of compensatory education services.* Washington, DC: U.S. Government Printing Office.

Kozol, J. (1991). *Savage inequalities: Children in America's schools.* New York: HarperCollins.

Kozol, J. (2006). *The shame of the nation: The restoration of apartheid schooling in America.* New York: Crown.

Ladson-Billings, G. (2006). From the achievement gap to the education debt: Understanding achievement in U.S. schools. *Educational Researcher, 35* (7), 3–12.

Lee, V.E., & Burkam, D.T. (2002). *Inequality at the starting gate: Social background differences in achievement as children begin school.* Washington, DC: Economic Policy Institute.

Lewin, T. (2008, November 8). Tough times strain colleges rich and poor. *The New York Times.* Retrieved from http://www.nytimes.com November 30, 2008

Lindsey, D. (2009). *Child poverty and inequality: Securing a better future for America's children.* New York: Oxford University Press.

Liu, G. (2006). How the federal government makes rich states richer. *Funding gaps 2006* (pp. 2–4). Retrieved from www.edtrust.com.

Liu, A., & Plyler, A. (2008). *The New Orleans index anniversary edition: Three years after Katrina.* Washington, DC: Brookings Institution Metropolitan Policy Program & Greater New Orleans Community. Retrieved from http://www.brookings.edu/reports/2007/08neworleansindex/aspx.

Long, B.T., & Riley, E. (2007). Financial aid: A broken bridge to college access? *Harvard Educational Review, 77* (1); 39–47.

National Access Network (2008). ACCESS. Teachers College, Columbia University. Retrieved from http://www.schoolfunding.info/litigation/litigation.php3.

National Association of Child Care Resource and Referral Agencies (2007). *Parents and the high price of child care.* Arlington, VA: Author. Retrieved from http://www.naccrra.org/docs/press/price_report.pdf.

National Association of State Student Grant and Aid Programs (2006). *Thirty-sixth annual survey report on state sponsored student financial aid: 2004–05 academic year.* Washington, DC: Author.

National Center for Public Policy and Higher Education (2008). *Measuring up 2008: the national report card on higher education.* Retrieved from www.highereducation.org.

Navarro, M. (2008, Dec. 11). Ground zero lawsuits are to being in 2010. *The New York Times.* Retrieved from http://www.nytimes.com December 31, 2008.

New York State Education Department (2008). *New York State school report cards for the 2006–2007 school year.* Retrieved from http://www.emsc.nysed.gov/irts/reportcard/2007/home.shtml.

Peske, H., and Haycock, K. (2003). *Teaching inequality: How poor and minority students are shortchanged on teacher quality.* Washington, DC: The Education Trust. Retrieved from http://www.edtrust.org.

Planty, M., Hussar, W., Snyder, T., Provasnik, S., Kena, G., Dinkes, R., KewalRamani, A., and Kemp, J. (2008). *The Condition of Education 2008.* NCES 2008–031. Washington, DC: National Center for Education Statistics, Institute of Education Sciences, U.S. Department of Education.

Polakow, V. (2007). *Who cares for our children? The child care crisis in the other America.* New York: Teachers College Press.

Richardson, J. W. (2005). *The cost of being poor: Poverty, lead poisoning, and policy implementation.* Westport, CT: Praeger.

Rimer, S. (2003, May 8). Cambridge schools try integration by income. *The New York Times.* Retrieved from http://www.nytimes.com.

Roza, M. (2006). How districts shortchange low-income and minority students. *Funding gaps 2006* (pp. 9–12). Retrieved from www.edtrust.com.

Rural School and Community Trust (2008, December). Graph: Total Title I funding per eligible child, 2008–09 school year. *Rural Policy Matters, 10* (12). <Au: Please provide page number.>

Sewing up the safety net (2008, November 27). Editorial. *The New York Times.* Retrieved from http://www.nytimes.com

Shonkoff, Jack P. (2005). The non-nuclear option: strong families and healthy children require social investment to complement the heroics of modern parenting. *American Prospect* (May).

Stebbins, H., & Scott, L.C. (2007, January). *Better Outcomes for all: Promoting partnerships between Head Start and state pre-K.* Washington, DC: Center for Law and Social Policy. Retrieved from http://www.preknow.org/documents-/HeadStartPre-KCollaboration_Jan2007.pdf January 31, 2007.

Swanson, C. B. (2008, April 1). *Cities in crisis: a special analytic report on high school graduation.* Bethesda, MD: Editorial Projects in Education Research Center. Retrieved from http://www.americaspromise.org/uploadedFiles/AmericasPromiseAlliance/Dropout_Crisis/SWANSONCitiesInCrisis040108.pdf April 30, 2008.

UNICEF (2007). *Child poverty in perspective: An overview of child well-being in rich countries.* Report Card 7. Florence, Italy: UNICEF Innocenti Research Center.

United Nations Human Rights Committee (2006, July 28). *Consideration of reports submitted by state parties under Article 40 of the Covenant: United States of America.* Retrieved from http://www.unhcr.org/refworld/type,CONCOB-SCOMMENTS,,USA,47bbf3662,0.html

U.S. Census Bureau (2006, August 29). POV03. People in Families with Related Children Under 18 by Family Structure, Age, Sex, Iterated by Income-to-Poverty Ratio and Race. Washington, DC: Author. Retrieved from http://pubdb3.census.gov/macro/032005/pov/new03_100htm September 30, 2006.

U.S. Census Bureau (2008, April). *Public education finances.* Washington, DC: Author. Retrieved from http://ftp2.census.gov/govs/school/06f33pub.pdf May 30, 2008.

U.S. Department of Health and Human Services (2000). *Oral health in America: A report of the surgeon general.* Rockville, MD: U.S. Department of Health and Human Services, National Institute of Dental and Craniofacial Research, National Institutes of Health.

U.S. Department of Health and Human Services, Administration for Children & Families (2006, February 9). Welfare rolls continue to fall. *HHS News.*

U.S. Department of Health and Human Services, Centers for Disease Control and Prevention (2008). General lead information: Questions and answers. Retrieved from http://www.cdc.gov/nceh/leqad/faq/about.htm. Updated July 8, 2008.

U.S. Department of Labor, Bureau of Labor Statistics (2008, May 30). Employment characteristics of families in 2007. *News.* Washington, DC: Author.

Wilkinson, R. (2008). *Aiding students, buying students: Financial aid in America.* Nashville, TN: Vanderbilt University Press.

Winerip, M. (2008, November 30). Filling a gap in child care, a few families at a time. *The New York Times.* Retrieved from http://www.nytimes.com December 31, 2008.

CHAPTER ELEVEN

Sexualization of Children in Contemporary Australian Media

SUSAN GRIESHABER

The release of a report by the Australia Institute called *Corporate Paedophilia: Sexualisation of Children in Australia* (Rush & La Nauze, 2006a) put the commercial exploitation of children's sexuality on the public agenda and claimed there was a need for sustained public debate about it in Australia. The two most significant claims made in the report are first, that sexualizing children in the media suggests it is a normal practice; and second, that it will encourage "paedophilic desire for children" (p. 2). *Corporate Paedophilia* succeeded in producing a short-lived but frenetic public discussion in the Australian national media and was the subject of heated debate on several blogs across the country (Egan & Hawkes, 2008). It was also accused of encouraging a moral panic about "virtual paedophilia" (Lucy & Mickler, 2007), and the retail department store David Jones took legal action against the Australia Institute, allegedly in an effort to gag informed debate about corporate activity (Media, Entertainment and Arts Alliance, 2007). As a result of this and other activity, a Senate inquiry into the sexualization of Australian children in the contemporary media began in March 2008. The inquiry acknowledged the "significant cultural challenge" of "preventing the premature sexualization of children" and in its 13 recommendations left no doubt that responsibility lies with "broadcasters, publishers, advertisers, retailers and manufacturers to take account of these community concerns" (Commonwealth of Australia, 2008, p. v).

This chapter investigates and critiques the idea of the sexualization of children in the contemporary media with a focus on recent events in Australia. It begins by commenting about aspects of *Corporate Paedophilia: Sexualisation of Children in Australia* (Rush & La Nauze, 2006a) and then investigates relevant literature about consuming bodies to provide a frame for discussing consumer culture, children, and childhood. Following this, the sexualization of children in the contemporary media is explored from the perspective of moral panics and the discourses of neoliberal tolerance and intolerance. The chapter concludes that although the idea of children being sexualized in contemporary media is contested, there can be no simple explanations and that a multiplicity of factors need to be taken into account that exist outside of media discourses.

Sexualization of Children in Contemporary Media?

The use of the term *Corporate Paedophilia* in the title of their initial paper makes a strong statement and suggests that the authors (Rush & La Nauze, 2006a) wanted to draw the attention of the Australian public to what they considered to be a serious issue and one in need of public discussion. Corporate pedophilia is a metaphor coined by Australian social commentator Phillip Adams to refer to selling products to children before "they are able to understand advertising and thus before they are able to consent to the process of corporate-led consumption" (Rush & La Nauze, 2006a, p. 1). The metaphor is explained as drawing a parallel between "actual paedophilia, the use of children for the sexual pleasure of adults, and corporate use of children for the financial benefit of adults who own and manage corporations" (p. 1). Rush and La Nauze (2006a) describe their use of the term as quite specific, stating that they are referring

> …only to advertising and marketing that either seek to present children in sexually suggestive ways, or seek to sell products to children using overt forms of adult sexuality. It encapsulates the idea that such advertising and marketing is an abuse of children and contravenes public norms. (p. 1)

Children are defined as aged 12 years and younger, and the authors acknowledge that their concern is "particularly girls" (p. vii) because of the way that they are "dressed, made up and posed in the same way as sexy adult models" (p. vii). They claim that what is different now is that it is children themselves who are used to model sexy adults, whereas in the past children have been exposed to representations of teen or adult (and not child) sexuality in advertising and popular culture. Rush and La Nauze say that there is now a lot more pressure on children to adopt a "sexualised appearance and behaviour at an early age" (p. vii) not only because of the representations of adult and teen sexuality but also because of what they call the "direct sexualisation of children" (p. vii). The flurry of activity produced by the release of *Corporate Paedophilia* culminated in a Senate[1] inquiry into the sexualization of children in contemporary media.

The Senate inquiry received a total of 167 submissions from 113 individuals and 52 groups or organizations as well as 900 standard or form letters that were sent via a Web site from the group called "Kids Free to Be Kids" (Commonwealth of Australia, 2008). All submissions indicated support for the inquiry, and it could be said that all were opposed to the sexualization of children in the media. However, the definition of and understanding attached to what was meant by the "sexualization of children in the media" was contested and varied widely. Lumby and Albury (2008b) challenged "the majority of submissions" (p. 81) made to the Senate inquiry because in their view the majority accepted without question that girls and young women were being "harmed by sexualized media images and that no further research was required to establish this fact" (p. 81). As far as Lumby and Albury were concerned there was no research evidence provided to indicate that sexualized media images were causing harm to girls and young women. Others took issue with the content of *Corporate Paedophilia* and engaged in what could be called more academic debate (e.g., Australian Psychological Society, 2008; McKee, 2008; Simpson, 2008). Table 11.1 shows the number of organizations and individuals that indicated support for the document in their submissions and those that did not.

In discussing some of the submissions further, my aim is to highlight key points of critique and significance in an attempt to understand these events from perspectives informed by theories of consumption and the context of neoliberalism in contemporary Australian society.

Table 11.1: Support for *Corporate Paedophilia*

	Total	Supported *Corporate Paedophilia*	Did not support
Organizations	52	39 Examples: Australian Childhood Foundation Australian Christian Lobby Australian Family Association Australian Psychological Society Catholic Archdiocese of Sydney Human Rights Commission Parents for a Real Choice The Australia Institute Women's Health Young Media Australia	13 Examples: Advertising Standards Bureau Australian Human Rights and Equal Opportunity Commission Australian Publishers' Bureau Australian Press Council Australian Subscription Television and Radio Association Australian Toy Association Commercial Radio Australia Family Planning Queensland Free TV Australia (Revised) Pacific Magazines and ACP Magazines Screen Producers Association of Australia
Individuals	113	105	4
Other	1	Standard letters and standard letters with correspondence (900)	
	1	Confidential	
Total	167		

Source: Rush & La Nauze, 2006a

In his Senate submission, academic and cultural studies theorist Alan McKee (2008) refuted the idea that there were representations of children in the contemporary media that sexualized them. He made the point that due to a range of enforceable laws there were "currently no representations in the mainstream media environment that a reasonable adult would perceive as 'sexualisation of children'" (p. 2). The opposite of this position, or seeing representations as sexualizing children, is an adult who is unreasonable. The issue of "reasonable adult" is addressed further in the section about neoliberal tolerance and intolerance. According to McKee, nine pieces of federal, state, and territory legislation in Australia prevent the sexualization of children in the media—a claim made on the basis of a textual analysis McKee had undertaken using examples referred to by Rush and La Nauze (2006a) as well as others in debates about the sexualization of children in the media (e.g., Bratz dolls, *Total Girl*, *Disney Girl*, *Barbie Girl* magazines, the Australian television soap *Home and Away*, the David Jones catalogue). McKee also addressed the issue of public confusion, which he said occurred in relation to eight issues in *Corporate Paedophilia* and included among others, consumer capitalism; younger children becoming sexually active at an earlier age; body image disorders in girls and young women; and the reprehensible act of highjacking the child sexual abuse and pedophilia agendas. The way in which McKee explained this last issue was that groups and individuals were using the sexualization of children in the media to make their agendas seem more important and in the process distract attention and divert resources from the real fight against child sexual abuse and the production and distribution of pornography.

As well as McKee finding no evidence of sexualized images of children, academics Lumby and Albury (2008a) and Simpson (2008) took issue with the credibility of the analysis undertaken by Rush and La Nauze (2006a), specifically the sample of advertising materials, television programs, and girls' magazines that were used. Lumby and Albury held that the sample of a total of 14 advertisements and examples of marketing material was far too small. They were also contemptuous of the so-called content analysis of three single issues of three different magazines read by girls aged 10–12 years, mainly because the categories of analysis (beauty, fashion, celebrity, crush) were "so broad as to be virtually meaningless" (p. 81). Simpson (2008) was also critical of the categories used, alleging that they were based on value judgments and because of this, should not be seen as scientific analysis. Simpson is not against using values per se; he stated that if values are used, then they should be "clearly articulated and explained" (p. 6). He called on those who want regulation in regard to the sexualization of children to explain their ideas of childhood and "the relationship between childhood and sexuality" (p. 6).

In anticipation of critique, Rush and La Nauze (2006a) preempted and refuted a number well-known arguments that they thought might be advanced in response to *Corporate Paedophilia*. These included rebutting the idea of moral panics, children's sexual development, changes in society, changing definitions of childhood, and the idea that fear and suspicion lead to "increased surveillance and control" (Kleinhans, 2004, p. 19). They reject each in turn, which culminated in an argument that the sexualization of children is a trend. They cite research from the United States (Rich, 2005) that supports their claims and emphasize that the trend must be stopped. A small section of the discussion paper deals with the sophistication of advertising and marketing techniques, but Rush and La Nauze (2006a) do not engage with any theoretical perspectives that deal with consumption and consumer culture.

Consuming Bodies

Consumer culture, or the mass production and consumption of goods and services in capitalist societies has brought an increasing focus on consumers and consuming bodies. Complicit in consumer culture of the early twenty-first century are neoliberal principles of free markets and free trade, relevant here because the concept of free markets and free trade means transferring (in principle) part of the control of the economy from the state to the private sector. The underlying premise is that government becomes more efficient, and the economy improves when the private sector plays a greater role. However, the daily reality seems to be that the market rules and that "culture has become something we consume rather than create" (Giroux, 2008, p. 104). Ritzer (1993) described the process of market exchange and its effects on daily life as the "McDonaldization of Society" (see also Kincheloe's [2002] discussion about McDonalds). He explained that the founder of MacDonalds applied the principles developed by Henry Ford for the car production line to the production and service of food. McDonaldization is about the increasing rationalization of the routine tasks of everyday life and the "process by which the principles of the fast-food restaurant are coming to dominate more and more sectors of American society as well as of the rest of the world" (Ritzer, 1993, p. 1).

Critics of neoliberalism and its effects on contemporary society attack it from all directions: economic, social, cultural, political; for its promise that economic growth "will cure social ills" (Giroux, 2008, p. 104); for being antidemocratic, for lacking ethics and a concern for citizenship; for its inequity, utilitarianism, commodification, deregulation and individualism; for its replacement of civic values with market values, and more. In her assessment of *Corporate Paedophilia* (Rush & La Nauze, 2006a), Abigail Bray (2008) acknowledged that the document adds to the "growing international dialogue about the importance of critiquing the neoliberal commodification of kids" (p. 326). But she also underscores the complexity and multifaceted nature of neoliberalism and the relationship between neoliberalism, consuming bodies, children and allegations of the sexualization of children in contemporary media.

Whether we like it or not, consumption and participation in commercial market activity are a significant part of the everyday lives of many children in the western world. It may occur through "pester" power where parents, caregivers, and family members are subjected to repeated requests for desirable items or through the escalating spending resources of children themselves, that is, through allowances ("pocket" money) or part-time jobs. While children's direct spending power may have been reduced with the recent global financial crisis that began in 2008, Dotson and Hyatt (2005) report that the number of children in the United States spending their own money has increased for the past three decades and that it tripled in the 1990s. Estimations indicate that in the United States in the year 2000, children under the age of 12 had a direct indirect influence on how nearly $300 billion was spent (McDonald & Lavelle, 2001). Kanner (2006) claims that budgets for advertising to children in the United States rose from $100 million in 1983 to $16 billion in 2004. In Australia, the tween[2] market is estimated to be worth more than $10 billion, with between $250 million and $1 billion being spent on clothing (Wells, 2006). There is no doubt that the child market is highly lucrative, and Kleinhans (2004) and Kanner (2006) claim that the continual drive for new markets has found a new home in the sexualization of children in contemporary media.

The absence of children from theories of consumer society and culture has been noted by Cook (2008) and Martens, Southerton, and Scott (2004). Apart from the fact that such theories were originally written from the perspectives of men and did not include women and children, the invisibility of children in theories of consumer culture seems to be due to the fact that children "pose analytic, ontological and epistemological problems to the theorizing of…most any kind of social action, economic or otherwise—precisely because their agency, being-in-the-world and ways of knowing are at issue" (Cook, 2008, p. 230). But this is no excuse to preclude attempts to theorize relationships among children, consumer culture and society. The book *Kidworld* (Cannella & Kincheloe, 2002) began this work by introducing ideas about the complexity of relationships that exist among children, consumer culture, and colonization. Despite the silences about children, three groups of theories in the sociology of consumption have been used to explain consumption: production of consumption; mode of consumption, and consumption as aesthetics, or how consumption exemplifies individualization (Martens et al., 2004). Each of these groups is now discussed.

Production of Consumption

Theories about the production of consumption include early work that investigated the production and distribution of products (such as toys), as well as the products themselves. These approaches did not take users of the products into account, which meant that they focused on the market to the exclusion of consumers (such as children and parents), and the conditions and location of use of the goods (Martens et al., 2004). Thus they are limiting because they take only part of the process of consumption into account. Another shortcoming is that because children have not been conceptualized as part of the theories, they are constructed as not-knowing and in need of guidance from adults about products such as toys. Production approaches are also problematic because "consumer behaviour is often read off from production trends" (Martens et al., 2004, p. 160). The difficulty with this is that because consumers are not consulted, inaccurate understandings often result about the reasons why consumers want certain products and the ways in which they use them. Where the assumed relationship between the product and the consumer is one of products dictating consumer behavior, it constitutes what has been called effects research.

Early effects research is based on behaviorism and assumes a simplistic cause and effect relationship between media consumption and human behaviour. More recent research into effects has challenged this simplistic approach with Buckingham (2000) developing an argument that new strategies are needed to protect the rights of children as consumers and citizens. To understand current patterns of consumption, it is important to include everyday consumption practices about choice and use, the influence of family and friends on everyday practices, how consumption becomes meaningful in the practice of everyday life, and how children learn to consume. In their analysis of the submissions to the Senate inquiry into the sexualization of children in contemporary Australian media, Lumby and Albury (2008a) argued that a media effects approach dominates the way many people (including professionals) understand youth media consumption. They said that submissions to the inquiry indicated that critiques of the media effects literature have had little if any effect on public policy and debate, which has resulted in the media effects model defining not only "popular media frames of reference but the very terms in which Australian public policy debates about the psychological and physical health of girls and young women are being conducted" (p. 82). As an example of the lack of uptake of the critiques of media effects, Lumby and Albury referred to the submission from the Australian Psychological Society (APS).

The APS is the peak body for professional psychologists in Australia. According to Lumby and Albury (2008a), its submission to the Senate inquiry was based on a "highly reductive and selective reading" (p. 82) of a report by the American Psychological Association (2007) about the sexualization of girls. The APS submission linked particular effects "directly and indirectly" to media consumption by girls (p. 82), stating for instance that the cognitive effects of "sexualising messages can lead girls to think of themselves in objectified terms" (p. 3). Self-objectification was described as a "process in which girls learn to see and think of their bodies as objects of others' desire, to be looked at and evaluated for its appearance" (p. 3). The submission also stated that girls are more likely to "encode and enact" what they have viewed when it is consistent with their own experiences and environment. Other effects linked to the sexualization of children in the APS submission include eating disorders, low self-esteem, and depression (p. 3). McKee (2008) resists the causal association of effects with body image disorders such as anorexia although he does acknowledge the rise in rates of reporting and associated public concern. He cites recent research to support the claim that the best predictors of girls and young women becoming anorexic are that they are high achievers and perfectionists, come from a middle class background, and have parents who tend to be controlling (p. 20). McKee says that the issue is the confusion of "correlation with causality," where there is an assumption of a causal link that the researcher sets out to prove and subsequently finds "only weak correlations in the process" (p. 20). The APS submission is an example of how a more critical understanding of media effects is required not only for the public, but for peak bodies that have significant influence on the community.

A final issue of concern about production modes of consumption is critical media education. Critical media education aims to teach consumers critical viewing skills and habits and is recommended by the Australian Psychological Society (2008) in its submission to the Senate inquiry. The APS indicated that critical media education would reduce the likelihood that young girls in particular will take up ("encode") "sexualized scripts" (p. 6). Critical media education is the approach used in the United States to teach media in schools and has been called an "inoculation model" (Lumby & Albury, 2008a, p. 82) because of its preventive and protective aims. Children and young people are "taught to identify and decode harmful media messages" (p. 82). But the difficulty is that this model

> …gives no recognition to the pleasures children and young people might take from popular media consumption which is not self-consciously "pro-social," let alone the pleasures they might take from media which are consciously irreverent and subversive of adult ideas of what they should be doing and thinking. (p. 82)

In other words, the model fails to recognize that consuming popular media is a significant part of the everyday lives of many children in the western world and that as the consumption as aesthetics approach suggests (see later section), it can be a defining part of who children are, what they do, and how they engage in daily life as individuals as well as with family, friends, and peers.

Mode of Consumption

Theories about the mode of consumption attempt to discern differences in how products are used and the way such use emphasizes distinctions between social groups. In this regard, French sociologist Bourdieu (1984) has been prominent in defining a sociology of the body that is class based. His theory of social stratification is founded on aesthetic taste and disposition, which are said to be learned at an early age from class upbringing and education. The aesthetic senses of different groups' social positions and their associated lifestyles are defined in opposition to each other and are linked directly to economic and cultural capital (Waquant, 1998). To Bourdieu, class distinctions are realized in the shared positions of social space and the way dispositions are enacted in consumption. For each major social position in French society (bourgeois, petty-bourgeois, popular) is a corresponding class habitus, which is the producer and "the product of internalisation of the division into social classes" (Bourdieu, 1984, p. 170). Bourdieu's concept of habitus has been used widely in sociology and beyond.

Despite the fact that Bourdieu's theory has not been applied to children's consumption specifically, the assumption is that there is an "intergenerational transfer of capital and internalization of habitus…through conceptually vague processes of socialization" (Martens et al., 2004, p. 163). In other words, what is not known is how cultural capital is transferred from one generation to the next and "through what processes the habitus becomes internalized" (p. 163). As well as these "unknowns," other questions arise, some of which are similar to those raised in the production approach to consumption: how and from whom do children learn to consume; how do reproduction and social change occur in relation to consumption; and how are the categories of "consumer," "adult," and "child" constructed in contemporary society? Theories of social classification and stratification are limited in their applicability to consumption in contemporary society because of the proliferation of goods and services. Further, in contemporary society, classification is far from straightforward because of the availability of a huge range of commodities and the difficulty in ascribing possession to a given social status.

Consumption as Aesthetics

In Giddens' (1991) view, late modernity is characterized by a loss of traditions and shared meanings and as a consequence in posttraditional societies, individuals must continually construct their own identities and in the process convey these meanings to others. Shilling (2005) claims the body has become a project and that what we do to our bodies and how we do it is the way that we achieve personal identity. Recent consumer culture, which has focused attention on adult body maintenance in terms of diet, exercise, cosmetic surgery, and body modification such as tattooing and piercing, is an example of what Shilling means. Children's bodies are no exception and they too have become a project, with many children and tweens continually fashioning and appropriating their identities through choices about clothes, hair, leisure, and associated accessories such as cell phones and miniature music players. Consumption then becomes more than choosing goods and services: it concerns lifestyle and choices about who we are and how we are seen by others, but ironically it is also about the lack of choice, because consumers have "no choice but to consume" (Giddens, 1991, p. 81). This theoretical perspective again raises questions of agency for both adult and child consumers.

Children and Agency

Changing ideas about children and childhood have witnessed an increase in the academic literature of approaches such as new childhood studies (e.g., Prout & James, 1997). This theoretical perspective has firmly established children as active, agentic, and competent as opposed to the passive, innocent, and immature child of developmental psychology (see Silin, 1995). Thus conceptions and images of children and childhood remain contested. Evidence of children being constructed as innocent and vulnerable was found in submissions from eight organizations and 45 individual submissions to the Senate inquiry, which means that innocence and/or vulnerability was mentioned in nearly one-third of all submissions (see Table 11.2). Submissions were categorized according to the language used. For example, if the submission mentioned that children were innocent and/or vulnerable, then it was recorded as such in tabular form. The categories "innocent" and "robbed of childhood" were used because of the frequency of which they were mentioned in submissions. Other categories were support for *Corporate Paedophilia* and risks. The risk categories are consistent with the headings used in *Corporate Paedophilia*: physical, psychological, and sexual harm; the "opportunity" cost of sexualization and ethical effects. "Opportunity" cost refers to what Rush and La Nauze (2006a) describe as the "cost to children of focusing on developing a sexualised appearance and personality...[and because of that] they will thereby have less time to devote to other things" (p. 44). Table 11.2 details these categories and the numbers of submissions classified in each according to whether they were submitted by individuals or organizations.

Table 11.2 Analysis of Submissions to Senate Inquiry

	Supported *Corporate Paedophilia*	Robbed of childhood	Innocent	Risks				
				Physical harm	Psychological	Sexual	Opportunity cost	Ethical
Individual	109	28	45	24	24	48	13	18
Organization	39	12	8	26	27	28	12	15
Total	148 (167)	40	53	50	51	76	25	33

As can be seen from Table 11.2, most concern was expressed in relation to the risk of sexual harm caused by the sexualization of children (mentioned in 76 submissions). The Senate inquiry (Commonwealth of Australia, 2008) concluded that in many private submissions, there were anecdotal claims suggesting that "many people believe exposure to sexual imagery in the media is harmful to children's development" (p. 48). The inquiry contrasted these anecdotal claims with the lack of research about the effects of premature sexualization on children. It took the advice of Professor Elizabeth Handsley, Vice President, Australian Council on Children and the Media who noted the "uncertain state of knowledge on the effects of the media on children's development" (p. 48) and recommended a precautionary approach. In light of this, the Senate made a number of recommendations to increase regulation of the media in relation to advertising and content directed at children. This is despite evidence from a UK study of children's attitudes and reactions to contemporary media, which showed that children are "not the incompetent or naïve consumers they are frequently assumed to be…children's response to sexual imagery in advertising or music videos displayed a well-developed understanding of how such images are constructed and manipulated" (Buckingham & Bragg, 2004, p. 238). Children apparently do develop the ability to make critical judgments about sexual content but understandably, this ability develops with age and experience. The same study found that parents play an important role in how children learn to process and interpret media images, which is something that children start at a relatively young age and that children find it difficult to understand sexual connotations and references. Of significance is the point made by the American Psychological Association (2007) that the media are not the only influence on children and as such "do not have an autonomous ability to either sexually corrupt children or to sexually 'liberate' them" (p. 4). Given the title of the document (*Corporate Paedophilia*) and some of the claims made by Rush and La Nauze (2006a), it is not surprising that nearly half of all submissions mentioned the sexual risk to which they thought children were exposed.

In terms of marketing and consumption, the child of development psychology is constructed as exploited or exploitable; innocent, not yet competent; and not yet a complete social actor, who is therefore at risk (see Cook, 2005). The empowered and knowing child of the new childhood studies is deemed to be far less vulnerable to exploitation, not innocent and an empowered social actor. However, the active agentic child of the new childhood studies is problematic from the consumption perspective. It makes critique of consumer culture difficult because the idea of the empowered and competent child as per the new childhood studies is antithetical to exploitation. Yet many adults (as well as children) have been and continue to be exploited by the power and seduction of sophisticated marketing techniques. The situation of experiencing both competence and lack of competence in media transactions suggests that multiple identities are at play and that at times, children, as well as adults can be positioned more powerfully and at other times, less powerfully in their dealings with and understandings of contemporary media.

Bodies are sites of constant production and regulation and are indicative of the power relations that are operating in society (Foucault, 1994, 1995). To Turner (2008), societies not only regulate populations but also control and manage bodies in social spaces, restrain citizens, and organize and manage bodily representation. He suggests that the body is a means of both consumption and expression. In her call for critiques of the neoliberal commodification of kids, Bray (2008) argued for a better understanding of the "disciplinary effects" of corporate culture on children (p. 326). Apart from those who expressed concern in submissions to the Senate inquiry into the sexualization of children in the contemporary media, Kanner (2006) and Kleinhans (2004) have claimed that the ways in which children's bodies are used as a means of marketing the consumption and expression of sexuality, and the corporate production and regulation of the sexuality of these child bodies have made it increasingly clear that the continual drive for new markets has found a new home in the sexualization of children in contemporary media. And as Bray has pointed out, "One would need a great deal of faith in the ethics of the 'free' market to assume that the corporate sexualisation of kids does not invoke a pae-dophilic imaginary" (p. 326). The question then becomes whether the release of *Corporate Paedophilia* and subsequent events qualify for what could be called a moral panic, created in fear of a pedophilic imaginary.

A Moral Panic?

Moral panics tend to occur when something happens to threaten the established social and moral order (Cohen, 1973/2006). They can produce social tension and create heated debate because the top-ics are controversial and because accepted ways of doing things are questioned. They are often engi-neered by conservative groups to protect established ways of doing things and more often than not involve issues that have been silenced or regarded as "taboo" and which have previously not been open for public debate. In this case, the claim has been made that what has changed is the use of children to model sexy adults, whereas previously teen or adult (and not child) models have been used in adver-tising and popular culture (Rush & La Nauze, 2006a). According to Cohen (1973/2006), this could be described as a new condition to emerge that poses a threat to society. But the submission from Brian Simpson (2008) to the Senate inquiry argued that "Whether intentional or not, the focus on the sexualisation of children and advertising fans a moral panic about children and sex generally" (p. 11).

In Goode and Ben-Yehuda's (1994/2006) model, there are five elements that can be used to judge and classify an event as a moral panic: concern, hostility, consensus, disproportionality, and volatili-ty. The release of *Corporate Paedophilia* (Rush & La Nauze, 2006a) prompted a great deal of concern about the sexualization of children in the contemporary media. It resulted in a second paper by the same authors, *Letting Children Be Children* (Rush & La Nauze, 2006b) and identified the action that needed to be taken to stop the sexualization of children. In early 2007, a new group of concerned par-ents founded Kf2bf (Kids free to be kids) and subsequently initiated an alliance with Young Media Australia (YMA). Later in 2007, YMA released a new Fact Sheet: *Too Sexy, Too Soon*. In all of these publications, hostility was directed toward the media, mainly because of the threat of pedophilia caused by representations of children as "sexualised commodities" and for robbing children of their child-hood and failing to protect their innocence (see the YMA Fact Sheet, 2007). A strategy typical of interest groups was used, which was to paint the issue "in terms of good versus evil" (Thompson, 2006, p. 61). The language indicated "moral indignation," and the evil other was depicted as typical and rep-resentative of the worst case scenario (p. 61). So the threat of pedophilia was pitted against the moral fabric of society, and urgent action was deemed necessary to control and manage the threat. And as Goode and Ben-Yehuda (2006) noted in their analysis of moral panics, there tends to be a need to "punish the perpetrators, and repair the damage" (p. 50).

Volatility was assured because of the emotive and sensitive nature of the claims and because the issue concerned children, sex, sexuality and pedophiles. Release of the YMA Fact Sheet (2007) coin-cided with a motion put to the Senate urging the government to establish an expert advisory group because of the growing body of evidence about the harmful effects of sexualization of children in the media. Around this time, Rush (2007) released another document: "Child Sexualisation Is No Game" and by March 2008, consensus was achieved across political parties with the announcement of the Senate inquiry into the sexualization of children in the contemporary media. Where moral panics are concerned, disproportionality concerns the amount of exaggeration and distortion that occurs, as well as what is ignored or left out of the argument (Goode & Ben-Yehuda, 2006). Goode and Ben-Yehuda state that the concept of moral panics "*rests* on disproportionality" (p. 55; emphasis in original) and that it implies that public concern is "in excess of what is appropriate if concern were directly proportional to objective harm" (p. 53). Simpson's (2008) comments to the Senate inquiry reflect a similar position: when the topic is the sexualization of children and advertising, there is a high probability that a moral panic about children and sex will occur. Simpson might have the right idea, but these days what might be called moral panics are more complex than the original analyses of what occurred in the 1970s. Moral panics associated with child sexual abuse have been around for a long time. Long enough, says Abigail Bray (2008), for them to have developed the reputation that they are "reactionary lower-middle-class social movements" (p. 324). However, Bray moves beyond such premises to propose links between neoliberalism, tolerance, intolerance, child sexual abuse and the corporate sexualization of girls within post-feminism.

Neoliberal Tolerance and (In)tolerance

Some of the basic characteristics of neoliberalism and the ideas of its critics have been discussed briefly in the earlier section "Consuming Bodies." A further analysis here focuses more specifically on aspects of the neoliberal state that are problematic and relate to tolerance and intolerance. Because of the way that the neoliberal state has developed, in many cases it has departed from "the template that theory provides" (Harvey, 2005, p. 64). This in turn has led to the suggestion that the neoliberal state may be "an unstable and contradictory political form" (p. 64). Certain versions of neoliberalism have promoted the development of stronger state structures and more centralized control and regulation. For instance, to Giroux (2008), neoliberal conceptions of democracy are "an extension of market principles," and citizens are seen as "hyperconsumers or unthinking patriots" (p. 175). Or, as Olssen, Codd and O'Neill (2004) put it, the state "actively constructs the market," and neoliberalism becomes a "new authoritarian discourse of state management and control" (p. 172). And this is despite the neoliberal principle of minimizing state control through privatizing resources and decentralizing social services. One of the contradictions of neoliberalism identified by Harvey (2005), social incoherence, is now investigated along with the notions of tolerance and intolerance.

Following Harvey's (2005) thesis and operating at what he calls the popular level, the free market can easily become out of control due to "the commodification of everything" (p. 80). The example of McDonaldization (Ritzer, 1993) provided earlier illustrates the concept as does Giddens' (1991) explanation of the loss of traditions and the subsequent focus on the construction of individual identity through consumption. As such there is a loss of coherence in society. The resultant threat to the social order and the corresponding "reduction of 'freedom' to 'freedom of enterprise'" (Harvey, 2005, p. 80) paves the way for antisocial behavior such as criminality and pornography (corporate pedophilia?). To Harvey (2005) and Brown (2006), neoliberalism has become the new common sense and the logic of the market has become a dangerous form of rationality. The threat to the social order is filled by the restoration of class power, which Harvey says is based on economics and characterized by "elite-led advocacy groups for various kinds of rights" (p. 78). These groups are not elected but are organized collectively and motivated to take action. They manifest in group solidarity on the basis of religion and morality, as well as rights and citizenship, and contravene basic principles of democracy because of their location in the politics of class and associated economic power. Their aim is to counteract the loss of coherence in society produced by defining individual identity through consumption and the subsequent chaos that this brings. This then is one explanation and provides an alternative understanding to the moral panic thesis for what resulted following the release of *Corporate Paedophilia* (Rush & La Nauze, 2006a).

Using Harvey (2005), what happened following the release of *Corporate Paedophilia* (Rush & La Nauze, 2006a) was that class-based advocacy groups, acting on the basis of collective concern over the perceived threat to the moral order, were able to garner enough public support and political clout to deliver a Senate inquiry into the sexualization of children in the media. This is what Harvey (2005) might call a neoconservative response to social incoherence. In the United States, neoconservatism is exhibited through moral values that are "centered on cultural nationalism, moral righteousness, Christianity (of a certain evangelical sort), family values and right-to-life issues, and on antagonism to the new social movements such as feminism, gay rights, affirmative action, and environmentalism" (Harvey, 2005, p. 84). Harvey makes it clear that this type of neoconservatism is not restricted to the United States. Neoliberalism has been a feature of Australian politics for nearly two decades and using Harvey's definition, several neoconservative social movements lodged submissions to the Senate inquiry. (The Family First party was so dissatisfied with the recommendations of the inquiry that it provided "Additional Comments," stating that the recommendations were insufficient to address the issue of sexualization of children.) But Giroux (2008) thinks that Harvey does not go far enough in explaining how neoliberal hegemony works, arguing that a more thorough analysis is needed of relationships among politics, culture, and class, and how the production of "neoliberal consent" occurs (p. 171). Perhaps Olssen et al. (2004) are closer to the mark, seeing neoliberalism as a form of governmentality operating as a "political doctrine of control" (p. 172), which is accompanied by a corpus of technologies of organization, classification, and regulation. Notwithstanding the complexity of these relationships, Brown's (2006) analysis of neoliberalism as a form of governmentality provides further insight.

Similar to Olssen et al. (2004), Brown (2006) sees neoliberalism as a form of governmentality that is all encompassing. But to Brown tolerance is a discourse of power and a "moral-political practice of governmentality" (p. 9). It works tacitly, subversively, and normatively, "posing as both a universal value and an impartial practice, designates certain beliefs and practices as civilized and others as barbaric…it operates from a conceit of neutrality that is actually thick with bourgeois Protestant norms" (p. 7). Both tolerance and intolerance of difference and diversity are produced hegemonically, marking who and what differs from normality. Tolerance operates as a discourse of power, perpetuating the idea of societies and communities being tolerant of racial, sexual, cultural, ethnic, economic, and religious differences but conveniently papering over any semblance of the historical construction of these differences and how they came to be. To Brown, tolerance is also a discourse of depoliticization because it nullifies claims for political justice by locating them in the realm of the personal, thereby reducing the political to the level of individual responsibility, to behavioral and emotional components of identity:

> …substituting a tolerant attitude or ethos for political redress of inequality or violent exclusions not only reifies politically produced differences but reduces political action and justice projects to sensitivity training, or what Richard Rorty called an 'improvement in manners.' A justice project is replaced with a therapeutic or behavioral one. (Brown, 2006, p. 16)

In this neoliberal regime, tolerance assumes virtues that are taken-for-granted as being of benefit for the greater good of society. But the depoliticization of tolerance dictates that only certain forms are acceptable, and in this respect, it seems that "good" versions of tolerance are associated with "politically sophisticated, neoliberal middle-class subjectivity, while intolerance is associated with the vulgar emotional instability of the reactionary lower-class other" (Bray, 2008, p. 325). The connection with the sexualization of children in contemporary media occurs for Bray when moral panics erupt about child sexual abuse.

The thesis of intolerance comes into play when moral panics about child sexual abuse are discursively constructed as "populist intolerance" and particular identities cast as "emotionally dangerous others" (Bray, 2008, p. 325). The question then for the submissions to the Senate inquiry into the sexualization of children (and those who were invited to make personal representations to the inquiry) is whether claims of moral panic, such as those by Simpson (2008) are in fact being constructed by such academics as populist intolerance by the reactionary lower-class other. This explanation locates academics such as Simpson as belonging to the tolerant and politically sophisticated neoliberal middle class and coincides with Bray's (2008) ideas about overcoming fear as the basis for tolerating difference. Put simply, once fear of any sort of difference is put to bed (sexual, racial, ethnic, and so on), so-called democratic tolerance reigns. Those who have not managed to control their fear, who remain afraid and angry are positioned as intolerant. Thus those fearful of pedophilia because of what they call the sexualization of children in contemporary media are considered intolerant.

Sexualization of Children?

Another way of seeing the argument that there are no representations of the sexualization of children in current mainstream media in Australia (McKee, 2008) is that it is part of the way in which intolerance toward the neoliberal system is marginalized and regulated by the politics of tolerance toward difference (see Brown, 2006). Intolerance to what might be called the sexualized representations of children in contemporary media has been associated with moral panics and in turn with conservative and right-wing thinking. The moral panic view is not sophisticated enough to accommodate the complexities of the market and consumption-driven neoliberal state. To some extent, the position of intolerance can be reconciled with Harvey's (2005) thesis of neoconservatism because of the antagonism (intolerance) toward new social movements such as feminism, gay rights, affirmative action, and environmentalism. Bray's (2008) argument about feminism as a discourse of intolerance is a case in point. In fact, Bray identifies her own responses to what she sees as the sexualized representations of children as aversion and intolerance, the result of an "oppressive politics" that produces in her very being a "conservative feminist moral panic power" (p. 328). The point is how it might be possible to move beyond the political effects of associating fear and anger with intolerance; of how to avoid "intolerance being pathologised and individualized as a symptom of the 'unreasonable-adult'" (Bray, 2008, p. 336). Neoliberalism and the politics of consumption demand that we do.

Notes

1. The Senate is one of two houses of the Australian Federal Parliament, and it has about the same amount of power to make laws as the other house of parliament. It is elected by proportional representation so that its composition closely reflects the voting pattern of the electors.

2. According to Rush and La Naze (2006a), *tweens* "are pre-adolescents who are claimed by marketers to be 'between' childhood interests and teenage pursuits" (p. 3). Wells (2006) says the tween market caters to those aged 7–13 years.

References

American Psychological Association. (2007). *Report of the APA Task Force on the sexualization of girls.* Washington, DC: APA.

Australian Psychological Society. (2008). *Submission to the Senate inquiry into sexualisation of children in the contemporary media.*

Bourdieu, R. (1984). *Distinction: A social critique of the judgement of taste.* London: Routledge & Kegan Paul.

Bray, A. (2008). The question of intolerance. *Australian Feminist Studies, 23*(57), 323–341.

Brown, W. (2006). *Regulating aversion: Tolerance in the age of identity and empire.* Princeton, NJ: Princeton University Press.

Buckingham, D. (2000). *After the death of childhood: Growing up in the age of electronic media.* Cambridge: Polity Press.

Buckingham, D. & Bragg, S. (2004). *Young people, sex and the media: The facts of life?* Basingstoke: Palgrave Macmillan.

Cannella, G. S. & J. Kincheloe (Eds.) (2002). *Kidworld: Childhood studies, global perspectives and education.* New York: Peter Lang.

Cohen, S. (1973/2006). Deviance and panics. In C. Chritcher (Ed.), *Critical readings: Moral panics and the media* (pp. 29–40). Maidenhead, England: Open University Press.

Cook, D. T. (2005). *How food consumes "the child" in the corporate landscape of fun: Commerce, agency and social meaning in contemporary children's culture.* Unpublished paper.

Cook, D. T. (2008). The missing child in consumption theory. *Journal of Consumer Culture, 8*(2), 219–243.

Commonwealth of Australia. (2008). *The Senate standing committee on Environment, Communications and the Arts: Sexualisation of children in the contemporary media.* Canberra: Senate Printing Unit, Parliament House.

Dotson, M. & Hyatt, E. M. (2005). Major influence factors in children's consumer socialization. *Journal of Consumer Marketing, 22*(1), 35–42.

Egan, G. & Hawkes, G. (2008). Girls, sexuality and the strange carnalities of advertisements. *Australian Feminist Studies, 23*(57), 307–322.

Foucault, M. (1994). *The birth of the clinic: An archaeology of medical perception.* New York: Vintage Books.

Foucault, M. (1995). *Discipline and punish: The birth of the prison.* New York: Vintage Books.

Giddens, A. (1991). *Modernity and self-identity.* London: Sage.

Giroux, H. A. (2008). *Against the terror of neoliberalism: Politics beyond the age of greed.* Boulder, CO: Paradigm Publishers.

Goode, E. & Ben-Yehuda, N. (1994/2006). Moral panics: An introduction. In In C. Chritcher (Ed.), *Critical readings: Moral panics and the media* (pp. 50–59). Maidenhead, England: Open University Press.

Harvey, D. (2005). *A brief history of neoliberalism.* Oxford: Oxford University Press.

Kanner, A. (2006). The corporatized child. *The California Psychologist, 39*(1), 1–2.

Kincheloe, J. L. (2002). The complex politics of McDonald's and the new childhood: Colonizing childhood. In G. S. Cannella, & J. L. Kincheloe (Eds.) (2002). *Kidworld: Childhood studies, global perspectives and education* (pp. 75–121). New York: Peter Lang.

Kleinhans, C. (2004). Virtual child porn: The law and the semiotics of the image. *Journal of Visual Culture, 3*(1), 17–34.

Lucy, N. & Mickler, S. (2007). The postmodern left: Part two. *Online Opinion*, March 29. Accessed January 2, 2009. http://www.onlineopinion.com.au/view.asp?article=5680&page=1

Lumby, C. & Albury, K. (2008a). Homer versus Homer: Digital media, literacy and child protection. *Media International Australia, 128*, 80–87.

Lumby, C. & Albury, K. (2008b). Submission of Professor Catharine Lumby, Director of the Journalism and Media Research Centre and Dr Kath Albury, ARC Postdoctoral Fellow, Journalism and Media Research Centre, UNSW to The Senate Standing Committee on Environment, Communication and the Arts Inquiry into the sexualisation of children in the contemporary media environment. April 23, 2008.

Martens, L., Southerton, D., & Scott, S. (2004). Bringing children (and parents) into the sociology of consumption: Towards a theoretical and empirical agenda. *Journal of Consumer Culture, 4*(2), 155–182.

McDonald, M. & Lavelle, M. (2001). *Call it 'kid-influence.'* U.S. News and World Report. Nation and world. Accessed February 7, 2009. http://www.usnews.com/usnews/biztech/articles/010730/archive_038048.htm

McKee, A. (2008). The Senate standing committee on the environment, communication and the arts: Inquiry into the sexualisation of children in the contemporary media environment.Media, entertainment and arts alliance. (2007). *Caveat emptor? David Jones gags debate.* Media release February 5. Accessed January 2, 2009. http://www.alliance.org.au/images/stories/070205pr_david_jones.pdf

Olssen, M., Codd, J. & O'Neill, A.M. (2004). *Education policy: Globalization, citizenship and democracy.* London: Sage.

Prout, A. & James, A. (1997). A new paradigm for the sociology of childhood? Provenance, promise and problems. In A. James & A. Prout (Eds.), *Constructing and reconstructing childhood: Contemporary issues in the sociological study of childhood* (pp. 7–33). London: Falmer.

Rich, M. (2005). Sex screen: The dilemma of media exposure and sexual behaviour. *Pediatrics Supplement, 116*(1), 329–331.

Ritzer, G. (1993). *The McDonaldization of society*, Newbury Park, CA: Pine Forge Press.

Rush, E. (26 Sept. 2007) Child sexualization is no game.Online Opinion: Australia's e-journal of social and political debate. From http://www.onlineopinion.com.au/view.asp?article=6422. Retrieved 2/16/010.

Rush, E. & La Nauze, A. (2006a). *Corporate paedophilia: Sexualisation of children in Australia.* Working paper no. 90. Canberra, ACT: The Australia Institute.

Rush, E. & La Nauze, A. (2006b). *Letting children be children: Stopping the sexualisation of children in Australia.* Working paper No. 93. Canberra, ACT: The Australia Institute.

Shilling, C. (2003) *The body and social theory* (2nd ed.). . London: Sage.

Silin, J. G. (1995). *Sex death and the education of children: Our passion for ignorance in the age of AIDS.* New York: Teachers College Press.

Simpson, B. (2008). *Submission to the senate inquiry into sexualisation of children in the contemporary media environment.*

Thompson, K. (2006). The history and meaning of the concept. In C. Chritcher (Ed.), *Critical readings: Moral panics and the media* (pp. 60–76). Maidenhead, England: Open University Press.

Turner, B. S. (2008). *The body and society: Explorations in social theory* (3rd ed.). London: Sage.

Young Media Australia. (2007). *Too sexy, too soon: The sexualisation of children in the media.* Fact Sheet. August. Accessed November 24, 2008. http://www.youngmedia.org.au/mediachildren/03_15_too_sexy_index.htm

Wacquant, L. J. D. (1998). Pierre Bourdieu. In R. Stones (Ed.), *Key sociological thinkers* (pp. 215–229). Basingstoke: Macmillan.

Wells, R. (2006). Very little women. *The Sunday Age*, May 7.

CHAPTER TWELVE

Cyber-Childhoods, Popular Culture and Constructing Identities

Nicola Yelland and Greg Neal

Abstract

In this chapter we consider childhood and the role of new technologies in children's lives. We report on a project that provided children (and their families) with computers and connection to the Internet. There is an increasing awareness that living in the twenty-first century involves using and interacting with a range of new technologies, also referred to as information and communications technologies (ICT). However, for many children and their families this is not possible because they do not have the capacity to purchase them. The Computer for Every Child project (CFEC) was a first attempt to bridge the "digital divide" by providing computers so that a group of families in the western suburbs of a large metropolitan city could participate in the Information Age. The families were mainly immigrants and refugees from the Africa and Asian region but also included those from European origins. We surveyed the children and their family members to determine the extent of their use of new technologies before and after receiving the computer and created case studies to explore the ways in which having a computer and experiencing online communications and communities created a context for them to experience a cyber childhood. In this chapter, we will describe what we observed and link this to current research on identity, learning and the role of popular culture.

Introduction

Many of the "Millennial Generation" (Howe and Strauss, 2000), that is those children born post-1985, inhabit digital spaces and communicate regularly with peers, family, and acquaintances for a variety of purposes using many devices. A large number of homes have a variety of media options that include TVs, mobile phones, computers, iPods, mp3 players, DVD machines, digital cameras, interactive toys and games, and video game consoles and mobile devices. This was made evident in a major study of birth to six-year-olds use of electronic media, Rideout, Vandewater, and Wartella (2003) reported that 99 percent have a TV at home and 36 percent have one in their own bedroom. Nearly a half of the group sampled had a video game player and 63 percent lived in a home that had Internet access. Additionally, nearly half (48 percent) of the group under six years of age have used a computer and 30 percent of them played video games. Their parents reported that they spend approximately 2 hours a day using screen media, about the same amount of time that they spent playing outdoors, and three times as much time as they spent reading (a book) or being read to.

It was also reported that many of the toddlers and preschoolers surveyed were not passively consuming media that has been purchased by their family. They were actively seeking out information or helping themselves to acquire it with the various electronic media at their disposal. Seventy-seven percent are turning on the TV by themselves, asking for particular shows (67 percent) using the remote control to change channels (62 percent) playing their favorite DVDs (71 percent) turning on the computer by themselves (33 percent), and loading CD-ROMS with games on (23 percent). The study revealed that listening to music (and dancing/ acting) is one of the most popular pastimes for young children in this age range with 79 percent listening to music daily with just under half (42 percent) owning their own CD so they can listen when they want to. If these young children are fluent in their use of new media, we would expect that older ones have lives that are characterized by extended uses of information and communications technologies (ICT) for an even wider range of activities. A later study by Rideout, Roberts, and Foehr (2005) found similar levels of use.

It has also been noted that over 2 million American children in the age range 8 to 16 years have created their own website (Grunwald, 2004), and there are similar trends in the United Kingdom (Gibson, 2005). The evolution and proliferation of social media such as MySpace, Facebook, and the growing use of blogs, wikis, and instant messaging enable young people to be in touch almost constantly with all their friends and families. They require us to reconceptualize skills of communication and identity formation that are so essential for effective learning in schools in light of the revolution that we have experienced in terms of being able to use and access such new technologies. These machines play different roles in the lives of many children for different purposes at different junctures in time and in a variety of communities of practice (Lave, Smith et al., 1988).

Yet there are still those children and families who are not able to participate in the so-called "digital revolution" for a variety of reasons that tend to be closely aligned to social and economic circumstances. Studies conducted regarding the links between social and digital engagement, especially with reference to Internet use, increasingly show that those individuals who have access to ICT generally come from families that have more schooling, higher incomes, and high-status occupations (Helsper, 2008). In discussing digital and social advantage, Helsper noted that "those who are most deprived socially are also least likely to have access to digital resources such as online services." (p. 9) Further, Helsper reported that when those from these demographic groups do participate in digital activity, it tends to be at the basic level and involve information seeking, obtaining leisure information, making purchases on line, and for individual communication with families and friends at a distance. In contrast, Helsper indicated that the advanced levels of activity characterized by social networking and civic engagement that allow participants to interact beyond their immediate networks, for example, are only conducted by 8 percent of the population. This then reinforces a gap since this qualitative difference in use enables those with more advanced technologies and applications to participate in activities that facilitate and extend their capabilities in cyber contexts, which are becoming increasingly important to be fluent in. In this way, simply providing access via machines is not enough. There needs to be opportunities for learning about the variety of uses beyond the basic applications that might address the important social inclusion issues that surround digital exclusion. This can often be problematic since new technologies are rapidly evolving and what constitutes digital inclusion changes accordingly. What was considered as advanced three years ago would now be generally considered as basic to the lives of many citizens. Studies have revealed that the main factors for digital inclusion are relevance, the nature of the experience, and empowerment (Helsper, 2008) This basically means that digital experiences have to be connected to the lives and needs of users and will only be perpetuated if they are positive and make life easier for them.

The Digital Divide

This is not a new phenomenon. During the initial stages of Internet use, there was a wide spread belief, or perhaps hope, that it would act as an equalizing force politically socially, and economically. It was noted (e.g., Anderson et al., 1995; Hauben and Hauben, 1997) that the Internet had the potential to disseminate knowledge and information to large audiences at a low cost. Based on these assumptions, it was further thought that the Internet would also bring about a revolution in democracy by providing people from all walks in life with political resources and information and a chance to openly debate all sorts of issues that related to politics and/or the government (e.g., Anderson et al., 1995).

However, this initial optimism was not sustained since it became apparent that the Internet was causing yet another divide within society; this is what came to be known as the "digital divide." The primary cause of this digital divide was initially identified as the unequal distribution of computers and Internet connections (NTIA 1998; Hoffman & Novak 1998). The groups that were on the privileged side of this divide were those who were already advantaged by higher levels of participation in education (Hoffman & Novak 1998; 1999) and economic wealth. In addition those who had access to and were using the Internet were using it in addition to traditional media and, in this way, the digital divide built upon an existing inequality within society, namely, between those who had access to traditional media and those who did not (Robinson, Levin and Hak, 1998). The introduction of the Internet could thus be said to have exacerbated and extended existing disparities caused by technology within society. This resonates with the notion that economic wealth and education are strong predictors of how quickly a person will adapt to and adopt new technologies.

Thus, the digital divide was traditionally described in relation to physical availability of the computer and access to the Internet. Scholars responded to this understanding of the computer and Internet and created a binary approach to this digital divide, which distinguished between those who had physical access to a network in their home and/ or work place and those who did not. "Access" was literally to refer to whether a person had the means to connect to the Internet if s/he wanted to (DiMaggio & Hargittai, 2002). Those who did have the means to use a computer and Internet were called the "haves" and those who did not were referred to as the "have nots." The common belief thus became that the ways to breach or eliminate the digital divide required that energy was needed toward provide machines for people (Yelland 2007, 11).

Digital Inclusion

The digital divide was then, initially, a useful and practical way of dealing with equity issues and access to the Internet. It highlighted a problem, namely, the inequality of computer and Internet use, in terms of the "haves" and the "have nots" and thus made access to new technology an issue. And this, in turn, prompted inquiries and discussions about equity and social justice (Yelland, 2007, 11). As DiMaggio et al. noted, the binary understanding was a natural and appropriate initial understanding of the divide (DiMaggio et al., 2001, 2).

As time progressed, it became clear that more people had access to the Internet than used it (NTIA, 1998), and thus we were urged to look beyond the statistics that documented numbers to address questions related to the nature and quality of this use; in other words, the issue became: how are people using the Internet? In this way, the focus changed from attempting to understand the inequality in provision to the nature of use whereby those from lower socioeconomic groups tended to use the machines for lower-order tasks rather than those that required higher-order thinking skills. As DiMaggio et al. stated:

> As the technology penetrates into every crevice of society, the pressing question will be *not* "who can find a network connection at home work, or in the library or community centre from which to log on?," but instead, "what are people doing, and what are they *able* to do, when they go on-line?"

Reconfiguration of the term "access" became the focus of literature that aimed to re-work the idea of the digital divide. It was conceived that the idea of "access" needed to be redefined in social as well as technological terms.

Warschauer (2004, 8) noted that technology "is woven in a complex manner into social systems and processes," and Yelland (2007, 11) echoes this view when she claims that a consideration of the various social contexts and applications of the computer and the Internet are essential and that by failing to address this issue reveals a lack of insight into how individuals make sense of their world and acquire the social and cultural capital relevant to participating effectively as citizens. Building on this idea, Castells (1996) claims that technologies are processes that affect our sense of the world, and according to this logic it would be illogical and ineffectual to try and separate an individual's use of technology from his or her perception of the world.

DiMaggio and Hargittai (2001, 17) highlight the role that society plays in affording all people access to the Internet by noting that the policies of public institutions shape patterns of inequality and effective Internet access and use. Everyone can potentially benefit from such policies and thus it becomes increasingly important for public institutions and agencies to consider the issues around access and use of new technologies. Further, as technologies become more pervasive in our lives we also need to provide mechanisms by which assistance can be provided, both formally and informally, so that individuals and groups may participate in online experiences (DiMaggio et al., 2001: 12). Formal assistance may include backing from public organizations such as the library or private organizations such as the workplace. Personal assistance is likely to be sought from family, friends, and colleagues.

There are several factors that can limit the autonomy of an individual's use of a computer and Internet. Warschauer (2004) contends that technologies are not neutral. There are numerous biases built into the Internet itself; specifically it is primarily based on the English language, and its design specifications may suit a certain type of person more than another (Yelland, 2007). The issue of regulation (filtering or monitoring information) also arises, as some workplaces or families choose to place restrictions on the type of information that can be retrieved (Yelland, 2007), and if a person is not able to gain the information he/she requires readily it is clear that his or her autonomy is being compromised.

Background to the Computer for Every Child Project

The first Computer for Every Child (CFEC) project was established in Israel in 1995. It aimed to provide computers for families who could not afford them, and it received funding from businesses and individuals who supported increasing equity opportunities in the community. One of the main goals of putting computers in homes was so that the families could support each other in their learning as well as create opportunities for e-learning in communities. In this way it provided contexts for children and families to participate in cyber worlds from which they were previously excluded.

The CFEC project in Australia started in 2006. It was believed that access to computer and Internet technologies at a young age has become a *critical* requirement for every child so they can fulfill their true learning potential. Being part of the information age with all the relevant equipment and information privileges particular people in society, and this was of concern in terms of equity and social justice. Aligned with this notion was the belief that developed economies, such as Australia's, are increasingly becoming knowledge-based economies in which information in all its forms plays a crucial role in economic processes, including growth and job creation. It is also evident that particular groups of people in Australian society are at high risk of poverty. These groups have limited or no access to computers or the Internet. Having no access creates a "digital divide" between children that have access and those that do not. This in turn places additional barriers to their ability to make their own choices about the direction of their lives. The aims of the computer for every child (CFEC) project is to target the digital divide in Australia. CFEC is providing eligible children with a computer for use in their home. The package includes software, Internet connection and access to a Help Desk. Basic computer training is also provided to the student and family members. It was hoped that providing the equipment and basic support would enable the participants to experience a range of technological opportunities and activities that would not otherwise be available to them.

Since we were interested in finding out if the presence of the machines might make a difference to the lives of those participating we sought information from them in the form of a survey, before and after they received the computers, and also created case studies of three families to provide richer insights into the lives of the families and their use of new technologies and participation in cyber worlds.

Children and Their Families

The CFEC project is based in primary schools in the Western Metropolitan region of Melbourne. Most of the families in the project had English as their second language. As previously stated the families did not have an existing Internet-connected computer but might have had a stand-alone machine that they mainly used for playing games and word processing. Thus, their opportunities for participating in online experiences was limited. If they had used the Internet, it was in a library or in the home of a friend or relative. The initial two training sessions provided participants with a basic introduction to the features of the machines and peripherals and then proceeded to show them how to use programs like Microsoft Word and the various Internet browsers. Many of the children had familiarity with these from their school use of computers and were in a position to assist their parents in their home language to use the applications.

Initial Data Sought from Participants

We sought information about the family's current use of new technologies, particularly computers, in their school, home, and community settings (S1). The same survey was given as a follow-up (S2), six months into the project to compare the effects of the provision of the computer and to capture what participants had experienced after their initial training period as well as what they used it for in their home.

The data showed that family members demonstrated a significant increase in the average frequency of their computer use on all items. Over 66 percent of family members indicated that they now used a computer with some degree of frequency. This is quite significant given the majority of participants did not previously use a computer with any sort of frequency. The computer was shared by at least three family members, and it was also noted that they did not report being unable to use the machine when they wanted or needed to.

New Technologies in the Home

When we first surveyed the 60 families they did not report substantial ownership of the various digital technologies available on the market. However, in the intervening six months, there was a significant change in the number of various technological items owned by the families. Many had purchased digital cameras, CD, or mp3 players and DVD players, which they used with the new machines. For example, apart from the new computer with Internet access, many had purchased printers/ scanners to use with it. At the six-month mark of the project, all families owned at least one or more computers, 17 families owned at least one printer, and 11 families owned at least one scanner.

Children's Participation in Cyberworld

In the first six months of the project the children played Internet games on the computer at home more frequently than before. The average use increased from less than once a month to about once a week (S1=1.36, S2=3.36, $p<.000$). The children also wrote on the computer at home more frequently over the two occasions. The average use increased from less than once a month to about once a week (S1=1.03, S2=2.84, $p<.000$). Additionally, the children drew or played with images on the computer at home more frequently as well. The average use increased from less than once a month to at least once a month (S1=.73, S2=1.92, $p<.005$). Other activities that increased were the children making or recording music, looking up information on the Internet, and using the computer/Internet "just for fun," that is, checking out different entertainment websites, reading the news and searching for information about hobbies.

Apart from an increase in participation in cyber activity via the Internet the children also used the computer at home for schoolwork more frequently over the six-month period. The average use increased from less than once a month to once a week (S1=1.26, S2=3, $p<.000$). The children were now able to use the Internet at home more frequently for finding out information for school projects and in some instances were able for the first time to enter their school's website. The average use increased from never, to at least once a month (S1=1.03, S2=2.84, $p<.000$). This translated into 76 percent of the students using the Internet once a week or more frequently to search for information that was related to school tasks. The percentage remained similarly high for Internet searches undertaken for their own interests, which suggests that for these students the Internet was a highly regarded resource for home use.

Summarizing Statements for Survey Data

In this way it was evident that family members were able to

- use a computer to access the Internet for school-work and leisure more easily;
- use the computer for activities such as downloading photos and music and playing games from CDs more often;
- negotiate the successful use of the computer between family members; and
- extend their frequency of use of computer-related activities to include a number of peripherals for both school and leisure-based activities.

These data gave us a useful broad picture of the ways in which the provision of the computer had enabled the children and their families to participate in cyber worlds. However, it did not reveal what specific types of things they were doing in more detail. We wanted to have a better picture of how the kids were participating online and to ask them if they thought this was what they wanted. So, we also conducted case studies of four families and two are presented to reveal the ways in which they were able to play in cyber worlds that were not previously available to them.

Case Study: Jelani

Jelani was an 11-year-old boy in Grade 5 at a metropolitan primary school. He is the oldest child of four, and he has three younger sisters. He and his family have been in Australia for two years after fleeing their homeland (Sudan) into Egypt and being successful in their migration application. The family speaks Dinka at home.

Jelani and the oldest of his sisters were born in Khartoum (Sudan). They left the Sudan and moved to Egypt when Jelani was 5 years old. Jelani had no schooling in Egypt and mainly stayed at home with his mother and father. Jelani was frequently unwell when he lived in Egypt. However, since medical facilities were limited the illness went unchecked, and he now has quite serious hearing and sight problems. Jelani cannot speak or understand Arabic and therefore could not communicate with the Arabic-speaking Egyptian children during their time in that country. The third child, a daughter, was born in Egypt. The family travelled to Australia after spending a period of three and a half years in Egypt. The youngest child was born in Australia. The family lived in their rental house for one month. The (CFEC) computer was located in the third bedroom where the father and the second youngest daughter sleep.

Jelani told us that he uses the computer at home about once or twice a week. He said that at school he plays games and writes on the computer with a word processor. On one visit, Jelani opened a picture file in paint and began editing it. The file had multicolored blocks arranged in stripes running vertically down the page. He used the eraser function to clear the page. Jelani also drew a window in the roof of the house, like the one he had seen on ABC Kids. While drawing this he sang a song about Louie drawing from ABC kids. Jelani also enjoys drawing the Sudanese flag and filling it in with the correct colors. He has many saved versions of the flag on his desktop (Figure 12.1). Thus, his computer activity provided a context for linking his life prior to Australia with what he was currently experiencing. It also constituted a medium in which he was able to represent his ideas about various things that were important to him.

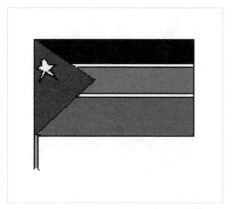

Figure 12.1: The Sudanese flag by Jelani

Figure 12.2: A house by Jelani

Jelani said he likes to play Solitaire and pinball on the computer. During one of the visits to his home (Figure 12.2), Jelani was playing Solitaire and writing his name into the dialogue box in the Hearts card game. However, he did not appear to know how to play and was just clicking at random on the cards. We showed Jelani how to put a card of the same suit from his hand as the one on the table and he followed the instructions well. When he finished a round of the game Jelani and his sister, Nailah read the scores and talked about how they might do better next time.

Jelani likes to type the words that he learnt on the *200 Words* program at school using the Microsoft Word program. He types words such as, "no, my, but, not, get, the, big, now, hello, about, air, house, computer."

When Jelani wanted to type a story, he started by typing: "On Monday I read my book." He also typed, "On Tuesday we went to Deng's house and we played soccer." Jelani knows how to use capital letters in their correct context. This became evident after he accidentally hit the Caps Lock key on a couple of occasions and corrected his mistake. He said he liked to type on the computer in preference to using a pen or pencil. This had also been noted with a number of other children, and it would seem that creating text on a computer with its easy correction facilities is very attractive to children who strive to create a final product that meets the approval of their teacher.

Jelani's sisters Nailah and Anana like to use the paint program to draw pictures. On one occasion Nailah drew a picture of a zoo (Figure 12.3) and Anana was copying Jelani's drawings of the Sudanese flag and a house (Figures 12.4 and 12.5).

Jelani started school in Australia in August 2004. He was placed in "Year Three" according to his chronological age. When he first arrived, he attended the Western English Language School organized via St. Albans Primary School. The Western English Language school offers an intensive language program, which focuses on English, socialization, and settlement. There are a small number of students in each of the language school classes. After 12 months, Jelani entered the mainstream primary school class. At the time of coming into the project, he had been in regular schooling for two years. Jelani's spoken English was not very strong and a lot of the time he has great difficulty expressing himself. His could read English slowly.

Jenny, the "Disability Officer" at the Primary school advised us that Jelani had "learning difficulties." He also has a hearing problem and very poor sight in one eye. The school was in the process of submitting an application for disability form on Jelani's behalf so that he could receive funding for extra assistance in school.

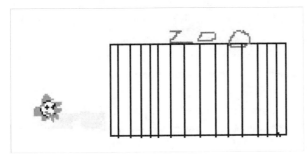

Figure 12.3: A zoo by Nailah

Jelani's class has access to four computers housed in a small room that is attached to their classroom. Peter, Jelani's teacher, noted that recently Jelani academic abilities have improved considerably. Jelani works with a small literacy group and Peter believes that this is helping Jelani's literacy. On a visit to his classroom, Jelani was observed reading a book called *Mother Sea Turtle* in a small group of three. Peter says that Jelani has not used the computer much this year as, as a class they have largely been concentrating on reading books but that he was planning to increase his time on creating text with computers as he had noted his enthusiasm for using computers and thought this would encourage him to express his ideas more clearly.

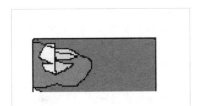

Figure 12.4: An example of Anana's drawing (a version of the Sudanese flag)

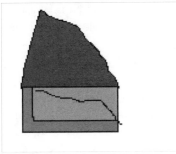

Figure 12.5: A house by Anana

Summary Statements about Jelani's Participation in Cyberworld

The presence of the computer in the home enabled Jelani to participate in activities that were not possible when the family did not have a computer. However, the activities were, as Helsper (2008) noted, at a basic level; we did not observe him engaged in online activities, but rather it seemed that having the computer had provided him with a means to represent his ideas and print them out to show others.

Heppell (1993) identified three learning stages that are apparent in students' use of ICT: a narrative stage characterized by observing and listening to things on the technology, an interactive stage where there are opportunities to explore (e.g., the Internet) and collate information and finally a participative stage in which the learner is able to create new media as a result of investigations. When we visited Jelani, we saw him exploring and building on his emerging English language skills, and he was creating new media by representing his flag, home, and experiences in other media in this modality. Jelani had a wide range of experiences that most young boys had not in his life, and in coming to Australia his family had stated that they wanted to participate in using new technologies. Teachers had noted an increased interest by Jelani, which while we cannot attribute to simply having the computer at home, he advised us that it was 'great' to have and he thought it was lots of 'fun.'

Case Study: Waseme

Waseme is a ten-year-old girl in Year 5 at another metropolitan primary school that is also part of the project. She lives in a house in an outer suburb of Melbourne, with her extended family. Her mother is the primary caregiver. Her father is deceased. She has one older brother, Aitan, and one younger sister, Arziki, both of whom live at home. Also residing in the house are an older male and female cousin (their parents are absent), along with Waseme's maternal aunt. The family primarily speaks Dinka at home, but Swahili and English are also used on occasion.

Waseme and her family have been in Australia for three years. The family was originally from the Sudan. Although the town in which they lived was peaceful, war was present in the neighboring towns. While in the Sudan the family lived in what Waseme described as a "hut," which had no electricity. The children said there were few houses around and grass was sparse. In these harsh, basic conditions, the family struggled to survive. The family settled in Ethiopia briefly before fleeing to Nairobi, in Kenya, via Sudan. In Nairobi, the family lived in a house in the city center.

The children had used a computer before they received their computer from the project. They had used their auntie's laptop occasionally and they also used the computers at school. The computer Waseme received as part of the CFEC project was located in Aitan and Dakari's (her brother and cousin's) bedroom. Waseme would like the computer to be located in her room but the boys insist on keeping it in their room. Waseme said that she enjoys using the computer and said, "When I get bored I go on the computer!"

At home, the children mainly use the following programmes: Kahootz, Microsoft Windows, iTunes, Windows Media Player, and Solitaire. The children have a collection of 80 songs predominantly by contemporary R&B bands. They also enjoy downloading video music clips. Waseme proudly shared a story written by her and her cousin, which included a special "bubble writing" heading and images that she had imported from clip art. The children do not use the Internet as much as they would like to because they had a dial-up connection and the telephone keeps interrupting the connection and distracting them. However, Dakari and Aitan do use email to send their teachers assignments. They also each have individual screen savers, which they downloaded from the Internet, and on one visit Aitan was looking up www.bling.com.au for ringtones on the Internet for his mobile phone.

Their mother gives her children money to buy games for the computer. Aitan bought Shrek for Arziki and a racing car game for himself with his money. On one visit the children were all helping Arziki play Shrek by telling her when to grab the letter of the alphabet specified by the game. Aitan told Arziki that she had done "Good work," when she got the correct letter.

Waseme said that she thinks the computer is helping her with her school work. Her class teacher also commented that Waseme is generally quite bright and is an average to above average student. She had some exposure to computers in English language school, but it was not up to the level of the other kids in mainstream classes.

Waseme's class teacher observed that her confidence has increased since she had a computer at home. Her literacy benchmark behaviors have increased and her fluency in spoken language and reading has improved. She has gone up 3 or 4 levels in Smart Words (a computer spelling game) and she now manages to keep up with the rest of the class. Waseme is comfortable with using the Maths 300 program, a curriculum program available on the Internet.

Waseme uses the computer for her extension projects which they research using the Internet. Her teacher noted that her projects are prepared using a word processor and that her use of formatting is appropriate. Waseme's teacher described her as being a good Internet researcher. On one visit to Waseme at school, she said that they were researching the question of; what pest animals do to the environment, and why people do not like them. They then had to summarise the information they had found and make a PowerPoint presentation. We watched as Waseme searched the Internet. She used the Google search engine and found the information she required. She was then able to put it into her own words and create the presentation as stipulated by the teacher.

Both her parents and teachers agreed that Waseme had gained confidence due to her increased proficiency with computer skills, and this increase in her self-esteem enabled her to extend her capacities in all areas of her school work. She shares the computer with her extended family members in a collaborative environment, and they play games that they have purchased for each other in a supportive way. As with Jelani it was evident that Waseme was still exploring the use of the computer and the Internet at an introductory level and would benefit from extended ideas for usage as well as a broadband Internet connection that was faster and would support more advanced uses.

Summary of Waseme's Activities with the Computer

Like Jelani, Waseme was using the computer at home in a basic way but her experiences with Kahootz enabled her to move into the participative stage that Heppell (1993) outlined, albeit in a semistructured environment. Her teacher had noted her increased levels of confidence in a range of areas, and this seemed to have impacted on her self-esteem and her ability to attempt and succeed in tasks at a higher level of attainment than previously. Having older family members meant that she had access to new ideas for using the computer online and she said that she enjoyed doing this.

Conclusions

Initially the CFEC project wanted to address issues of access to new technologies for those families who could not afford a computer. The survey and case studies of children and their families indicate that this aspect of the project has been achieved with more use of computers to access the Internet, for different purposes, related to both schoolwork and for leisure. Implicit in these statements is the notion that participation in cyber activity is not only valued in contemporary society but also desired by those, such as the families in this project, who did not previously have access to it. Our preliminary data illustrate that once access to computer use is provided the primary use of the computer seems to be for searching what is available on the Internet, playing games that have come with the computer (e.g., Solitaire) and using it for homework tasks that require the use of a word processor.

However, as time proceeds it is evident that we need to ask families what additional items and support that they might need in order to increase both the frequency and type of interactions they might experience in cyber worlds. The main barrier to more advanced uses was dial-up connections. However, more families are now being connected via a broadband. Indeed, the new digital divide seems to be connected to access via dial-up or broadband, with the former restricting possibilities considerably.

Our work with the families has illustrated that they have embraced the new media to represent their ideas and make meanings and representations with the resources available to them. In turn, this has given them increasing confidence to use computers in school more frequently. Teachers have reported an increase in self-esteem that has in turn provided them with additional avenues for expressing their ideas. Having a sense of belonging or connectedness is an important aspect of learning (e.g., Yelland, Cope, & Kalantzis, 2008), and our conversations with the children and their families have led us to believe that they now feel that they can appropriate the machines to conduct their school work as well as play games and listen to popular music with a new sense of confidence. On the practical side, the presence of the computers has decreased stress in the families who previously had to rely on trips to libraries and the houses of relatives and friends in order to complete some basic school tasks.

The teachers of the children have summarized four main areas in which they think the benefits of the project have been considerable:

- The increasing confidence displayed by the children not only in computer-based activities but in their general classroom participation and interactions
- Their broadened capacity to find relevant information from a variety of sources including electronic, which has enhanced their ability to acquire and use new knowledge
- A higher level of skills in using the computer and Internet to seek out information that would previously have been unavailable to them. The teachers noted that now they had computers and access, the students were able to follow up on topics or areas of interest easily whereas before they could not
- An increasingly wider range of opportunities for families to support each other with the new technology. Children would mentor their parents about possibilities, and they would discuss what they might do with the computer. In this way the teachers felt that the computer was central to shared experiences which were not available to them prior to its acquisition.

Wyn & Cuervo (2005) stated that identities have "become an important medium through which children and young people learn about themselves, their relationship to others in the world and through which meaning is constructed." (p. 3) Hughes and MacNaughton (2003) noted that "individuals actively and continuously construct and reconstruct their identity(ies) or sense(s) of self…(p. 127). In the twenty-first century, new technologies create contexts in which identities are explored and shaped in diverse ways. If children are excluded from them, they are missing vital experiences that are pervasive and ubiquitous in the lives of others. This is not to suggest that all such experiences are positive, but certainly they impact on identities and in turn this affects self-esteem and the potential for learning for students in our schools. In fact, it becomes essential to ensure that students are aware of the potential for major corporations to enter the technological spaces in order to promote consumption and capitalism. Critical literacy and interrogation of ideas support individuals to ask questions and analyze potential advantages and hindrances. It is clear from the work in CFEC that having a computer in their homes has enhanced the self-esteem and confidence of the students, but the extent to which this is dependent on the various types of activities that they are engaged with is not clear. What is apparent is that they still have a long way to go in terms of addressing the new digital divide since the activities that they are participating in are still at the basic level. It may be necessary to address this in schools so that both teachers and students are aware of the ways in which they might become co-constructors of knowledge.

References

Anderson, R. H., Bikson, T. K., Law, S. A. and Mitchell, B. M. (1995). *Universal Access to E-Mail—Feasibility and Social Implications*. Santa Monica, CA: Rand.

Castells, M, (1996) *Rise of the Network Society: The Information Age: Economy, Society And Culture.* New York: Blackwell.

DiMaggio, P., Hargittai, E.C., Celeste, C., and Shafer, S. (2001). From Unequal Access to Differentiated Use: A Literature Review and Agenda for Research on Digital Inequality. Available: http://www.eszter.com/research /pubs/dimaggio-etal-digitalinequality.pdf. (Accessed 10/01/07)

DiMaggio, P. & Hargittai, E. (August 2002). The new digital inequality: Social stratification among internet users. Paper presented at the American Sociological Association Annual Meeting. Chicago

Gibson, O. (2005). Young blog their way to publishing revolution. *The Guardian,* Friday, October 7, p. 9.

Grunwald, P. (2004). *Children and Their Families.* Bethesda, MD: Grunwals Association.

Hauben, M., and Hauben, R. (1997). *Netizens: On the History and Impact of Usenet and the Internet.* Washington, DC: IEEE Computer Society Press.

Helsper, E. J. (2008). Digital inclusion: An analysis of social disadvantage and the information society. Department for Communities and Local Government. www.communities.gov.uk/documents/.../pdf/digitalinclusionanaly-sis [Accessed August 18, 2009].

Heppell, S. (1993). Eyes on the horizon, feet on the ground? In C. Latchem , J. Williamson & L. Henderson-Lancett (Eds.), *Interactive Multimedia: Practice and Promise.* London: Kogan Page Ltd.

Hoffman, D. L. and Novak, T. P. (1998) *Bridging the Digital Divide: The Impact of Race on Computer Access and Internet Use.* Available: http://www2000.0gsm.vanderbilt.edu/Research/papers/Bridging%20the%20Digital%20Divide %20-%20The%20Impact%20of%20Race%20on%20Computer%20Access%20and%20 Internet%20Use%20%5BHoffman,%20Novak%20-%20Feb%201998%5D.pdf. (Accessed January 15, 2007).

Hornbeck, D. W. (1992). By all measures: The true road to equity. *Education week,* May.

Hughes, P. and MacNaughton, G. (2003) Building meaningful partnerships between staff and families, in Edward Caruso (ed.), *Enhancing Children's Development* (pp. 222–248), Victoria, Australia: Tertiary Press.

Lave, J., Smith, S., & Butler, M. (1988). Problem solving as everyday practice. In R. I. Charles & E.A. Silver (Eds.), *The Teaching and Assessing of Mathematical Problem Solving* (pp. 61–81). Reston, VA: National Council of Teachers of Mathematics.

Lean, O. (1948). Oliver Twist [Film]. United Kingdom: Pinewood Studios.

NTIA (1998) *Falling Through the Net II: New Data on the Digital Divide.* Washington, D.C.: U.S. Department of Commerce.

Rideout, V., Roberts, D.F., & Foehr, M.A. (2005) *Generation M: Media in the Lives of 8–18 Year Olds.* Kaiser Family Foundation: www.kff.org

Rideout, V. J., Vandewater, E. A., & Wartella, E. A. (2003). *Zero to Six: Electronic Media in the Lives of Infants, Toddlers, and Preschoolers.* Menlo Park, CA: Kaiser Family Foundation.

Robinson, J.P., S. Levin, & B. Hak (1998). Computer time. *American Demographics*: 18—23.

Warschauer, M. (2004). *Technology and Social Inclusion: Rethinking the Digital Divide.* Cambridge, MA: MIT Press.

Wyn, J., & Cuervo, H. (2005). *Young People, Well Being and Communication Technologies.* Report for the Victorian Health Promotion Foundation. Melbourne, Victoria.

Yelland, N. J. (2007) *Shift to the Future: Rethinking Learning with New Technologies in Education.* New York: Routledge.

Yelland, N., Cope, W. and Kalantzis, M. (2008) Learning by design: Creating pedagogical frameworks for knowledge building in the 21st century. *Asia Pacific Journal of Teacher Education.* Special Invited Issue. 36(3), 197–213.

CHAPTER THIRTEEN

Cinematic Representations of Childhood

Privileging the Adult Viewer

SANDRA CHANG-KREDL

Abstract

The author explores how childhood images in films position the adult spectator. The chapter's speculations reveal how child protagonists in films disturb the adult's comfortable position of protecting the child (Lury, 2005), by constructing for the adult viewer an "in-between" or liminal experience of "being-adult while also being-child" (Powrie, 2005, p. 350). This experience returns the adult to his or her remnants of childhood emotions. Illustrations of these instances are presented through film genres that typically depict children in significant roles.

My research has focused primarily on cultural formations targeting children. For example, I've analyzed how a cartoon series, such as *The Powerpuff Girls*, appropriates the discourse of girl empowerment in a way that repositions girls into conventional feminine roles as consumers (Chang-Kredl, 2007). I also examined the pretense narratives that five-year-olds generated while playing with media-based character toys (Chang-Kredl & Howe, in press). Recently, however, I read a special issue of *Screen* journal (Lury, 2005), in which the issue's authors explored how images of childhood are applied in films more typically viewed by adults. These articles jolted me into re-imagining my own connection with childhood culture and my own interest in studying media phenomena purportedly created for a category (children) living in a different (non-adult) time and space. As such, I will explore how childhood images in films position the adult spectator and then walk through a selection of movies, from war films to horror films, that exemplify ways that films make use of this powerful symbol of childhood.

Does Jacqueline Rose's (1998) tenet that "children's fiction is impossible" (p. 58) hold for images of childhood created *not* for the child, but for the adult? Rose's argument is that children's fiction hangs on the impossible connection between child and adult, where the adult comes first, as author and giver, and the child comes next, as reader and receiver, with neither entering the space in between. Nevertheless, fictional representations of childhood, in terms of popular literature or cinema, are *always* representations of adult's fantasies and interests—projections of their desires—whether the images are meant to either secure the actual child who is outside the image, or to regulate the 'childlike' characteristics in the adult's identity. And just as Rose warns us to be suspicious about the notion of children's fiction, there must also be something "impossible" about the creation of childhood images for adults. What is revealed about the adult's desire "in the very act of construing the child as the object of its speech" (Rose, 1998, p. 59)?

Positioning the Adult Viewer

Drawing on Jean-Francois Lyotard's interest in the discourse of childhood as a formation in process, Jonathan Bignell (2005) writes that "the concept of childhood is invoked as the determinant of adulthood, where childhood is projected retrospectively as an other epoch in which adulthood was already being prepared for but whose meaning can only be understood subsequently" (p. 382). The notion of childhood inhabits the same discursive space as Lyotard's concept of postmodernism—each is 'projected backwards' as the founding moment for a later state: a subsequent adulthood and a subsequent modernity. Perhaps it is through this retrospective space of the child (as symbol) that the adult filmmaker offers the adult spectator "different way[s] of seeing" (Powrie, 2005), ways that cannot be established through the viewing positions offered by adult or even teen lead characters.

Powrie (2005) borrows Foucault's concept of "heterospection" to suggest that the child protagonist in films constructs and offers "a combination of dislocation in time and space" (p. 350). Heterotopic space is not just a fusion of utopian and dystopian spaces. It is a different space, marked by defamiliarization—the child's perspective defamiliarizing the adult's world (p. 351). Applying Freud's concept of the uncanny, or the *unheimlich*, heterotopic space makes the familiar unfamiliar. The child's point of view allows the spectator to inhabit both here and there, now and then, recognizable and unrecognizable. As spectators, we look back to our own past and look forward to our present viewing.

Foucault (1967/1986) described an epoch of space, simultaneity, juxtaposition, 'near and far,' 'side-by-side,' 'a placeless place.' Powrie (2005) explains how the child protagonist increases the spectator's sense of being 'over there.' In other words, the space of films is more liable to be experienced as a heterotopic space where the spectator is asked to take the viewing position of the child, of the past. Heterospection is "being-adult while also being-child, inhabiting two different but complementary space-times" (p. 350). Children in films allow the adult spectator to *simultaneously* experience (and not just view) innocence *and* escape from the pain of innocence.

As Lury puts it, "[s]eeing is what children do; showing is what adults do for children" (2005, p. 309), and filmic representations of childhood can provoke emotive responses in adults in which they feel like children rather than protective adults. Lury uses the example of *The Sixth Sense* (dir: M. Night Shyamalan, 1999), in which the boy protagonist, Cole, *sees*, in a spontaneous, dangerous, and messy manner which he himself cannot understand. Seeing implies an unregulated gaze, a fascination, and a closeness between what is seen and what is felt. The function of the adult protagonist, child psychologist Malcolm Crowe, is to *show* Cole "how to cope with this gift of seeing" (p. 309). Showing is the directed and purposeful gaze which names, classifies and links cause to effect. The "trick of cinema" is to present 'showing' as 'seeing' and to recall the fears and pleasures of seeing (Lury). Lury describes the child's agency as "disruptive, impossible, unintelligible" when represented in film and in television, disturbing the adult's comfortable position of 'showing' (p. 308).

The concept of childhood 'reverie,' as a time and a place of idleness, daydreaming, and absorption also offers symbolic power to child protagonists (Bachelard, 1969). Through the concept of retrospection, feelings of innocence and nostalgia function together in films with child protagonists (Powrie, 2005, p. 348). Richard Coe (1984, p. 40) wrote that the Romantics were unable to distinguish between their actual child selves and the idealized, sentimentalized representations of childhood innocence. Nostalgia is experienced by the spectator of the child film, mixed with either self-pity ("I wish I could find that state of innocence again") or with pity ("thank God, my childhood was not like that") (Powrie, p. 343). Either way, there is a retrospection, or a look backwards, at childhood as pure and free, and in opposition to the constrained and materialist adult world.

The etymology of 'innocence' links the word to the concept of 'death': 'the one who is not guilty of harming' or of bringing about death (Powrie, 2005, p. 343). This feeds into the utopian notion that children are incapable of causing or inflicting harm. The viewers of child films are invited to relocate themselves into some past place, one meant to be desexualized and free from violence, an experience that Powrie describes as an "oddly fractured spectatorial position" (p. 345). Reality and fantasy are mixed in this 'in-between space' (p. 348), this threshold where adult viewers look backward in nostalgic identification with the child protagonist ("I was once that child"), but also look forward ("that child will be what I am now") (p. 348). The interruptions that are evoked by the child seen on the screen provide moments of connection between past selves and present selves.

Childhood Emotions

The "capacity to generate emotion in audience" is a crucial element in melodramatic films (Williams, 1988, p. 44). Images of childhood (or women or racial minorities) act as representations of weakness, vulnerability, and moral goodness in ways that are inexpressible through language. Melodrama begins and ends, or wants to end, in innocence and incites a moral feeling of righteousness achieved "through the sufferings of the innocent" (p. 62). The quest for "moral legitimacy" is critical, focusing on and recognizing the virtuous 'victim-heroes.'

Emma Wilson (2005) writes about how the emotions of children represented in films resemble and connect to their adult counterpart. Martha Nussbaum (2001) examined the cultural sources of emotions, and their foundations in childhood, in other words, how childhood emotions shape adult emotions. Adult emotions are densely involved with the remnants of childhood experiences of attachment, happiness, need, and anger. This accounts for the discomfort that representations of childhood emotions in films might provoke in the adult spectator. A temporarily 'dispossessed' adult may feel vulnerable while experiencing (on screen) the child's lack of control, and in the overwhelming experience, may involuntarily return to the childlike state of helplessness.

Wilson (2005) cites contemporary filmmakers who co-opt this sense of "involuntary emotion," or lack of mastery, in creating cinematic representations of childhood. She writes that in moving the adult through the "involuntary seizure of the emotions, in restoring momentarily an awareness of helplessness," filmic representations of childhood may serve to sensitize the spectator to the suffering or experience of childhood, and perhaps change the spectator's perception of childhood (p. 330).

Genres with Childhood Representations

How are societal beliefs about childhood reflected and constructed in films? Neil Sinyard's (1992) overview of genres of children's films, from mostly a Hollywood perspective, is useful in illustrating the types of films that have been produced with child protagonists. Neil Sinyard (1992) questioned who films about childhood are made for, what meaning film artists and producers derive from their reflections on childhood, and what the producers' attitudes towards childhood reflect and reveal about our society's condition. He suggested that many filmmakers, from Bergman to Spielberg, have focused their films on childhood because "the one thing the audience all [have] in common is that they had all been children."

Adapting Sinyard's account with other inquiries into children's films, I now consider some film genres that typically, and perhaps surprisingly, depict children in significant roles: adventure films, war films, 'human development' films, nostalgia films, horror films, and family films.

Fantasy and Adventure Films

Sinyard described the most popular children's genre as the adventure or fantasy film, the archetype being *The Wizard of Oz* (Dir: Victor Fleming, 1939). He wrote that many children's films are structured as a dream, in which a child (defined in juxtaposition to adulthood) escapes from his or her world into an adventurous other world, as Dorothy does in Oz. The escape may be temporal, as in Robert Zemeckis's *Back to the Future* (1985), where Marty McFly time travels into the past and into the future with the help of an eccentric scientist. Adult-child reversals are another cinematic means into escape fantasy. In Penny Marshall's *Big* (1985), 12-year-old Josh wishes to a fairground wish machine to be "big" and wakes up the next morning transformed into a 30-year-old. In *13 Going On 30* (dir: Gary Winick, 2004), Jenna wishes with magic wishing dust on her thirteenth birthday to be "thirty, flirty, and thriving," and wakes up as a successful 30-year-old magazine editor. An incompatible mother and daughter switch bodies in Disney's *Freaky Friday* (1976, remake 2003)

The dream or fantasy structure is an effective transition into an imaginary narrative, with little need to keep up a naturalistic drama. These films profess a superior imagination to the child, in his or her ability to fancifully travel in place or time. Often, these fantasy films reveal something about the child's real world: Dorothy in *The Wizard of Oz* realizes "there's no place like home"; Jenna in *13 Going On 30* realizes that true friendship is more important than popularity, and the mother and daughter in *Freaky Friday* realize that life in the other's place (child/adult) is not as easy as they thought. The implication is that these insights are brought about through the transformative power of childlike imagination. Penny Marshall drew on the myths of childhood innocence and adult-child juxtaposition to describe the narrative of her film, *Big*: "The story is how a child's innocence can touch people and make them realize certain things about themselves that, getting caught up in the rat race of life, they forget" (quoted in Sinyard, p. 21).

War Films

Children are the most convenient symbols of innocent victimhood in films. When a director wants to register an immediate and amplified emotional response from an adult viewer, a zoom in to an injured or frightened child in a wartime situation is straightforward and effective (an image that television news programs have also taken advantage of). One of the most famous wartime films focusing on a child's response to war is George Stevens's *The Diary of Anne Frank* (1959), a film version of the 13-year-old's personal account of her family's two years spent hiding in a cramped Amsterdam attic. Alan J. Pakula's *Sophie's Choice* (1982) provides the image of war breaking the human spirit with a climactic scene of a mother in Auschwitz being given the choice between the life of her son or her daughter.

Invoking the myth of innocence, Patricia Holland (2004) writes that "pictures of sorrowing children reinforce the defining characteristics of childhood—dependence and powerlessness" (p. 143). The children's displayed vulnerability on screen encourages adult viewers to want to protect them, giving rise to the satisfactory emotions of compassion and tenderness. Wilson (2005) argues that contemporary filmmakers both support and undermine the power dynamics existing between adult and child. She examines the types of identification with childhood that are possible, questioning whether the spectator can identify as the parent, the child, both, or somewhere in between.

Wartime films also offer a handy critique of the absurdity of adults. In Volker Schlöndorff's *The Tin Drum* (1980), Oskar, on his third birthday, and in response to the duplicity of the adults he sees around him during the eve of the Second World War, decides to will himself not to grow up and, over the next two decades of the story, stays frozen in time as a three-year-old.

Wartime representations of childhood can also collapse the distinction between adults' and children's lives—they are all 'just lives' (Kroll, 2002). In Roberto Benigni's *Life Is Beautiful* (1998), there is a merging and at times, reversal, of father and son, adult and child, in the characters of Guido and Giosue. Benigni, as filmmaker, complicates the division and connections between adulthood and childhood by creating both a child's fable (with Benigni's physical comedy and the parents being nicknamed Prince and Princess) and an adult's political tragedy (wartime).

Filmmakers take advantage of the way war incites adults to feel what children feel, and often depict the lesson that adults have something to learn (and must learn) from what children feel. The primary feeling during wartime is one of loss—loss of control, loss of mastery—a feeling familiar to children (Kroll, 2002). Pamela Kroll writes that "subjected to the wills and whims of more powerful authorities…the adult living in wartime does indeed 'quite naturally know' what the child feels" (p. 33). It is then left to the child to teach the adult how to cope in such a circumstance, through imagination, the ability to focus above all else on one's needs or desires, playful experimentation, open-heartedness, and the drive to figure out how to master situations. In *Life Is Beautiful,* the father's childlike and mischievous personality is what protects his son in a wartime internment camp. For example, the father translates the commander's rules of the camp to his son from: "1) Never attempt escape, 2) Obey all orders without asking questions, and 3) Any attempt at organized rioting is punished by hanging" into a game of: "You lose all your points 1) if you cry, 2) if you ask to see your mother, and 3) if you're hungry and you ask for a snack" (Kroll, p. 39). The prize of being given the birthday present of a real truck keeps Giosue, the young son, in the game.

'Human Development' Films

In human development films, the child's difficulties in learning to cope on the most basic level are often juxtaposed to the adult character's inability to function on a meaningful level. Alexander Mackendrick's *Mandy* (1952) and Arthur Penn's *The Miracle Worker* (1962) deal with childhood pain in the form of severe physical disability and misunderstanding. But Helen Keller's struggles to communicate ("wa-wa") and to let Teacher (Annie Sullivan) enter her world are comparable to her military father's obtuse shutting out of any view that threatens his own paternalistic one and to Teacher's struggles to come to terms with her own childhood suffering.

Children are often used in films to incite the adult to grow up. In the Czechoslovakian film *Kolya* (dir: Jan Sverák, 1996), a money-making scheme ends up with 50-year-old bachelor and lady's man, Franta, becoming stepfather to a five-year-old boy, Kolya. This unexpected responsibility leads Franta to discover a life of grown-up meaning, responsibility, and, in this film, satisfaction. Alejandro Agresti's *Valentín* (2002) follows the story of a nine-year-old boy, Valentin, who uses his child's sense to tackle his family's problems. Robert Benton's *Kramer vs Kramer* (1979) touches on the impact of divorce on a child but focuses on the parenting development of the father (Dustin Hoffman). The child's presence in these films forces the adults to differentiate themselves from childhood—to 'grow up.'

Francois Truffaut's *The Wild Child/L'enfant sauvage* (1969) follows a scientist's adoption of a child deprived of human contact. *L'enfant sauvage* may be interpreted as an allegory of Romantic ideals of childhood, with the wild boy the symbol of the natural, innocent child living on instinct and vitality and the scientist as the educative and social force integrating the child into society. Or the wild boy may be an example of Victorian education as the civilizing process linking ontology and phylogeny and ensuring the effective development of the animalistic child to the civilized adult (Walkerdine, 1986).

Nostalgia Films

Although there is only one childhood scene in Orson Welles's *Citizen Kane* (1941), it has been said that this is "the most important scene in one of the cinema's most important movies" (Sinyard, 1992, p. 135). The film begins with Kane's dying word 'rosebud,' and the rest of the film narrates the search for the significance of the word, a word which we find out represents the whole of Kane's childhood and the loss of his mother's love. As Andre Bazin wrote: "Kane admits before dying that there is no profit in gaining the whole world if one has lost one's childhood" (1978, p. 66). It is through the use of flashbacks that Charles Kane's childhood trauma is revealed. *Citizen Kane* plays on the notion that the roots of adulthood are contained in childhood, that we all carry traces of our childhoods and past selves, and that childhood is the 'investment in our future.'

Alan Wright (1996) describes the cinematic child's transformative effect on a film's narrative. Referring to the flashback sequences in *Citizen Kane* (1941), he describes flashbacks as vehicles to cinematically depict memory in a unified subject living across different spaces and times. Wright points to film directors, such as Bergman, Fellini, and Woody Allen, who devote considerable screen time to presentations of memories motivated by nostalgia.

In Jane Campion's *The Piano* (1993), the child acts as the mother's double—externalizing words when the mother cannot speak, and externalizing her mother's joy through dance. A number of scenes in the film present the mother and daughter in uncannily similar poses. Similarly, Charlie Chaplin's *The Kid* (1921) presents a number of doubling scenes between the tramp (Charlie Chaplin) and the five-year-old (Jackie Coogan). This eerie presentation of dualism, linking parent and child, emphasizes the mysterious connection between one's childhood and one's adulthood (and between parent and child).

Horror Films

As described, innocence is a theme that many writers of children's cinema base their analyses on, whether it be myth of innocence, violation of innocence, or loss of innocence. Films with children as the source of horror, seen in Jack Clayton's *The Innocents* (1961), William Friedkin's *The Exorcist* (1973), and Richard Donner's *The Omen* (1976), challenge and reverse the notion of childhood innocence, endorsing instead the idea of original sin. Sinyard (1992) questions for whom spectacles of evil and suffering children, or the fascination with the uncanny and sinister child, are made and what they reveal about adult society's views of childhood. In a more amplified way than in human development films, the evil children in horror films play a disruptive role in their parents' seemingly stable worlds.

Horror films may reflect the hostility that adults feel towards real children, perhaps because actual children are 'impossible': "They want more than they can have. And, at least to begin with, they are shameless about it" (Phillips, 1998, p. 119). Another explanation is that the child's perspective brings the adult viewer back to an intense feeling of terror. Charles Dickens once noted that a fair portion of childhood is lived in an apprehensive state of fear. This terror is amplified in, for example, David Lean's *Oliver Twist* (1948), in which Oliver is made to sleep in the bedroom where the coffins are kept.

Family Films

The family film aims for universal appeal, drawing on or reversing the assumedly shared ideology of childhood innocence and purity, and the universality of childhood—that all children are the same, the world over. Neil Sinyard (1992) wrote that Spielberg understood the Disney formula for the successful family film, namely, "the use of a broadly realistic setting into which one fantastic element or ingredient is introduced" (p. 32). In Spielberg's case, the ingredient might take the form of an extraterrestial named E.T. The significance of childlike fantasy is belabored in the head scientist's response to encountering E.T.: "I've been wishing for this since I was ten years old."

Finally, John Hughes' *Home Alone* films are examined by Joe Kincheloe (2004), who wrote about American society's ambivalent feelings toward children. He described these family films as comedic parallels to horror films that reflect adult hostility toward the child, by projecting evilness onto children. He wrote about postmodern childhood as comprised of a blend of child abandonment (latch-key kids) and parent-child alienation, where "children become 'adultified' (the child in *Home Alone* fending for himself against robbers) and adults become 'childified'" (2004, p. 244). Reflecting Zizek's (see Myers, 2003) description of postmodern "post-ideological" knowingness, *Home Alone* films confuse the roles of childhood and adulthood under the cloak of cynicism, or in 8-year-old *Home Alone* Kevin's words, "Families suck."

Conclusions

I've examined how images of childhood are applied in films in order to question my own interest in studying childhood culture. As educators, we regularly juggle between conceptual children and actual children. Perhaps, taking a moment to reflect on what the category of childhood (theoretical or actual) means to those of us living in the category of adulthood (theoretically or actually) may lead to surprising ways of thinking about why we do what we do.

What can this chapter's speculations on the privileging of the adult viewer reveal about the adult who constructs and views cinematic images of childhood? For one, the images disturb the adult comfortable position of "showing" (Lury, 2005), by evoking involuntary emotions of childhood, such as: lack of control, vulnerability, and overwhelming helplessness (Wilson, 2005). It may be that the adult is driven to return to his or her remnants of childhood emotions because, as Nussbaum (2001) suggests, the foundation of adult emotions is located in childhood. To continue the speculations more productively, perhaps these returns, these "in-between" or theshold experiences (Powrie, 2005), allow the adult to learn to distinguish between his or her child self in the past, idealized representations of childhood, and actual children in the adult's present life. The adult is then released from unconsciously replaying his or her childhood emotions and more able to "see" and learn from actual children.

Finally, this chapter addressed the Othering of the child, as represented by the adult filmmaker, as a form of dualism between adulthood and childhood. However, the issues of how race, class, and gender intersect with childhood require further examination. As revealed in the examples of childhood film genres in the chapter, childhood is often imagined and represented as European, middle-class, and skewed toward boyhood, perspectives and ommissions that further entrench the sense of racialized, classed, and gendered marginalization.

References

Agresti, A. (2002). *Valentin* (Film). Argentina: Miramax Films.

Bachelard, G. (1969). *The poetics of reverie: childhood, language and the cosmos.* Boston: MA: Beacon Press.

Bazin, A. (1958–1962/2005). *What is cinema?* (Selected by Hugh Gray, Trans.). Berkeley: University of California Press.

Benigni, R. (1997). *Life Is beautiful/La vita e bella* (Film). Italy/United States: Miramax Films.

Benton, R. (1979). *Kramer vs Kramer* (Film). United States: Columbia Pictures.

Bignell, J. (2005). Familiar aliens: *Teletubbies* and postmodern childhood. *Screen, 46* (3): 373–388.

Campion, J. (1993). *The piano* (Film). United States/Australia: Miramax.

Chang-Kredl, S. (2007). The construction of girl power in Cartoon Network, in Macedo, D. & Steinberg, S. (eds.) *Media literacy: A reader.* New York: Peter Lang.

Chang-Kredl, S., & Howe, N. (in press). Children's pretend play with media-based toys. *Play and Culture*, Vol. 10.

Chaplin, C. (1921). *The kid* [Film]. United States: First National; Warner Home Video.

Clayton, J. (1961). *The innocents* [Film]. United Kingdom: 20th Century Fox.

Coe, R. (1984). *When the grass was taller.* New Haven, CT: Yale University Press.

Donner, R. (1976). *The omen* [Film]. United Kingdom: 20th Century Fox.

Fleming, V. (1939). *The Wizard of Oz* [Film]. United States: Metro-Goldwyn-Mayer.

Foucault, M. (1967/1986). Of other spaces. *Diacritics, 16* (1): 22–27.

Friedkin, W. (1973). *The exorcist* [Film]. United States: Warner Bros.

Holland, Patricia (2004). *Picturing childhood: The myth of the child in popular imagery.* London: IB Tauris.

Howe, N. & Strauss, W. (2000). Millenials rising: The next great generation. New York: Vintage Books.

Jenkins, H. (Ed.) (1998). *The children's culture reader,* pp. 1–37. New York: New York University Press.

Kincheloe, J. L. (2004). *Home Alone* and bad to the bone: the advent of a postmodern childhood. In Steinberg, Shirley R. and Joe L. Kincheloe, eds. (2004).*Kinderculture: the corporate construction of childhood,* 2nd ed., (pp. 228–253). Boulder, Colorado: Westview Press.

Kroll, P. L. (2002). Games of disappearance and return: War and the child in Roberto Benigni's *Life Is Beautiful. Literature Film Quarterly* (pp. 29–45).

Lury, K. (2005). The child in film and television: introduction. *Screen, 46* (3): 307–314.

Mackendrick. A. (1952). *Mandy* [Film]. United Kingdom: Ealing Studios.

Marshall, P. (1988). *Big* [Film]. United States: 20th Century Fox.

Myers, T. (2003). *Slavoj Zizek.* NY: Routledge.

Nussbaum, M. C. (2001) *Upheavals of thought: The intelligence of the emotions.* Cambridge: Cambridge University Press.

Pakula, A. (1982). *Sophie's choice* [Film]. United States: Universal Pictures.

Penn, A. (1962). *The miracle worker.* United States: United Artists.

Phillips, A. (1998). *The beast in the nursery.* London: Faber & Faber.

Powrie, P. (2005). Unfamiliar places: 'heterospection' and recent French films on children. *Screen, 46* (3): 341–352.

Rose, J. S. (1998). The case of Peter Pan: the impossibility of children's fiction.   In Henry Jenkins, ed. *The children's culture reader*, pp. 58–66. New York: New York University Press.

Schlöndorff, V. (1979). *The tin drum* [Film]. Germany; United States: Artemis Productions.

Shyamalan, M. N. (1999). *The sixth sense* [Film]. United States: Buena Vista Pictures.

Sinyard, N. (1992). *Children in the movies.* New York: St. Martin's Press.

Stevens, G. (Director). (1959). *The diary of Anne Frank* [Film]. United States: Twentieth Century-Fox Film Corporation.

Sverak, Z. (1996). *Kolya* [Film]. Czech Republic: Space Films.

Truffaut, F. (1970). *The wild child* [Film]. France: United Artists.

Waters, M. (Director). (2003). *Freaky Friday* [Film]. United States: Buena Vista, Walt Disney Pictures.

Welles, O. (1941). *Citizen Kane* [Film]. United States: RKO Pictures.

Williams, Linda (1988). Melodrama Revisited. In N. Browne's (ed.) *Refiguring American film genres: History and Theory.* Berkeley: University of California Press.

Wilson, E. (2005). Children, emotion and viewing in contemporary European film. *Screen, 46* (3): 329–340.

Winick, G. (2004). *13 going on 30* [Film]. United States: Revolution Studios/Columbia Pictures.

Wright, A. (1996). A wrinkle in time: the child, memory and the mirror. *Wide Angle, 18* (1): 47–68.

Zemeckis, R. (Director). (1985). *Back to the future* [Film]. United States: Universal Pictures.

Section Three

Unquestioned Discourse and the Universalization of Childhoods

Diversity, Linguistics, and the Silencing of Social Justice in Education and Care

L OURDES D IAZ S OTO, S HARON H IXON AND C LARE H ITE

Abstract

This chapter begins by framing our concern for social justice and human rights in light of the global complexities affecting children and families. In spite of the Universal Declaration of Human Rights approved by the United Nations over 60 years ago, children and families throughout the world are living in oppressive and intolerable conditions. We examine the many ways marginalized peoples, particularly children in educational settings, have been denied equitable rights to education by forces that silence their voices. Such silencing is evidenced in girls, in children with learning differences, and in children whose cultural ways of knowing do not conform to the mainstream, among others. The chapter continues with an examination of the denial of linguistic human rights in post-colonial settings (e.g., India, Malaysia, Singapore, and Kenya) and among selected minority cultures and the negative consequences of language-in-education policies on not only marginalized peoples but also on the very countries imposing such policies. We conclude with a discussion of the need to prioritize our ethical responsibilities to address this concern.

Concern for Social Justice and Human Rights

For progressive early childhood educators willing to advocate on behalf of young children, these may appear to be daunting times. I am thinking about our early childhood colleagues across the globe from New Zealand, Australia, Norway, Sweden, United States, Canada, India, Africa, and many other countries who have toiled and struggled to support "minority" groups, women's and children's issues, human rights, poverty, linguistic human rights, antiviolence campaigns, peaceful nonviolent efforts, crimes against humanity, and even genocide. For most of us, the idea of social justice is not just prevention but prevention coupled with action. When Mahatma Gandhi asked us to become the change we wish to see happen, he was asking us to embody the very idea of equity, human rights, and social justice by our actions, by our behaviors in nonviolent ways. When Martin Luther King asked us to remember that it is only with the coupling of our minds and our hearts that true liberation will be reached, he was also asking for our thoughtful engagement on these matters.

But what happens when early childhood educators are faced with "totalitarian" environments, inhumane settings, rampant war devastating young children before our very eyes? What is our ethical responsibility when selected power brokers are intent on silencing the very voices that can shed light on these issues? Most of Lourdes's work has centered on issues of language and culture, but in a recent piece she focused on the proliferation of war (Soto, 2008) since that is the ultimate way to silence a group of people.

We are reminded that The *Universal Declaration of Human Rights* in United Nations (1948, www.un.org) long ago related some basic principles including but not limited to:

> recognition of the inherent dignity and of the equal and inalienable rights of all members of the human family is the foundation of freedom, justice and peace in the world human beings shall enjoy freedom of speech and belief and freedom from fear and want has been proclaimed as the highest aspiration of the common people.

In article 2 it states

> Everyone is entitled to all the rights and freedoms set forth in this Declaration, without distinction of any kind, such as race, colour, sex, language, religion, political or other opinion, national or social origin, property, birth or other status. Furthermore, no distinction shall be made on the basis of the political, jurisdictional or international status of the country or territory to which a person belongs, whether it be independent, trust, non-self-governing or under any other limitation of sovereignty.

It was not until 1959 that the United Nations ratified the UN Convention on the rights of the child stating in article 19

> Children have the right to be protected from being hurt and mistreated, physically or mentally. Governments should ensure that children are properly cared for and protect them from violence, abuse, and neglect by their parents, or anyone else who looks after them...any form of discipline involving violence is unacceptable...

Yet Pinheiro (2006) in a report to the United Nations General Assembly found that this is a global problem that has only recently been revealed (p. 8). Children and the adults who care for them are silenced by fear so that often incidents go unreported. The complexity of these issues includes many factors including personal characteristics, cultural, and physical contexts. Society's acceptance of violence, income, and education, and the fear of authority figures can play a large role in how children can gain access to safety and equity. There are groups of children that are especially vulnerable, for example, children with disabilities, ethnic minorities, children from marginalized groups, street children, refugee, and displaced children. Boys are at a greater risk for physical violence while girls face greater risks for sexual violence, neglect, and forced prostitution (Pinheiro).

Young children receiving early care and education are not necessarily immune from the spectacle of violence and abuse. Children enter the world as vulnerable entities needing our protection, love, and care. What happens when the adults are incapable or unwilling to provide what is in the child's best interest?

Our own field of early care and education and early childhood teacher education itself can re-examine its fixation on developmental models and dust-collecting research. How often do we find ourselves as transfixed mannequins talking, talking, talking while neglecting to prioritize our ethical responsibility for children's well-being? By focusing on social justice, our own scholarship can continue to lead the way in ameliorating the complexities children and families are facing in the global sphere.

Silencing

Silencing is a term that is often used by feminist and critical researchers and educators. Silencing has been defined or described in a variety of manners. Taylor, Gilligan, and Sullivan (1995) liken silencing to the act of "the slow slipping into a kind of invisible isolation" (p. 3). Fine (1991) suggests that "silencing signifies a terror of words, a fear of talk" (p. 32). Giroux (1988) believes that the "voices" (p. 174) of those deemed to be the "Others" (p 174) come "from the subordinate groups" (p. 174), and these "voices" (p. 174) are "marginaliz[ed]" and "exclude[ed]" (p. 174) in myriad ways.

Silencing in Education and Care

Who is silenced? Basically, anyone can be silenced by someone who holds more power than the silenced. The less powerful have been silenced throughout history and across cultures (Cammarota & Romero, 2006). Fine (1991) believes "silencing shapes low-income public schools more intimately than relatively privileged ones" (p. 34). Cammarota and Romero boldly claim that "school-sponsored silencing is exercised and experienced through the curriculum, teacher and student relationships, and racist discourse" (pp. 16–17). Struggling children or children with learning differences have been silenced (Hankins, 1999; Matthews & Kesner, 2000). Girls have been silenced (Dalley-Trim, 2006; Taylor et al., 1995), and boys from cultural backgrounds different from the mainstream culture have been silenced (Kendrick & McKay, 2002). Students from minority groups have been silenced (Benham & Heck, 1998; Cammarota & Romero, 2006; Fine, 1991). The writings of all students who stray from what an individual teacher considers to be normal or acceptable have the potential of being silenced (Kendrick & McKay, 2002; Schneider, 2001).

Silencing Children with Learning Differences

For the first-grade boy in the Matthews and Kesner (2000) study, silencing took place because of cooperative literacy activities with peers. Unlike many of the other examples of silencing discussed in this article, Matthews and Kesner suggest the silencing taking place in their study usually occurred because the other children were attempting to assist Sammy as he struggled with the tasks. The children offered to write for him or offered to help him sound out words and so forth. In other instances, the silencing was more deliberate as children ignored his suggestions and/or refused to listen to him read. Thus, in this situation, silencing of Sammy's voice can be attributed to his learning difficulties and the nature of the literacy activities.

Hankins (1999) suggests that labeling children such as Sammy in the Matthews and Kesner study as "at risk" (p. 64) can effectively silence them. Often times, Hankins argues, these children cease to have names as they become "Title kids, at-risk kids, [or] the low kids" (p. 64). She suggests these names "shape our opinions and expectations" (p. 64); thus, teachers have effectively marginalized and silenced the children even if this was not their intent. When Hankins suggests that labeling children can produce a silencing of their voices, these ideas coincide with Giroux's (1988) ideas that "difference is constructed through various representations and practices that name, legitimize, marginalize, and exclude the cultural capital and voices of subordinate groups in American society" (p. 174).

Silencing Girls

Within the last 20 years, some attention has been given to the silencing of girls (Dalley-Trim, 2006; Taylor et al., 1995). Girls might choose silence in schools as a method for assimilating into the target group (Taylor et al., 1995) or if they perceive their words as having no value (Taylor et al., 1995). They can be silenced by male classmates who call forth attention to their physical attributes (Dalley-Trim, 2006). Male classmates may also directly command them into silence (Dalley-Trim, 2006).

Taylor et al. (1995) suggest that girls might choose "to change their voices and give up their questions" (p. 3) if they hold the overriding belief that "the bounties of the world" (p. 3) are within their grasp, but in order to get them, they must first conform or at least attempt "to blend in or harmonize with" (p. 3) the majority. Taylor et al. (1995) also believe that the girls in their study did not give into this push toward conformity, but they were silenced because they perceived that others had no interest in what they had to say.

Another manner in which silencing of female voices can take place is through educational research itself. In other words, Taylor et al. (1995) believe that the participants' voices may be silenced during the interview or the analysis portions of the research if the researchers are not listening.

When boys are constructing their "hegemonic versions of masculinity" (Dalley-Trim, 2006, p. 29) by overtly calling attention to girls' physical appearance, they vociferously demonstrate their "masculine power" (Dalley-Trim, 2006, p. 29) and effectively silence girls at the same time. In instances like these, girls are now objects and not thinking beings. While Dalley-Trim (2006) studied ninth graders in North Queensland, boys do make sexual references at even younger ages. I once witnessed a fourth grade boy who had upset an entire female portion of the class because he called them *sexy*. The young girls in the class considered this to be a *bad word*. Boys can also construct "hegemonic versions of masculinity" (Dalley-Trim, 2006, p. 29) when they feel the need to demonstrate badness. The girls in the Dalley-Trim study were systematically silenced when the boys called them names or made fun of them. The boys even directly silenced the girls by telling them to "Shut up" (Dalley-Trim, 2006, p. 30). Upon occasion, the teacher intervened, but this did not always happen.

This silencing of girls takes upon another layer in complexity when one considers the idea that the behaviors required to construct "hegemonic versions of masculinity" (Dalley-Trim, 2006, p. 29) are often seen as "just boys being boys" (Dalley-Trim, 2006, p. 26). If teachers and other significant adults categorize the behaviors described as typical masculine behaviors, then Dalley-Trim suggests that this can lead to the further marginalization of girls. Indeed, Dalley-Trim believes that the educational policies of Australia have become one of "focus exclusively on boys" (p. 31) and not on "gender equity" (p. 31). Furthermore, Dalley-Trim correlates such a change in focus with the furthering of the stereotyping myth that "boys will be boys" (p. 26).

Silencing Ways of Knowing

Lopez and Hall (2007) suggest that children of Native American decent may come from cultures where the written word and the reading of literature were not the typical way of acquiring information. Instead, these children may come from a cultural background where watching one's elders demonstrate knowledge and skills over a long period of time was the way knowledge was passed from person to person and generation to generation. Thus, in the typical Western classroom where we want children to read for information or learn from a particular person teaching a subject or skill, we could be silencing that child's preferred or typically used method of knowing. Lopez and Hall suggest that this subjugation of creativity and other means of self-knowledge is even prevalent in tribal schools.

Benham and Heck (1998) suggest that the colonization of Hawai'i and the governmental policies that have occurred over the last several hundred years have fostered the marginalization of the native Hawaiians' culture and language. Thus, their voices have been too often silenced in the policy-making and the classroom. This silencing was especially true from the early 1880s through the 1960s. Benham and Heak (1998) refer to this as "the silence of the colonized mind" (p. xvi).

Benham and Heck (1998) argue that Hawaiian children may come to know information differently than their Anglo peers; for example, some Hawaiians may teach their children "the value of family privacy" (p. 193); thus, it may be difficult for a native Hawaiian child to share family events with classmates because he/she has been taught that this is not appropriate. Their voices are being silenced because they are being asked to share something that cannot be shared whereas they could be asked to share information that is encouraged by their cultural beliefs. All too often teachers will ask children to link what they are learning with their own experiences; this is even a reading standard in most elementary grades in the state of Georgia because it is believed that such connections will help children relate to the new knowledge. However, it becomes obvious from the Benham and Heck suggestion that we teachers may be harming students who come from cultures that believe that family business is not shared until one trusts the listener/reader.

In addition, Benham and Heck (1998) suggest that native Hawaiian children use "talk story" (p. 193) to learn. Children's use of casual conversations that include the "exchanging of pleasantries and information" (p. 193) can be silenced by teachers who follow a more traditional Western slant to education and learning. Like the Diné children mentioned previously, the Native Hawaiian children have had their ways of knowing severed from the learning process in which they must engage.

Hankins (1999) beautifully illustrates a classroom situation where she, a White teacher, effectively silenced her "Black" (p. 67) students. Hankins saw herself as a teacher who was working hard to overcome the one-dimensional view of schooling that can result from seeing schooling through White, middle-class eyes. However, one day, she was rather frustrated in the direction that her students took the conversation about a story they were reading. All she could see was that their talk had turned to fighting. Basically, Hankins failed to see that the children in her classroom were constructing meaning from the text based upon their living situations and their styles of interaction. After listening to the tape of the conversation, she said, "I was too busy reading the text I was creating instead of listening to the text they collaboratively wrote" (p. 69). Since this playing and replaying of the tape took place after the interaction, at the time of the incident, she saw their conversation as "poor behavior" (p. 69) and was unable to see it as a means of joint construction of meaning. She was unfamiliar with this learning style or interaction style and lost the opportunity to further engage their voices in what could have been a teachable moment. In the end, Hankins asks, "How many misses does it take to strike out, to fail a child?" (p. 71)

Silencing Topics

Discussions of race, religion, and sexual orientation are often silenced (Copenhaver-Johnson, Bowman, Johnson, 2007; Kendrick & McKay, 2002; Schneider, 2001; Taylor et al., 1995). Sometimes, this silencing is unintentional and may be due to the "dominant cultural taboo" (Taylor et al., 1995, p. 16). Copenhaver-Johnson, Bowman, and Johnson (2007) suggest that the "curiosity" (p. 235) children face as they are undertaking discussions to "work through new and existing understandings about race" (p. 235) are often quashed by "well-meaning parents, caregivers, and teachers" (p. 235). Furthermore, Copenhaver-Johnson et al. (2007) believe that this "silencing of discussions of race and power has been long integrated into classroom practice" (pp. 235–236).

Subjects that relate to violence may be silenced also. For example, Kendrick and McKay (2002) found that at least one boy in their study felt that he was not allowed to write or draw about the events (i.e., shooting animals) that were important to him and a part of his everyday life because he felt there was a teacher-imposed ban on writing about topics that were connected to violence. Thus, Dustin (a pseudonym for a fifth-grade boy in the study) was unable to voice through writings or drawings an important cultural aspect of his life. Furthermore, Kendrick and McKay suggest that his inability to write about his hunting experiences with key male family members (i.e., his father and grandfather) denied him full access to his writing identity and denied him the ability to "acknowledge how he positioned himself as a member of his family" (p. 53). In essence, his connection to his family, his identity, and his culture was effectively invalidated because he felt as if his teacher wanted him "to write about sunny days and stuff like that" (Dustin as cited in Kendrick & McKay, 2002, p. 52) instead of writing about topics that were relevant to his life experiences.

Canada, the United States, and New Zealand all show a recognizable gap between the boys' performance on literacy indicators as compared to the girls' scores (Ministry of Education, 2008; Service Canada, 2004). This begs the question: Is silencing of topics related to violence a possible contributor to the gap in literacy scores for boys as compared to girls?

Ironically, Dustin (Kendrick and McKay, 2002) is silenced because he cannot share a family experience that is important to him while the native Hawaiian children that Benham and Heck (1998) discuss are silenced because they are asked to share parts of their family life that are not meant to be shared in their cultural world.

Schneider (2001) provides valuable insight from the teachers' perspectives to show how this silencing of topics may occur. According to Schneider's interviews with teachers of a variety of grade levels from early elementary school to high school, teachers will develop a writing program and react to children's writing based upon a individual's teacher's ideas about what is moral and what is not moral, his/her fear of reprisals from parents, his/her lack of understanding of the legal issues that address the freedom of expression or the discussion of topics that may be considered controversial by others or self, his/her concern for the feelings of the child who was writing, or his/her sensitivity to the children in the classroom who may read or hear the writer's opinions or stories. For example, a teacher may not allow writing about homosexual parents because homosexuality is immoral according to an individual teacher's belief system. Another teacher may not allow such writing or sharing of the writing because he/she fears that parents who disagree with this lifestyle may complain to the administration. Whatever the reason for the teacher to deny the child the ability to write about what is for this child an important part of his/her life, the child's choice of topic has been effectively disallowed, and the child's true voice has been silenced.

Voluntarily Accepting Silencing

Sometimes, children may accept the silencing of the dominant group because it is what they think they need to do in order to get by (Fine, 1991). When Fine (1991) interviewed high school dropouts, they were able to provide insights into their early school experiences that shed light onto how they responded to the silencing of their voices. A few of her interviewees suggested that they did not participate in class when they were young because they were "good" (Eartha, as cited in Fine, 1991, p. 36) children. Fine discloses that they kept silent in order to avoid the perception that they were "rude" (Fine, 1991, p. 36) or had "poor discipline" (p. 36).

The idea that one must become silent in order to fit in exemplifies Freire's (1994) notion of "banking education" (p. 54). In this model of education, children "adapt" (p. 54) to the program that has been created by the oppressive educational authorities. In essence, adapting is expected. If Eartha in the Fine study (1991) wanted to be viewed as a "good" (Eartha, as cited in Fine, 1991, p. 36) student by the school community, then she had to allow herself to be one of the "receptacles" (Freire, 1994, p. 53) "waiting to be filled" (Freire, 1994, p. 53) with "true knowledge" (Freire, 1994, p. 57) by the all-knowing teacher. Her participation, and thus her voice, was neither wanted nor needed in the classroom. In fact, Freire (1994) suggests that educators (knowingly or unknowingly) need to silence the voice of these students if they want to maintain the status quo and minimize the chances that the students may transform the world as we know it. The "banking concept" (Freire, 1994, p. 53) of education is an attempt "to preserve a profitable situation" (p. 54) that exists for the oppressors.

Resistance to Silencing

Not everyone is willing to adapt and capitulate to the wishes of the oppressive educational system. Finding ways to make one's voice heard or refusing to be silenced can be seen as acts of resistance against this oppression perpetuated by the educational system. When Dustin, in the Kendrick and McKay (2002) study, draws a picture of the buck he shot with the help of his father on his grandfather's farm, he waged what Kendrick and McKay refer to as "small act of rebellion" (p. 51). Basically, he took the opportunity offered to him by the researchers to draw something for the researchers that his teacher would not see, to let his voice proclaim an important part of his cultural and family identity that had been denied him in many previous writing assignments. Thus, he resisted the oppressive practices of his teacher.

Native Hawaiian children, according to Benham and Heck (1998), may show their resistance by speaking Hawai'i Creole English; this demonstrates their "need to be accepted by the non-*haole*" (p. 193) and their unwillingness to capitulate to the *haole*, "foreigner, often white foreigner" (p. 238).

Paradoxically, resistance can also take the form of silence. Taylor et al. (1995) suggest that adolescents may decide not to share their true thoughts or feelings with particular people. In other words, the adolescent would silence her own voice if she felt she was speaking to someone who belonged to the privileged group.

Silencing in the World at Large

While the previously mentioned and insidious instances of silencing are detrimental to children's self-esteem, sense of self, cultural identity, connections to family, and so forth, violence against children or children who live in a violent world are perhaps the most drastically affected by silencing.

Ashworth (1999) suggests that there are innumerable atrocities perpetuated against female children each and every day across the world, yet the voices of these "girl children" (p. 264) have often not heard because the language of human rights discourse has so often excluded women and girls from consideration because human rights were considered to be "gender neutral" (p. 259) and few investigated if the human rights discussed were being experienced by the female portion of the population until feminist scholars and others called into question the notion of gender neutrality and lack of specific evidence tying women's rights to reported and discussed human rights. Ashworth argues that the atrocities against these young females include but are not limited to sexual abuse, forced marriages before they are even 12 years old, child prostitution, killing of female (babies, fetuses, and children), and lack of educational opportunities offered. Perhaps what makes this silencing the most disturbing is that the silencing of females, be they adult or child, in the discourse of human rights has meant that the "facts and acts of silencing [have] also become invisible: without a visible victim, there is no crime, and without a crime there is no perpetrator" (Ashworth, 1999, p. 261).

How will the voices of these young female children be heard? Ashworth (1999) documents several organizations/events (Vienna World Conference on Human Rights (1993), The Global Leadership Center, and CHANGE, to name a few) that have opened a different type of discourse that attempts to have these voices heard, and they have made recommendations for accomplishing these goals. Perhaps the most effective tool to combat atrocities against female children and female adults and to combat the silencing of these females is the call for "re-education of the male population" (Ashworth, 1999, p. 267). In other words, Ashworth sees the recommendation as a means to urge governments to do more than implement strategies that help to heal the wounds of the victimized; in order to do this, they have to change the behaviors of men through "re-education" (Ashworth, 1999, p. 267). In addition, the education of females was put forth as a necessity if we want females to "gain control over their own fertility" (Ashworth, 1999, p. 269).

Silencing, be it the silencing of minority voices or be it the silencing of topics that make one uncomfortable, maintains the status quo. If girls are quiet in the schools, then the boys get the lead, and they and the girls may develop the notion that boys are indeed superior. If teachers will not talk about race, sexual orientation, and other subjects that may make them uncomfortable, then homophobic and racist ideas are not altered or challenged in any manner. If White, middle class teachers continue to view their ways of knowing the world as the way to know the world, then other worldviews are not incorporated into the classroom environment, and whole groups of children are effectively silenced and shut out of the learning process. Silencing will continue to be an insidious problem in our schools as long as educators continue to perpetuate it or accept it.

Language and Cultural Domination

Throughout history and across the globe, examples of cultural and linguistic domination of one group by another have been commonplace. Those in power, seeking to expand both their wealth and dominance, asserted their language and cultural traditions over the powerless in order to subjugate them. Early explorers to the Americas, for example, both enslaved indigenous peoples and used Christian missionaries to remake the "heathens" to more closely fit the European ways. In more recent history, educational institutions were viewed as a primary method of promoting the language and cultural traditions and beliefs of the dominant group in spite of a common belief that much of the process of education is merely the objective and neutral development of content knowledge and skills. A close examination of most educational systems reveals that they are controlled by those who hold political power (Spring, 2004; Tyack, 1974). Those in power, frequently the wealthiest and most educated, make decisions about the contents of the curriculum, how much education is provided and to whom, in what language is it taught, the necessary qualifications of the teachers, and the manner in which education is carried out (Soto & Kharem, 2006). Examples of the political nature of education abound from failures in many countries to provide education for females to the same extent as for males, to decisions about who runs the schools, and who has access to higher levels of education.

The political ideology of the elite rulers also controls choices about languages used in instruction and how languages other than those of the elite are treated in schools. In looking specifically at the impact of language-in-education (LIE) policies implemented by many countries in response to the increasing globalization of the economy, we will describe the LIE policies in several postcolonial countries where English has been viewed as a necessary means to the educational, economic, and technological advancement of these countries. In sum, English is viewed by these postcolonial governments as a highly valued type of linguistic capital that can help to modernize countries and improve lives. In such countries as India, Singapore, and Malaysia, where English was previously imposed by the colonizers, it is now being imposed from within, a phenomenon Lin and Martin (2005) refer to as the "postcolonial puzzle."

In colonial India, the language and curriculum were selected by the British-controlled government. Students were taught European values and knowledge, although generally in their native languages, so as to ensure adequately prepared workers within the colonial system (Annamalai, 2005). English was taught as a subject but, in most schools, was not the medium of instruction. However, many colonial leaders promoted what became known as the Anglicist position, which supported the idea of educating a small elite population fully in English. Even today, more than 60 years after gaining independence, the elite of India, through the cultural capital gained from family histories of education, and fluency, in English, have access to power, wealth, and status denied those of marginalized Indians (Annamalai, 2005). In recent years, more children are being educated in English. Increasingly, though, India's children are experiencing the challenging task of being educated in three different languages: English, Hindi (the national language), and a local language.

In postcolonial Singapore, English and Mandarin Chinese are privileged over Hokkien, the historic language of the Singaporese. As a result of neglect and relegation to a lower status, Hokkien is now a dying dialect. What has arisen is a denigrated creole referred to as Singlish with elements of Mandarin, Hokkien, Tamil, and English. Those who speak only Singlish and not standard English are generally those who are poorly educated and, therefore, powerless (Rubdy, 2005). Since the 1980s, English has been the medium of instruction in Singapore's schools and most young children grow up bilingual or even multilingual (Gupta, 1994). But it is not uncommon in Singapore to find children educated in the privileged languages now unable to communicate with grandparents and parents whose first language is Hokkien. In an effort to encourage the use of standard English over Singlish, the government has enacted a "Speak Good English" movement (Ministry of Education, 2009). The ministry's position is that the use of Singlish will negatively impact students' success in learning Standard English, which the government considers essential to the country's economic success. Others have argued that Singlish is a valued language variety that, due to its unique combination of elements of the main heritage languages of the Singaporese, should not be sacrificed to the "hegemonic forces of globalization" (Rubdy, 2003).

Singapore's neighboring country, Malaysia, has also enacted new language-in-education policies. In 2003, the government of Malaysia, in an effort to modernize the country and improve its position in the global economy, decided to use English as the medium of instruction in all science and mathematics classes, starting in first grade, due to the fact that English is currently the global language of science and technology (Heng & Tan, 2006). The Malay peoples make up approximately half of the country and Bahasa Melayu is the national language. There are also three other substantial groups: ethnic Chinese, Indians (usually Tamil-speaking), and various indigenous peoples (e.g., Iban, Kelabit, Penan, Sa'Ben) who each have distinct home languages, most of which do not have a literate tradition. In the short time that this new policy has been in effect, it appears that, for many children, educational levels may be negatively impacted. In an examination of teachers teaching in both English and Bahasa Melayu as a result of the government's 2003 language of instruction decision, researchers observed that teachers may be teaching science and math in English yet have extremely limited English capabilities themselves. Since they are discouraged from teaching bilingually in order to clarify and explain the content in the students' dominant language, the students may wind up learning very little of the content. The weak instruction in school is exacerbated by unequal access to English out of school among the poorer and rural people in Malaysia, resulting in the undereducation of these children because they are learning very little in English-medium classrooms. This is particularly true for those students whose first language is not Malay, the primary medium of instruction in subjects other than math and science, who at an early age are forced to simultaneously add on two new languages to their home language.

In Kenya, for the earliest grades (standards 1–3), the medium of instruction is either the indigenous languages (if dominant in the community) or Kiswahili, the national language, or English. If it is in Kiswahili, then English is introduced in standard 4. The children of the urban poor have little access to English outside school, and most major examinations are in English or Kiswahili, so teachers feel compelled to use English in instruction most often (Bunyi, 2005). Bunyi described her findings from a year-long qualitative investigation in two classrooms, standards 1 and 4, in a school in a rural community bordering Nairobi, Kenya's capital. With a dearth of first language materials, children had little access to their L1—Gicagi. The children learned very little and most standard 1 students could read little at the end of the year. Even many standard 4 students did not show evidence of literacy. Bunyi points out that the language practices could be a contributing factor in the high (44%) dropout rate before the end of primary (standard 8) and for the poor test results in English at the end of Standard 6. She goes on to theorize that the poor quality of instruction is partly due to the teachers' limited abilities in English and to a dependence on interaction patterns that are leftover from the colonial missionaries who emphasized rote memorization of religious texts. In other words, the students have little chance to use the new language in authentic ways.

A situation similar to that of Kenya's is seen in South Africa where English and Afrikaans are the main languages of instruction, especially after standard 3. For those students who have an L1 other than Afrikaans, achievement has been weak. For example, they underperform their native Afrikaans-speaking peers on the international TIMMs test (Brock-Utne, 2005). Likewise in Tanzania, English is the medium of instruction in schools, and the results have often been that students sit through classes learning little if anything (Brock-Utne, 2005). The "postcolonial puzzle" found in those countries in which English was formerly forced upon them but who have recently adopted it by their own volition may have unanticipated effects. The move toward incorporating English as a medium of instruction in an attempt to increase global competitiveness may have had the unexpected consequence of lowered educational levels, which will likely weaken, not strengthen, their competitiveness.

Even in countries where English has been the dominant language for more than a century, evidence of linguistic and cultural domination is seen in the political ideology upon which schooling is based. In its earlier days, the United States was actually quite tolerant of languages other than English.

Such tolerance can be found, for example, in the history of the medium of instruction. In publicly funded German schools in the Mid-west, students were taught all subjects in German (Toth, 1990). Likewise, in the parishes of Louisiana, the medium of instruction was frequently French (St-Hilaire, 2004). With the Native Americans, on the other hand, concerns about how to assimilate them and weaken their resistance contributed, in the mid-to-late nineteenth century, to a growing intolerance for linguistic and cultural difference. In a deliberate effort to eradicate the culture and language of many of the indigenous peoples, the government removed the children from their families and placed them in boarding schools where they were dressed as Whites and beaten for using their indigenous languages (Spring, 2007). With anti-immigrant sentiments increasing toward the end of the nineteenth century, linguistic freedoms enjoyed by many groups were reduced. Teaching in German and even teaching German was declared illegal (Toth, 1990). In 1921, the Louisiana constitution was revised to restrict the use of languages other than English in schools, and children were subsequently punished for using their French language (St-Hilaire, 2005). A similar situation is seen in the policies toward the use of Spanish in the United States. After annexing almost half of Mexico at the end of the Mexican-American War, and in spite of agreements otherwise about how language freedoms would be recognized, the United States made efforts to restrict the use of Spanish in commerce and education (Spring, 2007). Today, though less overt, Spanish is still restricted in many states and school districts. More recently, the entire "English Only" movement reveals the continued determination to restrict the use of all languages other than English (Macedo, 1997).

Language Loss

The language policies described herein have impacts on both the language itself and on those who speak, or whose families speak, those languages. Language policies, which privilege one language over another, often result in virtual death, or linguicide, of the least-favored language. Results of such efforts to force minority peoples to abandon their birth languages, or at least restrict their use both oral and written, can be found in the literature on language loss and attrition. Earlier, we noted the decline in Hokkien in Singapore. Another country in which the privileging of English has led to a diminution of the earlier national language is in Ireland. In spite of the nationalist spirit, which arose in Ireland after it gained independence, the Irish language is losing ground. In exploring the historic role of the Irish language, O Croidheáin (2006) looked for reasons to explain its decline relative to English and concluded that it is largely due to globalization and the political and economic needs of the Irish power elite.

In the United States, the loss of heritage languages by immigrants and their children, while having always occurred, appears to be doing so at an increasing rate (Wong-Fillmore, 2000). A look at such loss among speakers of Spanish, the largest linguistic minority in the United States, is very revealing. According to the Pew Hispanic Center, 95 percent of first-generation Latino immigrants report speaking Spanish very well. For second-generation Latinos/as, a marked loss is seen with 56 percent reporting they speak their home language very well. By the third generation, the effects of lack of support for native language instruction in schools reduce this percentage further to 29 percent. As would be expected from the absence of the home language in instruction, ability to speak English very well proceeds inversely to the decline of ability in Spanish. Of first-generation Hispanic immigrants, 23 percent report that they speak English very well. These figures increase to 88 percent, and 94 percent for second- and third-generation Latinos/as, respectively. This loss of the heritage language, as will be explained further on, has had negative impacts on the academic achievement of these children.

Another example of the negative impact of political decisions on heritage languages is found in the language of the Haida, an indigenous people who inhabit islands off the northwest coast of British Columbia where they have existed for over 10,000 years (White, 2006). The Haida, through increased interaction with the dominant English speakers and decisions by the government to send the children to residential schools, have seen the numbers of fluent speakers dwindle. Of the 5000 living Haida, only approximately 20 percent have some knowledge of the language and few of those are actually fluent (White, 2006). Similar tragic stories hold for many of the indigenous peoples of North America. This loss of language is directly tied to loss of culture and cultural identity.

Also in Canada, similar language loss has been found in the children of immigrants. In a qualitative study of parents' and early childhood educators, beliefs about the language development of the young children in immigrant families representing 14 different languages, Pacini-Ketchabaw and de Almeida (2006) found language loss common. Sadly, both the parents and educators who participated in the study considered English, not their heritage languages, to be the "natural and legitimate language of young people" (p. 313).

Wong-Fillmore (1991, 2000) writes of language loss and the terrible consequences of such loss to families. Not allowing children to both develop and use their home languages (L1s) results not only in the possibility of reduced literacy in English and lower academic achievement but also serves to separate children from their cultural traditions and from their parents' ability to pass on those values and traditions. Children may grow up unable to communicate with their extended families or, over time, as they increasingly resort to English and it becomes their dominant language, may even lose the ability to communicate in their home language even with their own parents. Clearly, a subtractive form of bilingualism is occurring as these families have, over time, lost a large part of their cultural identification as they lose the ability to communicate in their heritage languages.

Not only does language loss negatively impact those from minority language groups, but it also harms those countries by reducing the academic achievement, and thus productivity, of those for whom English is not the first language. This can be seen in studies on the impact on early childhood of first language loss. Researchers have clearly established that students who have well-developed first languages (L1) reach higher levels of achievement in academics and in the target language (the one being learned) than do students whose L1s are not well developed (Collier, 1992; Cummins, 1981). Students with well-developed L1s also have more success in learning English literacy and mathematics (Hakuta, 1986; Ramirez, 1992). Without a good foundation in the L1, students will become increasingly unsuccessful academically as they encounter more complex academic language (Cummins, 1981). Why then, we might ask, given the consequences of failure to support the continued development of home languages, would educational institutions across the globe choose not to do so? The answer to this is complex and multilayered, but a large part is attributable to political ideology and beliefs about what is most beneficial to a country rather than to the individual members. Ironically, though, those in power have apparently not understood that language-in-education policies do not have to be "win/lose." Rather, both the country and the linguistic minorities benefit when the heritage languages are valued and maintained in education.

For families that are part of the controlling elite, this politicization works in favor of their aspirations. For minority families, on the other hand, it marginalizes and generally prevents the children of such families from profiting. There are differences in how mainstream families and marginalized, minority families understand the political nature of schooling and their ability to use this understanding to their children's benefit. Middle class families possess the cultural capital to advocate for their children and interact productively with school personnel. They are comfortable challenging school practices and personnel. For example, they may readily complain about a teacher or question the choice of a novel assigned to the student. Likewise, they involve themselves in the schools, identify the "best teachers," and politic to be sure that their children have those teachers and are in the classes that will lead to higher levels of academic achievement (Baker & Stevenson, 1986). Further, they are able to "buy into" the best available schools by locating their homes in neighborhoods where schools are well resourced (Kozol, 2005).

Understandably, families that lack the cultural capital that comes with complete familiarity with the educational system may assume that all students have the same opportunities in education and may not realize the need to advocate for their children or, understanding the need, may not have the tools for doing so. African American, working class, and low-income families often believe that the school is the authority and that their own roles are limited. They also believe that less contact with schools is best and that their children are satisfactory sources of information about school events and news. So, they are not able to improve their children's chances of success (Lareau & Shumar, 1996).

Addressing Our Concerns

Our major concern centers on issues of power as well as how might we implement projects to alleviate the pervasive culture of silencing. Our own field has for decades now relied on education and practices that have not necessarily ameliorated the very daily lived realities of those we have most loved, our children. In spite of good intentions and difficult advocacy campaigns we are still seeing the heavy blanket of injustice for too many of the world's children. Patti Lather's vision (1991, 1993) and Lather and Smithies (1997) project where concerns for oppression, exploitation, and domination are an integral part of the research process can serve to guide our scholarship and research. Lather embraces the idea that social and educational inquiry can have ameliorative intention so that as inquirers we can contribute to improving people's existing and future lives. bell hooks notes

> The moment we choose to love,
> we begin to move against domination,
> against oppression.
> The moment we choose to love,
> we begin to move toward the freedom
> to act in ways that liberate others and ourselves.
> That action is the testimony of love as the practice of freedom.

With this work there is a need to pursue newly evolving qualitative and experimental paradigms that emphasize decolonizing models as well research capable of ameliorating oppressive dehumanizing conditions. As early childhood scholars we can continue to lead the way by allowing our scholarship to improve the lives of children, pursue issues of social justice and equity, human rights, children's rights, and families' well-being. Our projects are truly "projects from the heart" capable of reflecting our love for humanity.

References

Annamalai, E. (2005). Nation-building in a globalised world: Language choice and education in India. In *Language-in-education, policy and practice* (pp. 20–37). Buffalo, NY: Multilingual Matters.

Aronowitz, S. & Giroux, H. (1985). *Education under siege: The conservative, liberal, and radical debate over schooling.* South Hadley, MA: Bergin & Garvey.

Ashworth, G. (1999). The silencing of women. In Dunne & Wheeler (Eds), *Human rights in global politics* (pp. 259–276). Cambridge, UK: Cambridge University Press.

Baker, D.P. & Stevenson, D.L. (1986). Mothers' strategies for children's school achievement: Managing the transition to high school. *Sociology of Education, 59,* 156–166.

Benham, M.K. & Heck, R.H. (1998). *Culture and educational policy in Hawai'i: The silencing of native voices.* Mahwah, NJ: Lawrence Erlbaum.

Borman, K.M. (1998). *Ethnic diversity in communities and schools.* Stamford, CT: Ablex Publishing Corporation.

Brock-Utne, B. (2005). Language-in-education policies and practices in Africa with a special focus on Tanzania and South Africa. In A.M.Y. Lin & P. Martin (Eds.), *Decolonisation, globalisation: Language-in-education, policy and practice* (pp. 20–37). Buffalo, NY: Multilingual Matters.

Bunyi, G.W. (2005). Language classroom practices in Kenya. In A.M.Y. Lin & P. Martin (Eds.), *Decolonisation, globalisation: Language-in-education, policy and practice* (pp. 131–152). Buffalo, NY: Multilingual Matters.

Cammarota, J. & Romero, A. (2006). A critically compassionate intellectualism for Latina/o students: Raising voices above the silencing of our schools. *Multicultural Education, 14 (2),* 16–23.

Collier, V.P. (1992). A synthesis of studies examining long-term language minority student data on academic achievement. *Bilingual Research Journal, 16,* 187–212.

Copenhaver-Johnson, J.F., Bowman, J.T., & Johnson, A.C. (2007). Santa-stories: Children's inquiry about race during picture-book read-alouds. *Language Arts, 84(3),* 234–244.

Cummins, J. (1981). The role of primary language development in promoting educational success for language minority students. In *Schooling & language minority students: A theoretical framework.* Los Angeles: Evaluation, Dissemination, & Assessment Center, California State University.

Dalley-Trim, L. (2006). "Just boys being boys"? *Youth Studies Australia, 25(3),* 26–33.

Fine, M. (1991). *Framing dropouts: Notes on the politics of an urban pubic high school.* Albany, NY: State University of New York Press.

Foucault, M. (1980). *Power/knowledge.* New York: Pantheon.

Freire, P. (1994). *Pedagogy of the oppressed.* New York: Continuum.

Garcia, E.E. (2005). *Teaching and learning in two languages: Bilingualism and schooling in the United States.* New York: Teachers College Press.

Giroux, H.A. (1988). Border pedagogy in the age of postmodernism. *Journal of Education, 170* (3), 162–181.

Gupta, A. F. (1994). *The step-tongue: Children's English in Singapore.* Clevedon: Multilingual Matters.

Hakuta, K. (1986). *Mirror of language: The debate on bilingualism.* New York: Basic Books.

Hankins, K. (1999). Silencing the lambs. In J. Allen (Ed), *Class actions: Teaching for social justice in elementary and middle school* (pp. 61–71). New York: Teachers College Press.

Heng, C. & Tan, H. (2006). English for mathematics and science: Current Malaysian language-in-education policies and practice. *Language and Education, 20* (4), 306–321

Kendrick, M. & McKay, R. (2002). Uncovering literacy narratives through children's drawings. *Canadian Journal of Education, 27(1),* 45–60.

Kozol, J. (1991). *Savage inequalities.* New York: Crown Publishers.

Kozol, J. (2005). *The shame of the nation: The restoration of apartheid schooling in America.* New York: Crown Publishers.

Lareau, A. & Shumar, W. (1996). The problems of individualism in family-school policies. *Sociology of Education,* Extra issue, 24–39.

Lather, P. (1991). *Getting smart: Feminist research and pedagogy within the postmodern.* New York: Routledge

Lather, P. (1993). Fertile obsession: Validity after poststructuralism. *Sociological Quarterly,* 35, 673–694.

Lather, P. & Smithies, C. (1997). *Troubling the angels: Women living with HIV/AIDS.* Boulder, CO: Westview Press.

Lin, A.M.Y. & Martin, P. (2005). From a critical deconstruction paradigm to a critical construction paradigm: An introduction to decolonization, globalization, and language-in-education policy. In A.M.Y. Lin & P. Martin (Eds.), *Decolonisation, globalisation: Language-in-education, policy and practice* (pp. 1–19). Buffalo, NY: Multilingual Matters.

Lopez, A. & Hall, M. (2007). Letting in the sun: Native youth transform their school with murals. *Reclaiming Children and Youth, 16 (3),* 29–35.

Macedo, D. (1997). English only: The tongue-tying of America. In A. Darder, R. D. Torres, and H. Gutierrez (Eds.), *Latinos in education: A critical reader.* New York: Routledge.

Matthews, M.W. & Kesner, J.E. (2000). The silencing of Sammy: One struggling reader learning with his peers. *The Reading Teacher, 53(5),* 382–390.

Ministry of Education: Education Counts (2008). *Reading literacy achievement primary schooling.* Retrieved March 31, 2009, from http://www.educationcounts.govt.nz/indicators/indicator_page/literacy/74 8.

Ministry of Education, Singapore. http://www.moe.gov.sg/media/forum/2008/12/good-English-the-way-to-go.php. Retrieved February, 19, 2009.

NCES (1992). NELS 88: Second Follow-Up Parent Data. Washington, DC: Department of Education.

O'Croidheáin, C. (2006). *Language from below—The Irish language, ideology and power in the 20th-century Ireland.* Oxford: Peter Lang.

Pacini-Ketchabaw, V. & Armstrong de Almeida, A-E. (2006). Language discourses and ideologies at the heart of early childhood education. *The International Journal of Bilingual Education and Bilingualism, 9 (3),* 310–341.

Pew Hispanic Center. English usage among Hispanics in the United States. Retrieved January 26, 2009 from http://pewresearch.org/pubs/644/english-language-usage-hispanics.

Pinheiro, P.S. (2006). *Study on violence against children.* Report to the U.N. General Assembly. Sixty-first session item 62a: Promotion and protection of the rights of the child.

Ramirez, J. (1992). Executive summary. *Bilingual Research Journal, 16,* 1–62.

Rubdy, R. (2003). Creative destruction: Singapore's Speak Good English movement. *World Englishes, 20(3),* 341–355.

Rubdy, R. (2005). Remaking Singapore for the new age: Official ideology and the realities of practice in language-in-education. In A.M.Y. Lin & P. Martin (Eds.), *Decolonisation, globalisation: Language-in-education, policy and practice* (pp. 55–73). Buffalo, NY: Multilingual Matters.

Schneider, J.J. (2001). No blood, guns, or gays allowed! The silencing of the elementary writer. *Language Arts, 78(5),* 415–425.

Service Canada (2004). *Reading achievement in Canada and the United States: Findings from the OCED Progamme for International Student Assessment—May 2004.* Retrieved March 31, 2009 from http://www1.servicecanada.gc.ca/eng/cs/sp/lp/publications/2004-002611/page09.shtml.

Soto, L.D. & Kharem, H. (2006). A post-monolingual education (United States). *International Journal of Educational Policy,* Research and Practice: Reconceptualizing Childhood Studies, 7, pp. 21-34.

Soto, LD. (2008). Hearts of compassion: The concern for violence against children. *Contemporary Issues in Early Childhood, 3(9),* 234–240.

Spring, J. (2007). *Deculturalization and the struggle for equality: A brief history of the education of dominated cultures in the United States.* (5th ed.). Boston, MA: McGraw-Hill.

Spring, J. (2004). *Conflict of interest: The politics of American education.* Boston, MA: McGraw Hill.

St-Hilaire, A. (2005). Louisiana French immersion education: Cultural identity and grassroots community development. *Journal of Multilingual and Multicultural Development, 26(2),* 158–172.

Taylor, J.M., Gilligan, C., & Sullivan, A.M. (1995). *Between voice and silence: Women and girls, race and relationship.* Cambridge, MA: Harvard University Press.

Toth, C. (1990). *German-English bilingual schools in America: The Cincinnati tradition in historical context.* New German-American Studies, Vol. 2 (pp. 81–92). New York: Peter Lang.

Tyack, D. (1974). *The one best system: A history of American urban education.* Cambridge, MA: Harvard University Press.

White, F. (2006). Haida language research digitization project. In M. Kiyota, J. J. Thompson, & N. Yamane-Tanaka (Eds.), Papers for the International Conference on Salishan and Neighbouring Languages XLI. *University of British Columbia Working Papers in Linguistics,* Vol.18, 278–285.

Wong-Fillmore, L.W. (1991). When learning a second language means losing the first. *Early Childhood Research Quarterly, 6,* 323–346.

Wong-Fillmore, L.W. (2000). Loss of family languages: Should educators be concerned? *Theory into Practice, 39* (4), 203–210.

CHAPTER FIFTEEN

Racism and Imperialism in the Child Development Discourse

Deconstructing "Developmentally Appropriate Practice"

SADAF SHALLWANI

Abstract

In this chapter, it is argued that, as part of the modern Enlightenment project, the dominant discourse on "child development" reflects and reproduces racism and imperialism. In the first section, it is asserted that racism, as defined by Foucault (1975–76/2003), is found within the child development discourse, both in the regulation of children's bodies and the bodies and spaces with which children interact. Racism also serves to divide, classify, and "normalize" notions of childhood. Through the above, the discourse aims to produce useful and docile children who will become useful and docile adults. In the second section, it is argued that the child development discourse privileges and produces characteristics associated with the modern Western imperial subject. This includes imagined notions of progress toward civility and a fantasy of the White Subject who is scientist, conqueror, and explorer, citizen of democracy, and a contributor and consumer in a capitalist market economy. Moreover, the discourse emphasizes a Western imperial sense of "Self" versus "Other," both in the goals of child development, and in the discipline's representation of itself. These arguments are demonstrated empirically through a textual analysis of the official position statement of the U.S. National Association for the Education of Young Children (NAEYC, 1997), found in the guidebook entitled: *Developmentally Appropriate Practice in Early Childhood Programmes* (Bredekamp & Copple, 1997, pp. 3–30). This text is an example of the dominant child development discourse, and is highly influential in the design, development, and evaluation of programs, curricula, and pedagogical practices with young children, both in North America and around the world.

Knowledge, in particular knowledge of and about the social, is not produced in a vacuum. Knowledge producers are set in social milieus. The political economy and culture of their productive practices act upon the categories employed, and so they inform the knowledge being produced. By furnishing assumptions, values, and goals, this economy and culture frame the terms of the epistemological project. Once produced, the terms of articulation set their users" outlooks. The categories that now fashion content of the known constrain how people in the social order at hand think about things. Epistemological "foundations," then, are at the heart of the constitution of social power. (Goldberg, 1993, p. 149)

Knowledge in the human sciences in general, and in the study of the child in particular, is socially constructed. In this chapter, it is argued that, as part of the modern Enlightenment project, the dominant discourse on "child development" reflects and reproduces racism and imperialism. The text used as an empirical example is the official position statement of the National Association for the Education of Young Children (NAEYC, 1997) in the United States, found in the guidebook entitled *Developmentally Appropriate Practice in Early Childhood Programmes* (Bredekamp & Copple, 1997, pp. 3–30). This text is a typical example of the dominant child development discourse and is highly influential in the design, development, and evaluation of programs, curricula, and pedagogical practices with young children, both in North America and around the world.

The Modern Enlightenment Project

The modern Enlightenment project has been characterized by belief in the power of science to discover objective universal truth, belief that the pursuit and attainment of this knowledge can lead to a better life, and belief in a liberal democratic state founded on rationality and knowledge. As Harvey describes:

> The project of Modernity came into focus during the eighteenth century. That project amounted to an extraordinary intellectual effort on the part of Enlightenment thinkers to develop objective science, universal morality and law and autonomous art….The idea was to use the accumulation of knowledge generated by many individuals working freely and creatively for the pursuit of human emancipation and the enrichment of human life. The scientific domination of nature promised freedom from scarcity….The development of rational forms of social organisation and rational modes of thought promised liberation from the irrationalities of myth, religion, superstition, release from the arbitrary use of power as well as from the dark side of human natures. Only through such a project could the universal, eternal and immutable qualities of all humanity be revealed….The Enlightenment project took it as axiomatic that there was only one answer to any one question. (Harvey, 1989, 12, 27; as cited in Dahlberg, Moss, & Pence, 1999)

In this regard, the modern Enlightenment project has been built on mechanisms of social regulation and engineering—observing, classifying, regulating, and intervening on human bodies in order to attain human emancipation.

The Modern Enlightenment Project and the Child Development Discourse

Modernity's tasks of surveillance, measurement, classification and intervention have been carried about by different discourses of "knowledge," including discourses on children and childhood. Foucault (1977/1984) has described the problem of management of "childhood," with new and particular rules to regulate relations between adults and children. Nikolas Rose has more recently asserted,

> Childhood is the most intensively governed sector of personal existence. In different ways, at different times, and by many different routes varying from one section of society to another, the health, welfare, and rearing of children have been linked in thought and practice to the destiny of the nation and the responsibili-

ties of the state. The modern child has become the focus of innumerable projects that purport to safeguard it from physical, sexual and moral danger, to ensure its "normal" development, to actively promote certain capacities of attributes such as intelligence, educability and emotional stability. (Rose, 1989, p. 121, as cited in James, Jenks, & Prout, 1998, p. 7)

Developmental psychology, as part of the child development discipline, has been particularly occupied with the tasks of monitoring, regulating, and molding human beings in the earliest years of their lives (Burman, 2008).

Racism: Disciplinary and Regulatory Power in the Child Development Discourse

"Racism" is a way of dividing, normalizing, and hierarchizing groups within a population (Foucault, 1975–76/2003). It falls within the modern Enlightenment project's goals of social regulation. In this section, it is argued that this racism is found within the child development discourse, both in the regulation of children's bodies and the bodies and spaces with which children interact. It also serves to divide, classify, and "normalize" notions of childhood. Through all of the above, the discourse aims to produce useful and docile children who will become useful and docile adults.

Power, Race, and Knowledge

Michel Foucault has described modernity's goals of social engineering as resting on two major forms of state power (Foucault, 1975–76/2003): disciplinary power and regulatory power. Disciplinary power functions to render individual bodies useful and docile, and regulatory power—or biopower—functions to monitor and regulate populations. Both of these powers are served by strategies such as dividing, hierarchizing, and normalizing. The element of the "norm" in particular, can both discipline individual bodies and regulate populations:

> In more general terms still, we can say that there is one element that will circulate between the disciplinary and the regulatory, which will also be applied to body and population alike, which will make it possible to control both the disciplinary order of the body and the aleatory events that occur in the biological multiplicity. The element that circulates between the two is the norm. The norm is something that can be applied to both a body one wishes to discipline and a population one wishes to regularize. (Foucault, 1975–76/2003, pp. 252–253)

Foucault further discusses the "art of punishing" (1977/1984, p. 195) and the norm in the regime of disciplinary power:

> It brings five quite distinct operations into play: it refers individual actions to a whole that is at once a field of comparison, a space of differentiation, and the principle of a rule to be followed. It differentiates individuals from one another, in terms of the following overall rule: that the rule be made to function as a minimal threshold, as an average to be respected, or as an optimum toward which one must move. It measures in quantitative terms and hierarchizes in terms of value the abilities, the level, the "nature" of individuals. It introduces, through this "value-giving" measure, the constraint of a conformity that must be achieved. Lastly, it traces the limit that will define difference in relation to all other differences, the external frontier of the abnormal (the "shameful" class of the Ecole Militaire). The perpetual penalty that traverses all points

and supervises every instant in the disciplinary institutions compares, differentiates, hierarchizes, homogenizes, excludes. In short, it normalizes. (Foucault, 1977/1984, p. 195)

These techniques of dividing, hierarchizing, and normalizing populations and individuals work through "racism." Foucault has named racism in particular as a means of "…introducing a break into the domain of life that is under power's control: the break between what must live and what must die….It is a way of separating out the groups that exist within a population" (Foucault, 1975–76/2003, pp. 254–255). The "normal" depends on the existence of the "abnormal," the racialized Other, who is different, inferior, and excluded. As such, scientific knowledge is necessarily racialized, as it serves to justify the division and regulation of populations. As Goldberg explains,

> What I am calling "racial knowledge" is defined by a dual movement. It is dependent upon—it appropriates as its own mode of expression, its premises, and the limits of its determinations—those of established scientific fields of the day, especially anthropology, natural history, and biology. This scientific cloak of racial knowledge, its formal character and seeming universality, imparts authority and legitimation to it. Its authority is identical with, it parasitically maps onto the formal authority of the scientific discipline it mirrors. At the same time, racial knowledge—racial science, to risk excess—is able to do this because it has been historically integral to the emergence of these authoritative scientific fields. Race has been seen as a basic categorical object, in some cases a founding focus of scientific analysis in these various domains. This phenomenon has no doubt been facilitated by the definitive importance of difference in modernity's development of knowledge. (Goldberg, 1993, p. 149)

In this sense, knowledge is racial in the way it normalizes, categorizes, and hierarchizes groups of humans.

The child development discipline carries out the state goals of discipline and regulation by monitoring and regulating children's bodies as well as the bodies and spaces with which children interact (i.e., caregivers and settings). This disciplining and regulating are justified by appeals to modernity's belief in an empirical universal knowledge base and goals of emancipation and involves constant monitoring and regulating of bodies and systems.

Monitoring and Regulating Children's Bodies

The child development discourse justifies and promotes the monitoring and regulation of children's bodies, through the intertwined techniques of dividing practices (Foucault, 1977/1984, p. 195) and closely observing and training bodies to be useful and docile (Foucault, 1975–76/2003, p. 249).

> The classical age discovered the body as an object and target of power. It is easy enough to find signs of the attention then paid to the body—to the body that is manipulated, shaped, trained, which obeys, responds, becomes skillful and increases its forces. (Foucault, 1977, p. 136, as cited in James, Jenks, & Prout, 1998, p. 10)

The early childhood professional is required to closely observe and intervene to make the child's body docile and useful:

> Teachers continually observe children's spontaneous play and interaction with the physical environment and with other children to learn about their interests, abilities, and developmental progress. On the basis of this information, teachers plan experiences that enhance children's learning and development. (NAEYC, 1997, p. 17)

It is important to note that the early childhood professional is generally portrayed as an objective and separate observer. The importance of the early childhood professional's objective observation of the child in this technology has been underscored by Foucault:

> Disciplinary power, on the other hand, is exercised through its invisibility; at the same time it imposes on those whom it subjects a principle of compulsory visibility. In discipline, it is the subjects who have to be seen. Their visibility assures the hold of the power that is exercised over them. It is the fact of constantly being seen, of being able always to be seen, that maintains the disciplined individual in his subjection. (Foucault, 1877/1984, p. 199)

Monitoring and Regulating the People and Settings with Which Children Interact

The child development discourse advocates monitoring and regulating the bodies and spaces encountered by children in public and private spheres. Racialized knowledge produces particular notions of "normal" and "optimal," which are then imposed at population levels. For example, the NAEYC position statement asserts:

> Children's development in all areas is influenced by their ability to establish and maintain a limited number of positive, consistent primary relationships with adults and other children. (NAEYC, 1997, p. 15)

In this way, particular imagined (White, Western, middle class) models of caregiving and childrearing are normalized and prescribed as optimal for children's development, thus pathologizing and inferiorizing other models and arrangements.

In the public sphere of the early childhood institution (e.g., child care centre, preschool), the body of the early childhood professional is regulated in particular ways. Her body is required to engage in "appropriate" practices and avoid "inappropriate" practices; she is required to interact (and not interact) with children and families in particular ways deemed "normal" and prescribed as optimal. The body of the early childhood professional is under constant scrutiny in the hierarchy of observation, under the guise of professionalism and quality, which inscribe particular rules of social administration. The professional can only exist in contrast to the unprofessional (Bloch & Popkewitz, 2000, p. 23); high quality can only exist in contrast to low quality. This system requires ongoing monitoring and regulation to ensure standards are met; to identify, regulate, and exclude the unprofessional and the low quality. In the implementation of early childhood programs, the NAEYC recommends that comprehensive systems are in place to prepare, regulate, and evaluate the quality of staff and programmes (NAEYC, 1997, pp. 24–25). The NAEYC offers accreditation criteria and procedures for organizations wishing to train early childhood professionals. Appeals to "knowledge" and appeals to safety are made in justifying these particular rules of social administration:

> Of even greater concern was the large percentage of classrooms and family child care homes that were rated "barely adequate" or "inadequate" for quality. From 12 to 20% of the children were in settings that were considered dangerous to their health and safety and harmful to their social and cognitive development. An alarming number of infants and toddlers (35 to 40%) were found to be in unsafe settings. (NAEYC, 1997, p. 7)

The early childhood professional is both the effect and effector of disciplinary power and regulatory power. As she is expected to monitor and regulate the bodies of children, she is monitored and regulated by the early childhood discipline.

Dividing, Classifying, and "Normalizing" Childhood

The racialized knowledge base of the child development discipline engages in dividing practices (Foucault, 1977/1984, p. 195), through classification, individualization, normalization, and thus hierarchization and exclusion. First, the category of "the child" is differentiated from the category of "the adult," with the child conceptualized as vulnerable and primitive, and the adult conceptualized as savior and civilized. Justifications for intervention in children's lives often appeal to such notions of children's vulnerability:

> Because children's health and safety too often are threatened today, programs for young children must not only provide adequate health, safety, and nutrition but may also need to ensure more comprehensive services, such as physical, dental, and mental health and social services. (NAEYC, 1997, p. 15)

Second, the processes of children's development and learning are divided in a number of ways, such as (a) domains of development (e.g., cognitive, social, emotional, physical); (b) ages and stages of development; and (c) modes of learning/types of knowledge (e.g., emotional, spatial, rational). For example, the *Developmentally Appropriate Practice* guidebook charts developmental tasks in each domain that children are expected to accomplish at particular ages (e.g., Bredekamp & Copple, 1997, pp. 70–71: Developmental Milestones of Children from Birth to Age 3).

Finally, and most importantly, the process of "development" is normalized and racialized. Development is portrayed as a universal phenomenon, which is orderly, linear, progressive, and cumulative. "Normal" development thus creates "abnormal" development, whereby difference (deficiency, deviance) is located in and serves to exclude the individual (child). For example, the NAEYC asserts that, "Development occurs in a relatively orderly sequence, with later abilities, skills, and knowledge building on those already acquired" (NAEYC, 1997, p. 10). They further claim that there is a clear knowledge base about child development and learning—"knowledge of age-related human characteristics that permits general predictions with an age range about what activities, materials, interactions, or experiences will be safe, healthy, interesting, achievable, and also challenging to children" (NAEYC, 1997, p. 9). However, as articulated by Bloch and Popkewitz,

> That the norms, the natural, and the biological were those of middle-class, white, young boys and girls, as observed by "scientific" methods used by white, middle-class, "scientifically trained" men and women, was, in the 1920s-1940s, rarely discussed, and with some likelihood, rarely recognized. Nonetheless, these norms created a universalized girl or boy, what was normal and what was deviant, who was advanced, which children were retarded, in short, what normal childhood versus adolescence and adulthood were, what normal stages of progress were, what backwardness looked like, and what evolutionary ideals or "norms" for childhood should be. (Bloch & Popkewitz, 2000, p. 20)

In this way, particular imagined (White, Western, middle-class) characteristics and models are deemed to be the "norm" and prescribed as optimal for all children, thereby constructing the "abnormal," the "deficient," and the "other." Moreover, early childhood professionals are required to "adapt for and be responsive to inevitable individual variation" (NAEYC, 1997, p. 9), and individual variation is described in part as "the inevitable variability around the average or normative course of development" (NAEYC, 1997, p. 10). The repeated use of the word "inevitable" implies that deviance from the norm is something one would want to avoid but cannot. In this way, the norm is the imagined, the unreal, and yet the ideal, that cannot be attained. Ghassan Hage has described this imagined White as "the ideal of being the bearer of "Western" civilization. As such, no one can be fully White, but people yearn to be so. It is in this sense that "Whiteness is itself a fantasy position and a field of accumulating Whiteness." (Hage, 2000, p. 58).

Useful and Docile Children, Useful and Docile Adults

The child development discipline also occupies itself with training bodies to be docile, to be self-regulating and other-regulating, to give rise to docile adult bodies (Foucault, 1977, p. 136, as cited in James, Jenks, & Prout, 1998, p. 10). In this discourse, development is presented as natural and yet needing careful monitoring, regulation, and intervention to produce docile and useful bodies. As described in the NAEYC position statement:

> Development and learning are dynamic processes requiring that adults understand the continuum, observe children closely to match curriculum and teaching to children's emerging competencies, needs, and interests, and then help children move forward by targeting educational experiences to the edge of children's changing capacities so as to challenge but not frustrate them. (NAEYC, 1997, p. 15)

The child development discourse places particular emphasis on the "early years" for the believed malleability of children's brains during these years and the long-term outcomes expected from these early interventions:

> Current research demonstrates the early and lasting experiences of children's environments and experiences on brain development and cognition. (NAEYC, 1997, p. 6)

In this regard, a major focus of the child development profession has become the order and regulation of children's time, space, and bodies. Children's bodies are trained to behave in particular (White, Western, middle-class) ways: to function according to timetables and routines (e.g., eating or napping at the same time every day), and to behave differently in different spaces (e.g., thematic play areas, outdoors physical activity versus indoor pretend play, storytime seated on the floor versus eating at a table):

> Children experience an organized environment and an orderly routine that provides an overall structure in which learning takes place. (NAEYC, 1997, p. 17)

There is an emphasis on children learning self- and other-regulation, responsibility, and autonomy, as demonstrated in NAEYC's description of appropriate practice:

> Teachers set clear, consistent, and fair limits for children's behavior and hold children accountable to standards of acceptable behavior. To the extent that children are able, teachers engage them in developing rules and procedures for behavior of class members. (NAEYC, 1997, p. 19)

Similarly, the justifications for monitoring and intervention, as well as the outcome measures by which children are evaluated, reflect how docile and useful the child's body is; children are evaluated on how they function within school settings and how they integrate with "mainstream" society. For example, the NAEYC appeals to the perceived failure of racialized others to meet imagined White standards:

> Currently, too many children—especially children from low-income families and some minority groups—experience school failure, are retained in grade, get assigned to special education, and eventually drop out of school. (NAEYC, 1997, p. 7)

In this way, social control is performed through processes of "normalization" and exclusion (Dahlberg, Moss, & Pence, 1999, p. 65) of racialized other children. Despite its coding in the languages of class and minority status, race is the dividing factor, whereby Whiteness is normal, and racial others are abnormal and in need of intervention.

Imperialism: Child Development as the Production of the Western Imperial Subject

Imperialism is "characterized by an exercise of power, either through direct conquest or (latterly) through political and economic influence that effectively amounts to a similar form of domination" (Young, 2001, p. 27, as cited in Cannella & Viruru, 2004, p.15). Imperialism has been intertwined with modern Enlightenment and Western imperial notions of "humanity" (Young, 1990/2004) and "civility" (Coleman, 2006).

Foucault (1977/1984) asserted that power is constitutive and productive, as opposed to merely repressive. In this section, it is argued that the child development discourse privileges and produces characteristics associated with the modern Western imperial subject. This includes imagined notions of progress toward "White civility" (Coleman, 2006, p. 10), and a fantasy of the White subject who is scientist, conqueror, and explorer, citizen of democracy, and a contributor and consumer in a capitalist market economy. Moreover, the discourse emphasizes a sense of "Self" versus "Other," both in the goals of child development and the discipline's representation of itself.

Yearning for "White Civility"

First, the notion of "development" as "progress" implies a linear and progressive path from "the primitive" to "the civilized" (Coleman, 2006, pp. 10–11), and is thus tied up with moral and cultural ideas of White civilized superiority (Goldberg, 1993, p. 166). Whether the discourse is about countries or humans, it is implied that there is one path to "development," and all entities can be ranked on this continuum (e.g., under-developed, developing, developed). Goldberg asserts,

> This assumption has had to do, in part, with the self-identity of the West, of its self-confident superiority, its imperial successes, its dominant colonialism, and its postcolonial dominance. It has also had to do, at least in part, with the projection of European Enlightenment values as universal, as the standard against which all judgements should be measured. (Goldberg, 1993, pp. 166–167)

Goldberg (1993) describes the notion of "the primitive" as one hegemonic conceptual schema in the production of contemporary racialized knowledge:

> Formally, primitive societies were theorized in binary differentiation from a civilized order. (…) In popular terms, nonwhite primitives have come to be conceived as childlike, intuitive, and spontaneous; they require the iron fist of "European" governance and paternalistic guidance to control inherent physical violence and sexual drives. (Goldberg, 1993, p. 156)

Progress and improvement are thus conceived as the pathway from racialized and gendered Other—signified by "the under-developed/developing," "the primitive," "the child"—to the White man—signified by "the developed," "the civilized," and "the adult." Coleman cites Richard Dyer:

According to Dyer, enterprise is often presented as the sign of the White spirit—that is, to a valuation of energy, will, discovery, science, progress, the building of nations, the organization of labour, and especially leadership. "The idea of leadership," [Dyer] writes, "suggests both a narrative of human progress and the peculiar quality required to effect it. Thus white people [are understood naturally to] lead humanity forward because of their temperamental qualities of leadership: will power, far-sightedness, energy." (Coleman, 2006, p. 12)

Becoming a "White Subject"

The discourse both normalizes and prescribes "child development" as the development of the rational scientist, the conquering explorer, the citizen of democracy, and the member of a capitalist market economy—roles associated with the (White) Western imperial subject.

Rational scientist

First, the racialized discourse on child development, in line with the values of modernity and the yearnings for White civility, represents child development as a progressive evolution from dependence-attachment and irrationality-emotion (considered feminine and primitive qualities), to independence-detachment and rationality-objectivity (considered masculine and civilized qualities). Burman describes Piaget's depiction of the developing child as "…a budding scientist systematically encountering problems in the material world, developing hypotheses, and learning by discovery and activity" (Burman, 1994, p. 157). Along the same lines, in the NAEYC position statement, it is stated:

> Children need to form their own hypotheses and keep trying them out through social interaction, physical manipulation, and their own thought processes—observing what happens, reflecting on their findings, asking questions, and formulating answers (…). (NAEYC, 1997, p. 13)

The individual is conceived as separate, developing intellectually towards logic and rationality, epitomized within "the scientific method" of modern knowledge production. As noted by Burman, the reverence for activity and discovery carries with it colonial (and gendered) implications (Burman, 1994).

Explorer and conqueror

Second, the child development discourse perpetuates the imperial subject as explorer and conqueror by representing child learning and growth as exploration and achievement. Importance is given to motivation, curiosity, initiative, confidence, autonomy, and achievement, reflecting imperial and gendered nuances. Two assertions from the NAEYC position statement serve as examples:

> To strengthen children's sense of competence and confidence as learners, motivation to persist, and willingness to take risks, teachers provide experiences for children to be genuinely successful and to be challenged. (NAEYC, 1997, p. 19)

> Children continually gravitate to situations and stimuli that give them the chance to work at their "growing edge." Moreover, in a task just beyond the child's independent reach, the adult and more-competent peers contribute significantly to development by providing the supportive "scaffolding" that allows the child to take the next step. (NAEYC, 1997, p. 14)

There is a continuous reference to edges, frontiers, the "just beyond," which the child is constantly encouraged to attain. This language bears a striking resemblance to the language of imperialism and colonialism. Slotkin has described the usage of this metaphor as the "Frontier Myth," according to which,

> (…) the conquest of the wilderness and the subjugation or displacement of the Native Americans who originally inhabited it have been the means to our achievement of a national identity, a democratic polity, an ever-expanding economy, and a phenomenally dynamic and "progressive" civilization. The original ideological task of the Myth was to explain and justify the establishment of the American colonies; but as the colonies expanded and developed, the Myth was called on to account for our rapid economic growth, our emergency as a powerful nation-state, and our distinctively American approach to the socially and culturally disruptive processes of modernization. (Slotkin, 1992, p. 10)

Conquest and expansion are thus intertwined with progress, development, and the attainment of White civility.

Citizen of democracy

Third, the child development discourse reflects and promotes particular imagined roles the child will be expected to play as an adult in society. For example, citizens of a liberal democratic society are required to be self-governing and autonomous (Burman, 1994, p. 168). In this vein, children are expected to develop into docile, self- and other-regulating bodies. This is highlighted by a quote shared earlier from the NAEYC position statement:

> Teachers set clear, consistent, and fair limits for children's behavior and hold children accountable to standards of acceptable behavior. To the extent that children are able, teachers engage them in developing rules and procedures for behavior of class members. (NAEYC, 1997, p. 19)

Contributor and consumer in capitalist market economy

Finally, a capitalist market economy requires entrepreneurs and consumers, which the child development discipline aims to produce. As suggested in the NAEYC statement, consumer preferences and demands are cultivated:

> Teachers provide children with a rich variety of experiences, projects, materials, problems, and ideas to explore and investigate, ensuring that these are worthy of children's attention. (NAEYC, 1997, p. 18)

> Teachers provide children with opportunities to make meaningful choices and time to explore through active involvement. (NAEYC, 1997, p. 18)

In this way, consumer preferences and demands are cultivated and valued:

> From infancy onwards, the child is encouraged to characterize himself in terms of his favourite toys and foods and those he dislikes; his tastes, aversions and consumer preferences are viewed not only as legitimate but essential aspects of his growing individuality—and a prized quality of an independent person. (LeVine, 2003, p. 95)

Moreover, particular qualities associated with "entrepreneurship" are privileged:

[Children] need to understand that effort is necessary for achievement, for example, and they need to have curiosity and confidence in themselves as learners. (NAEYC, 1997, p. 8)

Teachers foster children's collaboration with peers on interesting, important enterprises. (NAEYC, 1997, p. 19)

However, these White "enterprising" qualities (Dyer, as cited in Coleman, 2006, p. 12) are not universal, and differ substantially from those qualities desired for those (and accessible to those) who work at the mass production levels (Bloch & Popkewitz, 2000, p. 29). As discussed earlier, non-White, non-middle-class children are thus excluded from White middle-class citizenship and economic participation (Fanon, p. 131, as cited in Young, 1990/2004, p. 163)

"Self" versus "Other"

The child development discourse also emphasizes the Western imperial (and racist) sense of "Self" versus "Other," both in the goals of child development, and the discipline's representation of itself.

First, successful child development has been conceptualized as children's learning to clearly develop a sense of "Self" (who is the universal Subject or agent) in opposition to "the Other" (who is different and objectified). The NAEYC position statement articulates:

Moreover, to live in a highly pluralistic society and world, young people need to develop a positive self-identity and a tolerance for others whose perspective and experience may be different from their own. (NAEYC, 1997, p. 8)

In this sense, the child grows to be the Self, an identity which depends on the designation of the Other, in whom difference is located (Ahmed, 2000, p. 7). This Self is considered to be the universal subject, the universal human; yet the values and ideals promoted are actually associated with a particular fantasy of Whiteness, which, as discussed earlier, is both yearned for and unattainable (Hage, 2000, p. 58).

Western bourgeois racial prejudice as regards the nigger and the Arab is a racism of contempt; it is a racism which minimizes what it hates. Bourgeois ideology, however, which is the proclamation of an essential equality between men, manages to appear logical in its own eyes by inviting the sub-men to become human, and to take as their prototype Western humanity as incarnated in the Western bourgeoisie. (Fanon, p. 131, as cited in Young, 1990/2004, p. 163)

"We" and "the Other" in the Child Development Discourse

Second, the discipline of child development portrays particular imagined notions of "We," as a subject/agent who encompasses leadership, legitimized authority, benevolence, and the power to include and exclude the Other.

In line with the rhetoric of the New World Order, in which the American government is responsible to lead due to its superior values of order, democracy, and freedom (Said, 1994, p. xvii), the Western child development discourse considers itself the leader in child development worldwide. This leadership is qualified by authority, legitimacy, and totality. For example, the NAEYC states,

> Based on an enduring commitment to act on behalf of children, NAEYC's mission is to promote high-quality, developmentally appropriate programs for all children and their families. Because we define developmentally appropriate programs as programs that contribute to children's development, we must articulate our goals for children's development…what we want for them, both in their present lives and as they develop to adulthood, and what personal characteristics should be fostered because they contribute to a peaceful, prosperous, and democratic society. (NAEYC, 1997, p. 8)

The White Western subject presumptuously claims to know and represent all children, all families, and all professionals, and brazenly confers itself the power to define that which is morally and socially desirable for all.

Moreover, this leadership comes from imagined moral superiority and corresponding responsibility (perhaps as Rudyard Kipling's white man's burden, as cited in Razack, 2004, p. 4). There is an appeal to a sense of danger and urgency, a need to save the children, and a capacity to save but only in the one way determined by the legitimized authority:

> Of even greater concern was the large percentage of classrooms and family child care homes that were rated "barely adequate" or "inadequate" for quality. From 12 to 20% of the children were in settings that were considered dangerous to their health and safety and harmful to their social and cognitive development. An alarming number of infants and toddlers (35 to 40%) were found to be in unsafe settings. (NAEYC, 1997, p. 7)

> (…) (W)hile early childhood programs have the potential for producing positive and lasting effects on children, this potential will not be achieved unless more attention is paid to ensuring that all programs meet the highest standards of quality. (NAEYC, 1997, p. 7)

The highest standards are, of course, determined by the White Western subject group. The implication is that there is potential, the children can be saved, but *only* if everyone's on board, only if everyone agrees to the standards and norms established by the White Western subject, only then can we save all the children.

Most fundamentally, the fantasy of the imagined "We" (the White Western Imperial Self) is defined by and depends upon "the Other," and upon the power of "We" to include or exclude the racialized Other. Difference and deviation are located in the Other, as opposed to the universal Self/We who responds to and has the power to (selectively) include the Other. In this vein, the child development discourse depicts families as deficient in caring for their children and the discipline/profession as the legitimate knowledge base regarding children and childhood:

> The program links families with a range of services, based on identified resources, priorities, and concerns. (NAEYC, 1997, p. 22)

> Increasingly, programs serve children and families from diverse cultural and linguistic backgrounds, requiring that all programs demonstrate understanding of and responsiveness to cultural and linguistic diversity. (NAEYC, 1997, p. 4)

> [Appropriate] curriculum provides opportunities to support children's home culture and language while also developing all children's abilities to participate in the shared culture of the program and the community. (NAEYC, 1997, p. 20)

Difference and need (culture, language, and disability) are clearly located in the racialized Other (individual, child, family, home, background), while the imagined "We" (all, shared, community) holds the responsibility and benevolence to respond, to include or exclude:

> Many different settings in this country provide services to young children, and it is legitimate—even ben-eficial—for these settings to vary in certain ways. However, since it is vital to meet children's learning and developmental needs wherever they are served, high standards of quality should apply to all settings. (NAEYC, 1997, p. 4)

> Teachers acknowledge parents' choices and goals for children and respond with sensitivity and respect to parents" preferences and concerns without abdicating professional responsibility to children. (NAEYC, 1997, p. 22)

Again, difference and deviation are located in the individual/child/family, and the imagined "We" of the child development discipline holds moral responsibility (the white man's burden) to intervene in the raising of children. Superficial input from parents is "allowed," but the profession remains the expert on the "real" issues. The state goals of social regulation rely fundamentally on this knowledge/power imbalance in the relationship between the discipline and the individual.

Sara Ahmed discusses the stranger fetishism involved in the rhetoric of inclusion, arguing that othering happens through acts of inclusion, and that this discourse is built around a fantasy of a national subject who has the power to define who should and should not be included (Ahmed, 2000, p. 112). Similarly, Hage describes the imaginary of the "nationalist manager" and the other as object: the nationalist's capacity to classify others as desirable and undesirable and manage both the nation-al space and the national object (Hage, 2000, p. 58).

Significantly, despite the repeated implicit references to the racialized Other, race itself is never explicitly acknowledged in this and most texts in the child development discourse. Toni Morrison has argued that coded language and significant omissions are required to maintain the frail construc-tions of the imagined nation (Morrison, 1992, p. 6). In the NAEYC statement, the closest one gets to race is "culture" or "class" (or in one situation, "minority status")—described by Goldberg as con-temporary masks of race (Goldberg, 1993, pp. 69–74). These codes for race are associated with codes for difference, deviance, and need; in short, the nonwhite is othered and excluded.

As it has been argued, the dominant discourse on "child development" reflects and reproduces racism and imperialism. The discourse regulates children's lives, "normalizes" and hierarchizes dif-ferent groups, divides and classifies childhood, and privileges particular White and imperial characteristics.

References

Ahmed, S. (2000). *Strange Encounters: Embodied Others in Post-Coloniality*. London: Routledge.

Bloch, M. N. & Popkewitz, T. S. (2000). Constructing the parent, teacher, and child: Discourses of development. In L. D. Soto (Ed.), *The Politics of Early Childhood Education*. New York: Peter Lang, pp. 7–32.

Bredekamp, S., & Copple, C. (1997). *Developmentally Appropriate Practice in Early Childhood Programmes, Revised Edition*. Washington, D.C.: National Association for the Education of Young Children.

Burman, E. (1994). *Deconstructing Developmental Psychology*. London: Routledge.

Burman, E. (2008). *Deconstructing Developmental Psychology*, 2nd edition. London: Routledge.

Cannella, G. S., & Viruru, R. (2004). *Childhood and postcolonization: Power, education, and contemporary practice*. New York: RoutledgeFalmer.

Coleman, D. (2006). *White Civility: The Literary Project of English Canada*. Toronto: University of Toronto.

Dahlberg, G., Moss, P., & Pence, A. (1999). *Beyond Quality in Early Childhood Education and Care: Postmodern Perspectives*. London: Falmer.

Foucault (1984). *The Foucault Reader* (P. Rabinow, Ed.). New York: Pantheon. (Original work published 1977)

Foucault, M. (1975-76; 2003*). "Society Must Be Defended": Lectures at the College de France, 1975–76*. D. Macey (Trans.). New York: Picador.

Goldberg, D. T. (1993). *Racist Culture: Philosophy and the Politics of Meaning*. Cambridge: Blackwell.

Hage, G. (2000). *White Nation: Fantasies of White Supremacy in a Multicultural Society*. New York: Routledge.

James, A., Jenks, C. & Prout, A. (1998). *Theorizing Childhood*. Cambridge, UK: Polity Press.

LeVine, R. (2003). *Childhood Socialization: Comparative Studies of Parenting, Learning and Educational Change*. Hong Kong: Comparative Education Research Centre.

Morrison, T. (1992). *Playing in the Dark: Whiteness and the Literary Imagination*. Cambridge, MA: Harvard University.

National Association for the Education of Young Children (1997). NAEYC Position Statement: Developmentally Appropriate Practice in Early Childhood Programs Serving Children from Birth through Age 8. In, S. Bredekamp & C. Copple (Eds.), *Developmentally Appropriate Practice in Early Childhood Programs*. Washington, DC: National Association for the Education of Young Children.

Razack, S. (2004). *Dark Threats and White Knights*. Toronto: University of Toronto.

Said, E. (1994). *Culture and Imperialism*. New York: Random House.

Slotkin, R. (1992). *Gunfighter Nation: The Myth of the Frontier in Twentieth-Century America*. Oklahoma: University of Oklahoma.

Young, R. (1990/2004). Disorienting Orientalism. In, *White Mythologies*. London: Routledge, pp. 158–180.

CHAPTER SIXTEEN

Modern Research Discourses Constructing the Postcolonial Subjectivity of (Mexican) American Children

Araceli Rivas

Abstract

Modern constructions of childhood created by the Western imagery are dismantled from a post-colonial critique of the enterprise of research. The enterprise of research is situated in a configuration of power, knowledge, and culture that has imbedded colonial structures. These colonial structures in educational research discourses are problematized for creating multiple subjectivities of (Mexican) American children as the Other. The historical and contemporary otherness of (Mexican) American children positions them as underperforming objects of the mental measurement machine and as a cultural entity whose differences from the dominant culture are the source of undereducation and incompatibility to the American educational system. Thus, educational research discourses reaffirm the construction of (Mexican) American children to an inferiority/superiority matrix and re-establish difference as a barrier or a problem to be solved. From a postcolonial critique, these discourses expose the colonial structures that privilege dominant perspectives about subjectivities of minority children as well as the privilege of researcher as author. Decolonization in educational research is advocated to take this practice beyond the Western vision of progress to a personal level toward social justice.

Introduction

Modern constructions of childhood can be projected into a map of histories, cultures, institutions, economies, politics, actors, and practices that interrelate to (re)produce Western assumptions of a universal child. Within this map lie many degrees of analysis that can critically deconstruct, oppose, contest, problematize, reform, or transform the axes that (re)define the modern and Western constructions of childhood. Critical analyses have examined developmental psychology (Burman, 1994), early childhood education (Cannella, 1997; Viruru, 2001; MacNaughton, 2005), corporate childhood (Steinberg & Kincheloe, 1997), multiculturalism (Spring, 2000; 2004), critical pedagogy (Apple 1990; McLaren, 2003), and comparative education (McGovern, 1999). Notwithstanding the aforementioned, there are other critical voices that counter dominant Western notions of childhood from multiple perspectives and locations. Whether analytical perspectives are feminist, poststructural, Marxist, postmodern, postcolonial, and the location of critique is (are) education, medicine, media, psychology, government, law, corporations, or the nation states, each contributes to a reflection about social equity and justice in the context of childhoods.

The present chapter connects with the critical voices that examine the (re)production of childhood in particular that of the (Mexican) American child.[1] The location of critique is research as it is a modern practice that has been produced from a Western perspective of the Other (Clifford & Marcus, 1986; Hallam & Street, 2000). While the principles underlying research are the production of knowledge and the liberal ideals of progress, research is not a neutral and objective endeavor. It is a practice embedded in a matrix of power, knowledge, and cultural configurations (Said, 1978) with colonial structures (Smith, 2002). Thus, this chapter examines the implication of academic research in the construction of (Mexican) American children from a postcolonial perspective. A postcolonial perspective provides the theoretical foundation for understanding past and contemporary, local and global consequences tied to geographical, economic, cultural, and intellectual colonization (Loomba, 1998). Postcolonial theorizing also contextualizes the transnational subjectivities of (Mexican) American children as an ethnic group that has a 500-year history of colonization—Spain (sixteenth century) and the United States (nineteenth century) (Acuña, 2000). Regardless of the geopolitical space, in Mexico (as Mexico Americanos) or in the United States (as Mexican Americans), this ethnic identity constitutes one of the oldest postcolonial subjectivities constructed by hegemonic (non-scientific and scientific) discourses within two historical periods.

While a critical postcolonial analysis of discourses produced by diverse institutions (media, government, religion, marketing) is necessary in the dismantling of the Western narratives of the Other, this chapter reflects upon "scientific" discourses that construct realities about (Mexican) American childhood in the context of educational research. The first section of the chapter expounds on postcolonial theory as it relates to oppressive Othering and colonial discourse. The second section reviews three axes of representation from historical and contemporary educational discourses about (Mexican) American children that exemplify the mechanisms of oppressive othering and the colonial discourse. The third section provides a postcolonial critique of educational research discourse as a colonial practice. The last section also discusses possibilities of decolonization within the enterprise of educational research. The intention is to open a critical space to examine educational research and its potential to perpetuate colonizing discourses that (re)construct childhoods from dominant Western perspectives of the Other.

Postcolonial Perspectives, Discourse Practices, and Constructing the "Other"

Under postcolonial theorizing, the conceptualization of colonialism encompasses "forms of subjugation of one people to another" through direct or indirect military, economic, political, or cultural domination (Young, 2001, p. 15). Consequently, postcolonial studies are an interdisciplinary and trandisciplinary undertaking that has multiple analytic approaches to theorize. Postcolonial studies also draw from different academic fields such as sociology, history, literature, and cultural studies. Seminal postcolonial critiques include the role played by various forms of representation and otherness (i.e., Said, 1978), nationality and identity (i.e., Fanon, 1963; Memmi, 1965; Nandy, 1988), transnational hybridity of cultures and peoples (i.e., Bhabha, 1994), the subaltern voice (Guha & Spivak, 1988), and resistance as oppositional (i.e., Bhabha, 1994; Fanon, 1967). Within the context of this chapter, the postcolonial approach follows the conceptualization of *Othering* and colonial discourse to examine the cultural process of othering as a research practice.

In postcolonial theorizing, the concept of *Othering* is central to describing the psychological and social phenomenon tied to the mentality of the *colonizer and colonized*. Otherness (alterity) is a state of difference while *othering* is the process where "the 'construction' of the subject itself" is "inseparable from the construction of its others" (Ashcroft, Griffiths, & Tiffin, 2000, p. 11). The subject/group derives its identity in a process of differentiation that excludes "us" from "them" based on racial, ethnic, geographical, economic, or ideological markers (Greenberg, 2003, para.1). The process of identification and differentiation is problematic when self- (group) identification depends on the disparagement of the Other and establishes dominant ideological frameworks to judge, classify, and order the Other (Greenberg, 2003). For instance, in South America othering *la raza* (the race) entailed the classification of its inhabitants and its natural environment along the axis of civilization, racial composition, gender, and geographical location while establishing and privileging North Euro-American identity as superior and civilized (Salvatore, 1996). Thus, oppressive othering is a mechanism that (a) "creates patterns of interaction that reaffirm a dominant group's ideology of difference;" (b) places another cultural group into inferior/superior axis (e.g. normal/deviant, centre/margin, core/peripheries); and (c) "turns subordinates into commodities" (Schwalbe, Goodwin, Holden, Schrock, Thompson, & Wolkomir, 2000, para. 17). Said's (1978) discourse analysis provides another example of the mechanisms of oppressive othering imposed by the West on the Orient.

Edward's Said work on *Orientalism* (1978) details the construction of the Other within a colonial discourse. The poststructuralist analysis of nineteenth and twentieth century texts reveals essentialized representations of the Oriental as "irrational, depraved (fallen), childlike, different" contrary to the rational, virtuous, mature European (Said, 1978, p. 40). The Orient as a geographic location was represented as feminine, timeless, bizarre, lustful, backward, and lazy—an imagined contrast to the civilized, masculine, moral, productive West. Further, the variety of text analyzed demonstrated how the West imagined the Orient through various political, social, scientific, religious discourses that sustained an otherness that reflected an imperialistic attitude and justified the colonial rule.

> Orientalism can be discussed and analyzed as the corporate institution for dealing with the Orient—dealing with it by making statements about it, authorizing views on it, describing it, by teaching it, settling it, ruling over it: in short, Orientalism is as a Western style of dominating, restructuring, and having authority over the Orient" (p. 3).

These discourses reflected a body of knowledge about the Orient/al character, culture, history, society, and traditions that made their "management easy and profitable" under the "all-embracing Western tutelage" (Said, 1978, pp. 35–36). They were represented "as something one judges (as in a court of law), something one disciplines (as in school or prison), something one studies and depicts (as in curriculum), something one illustrates (as in a zoological manual)" (Said, 1978, p. 40). The colonial discourse also accentuated the practice of surveillance experienced by the Other—"Westerns are informed observers and their complacent gaze reduces other peoples to be observed" (Fox-Genovese, 1999, p. 536). Thus, discourses about the Orient/al positioned them under surveillance and *statu pupillari* in need of civilization and saving by scholars, missionaries, business, military, and teachers of the West.

Beyond the constellation of representations, superiority/inferiority configurations, and the imperialistic attitudes of the West, *Orientalism* (1978) substantiates the framework of a colonial discourse where there is a relationship between culture, knowledge, and power (Young, 2001). The postcolonial inquiry by Said (1978) derives from Foucault's (1970; 1972) concept of discourse and the relationship between knowledge and power. For Foucault, discourse is produced by (a) "rules of production of statements" (conditions that allow statements to emerge); (b) "rules that delimit the sayable" (production and repeatability of what is considered legitimate and true); (c) "rules that create the spaces in which new statements can be made;" (sites of power) and 4)"rules that ensure that a practice is material and discursive at the same time"(social practices and language) (Kendall & Wickham, 1999, pp. 24–43). Applied to *Orientalism* (1978), the colonial discourse reveals that the Western "ways of knowing are themselves mechanisms of power" (Bauman, 1998, p. 79) in that regimes of knowledge and the discourses produced about the Orient demonstrate a *will to power* (Foucault, 1972). This *will to power* disciplines the sayable (regimes of knowledge) by excluding, silencing, marginalizing, ignoring, and prohibiting other types of knowledge. A *will to power* is "practiced" in the legitimation of what is considered to be true, valid, and valuable (Kendall & Wickham, 1999, p. 55). In turn, the social practices and processes that legitimate *what is true, valid, or valuable* reflect a *will to truth* from their respective sites of power (Foucault, 1972). Thus, the Western *will to knowledge* and the *will to truth* imposed on the Orient is also *a will to power* (Young, 2001).

In relation to the processes and mechanisms involved in the practice of modern research, the configuration of power, knowledge, and culture is inextricably applicable. The production of knowledge emerges from individual and institutional histories, cultures, interests, struggles, politics, as well as economics that shape the trends of what, why, how, and who is researched (e.g., Condliffe Lagemann, 2000). As a cultural practice, modern research contains Enlightenment notions of progress as depicted by its primary functions—to describe, explain, predict, and improve (Gall, Borg, Gall, 1996). Fundamentally, the *Western* cultural enterprise of science contains a multilevel metanarrative of progress where blocks of knowledge are built, revolutionary paradigms are created (Kuhn, 1996), and there is a positive social outcome of improvement and development. However, the cultural enterprise of science (modern research) embodies a historical project embedded within both imperial practices and continued colonial structures that have been questioned and challenged (Harding, 1998; Kavita, 1998; Smith, 2002). Across academic social science fields during the 1960s and 1970s, self-critical contentions reflected on the relationship between culture, knowledge, and power with assertions that "anthropology had been nothing but a tool of imperialism," "sociology an instrument of control of the working class and minorities," and "psychology a device for social discipline and the increase of productivity" (Haan, Bellah, Rabinow, & Sullivan, 1983, p. 5).

Furthermore, Smith (2002) problematizes the Western cultural enterprise of research for colonizing indigenous groups through its conceptual tools of writing, theory, and history. In the process of legitimatizing knowledge, the rights of the indigenous to conceptualize, theorize, act on, and represent their own reality have been silenced (Smith, 2002). As Stanfield (1994) corroborates, "the tendency for Western researchers to impose even their most enlightened cultural constructs on Others rather than creating indigenized theories and methods to grasp the ontological essences of people of color is, of course, legendary" (p. 176). Thus, academic research discourses can be implicated in the (re)colonization of indigenous groups and minority groups through its colonial tools of theorizing, conceptualizing, and writing about the Other—fundamentally, discourses that impose a linguistic order of the world (Foucault, 1970).

In summary, the postcolonial conceptualization of othering and colonial discourse contextualizes the critique of educational research discourse from multiple perspectives. It defines othering not only as a constellation of representations, but it also describes the relationship between the identification of self (colonizer) as an inseparable process from the differentiation of the Other (colonized). It is in this relationship of identification that the West projects an imagined, different, and separate Other that is to be observed, described, categorized, ordered, and positioned to an inferior/superior matrix. Further, the colonial discourse situates modern research practice as imbedded in the knowledge, power, and cultural configurations where the *ways of knowing* (theory, writing, history, research) are part of the will to knowledge, a will to truth, and will to power. The colonial discourse also frames its history to imperialistic structures (oppressive othering) that are culturally distinctive (the West) where there social practices and respective sites of power (e.g, religious, scientific, political, economic) legitimize and limit the sayable (discursive). The limitation of the sayable in research is reflected in the devaluing of indigenous knowledges (McGovern, 1999) or the silencing of the voices of the minority groups and children (Cannella, 1997) or in the lack of self-determination of indigenous groups to self-theorize and write their own reality as well as determine their own research goals and agendas (Smith, 2002). In all, the concepts of othering and the colonial discourse offer a framework to examine and challenge the "subjective, intersubjective, and normative reference claims" embedded in Western practices and discourses of research (Kincheloe & McLaren, p. 1994, p. 140).

(Mexican) American Children in Past and Present Educational Research Discourses

Based on the concepts of othering and the configurations of knowledge, power, and culture, this section illustrates the discourses that construct the otherness of (Mexican) American children in education as a product of the Western academies. A review of the *key* educational discourses is discussed from a historical and contemporary perspective. The historical perspective is based on a literature review while the contemporary perspective is based on a content analysis conducted by Rivas (2005) on 119 research documents from 1980 to 2003. Note that historical undertones contextualize the educational discourses discussed providing a backdrop of the multiple and significant issues in (Mexican) American education, the history of educational research, and the American history of minority groups. Further, the terms Chicano, Spanish-speakers, limited English proficient (LEP), Latinos, Hispanic, English language learners are used interchangeably due to the historical shifts in the labels used in educational research to describe (Mexican) Americans.

Mental Measurement as the Sorting Machine

Early educational discourses related to (Mexican) American children emerge from the testing movements where the constructions of the minority children were contextualized by medicalized discourses of psychology (Benjamin & Baker, 2004; Burman, 1994). One of the main goals of mental measurement was the classification of children in order to determine if they could be educated and subsequently, schooled so that they could become productive members of society. In the early history of the testing movement, the scientific faith in intelligence testing held the belief that it had the capacity to bring "tens of thousands of these high grade defectives under the surveillance and protection of society" and help decrease the "reproduction of feeble-mindedness and [would aid] in the elimination of an enormous amount of crime, pauperism, and industrial inefficiency" (Terman, 1916, cited in Donato, 1997, p. 24). Hundreds of comparative racial studies were produced in the United States claiming the intellectual superiority of the mythical white, middle class Anglo child while *scientifically proving* the inferiority of ethnic minority groups (Gonzalez, 1990). Eight studies were produced from 1920 to 1929 that specifically used (Mexican) American children as an object of study (cited in Valencia, Menchaca, & Donato, 2002, p. 86). These studies explicitly or implicitly attributed the low intellectual ability performance of these children to heredity. For instance, Garretson (1928) stated that (Mexican) American children were genetically inferior and that factors such as mobility patterns, irregular attendance, and linguistic differences contributed to their mental retardation (cited in Donato, 1997, p. 26). Other *scholars* such as Sheldon (1924) found that "Mexicans as a group possessed 85 percent of the intelligence of a similar group of White children" (cited in Donato,1997, p. 26). In summary, comparative studies from 1915 to 1950 that measured intellectual abilities and achievement consistently *found* that (Mexican) American children performed below the standard Anglo population (Gonzalez, 1990). Therefore, the early educational discourses that constructed (Mexican) Americans to an inferior intellectual position exhibited an otherness that projected cultural beliefs and practices based on the social eugenics ideologies and the scientific faith in measurement.

Contemporary educational discourses related to intellectual ability and testing continued in the second half of the twentieth century. These discourses shifted from inferior genetic ability to test fairness as related to the educational practices of overrepresentation in special education and underrepresentation in gifted education (e.g. Aloia, Maxwell, & Aloia, 1981; MacMillan, Gresham, Lopez, Bocian, 1996; Sacuzzo, Johnson, & Guertin, 1994). For example, Mercer (1973) examined unequal assessment practices resulting in a disproportional identification and placement of (Mexican) American children in special education classrooms for the mild retardation. In the early 1980s, a committee from the National Academy of Sciences confirmed earlier findings—a high percentage of minority students were placed in classrooms for the mentally retarded, trainable mentally retarded, and emotionally disturbed (Rueda, Artiles, Salazar, & Higareda, 2002). Government-funded research projects in California and Texas in the 1980s also found that children from Latino parents had a higher chance to be identified as disabled and that the referral and eligibility process to special education was influenced by limited English skills (Rueda et al. 2002).

Parallel to discourses of overrepresentation, educational research discourses also focused on test fairness. The most common objection to standardized testing argued against cultural test bias—for example, some researchers contended that cultural test bias stemmed from the experiential background of minority children that are "alien" (Rodriguez, 1989, p. 4) or "foreign" (Mishra, 1981b, p. 154) to the experiences of white, middle-class children. Other researchers contended test fairness from psychometric criteria: construct validity, predictive validity, factor analysis, item analysis, verbal loading saturation, and adequate norms. Some researchers argued that the test fairness should be challenged from construct and predictive ability since the existence of performance group differences (minority versus majority) jeopardized the placement and selection of minority groups (Mishra, 1983). From a practical perspective, educational discourses challenging standardized testing contended that traditional measures place too much emphasis on overall ability not on specific behaviors associated with academic tasks (Frontera & Horowitz, 1995) and that traditional testing does not account for second language acquisition process penalizing English language learners (e.g., Hansen, 1989; Beaumont, de Valenzuela, & Trumbull, 2002).

Related to the issue of test fairness in association to special education, contemporary research discourses on mental measurement also examined the issue of underrepresentation of minority children in gifted and talented education. These discourses proposed alternative conceptualizations of intelligence and methods of assessment for the identification and selection of minority children into gifted and talented programs. Some researchers support the theory of multiple intelligences as a reform to the concept of intelligence (e.g., Sarouphim, 2000) or the interpretation of cognitive styles as a more appropriate measure of ability (Kush, 1996). Still other researchers note cultural differences in the conceptualization of intelligence—parents and lay people define intelligence/giftedness by social emotional abilities in real life contexts while experts define intelligence based on traditional scholastic aptitude skills (e.g., Riojas-Clark & Gonzalez, 1998). In relation to methods of assessment, researchers propose information-processing analysis methods (Sacuzzo, Johnson, & Guertin, 1994), developmental approach based on Piagetan taks (Saito-Horgan, 1995), or a combination of qualitative and standardized measures (Gonzalez, 1994) as more unbiased methods for the identification of gifted minorities and the assessment of bilingual children.

In all, the educational discourse built from the cultural construct of intelligence creates and maintains the alterity (difference) of (Mexican) American children. The early roots of *scientific* mental measurement of (Mexican) American children project the colonial imagery of the Western, Anglo self as superior to other races. Within the historical social changes brought by the Civil Rights Movements as well as the litigation of minority groups in education, the discourse of ability measurement has transformed from characterizing (Mexican) Americans as inherently *less intelligent* to *mismeasured* subjects. The testing movement originally created to sort the feebleminded from the productive individuals was *found* to have a glitch in the system—it sorted a high percentage of (Mexican) Americans into the low end of the scale of intelligence. This glitch resulted in past and present legal cases as well as national and local struggles toward the fair testing of minority children. (Mexican) American children have been *mismeasured* and *misplaced* by the colonial establishments of the testing movement. This mismeasurement has led to *false negatives* in gifted and talented education and *false positives* in special education. Of course, to the children living the real consequences of the assessment systems (e.g., not being able to graduate for failing a state exam or being placed in inadequate instructional programs), the issue goes beyond the discursive. Furthermore, while other discourses created by the establishment of testing have not been exemplified in this section, the testing movement is well entrenched in the educational system with accountability structures for student achievement (No Child Left Behind Act) and testing companies that provide the tools to order, sort, and rank people and things. Thus, the representation of (Mexican) Americans in educational testing has been constructed from the Western *scientific faith* in measurement that adheres to the belief that "understanding is akin to measuring"(Smith, 2002, p. 42) and the practice of classifying students according to ability, academic, and emotional performance as well as English proficiency.

Shifting the Location of Blame and Change from the Child, to Culture, to Schools

In U.S. education, the issue of segregation has a long and complex history in the struggle for equal education for minority groups. During the twentieth century, (Mexican) American children *who attended public schooling* experienced educational segregation.[2] Early in the twentieth century, the segregation consisted of student placement into *Mexican classrooms* or entirely separate and unequal schools (Donato, 1997). For example, Texas had 122 segregated school districts within 59 counties that specifically had schools for (Mexican) American children (San Miguel, 2009). In the 1920s and 1930s, the issue of segregation of (Mexican) Americans became a topic of debate among scholars and students of education. Those that supported segregation argued that schools were ill prepared to provide an adequate instruction to children that did not speak English (Donato, 1997). Supporters of segregation also argued that limited or non-English students impeded the academic progress of Anglo children (Valencia, Menchaca, & Donato, 2002). Liberal educators supported segregation from the standpoint that the integration of (Mexican) Americans in the English classrooms could cause psychological damage—"as true believers, liberal teachers were convinced that ethnic integration created negative classroom environments and that it discouraged Mexican youth from staying in schools" (Donato, 1997, p. 14). Further, the Anglo public supported segregation because (Mexican) Americans were considered dishonest, immoral, and violent (Donato, 1997, p. 16). As an ethnic group, they were also characterized with low standards of cleanliness (San Miguel, 1987), as irresponsible, thriftless, sex conscious, and procrastinators (Maguire, 1938 cited in Donato, 1997). This type of oppressive othering of (Mexican) Americans was also held by educators as is mentioned below from a principal from Phoenix, Arizona:

> Much more classroom time should be spent teaching the [Mexican] children clean habits and positive attitudes towards others, public property, and their community in general....[The Mexican child] can be taught to repeat the Constitution forward and backward and still he steals cars, breaks windows, wrecks public recreational centers, etc., if he doesn't catch the idea of respect for human values and personalities. (Weinberg, 1977 cited in Gonzalez, 1990, p. 3).

In the interface of deculturalization programs (Spring, 2000), segregation was furthered justified by Americanization scholars who warned policymakers and educational reformers that increasing Spanish-speaking population presented a problem because they lacked educational ambition (Donato, 1997).

> A number of studies are available that point to the fact the educational status of the Mexican is low because of poor attendance, limited average grade completion, and frequent school failures. Some of this educational status may be explained in terms of high mobility, necessitated as transient workers, difficulties centering upon bilingualism, and perhaps a culture that values "living": rather than schooling (McDonaugh, 1949, cited in Donato, 1997, pp. 18–19).

This type of discourse classifying (Mexican) American students as culturally backward and linguistically deprived was held consistently by school officials with some supporting this classification from the mental, emotional, or language assessment practices (San Miguel, 2009). Not any different, state officials held the perception that (Mexican American) children needed to "correct cultural and linguistic deficiencies before mixing with their 'American' peers" (Donato, 1997, pp. 12–13).

In addition to the justification of segregation, the discourse on cultural deprivation also offered an explanation of the underachievement of (Mexican) Americans in U.S. education. The construct of cultural deprivation (also known as the culture of poverty theory) became a dominant framework in educational psychology shifting the balance from genetic inferiority to environmental determinism (Garcia & Wiese, 2002). Consequently, the location of blame for the undereducation of (Mexican) Americans shifted the emphasis from the individual to the culture and the community. By the

1960s, research about (Mexican) Americans typically included four research foci—the measurement of achievement within this group, the relationship of socioeconomic factors to achievement, the conditions associated with school failure, and curricular studies (Carter, 1970). The research literature typically ascribed (Mexican) American school failure to cultural factors. Particularly, the home culture was viewed as lacking educational tradition—it had few books, provided an improper diet, and lacked adequate motivation for the children to pursue educational career (Reissman, 1962, cited in Carter, 1970, p. 37). Further, the discourse of cultural deprivation was sustained by social practices aimed to counter the effects of poverty (e.g., Title I of the Elementary and Secondary Education Act) and compensate for such economic deficiencies.

> It is not inappropriate that the programs of special education for the disadvantaged have been described as compensatory. They are attempts to compensate for, to overcome, the effects of hostile, different, or indifferent backgrounds. Their aim is to bring children from these backgrounds up to the level where they can be reached by existing educational practices and it is in terms of this aim that we tend to judge their success or lack of it…The unexpressed purpose of the compensatory programs is to make disadvantaged children as much as possible like the kinds of children with whom the school has been [or perceives itself as] successful, and our standard of educational success is how well they approximate middle-class children in school performance (Gordon & Wilkerson, 1966, cited in Carter, 1970, p. 259).

Locating the deficits to the child and culture supported "adjust-the-child approaches" whose underlying goal was to transform "real" economic or "assumed" cultural deficiencies of (Mexican) Americans and other minority children (Carter, 1970, p. 259). Therefore, the otherness projected to (Mexican) Americans in early educational research discourses linked underachievement to perceived cultural deprivation and economic deficit but did not necessarily link such an underachievement to the deficits of educational systems or existing social inequalities. However, there were few voices in the educational discourse that examined the schooling experiences of (Mexican) Americans. In the early twentieth century, studies by Little (1944), Reynolds (1933), and Sanchez (1934, 1951) documented the inadequate schooling conditions of (Mexican) Americans (cited in Cortès, 1974). Later, also in the history of educational research, the educational system does come under scrutiny by some researchers shifting the educational discourses to a lesser focus on cultural deprivation. Nevertheless, the discourse of cultural factors and its relationship to (Mexican) American academic achievement continued to resonate in current educational research.

Recent educational discourses reinscribe the discourse of the achievement of (Mexican) American children to cultural factors. While contemporary discourses do not hold cultural factors to be the cause of academic failure, cultural factors are held as a source of variance in their academic success. Specifically, researchers consider family factors to exert a significant educational influence on children (e.g., Arzubiaga, Rueda, & Monzo, 2002; Delgago-Gaitan, 1992; Silverman, La Greca, & Wasserstein, 1995). According to this perspective, parents "are the child's first teacher" (Birch & Ferrin, 2002, p. 70) and the providers of early educational and social experiences (e.g., Cortese, 1982; Ortiz, 1993; Welsh, Doss, & Totusek, 1981). Research representing this type of discourse has *found* that Hispanic mothers with more education tend to promote more classroom behavior by stimulating in children conversational and inquiry strategies (Laosa, 1982 cited in Kush, 1996, p. 572). Therefore, the "intellectual disadvantage" observed in ethnic minorities can be explicated by the low parental level of education that in turn affects the parent–child teaching styles that "diverge from mainstream classroom practices" (Laosa, 1982 cited in Ortiz, 1993, p. 14). Research also links other parental behaviors to educational outcomes. For instance, (Mexican) American students with higher academic performance had parents that "spent time discussing their school activities" (Keith & Lichtman, 1994 cited in Hess & D'Amato, 1996, p. 355). Other educational research discusses parental involvement in school as a factor that contributes to student achievement (e.g., Okagaki & Frensch, 1998), the differences in Latino parent participation in school activities in comparison to white parents (e.g, Figueroa & Gallegos, 1980), or the different types of parent–school activities engaged in by Mexican American parents (e.g., Birch & Ferrin, 2002). Altogether, the discourses position the culture of parenting as an axis of representation in the education of (Mexican) American children.

Finding a location of change, the contemporary discourses of (Mexican) American children in education depart from solely locating the problem of undereducation to deficiencies within child and culture to include critiques of the educational system. These critiques include the teaching force, the curriculum, the quality of instruction, and cultural insensitivity. For example, Cardelle-Elawar (1990) *found* that Hispanic students do not receive instruction that supports higher order thinking skills resulting in learning handicap for students. Gutierrez (1992) also cited studies that *found* that minority students did not receive effective writing instruction. Similarly, Kuhlman et al. (1993) *found* that Spanish-speaking children received instruction that supported oral language development but not writing skills. In relation to the discourse on cultural sensitivity, Benjamin (1997) critiqued the school curriculum for disregarding (Mexican) American knowledge, language, and culture. Likewise, Moore (1988) argues that the formal and informal curriculum reinforces the dominance of the English language, the Anglo history, and its cultural norms. The critiques of teachers are based on the student–teacher interactions of minority students and white teachers or the instructional methods used by teachers to educate (Mexican) Americans. For example, Saito-Horgan (1995) critiques the mismatch of "developmentally appropriate" instruction given to (Mexican) American students as too abstract (p. 17). Other researchers discuss the low expectation of teachers toward minority students. Other critiques of teachers include the issues of multicultural education and claim that the teaching force is not trained adequately on student diversity or to teach language minority children (e.g., Rodriguez, 1981; Figueroa & Gallegos, 1980).

While contemporary research discourse critiques the educational system, researchers also offer utopian formulas to solve these educational deficiencies and *save* the (Mexican) American child. Researchers provide general suggestions to improve the quality of instruction—reduce class size; design greater individualization of instruction; stress content reading development for English language learners; or use concrete objects to teach science inquiry to language minorities. Researchers also discuss specific suggestions for classroom practices and environment with the underlying assumption that the classroom environment and practices can accelerate "the overall rate of academic development, especially in children divergent in socio-economic status (SES), achievement levels, and measured intelligence" (Arreaga-Mayer, Utley, Perdonomo-Rivera, & Greenwood, 2003, p. 30). Teacher improvement discourses include the professional development of teachers and administrators on issues surrounding student diversity (attitudes, resources, challenges, value systems, and learner variations). Recommendations also include discussions about parent and school collaboration. For example, Delgado-Gaitan (1992) and Arzubiaga et al. (2002) maintain that it is necessary for school systems to recognize the various ways (Mexican) American parents support their children's education so that collaboration and communication are effective. Baca, Bryan, McLean-Bardwell, and Gomez (1989) specifically recommend the establishment of educational programs for immigrant families that teach them the differences between Mexican and U.S. school systems. Overall, although recommendations to improve the quality of education exclude the voices of the affected and communities of schools, the discourses shift from emphasizing only the child as the source of academic failure to focusing on the educational system as an approach to change the outcomes of (Mexican) American children.

In summary, the early educational discourses othering (Mexican) American children constructed differences based on the *incompatibility* of children to the "American" school system. *Scientifically proven* that their intelligence was *not equal* to the white child, it was not fit to let them compete with their peers in the same classroom. Knowing that their character was immoral and their language un-American, (Mexican) American students had to be *separately* educated and reformed. Later, *finding* that the source of the problem for the undereducation of (Mexican) American children was cultural and economic, *change became a possibility*. Antipoverty interventions in schools could compensate for cultural and economic deficits. Nevertheless, while contemporary discourses no longer locate the blame of the undereducation of (Mexican) Americans to be inherent within child characteristics and home culture, the discourse of cultural incompatibility is sustained. Now reformation is necessary in the educational system—its teaching force, its curriculum, its quality of instruction, its cultural insensitivity, and its school-parent relationships—all to compensate for the (Mexican) American cultural and linguistic differences.

Does the (Mexican) American Child Speak English?

The issue of English language proficiency and bilingualism is both a historical and contemporary discourse in the education of (Mexican) American children that has strong social currents of politics, a legal history, and historical clashes in the struggle to an equal education and social justice. Historically, the colonial structures established by the deculturalization movements (Spring, 2000) devalued native languages of minority groups. This was reflected in the institutionalization of "No Spanish" rules in schools and in the belief that it was "un-American" to speak other native languages (Bernal, 1999, p. 80). In relation to early educational discourses, researchers adhered to the view that bilingualism represented a handicap, a detriment to cognitive development, and an obstacle to the education of (Mexican) American children (Carter, 1970, 1979).

> A large proportion of the investigators have concluded from their studies that bilingualism has a detrimental effect on intellectual functioning. The bilingual child is described as being hampered in his performance on intellectual tests in comparison with the monolingual child.[3] (Peal & Lambert, 1962 cited in Carter 1970, pp. 49–50)

Moreover, other studies such as the one conducted by the U.S. Commission on Civil Rights in 1975 concluded that the lack of English skills was the main reason for the failure of Chicano students (cited in Gandara, 1993, p. 139). Other studies challenged these scientific *findings* by refining the categorization of (Mexican) Americans in the research methodology. For example, Kimball (1968) and Lugo (1970) *found* no relationship between home language and the academic achievement of Mexican immigrant students (cited in Gandara, 1993, p. 139). Still, other studies *concluded* that there was a difference in the academic achievement of foreign and native-born (Mexican) Americans (e.g., Buriel, 1987; Valenzuela, 1999). Matute-Bianchi (1986) also *found* variability in the academic achievement of first-second-third generation minorities in the United States. Thus, as research constructs and methodologies have been modified, the discourses of difference have been fine-tuned to describe (Mexican) Americans children as a group.

Furthermore, contemporary educational discourses contextualizing the identity of (Mexican) American children continue to position language as a critical axis of representation and practice. Researchers regard language as an instrument of ethnic identification, social roles, and social cohesion. For instance, researchers regard language as a "means for entry into culture" (Weisskirch & Alva, 2002, p. 376) as well as a mechanism for social mobility (Stafford, Jenckes, & Santos, 1997). From a broader social perspective, other researchers discuss language as a form of historical and present oppression—the extermination of native languages in the U.S. educational system (e.g., Smith, 2002); the political push for all English (e.g., Baquedado-Lopez, 1997), and the inferior social status of native languages as experienced by minority students in schools (e.g., Stafford et al., 1997). Still other research discourses continue to link the role of language and thought to second language acquisition. Second language acquisition and cognitive functioning of bilingual students have been *found* to increase higher levels of cognitive ability, greater flexibility of thought/divergent thinking, and the development of metalinguistic and metacognitive skills. Moreover, there are other researchers that deemed second language acquisition in the curriculum as "perhaps one of the most important" aspects in the education of non-English speaking students (Escamilla, & Cogburn-Escamilla, 1980, p. 6). Research discourses also compare the development of reading and writing skills between English monolingual students and second language learners. For second language learners developing reading skills, background knowledge is *found* to be a highly significant educational factor given the dissonance between school and home culture (e.g., Beaumont et al., 2002; Langer, Bartolome, Vasquez & Lucas, 1990). Other researchers note that the development of reading and writing skills of second language learners is similar to "native speakers learning to write English" (Hudelson, 1984 cited in Kuhlman, Bastian, Bartalome, & Barrios, 1993, p. 6). Further, based on the *scientific* information on the development of reading skills of English language learners and the "mismatch between English difficulty and second language proficiency," some researchers recommend modification to reading instruction for these students (e.g., Langer et al., 1990, p. 428). These research samples exemplify the multiple functions language plays in the representation of (Mexican) American children that also highlight the colonial practice to compare the Other to *normalized students*—the English native.

Furthermore, discourses about (Mexican) American children not only include issues of language and academic achievement but also extend to a controversy about the provision of bilingual education. National attention to the issue of bilingual education surfaced when the Mexican American Education Study (MAES) conducted by the Civil Rights Commission (1972) found that in the Southwest states, few students were provided with adequate language instruction despite the fact that one in two first graders' needed bilingual education (cited in Valencia, 2002, p. 8). Consequently, the effectiveness of bilingual education research continued in the latter decades comparing monolingual programs and transitional programs (Zappert & Cruz, 1977; Troike, 1978; American Institutes for Research, 1978; Baker & Kanter, 1981; Willig, 1985; U.S. General Accounting Office, 1987; Ramirez, Yuen, Ramey, Pasta, 1990) yielding contradicting results and interpretations (cited in Cziko, 1992). On the other hand, studies conducted on programs that offered two-way (dual) bilingual education or the late-exit bilingual education (Ramirez et al., 1991; Rossell and Baker, 1996; Greene, 1997; Thomas and Collier, 1997; Salazar, 1998) provided support to the effectiveness of these types of bilingual programs (cited in Guerrero, 2002). Relevant to the postcolonial analysis is the position of controversy that (Mexican) American children's educability in the U.S. education system continues to depend on the provision of "meaningful and effective education" (Title VI, Civil Rights Act of 1964) and the provision to their special linguistic needs (Bilingual Acts of 1968 and 1974). Linguistic differences, therefore, also represent a problem to be solved.

In summary, any synopsis of the educational research discourses about (Mexican) American children and language delimit the complexity of the historical and current issues of social justice as well as the educational and linguistic rights of minority groups in the United States. Nonetheless, what can be concluded about the educational research discourses from this review is that linguistic differences constitute one of the primary axes of representation about (Mexican) American children. In addition, educational discourses maintain a comparative framework between non-English speakers and bilingual children, idealizing the *normal student*—the English native speaker proficient in expression and skill. The discourse of the (Mexican) American child learning to become proficient in English or not being proficient in English in research obscures the history of colonization and deculturalization where indigenous tribes and minority group cultures and languages were oppressed (Spring, 2000). Furthermore, the controversy and debates on the effectiveness of bilingual education silence global multilingual and multicultural perspectives in education (United Nations Educational Scientific and Cultural Organization, 2003). Thus, these educational discourses reflect a cultural projection limited to its geopolitical space and ethnocentric perspectives.

The Colonial Structures of Research Discourses

The discussed discourses exemplify an underlying colonial discourse present in educational research. The colonial discourse is characterized by the mechanism of reaffirming difference and simultaneously positioning others within a superior/inferior configuration. Early educational discourses explicitly affirmed the difference in the intellectual ability of (Mexican) American children while contemporary discourses reaffirmed the difference in how they are measured and classified in the multiple assessment systems. Discourses about cultural diversity also reinforced a construed distinction between civilized/uncivilized and educable/noneducable. *Scientific* discourses about the source of the (Mexican) American child's underachievement viewed the home environment and parental characteristics as less than optimal for the promotion of academic success as opposed to the white, middle class culture. Furthermore, the issue of linguistic diversity in educational discourses represented and represents the axis of the educability of (Mexican) American children. If they do not speak English it is an educational barrier. If they can speak English they can be educated. Thus, regardless of the axis of representation, whether it is language or culture, the discourses sustain the incompatibility of (Mexican) American children to the educational system.

The colonial discourse is also characterized by ordering and positioning Others within a superior/inferior axis. The intellectual inferiority and cultural deprivation ascribed to minorities are infamous. Of interest are the mechanisms that position minorities to inferior or worse positions. The mechanisms in research and education are reflected by the tools that order people and things. The tools can be educational practices such as the assessment systems or conceptual or theoretical constructs that delimit the postcolonial subjectivity of children. The constructs such as intelligence, theories of poverty, gifted and talented, and so on, *ascribe* people and cultures with substandard performance or values given their inherent comparative structures (e.g., psychometric theories). Other ordering tools exemplified in the discourse are the categorization and classification of people, cultures, and things. In research, this is illustrated by refining the techniques of categorization and classification (e.g., academic achievement by socioeconomic levels) while discursively *ignoring* the social inequalities or structures that may promote such hierarchies or differences.

Furthermore, the exemplified educational research discourses are implicated with the colonial structures of surveillance. The Western gaze is reflected in the discourses where the (Mexican)

American child is depicted, judged, categorized, classified, ordered, and positioned by constructs, theories, or practices meant to change, reform, and save. Discourses positioning the non-English child within the controversial debates on what are the most effective methods to educate them *dismiss* the issue that educational practices are not objective or rational processes. Schools are cultures of power and hierarchy. Furthermore, discourses on the reformation of schools or educational practices *displace* the power of children, parents, teachers, and communities for *change* to the expert—the researcher, policymaker, educator, or government. Thus, self-determination to define reality and bring change is not existent in these discourses.

The otherness of (Mexican) children constructed by educational discourses is not only about the constellation of representations and the mechanisms of othering in the colonial discourse. It also entails the configuration of culture, power, and knowledge where the researcher has the privilege to conceptualize, define, and write about the Other's reality. Thus, production of knowledge inherently provides the author/researcher with a power that is practiced on the researched (internal *will to knowledge*). At the personal level, research discourses project the researcher's own cultural imagery as she/he makes the decision about what to research, when, and how to research. In turn, the researcher partakes in the power-knowledge configurations at the respective sites of power (e.g., peer reviewed journals, the university, or research institute) that determine what is considered legitimate and valid research (external *will to truth*). This legitimized research endeavors then become part of the broader discursive formations and the bodies of *legitimized* knowledge at the exclusion of alternatives or non-Western possibilities.

In summary, the constructions of (Mexican) American children in educational discourses (re)create multiple axes of representation and subjectivities that have colonial structures. These colonial structures reproduce differences through mechanisms of oppressive othering and comparative frames of reference in relation to the dominant culture. The reproduction of difference does not mean that the (Mexican) child is "essentially an idea, or a creation with no corresponding reality" (Said, 1978, p. 5). There are children learning a second language, children living in poverty, and children not receiving meaningful and effective instruction in public education that are of Mexican ancestry. The intention is to expose the underlying colonial structure that produces differences based on a constant postcolonial subjectivity that is less than, behind, below the standards and values created by the dominant Western culture. Thus, research practice is a modern apparatus that reestablishes a colonial relationship where the minority child is observed, measured, judged, depicted, and classified under a Western imagery of constructs, theories, and writing. Lastly, modern research reflects colonial structures when it disempowers the researched voice, silences other forms of knowledge, and does not allow for self-determination.

Possibilities of Decolonization in Educational Research

It is not unexpected that construction of the alterity of (Mexican) American children holds a Western vision of science and education considering that most research is produced from universities—a colonial institution (Smith, 2002). After all, these Western imageries of science reflect particular ontological, epistemological, and methodological paradigms where the production of knowledge is culturally, socially, and politically situated (the matrix of power, knowledge, and culture). Furthermore, the foundations of educational research have been produced mostly from a white male research perspective and from the science models of medicine and psychology[4] (Benjamin & Baker, 2004; Condliffe Lagemann, 2000). The critical issues are the oppressive othering, the comparative framework, the hierarchies, the imposition of Western theories to explain and classify minority groups, the privilege to write about the postcolonial subject through the most *Enlightened constructs*, and the ethnocentrism that delimits other possibilities in the imagery of science (research practice) and the production of knowledge. While problematic issues reside in the practice of modern research, this essay does not propose that research is a futile enterprise. It attempts to bring light to its colonial vestiges and opens a critical space to reflect about other research possibilities that might reflect a critical, global, multicultural perspective to research that encompasses social justice and children. Most importantly, it advocates for a continued process of decolonization to dismantle Western narratives about the Other—the (Mexican) American child. The process of decolonization can occur at many possible levels—the researcher, university, academic fields, organizations, the media, government, and other social institutions involved in the production and consumption of research/knowledge/information.

From the researcher perspective, decolonization may start with the understanding of the historical formations of the scientific enterprise as a Western, modern practice that has colonial structures and preconceptual elements of classification, hierarchy, patriarchy, and racism (Rivas, 2005; Smith, 2002). The decolonization of the researcher's imagery may entail a study or deconstruction of the formations of the particular academic field of study and its normative assumptions, constructs, conceptualizations, and theories. Decolonization within the researcher may involve introspection about one's philosophical views, culture, and scientific imagery as a product of university training and life experiences—not a position of truth. Furthermore, decolonization also may evolve from one's own social construction outside of the university. As a (Mexican) American, I decolonized my cultural imagery as a mestiza (a colonial definition) to understand my indigenous roots and begin to learn about my ancestor's knowledge, knowledge not taught in the U.S. schools and universities. Thus, research is not about discovering but uncovering the self as a scholar.

Decolonization may also involve the consideration of relationship between the researcher and the researched as a position of power and privilege. This privilege of writing, conceptualizing, and determining a research agenda can be a joint democratic project with the people and communities involved (Smith, 2002). Decolonization in modern research includes the critical questions of who will benefit from such research projects, who is silenced, what knowledge systems are included or excluded (Cannella, 1997; McGovern, 1999). In addition, decolonization is also possible within the governing bodies (i.e., IRB; journal editors and reviewers, research institutions) that determine the "right" type of knowledge that should be produced by scientists. Opening critical spaces and accepting diverse ways of knowing reflect a decolonized scholarship. Most importantly, the decolonization of modern research is setting its purpose beyond the building of bodies of knowledge and using knowledge for social justice,

Knowledge that does not go beyond contemplating the world and observing it objectively without transcending given social conditions merely affirms what already exists. (McLaren, 2003, p. 197) Decolonization is about the courage to take a critical stand to the causes of social justice, equality, and respect for people and the environments.

Notes

1. The parentheses denote the geopolitical shift and fluid subjectivity of children from Mexican descent that come from families that lived in the United States prior to the U.S. colonization, U.S.-born children of immigrants,

migrants, and undocumented parents, recent immigrants, or children of Mexican indigenous descent.
2. A small percent of (Mexican) American children attended public schools in the first half of the twentieth century. The issue of educational access was more pronounced in this time period (San Miguel, 2009).
3. Peal and Lambert (1962) critiqued these studies based on the methodological problems in the conceptualization of pseudobilinguals and true bilingual children (cited in in Diaz, 1990, p. 93).
4. The field of psychology itself attempted to gain academic status as a *true science* through the medical model of science (Benjamin & Baker, 2004). Moreover, education was later influenced by these and other uprising academic fields (Condliffe Lagemann, 2000).

References

Acuña, R. (2000). *Occupied America: A history of Chicanos* (4th ed.). New York: Longman.

Aloia, G., Maxwell, J.A., & Aloia, S.D. (1981). Influence of child's race and EMR label on initial impressions of regular-classroom teachers. *American Journal of Mental Deficiency, 85*(6), 619–623.

Apple, M.W. (1990). *Ideology and curriculum.* New York: Routledge.

Arreaga-Mayer, C., Utley, C.A., Perdonomo-Rivera, C., & Greenwood, C.R. (2003). Ecobehavioral assessment of instructional contexts in bilingual special education programs for English language learners at risk for developmental disabilities. *Focus on Autism and Other Developmental Disabilities, 16* (1), 28–40.

Arzubiaga, A., Rueda, R., & Monzo, L. (2002). Family matters related to reading engagement of Latino children. *Journal of Latinos and Education, 1*(4) 231–243.

Ashcroft, B., Griffiths, G., & Tiffin, H. (2000). *Postcolonial studies: Key concepts.* London: Routledge.

Ashcroft, B., Griffiths, G., & Tiffin, H. (2001). *The empire writes back: Theory and practice in post-colonial literatures* (2nd ed.). New York: Routledge.

Baca, R., Bryan, D., McLean-Bardwell, C. & Gomez, F. (1989). Mexican immigration and the port-of-entry school. *International Migration Review, 23* (1), 3–23.

Baquedado-Lopez, P. (1997). Creating social identities through "Doctrina" narratives. *Issues in Applied Linguistics, 8* (1), 27–45.

Bauman, E. (1998). Redressing colonial discourse: Postcolonial theory and the humanist project. *Critical Quarterly, 40*(1), 79–89.

Beaumont, C., de Valenzuela, J.S., & Trumbull, E. (2002). Alternative assessment for transitional readers. *Bilingual Research Journal, 26*(2), 241–268.

Benjamin, R. (1997). *Si hablas espanol eres mojado* (if you speak Spanish you are a wetback): Spanish as an identity marker in the lives of Mexicano children. *Social Justice, 24*(2), 26–44.

Benjamin, L.T. & Baker, D.B. (2004). *From séance to science: A history of the professions of psychology in America.* Belmont, CA: Thomson & Wadsworth Learning.

Bernal, D. D. (1999). Chicana/o education from Civil Rights era to the present. In J. F. Moreno (Ed.) *The elusive quest for equality: 150 years of Chicano/a education* (pp. 77–108). Cambridge, MA: Harvard Educational Review.

Bhabha, H.K. (1994). *The location of culture.* New York: Routledge.

Birch, T.C., & Ferrin, S.E. (2002). Mexican American parental participation in public education in an isolated Rocky Mountain rural community. *Equity & Excellence, 31*(1), 70–78.

Buriel, R. (1987). *Academic performance of foreign-and native-born Mexican Americans: A comparison of first-, second-, and third generation students and parents.* Report to the Inter-University Program for Latino Research, Social Science Research Council.

Burman, E. (1994). *Deconstructing developmental psychology.* New York: Routledge.

Cannella, G.S. (1997). *Deconstructing early childhood education: Social justice and revolution.* New York: Peter Lang.

Cardelle-Elawar, M. (1990). Effects of feedback tailored to bilingual students' mathematics needs on verbal problem solving. *The Elementary School Journal, 91*(2), 165–175.

Carter, T. P. (1970). *Mexican Americans in school: A history of educational neglect.* New York: College Entrance Examination Board.

Carter, T. P. (1979). *Mexican Americans in school: A decade of change.* New York: College Entrance Examination Board.

Clifford, J. & Marcus, G.E. (Eds). (1986). *Writing culture: The poetics and politics of ethnography.* Los Angeles, CA: University of California Press.

Condliffe Lagemann, E. (2000). *An elusive science: The troubling history of education research.* Chicago, IL: University of Chicago Press.

Cortès, C. E. (1974). *Education and the Mexican American.* New York: Arno Press.

Cortese, A. (1982). Moral development in Chicano and Anglo children. *Hispanic Journal of Behavioral Sciences, 4*(3), 353–366.

Cziko, G.A. (1992). The evaluation of bilingual education: From necessity and probability to possibility. *Educational Researcher, 21*, 10–15.

Delgado-Gaitan, C. (1992). School matters in the Mexican-American home: socializing children to education. *American Educational Research Journal, 29*(3), 495–513.

Diaz, R. M. (1990). Bilingualism and cognitive ability: Theory, research, and controversy. In A. Barona & E.E. Garcia, (Eds.) *Children at risk: Poverty, minority status, and other issues in educational equity* (pp. 91–99). Washington, DC: National Association of School Psychologists.

Donato, R. (1997). *The other struggle for equal schools: Mexican Americans during the Civil Rights era.* Albany, NY: State University of New York Press.

Escamilla, M., & Cogburn-Escamilla, K. (1980). A comparison of English and Spanish syntactic language development in young Spanish speaking Mexican-American in maintenance bilingual-bicultural, and pull-out ESL programs. Paper presented at the 5th Annual Conference on Language Development (Boston, MA, 1980).

Fanon, F. (1963). *The wretched of the earth.* New York: Grove Press.

Fanon, F. (1967). *Black skins, white masks.* New York: Grove Press.

Figueroa, R. & Gallegos, E.A. (1980). Ethnic differences in school behavior. *Bilingual Education Paper Series, 3*(7). California State University, Los Angeles, CA. National Dissemination and Assessment Center.

Foucault, M. (1970). *The order of things: An archeology of the human sciences.* New York: Random House Inc.

Foucault, M. (1972). *The archeology of knowledge & the discourse on language.* New York: Pantheon.

Fox-Genovese, E. (1999). Ideologies and realities. *Orbis, 43(4)*, 531–539.

Frontera, L.S. & Horowitz, R. (1995). Reading and study behaviors of fourth-grade Hispanics: Can teachers assess risks? *Hispanic Journal of Educational Sciences, 17*(1), 100–120.

Gall, M.D., Borg, W.R., & Gall, J.P. (1996). *Educational Research: an introduction* (6th ed.). White Plains, NY: Longman.

Gandara, P. (1993). Language and ethnicity as factors in school failure: the case of Mexican-Americans. In R. Wollons (Ed.). *Children at risk in America: History, concepts, and public policy* (chap. 8). Albany, NY: State University of New York Press.

Garcia, E. E. & Wiese, A. (2002). Language, public policy, and schooling: a focus on Chicano English language learners. In R.R. Valencia (Ed.) *Chicano school failure and success: Past, present, and future* (pp. 149–169). New York: Routledge Falmer.

Gonzalez, G. G. (1990). *Chicano education in the era of segregation.* Cranbury, NJ: Associated University Press.

Gonzalez, V. (1994). A model of cognitive, cultural, and linguistic variables affecting bilingual Hispanic children's development of concepts and language. *Hispanic Journal of Behavioral Sciences, 16*(4), 396–421.

Greenberg, S. (2003). Chosenness. *Politics and policy archive.* Retrieved on March, 2003, from http://www.clal.org/pp44.html.

Guerrero, M.D. (2002). Research in bilingual education: moving beyond the effectiveness debate. In R.R. Valencia (Ed.) *Chicano school failure and success: Past, present, and future* (pp. 170–191). New York: RoutledgeFalmer.

Guha, R. & Spivak, G.C. (1988). *Selected subaltern studies.* New York: Oxford University Press.

Gutierrez, K.D. (1992). A comparison of instructional contexts in writing process classrooms with Latino children. *Education and Urban Society, 24*(2), 244–262.

Haan, N., Bellah, R.N., Rabinow, P., & Sullivan, W.M. (1983). *Social science as moral inquiry.* New York: Columbia University Press.

Hallam, E. & Street, B.V. (Eds). (2000). *Cultural encounters: Representing 'Otherness.'* New York: Routledge.

Hansen, D.A. (1989). Locating learning: Second language gains and language use in family, peer, and classroom context. *NABE: The Journal for the National Association for Bilingual Education, 12*(2), 161–180.

Harding, S.G. (1998). *Is science multicultural? Postcolonialisms, feminisms, and epistemologies.* Bloomington, IN: Indiana University Press.

Hess, R.S. & D'Amato, R.C. (1996). High school completion among Mexican-American children: Individual and family background variables. *School Psychology Quarterly, 11*(4), 353–368.

Kavita, P. (1998). English mud: Towards a critical cultural studies of colonial science. *Cultural Studies, 12*(3), 300–331.

Kendall, G., & Wickham, G. (1999). *Using Foucault's methods.* Thousand Oaks, CA: Sage Publications.

Kincheloe, J.L. & McLaren, P. (1994). Rethinking critical theory and qualitative research. In Denzin, N. & Lincoln, Y. (Eds.). *Handbook of qualitative research* (pp. 138–157). Thousand Oaks, CA: Sage.

Kuhlman, N.A., Bastian, M., Bartalome, L., & Barrios, M. (1993). Emerging literacy in a two-way bilingual first grade classroom. Proceedings from the National Association Bilingual Education Conferences (Tucson, AZ, 1990; Washington, DC, 1991).

Kuhn, T. S. (1996). *The structure of scientific revolutions* (3rd ed.). Chicago, IL: University of Chicago Press.

Kush, J.C. (1996). Field-dependence, cognitive ability, and academic achievement in Anglo-American and Mexican American students. *Journal of Cross-Cultural Psychology, 27*(5), 561–575.

Langer, J.A., Bartolome, L., Vasquez, O., & Lucas, T. (1990). Meaning construction in school literacy tasks: A study of bilingual students. *American Educational Research Journal, 27*(3), 427–471.

Little, W. (1944). Spanish speaking children in Texas. In C. E. Cortès, (Ed.) (1974). *Education and the Mexican American.* New York: Arno Press.

Loomba, A. (1998). *Colonialism/Postcolonialism.* New York: Routledge. Machida, S. (1986). Teacher accuracy in decoding non-verbal indications of comprehension and noncomprehension in Anglo-and Mexican-American children. *Journal of Educational Psychology, 78* (6), 454–464.

MacMillan, D.L., Gresham, F.M., Lopez, M.L., Bocian, K.M. (1996). Comparison of students nominated for pre-referral interventions by ethnicity and gender. *The Journal of Special Education, 30*(2), 133–151.

MacNaughton, G. (2005). *Doing Foucault in early childhood studies: Applying post-structural ideas.* London: Routledge.

Manuel, T. H. (1930). The education of Mexican and Spanish-speaking children in Texas. In C.E. Cortes (Ed.) *The Mexican American* (1974). New York: Arno Press.

Matute-Bianchi, M.E. (1986). Ethnic identities and patterns of school success and failure among Mexican-descent and Japanese Americans in a California high school: An ethnographic analysis. *American Journal of Education,* 233–255.

Mc Govern, S. (1999). *Education, modern development, and indigenous knowledge: An analysis of academic knowledge production.* New York: Garland Pub.

McLaren, P. (2003). *Life in schools: An introduction to critical pedagogy in the foundations of education* (4th ed.). Boston, MA: Pearson Education, Inc.

Memmi, A. (1965). *The colonizer and the colonized.* Translation by H. Greenfield. Boston, MA: Beacon Press.

Mishra, S.P. (1981). Factor analysis of the McCarthy Scales for groups of white and Mexican-American children. *Journal of School Psychology, 19*(2), 178–182.

Mishra, S.P. (1983). Validity of WISC-R IQs and factor scores in predicting achievement for Mexican-American children. *Psychology in the Schools, 20*(4), 442–44.

Moore, H.A. (1988). Effects of gender, ethnicity, and school equity on students' leadership behaviors in a group game. *The Elementary School Journal, 88*(5), 515–527.

Nandy, A. (1983). *The intimate enemy: Loss and recovery of self under colonialism.* Oxford: Oxford University Press.

Okagaki, L. & Frensch, P.A. (1998). Parenting and children's school achievement: A multiethnic perspective. *American Educational Research Journal, 35*(1), 123–144.

Ortiz, R. W. (1993). Unpacking the effects of generation and SES on early literacy practices of Mexican American fathers. Paper presented at the Annual Meeting of the American Educational Research Association (Atlanta, GA, 1993).

Reynolds, A. (1933). The education of Spanish-speaking children in five Southwestern states. Washington, DC (U.S. Department of the Interior Bulletin 1933, No. 11). In C. E. Cortes (Ed.) *The Mexican American* (1974). New

York: Arno Press.

Riojas-Clark, E. & Gonzalez, V. (1998). Voices and voces: Cultural and linguistic dimensions of giftedness. *Educational Horizons, 7* (1), 41–47.

Rivas, A. (2005). *Postcolonial analysis of educational research discourse: Creating (Mexican) Americans as the Other.* Dissertation from A & M University, Texas.

Rodriguez, R.F. (1989). The effects of sociocultural factors on the achievement of minority children. In *Education and the changing rural community: Anticipating the 21st century.* Proceedings of the 1989 ACRES/NRSSC Symposium. RC 017 257.

Rodriguez, R.J. (1981). A longitudinal study of bilingual English syntax. *Aztlan—International Journal of Chicano Studies Research, 12*(1), 75–87.

Rueda, R., Artiles, A.J., Salazar, J. & Higareda, I. (2002). An analysis of special education as a response to the diminished academic achievement of Chicano/Latino students: An update. In R. R. Valencia (Ed.) *Chicano school failure and success: Past, present, and future* (pp. 310–332). New York: RoutledgeFalmer.

Sacuzzo, D.P., Johnson, N.E., & Guertin, T.L. (1994). Information-processing in gifted versus non-gifted African-American, Latino, Filipino, and white children: Speeded versus non-speeded paradigms. ERIC Document Reproduction Service No. ED 368 099.

Said, E. (1978). *Orientalism.* New York: Random House Inc.

Saito-Horgan, N. (1995). Rates of cognitive development among bilingual Latino children. Paper presented at the Annual Meeting of the American Educational Research Association (San Francisco, CA, 1995).

Salvatore (1996). North American travel narratives and the ordering/othering of South America (1810–1860). *Journal of Historical Sociology, 9*(1), 85–110.

Sanchez, G. I. (1934). The education of bilinguals in a state school system. In C. E. Cortès, (1974). *Education and the Mexican American.* New York: Arno Press.

Sanchez, G. I. (1951). Concerning segregation of Spanish-speaking children in the public schools. In C.E. Cortès (Ed.) (1974). *Education and the Mexican American.* New York: Arno Press.

San Miguel, G. (1987). *"Let all of them take heed": Mexican Americans and the campaign for educational equality in Texas, 1910–1981.* Austin, TX: University of Texas Press.

San Miguel, G. (2009). Mexican Americans and Education. The online handbook of Texas. Retrieved January 12, 2009: http://www.tshaonline.org/handbook/online/articles/MM/khmmx.html.

Sarouphim, K.M. (2000). Use of the DISCOVER Assessment for identification purposes: Concurrent validity and gender issues. Paper presented at the Annual Meeting of the American Educational Research Association (New Orleans, LA).

Schwalbe, M., Goodwin, S., Holden, D., Schrock, D., Thompson, S., & Wolkomir, M. (2000). Generic processes in the reproduction of inequality: An interactionist analysis. *Social Forces, 79* (2), 419–453.

Silverman, W.K., La Greca, A.M., & Wasserstein, S. (1995). What do children worry about? Worries and their relation to anxiety. *Child Development, 66,* 671–686.

Simpson, C. (Ed). (1998). *Universities and empire: Money and politics in the social sciences during the cold war.* New York: The New York Press.

Smith, L. T. (2002). *Decolonizing methodologies: Research and indigenous peoples.* New York: Zed Books Ltd.

Spring, J. H. (2000). *Deculturalization and the struggle for equality: A brief history of the education of dominated cultures in the United States.* Boston, MA: McGraw-Hill.

Spring, J.H. (2004). *The intersection of cultures: Multicultural education in the United States and the global economy.* Boston, MA: McGraw-Hill.

Stafford, M.E., Jenckes, L.B., & Santos, S.L. (1997). Hispanic children's recognition of languages and perceptions about speakers of Spanish, English, and Chinese. *Bilingual Research Journal, 21*(2 &3), 255–271.

Stanfield, J.H. (1994). Ethnic modeling in qualitative research. In N.K. Denzin & Y. S. Lincoln (Eds.) *Handbook of qualitative research* (pp. 175–188). Thousand Oaks, CA: Sage.

Steinberg, S.R. & Kincheloe (1997). *Kinderculture: The corporate construction of childhood.* Boulder, CO: Westview Press.

United Nations Educational Scientific and Cultural Organization NESCO (2003). Education in a multilingual world. Paris, France: United Nations.

Valencia, R. R. (2002). The plight of Chicano students: An overview of schooling conditions and outcomes. In R.R. Valencia (Ed.), *Chicano school failure and success: Past, present, and future* (pp. 3–51). New York: Routledge Falmer.

Valencia, R. R., Menchaca, M., & Donato, R. (2002). Segregation, desegregation, and integration of Chicano students: Old and new realities. In R.R. Valencia (Ed.), *Chicano school failure and success: Past, present, and future* (pp. 70–113). New York: Routledge Falmer.

Valenzuela, A. (1999). *Subtractive schooling: U.S. Mexican youth and the politics of caring.* Albany, NY: State University of New York Press.

Viruru, R. (2001). *Early childhood education: Postcolonial perspectives from India.* New Delhi; Thousand Oaks, CA: Sage Publications.

Weisskirch, R.S., & Alva, S.A. (2002). Language brokering and the acculturation of Latino children. *Hispanic Journal of Behavioral Sciences, 24*(3), 369–378.

Welsh, D.J., Doss, D.A., & Totusek, P. (1981). Title I parents as compensatory reading instructors: Is there no place like home? Publication No. 80.58. Paper presented at the Annual Meeting of the American Educational Research Association (Los Angeles, CA, 1981).

Young, R. J. C. (2001). *Postcolonialism: An historical introduction.* Malden, MA: Blackwell Publishers.

CHAPTER SEVENTEEN

The Ambivalence of Citizenship in Early Childhood Education

Antiracist, Transnational Feminist, and Postcolonial Contributions

VERONICA PACINI-KETCHABAW AND RADHIKA VIRURU

Abstract

Using antiracist, transnational feminist, and postcolonial critiques of citizenship, the chapter argues that existing discussions on citizenship in early childhood need to be expanded to integrate connections to histories of racialization, citizen–subject formation, gender, and colonialism. We ask: What does it mean to speak of citizenship in the age of Empire? Is speaking of citizenship part of the process of the creation of Empire? Given that many surveys of young people in "established" democracies show an increasing disenchantment with the concept of citizenship, why should it continue to be important in early childhood education? The chapter shows that the concept of citizenship, as it is mostly presently defined, belongs mostly not only to Euro-Western ways of viewing the world but also to frameworks that seem somewhat outdated in a world where citizenship for many is no longer moored to principles like belonging and loyalty. The transnational nature of participation in the world does not fit within traditional definitions of what citizenship is. In light of all of these observations, we raise the questions of whether or not discussions of citizenship belong in early childhood. Does centering on this concept close the door on other meaningful discussions and silence other voices? What meanings do the notions of multilayered and flexible citizenships hold in early childhood discourses? Are children subaltern-citizens?

> It is important that our analysis of citizenship specify the situated nature of enunciations in a field of space–time interrelationships without relying on a telos of predetermined inevitability. The situated entanglements of geopolitics, market logic, exceptions, and ethical discourses require a conceptual openness to contingency, ambivalence, and uncertain outcomes. (Ong, 2006, p. 18)

The main argument of this chapter is that existing discussions on citizenship in early childhood need to be expanded to integrate connections to histories of racialization, citizen-subject formation, gender, and colonialism. We present our arguments with the hopes that they instigate future discussions on early childhood research, pedagogical and policy discourses, and to further the process of what Dietz (2003) has described as becoming "less unthinkingly Western and more thoughtfully Western, more global, more comparative, and more democratic in its efforts to grasp the complexities of human cultures, social orders, and practices as it addresses [children] in the world" (p. 400). Hardt and Negri (2000) have suggested that, right in front of our eyes, new forms of Empire are constantly being created. Therefore, we ask, what does it mean to speak of citizenship in the age of Empire? Is speaking of citizenship part of the process of the creation of Empire? Given that many surveys of young people in "established" democracies show an increasing disenchantment with the concept of citizenship, why should it continue to be important in early childhood education?

We use antiracist, transnational feminist, and postcolonial critiques of citizenship to argue for the expansion of discourses on citizenship regarding young children. Postcolonial scholars, for example, have argued that citizenship as a construct reflects mostly Euro-Western perspectives on what it means to be a citizen. The limitations of this concept are all the more problematic in a world where citizenship has started to become less of an expression of belonging or loyalty and more of an assertion of the ability to participate in labor markets (Ong, 1999, 2006). To further complicate the picture, other scholars (Hardt & Negri, 2000) have suggested that in an age of Empire, nation states are no longer an extremely significant part of the apparatus of the Empire; on the contrary, it is through the process of deterritorializing and decentering, that the globe comes within its realm. Other scholars, however, have focused on the role of boundaries in the creation of citizenship(s): just as there are theoretical boundaries, that have excluded or denied recognition to non-Western perspectives in defining what citizenship is, those from the non-West have also had to face the physical boundaries created by discourses of citizenship. Postcolonial scholarship highlights how both the physical and theoretical boundaries have become spaces for transgression and transnationalisms. Recent work has also discussed the concept of subaltern-citizenship: how is citizenship redefined when subalterns become citizens? In this chapter, we explore how such perspectives can help redefine/reconstruct citizenship in early childhood contexts.

The literature on citizenship is quite extensive, multifaceted, and contentious, and this chapter does not intend to either provide a detailed review of what the arguments in the literature are nor to "solve" those arguments. Rather, we propose to bring "stutters" into ongoing conversations around citizenship and young children. We begin with a brief review of the theorizing currently underway in early childhood education regarding citizenship. We focus on how citizenship has been conceptualized from a participatory perspective. Next, we address some of the limitations of liberal discourses of citizenship participation that are prevalent in early childhood. The last two sections of the chapter propose that antiracist, transnational feminist, and postcolonial perspectives on citizenship could add valuable insights into early childhood discussions on citizenship.

Theorizing Citizenship in Early Childhood

Within the early childhood education literature, citizenship is presented in relation to participation, listening to children's voices, and involving children in decision-making processes (Millei, 2008). Children are increasingly being perceived as highly capable beings who are more able to participate as citizens than ever before. They are also seen as active agents of their own environments and therefore as active contributors to their own positioning as citizens. These discussions come as an interesting juxtaposition to other scholarship on citizenship, which focuses on the trend toward declining civic engagement (Dahlgren, 2007) and the idea that Western democracy is in trouble, as adults seem less inclined to participate in society and to vote. Suggested reasons for this disengagement include the institutionalized nature of modern democracies; a widening gap between citizens and their elected representatives and the expanding role of the corporate sector in making decisions that impact people's lives (Putnam, 2000; Bennett, 2007; Dahlgren, 2007; Hasebrink & Paus-Hasebrink, 2007). According to Bennett (2007), the generation commonly known as the Millennials (approximately those turning 21 around the year 2000) or the "dotnets" (a term used more in the United States than in Europe, but referring approximately to the same demographic) are disinterested in traditional models of politics, preferring to exhibit civic participation through engagement in activism around specific issues, "political consumerism and protest activities" (Keefer et al., 2002). It should be pointed out that the recent U.S. presidential election was seen as representing a significant change in this trend, as many more younger voters participated than in the past (Dahl, 2008).

Another relevant body of knowledge on children and citizenship emerges from citizenship studies. Although this body of knowledge does not claim to necessarily focus on young children, it is worth reviewing as it helps to contextualize the literature on citizenship in the early years. The main concerns within the literature on citizenship and children are how children can be accommodated in definitions of adult citizenship, and how to develop child-sensitive conceptualizations and practices of citizenship. Citizenship is often conceptualized and put into practice in relation to children's membership to a community; participation rights ("the right of participation in decision-making in social, cultural and political life"); contributions that children make to society (e.g., helping, being a good neighbor); and their status, respect, and recognition in society (Lister, 2008, p. 10). Lister (2008) argues:

> Much of the literature that is making the case for recognition of children as citizens is not so much arguing for an extension of adult rights (and obligations) of citizenship to children but recognition that their citizenship practice (where it occurs) constitutes them as de facto, even if not complete de jure, citizens. It is also calling for adults to transform their relationship to children particularly in terms of respectful behaviour and changes in the way participatory citizenship is practiced in order to accommodate children. (p. 18)

Another important strand of this body of work links children's citizenship with the UN Convention on the Rights of the Child. In particular, citizenship scholars like Stasiulis (2002) engage in discussions regarding the way in which governments respect children's rights to citizenship. In her well-cited article she says:

> While it is now commonplace for adult politicians and advocates for children's rights to parrot aphorisms such as "children are now social actors, subjects in their own right, and active citizens, merely than objects of adult concern and intervention," this view is not borne out in Canadian formal policies or governance practices. The rhetoric about the "future potential" of children and youth "conceals a more fundamental set of closed-mind attitudes that acts as a barrier to young people who want to get involved in civic life and contribute to policy-making. (p. 531)

Stasiulis (2002) continues to propose that "in order to understand the directions that active children's citizenship might take, it is instructive to listen to children's voices and to see how children are doing it for themselves" (p. 532).

Although we appreciate the contributions of these strength-based approaches to citizenship, we are cautious about the implications of these one-sided solutions to the integration of children into "adult worlds." In order to substantiate our argument, we begin with a review of some useful critiques that have been put forward in the early childhood literature. We use these as initial points for an analysis that considers citizenship as a socio-cultural process of citizen–subject formation.

Problematizing Liberal Discourses and Practices of Citizenship

Our critical reflection on discourses of citizenship in early childhood education is inspired by discussions that begin to problematize the ways in which citizenship has been conceptualized and practiced. As mentioned above, citizenship is related to participation, the inclusion of children's views, rights and voices into practices and policy development. Models are inclusionary, attempting to include children into "adult," "public" discussions. The overall intention is to bring children to discussions and treat children as contributing members of society. Several scholars have critiqued the participatory approach toward citizenship and proposed that these approaches to more fully engage young children favor liberal concepts of justice and equality.

For example, Millei (2008) conducted a Foucaultian analysis of government that problematizes notions of citizenship and participation in early childhood education. She argues that although children's participation and involvement in decision-making processes are thought of as forms of liberation, they are in fact technologies of government. "Children are regulated through their freedom. They are assigned to participate by the same discourses that aim to liberate their conduct from adult domination" (p. 49). Millei cautions us that discourses of participation transform adult-power relations but do not make those relations disappear. Therefore, she concludes, "children's participation and citizenship should be considered as open for contestation and debates according to particular events and shifting power relations in order to maintain their empowering potential" (p. 52).

Coleman (2007) has also commented on how governmentality impacts the construction of citizenship in children. Political elites define what does and does not construct the "good" citizen, engendering self-disciplinary conduct in "citizens." Thus citizenship becomes a process of actively embracing defined protocols and ideologies: this also happens at a collective level, as like-minded "citizen" groups provide support for behavior that conforms to these ideologies (for example, neighborhood watch groups). Coleman also points out that these kinds of activities tend to be dominated by older males in society. As an alternative, Coleman suggests that new mass-produced technologies such as easily available camcorders and cellular phones can enable younger people (especially females) to participate in civic engagement, even if it is of an unconventional nature such as participation in certain reality shows on television. Bennett (2007) has pointed out that more young people voted in regards to the TV show *Big Brother* in the United Kingdom than in the general elections. He cautions, however, that due to the possibility of casting more than one vote, the TV voting figures may not be accurate. While recognizing the "produced" nature of such shows, Coleman points out that they do provide new models of participation. Eliasoph (1998) has said that for younger people to participate more as citizens, it is necessary to do away with the misconceptions that political conversations are somehow dangerous and will "disrupt meetings and rip friends apart and intimidate neighbors and evacuate meetings of healthy community volunteers and ruin good jokes and not do any good" (p. 37). Citizen engagement in the political process, she argues, takes place on many levels and through many conversations: the more that one can seek out these alternative spaces of engagement and recognize their legitimacy, the more children will become involved in the political processes that are at the heart of citizenship (Coleman, 2007).

Another important critique of the participatory approach toward citizenship is that provided by Kjorholt (2005), who problematizes Scandinavian policies and practice traditions of viewing children as "fellow citizens." Also using a Foucaultian analysis of discourse, she points to problematic age-related social orders reinscribed in participation narratives where "children are presented as autonomous and recognized as *equal* to adults in certain respects, but on the basis of being *different*" (p. 159). For example, she argues, children are presented as having the right to engage in play activities because "they are seen as human beings belonging to a particular cultural group" that shares specific characteristics (p. 159). The differences between children and adults as well as the solutions that are enacted to solve those differences are based on narrow understandings of power relations that assume power as an individual property.

Kjorholt (2005) also problematizes the discourses of individualism and self-realization that some early childhood conceptions of citizenship embed. Drawing on the work of Charles Taylor she argues:

> The moral space in which children are placed seems to be a space that constructs self-determination and negative freedom as overarching values. This is problematic for many reasons. Taylor argues that "the subject himself cannot be the final authority on the question whether he is free; for he cannot be the final authority on the question whether his desires are authentic, whether they do or do not frustrate his purposes" (Taylor, 1985, p. 216)…The subject's individual autonomy is closely intertwined with dependency since it is constructed within a web of social relationships. (p. 164)

Kjorholt (2005) questions the autonomous subject as a limiting assumption of citizenship discourses of childhood. She argues that citizenship discourses fail to acknowledge the ways in which individuals' (including children's) subjectivities are created. As mentioned above, citizenship discourses assume coercion, forgetting that subjects are constituted through liberal principles of governing that emphasize the idea of self-regulated subjects. The choices and actions provided to children within the citizenship literature forget that children are working within a limited repertoire of discourses.

James, Curtis, and Birch (2008) have also critiqued contemporary concepts of childhood and citizenship, as "actively repositioning children as both irresponsible and vulnerable, a representation that lessens their opportunities for active citizenship" (p. 85). According to these scholars, there has been an increasing trend to characterize late modern societies as places of risk for children; this trend has contributed toward a tendency to focus on the need to construct childhood as a period defined by the need for protection. As Ansell (2005) has shown, the Dionysian view (as little devils) and the Apollonian view (as little angels) of childhood represent a binary axis around which contemporary discourses about childhood revolve. Both views, however, have contributed to the discourse of risk and protection, which are a part of common understandings of childhood. From one point of view, children need protection from themselves, or else their inner devils will be unleashed, causing harm both to themselves and others. From the "little angel" point of view, children need not only protection from dangerous forces such as dysfunctional families and child molesters but as the embodiment of innocence, become worthy of protection as symbols of innocence. As James et al. (2008) elaborate, both these points of view limit the possibilities for children to participate as citizens.

James et al. (2008) support their claims with data from a recent study of children's perceptions of hospital space. The study was designed to elicit children's perceptions of what they would consider as child friendly spaces in hospitals. The researchers conducted 120 interviews with children between the ages of 4 and 16. Their findings revealed that children overwhelmingly argued, that they, as children, needed supervision in hospital spaces, perceiving themselves as both "vulnerable and irresponsible" (p. 91). The children mostly expressed the view that they should be accompanied by adults at all times in the hospital, even in what are considered private spaces such as the toilets. As the authors comment, they seemed to look at the environment through a frame of risk: they were very aware of the ways in which they might hurt themselves, such as by falling off of a bed, or through ingesting medicines improperly. They were also very aware of what they seemed to consider their own ability for irresponsibility, producing a list of all the dangerous things that they might do if left unsupervised (grab something, break something, or ruin equipment, for example). James et al. (2008) see their study as raising two questions that are relevant to the study of childhood and citizenship: (a) why should children and young people have such negative views of childhood as a social category and (b) what consequences does this have for their sense of self? We would further ask the question as to whether it is possible for the discourse of citizenship for children to co-exist with such extreme discourses of risk?

In short, the reviewed critiques point to the problematic adult/child binary assumed in liberal conceptualizations of citizenship. Many postcolonial scholars (Schueller, 2009; Mignolo 2000) have commented on how binary ways of thinking contradict the life experiences and ways of viewing the world of "others." Mignolo (2000) has commented that "colonial discourse was one of the most powerful strategies in the imaginary of the modern/colonial world system for producing dichotomies that justified the will to power" (p. 337). In early childhood contexts, this is exemplified through the construction of the dichotomy between children and adults. As has been suggested elsewhere, this (artificial) separation, based on what is supposed to be scientific fact, creates a privileged position from which adults function (Cannella & Viruru, 2004). The distinctions between children and adults further revolve around a series of binaries: ignorant/knowledgeable; innocent/worldly; small/large; becoming/being; sexually immature rather than mature to name but a few (Lee, 2002; Jenks, 1996). As James, Curtis, and Birch (2008) have said, this dichotomy has also led to the construction of dichotomous institutions and cultural practices for children and adults such as school/work and cartoons/horror films. As these authors point out, children who do not experience such separate worlds are thought to have lost their childhoods (Buckingham, 2000). These binaries have, however, been contextualized by critical scholarship, such as that of Silin (1995) who provides a profound example of problems with the creation of an adult/child dichotomy in his discussion of illness and death (Cannella & Viruru, 2004). When faced with situations involving life, death, and illness, Silin found that it was those who are younger who seemed to deal with death and illness in more knowledgeable ways. Cockburn (1998) has suggested that for the concept of citizenship to become more inclusive, it has to be fundamentally rethought based upon the recognition that "by seeing children and adults as mutually dependent on one another through recognition of the essential interdependence of all human beings" (James et al., 2008, p. 87). Thus according to Cockburn (1998), citizenship is not something that one has to qualify for (for example, at a certain age) but a preexisting right of all human beings.

Adult/child binaries are not the only ways in which liberal discourses of citizenship mask colonial reasonings. The other dichotomies that are reinstated in citizenship and participation discourses are those that separate private/public spheres (often problematized by feminist citizenship scholars). Definitions of citizenship privilege the public as the only social sphere for children to participate and therefore become full citizens. "The mainstream ideal of citizenship is defined precisely in terms of an identity status based upon rights and activities enacted in the national public arena *as against* those merely private personal activities in the domestic sphere" (Beasley & Bacchi, 2000, p. 340). These are equality-based conceptions of citizenship that, Dietz (2003) argues, emphasize an essentialist approach.

> Mainstream accounts of citizenship therefore ignore the dependence of public activities upon private ones, as well as the related difficulties attached to regarding them as entirely separate (Mouffe, 1993), and by impli-cation effectively exclude the private sphere…to the extent that citizenship is equated with the public sphere, feminist writers therefore argue that women [and children] are not and cannot be "full citizens." (Beasley & Bacchi, 2000, p. 340)

Overall, liberal conceptualizations of citizenship are wellintentioned as they try to move beyond legalistic (formal rights) perspectives of citizenship and re-conceptualize citizenship as social and political participation. We agree with Beasley and Bacchi's (2000) argument that these kinds of approaches to citizenship were developed in response to "the long shadow cast by national histories of openly exclusionary social practices" (p. 339). The problem with these approaches, however, is that the dualities between adult/child and public/private are not necessarily displaced, but they remain stable, spatial, and fixed (Dietz, 2003; Kjorholt, 2005; Beasley & Bacchi, 2000). Furthermore, citizenship approaches that remain within dualistic divisions also remain links to exclusionary pasts of citizenship (racist, property-based, etc.).

There is much to learn from governmentality and feminist analyses that problematize the narrowness of liberal understandings of citizenship and participation. These are, in fact, significant contributions that should be taken into consideration as we engage in research, pedagogical practices, and policy development regarding young children's citizenships. While we acknowledge their usefulness in early childhood education, we believe that the problematization of citizenship in early childhood education should also attend to the connections, limitations, and problematics posited in antiracist, transnational feminist, and postcolonial critiques of citizenship. The next two sections problematize citizenship in relation to racisms, nation-state formation, and colonialism.

Antiracist and Transnational Analyses of Citizenship

In our review of the literature, we have noticed that the majority of the citizenship literature regarding children does not include the now large body of knowledge around citizenship that emerges from scholars who discuss citizenship in relation to racialization, colonialism, and migration. These discourses, however, are of great importance in early childhood as most Western societies are now imagined as pluralistic and multicultural as they accept a large number of immigrants every year. This specific issue remains silenced in the citizenship literature regarding young children. Miller, in his problematization of citizenship definitions in the early years, asks: "Do participation and citizenship create 'equal playing fields' for all children?" We believe that the work of antiracist, transnational feminist, and postcolonial scholars provide useful ideas for engaging with Miller's question.

Transnational feminist scholar Aihwa Ong challenges two lines of inquiry present in traditional studies of citizenship regarding immigration. First, she argues that the meaning of achieving citizenship has long rested on a set of expectations that scholars [of citizenship] refer to as "ethnic succession" (Ong, 2003, p. 3). This model of ethnic succession, Ong argues, "holds that as the moral capital of suffering and contribution is built up from generation to generation, each minority or immigrant group should be absorbed into a higher rank" (p. 3). Ong continues to say that the result of "achieving citizenship is an ending process of struggles against undemocratic exclusions based on ethnicity and race, with the assumption that the social status of a particular minority group will improve over time with cumulative increases in experiences of adversity and material gains, and will in turn lift up the individuals belonging to that group" (p. 4). Second, Ong (2003) challenges "the right to be different" discourse found within multicultural and pluralistic discussions. She argues that "while the prevailing pluralist discourse accepts 'difference' as an object of analysis,…'culture' (or 'race,' ethnicity,' or 'gender') is not the automatic or even the most important analytical domain in which to understand how citizenship is constituted" (p. 6). How are we challenging ethnic succession beliefs (the valorization of cultural difference) in early childhood conceptualizations and practices of citizenship?

A challenging example of alternative meanings of citizenship is offered by Habashi's (2009) analysis of how the concept of citizenship in Palestinian contexts necessarily includes resistance to Israeli oppression. Given the political conditions in the region, Palestinian children are often engaged in resistance in the fight against colonization, which in itself is a symbol of global power. As Habashi (2009) has put it, "now more than ever, global power/discourse is not isolated from local colonized reality and the practice of exploitation is unencumbered by boundaries. Imperialism and colonial realities are extensively woven into the social political fabric of the Palestinian legacy and are circulated through intergeneration narratives" (p. 5). According to Habashi, children's perspectives on resistance are a valuable testimony as to how the intergenerational narratives of resistance are continued and reshaped. Zureik (2003), for example, has recommended that it is important that while doing research with Palestinians, part of capturing the multiple realities of their existence(s) is to include intergenerational narratives of survival and resistance. Thus citizenship, in this context, exemplifies a rewritten continuity, which values children's experiences just as much as adults.

To link these problematics to our previous discussion of feminist critiques of public/private dichotomies, while earliest feminist analyses of citizenship were based on a critique of gender erasures, minority feminist scholars further demonstrate that feminist scholarship on citizenship has often been blind to factors beyond gender. In constructing borders around who is to be included or excluded in categories of citizenship and who is considered a worthy contributor to social and market economies, the state deploys multiple signifiers of group differences beyond gender, such as age, race, ethnicity, language, religion, abilities, and sexual orientation in interaction with gender and class (Anthias, Yuval-Davis, 1992). When taken as a given and naturalized, the deployment of these signifiers help nations and their governments to distinguish among competing claims for citizen welfare rights and benefits and to differentially allocate these resources. Consequently, when young children engage in everyday practices, they confront particular social, legal, cultural, and political issues concerning their citizenship rights, responsibilities, and identities.

Nira Yuval-Davis' (2000) work on citizenship is of great interest as we believe it has much to offer to citizenship discussions in early childhood education. In particular, we want to highlight her construct of multilayered citizenship. In her definition of multilayered citizenship, she problematizes the closed aspect of traditional definitions of citizenship in relation to the nation-state. She says:

> Citizenship needs to be understood as a multi-layered construct, in which one's citizenship in collectivities in the different layers—local, ethnic, national, state, cross- or trans-state and supra-state—is affected and often at least partly constructed by the relationships and positionings of each layer in specific historical context. This is of particular importance if we want to examine citizenship in a non-westocentric way.

The constraints on the state in many of the post-colonial states, by local and traditional communities on the one hand and multinationals and international agencies on the other hand, would be even more notice-able than in the West. (p. 122)

To assist in conceptualizing citizenship identity formation, we also find attractive Aihwa Ong's (1996) theory of "flexible and cultural citizenship" because it links subject formation to regulatory effects enacted in the local but linked to the global. As hinted in the introductory quotation, Aihwa Ong (2003) argues that citizenship should be viewed

in terms of the effects of multiple rationalities (biopolitical, class, ethno-racial, gender) that directly and indi-rectly prescribe techniques for living for independent subjects who learn how to govern themselves. Instead of considering citizenship solely in terms of the state's power to give or deny citizenship, I look at social policies and practices beyond the state that in myriad mundane ways suggest, define, and direct adherence to democratic, racial, and market norms of belonging (p. 15)

Drawing on the work of philosopher Michel Foucault, Ong (2003) further argues that:

'Bio-power' [is] the central concern of the modern liberal state in the fostering of life, growth, and care of the population. The biopolitical rationality makes strategic use of bodies of knowledge that invest bodies and populations with properties that make them amenable to various technologies of control. This power over life is exercised with the purpose of producing subjects who are healthy and productive, goals that redound to the security and strength of the state. But the state itself has no essence: "the state is nothing more than the mobile effect of a multiple regime of governmentality." Studying the government of a pop-ulation thus entails a study of the diverse techniques arising from multiple sources that act on the body, the mind, and the will, dedicated to making individuals, families, and collectivities "governable." A repertoire of techniques of power, informed by the human sciences, comes to constitute "the social," defining cate-gories of [Other], in opposition to what is thereby considered "normal" society. Such social norms define which category of subjects is more or less valued as citizens of the nation. (pp. 8–9)

By analyzing citizenship as culturally constituted through cultural practices—of becoming and being made—the lived realities of young children's lives in discourses on citizenship and belonging can be more clearly viewed and understood (Mohanty, Russo, & Torres, 1991; Ong, 1996, 1999; Razack, 1998; Yuval-Davis, 2000).

Ong's (1999) ethnography of transnational practices and linkages embeds a theory of practice within, not outside of or against, political-economic forces. These perspectives link everyday routines, not only as embodiments and enactments of norms, values, and conceptual schemes about time, space, and the social order so that everyday practices endorse and reproduce these norms, but also as important links to the everyday rituals of life—"to the regulatory effects of particular cultural insti-tutions, projects, regimes and markets that shape people's motivations, desires, and struggles and make them particular kinds of subjects in the world" (Ong, 1999, p. 6).

We posit that citizen identities are forged in everyday interactions and lived environments that are hierarchically organized and mediated by dominant "white" and other ethnic minority cultural formations. Identity formation is not only a matter of gender, age, and stage, but also an outcome of young children's community histories, dominant and resistant discourses and material practices, local community contexts and structures, and individuals' and groups' own social positionings and sense of self-making. Recent transnational feminist theories of citizenship and belonging also help us to question and more fully account for mobile identities that move across national borders and boundaries yet are embodied in specific times and places (Alexander & Mohanty, 1997; Anthias & Yuval-Davis, 1991; Friedman, 1998; Grewal & Kaplan, 1994; Ong, 1999; Yuval-Davis, 2000). By approaching citizenship through culture (as opposed to philosophy, ethics, or law), what we are asked to do is to open up possibilities for studying issues of identity formation in young children's relationships to citizenship and democracy.

In these approaches to citizenship, identity is to be understood as socially constructed, mobile, multiple, and always in a process of formation, emerging through discourse and representation in relation to changing social contexts and to others in the lived environment (Hall, 1997). Yet, as culturally formed and forming subjects who live in a hierarchically ordered cultural world, young children are not to be seen as entirely free to choose or mold their identities. On the one hand, their sense of identification with the adopted nation is "flexible," "in transition," and "negotiated." On the other hand, citizen identity, as a relational process linked to power, is also always being imposed and regulated. In other words, identities of citizenship are an outcome of numerous complex forces (Ong, 1999).

According to some researchers, young children are not passive receptacles of dominant discourses and controlling practices. They are also actively engaged in producing their own identities (Grieshaber & Cannella, 2001). Yet, the actual everyday practices that are involved in producing these hybrid, multicultural, and transnational identities are still relatively poorly understood. What is involved in constituting ever-shifting identities of young children as citizen-subjects? What practices are involved in producing hybrid, fluid, and adaptive citizenship-identities and what difference do changing cultural contexts make to identity formation (Anthias, 2002; Hall, 1992)?

To summarize, antiracist and transnational feminist scholarship on citizenship, a rich and diverse field as exemplified above, highlights negotiated and strategic citizenship strategies as they affect young children and early childhood education. What this literature asks for is that researchers, practitioners and policymakers pay close attention to historical forces such as colonialism, globalization, national immigration and citizenship policies, diasporic communities, and migration chains, while also inquiring into strategies of agency and resistance. In particular, they call into question Western notions of children's identity formation that view identity as a private arrangement that has no place in the spheres of social policy and market economies. In fact, these theories propose that children's identity formation is a major political economic arrangement directly supporting global economies (Penn, 2005). To develop more complex understandings of the lived realities of child engagement with citizenship, we need to attend to the different ways that children respond to the demands of economies and nation states in their daily lives and perhaps spend less time trying to make children fit into already defined categories of citizenship.

Postcolonial scholars have also suggested that one must rethink the concept of citizenship in an age of Empire, where the very concept of the nation-state is being questioned. Furthermore, in the hybrid cultures of the global world, where multimedia technologies play an increasingly complex role, citizenship as participation is being redefined and enacted very differently than previously understood. We turn our attention to these arguments in the next section of the chapter.

Postcolonial Analyses of Citizenship

Postcolonial critiques of the concept of citizenship have been wide-ranging. One of the most fundamental critiques is that mainstream literature on citizenship has focused on Euro-Western constructions of what it means to be a citizen. Ownership of the concept of citizenship has been credited to European civilizations, ignoring the influence of events such as the Haitian revolution, which is thought to have greatly influenced the meanings of citizenship in the West (Cooper, 2005). The roots of the political agenda of what might be termed "western thought" emerges from the 1400s onwards, the period of the Spanish and Portuguese expansionism (Cannella & Viruru, 2004). An essential part of this process was the idea of nation building, which took on very different forms in different parts of the world. In the west, the focus was on defining the rights of citizens and setting up systems of parliamentary democracies. On the other side of the world, however, the process of nation building (imposed by the west) consisted more of enforcing imperial rule and subjecting citizens to authoritarian rules within their own countries, all supposedly in the name of establishing the foundation for their own development. Thus the history of the evolution of Western models of citizenship is also a history of domination and oppression (Cannella & Viruru, 2004). As Hansen and Stepputat (2005) have said, colonial and postcolonial states have at least two faces. The benevolent face of this apparatus allowed "respectable" citizens to exercise their rights, to form what was seen as the nucleus of a civil society in uncivilized places and even to protest against perceived inequities. This laid the foundation for the kinds of national citizenships that people were expected to assume, as their nations achieved independence from colonization. The more brutal face of the state, however, was shown to its "not quite citizens": communities excluded from the mainstream, who nevertheless have to work with the state to ensure their livelihoods. Chatterjee (2005) characterizes this sphere as "political society," composed of those whose "forms of community life and rationalities" are "radically different" from other citizens, yet who still, if only nominally, hold the status of citizens of a particular nation. Mamdani (1996) has also commented on how the aftermath of colonial rule led to the creation of what were essentially differentiated citizenships, based on various systems of categorization such as social class and race.

As Chatterjee (2005) puts it, in postcolonial India, all its people can be considered "citizens," however, "most of the inhabitants of India are only tenuously, and even then ambiguously and contextually, rights bearing citizens in the sense imagined by the constitution" (p. 83). These "citizens," although they may not be always allowed to participate in the democratic processes of the state, have to be both taken care of by the state, if only for purposes of control: as such their relationship can be considered more political than civil. An example of such a group could be a community of squatters in a city, who are considered to have occupied their land illegally: since their occupation is illegal, their relationship with the state is necessarily somewhat tense. On the other hand, the state cannot refuse to have a relationship with them, and in fact recognizes that these inhabitants have some claims to welfare protection from the government. Yet, these are not the interactions that would be typically defined as relationships with one's own "citizens."

Comaroff and Comaroff (2005) have commented that most postcolonies have gone through two epochal phases: the first phase encompassed actual liberation from colonial rule but also its immediate aftermath, which included grappling with the realities of neocolonialism, such as debt and dependency. This phase is seen as belonging to the "old" political order, dominated by nation-states and their relationships with one another. In the second epoch, postcolonies started to experience the effects of the "new" world order of a "more fluid, market-driven, electronically articulated universe" (p. 125). In such a world order, the state is perpetually in crisis as it struggles to legislate in the face of complex flows of capital and people, and its authority is continually challenged. In this second epoch, which Comaroff and Comaroff (2005) see as extending through the present, although most human beings live as citizens in nation states, they "tend only to be conditionally, partially and situationally citizens of nation-states" (p. 127). Thus, from a postcolonial point of view, the concept of citizenship is laden with fractured meanings and imperial histories that continue to define the ways in which "citizens" live their lives.

We would also like to comment briefly on scholarship around the concept of Empire (as defined by Hardt & Negri, 2000) and how that relates to ideas about citizenship. These ideas not only occupy a unique if contested place within postcolonial scholarship but also offer possibilities for reconceptualizing ideas about citizenship in early childhood. The concept of Empire, as put forward by Hardt and Negri (2000), differs from other forms of imperialism in that it is not bound by physical boundaries: it encompasses all of the "civilized world" without distinguishing between nation-states. Hardt and Negri see this not only as a new world order, but a permanent one: it is here to stay, and thus does not recognize temporal as well as physical boundaries. This form of Empire eschews political control in favor of control over human nature. Paradoxically, although its processes can include violence, it claims to be working toward world peace. Hardt and Negri (2000) also discuss strategies of resistance to the all-encompassing concept of Empire, among which is the concept of nomadism and miscegenation: by the multitude as an alternative to citizenship. Sassen (2004) has commented that the deterritorialization associated with Empire has resulted in new forms of citizenship, specifically what she calls "denationalized forms" of citizenship (p. 180). For example, Sassen (2004) points out that in a globally competitive world, there has been a movement to reduce the entitlements of citizens. Further, loyalty is less valued as a commodity, as, due to technological advancements, winning wars no longer depends solely on loyal citizen-soldiers. Deterritorialization has also generated realities that in turn have generated new kinds of citizenship, such as that displayed by the many illegal immigrants to the West, who despite lacking the status of citizens, perform many of the same actions such as raising families and schooling children.

Postcolonial scholars have also explored issues of citizenship from subaltern perspectives. As Pandey (2008) has said (and to us, this is reminiscent of the processes of deterritorialization and nomadism discussed above), it is important to explore the "potential that the subaltern possesses (or the threat s/he poses) of becoming a full member of the community, the village, the ward and the polis" (p. 275). Pandey (2008), however, believes that in using the term "subaltern-citizens," it is citizen that qualifies subaltern and not the other way around. In other words, the study of subaltern citizenship asks the question as to how citizenship can be reconceptualized through subaltern eyes? Pandey (2008) believes that using the term subaltern-citizens in itself can be helpful, as it removes artificial "us/them" barriers, and thus creates a space where dialogue can take place.

Conclusion

In this chapter, we have argued for the need to critically reflect on the concept of citizenship as ambiguous and contentious. As many of the above analyses suggest, the term citizenship and the realities that it embodies are filled with contradictions and possibilities. While it has traditionally been used as a tool to guarantee (to some) rights and freedoms, it has simultaneously been used as an instrument of exclusion. At times it has been simplified down to an essence (the right to vote), an idea which, as suggested above, has lost the power to resonate with citizens themselves. The concept of citizenship continues to be associated in the West with ideas that center around participation in one's neighborhood/community/country and the guarantees of certain fundamental rights and protections.

As the field of childhood studies and other related disciplines have expanded and challenged established notions of what participation and rights are, attempts have been made to include them in these discourses. However, these discourses continue to be based on foundational beliefs of individualism, the importance of self-realization and a dichotomous perspective that separates adults and children, as well as the ethnic succession principle discussed above. These practices do not take into account either the complex lived experiences of many "citizens" nor the expanding literature on citizenship, particularly those coming from feminist, transnational, antiracist, and postcolonial perspectives. Scholars from these domains illustrate how citizenship must be understood as much more than an entity that uncomplicatedly expresses where one belongs and what one's rights are. As the concepts of multilayered and flexible citizenships underline, the mere right to vote is a minimal part of citizenship, as it is something that people live with and engage/contest with in their daily lives. In a world where the concept of the nation-state itself is seen as having waning importance, some scholars have suggested that citizenship has become less relevant, as nation/states become less able to "protect" the rights of their citizens. Furthermore, as the experiences of many show, nominally holding the title of citizen has not always opened up pathways of empowerment.

In light of all of the above, we raise the questions of whether or not discussions of citizenship belong in early childhood? Does centering on this concept close the door on other meaningful discussions and silence other voices? What meanings do the notions of multilayered and flexible citizenships hold in early childhood discourses? Are children subaltern-citizens?

One of the first ideas that struck us as we explored the literature on children and citizenship is its framing on the process of becoming: citizenship is seen as an area where children are newly being admitted; even as they are admitted to this new arena, it is underlined that their participation cannot be seen as the "full" and "knowing" participation of adult citizens. To us, this contradicts the reality that children already are citizens, whether or not that "legal" status has been accorded to them. It is reminiscent of what Guha (1997) and Chakraborty (2000) have seen as the characteristics of a colonial state: that it had subjects not citizens. Many children around the world contribute to the economy, through both paid and unpaid labor; they resourcefully participate in tasks such as raising other children and running households and play an active role in communities as they care for others, whether those be other children or adults. Thus the idea of the exclusion of children from discussions about citizenship as "new" does not respect the realities of children around the world.

As many of the analyses presented above have shown, the concept of citizenship, as it is mostly presently defined, belongs mostly not only to Euro-Western ways of viewing the world but also to frameworks that seem somewhat outdated in a world where citizenship for many is no longer moored to such principles as belonging and loyalty. The transnational nature of participation in the world does not fit within traditional definitions of what citizenship is. As Odem (2008) has shown in relation to the positioning of Mexican immigrants to the United States, one can be officially a "citizen" of one country, while fulfilling the traditional rights and responsibilities of another. Within what has been traditionally defined as the West, many children already experience citizenship as a contested and difficult terrain (for example, as through virtue of being born in the United States, they may be considered U.S. citizens and be entitled to certain things that their parents are not). Thus, to present citizenship in early childhood as a benign journey during which one gradually realizes one's responsibilities and gains understanding of one's rights is denigrating to the many children who engage with these concepts every day and who construct their own understandings of what citizenship is(n't). As Habashi (2009) has pointed out, for some children, resistance may be an essential part of participation as a citizen.

References

Alexander, M. J., & Mohanty, C. T. (1997). *Feminist genealogies, colonial legacies, democratic futures*. New York: Routledge.

Ansell N (2005). *Children, youth and development*. Routledge, London.

Anthias, F. (2002). Where do I belong? Narrating collective identity and translocational positionality. *Ethnicities, 2*(4), 491–514.

Anthias, F., & Yuval-Davis, N. (1991). Connecting race and gender. In F. Anthias & N. Yuval-Davis (Eds.), *Racialized boundaries: Race, nation, gender, colour, and class and the anti-racist struggle* (pp. 96–131). London: Routledge.

Beasley, C., & Bacchi, C. (2000). Citizen bodies: Embodying citizens—a feminist analysis. *International Feminist Journal of Politics, 2*(3), 337–358.

Bennett, W. L. (2007). Civic learning in changing democracies: Challenges for citizenship and civic education. In P. Dahlgren (Ed.), *Young citizens and new media* (pp. 59–78). New York: Routledge.

Buckingham, D. (2000). *After the death of childhood*. Cambridge: Polity Press.

Cannella, G.S. & Viruru, R. (2004). *Childhood and postcolonization: Power, education and contemporary practice*. New York: Routledge.

Chakraborty, D. (2000). *Habitations of modernity: Essays in the wake of subaltern studies*. Chicago, IL: University of Chicago Press.

Chatterjee, P. (2005). Sovereign violence and the domain of the political. In T.B. Hansen & F. Stepputat (Eds.), *Sovereign bodies: citizens, migrants and states in the postcolonial world* (pp. 82–102). Princeton, NJ: Princeton University Press.

Cockburn, T. (1998). Children and citizenship in Britain: A case for a socially interdependent model of citizenship. *Childhood, 5*(1), 99–117.

Coleman, S. (2007). From Big Brother to *Big Brother*: Two faces of interactive engagement. In P. Dahlgren (Ed.), *Young citizens and new media* (pp. 21–40). New York: Routledge.

Comaroff, J. & Comaroff, J. (2005). Naturing the nation: Aliens, apocalypse and the postcolonial state. In T.B. Hansen & F. Stepputat (Eds.), *Sovereign bodies: Citizens, migrants and states in the postcolonial world* (pp. 120–147). Princeton, NJ: Princeton University Press.

Cooper, F. (2005). *Colonialism in question: Theory, knowledge and history*. Berkeley, CA: University of California Press.

Dahl, M. (2008). *Youth vote may have been key in Obama's win: Young voters had "record turnout," preferred Democrat by wide margin*. Retrieved March 12, 2009, from *http://www.msnbc.msn.com/id/27525497*

Dahlgren, P. (2007). Introduction: Youth, civic engagement and learning via new media. In P. Dahlgren (Ed.), *Young citizens and new media* (pp 1–18). New York: Routledge.

Dietz, M. G. (2003). Current controversies in feminist theory. *Annual Review of Political Science, 6*(1), 399–431.

Eliasoph, N. (1998). *Avoiding politics: How Americans produce apathy in everyday life*. Cambridge: Cambridge University Press.

Friedman, S. S. (1998). *Mappings: Feminism and the cultural geographies of encounter*. Princeton, NJ: Princeton University Press.

Grewal, I., & Kaplan, C. (Eds.). (1994). *Scattered hegemonies: Postmodernity and transnational feminist practices*. Minneapolis, MN: University of Minnesota Press.

Grieshaber, S., & Cannella, G. S. (2001). From identity to identities: Increasing possibilities in early childhood education. In S. Grieshaber & G. S. Cannella (Eds.), *Embracing identities in early childhood education diversity and possibilities* (pp. 3–21). New York: Teachers College Press.

Guha, R. (1997). *A subaltern studies reader, 1986–1995*. Minneapolis, MN: University of Minnesota Press.

Habashi, J. (2009). *Manifesto of religious reinvention: Unexpected paths to solidarity*. Paper presented at the Research Seminar on Living Rights, IUKB, Sion, Switzerland.

Hall, S. (1997). Introduction. In S. Hall (Ed.), *Representation: Cultural representations and signifying practices* (pp. 1–12).

London: Open University Press and Sage.

Hall, S. (1992). New ethnicities. In J. Donald & A. Rattansi (Eds.), *"Race," culture, difference* (pp. 252–259). London: Sage.

Hansen, T. B. & Stepputat, F. (2005). Introduction. In T.B. Hansen & F. Stepputat (Eds.), *Sovereign bodies: Citizens, migrants and states in the postcolonial world* (pp. 1–38). Princeton, NJ: Princeton University Press.

Hardt, M. & Negri, A. (2000). *Empire*. Cambridge, MA: Harvard University Press.

Hasebrink, U. & Hasebrink, I. P. (2007). Young people's identity construction and media use: Democratic participation in Germany and Austria. In P. Dahlgren (Ed.), *Young citizens and new media* (pp. 81–102). New York: Routledge.

James, A., Curtis, P. & Birch, J. (2008). Care and control in the construction of children's citizenship. In A. Invernizi & J. Williams (Eds.), *Children and citizenship*. Thousand Oaks, CA: Sage.

Jenks, C. (1996). *Childhood*. London: Routledge.

Keeter, S., Zukin, C., Andoline, M. & Jenkins, K. (2002). *The Civic and Political Health of the Nation: A Generational Portrait*. Center for Information and Research on Civic Learning and Engagement. Retrieved March 12, 2009, from www.civicyouth.org

Kjorholt, A. T. (2005). The competent child and "the right to oneself": Reflections on children as fellow citizens in an early childhood centre. In A. Clark, P. Moss & A. T. Kjorholt (Eds.), *Beyond listening children's perspectives on early childhood services* (pp. 151–174). Bristol, UK: Policy Press.

Lee, G. (2002). Young gifted girls and boys: Perspectives through the lens of gender. *Contemporary Issues in Early Childhood, 3*(3), 383–399.

Lister, R. (2008). Unpacking children's citizenship . In J. Williams, A. Invernizzi (Eds.), *Children and citizenship*. Thousand Oaks, CA: Sage.

Mamdani, M. (1996). *Citizen and subject: Contemporary Africa and the legacy of late colonialism*. Princeton, NJ: Princeton University Press.

Mignolo, W. (2000) *Local histories/Global designs: Coloniality, subaltern knowledges and border thinking*. Princeton, NJ: Princeton University Press.

Millei, Z. (2008). Problematizing the concepts of "citizenship" and "participation" in early years discourses: Are they so empowering? *International Journal of Equity and Innovation in Early Childhood, 6*(2), 41–56.

Mohanty, C. T., Russo, A., & Torres, L. (Eds.). (1991). *Third world women and the politics of feminism*. Bloomington, IN: Indiana University Press.

Odem, M. E. (2008). Subaltern immigrants: Undocumented workers and national belonging in the United States. *Interventions: The International Journal of Postcolonial Studies, 10*(3), 359–380.

Ong, A. (1996). Cultural citizenship as subject-making: Immigrants negotiate racial and cultural boundaries in the United States. *Current Anthropology, 37*(5), 737–763.

Ong, A. (1999). *Flexible citizenship: The cultural logics of transnationality*. Durham, UK: Duke University Press.

Ong, A. (2003). *Buddha is hiding: Refugees, citizenship, the new America*. Berkeley, CA: University of California Press.

Ong, A. (2006). *Neoliberalism as exception. Mutations in citizenship and sovereignty*. Durham, NC: Duke University Press.

Pandey, G. (2008). Subaltern citizens and their histories. *Interventions: The International Journal of Postcolonial Studies, 10*(3), 271–284.

Penn, H. (2005). *Unequal childhoods: Young children's lives in poor countries*. London: Routledge.

Putnam, R. (2000). *Bowling alone: The collapse and revival of American community*. New York: Simon & Schuster.

Razack, S. H. (1998). *Looking White people in the eye*. Toronto, ON: University of Toronto Press.

Sassen, S. (2004). The repositioning of citizenship: Emergent subjects and spaces for politics. In P. Passavant & J. Dean (Eds.), *Empire's new clothes: Reading Hardt and Negri*. New York: Routledge.

Schueller, M. J. (2009). *Locating race: Global sites of postcolonial citizenship*. Albany, NY: SUNY Press.

Silin, J. G. (1995). *Sex, death, and the education of children: Our passion for ignorance in the age of AIDS*. New York, NY: Teachers College Press.

Stasiulis, D. (2002). The active child citizen: Lessons from Canadian policy and the children"s movement. *Citizenship*

Studies, 6(4), 507–538.

Yuval-Davis, N. (2000). Citizenship, territoriality and the gendered construction of difference. In E. F. Isin (Ed.), *Democracy, citizenship and the global city* (pp. 172–188). London: Routledge.

Zurieik, E. (2003). Theoretical and methodological considerations for the study of Palestinian society. *Comparative Studies of South Asia, Africa and the Middle East, 23*(1 & 2), 152–162.

CHAPTER EIGHTEEN

The Denial of Sexuality and the Power of Censorship

CORRINE WICKENS

Abstract

In the modern period, calls for the censorship of books and other materials geared for younger children are largely related to the romanticized notion of childhood innocence, constructed in opposition to adult knowledge, corruption, and mostly (homo)sexuality (Robinson, 2002; Sears, 1999). In this chapter, I contend that such a dialectic can only be maintained through three interrelated functions as part of the cultural struggle over children's bodies and minds, most particularly their sexuality: (a) adult disregard and denial of children's physicality and innate sexuality, (b) privileging of a (hetero)narrative of childhood, and (c) the use of censorship in children's and young adult fiction and nonfiction, connected to children's physical and sexual selves. These practices originate from "developmentally appropriate" models that deny children's physiological and sexual selves, as well as information and literature that support and embrace children's healthy exploration of those selves.

Censorship has a long history, dating back to the fifth century B.C.—when Plato called for the ban of plays and poetry, arguing that fiction and drama confused young people by blurring the lines between reality and fantasy (Nilsen & Donelson, 2001). However, in the modern period, calls for the censorship of books and other materials geared for younger children can be associated with romantic notions of childhood and children: children as "pure" and "innocent," "unknowledgeable of adult behaviors," and "asexual."

In these associations, childhood innocence is constructed in opposition to adult knowledge, corruption, and mostly sexuality, including and most especially homosexuality (Robinson, 2002; Sears, 1999). However, I contend that such a dialectic can only be maintained through three interrelated functions as part of the cultural struggle over children's bodies and minds, most particularly their sexuality: (a) adult disregard and denial of children's physicality and innate sexuality, (b) a privileging of a (hetero)narrative of childhood, and (c) the use of censorship to children's and young adult fiction and nonfiction, connected to children's physical and sexual selves. To understand and unpack the interrelationships of these functions, I will explore first the cultural myth of innocence, and its origins; the contradictory, yet complicit, discourses of children as innocents and asexual, and children as "naturally" heterosexual; the growing body of scientific research demonstrating normative sexual behaviors among young children; and finally shifting trends in, and censorship of, children's literature as a pivotal point in this struggle.

Industrialization and Origins of the Myth of Childhood Innocence

To begin, we must understand that current conceptualizations of children and childhood in general are recent, modernist constructions. Prior to industrialization and ensuing modernization, children maintained a highly ambiguous identity, based not on specific notions of "children," but their ability to contribute to household incomes. Although younger people were relegated to the bottom of the social stratum, they were not segregated from the adult world as is common today. "Certainly there was no separate world of childhood. Children shared the same games with adults, the same toys, the same fairy stories. They lived their lives together, never apart" (Plumb, 1971, p. 7). Moreover, prior to the Victorian era, living, working, and sleeping spaces were largely communal, such that children were exposed to all the same experiences that adults were, including aspects of adult sexuality. "Not only was there no possibility of protecting children from any of the harsh realities of adult life, but the idea that it might be desirable to do so does not appear to have existed" (Jackson, 1990, p. 31). Likewise, sex (as intercourse) and sexuality as a private matter, especially something to be "concealed" from children, is also a modern concept that developed with construction of segregated living spaces. Thus, the lack of sexual privacy was associated with open discussions of sexual matters, "indicating that sex was taken for granted as a routine part of everyday life" (Jackson, 1990, p. 32).

However, the advent of industrialization brought about numerous momentous changes in social structures, family structures, and the care and conception of children. For instance, the construction of factories caused a separation between the workplace and the household, creating a new division of public and private spheres and insularity around all things "private" (Jackson, 1990; Cherlin, 1983). Given the shifts in these physical and social geographical dimensions (from paid labor being performed primarily in the household to paid work being performed primarily outside of the household), the shape of families shifted from a more nebulous group of individuals living and working within a given household to more exclusive, nuclear kin groups (Jackson, 1990; Cherlin, 1983). New divisions of labor ensued as well, with men leaving the house to work and women taking charge of household concerns, including the ultimate care of children.

At this same time, shifts in the conceptions of children were occurring rapidly as well. As noted previously, children used to live and work directly alongside adults and treated as "miniature adults" (Plumb, 1971). During the Puritan era, however, children were conceived not only as miniature adults but also innately sinful and savage. Thus, discipline and punishment were exacted as coercive forces for self-control, molding children into adult standards of righteousness (Illick, 2002). Then, with industrialization and increasing numbers of immigrant children, increased concern over unsafe child labor conditions, children became something to be "protected" (Burman, 1994). New compulsory laws in elementary education also served to reinforce the concept of "childhood" as a distinct stage in life development requiring special safeguards from caring adults.

As part of a larger social purity movement, these social reformers also campaigned against any outward displays of indecency and/or obscenity (D'Emilio & Freedman, 1997). Jackson (1990) contends that one of the most critical developments of this era was that "moral regulation was no longer applied only to sexual conduct, but was extended to what could be *said* about sex" (p. 37, emphasis added). Prior to the mid-nineteenth century, there were no legal proscriptions against sexually explicit material, only moral codes of decency (D'Emilio & Freedman, 1997). Anthony Comstock, however, initiated one of the most sweeping antiobscenity campaigns, designed to restrict sexual expression as anything outside reproductive purposes and underscore association of sexuality with the private sphere. Thus, "any public expression of sexuality was considered, by definition, obscene" (D'Emilio & Freedman, 1997, p. 160). As part of this larger campaign, Comstock orchestrated a pervasive censorship campaign of young adult literature, purportedly on behalf of the nation's children (Beisel, 1997; Nilsen & Donelson, 2001). He contended that obscenity in children's literature led to "laziness, immorality, lustfulness, criminality, and sometimes death among youth" (Beisel, 1997, p. 53). Furthermore, in the third annual report to the New York Society for the Suppression of Vice, Comstock asserted that obscene literature provoked corruption in school and in homes by "exciting the imagination…and passions of the youth into whose hands they may come" (cited in Beisel, 1997, p. 53).

Significant to this antiobscenity crusade was the belief in the harmful mental and physical repercussions associated with male masturbation. Numerous advice books were written detailing such harm that would come to young boys who engaged in such onanistic behavior (see Kimmel (2006) for detailed discussion of these texts). These advice books commonly asserted "men's need for self-control over passion, temperance, and masturbation, which would sap their energies and leave 'effeminated' men's bodies" (Kimmel, 2006, p. 32). Foucault (1978) likewise well documented the incessant concerns about male masturbation, prompting utmost vigilance and surveillance by parents and educators for any potential signs of such tendencies. This was part of a greater set of discourses with the outward intent to root out sexual thoughts and actions, which he refers to as the "repressive hypothesis." However, these acts in fact served to foreground sex and sexuality and create more talk around and about sex than ever before. Given that these measures were conducted in name of the "good of the child," concerns about sexuality and sexual dysfunctions and children became inextricably linked (Foucault, 1978).

Normative Descriptions of Children's Sexual Knowledge and Behavior

One problem we have with thinking about children and children's sexuality is the multiple meanings for sex and sexual. The concept of "sex" itself is commonly understood in two major ways: (a) the constitution of male and female based on respective, dimorphic (the fact that humans usually come in two forms) reproductive organs and (b) the act of sexual intercourse (Cameron & Kulick, 2003). In the first definition, sex is a noun, frequently used interchangeably with gender; in the second, sex enacts a verb, generally referring to sexual intercourse.

Thus, the understanding of sex as intercourse implies the first: two sexes engage in sex for purposes of reproduction. The very suggestion of homosexuality takes issue with both of these: the constitution of men and women hinges on their sexual desire for and sexual intercourse with the opposite "sex," and the constitution of sex denotes intercourse necessarily conducted between women and men (Cameron & Kulick, 2003). Thus, a woman must desire and engage in sexual behaviors with the opposite sex and vice versa; to do otherwise is to be considered not a real woman or a real man (Butler, 1990).

Although adults tend to associate genital stimulation with sexual arousal, some early research has demonstrated that genital activation begins as an automatic process in the womb. In fact through ultrasound technology, male fetuses have been shown to have penile erections as early as the seventeenth week (Martinson, 1994). In this way, the penile erections result from a responsive reflex in the same manner of sucking, also known to occur *in utero*. Then upon birth, penile erections result from both this responsive reflux, e.g., during REM sleep, and from accidental or intentional stimulation (Langfeldt, 1990; Martinson, 1994). Given that genital activation in girls is more difficult to observe, scientific and medical studies for girls are more limited; nevertheless, at birth genital swelling and vaginal lubrication has been observed. (Langfeldt, 1990; Pollard, 1993). Thus, Nettie Pollard (1993) contends that it is now "indisputable that everyone is sexual, even before birth" (p. 108). Infant boys generally find their penis between the sixth and seventh month and infant girls between tenth and eleventh month (Galenson, 1990). Once the children gain upright mobility, infants more intentionally explore other parts of their body, including their genitalia. Children's sexed physiology holds great fascination for them largely because it is usually concealed underneath a diaper.

Gordon, Schroeder, and Abrams (1990b) tested 130 children ages 2–7 about their knowledge of sexuality, which included the topics gender identity, sex body parts, nonsexual body parts, sexual behavior, pregnancy, and private parts (a variable used to assess if children could identify their "private parts" and who was allowed to touch them for abuse prevention). Their research demonstrated a positive correlation with sexual knowledge and age, such that the two- and three-year-olds knew significantly less about sexuality than did the older children. While the two-year-olds answered correctly 40–50% of the questions about gender identity and nonsexual body parts, most of the children did not demonstrate knowledge of sexual behavior or pregnancy until six years of age. In fact, of the 130 children assessed, only eight demonstrated any knowledge of sexual intercourse. This affirms Waterman's (1986) position that children do not appear to demonstrate much knowledge of adult sexual behavior.

Interestingly, in a closely related study, Gordon, Schroeder, and Abrams (1990a) failed to observe any significant difference of knowledge or understanding of sexual behavior between sexually abused and nonabused children. Although some of the children may have been exposed to inappropriate sexual experiences, and in some cases quite severe, they lacked knowledge and understanding of the meaning of these behaviors.

In the last ten years, a growing body of scientific research has sought to determine a range of sexual behaviors most commonly occurring among young children. Sexually explorative behaviors, such as touching a mother's breasts and "playing doctor," has been found to be most common in children two to six years of age (Friedrich, Fisher, Broughton, Houston, & Shafran, 1998; Larsson & Svedin, 2002; Lindblad, Gustaffsson, Larsson, & Lundin, 1995; Sandnabba, Santilla, Wannäs, & Krook, 2003). In fact, an earlier study noted that up to 75% of children aged six and younger may engage in sexually explorative behavior (Friedrich, Grambisch, Broughton, Kuiper, & Bielke, 1991). Touching one's genitals, looking at other people when they are nude, masturbating, showing interest in the opposite sex, incorporating sex/romance into play activities all have been shown to be relatively common behaviors among young children. However, such behaviors tend to peak around five years of age and then decline for the next seven years (Friedrich, Fisher, Broughton, Houston, & Shafran, 1998).

Children quickly learn the powerful social mores around sexuality, including understanding of private versus public spheres. For instance, in comparative studies of children's sexual behaviors in daycares and at home, researchers noted children's increased likelihood of such exploratory and voyeuristic behaviors (trying to look at other children's genitals) at home rather than at daycare. Furthermore, they demonstrated a wider range of sexual behaviors and more often: they walked around naked indoors, talked about sex, were hugging adults outside the family, exhibited genitalia to adults (within the family), masturbated, and tried to touch other children's genitalia (Larsson & Svedin, 2002). While the frequency varied for each ranging from once or twice, to sometimes, to often, this suggests children may have increased opportunity and freedom to explore their bodies as well as others' at home as compared to daycare centers.

Given the resilient ideologies of children as innocent and sexuality as somehow an adult characteristic, to observe children using sexual language or engaging in sexual explorative play may disturb adults. Rothbaum, Grauer, and Rubin (1997) contend that adult anxiety about childhood sexuality stems from misunderstanding about its meaning and attributing adult meanings. In general, childhood sexual behavior is driven by curiosity and play, evokes spontaneity and openness, and underscores a child's own sensual pleasure. In contrast, adult sexuality tends to be intentional and goal-oriented, self-conscious, and desirous of privacy, and centered around passion and eroticism. For instance, childhood masturbation tends to evince a soothing effect for children, and for most does not appear to be associated with orgasm (Rothbaum, Grauer, & Rubin, 1997). Another common behavior among young children is touching of adult genitals (especially that of mothers), which Waterman (1986) suggested involved "determined curiosity, attempts at humor, and limit testing but not erotic fulfillment" (23). "Eroticism," Waterman (1986) continued, "is more than a physical sensation; it is an awareness and understanding of these sensations" (p. 25). Although some children's behaviors may on the surface appear quite adult-like, Rothbaum, Grauer, and Rubin (1997) reiterate the distinction in purpose and meaning.

The Question of (Hetero)sexuality

While the dominant narrative characterizes younger persons as both innocent and asexual, a parallel narrative underscores children's implicit and presumed heterosexuality. This potential paradox is tempered by modern psychological theories of childhood development, in which children are in a state of becoming (Piaget, 1955; Freud, 1938; Erikson, 1968). Children progress through a series of stages in regard to their cognitive, psychosocial, and sexual development. Specifically according to Freud, children must separate their affinities for their same-sex parent and transfer them to their opposite-sex parent in order to eventually demonstrate mature gender and heterosexual identities (1938).

Ironically, given the specialized nature of childhood, children who appear to be heterosexual or demonstrate heterosexual tendencies, e.g., through young girl-boy romance, and children who do not, by defying gender norms, for example, boys playing with dolls, or sexual norms, for example, a girl kissing a girl on the cheek, are given unusual latitude by adults. While "cute boy-girl romance reads as evidence for the mature sexuality that awaits them, any homoerotic behavior reads as harmless play among friends or as a mistake that can later be corrected by marriage" (Bruhm & Hurley, 2004, p. ix). Childhood thus is a state of temporal displacement, in which Bruhm and Hurley contend adults spend more time worrying about what *will* become of the child than worrying about how the "child exists as a child" (p. xiv). "The utopian projection of the childhood into the future actually opens up a space for childhood queerness—creating space for the figure of the child to be queer as long as the queerness can be rationalized as a series of mistakes or misplaced desires" (p. ix).

While adult projections of children can "forgive" childhood transgressions, recent research of children and young adults demonstrate their potency as sexual agents and regulators of powerful gender and sexual norms. Garvey (1984) documented the practice of teasing other children by mislabeling gender as frequent behavior among three- and four-year-olds. Elementary school students frequently enforce strict regulation of narrow gender roles through homophobic harassment and name-calling (Renold, 2000; Rofes, 1995. As such by middle school, girls and boys have learned the synonymy of gender identity with heterosexual behavior and the importance of maintaining appearances of heterosexuality (Harris and Bliss, 1997; Mac an Ghaill, 1994; Renold, 2003).

Censorship

Since the Puritans, children's and young adult literature has been used to mold the minds and spirits of their audiences. The literature has been heavily laden with moralistic messages meant to teach and instill proper manners and behaviors (Lesesne, 2004). For most of the history of children's literature, the primary organizations and personnel in charge of publishing and distributing children's literature were a homogenous group and did not purchase or promote books that they deemed inappropriate for young children. As such, they served as significant gatekeepers and regulators of children's literature, determining what was "good" and what was "bad" for children to read (Simmons, 2000). In fact as some researchers have noted, adults have always controlled access to children's literature, mediating what is accessible for children to even read (Anderson, 2004; MacLeod, 1994; Simmons, 2000). "Books that were bought were those the grown-ups thought the child *should* read; later, toward the end of the nineteenth century, that sentence would become 'what the grown-ups thought the child *liked* to read" (Anderson, 2004, p. 3).

However, cultural shifts in the publishing of children's literature in recent years have increasingly challenged what constitutes as "appropriate" for children to read. There may be no greater demonstration of this than the recent increase of publishing—and likewise censorship—of children's books that include of diverse family formations and emphasize the physicality of children's bodies (ALA, 2008). For instance, the realistic children's picture book *And Tango Makes Three* (Parnell & Richardson, 2005), which describes two male penguins who raise a chick as their own in the Central Park Zoo, topped the most challenged list of 2006 and 2007, with reasons cited as "homosexuality, anti-family, and unsuited to age group" (ALA, 2008). Then, of the 100 most frequently challenged books between 1990 and 2000, *Daddy's Roommate* (1990) by Michael Willhoite, a picture book about a child and his two dads, ranked second. *Heather has Two Mommies* (Newman, 1990) just missed the top ten list, ranking the eleventh most challenged book of the decade. Although Willhoite's book fell off the top 100 list for the years 2000–2007 and Newman's title fell to 100, Richardson & Parnell's picture book ranked ninth and *King and King* (de Haan & Nijland, 2002), a colorful picture book about a prince who refuses to marry a princess and marries another prince instead, ranked eighteenth.

Another powerful example of this trend to sanitize children's lives of any suggestions of sexuality, whether subtle or overt, is the censorship of books that mention any form of genitalia. Most notably Robie Harris' nonfiction texts that address children's changing bodies have been widely challenged for their "suitability" and "appropriateness." For example, *It's Perfectly Normal* (Harris, 1994), a book geared for 10- to 14-year-olds, discusses in frank and biologically correct terms sex, reproduction, and other physiological, emotional, and social changes that occur during puberty. As such, it has been challenged due to censors' concerns about "homosexuality, nudity, sex education, religious viewpoint, abortion and being unsuited to age group" (ALA, 2008). As a result, it has moved from its ranking of 15 between the years 1990–2000 to the eighth most challenged book between 2000 and 2007 (ALA, 2009). Strikingly, in 2005, Robie Harris's illustrated books both *It's Perfectly Normal* (Harris, 1994) and her related text for younger children *It's So Amazing!* (Harris, 1999) ranked first and tenth, respectively, on the list of most frequently challenged books in America.

Ironically, the inclusion of a single word that evokes sexual genitalia appears to be sufficient cause for censoring a novel, as in the case with the publication of Susan Patron's (2006) Newbery award winner *The Higher Power of Lucky*. After it won the Newbery, much attention and controversy were drawn to the book, particularly her use of the word "scrotum" on the first page. The main character, Lucky, listens through a hole in a wall as another character describes how a rattlesnake bit his dog on the scrotum. Although the novel did not make ALA's top ten list for 2007 of the most challenged books, the *New York Times* reported that the book had been banned from school libraries in a number of states in the South, West, and Northeast because of the use of that single word (Bosman, 2007, February 18). "The inclusion of the word has shocked some school librarians, who have pledged to ban the book from elementary schools, and reopened the debate over what constitutes acceptable content in children's books" (para. 4).

Repeatedly in these challenges, would-be censors refute the claim that they are "censoring" books, but rather protecting the innocence of children. In an effort to put forth a bill that would remove public funding for any library or school that included texts about gays or lesbians or by gay or lesbian authors, Alabama Representative Gerald Allen, contended, "I don't look at it as censorship. I look at it as protecting the hearts and souls and minds of our children" (Holguin, 2005, para. 4). Then, Jeff Issa, along with his wife Eileen, requested that their local library, Lower Macungie (Pa.) Library, remove the book *King and King* (de Haan & Nijland, 2002) from circulation due to its homosexual content. "I just want kids to enjoy their innocence and their time of growing up," Issa said. "Let them be kids and not worry about homosexuality, race, [or] religion" (ALA, 2008b, "*King and King*," para. 2). While censorship takes many forms, it is interesting that one reviewer of *And Tango Makes Three* (Parnell & Richardson, 2005) challenged on the publisher's (Simon and Schuster) website its publication in the first place:

> I cannot believe that this is a children's book. The story, albeit true, is about two male penguins who find "true love" in a male/male g.a.y. relationship. The zoo keeper provides them with an egg that they hatch and make a "family." If this is what people today want to teach their kids, that's fine, but do not promote this as a children's book. (Simon & Schuster, Books, *And Tango Makes Three*, 2009)

Interestingly, the author recognizes the veracity of the story but disputes its telling in a children's picture book. Again, the inference is that such a story is inappropriate for children, because children cannot understand homosexuality, of love between two same-sexed persons or creatures, or possibly more significantly that they should not be introduced to such possibilities at all.

Discussion and Conclusions

Developmentally appropriate models are modernist concepts that view children as not fully developed, rather than complete individuals just as they are at any given point in time. This mythos contrives children as innocent and asexual, and as such, needing special protection. This same set of ideologies has constructed sexuality, especially homosexuality, as something private, something to be concealed, something restricted within the adult realm. Yet, children are infused in a world, movies, commercials steeped in sexual innuendo and imagery. As such, they are exposed to sex and sexuality frequently in their daily lives yet given no education or information about such images.

Moreover, recent research from multiple Western countries has demonstrated normative sexual behaviors in children ranging from 2 to 7 years, including touching of adult genitals (usually the mother's), self-stimulation, use of sexual language, and some sex play ("playing doctor"). These behaviors have been attributed to children's healthy exploration of themselves and their world. Furthermore, affirming parental responses to these behaviors have shown to aid in children's positive self-concept.

By and large in contemporary society, children are given diverse information and modeling about body parts, proper hygiene, social interaction, except for aspects relating to their sex. Similarly, increased emphasis has been placed on children learning about diverse racial and ethnic cultures and diverse family formations (generally single or adopted), while information about sexual diversity, including gay- and lesbian-headed households remains overtly restricted. Although many adults and youth have understood themselves to be "different" in regards to sexual and gender orientations from very young ages, and according to the Census Bureau 270,313 children under the age of 18 are growing up in same-sex households, discussion of these topics remains off limits (Romero, Baumle, Badgett, & Gates, 2007).

Censorship of children's and young adult literature is a central apparatus derived from and reinforcing of these same modernist ideologies. Books that seek to dispel misinformation about children's physiological and sexual bodies, such as Robie Harris' *It's Perfectly Normal* (Harris, 1994) and *It's So Amazing* (Harris, 1999) or incorporate broader conceptions of family, such as *Heather Has Two Mommies* (Newman, 1990) or *And Tango Makes Three* (Parnell & Richardson, 2005) have been widely challenged and censored for doing so. Of the top three reasons for a book challenge, "unsuited to age group" appears to be used most broadly across age groups, especially for literature published for younger children.

Challenges to reexamine "developmentally appropriate" models and their ensuing ideologies are not new (Cannella, 1997, 2001); yet, they fiercely persist. But in doing so, they deny children's physiological and sexual selves, as well as information and literature that supports and embraces children's healthy exploration of those selves. Unfortunately, this avoidance, this denial likely says more about adults' continuing awkwardness about the broad scope of human sexuality than it does about children's.

References

American Library Association. (2008a). ALA unveils most-challenged books of 2005. Retrieved http://www.ala.org/ala/alonline/currentnews/newsarchive/2006abc/march2006ab/challenge05.cfm

American Library Association (2008b). *King and King* reigns in Pennsylvania. Retrieved http://www.ala.org/ala/alonline/currentnews/newsarchive/2007/december2007/kingreigns.cfm

American Library Association. (2009). Frequently challenged books. Retrieved http://www.ala.org/ala/aboutala/offices/oif/bannedbooksweek/challengedbanned/frequentlychallengedbooks.cfm

Anderson, V. (2004). *The dime novel in children's literature.* Jefferson, NC: McFarland & Company, Inc.

Beisel, N. K. (1997). *Imperiled innocents: Anthony Comstock and family reproduction in Victorian America.* Princeton, NJ: Princeton University Press.

Bosman, J. (2007, February 18). With one word, children's book sets off uproar. *New York Times*. Retrieved http://www.nytimes.com/2007/02/18/books/18newb.html

Bruhm, S. & Hurley, N. (2004). Curiouser: On the queerness of children. In S. Bruhm & N. Hurley (Eds.) *Curiouser: On the queerness of children* (pp. ix–xxxviii). Minneapolis, MN: University of Minnesota Press.

Burman, E. (1994). *Deconstructing developmental psychology*. London: Routledge.

Butler, J. (1990). *Gender trouble*. New York: Routledge.

Cameron, D. & Kulick, D. (2003). *Language and sexuality*. Cambridge, MA: Cambridge University Press.

Cannella, G.S. (1997). *Deconstructing early childhood education: Social justice and revolution*. New York: Peter Lang.

Cannella, G.S. (2001). Natural born curriculum: Popular culture and the representation of childhood. In J.A. Jipson & R.T. Johnson (Eds.), *Resistance and representation: Rethinking childhood education* (pp. 15–22). New York: Peter Lang.

Cherlin, A. (1983). Changing family and household: Contemporary lessons from historical research. *Annual Review of Sociology, 9*, 51–66. doi:10.1146/annurev.s0.09.080183.000411

de Haan, L. & Nijland, S. (2002). *King and king*. Berkeley, CA: Tricycle Press.

D'Emilio, J. & Freedman, E.B. (1997). *Intimate matters: A history of sexuality in America*. Chicago, IL: University of Chicago Press.

Erikson, E.H. (1968). *Identity, youth, and crisis*. New York: W.W. Norton.

Foucault, M. (1978). *The history of sexuality*, Vol.1. New York: Pantheon Books.

Freud, S. (1938). *The basic writings of Sigmund Freud*. New York: The Modern library.

Friedrich, W.N., Fisher, J., Broughton, D., Houston, M., & Shafran, C.R. (1998). Normative sexual behavior in children: A contemporary sample. *Pediatrics, 101*, 4, e9.

Friedrich, W.N., Grambsch, P., Broughton, D., Kuiper, J., Bielke, R. (1991). Normative sexual behavior in children. *Pediatrics, 88*, 456–464.

Galenson, E. (1990). Observation of early infantile sexual and erotic development. In J. Money & H. Musaph (Eds.), *Handbook of sexology* (pp. 169–178). New York: Elsevier.

Garvey, C. (1984). *Children's talk*. Cambridge, MA: Harvard University Press.

Gordon, B.N., Schroeder, C.S., & Abrams, J.M. (1990). Age and social-class differences in children's knowledge of sexuality. *Journal of Clinical Child & Adolescent Psychology, 19*, 1, 33–43.

Gordon B.N., Schroeder C.S., & Abrams J.M. (1990). Children's knowledge of sexuality: A comparison of sexually abused and nonabused children. *American Journal of Orthopsychiatry, 60*, 2, 250–257.

Harris, R.H. (1994). *It's perfectly normal : a book about changing bodies, growing up, sex, and sexual health*. Cambridge, MA: Candlewick Press.

Harris, R.H. (1999). *It's so amazing!: A book about eggs, sperm, birth, babies, and families*. Cambridge, MA: Candlewick Press.

Harris, M. & Bliss, G. (1997). Coming out in a school setting: Former students' experiences and opinions about disclosure. In M. Harris (Ed.), *School experiences of gay and lesbian youth: The invisible minority* (pp. 85–110). New York: Haworth Press.

Holguin, J. (2005, April 25). Alabama bill targets gay authors. Retrieved from http://www.cbsnews.com/stories/2005/04/26/eveningnews/main691106.shtml

Illick, J. E. (2002). *American childhoods*. Philadelphia, PA: University of Pennsylvania Press.

Jackson, Stevi. (1990). Demons and innocents: Western ideas on children's sexuality in historical perspective. In M.E. Perry (Ed.) *Handbook of Sexology, Vol. 7: Childhood and Adolescent Sexology* (pp. 23–49). Amsterdam, Netherlands: Elsevier Science Publishers.

Kimmel, M. (2006). *Manhood in America: A cultural history*. New York: Oxford University Press.

Langfeldt, T. (1990). Early childhood and juvenile sexuality: Development and problems. In J. Money & H. Musaph (Eds.), *Handbook of sexology*. New York: Elsevier.

Larsson, I. & Svedin, C.G. (2002). Teachers' and parents' reports on 3- to 6-year-old children's sexual behavior—a comparison. *Child Abuse & Neglect, 26*, 3, 247–266.

Lesesne, T.S. (2004). Young adult literature comes of age. In L. Pavonetti (Ed.), *Children's literature remembered: Issues, trends, and favorite books* (pp. 211–224). Westport, CT: Libraries Unlimited.

Lindblad, F., Gustafsson, P.A., Larsson, I. & Lundin, B. (1995). Preschoolers' sexual behavior at daycare centers: An epidemiological study. *Child Abuse & Neglect*, 19, 5, 569–577.

Mac an Ghaill, M. (1994). *The making of men: Masculinities, sexualities, and schooling*. Buckingham, UK: Open University Press.

MacLeod, A.S. (1994). *American childhood: Essays on children's literature of the nineteenth and twentieth centuries*. Athens, GA: University of Georgia Press.

Martinson, F.M. (1994). *The sexual life of children*. Santa Barbara, CA: Bergin and Garvey.

Newman, L. (1990). *Heather has two mommies*. New York: Alyson Publications.

Nilsen, A.P. & Donelson, K.L. (2001). *Literature for today's young adults*, 6th ed. New York: Longman.

Parnell, P. & Richardson, J. (2005). *And Tango Makes Three*. New York: Simon & Schuster.

Patron, S. (2006). *The higher power of Lucky*. New York : Atheneum Books for Young Readers.

Piaget, J. (1955). *The Child's construction of reality*. London: Routledge and Kegan Paul.

Plumb, J.H. (1971). The great change in children. *Horizon, 13(1)*, 4–12.

Pollard, N. (1993). The small matter of children. In A. Assiter & N. Pollard (Eds.), *Bad girls and dirty pictures: The challenge to reclaim feminism* (pp. 105–111). Boulder, CO: Pluto Press.

Renold, E. (2000). "Coming out": Gender, (hetero)sexuality and the primary school. *Gender and Education, 12(3)*, 309–326.

Renold, E. (2003). 'If you don't kiss me, you're dumped': Boys, boyfriends, and heterosexualised masculinities in the primary school. *Educational Review, 55(2)*, 179–194.

Robinson, K. H. (2002). Making the invisible visible: gay and lesbian issues in early childhood education. *Contemporary Issues in Early Childhood*, 3, 3, 415–433.

Rofes, E. (1995). Making schools safe for sissies. *Rethinking Schools 9(3)*, 8–9.

Romero, A.P., Baumle, A.K., Badgett, M.V.L., Gates, G.J. (2007, December). *Census snapshot: United States*. Los Angeles, California: The Williams Institute. Retrieved from http://www.law.ucla.edu/williamsinstitute/publications/USCensusSnapshot.pdf

Rothbaum, F., Grauer, A., & Rubin, D.J. (1997). Becoming sexual: Differences between child and adult sexuality. *Young Children, 52(6)*, 22–28.

Sandnabba, K.N., Santtila, P., Wannäs, M., Krook, K. (2003). Age and gender specific sexual behaviors in children. *Child Abuse & Neglect, 27*, 6, 579–605.

Sears, J. (1999). Teaching queerly: Some elementary propositions. In W.J. Letts IV & J.T. Sears (Eds.), *Queering elementary education: Advancing the dialogue about sexualities and schooling* (pp. 3–14). Lanham, MD: Rowman & Littlefield Publishers.

Simon & Schuster (2009). "Books, *And Tango Makes Three*" Retrieved http://books.simonandschuster.com/9780689878459

Simmons, J.S. (2000). Middle schoolers and the right to read. *ALAN Review, 27(3)*, 45–49.

Waterman, J. (1986). Developmental considerations. In K. MacFarlane & J. Waterman (Eds.), *Sexual abuse of young children: Evaluation and treatment* (pp. 15–29). New York: Guilford.

Willhoite, M. (1990). *Daddy's roommate*. Boston, MA: Alyson Wonderland.

CHAPTER NINETEEN

Critical Politics of Play

LIZ JONES, RACHEL HOLMES, CHRISTINA MACRAE AND
MAGGIE MACLURE

Abstract

The aim of this chapter is to consider how we, as researchers, might begin to contemplate the politicisation of children's representative gestures that are carried by and through different forms, manifestations and expressions of their playfulness. In particular, we mark out four 'reception classes' (described below) that were of central interest in the study. We argue that while each is assembled in ways that make them easy to identify as contemporary places for the young, they are nevertheless infected with spectres, mutations and the not quite absent past. As the chapter develops we brush against shadows, including Rousseau and Piaget so as to appreciate how play, while seemingly alive and well within each room nevertheless is tied to philosophical and political reverberations. These include among others 'the child' as manifested within child-centred progressive education with its utopian longings for the rational subject (Walkerdine, 1984; Burman, 1994, 2008). Through the data, we illuminate how it is possible to be discursively enmeshed within and at times shackled by the past yet simultaneously deeply conscious of more recent bodies of thinking. This chapter also seeks to set our own methodological foraging into play so as to forestall our customary ways of knowing the young child. By methodologically interfering with the data, it becomes possible to perceive play as a means of satisfying the hunger of both living and more ghostly discourses where young people are enveloped, entombed and enshrouded within stratifications of normalisation. In fathoming the interplay between play and politics at times we find resonance with Foucault's concept of 'heterotopias' (1967, 1986, 1998) where certain places, including in this instance the 'reception classroom,' bring together disparate objects from different times in a single space so as to offer protection from the erosion of 'real' time.

Introduction

The aim of this chapter is to mark out both consider how we, as researchers, might begin to contemplate the politicisation of children's representative gestures that are carried by and through different forms, manifestations and expressions of their playfulness. Because we will be drawing on data from a research project[1] that we were all involved with we will begin by offering a brief description of this. In particular we mark out four 'reception classes' that were of central interest in the study. Within these spaces, we make an uncanny move by suggesting that ideological echoes and discursive shadows haunt them. We argue that while each is assembled in ways that make them easy to identify as contemporary places for the young, they are nevertheless infected with spectres, mutations and the not quite absent past. As the chapter develops we brush against shadows, including Rousseau and Piaget so as to appreciate how play, while seemingly alive and well within each room nevertheless is tied to philosophical and political reverberations. These include among others 'the child' as manifested within child-centred progressive education with its utopian longings for the rational subject (Walkerdine, 1984; Burman, 1994, 2008). Through the data we illuminate how it is possible to be discursively enmeshed within and at times shackled by the past yet simultaneously deeply conscious of more recent bodies of thinking. Such bodies include 'the child' as apparent within the 'Every Child Matters'[2] (2005) agenda as well as the one who lingers within the standards culture where its lifeblood is kept in circulation through testing and auditing.

This chapter also seeks to set our own methodological foraging into play so as to forestall our customary ways of knowing the young child. By methodologically interfering with the data, it becomes possible to perceive play as a means of satisfying the hunger of both living and more ghostly discourses where young people are enveloped, entombed and enshrouded within stratifications of normalisation. In fathoming the interplay between play and politics at times, we find resonance with Foucault's concept of 'heterotopias' (1967, 1986, 1998) where certain places including in this instance the 'reception classroom' (described below) bring together disparate objects from different times in a single space so as to offer protection from the erosion of 'real' time.

The Research Context

In order to cover a range of student populations and provisions, the research project was located in four mainstream Manchester primary schools: a 'faith' school with students of mainly white-British heritage and a high entitlement to free school meals; an inner-city school with a multiethnic intake (c. 30 family languages spoken) including asylum seekers and refugees; a school in a 'leafy suburb' of moderately affluent homes; a city school in an area of social deprivation. Three members of the research team each spent one day a week in each of the four schools. The majority of research time was spent in what are referred to in England as the 'reception class.' Reception classes are the first stage of compulsory schooling in the UK, at age 4–5 years. As well as undertaking observations each researcher videoed certain events. Besides tracking actions within the classroom, time was also spent observing children's interactions in the playground, lunch queue and other settings within school so as to understand how children act and are perceived when outside the classroom. Fieldwork was collected over a period of eighteen months. This enabled us to closely observe the young people as they strove to negotiate the complexities that are involved when starting school as well as track their progression to the next stage of schooling.

Summoning the 'Paper Child'

Observation field-note:

> Every child is to be observed while at play…It is strange as the children are sorted out for the morning session because all the adults are observing children, armed with clipboards and pens…not much adult interaction with the children, and I don't feel out of place at all. (Christina MacRae, 26 September 2006)

The reception class within mainstream school embraces two pivotal moments. First it marks a point of departure for the child as she begins her journey through statutory education. It is a journey where in terms of the child's learning little will be left to chance. Various technologies including assessment and testing procedures will be used to regularly monitor and calibrate her overall educational development. Thus it is within such a departure that the second key event happens. The 'paper child' is born. Of course within the United Kingdom, various manifestations of the 'paper child' have had to be summoned at particular historical junctures for particular sets of reasons. However our interest does not so much lie in tracing historical demonstrations[3] of this particular phenomenon; rather our focus is on the interrelationship between the means by which the 'paper child' has been morphed in each of the reception classrooms and the relationship between this species and play.

As we have noted, the reception classroom is the first stage of statutory schooling, and it is not too surprising that the practitioners had to spend some time of the new academic year familiarising themselves with the young people. One orthodox means by which this is done is by establishing a 'base line assessment.' In English schools, the practice of undertaking a baseline assessment was 'originally devised to provide a fixed point from which progress could be assessed,' but more recently 'they have been seen as providing teachers with a detailed profile of their pupils from which to plan an appropriate curriculum and against which progress can be measured' (Tymms and Merrill, 2004: 107). MacRae's observation that is cited above provides a brief instance when children's play was being used as a form of assessment where it will assist in establishing 'what they [i.e. the children] know and can do at the point of entry [i.e., into school]' (Tymms and Merrill, 2004: 108). However, we want to consider how we might rethink children's play in political yet destabilising ways. We want to argue that while the 'paper child' can be understood as an exercise in total panoptic control, she nevertheless has to share spatial and temporal experiences with other discursive manifestations. Such existences linger within and emerge from ideological echoes and discursive shadows that haunt these classrooms. In seeking to develop an understanding of such affiliations as they were played out within the complexities of time and space we have found it productive to see the reception classroom as heterotopia (Foucault, 1967, 1986, 1998). From our perspective, heterotopias offer a means for appreciating spaces—including the reception classroom—as complex, often ambiguous sites where individuals are both controlled yet can control the organisation.

Foucault (1986) sought to develop a typology of heterotopias. As places, they are characterised as being connected to other places and yet outside of them. Think here of children's inventive play where the makeshift tent within the classroom or a den in the school grounds produces a different space that at the same time mirrors what is around them. Thus a tent or a den is a space that reflects and contests simultaneously. Moreover 'heterotopias are places that are situated in and across time, places that hold multiple, seemingly contradictory and exclusive, meanings to individuals at one and the same time…in some way they are capable of juxtaposing, in one real place, several different spaces' (Cairns et al., 2003: 135).

We propose to work within the scope of one of Foucault's examples of the heterotopia, that is, 'the mirror.' For Foucault, mirrors are intriguing because they completely disrupt one's spatial position where 'the space occupied is at the same time completely real and unreal, forming an utter dislocation of place' (Foucault, 1998: 179). Similarly echoes and shadows can create a disarming sense of distortion of both temporality and place as they dislocate themselves from what is 'original' in order for them to exist. The echo dislocates from the 'original' voice and the shadow falls away from its 'original' object. Thus we want to both dispel any notion of 'original' as well as open up the idea of reflection, echoes and shadows as simulacra that simultaneously throw back and contest. Accordingly, we will take examples of data and subject these to various forms of echolalia, shadowing and mirroring. As a first step we want to enact a dislocation by using examples of data derived from two of the other schools that were in the project and which had been collected by Jones and Holmes, respectively. In terms of 'real' time, the examples were collected at a similar point in the school term when MacRae was undertaking her observation of the teachers that were compiling profiles. Thus the children that feature in the subsequent data were in the second to third week of their respective reception classes. Our second step is to shadow the teachers or put a little differently mimic or mirror the teachers' actions by reading two examples of data within the framework of the 'Practice Guidance for the Early Years Foundation Stage' (Department for Education and Skills (DfES), 2007). For it is this document that the teachers themselves were using when compiling baseline profiles for the children. Moreover, this guidance is also an integral part of the 'Every Child Matters' agenda, a government-led initiative where children from 'all backgrounds' and 'all circumstances' will be pivotal in bettering society. The 'Practice Guidance for the Early Years Foundation Stage' benchmarks the age of the child with expected possibilities of behaviour, thereby authorising the notion that what is seen can be 'easily' matched with a series of developmental milestones. Our third move is to work with both the data and Foucault's notion of the mirror so as to 'see' ourselves. In describing the mirror, Foucault writes, 'I see myself where I am not, in an unreal, virtual space that opens up behind the surface; I am over there, there where I am not, a sort of shadow that gives my own visibility to myself, that enables me to see myself where I am absent' (Foucault, 1967: 3). Curiously Holmes, Jones and MacRae had each taught reception aged children so there is for each of them a strong sense of 'seeing themselves' as 'a sort of shadow' in a 'virtual space.' Put a little differently we want to dislocate attention away from the teachers so as to chase our own shadows and in so doing make visible some of the orthodoxies that surround early years education and which inevitably impact upon our own framing mechanisms.

The 'Child' and the 'House'

Observation field notes:

> Shahed meticulously rests the cloth so that it is on the table exactly as she wants it. She then proceeds to take out various items from the cupboard under the sink. She places knives, forks and spoons painstakingly on the table. Flowers are placed at the exact centre of the table. Each plate is given a selection of food and these are carried one by one to the table and set appropriately. The chairs are then aligned. On each a soft toy is made to sit up. The dog is then put into the basket and food is prepared for it and a bowl is set down. (Liz Jones, 28 September 2006)

If we examined 'the child' within this observation under the rubric of the 'Practice Guidance for the Early Years Foundation Stage' (DfES, 2007) we could make a number of statements in terms of

Shahed's current development. We might, for example, make mathematical judgements where her 'painstaking' activities with the cutlery points to a child who can estimate accurately so that each soft toy has the requisite number of implements. From this base, one potential next step would be to encourage Shahed to 'experiment with a number of objects, the written numeral and the written number' and that she would develop this 'through matching activities with a range of numbers, numerals and a selection of objects' (p. 67). Meanwhile under the category of 'Developing imagination and imaginative play' our recordings might refer to Shahed's capabilities in noticing 'what adults do' so that she is able to spontaneously imitate 'when the adult is not there' (p. 113). Given this 'starting point' our role, would be to 'support [Shahed's] excursions into imaginary worlds by encouraging inventiveness, offering support and advice on occasions' and 'ensuring that [she] has experiences that stimulate [her] interest' (p. 113). Additionally our observations might predispose us to record that she can 'respond in a variety of ways to what she sees, hears, touches and feels' (p. 107) where our next task would be make ourselves 'alert to [Shahed's] changing interest and the way [she] responds to experiences differently when [she] is in a happy, sad or reflective mood' (p. 107).

Effectively it is possible to read the above description of the home as an embodiment of rational and normal behaviour. The virtual space that the observation creates allows us to see a child whose affinities, mastery and connections with the house and its objects alludes to a domestic pedagogy where it is highly likely that the 'mother as teacher' (Walkerdine & Lucey, 1989) has provided Shahed with a solid foundation upon which subsequent learning can be built. Within her own home, Shahed has evidently been busy 'doing' and as a consequence of hearing, seeing and remembering she has developed understanding. Wittingly or unwittingly Shahed's family home has provided a space where its pedagogic practices in the form of domestic rituals have gone straight to the heart of child centred pedagogy where doing and understanding are the cornerstones of both effective and normalised learning. It is possible to perceive within the simulation of the classroom home what James et al. (1998) refer to as 'the unholy alliance between the human sciences and human nature' (p. 17). As an alliance it was one that was significantly orchestrated by Piaget whose linear and ordinal model would have the child moving along a continuum whose stages are ordered temporally and arranged hierarchically. As a 'little woman/mother' each of Shahed's actions can be read as evidence of or clue to her overall normal development. As her teacher, we can use her play to fill in various categories where 'there are no facts, no knowledge stated outside the terms of a developmental accomplishment' (Walkerdine, 1984: 158; see also Burman, 1994, 2008; Morss, 1990).

In his early work, Piaget employed the concept of the 'circle of science' (1972) where knowledge is assured and logic will work at warding off 'metaphysical disappointments' (Gruber and Voneche, 1977: 42). In turning back again to Liz Jones' observation, it is interesting to note how in describing the scene Liz seemed intent on conveying the preciseness and the procedural qualities of the young girl's play. Given the kinds of words that she has used including for instance ones such as 'meticulously,' 'exactly,' 'painstakingly,' 'appropriately' and 'aligned' Liz was driven to both record and express the carefulness of the play in ways that might circum/scribe it within a 'ring of truth.' It is we think possible to perceive Shahed's play as a manifestation of a ring of truth or science where her psychological and physical experiences produce a body that evokes a singular and universal notion of what it means to be 'a house/wife.' Rousseau's (1979) contributions to political philosophy in general and early years education in particular also finds resonance here with Shahed's mirroring activities. A central idea within Rousseau's work was that 'man' is by nature good but that he (sic) is corrupted and depraved by society. In the work, Emile Rousseau set out an agenda for living righteously. Here the child can take the lead from and follow a 'guardian' so that the task of living in the 'right' way is accomplished. In the above discussions, we have suggested that it is likely that Shahed is shadowing and imitating her own mother when playing in the home. We would suggest that her mother has taken on the mantle of the 'guardian' and has given her daughter knowledge that includes knowing how kitchens work but also how 'others,' including in this instance soft toys and a dog, must have their needs met. If we now return to the 'Practice Guidance for the Early Years Foundation Stage,' it is possible to discern how both Rousseau's notion of the guardian as well as Piaget's 'circle of science' is still operational. Above we have already indicated how it is the practitioner's professional responsibility to support Shahed's excursions 'into imaginary worlds' to give 'support and advice' as well as ensuring that she will have experiences that will 'stimulate [her] interest.' Elsewhere this document also reiterates how practitioners must work with the child so as to 'practice and build up ideas, concepts and skills' (p. 24). As such there is an elision between the natural, innocent child who must be supported and advised with the scientific child who through developmentally appropriate practice (Bredekamp, 1987) will 'make sense of the world.' Within the Every Child Matters agenda the notion of guardian is still a forceful presence where teachers together with other agencies are mandated to guard children's maturation so that they grow in ways that will contribute towards the 'good society.'

The 'House' as Mutually Repellent Spaces

As we have noted earlier in the chapter, the teachers' observations were directed at assessing children's play so that individual profiles for each child could be constructed. Our own mirroring activities led us to read Shahed's play using an example of curriculum guidance. While arguably minimal attention has been given to this document, it is nevertheless apparent that it is a mechanism for looking at the present so as to determine the future. If we fancied we could see it as a glass ball. But as we shall subsequently argue it is a glass ball with significant shortcomings because it offers a singular, straight and narrow conceptualisation of young children. In turning to our next examples of play we want to shake the ball and turn its contents into ghostly, milky shapes where rather than pure perception we have to make do with glimpses, vibrations or what Deleuze describes as the 'out-of-field' (1986: 17). Here Deleuze is referring to the work of the camera. So in watching a cinematic image, we see what is in the frame, but we are also attuned to events or other features that are not immediately within our sight lines. Think here of the camera roving over Shahed's play but where additionally both Liz Jones and Shahed herself would still be hearing the calls, cries, exclamations of those other actors who circulate around them both. Thus the 'out-of- field' is the stuff that is not within immediate perception or directly reflected back to us but which lies outside of the frame. While absent, it nevertheless has presence. With the following extracts of data, it is interesting to think further about absence, reflections, echoes and shadows at work.

Observation field note:

> 'It's so lovely seeing so many of you playing fairly in the house, especially you Ricky. You're playing properly…' (teacher) (Rachel Holmes, 2 October 2006)

Within this extract, we can observe the teacher affirming classroom doctrines. Thus play not only displays children's capacities to display fairness, but it also reflects their growing awareness of how to 'play properly.' This moment seems to reassure the teacher (and the researcher who notes this incident as an example of 'good behaviour') that 'the paper child' (en)lightened by dominant early years classroom narratives is (im)potently evoking 'correct play.' The teacher's efforts to nurture appropriate ways of the children 'being' with each other, as well as enacting suitably compliant interpretations of play, create something of a solid presence that is reified by, and in turn reifies the curriculum documents. However, also of interest to us is the child that simultaneously inhabits heterotopic worlds, where the elicit shadows cast behind an unsettling presence and the ways those shadows render the child as an ideological echo within (dis)located heterotopias.

These data offer us an excerpt of play that could be understood to move among murkier shadows. By using the metaphorical spaces of the shadow and echo, we find ways to dislocate ourselves as researchers from what could be understood as the classroom rhetoric and practices being analysed in obvious ways. As the echo dislocates from the 'original' voice, the shadow falls away from its 'original' object, but they both make use of 'lean-to' mechanisms (Stronach, 2008) in order for them to be understood as shadows or echoes. For example, the shadow needs to lean-to a solid presence in order to be a shadow; the echo needs to lean to, yet simultaneously menace the voice in order to avoid being just another voice. Thus we want to firstly dispel any notion of 'original' and secondly open up the idea of reflections, echoes and shadows as simulacra that simultaneously throw back and contest. We will begin by observing that in some ways this is an out-of-kilter home.

Observation field notes:

> Outside in the home corner, children are role playing—bulldogs, puppy dogs and cats. There is a mum who is looking after the animals. Joshua, Olivia and Tyler are animals, all eating everyone else's (sic) food. 'That's the last of the dog food' said Joshua. He takes a teapot and says to Olivia, 'I'm pouring boiling water all over you.' Olivia responds, 'I'm telling my cousin, my BIG cousin of you.' Joshua stops pouring. 'I'm telling him' says Olivia (Rachel Holmes, 25 September 2006)

Certain elements such as a mum sorting out food are comfortably familiar to us but it is concurrently a dangerous space where cruelty and latent violence sit alongside sharing 'everyone else's food.' The anthropologist Mary Douglas notes that:

> …from all possible materials, a limited selection has been made and from all possible relations a limited set has been used. So disorder by implication is unlimited, no pattern has been realised in it, but its potential for patterning is indefinite. This is why, though we seek to create order, we do not simply condemn disorder. We recognise that it is destructive to existing patterns; also that it has potentiality. It symbolises both danger and power (Douglas, 1966: 94).

If disorder has potentiality, might we gain something from thinking about this home in terms of being a mutually repellent space where peculiar and repugnant relations are aired? Above we noted how Christina MacRae did not feel 'out of place at all' because both she and the teachers were similarly employed in watching and recording. Meanwhile, there are elements of oddness and strangeness within Rachel's description where it has a sense of being 'all over the place.' Her observation is rich in that it carries aspects of children's lives that are denied or are less readily available to us than within the description of Shahed's play. But it is opaque in that it is difficult disentangling certain threads. Who for instance is the bulldog? Do we guess that it's a role that was undertaken, even snapped up by one of the boys? What about the mum? Is this a mum in the guise of one of the animals? Or has she retained a human form? Are we even right to assume that she is indeed a she? Rachel herself adds further to our confusion where she slides between using 'else' as in 'everyone else's food' and the 'fact' that it is animals eating the 'dog food.' Would it be possible to use our previous strategy and read this play against 'The Practice Guidance for the Early Years Foundation Stage'? Can we make explicit statements or neat judgements on our clipboards? A more generative approach might be to offer an 'out of place' or even an 'all over the place' reading of this disorderly house where additionally children are also understood as being 'all over the place' rather than caught within a linear notion of maturation. Taylor and Richardson (2005: 166) argue that the home within reception classrooms is a 'sign-laden' space that has a 'decidedly straight, white and middle class aesthetic.' The effect of which is to reproduce 'a universalised ideal of utopian domestic space and normative family relations that are suitable for children to emulate.' Certainly the observation that Liz Jones made of Shahed's play sits quite comfortably within this analysis. Similarly if we were to follow the philosophical inclinations of Froebel in relation to play it would be possible to perceive Shahed's as being the site where 'not only the germ, but also the core of his (sic) [her] whole future life…individuality, selfhood, future personality' was being constituted (1826:4). Likewise within the Montessori tradition, Shahed's play would be understood as 'spontaneous manifestations of the child's nature' (Montessori, 1964: 28). However, in taking note of Douglas, we want to juxtapose the scrupulous ordering that occurs within Shahed's play against the more intangible efforts of the children-as-animals. In so doing, we seek to make ourselves more open to other possibilities where our previous reading of Shahed can be trifled with. Accordingly we will return to Foucault's theories in relation to the heterotopias so as to both read the orderly and the disorderly within curious spaces.

Ideological Echoes and Discursive Shadows

In Greek mythology, Echo was a nymph who was condemned by Hera to speak only when echoing the words of others. She fell hopelessly in love with Narcissus and pined away in unrequited passion until only her voice was left (Zissos, 2000). Derrida's reflections quoted in Dick et al. (2005) on this myth are helpful because he directs our attention to the image that lies embedded within it. He notes that 'one sees the myth as about the relationship between specular image and voice, between sight and voice, between light and speech, between the reflection and the mirror.' We consider how in not too dissimilar ways we too are trying to grapple with such relationships when for instance we make the move between 'seeing' an example of play and making sense of it. Put a little differently while we want to shed light on the politics of play we nevertheless realise how our own spectating practices suffer from narcissistic tendencies where such seeing is never innocent and always blinded by our own personal investments. As Derrida forewarns, '…Narcissus realizes that he can only see himself, that it's only his own image he is seeing in the water. To see only oneself is a form of blindness. One sees nothing else' (2005: 94). Thus our methodology when examining the reception classroom tries to evoke rather than pin down where by playing among the discursive shadows that reside within the early years classroom, we want to tentatively voice some of the work that these insubstantial yet powerful bodies perform.

We suspect that in looking in at Shahed's play most of us would in all likelihood see it as ordinary, common place and quite predictable. It is in this way that it comes to be seen as natural. Of course, what has been overlooked within this reading is that the 'home' in which Shahed plays is a 'specific kind of adult world.' It is an embodiment of an ideal but it is also what Defert refers to as 'a spatio-temporal unit' (1997: 275) where as an emplacement both time and objects have been meticulously arranged. It is akin to another of Foucault's heterotopias, the prison where time both mirrors real time so night and day exists but where it also carries notions of suspension, of 'doing' time or having 'time out.' Similarly it echoes another heterotopia, that is, the Jesuit colonies in South America where all aspects of life were regulated in minute detail (Johnson, 2006). Both prisons and religious communities are practices in colonising 'deviants' or 'savages/natives' so as to 'return' the individual to some presumed notion of normal or 'original' state. The house as heterotopia or to use a term favoured by Derrida (1976), the house as palimpsest bears 'traces' of various philosophical traditions and political intentions aimed at summoning 'the child' who while a simulacrum nevertheless is made substantial or embodied through being 'written upon.' The lingering assumption is that beneath these graphics or tracings lies an original. The following quotation echoes our thinking:

> In the move from common-sense assumption to full-blown philosophy, realism relies upon the projection of a picture or metaphor. It takes the characteristics of immediacy, solidity, familiarity, externality and objectivity of the physical world around us, the everyday world in which we lead our lives, have breakfast, go to school, make discoveries and develops the picture into a model of reality itself (Parker, 1997: 81).

If Shahed isn't real then who is she? In a sense any attempts at articulating an answer has to be undertaken or at least considered within the discourse that we are seeking to sustain or according to the path that we choose to follow (Derrida, 1976). Hence if we were to read Shahed through the filament of Freud's psychoanalytical theory for instance our description might alter. We might for example describe her as precocious where her obsession with order is almost creepy. Following Stockton (2004), we could compare her to 'the child' within Victorian fiction where a splitting has to be undertaken so as to allow 'mother-wife conglomerations' (p. 291), allowing daughters to play both mother and wife to their fathers.[4] Of course, in the absence of a husband or a father we don't know in any sort of conclusive way how Shahed might actually relate to either. We could hazard however in an 'out of field' fashion that within her house husbands, like soft toys, might be brought into some kind of Freudian alignment where 'marriage is not made secure until the wife has succeeded in making her husband her child' (Freud, 1974: 134). Alternatively, we could pause for a moment so as to consider how traditionally for numerous cultural, political and economic reasons the home has been aligned with the feminine and has accordingly been perceived as a place of exclusion from the 'real.' This prompts us to ask whether Shahed was pushed or pulled in terms of playing in the home? We will return to this question subsequently.

So, if our strategy in perceiving Shahed within these more fanciful terms is to both foreground while simultaneously detract from the more immediate, ordinary and habitual ways of seeing her play what sorts of 'all over the place readings' can we offer in relation to the house that is home to the children-as-animals? Interestingly one of the reasons for the teachers watching the children while at play was to identify what sorts of learning and knowledge they bring into school. What is interesting here is that there is a tacit recognition that the children have 'pasts.' Yet as Stockton (2004) notes the idea of children having a past is 'antithetical' to universal notions of childhood. She writes, 'The child is spectre of who we were when there was nothing yet behind us.' This, as she goes on to explain 'is the normative child—or the child who, on the path to normativity, seems safe to us and whom we, consequently seek to safeguard at all cost' (p. 296). As referred to previously schools and other agencies are integral to the overall success of the 'Every Child Matters' agenda. The growth of this child, that is, the one who comes from all communities and all backgrounds represents our collective efforts to seize hold of time so that growth or maturation can be disciplined, managed and tamed. What links the child-from-all-backgrounds and all-communities is its (presumed) 'innocence.' Stockton describes such innocence as a 'form of normative strangeness' because it is what we adults apply to the child which—while 'lost' to us and is thus 'alien'—we nevertheless 'retrospect it through the gauzy lens of what [we] attribute to the child.' She summarises the conundrum that we adults face where we 'must walk the difficult line of keeping the child at once what it is (what adults are not) and leading it toward what it cannot (at least, as itself) ever be (what adults are)' (p. 297).

Joshua, Olivia and Tyler's play does convey a sense of their past where it hints at what Probyn

(1996: 324) refers to as the 'perplexity of living.' Within the home the children's play fluctuates between relatively (straight) forward performances (mums getting food) with more weird or curious ones where envisaged acts of violence are suddenly aired. This place recalls what Freud (1974: 86) refers to as the 'uncanny' aspects of social life with its complex shuttling between the heimlich and the unheimlich, that is the homely and the unhomely where each glances off each other in perplexing ways. Within this framing mechanism we could ask: Is this a space of protection or one of (possible) death? What forms of maturation or growth will occur in this space where there seem to be more schisms than unity? Such questions are a little different than those that we posed earlier when being guided by an orthodoxy but our persistence in asking is driven by its aspirations where our role as the teacher is envisaged as supporting children's 'excursions into imaginary worlds by encouraging inventiveness, offering support and advice on occasions' (p. 17). So what kinds of advice do we give a boy who wants to pour boiling water on someone? What actions do we take when the BIG cousin is summoned to settle an infringement or an old score?

Metaphorical Movements and Time

As a starting point, we might consider why the children are choosing to be animals and importantly why they are choosing to be animals within a space that is designated as a 'home.' Taking our lead from Stockton (2004), we can perceive children becoming animals as a metaphorical move undertaken to allow for ' growth.' This is not, however, growth as understood in terms of growing up but 'growing sideways' (p. 279). Stockton's thoughts around 'growth' have been partly influenced by Deleuze and Guattari's (1980) work *A Thousand Plateaus*, where one example they give of a plateau or a state of 'intensity' is 'becoming an animal.' While 'becoming an animal' within Deleuze and Guattari's frame has nothing to do with either sentimentality or domestic ties it nevertheless has an interesting relationship with movement and time. They write that 'becoming an animal is an assemblage that a child can mount in order to solve a problem from which all exits are barred him (sic)' (1980: 260). Given these thoughts in relation to 'becoming an animal' and returning once again to both our children-as-animals and the solitary Shahed we want to ask: what is their 'problem,' what is it they are 'trying to solve,' what are the 'exits' (to the problem) and why are they currently 'barred'?

In the above discussion, we have already alluded to the children's growth in terms of 'growing sideways' where a horizontal notion of both time and movement is interrupted. We want to carry on working around the dimension of time so as to address the above questions and in so doing foreground the interrelationship between the above enquiries and politics. In the absence of knowing with any degree of 'certainty' just what the children's own reasons were for assuming their animal guises we nevertheless want to continue the analysis by staying within the methodological spirit provided by an 'out of the field' and 'out of place' way of working. As a first step, we want to propose that in becoming animals the children are executing a metaphorical shift. Such a step allows us to develop an analysis of children's play and its links with their maturation in ways that both recognises the attraction of Modernist notions of 'good' including the hope for a 'better' society while simultaneously maintaining a deep scepticism in relation to those normalised relations that are currently used in pursuit of the ideal.

In part, we understand 'the problem that has no exit' in terms of an obsession with 'fixing' children within an idealised notion of what it means to be a child. The gaze that Liz Jones cast upon Shahed and the resultant text that emerged from that gaze situated her play within a set of blindingly obvious binaries where Shahed personified everything that is not male so as to be female and where as a consequence order prevailed over disorder. Previously it was noted how 'the house' and its objects also work at scripting what is and is not possible in terms of 'being.' As such both Liz's observation and 'the house' conspire so as to 'stitch' (MacLure, 2003: 9) the young girl so that she is pinned or 'positioned within a particular moral universe' and in turn 'invested with a particular identity' (MacLure, ibid: 9). This begs the question: must Shahed be stitched up in this way? We will let this question hang momentarily.

Previously, we have noted the disjointed qualities of Rachel Holmes' observation. Whilst recognising that it could be critiqued on the grounds that it does not provide us with an accurate picture, we nevertheless savour its inability to tell the whole story. It provides gaps where it becomes possible to think beyond that which is habitual. Homes are where acts of growing-up are undertaken. But the children-as-animals that are within Holmes' description muddle some of our more tightly held notions about maturation. Following Stockton, we suggest that the guise of animal performs 'a metaphorical pause' (Stockton, 2004: 299) where customary notions of 'being' are suspended. It is in this sense that the dog or the puppy or the cat becomes a 'political animal,' one that within 'modernist abstractions of time' grants to children 'a precious kind of shelter for their feelings and their growth' (Stockton, 2004: 299). As Douglas notes above, 'order implies restriction' and certainly with Shahed's play there is a deep sense of restriction where one suspects that because of the crippling effects of her child-as-mother persona her play is destined to be reiterative where exits to a different way of being, that is, to experience herself within multiple subject positionings (see Davies, 1989; Brown and Jones, 2001; Jones and Brown, 2002) will be frustrated and maybe even barred. The 'animal as shelter' that is offered to the children in Holmes' description allows for a momentary departure from normalised play patterns. Take the incident where they are all 'eating everyone else's food.' While this could be considered a form of sharing is it we wonder the kind of sharing that is promoted within early-years education? Arguably, within this arena it is the discourse of liberal humanism that still pervades where young children are often exhorted to be kind to one another and to share. A different and maybe a more generative way of seeing the performance of children-as-animals eating is to frame it within what Deleuze (1986) refers to as the 'milieu.' Thus it is the 'milieu' within which the children find themselves that 'actualises' what Deleuze describes as 'several qualities and powers' including 'impulse' (p. 127). It is the qualities, powers and impulses of the milieu itself that 'leads each to choose its part, await its moment, defer its gesture, and borrow the outlines of form which will best enable it to perform its act' (p.28). Significantly what is absent from the milieu is the idea that the actor or character will appeal to some external notion of how to act. Thus if we look back at the performance of Joshua, Olivia and Tyler as animals where they are all eating 'everyone else's food' there is a sense of 'muddling through' rather than sharing against some rational constitution of fairness.

If the child-as-animal is provided with some kind of metaphorical pause or respite from normative notions of maturity what sort of metaphorical play can be evoked from the child who wants to pour boiling water onto another member of the house. Similarly what about the insertion of the BIG cousin into the play? If as Lacan posits we are 'born into language' (1977:103) what might we infer from children who are articulating intentions that are cruel, painful and dangerous? Are we witnessing forms of play that are the by-products of growing up in impoverished communities where parents are failing in their duty to nurture their children properly? Does such play sit easily within the 'Every Child Matters' agenda where the young child is perceived as the salvation of society (Baker,

1998; Rose, 1999, Wagner, 1994)? Are these children getting what is referred to in government rhetoric as a 'good start in life'? Will these young people mature into citizens who will contribute towards the 'nation's social and economic interests?' (DES; DWP & DTI, 2004).

If we were to read Joshua within the terms of his play being somehow 'improper' then our responses to him as his teacher would inevitably have to involve a whole gamut of practices predicated on the idea of ensuring he understood there were right ways of behaving, which in turn is predicated on the notion of there being a right way of being. Effectively we would be legitimising the kinds of play that could or could not go on within the home. Our argument does not involve legitimising cruelty but it does recognise what we referred to earlier as the 'perplexities' of living. Within such perplexities, children 'are 'subjected' to a variety of different often conflicting, discourses, with differing criteria of authenticity and truth' (MacLure, 2003: 19). The 'passivity' of Shahed's soft toy family meant that her authority in the home was never disputed. Within this space she could assume a particular position that didn't have to be negotiated, wrangled with or fought over. What Joshua's boiling water and Olivia's BIG cousin allow us to see is that 'identity is complex, confusing and, above all, an ongoing struggle' (MacLure, 2003: 19). While we cannot explain why Joshua made a shift from becoming-animal to becoming potentially cruel, we nevertheless need to recognise that within this space and within his terms he was trying to execute a renegotiation or reconfiguration of who he might become. Momentarily we can see him trying on a guise that is slightly different to the child who notes, 'That's the last of the dog food.' So, holding the teapot, he states that he is going to pour boiling water on Olivia. Having destabilised the children-as-animals play and in that sense interrupted the discursive practices that surrounded this particular performance he obliges Olivia to also assume a different set of practices. She could have run to an adult and sought their help in admonishing Joshua. Instead she sought refuge in her own current understanding of how the world works and as a consequence evoked the spectre of a BIG cousin. And whilst Joshua is immediately quelled this is not quite sufficient to satisfy Olivia who sensing that she has got Joshua on the (metaphorical) run persists in her own ways of turning the screw where she echoes the threat of 'still telling.' The BIG cousin is clearly not present but lurks in an out-of-field way so while not in the frame can nevertheless exert control. What this play allows us to see is the fluidity surrounding notions of being where the children had to undertake 'discursive work' so as to negotiate 'the rapids of desirable and undesirable identities' (MacLure, 2003: 19) that each encountered in the heterotopic space. We could say that by holding the teapot and threatening malpractice Joshua created an impasse for Olivia and maybe even for himself. However, Olivia by threatening to 'tell' breaches or suspends the social world that they had hitherto been inhabiting and it is in this sense she mounts or executes some sort of exit to 'the problem.'

In using the heterotopia, we aimed to examine brief examples of play with an intensity that sought to magnify or to go beyond what is ordinarily seen with the naked eye. But while we wanted to look differently, we nevertheless recognise how our own account(ing) practices have slipped dangerously close to valorising the more transgressive play of the children-as-animals over Shahed's solitary performance. Thus in our efforts to ward off some of the effects of positioning Shahed as the negative 'other' to the (positive) animals-as-children we want to return to the two questions that we left dangling when we asked 'Was Shahed pushed or pulled in terms of playing in the home?' and 'Must Shahed's identity be 'stitched up' in a particular way?'

We want to suggest that the two questions are interrelated where notions of 'push,' 'pull' and 'identity' cannot be separated out from 'desire' embedded within the complexities of what it could mean to 'be.' So on the one hand Shahed is pulled into the home because it might well resemble the real and in that sense she is drawing comfort and inspiration from its normative depiction of [her] social life. In terms of 'push' we wonder whether this might be understood as forms of 'pushing out' where her painstaking and meticulous practices are aimed in part at 'repelling' others? In other words, might her play be understood as asserting some kind of temporary privacy or respite from the forced sociality within the reception classroom where 'playing with others' is understood as a natural part of what it means to be a social body? Within organisational research, there is a phenomenon that is described and referred to as 'occupation rights.' Public libraries are a good example of where 'occupational rights' are practiced where certain users work hard at creating 'no-go zones' aimed at deterring other users. So personal artefacts will be aligned in ways that create barriers against others and or rights to particular chairs will be established by regularly occupying them for significant periods of time (Sommer, 1969). As Cairns et al. note (2003: 129), 'in organizational settings these rights manifest themselves in the personalisation of the working area as a visible expression of an individual's identity, interests and ownership.' They elaborate further, 'such territorial rights are jealously guarded often in spite of formal management policies.' Thus we can perceive the home as being both a place of freedom and control. So on the one hand, it offers an exit from the disciplinary collective of the classroom but in order to safeguard her sanctuary, she has to perform what almost looks like a ritual process so as to ward off other 'users.'

Concluding Remarks

Taking our own observations of play as a point of departure we have tried to echo, mirror and at times imitate conventional practices that are undertaken within the reception classroom. We tried to illustrate the relationship between conventions and inventions that in this instance materialises the 'paper child.' The documentation of children within a normative trajectory is both a way of knowing the child in terms of the present but it is additionally a form of tagging, labelling and classifying for future economic and political purposes. As such, play becomes part of the surveillance machinery aimed rendering children transparent where their regulation can be directed towards some fixed point.

Working with/in Foucault's conceptualisation of heterotopias has allowed us to take those necessary steps in which to see something a little differently. In worrying our own descriptions of children's play we sought to both foreground the relationship between play and political imperatives. But we have also sought to meddle with our own representational practices and in that sense we perceive heterotopias as practices in what Johnson describes as 'drawing us out of ourselves' (Johnson, 2006: 84). In drawing ourselves out of ourselves we have come to see the reception classroom as a place where hope, including hope for a better society coexists with normative and repressive practices; where notions of what it means to 'grow' oscillate between linearity, ambivalence and contradiction; where 'the child' is written upon so as to reflect an external fantasy but where she strikes back so as to displace, invert and overall remind us that there are other contestations of what it might mean 'to be' a child.

Notes

1. The research that underpins this chapter was supported by funding from the UK Economic and Social Research Council (Becoming a Problem: How and Why Children Acquire a Reputation as Naughty in the

Earliest Years at School, ref: RES—062–23–0105).

2. 'Every Child Matters' is a government programme for a national framework to support the 'joining up' of children's services including education, culture, health, social care and justice. The government's aim is for every child, whatever their background or circumstances, to have the support they need to: be healthy; stay safe; enjoy and achieve; make a positive contribution and achieve economic well-being.

3. See Broadfoot, P. (1996) *Education Assessment and Society*. Buckingham: Open University Press; Gipps, C. (1994) *Beyond Testing*. London: Falmer Press; Torrance, H. (2000) 'Postmodernism and educational testing,' in Filer, A. (Ed) *Assessment and Social Practice*. London: Falmer Press.

4. See, for example, Charlotte Bronte's Villette.

References

Baker, B. (1998) Childhood-as-rescue in the emergence and spread of the U.S. public school. In (eds) Popkewitz, T.S. & Brennan, M.D. *Foucault's Challenge: Discourses, Knowledge, and Power in Education*. New York: Vintage Books.

Bredekamp, S. (Ed.) (1987) *Developmentally Appropriate Practice in Early Childhood Programs Serving Children from Birth through Age 8*. Washington, DC: National Association for the Education of Young Children.

Brown, T. and Jones, L. (2001) *Action Research and Postmodernism: Congruence and Critique*. Buckingham: Open University Press.

Burman, E. (1994) *Deconstructing Developmental Psychology*. London: Routledge.

Burman, E. (2008) (2nd ed.) *Deconstructing Developmental Psychology*. London: Routledge.

Cairns, G. McInnes, P. and Roberts, P. (2003) Organisational space/time: from imperfect panoptical to heterotopian understanding. Ephemera: Critical Dialogues on Organisation. Vol 3 (2), pp. 126–139.

Davies, B. (1989) *Frogs, Snails and Feminist Tails: Preschool Children and Gender*. Sydney: Allen and Unwin.

Defert, D. (1997) Foucalt, space, and the architects, in politics/poetics. Documenta X-The Book. Ostfildern-Ruit: Cantz Verlag.

Deleuze, G. (1986) *Cinema 1*. Trans. H. Tomlinson & B. Habberjam. London: Continuum.

Deleuze, G. and Guattari, F. (1980) *A Thousand Plateaus: Capitalism and Schizophrenia*, Trans. B. Massumi. Minneapolis, MN: University of Minnesota Press.

DfES (Department for Education and Skills) (2005) *Every Child Matters: Change for Children*. London: HMSO.

DfES (Department for Education and Skills (2007) *Practice Guidance for the Early Years Foundation Stage*. London: HMSO.

DfES (Department for Education and Skills), DfWP (Department for Work and Pensions) and DfTI (Department for Trade and Industry) (2004) *Choice for Parents, the Best Start for Children: a Ten Year Strategy for Childcare*. London: HMSO.

Derrida, J., (1976) *Of Grammatology*. Trans G.C. Spivak. Baltimore & London: Johns Hopkins University Press.

Dick, K., Kofman, A.Z., Hartman, G., Royle, N., Kofman, G. and Derrida, J. (2005) *Screenplay and Essays on the Film*. Manchester: Manchester University Press.

Douglas, M. (1966) *Purity and Danger*. London: Routledge

Foucualt, M. (1967) Of Other Space. Trans. J. Miskowiec. Available at: *www.foucault.info/documents/heteroTopia /Foucault.heterotopia.en.html*

Foucualt, M. (1986) Of other spaces. *Diacritics* 16, 22–27.

Foucault, M. (1998) Different spaces. In J. Faubion (ed) *Aesthetics: the Essential Works*, 2 London: Allen Lane.

Freud, S. [1919] (1985) The uncanny. In Dickson, A. (ed) *Art and Literature: Jensen's Gradiva, Leonardo da Vinci and Other Works, The Pelican Freud Library*, vol. 14 Harmondworth: Penguin.

Freud, S. (1974) Feminity. In *New Introductory Letters on Psychoanalysis*. Trans & ed. J. Strachey. London: Hogarth.

Froebel, F. (1826) *The Education of Man*. Keilhan/Leipzig: Wienbranch.

Gruber, H.E. and Voneche, J.J (eds) (1977) *The Essential Piaget*. New York: Basic Books.

James, A.; Jenks, C. and Prout, A. (1998) *Theorizing Childhood*. London: Polity Press.

Johnson, P. (2006) Unravelling Foucault's different spaces. *History of the Human Sciences*. 19 (4), 75–90.

Jones, L and Brown, T. (2002)'Reading' the nursery classroom: a Foucauldian perspective. *Qualitative Studies in Education*, 14 (6), 106–202.

Lacan, J. (1977) *Ecrits: A Selection*. Trans. A. Sherridan. New York: Norton.

MacLure, M. (2003) *Discourse in Educational and Social Research*. Buckingham: Open University Press.

Montessori, M. (1964) *The Montessori Method*. New York: Schocken Books.

Morss, J. (1990) *The Biologising of Childhood: Developmental Psychology and the Darwinian Myth*. London: Lawrence Erlbaum.

Parker, S (1997) *Reflective Teaching in the Postmodern World: a Manifesto for Education in Postmodernity*. Buckingham: Open University Press.

Piaget, J. (1972) *Psychology and Epistemology*. Trans. P. Wells, Harmondsworth: Penguin.

Probyn, E. (1996) *Outside Belonging*. London: Routledge.

Rose, N. (1999) *Governing the Soul: The Shaping of the Private Self*, 2nd ed. London: Free Association Press.

Rousseau, J. J. (1979) Emile, or on education [1762]. Trans. A. *Bloom*. New York: Basic Books.

Sommer, R. (1969) *Personal Space: the Behavioural Basis of Design*. Englewood Cliffs, NJ: Prentice Hall.

Stockton, K. B. (2004) Growing sideways, or versions of the queer child: the ghost, the homosexual, the Freudian, the innocent and the interval of the animal. In (eds) Bruhm, S. & Hurley, N. *Curiouser: on the Queerness of Children*. Minneapolis, MN: University of Minnesota Press.

Stronach, I. (2008) Rethinking words, concepts, stories and theories: sensing a new world? Key note address at the 8th International Congress of Qualitative Inquiry. Urbana, IL: Champaign.

Taylor, A and Richardson, C. (2005) Queering home corner. *Contemporary Issues in Early Childhood*, 6 (2), 163–173.

Tymms, P. and Merrill, C. (2004) On-entry baseline assessment across cultures. In (eds) Anning, A., Cullen, J. and Fleer, M. *Early Childhood Education: Society and Culture*. London: Sage Publications.

Wagner, P. (1994) The *Sociology of Modernity*. New York: Routledge.

Walkerdine, V. (1984) 'Developmental psychology and the child-centred pedagogy: the insertion of Piaget into early education.' In (eds) J. Henriques, W. Holloway, C. Urwin, and V.Walkerdine. *Changing the Subject*. London: Methuen.

Walkerdine, V. and Lucey, H. (1989) *Democracy in the Kitchen: Regulating Mothers and Socialising Daughters*. London: Virago Press.

Zissos, A. (2000). Ovid's Rape of Proserpina (Met. 5.341–661): *Internal Audience and Narrative Distortion*. Phoenix 53, pp. 97–113.

Section Four

Childhoods and Unthought
Struggles for Social Justice

CHAPTER TWENTY

Mapping Globalization and Childhood

Possibilities for Curriculum and Pedagogy

Iris Duhn

Abstract

The territory of globalization and childhood is charted through a double movement: identification of some of the forces that are currently shaping discourses, and a proposal that these forces, once recognized, can be redirected toward new ends. The intention is to foreground the potential for creative engagement that is generated when globalization and childhood are theorized as discursive networks which produce specific effects and power relations.

The questions that inform this chapter are framed around the difficulty of finding ways of complex engagement with "big" global issues, such as climate change and consumerism, in the context of early childhood education. A critical engagement with globalization offers possibilities for re-thinking early childhood pedagogy as an effect of the interplay between the global and local, space and place, self and other, and nature and culture. Such a conceptualization of globalization draws on questions such as: "How is the global imagined? Through what forms of knowledge and expertise? How are problems to be addressed and by whom? What spatialities and subjectivities are assumed?" (Larner & Walters, 2002, p. 3). These kinds of questions enable the theorization of globalization as a multitude of forces and processes and emphasizes that globalization affects people, places, and things in intricate ways.

Rather than romanticizing concepts such as "place" and "the local" as potential counter points against globalization, this chapter explores how the global/space and local/place can be conceptualized as constituting each other, and how the space/place interconnection may be relevant to pedagogy in early childhood education. The chapter makes reference to a current two-year qualitative research project, which focuses on ecological sustainability and the notion of care for self, other and the environment to illustrate the relevance of critical engagement with globalization in early childhood education. A pedagogy that encourages complexity may enable children and adults to understand themselves as becoming critical global citizens and global consumers.

The chapter charts the territory of globalization and childhood through a double movement: firstly, by identifying some of the forces that are currently shaping discourses, and secondly, by proposing that these forces, once recognized, can be redirected toward new ends. The intention is to foreground the potential for creative engagement that is generated when globalization and childhood are theorized as discursive networks, which produce effects and power relations (Dean, 1999; Rose, 1999). The mapping of the intersections of globalization and childhood is not only a theoretical exercise but has material effects, as the second part of the chapter will demonstrate.

Contemporary Discourses

Mapping the Global

Hardt and Negri (2000) argue that in order to develop a sense of control and agency in times of rapid change, it is no longer sufficient to resist and oppose meta-narratives, such as globalization and neoliberalism. Instead, the political task is to identify how global discourses affect identities and places, and to find new ways of understanding self and other (including nonhuman) in place and space (Haraway, 2008). The emphasis lies on becoming-other, on transformation, on nonlinearity, and on an acceptance of complexity (Brah, Hickman, & Mac an Ghaill, 1999; Callejo Perez, Fain, & Slater, 2004; Smith, 2001). Resisting change can produce nostalgic longings for an imagined simpler, more stable past, whereas an engagement with global discourses as productive multiplicity generates desire for learning to think differently—about self, other, the world.

Theorizing globalization as a process that is web-like, fragmented and polycentered disrupts the meta-narrative of neoliberal political rationality with its focus on smooth and linear discourses of economic globalization. The metanarrative of globalization perpetuates discourses that separate the global and the local, or space and place. The global economy for instance seems to operate "somewhere else" in some invisible space, which dominates and regulates everyday "places" through trickle down effects that impact on peoples' life. A mapping of globalization that makes its contradictory multifaceted nature visible and highlights the interplay between space and place, demystifies "the global": cartographies map power relations and highlight tensions, exclusions, and possibilities (Braidotti, 2006). Considering globalization as web-like, fragmented and poly-centered stresses how inevitably complex analysis has to be in its attempt to map effects, such as "the homogenization of commodity culture in terms of consumerist practices" (Braidotti, 2006, p. 31), as well as in the mapping of possibilities for multiple other ways of engaging with consumerist practices. Understanding global forces and discourses is the precondition for a redirection of those forces.

Childhood and Capitalism, the Local and the Global

Throughout modernity, "the child" as a discursive construct has functioned as a largely unacknowledged "foundational product of the modern episteme" (Wallace, 1995, p. 284). According to Sharon Stephens (1995), childhood is a constitutive discourse of modernity and of the liberal capitalist world order. In neoliberal global discourse childhood as a domain retains its constitutive function; the child-subject continues to represent potentiality, which requires intense regulation, monitoring, and control. Global capitalism, however, has discovered the child-subject as a "malleable entity in the making" (Castaneda, 2002, p. 4), which produces the child-as-consumer. As a consumer, the child-subject disrupts and reorganizes some of the markers of modern childhood. The child-as-consumer demands and chooses, and is well aware of its rights to resources. Following on from Stephens, geographer Sue Ruddick (2003) argues that instead of thinking of childhood as a category that is being re-organized in neoliberal global economies, childhood as a concept has to be considered as deeply entangled with the economic and political order (Ruddick, 2003; Stephens, 1995). From this perspective contemporary childhood is produced by and produces changing understandings of what it means to be a "global subject," such as a global consumer.

However, Ruddick (2003) suggests that childhood has largely been excluded from critical analyses of global shifts in political and economic rationalities. According to Ruddick, this is an indication of the positioning of childhood at the local level where childhood "has often been relegated to the private and/or domestic sphere" (p. 334). In the meta-narrative of globalization, the private and/or domestic sphere seems far removed, and thus irrelevant, for analyses of macro change such as the restructuring of national economies on a global scale. Childhood, if conceptualized within modernist theoretical frameworks, largely remains a local or national issue, unless it is discussed as a global project, as, for example, in international debates on child labor.

The division into private and public and/or local and global is a remnant of older, "pre-global" political rationalities. Ruddick (2003), much like Nikolas Rose (1999), argues that political power in the twenty-first century can no longer be adequately analyzed by using the well-tested theoretical frameworks of political analysis that were effective for much of the twentieth century. Political analysis has traditionally been "forged in the period when the boundaries of the nation state seemed to set the natural frame for political systems, and when geo-politics seemed inevitably to be conducted in terms of alliances and conflicts among nation states" (Rose, 1999, p. 1). Geopolitics now are about how flows of people and things are regulated, controlled, organized across boundaries of nation states (Lash & Urry, 1994). Investigating the relationship between geopolitics and childhood offers the potential of challenging the perceived gulf between "big" global issues and local manifestations of global discourses.

Ruddick (2003) suggests that much of the contemporary social and cultural imagination is still locked in conceptual spaces that are framed by traditional grids. In this imaginary, the global refers to the "smooth space of international capitalism" (Deleuze & Guattari, 1988) where funds are being moved through invisible networks at lightning speed. The global appears as a force that is untouchable; however, like a scalpel-sharp laser it descends on "places" to leave its mark. National economies are being reformed to create openings for "global actors such as multinational corporations and to global institutions such as the IMF" (Larner, 2003, p. 509). Nation states are now competing for a place in the global economy and its fast networks of international capitalism. In New Zealand for instance, many of the recent neoliberal reforms aimed to ensure easy access to national markets for international actors (Kelsey, 1995; Larner, 2002). In this serious, fast, and powerfully cutting world of global capitalism, childhood seems seriously misplaced.

An imaginary in which space dominates place produces specific identities. For example, it is easy enough to conceptualize the global as a playground for the rich and powerful in contrast to the local as community oriented and more humane. In this imagination, the global sounds glamorous, remote, and strangely sanitized whereas the local evokes a sense of the messiness of life, including conflict, as well as familiarity and attachment. Childhood as constitutive category of modernity is conceptually tied up with the notion of dependency, the private, home, and family (Cannella, 1997). The meta-narrative of globalization reproduces traditional discourses of childhood—the smooth global imaginary goes hand in hand with the smooth, innocent and dependent child of western discourses (Kincaid, 1998).

Global capitalism and childhood, however, may be in far closer proximity than current imaginings of "smooth space" allow. For starters, both capitalism and childhood are historically and culturally specific constructs. Childhood, like capitalism, "is also globally mobile, generating new variations of itself as it moves" (Chin, 2003, p. 309). This is illustrated by changes in discourses of childhood in Aotearoa/New Zealand; the "bicultural child" in the national early childhood curriculum is a case in point (Duhn, 2008; Ritchie, 2002, 2003).

A culturally and historically specific variation of capitalism in New Zealand is the accelerated spread of a new site of consumption in the form of shopping centres. New Zealand, often considered in terms of tourism marketing slogans as "clean and green," has 20 percent per capita more consumption space than Australia (Larner & Le Heron, 2002). These new spaces of capitalism are particularly aimed to appeal to the young; in fact, "the developers have explicitly targeted young people" (Larner & Le Heron, 2002, p. 766). Contemporary childhood is discursively and materially entangled with global capitalism. Youthfulness is highly desirable and a commodity in itself (Ruddick, 2003), as the incredible selling power of Hannah Montana demonstrates. The smooth child and smooth capitalism have joined forces.

Globalization and Curriculum in New Zealand

In an indirect or rather, unacknowledged way, globalization has informed pedagogy in New Zealand for more than a decade. The early childhood curriculum, Te Whāriki (Ministry of Education, 1996) has been hailed as a progressive curriculum that was ahead of its time (Hedges & Nuttall, 2008; Nuttall, 2003); with its focus on life-long learning and problem-solving, and its articulation of the learner as capable, as a good communicator, who contributes, participates and makes choices, it also paved the way for cosmopolitan pedagogy in New Zealand (Duhn, 2006). Cosmopolitan pedagogy aims to produce the self-governing, autonomous, problem-solving global subject who works collaboratively in a wide range of contexts (Burbules & Torres, 2000; Fendler, 1998; Hultqvist, 1998; Popkewitz, 2004). The New Zealand Curriculum addresses global change through an outline of attributes, particularly in its section on values and through key competencies (Ministry of Education, 2007, p. 10, 12) that draw on cosmopolitan pedagogy. Some of these attributes have already been introduced into educational discourse through Te Whāriki. The same can be said in relation to the focus on social and cultural contexts for learning and the emphasis on "place" as the basis for belonging which is integral to Te Whāriki (Ministry of Education, 1996, p. 56). Like Te Whariki, The New Zealand Curriculum also aims to encourage diverse, "place-based" responses to local school curriculum interpretation and implementation; schools have "considerable flexibility when determining the detail" of curriculum (Ministry of Education, 2007, p. 37). Clearly, place is important, and so is globalization. It is not clear, however, how the two are connected.

Despite the evidence of global discourses in curricula, there is no research that investigates how cosmopolitan pedagogy affects teaching and learning. Globalisation in general only finds its way onto the research agenda in the form of "trickle down" effects, for example under the guise of the increasing awareness of multiculturalism and bilingual children's needs (Teaching and Learning Research Initiative, 2008, p. 3).

Considering globalisation as an issue that "creeps" on the agenda or, in the case of education into the curriculum, rather than considering curriculum as a site where discourses of globalization are pro-duced draws on particular understandings of globalization. It is the story of inevitable global change that eventually becomes visible at the local level. This story has limitations, one of which is the con-struction of "the global," which is distinctly different from "the local." This distinction is significant; an understanding of globalization as "happening elsewhere" creates particular power relations that make a focus on the global seem irrelevant. A recent Australian/New Zealand survey on climate change, probably one of the most dominant "global" issues, illustrates this point: at least 10% of New Zealanders believe it is too late to make a difference to climate change (Gregory, 2008). Changing daily practices and habits consequently makes no difference—global change seems uncontrollable, inevitable, and coming from "above." For teachers this means that they are left to their own devices when trying to find ways of addressing global issues. The curriculum reinforces the meta-narrative of smooth globalization, which leaves teachers with the task of dealing with complex global issues "on the ground."

Theorizing Globalization in Education

The possibilities, demands, and challenges that critical engagement with globalization poses are enor-mous (Beck, 2004; Grewal & Kaplan, 1994; Hardt & Negri, 2004; Larner & Walters, 2004). In the wider educational context, the impact of globalization has been theorized in relation to policies and systems (Dale, 2008; Lingard & Ozga, 2007; Olssen, Codd, & O'Neill, 2004), but increasingly also with a focus on pedagogies and power relations (Apple, Kenway, & Singh, 2005; Burbules & Torres, 2000; Edwards & Usher, 2008). It is the second body of work that I am interested in because it offers the opportunity to theorize globalization through unsettling the global/local discourse (Foucault, 1994; Lather, 2004). For the meta-narrative of globalization this means that the focus shifts from analyz-ing how the "trickle down" effects of globalization are managed "on the ground." Instead, place and space, or the local and the global, become the sites that produce each other.

Some recent theorization of globalization have produced new perspectives of learning and teaching that focus on the connection between space and place, self, and other (Edwards & Usher, 2008), places of learning (Ellsworth, 2005), and a pedagogy of place (Callejo Perez et al., 2004). This emphasis on identities, on the materiality of places and bodies, and on situated knowledges can gen-erate powerful ways of understanding globalization as multiple, complex forces and as processes that re-create the local, the global, self, and other in a complex interplay. Globalization no longer is what happens "somewhere else"; instead, attention is paid to how discourses, practices, ways of being and doing, and understandings of the global and the local re-shape the here and now in interplay.

Shifting away from the familiarity of the meta-narrative can be unsettling. In many ways, glob-alization offers possibilities for re-thinking the validity of what is assumed and for disturbing the pat-terns that govern thought (Gordon, 1991; Rose, 1999). This is a highly political activity, because it focuses attention on power relations. Aimed at transformation based on critical analysis, it requires the ability to work simultaneously in a critical and deconstructive, as well as in a constructive and ethico-political manner (Hardt & Negri, 2000). The challenge is to find ways of thinking globaliza-tion in such a way that global forces become recognizable in everyday life and to use them. How important it is to develop such two-pronged projects becomes immediately apparent in New Zealand with its historical focus on biculturalism (O'Sullivan, 2007; Pearson, 2005). Without the commit-ment to complex critical engagement, a focus on globalization may appear as a threat to indigenous politics with its specific focus on "place."

Maori have long claimed special rights based on their status as *tangata whenua* (the people of the land). The binary opposition of space and place in the meta-narrative of globalization mirrors postcolonial politics with its incessant tension over land rights and belonging, which continues to play out between the Crown/ government and local *iwi* (tribes). In the New Zealand context, it may be comforting to think that local resistance and local politics offer a respite from global demands. An indigenous keynote speaker at an early childhood conference summed this up in the following way: "Why pretend to be multicultural, if bicultural doesn't work?" (May & Reedy, 2003). Underlying this question may be the fear that globalization pushes "sameness" and homogeneity at the cost of local diversity. From this perspective, place-based politics are about establishing distinctive local identities as a form of resistance against the global tide. These kinds of politics inadvertently reinforce a global/local split, and contribute to the meta-narrative of globalization as macro level change, only in this version "place" is romanticized as a site that diverts or resists the global flow—at least for the moment. At the same time, it is of critical importance to recognize the difference in perspectives, and to continuously pay attention to shifting power relations. Understandings of place and space differ. Through the recognition of, and respect for, difference, new political patterns can emerge.

Redirecting Curriculum: Early Childhood Education as Transformative Engagement in Global Context

Yearning for Difference

The narrative of the child as becoming consumer is embedded in a research project with a focus on ecological sustainability through caring for self, other and the environment from western and Maori perspectives. The idea for this research emerged out of a conversation with an early childhood teacher, Tian, about 18 months ago. Tian's interest at the time was focused on climate change and her awareness that children, even more than adults, will have to be able to live with rapid and potentially life-changing change. Tian felt strongly that it was her responsibility as a teacher to integrate this global issue into her teaching. She also realized that this could not be done alone, and that it required a willingness to examine and unsettle existing patterns of thought and practice.

Tian organized a staff meeting in the centre she co-owns where she wanted to share her thoughts with her colleagues by watching Al Gore's *Inconvenient Truth*. During the meeting, it became obvious that the other teachers could not quite fathom how such a huge global issue could have anything to do with early childhood education. Tian, however, insisted that global warming was an issue of immense importance to early childhood education, and she was searching for ways of understanding the implications for pedagogy. Her initial desire to transform thinking and practice sparked a two-year research project, now in its second year, that includes ten kindergartens and early childcare centres from across New Zealand. As a group of four researchers, we are committed to Tiriti o Waitangi, the Treaty of Waitangi, which is embedded in our project design with its bi-focus on indigenous and western politics and perspectives. One of our initial aims was to ensure that the project would not be type-cast as "about worm farms and compost" only. Our theoretical framework is built around the notion of care—for the self, the other and the environment. This broad approach grounds the research in the principle of *kotahitanga*, a commitment to more than one, to collectivism, and the understanding that the individual is always embedded in relationships with "people, places and things" (Ministry of Education, 1996, p. 11), as the New Zealand early childhood curriculum so aptly puts it. Developing a pedagogy that does justice to the complexity of those relationships is part of the challenge of this project.

Understanding the Global in the Local Context

Tian's teaching team remained unsure about the relevance of global issues to pedagogy. The teachers found it difficult to reconcile issues such as global warming with young children's learning, even if the young child is conceptualized as a "competent and confident learner(s)" (Ministry of Education, 1996, p. 9). In many ways, the focus on global warming made the power of the meta-discourse of the global visible: teachers felt overwhelmed by the urgency and enormity of global warming, which had a paralyzing effect. As caring teachers they wanted to protect children from this unsettling and potentially devastating knowledge. Faced with the demands of action, the interconnection of globalization as "happening elsewhere" and being an invisible, untouchable but powerful (almost omnipotent) force and the discourse of the innocent, dependent child had the effect of deeply unsettling them. They were not sure what to do, and what to think. In terms of pedagogy, it was puzzling to conceive of a framework for learning and teaching that would enable the teachers to feel enthusiastic and inspired about global warming and climate change.

Global warming as the initial focus for the overall research focus on ethics of care and environmental sustainability led to the teachers' interest in recycling as an issue that was relevant to the children. Many children in childcare bring elaborately packaged lunches, and packaging is not always easy to dispose of—plastic containers do not lend themselves to composting. The idea was to integrate recycling into daily pedagogical practices. By doing something on a regular basis and building it into the daily rhythms of the centre, children had time to get used to new ways of doing things. They began to sort their left-overs into compostable, recyclable and nonrecyclable piles and began to take interest in the processes of disposal. The connection between composting and left-over food was an interesting one, and the children could see how one was connected to the other.

The pedagogy of place that the teachers worked with had a strong emphasis on doing and on building up intensities. The plastic recycling left everyone feeling rather flat—it is all very well to know that someone collects the plastic, and it's possible to find out where it goes to be recycled. However, left-over food went into the compost and ended up doing its work for the center garden. Plastic just disappeared. Instead of sitting down with the children at mat time to talk about plastic rubbish and the difficulty of re-using plastic effectively, teachers and children began to use plastic more consciously. It became a resource, to be used in the centre or to be taken home to be reused. Someone came up with the idea to take part in the nationwide *Junk to Green Funk* competition, organized by TradeAid. The competition provided the opportunity to build relationships between the wider community and children, teachers, and parents. The paralysis of the global meta-narrative was shaken off by a joyful and vigorous engagement with the project. Children collected plastic containers. Instead of sending plastic off to an unknown destination, plastic was redirected to the center.

For weeks, the center was abuzz with plastic curtain making, which involved threading, punching holes, sorting plastic, deciding on design, forming and disbanding teams, talking about and researching where the plastic comes from and where it ends up, and finally eventually the curtain off as a competition entry. Children went home to their parents to talk about plastic recycling, and parents with their children, and other family members, could go on to the TradeAid website to see the entries. In the process of doing so, they had the opportunity to talk, read and see more of TradeAid's work with communities worldwide. TradeAid became a permanent aspect of weekly centre and home routines when a roster for ordering goods was organized and run by parents. Children, teachers, and families are now part of a global network of production and consumption that disrupts the discourse of hyperconsumption by valuing small scale production and by becoming aware of the preciousness of resources that are used to produce, to consume and, in the case of some of the TradeAid communities involved, to survive.

Adults and children were engaged in conversations that continuously crossed from the global to the local, and in the process created a sense of belonging to "place." "Place" involved the early childcare center, but also the *Junk to Green Funk* curtain entry, the website, lots of plastic containers and learning about rubbish. It involved at least a fleeting awareness of other families in far away places whose children had to work hard to ensure survival. The local and the global, adults and children, consumers and producers, the childcare centre and families' homes became entangled in a complex geopolitical encounter. This encounter sits alongside weekly shopping routines to the mall where differences become entrenched again in opposition to each other, or where they become invisible; hyperconsumerism depends on discourses that create the illusion of smoothness, both in relation to consumption and production (Harvey, 1998).

The shaping of relationships between people, places, and things is also the shaping of "place" in the context of discourses of globalization. "Aotearoa Kids" becomes the place where subjectivities and practices re-shape and emerge, where pedagogy is re-thought. The catalyst for change is "the global" in its encounter with the "the local." New subjectivities and practices in turn create new possibilities for understanding learning and teaching as transformative actions in global times. This is what Ellsworth (2005) refers to as pedagogy as knowledge-in-the-making, based on "experiences of being radically in relation to one's self, to others, and to the world" (p. 2). Gruenewald and Smith (2008) argue that learning is about increasing awareness of the self-other-world relationships. A pedagogy of place emphasizes the relational and embodied nature of learning; with an increasing awareness of global issues, this focus has the potential to produce transformative change. With its focus on effects on self-other-world relationships, it is a pedagogy of situated knowledge in the making. It counters the paralyzing effects of meta-narratives of globalization through its embodied, material engagement with learning and teaching. A pedagogy of place creates complexities, and an awareness of the many layers that unfold when one starts paying attention to the self as deeply embedded in relationships with its many others in the world.

References

Apple, M. W., Kenway, J., & Singh, M. (Eds.). (2005). *Globalizing education: Policies, pedagogies, and politics*. New York: Peter Lang.

Beck, U. (2004). The truth of others: a cosmopolitan approach. *Common Knowledge, 10*(3), 430–449.

Brah, A., Hickman, M., & Mac an Ghaill, M. (Eds.). (1999). *Global futures: Migration, Environment and globalization*. New York: St. Martin's Press.

Braidotti, R. (2006). *Transpositions*. Cambridge, UK: Polity Press.

Burbules, N., & Torres, C. (Eds.). (2000). *Globalization and education: Critical perspectives*. London and New York: Routledge.

Callejo Perez, D., Fain, S., & Slater, J. (Eds.). (2004). *Pedagogy of place: Seeing space as cultural education*. New York: Peter Lang.

Cannella, G. (1997). *Deconstructing early childhood: Social justice and revolution. New York:* Peter Lang.

Castaneda, C. (2002). *Figurations: Child, bodies, world*. Durham and London: Duke University Press.

Chin, E. (2003). Children out of bounds in globalising times. *Postcolonial Studies, 6*(3), 309–325.

Dale, R. (2008). Globalisation and education in Aotearoa/New Zealand. In V. Carpenter, J. Jesson, P. Roberts & M. Stephenson (Eds.), *Nga kaupapa here: Connections and contradictions in education* (pp. 25–35). Melbourne: Centage.

Dean, M. (1999). *Governmentality: power and rule in modern society*. London: Sage Publications.

Deleuze, G., & Guattari, F. (1988). *A thousand plateaus: capitalism and schizophrenia* (B. Massumi, Trans.). London: Athlone Press.

Duhn, I. (2006). The making of global citizens: Traces of cosmopolitanism in the New Zealand early childhood curriculum, Te Whaariki. *Contemporary Issues In Early Childhood, 7*(3), 191–202.

Duhn, I. (2008). Globalising childhood: Assembling the bicultural child in the New Zealand early childhood curriculum, Te Whaariki. *International Journal of Critical Childhood Policy Studies, 1*(1), 82–105.

Edwards, R., & Usher, R. (2008). *Globalisation and pedagogy: Space, place and identity* (Second ed.). London and New York: Routledge.

Ellsworth, A. (2005). *Places of learning: media, architecture, pedagogy*. New York: RoutledgeFalmer.

Fendler, L. (1998). What is it impossible to think? A genealogy of the educated subject. In T. Popkewitz & M. Brennan (Eds.), *Foucault's challenge: discourse, knowledge and power in education* (pp. 39–62). New York: Teachers College Press.

Foucault, M. (1994). Governmentality. In J. Faubion (Ed.), *Michel Foucault: power. Essential works of Foucault 1954–1984* (pp. 201–222). London: Penguin Books.

Gordon, C. (1991). Governmental rationality: an introduction. In G. Burchell, C. Gordon & P. Miller (Eds.), *The Foucault effect. Studies in governmentality* (pp. 1–52). London: Harvester Wheatsheaf.

Gregory, A. (2008, 21 August). Many think it's too late for climate, survey finds. *The New Zealand Herald*, p. A4.

Grewal, I., & Kaplan, C. (Eds.). (1994). *Scattered hegemonies: postmodernity and transnational feminist practices*. Minneapolis, MN: University of Minnesota Press.

Gruenewald, D., & Smith, G. (Eds.). (2008). *Place-based education in the global age: Local diversity*. New York: Taylor & Francis.

Haraway, D. (2008). *When species meet*. Minneapolis: University of Minnesota Press.

Hardt, M., & Negri, A. (2000). *Empire*. Cambridge, Massachusetts: Harvard University Press.

Hardt, M., & Negri, A. (2004). *Multitude: War and democracy in the age of empire*. New York: Penguin Press.

Harvey, D. (1998). *The condition of postmodernity*. Oxford: Blackwell.

Hedges, H., & Nuttall, J. (2008). Macropolitical forces and micropolitical realities: Implementing Te Whaariki. In V. Carpenter, J. Jesson, P. Roberts & M. Stephenson (Eds.), *Nga kaupapa here: Connections and contradictions in education* (pp. 77–87). Melbourne: Cangage.

Hultqvist, K. (1998). A history of the present on children's welfare in Sweden: from Froebel to present-day decentralisation projects. In T. Popkewitz & M. Brennan (Eds.), *Foucault's challenge: discourse, knowledge, and power in education* (pp. 91–116). New York: Teachers College Press.

Kelsey, J. (1995). *The New Zealand experiment: a world model for structural adjustment?* Auckland: Auckland University Press with Bridget Williams Books.

Kincaid, J. (1998). *Erotic innocence: the culture of child molesting*. Durham and London: Duke University Press.

Larner, W. (2002). Globalisation, governmentality and expertise: creating a call centre labour force. *Review of International Political Economy, 9*(4), 650–674.

Larner, W. (2003). Neoliberalism? [Guest Editorial]. *Environment and Planning D: Society and Space, 21*(5), 509–512.

Larner, W., & Le Heron, R. (2002). The spaces and subjects of a globalising economy: a situated exploration of method. *Environment and Planning D: Society and Space, 20*, 753–774.

Larner, W., & Walters, W. (2002, 7–13 July 2002). *Globalisation as governmentality*. Paper presented at the International Studies Association Congress, Brisbane, Australia.

Larner, W., & Walters, W. (Eds.). (2004). *Global governmentality: Governing international spaces*. New York: Routledge.

Lash, S., & Urry, J. (1994). *Economies of signs and space*. London: Sage.

Lather, P. (2004). Foucauldian "indiscipline" as a sort of application: qu(e)er(y)ing research/policy/practice. In B. Baker

& K. Heyning (Eds.), *Dangerous coagulations? The use of Foucault in the study of education* (pp. 279–303). New York: Peter Lang.

Lingard, B., & Ozga, J. (Eds.). (2007). *The RoutledgeFalmer reader in education policy and polics*. London and New York: Routledge.

May, H., & Reedy, T. (2003). Keynote address at Te Whaariki hui o Orakei marae [video]. Auckland: University of Auckland, Faculty of Education.

Ministry of Education. (1996). *Te Whariki: he whaariki maatauranga mo ngaa mokopuna o Aotearoa*. Wellington: Learning Media.

Ministry of Education. (2007). *The New Zealand curriculum*. Wellington: Learning Media.

Nuttall, J. (2003). Introduction: weaving *Te Whaariki*. In J. Nuttal (Ed.), *Weaving Te Whaariki: Aotearoa/New Zealand"s early childhood curriculum document in theory and practice* (pp. 7–15). Wellington: New Zealand Council for Educational Research.

O"Sullivan, D. (2007). *Beyond biculturalism: The politics of an indigenous minority*. Wellington, New Zealand: Huia Publisher.

Olssen, M., Codd, J., & O'Neill, A. (2004). *Education policy: Globalization, citizenship and democracy*. London: Sage.

Pearson, D. (2005). Citizenship, identity and belonging: Addressing the mythologies of the unitary nation state in Aotearoa/New Zealand. In J. H. Liu, T. McCreanor, T. McIntosh & T. Teaiwa (Eds.), *New Zealand identities: Departures and destinations* (pp. 21–37). Wellington, New Zealand: Victoria University Press.

Popkewitz, T. (2004). The reason of reason: cosmopolitanism and governing of schooling. In B. Baker & K. Heyning (Eds.), *Dangerous coagulations? The uses of Foucault in the study of education* (pp. 189–224). New York: Peter Lang.

Ritchie, J. (2002). Bicultural development: innovation in implementation of *Te Whaariki*. *Australian Journal of Early Childhood, 27*(2), 23–41.

Ritchie, J. (2003). Bicultural development within an early childhood teacher education programme. *International Journal of Early Years Education, 11*(1), 39–52.

Rose, N. (1999). *Powers of freedom: reframing political thought*. Cambridge: Cambridge University Press.

Ruddick, S. (2003). The politics of aging: globalisation and the restructuring of youth and childhood. *Antipode, 35*(2), 334–362.

Smith, M. (2001). *An ethics of place: Radical ecology, postmodernity, and social theory*. Albany: State University of New York Press.

Stephens, S. (1995). Children and the politics of culture in "late capitalism." In S. Stephens (Ed.), *Children and the politics of culture* (pp. 3–48). Princeton: Princeton University Press.

Teaching and Learning Research Initiative. (2008). Research needs in the early childhood sector: An interview with Dr. Anne Meade. *Background Papers 2008*, from http://www.tlri.org.nz/pdfs/background-paper-pdfs/early-childhood-sector.pdf

Wallace, J.-A. (1995). Technologies of "the child": Towards a theory of the child-subject. *Textual Practice, 9*(2), 285–302.

CHAPTER TWENTY-ONE

Appropriating Reggio Emilia

From Cults to Cultural Constructions

HAROLD GOTHSON

Introduction

What happens with ideas and narrating of experiences when they travel from one context to another? What happens with the idea and what happens with the receiving context? In a time defined as globalized, it is reasonable that these questions could be useful for creating a hypothesis of what is happening when ideas travel and are exchanged also within the educational fields of the world.

With this general viewpoint, I wish to contribute to the dialogue about a strong inspiration of my own—the inspiration I have got from the world-famous preschools of the north Italian city—Reggio Emilia. My voice is not a neutral voice as I am one of the initiators of the Swedish Reggio Emilia Institute in Stockholm in 1992. I agreed to give my viewpoints on this paper at the Reconceptualizing Early Childhood Education Conference in Hongkong in December 2007 because one of my main answers or clues to avoid simply a cargo of methods or a construction of a cult is to accept that this is a risk in all processes of inspiration.

To be inspired by Reggio Emilia therefore initially, in my opinion, is to invite the complex and contradictory reality that surrounds every decision of action and thinking in general. This means to invite that risks and possibilities often are at place together—interwoven and always in need of being interpreted with multiple strategies. To act and to think are not innocent; they are always related to ethical choices and responsibilities—also relating to your chosen points of reference. Risk and possibilities—you always have to find a balance—and make a choice. In this case the reference point is Reggio Emilia and the encountering part is the educational context of Sweden.

What is Reggio Emilia? Who Can Tell?

Reggio Emilia has over the last decades become a voice in the didactical discussion about early childhood education and care all over the globe. But who can tell what Reggio Emilia is about? My starting point is that this should be the first level of problematizing. I think that this issue has been very delicate for our friends and colleagues in Reggio Emilia to handle over the years. They have seen many starting to tell their story—the interpreted story of Reggio Emilia told as a true story, guided with images—as messages of proof. But, there is no essential "true" Reggio Emilia; all narrations are built on interpretations, choices, and interests. The problem occurs when this issue is not addressed. Then I understand that my colleagues sometimes reject being defined as the "shadow of the shadow of the shadow."

For me who wishes to build a conversation and cooperation with Reggio Emilia it is important to respect that I can only tell my story as a person not being a part of their experience but of other experiences in my context. My narration is therefore a story of what I have seen with my Swedish eyeglasses. We Swedes talk about our Swedish challenge and what we construct as an answer to the question: What can we learn from Reggio Emilia? We then have to make choices of questions directed toward both Reggio Emilia and toward our own context.

If each messenger delivers their story with that label, this is my or our story, then it is interesting to understand the picks made from Reggio Emilia foremost as a description of the context of the storyteller. What makes his story of Reggio Emilia a contribution to the understanding of another's own context? Now it can be interesting to discuss how different reference points to Reggio Emilia in different countries have made their interpretations of Reggio Emilia. How have they used Reggio Emilia—or perhaps not used Reggio Emilia? At the same time, it is interesting to ask us what could be the same and what has to differ dependent on context considerations? Then it becomes interesting to understand what our different interpretations have provoked in our different contexts.

In this understanding, we need critical voices from outside. These critical voices help us to be aware of not becoming too overwhelmed and impressed. But mostly it helps us to think of what in our own context produces a risk for lacking in critical viewpoints and analysis. It helps us to think of risks and possibilities, and where is the balance?

In the late 1980s, I was responsible for a project at the Swedish National Board of Health and Welfare concerning the development of the leadership in Swedish childcare. In this project I encountered Reggio Emilia for the first time. I then mostly reflected on how the organization in Reggio Emilia was related so strongly to the pedagogical philosophy it wished to support.[1]

From my perspective I find some superficial standpoints to the issue of possibly naming a didactic effort as that of Reggio Emilian. Firstly I remember a question from a Swedish colleague to the late former head of the preschools Loris Malaguzzi on his opinion of Maria Montessori. He answered rhetorically: "Maria Montessori is our mother but we reject to become montessorians." Later when he opened our Reggio Emilia Institute he said that our destiny is to die and then something of the same will rise somewhere else. My interpretation was that his understanding of educational history made him very aware of that good experiences often will turn into methods and leave the ongoing reconstruction that is needed. In all inspiration and in all times, it should be important to reject constructing ourselves as Reggio Emilians. But still this happens all the time in all processes of inspiration. But in Stockholm and Sweden, this is not the only story.

Loris Malaguzzi encouraged in his late years a more intense international cooperation—creating a Children's International—and probably he saw this as a contradicting force toward superficiality and rigidity in the inspiration from Reggio Emilia.

To Create Stockholm Didactics in Stockholm Is to Be Reggio Emilia Inspired

I find it amusing to think that if Reggio Emilia should label a didactics, it is with the name of a city, a context, and not of a hero, often a lonely man in social, cultural, and educational movements in modern times. This can be used as a message: relate to your own context with the same passion as Loris Malaguzzi and our colleagues in Reggio Emilia have been doing. This is to accept the challenge that the director of the preschools of Reggio Emilia, Sergio Spaggiari, sometimes at his ending speech at study tours to Reggio Emilia has said: "Go home and forget us, and use the inspiration you have got to put your strength into the challenges of the childhoods you are a part of." To be inspired from Reggio Emilia in Stockholm is then to develop a Stockholm didactics. Therefore we called our initiating project in the 1990 for the Stockholm project[2] as we were working with preschools in Stockholm.

This contextualized way of relating to Reggio Emilia prevents us from trying to become the same or becoming "the other." Instead it focuses on diversity and accepting "the other" as not the same but as radically different, not looking for confirmation but for disturbances. If my starting point was to stress the interdependent but subjective voice of all understanding I now turn to defining encounters as not a matter of finding sameness but alterity and diversity. This is also what we wish education could be—a place for encountering diversity that challenges my subjective eye and ear of consciousness—a challenge to my discourse for understanding the world. This is what we early defined as the role of Reggio Emilia in Sweden—to be accepted as different, and therefore as a challenger that made us recognize what we have taken for granted.

Seen in this way, the meeting with Reggio Emilia was and is to cross boarders; it offers the challenge to visualize my own and my cultures taking for granted. To construct a crisis is to invite otherness and reject confirmation. But it is necessary to be aware of that this is to invite not only the possibility of cultural development but also the risk of creating a cultural cargo and an educational cult.[3]

We can now summarize that it is important to turn your eyes from Reggio Emilia toward your own context if you want to be Reggio Emilia–inspired. Therefore we should not put too much effort into describing Reggio Emilia but ourselves. We should describe our own society and its distribution of power for childhoods, our own pedagogical traditions as tools and obstacles for change but mostly our own political and social and culture issues that should be related to the creation of a democratic citizenship in our time. In this cause, we have to find not only possibilities but also risks with our inspiration.

It is important to point out that Reggio Emilias themselves all the time are looking for other contexts for challenges that makes them uncomfortable and forces them to reconstruct and develop their ideas. In this attitude, we wish to share and being the same in the ongoing effort to find new confusing and provoking encounters to make it possible to create resistance against the taken for granted.

Still it is sincerely difficult with strong inspiration; you easily lose your own ideas in comparing. Suddenly we ourselves have constructed a new normative storytelling in which Reggio Emilia knows all the answers. This is the root for developing a cult and a cargo of methods. It usually comes in formulations as: "we haven't come so far" or worse "is this way of thinking and acting acceptable as Reggio Emilia inspiration." The balance we need to face is to both be self-critical and self-respecting. We have to go on believing in dialogue as listening but also as disagreeing. To do so, we need to cross the boarders to others in our own context that not always agrees but questions our position.

A conclusion of this is that in our context in Sweden we do not look upon our cooperation with Reggio Emilia as a matter of implementing a Reggio Emilia approach. Instead we have from the beginning talked about Reggio Emilia inspiration. After many years of work, we now wish to describe our collaboration with the words:" In dialogue with Reggio Emilia." In this dialogue we also wish to discuss questions where we differ. This has not weakened our respect for Reggio Emilia. It is simply stressing the importance of reciprociality as a matter of taking responsibility for your own development and choices of cultural construction. As a matter of fact few of us have experienced such a strong social, cultural, didactical, and a political force supporting children as part of building democracy. This should also make us eager to ago on using Reggio Emilia as a reference point as something to listen to as something remarkable. This we have to remind us of when we sometimes think that we have created our progress of ourselves. You seldom do something new without a strong interdependency on others.

So what is the Swedish society challenged by as a culture and society and as an educational system?

A Swedish Challenge: To Question Our Cultural Construction of Identity

Sweden is a country of only 9 million inhabitants. A hundred years ago we were one of the poorest countries in Europe. Today we are a welfare state based on export, in later years in high technology, but still a country with growing challenges. Globalization has in less than 50 years turned Sweden into a multiethnic, multireligous, and multipolitical country.

A contradiction to face is the tension between the past and the present. Sweden is a country with traditionally a rather homogeneous ethnical culture. The country has since almost 500 years been a nation strongly governed from above, firstly by royalty but in modern times within a strong welfare state. Besides the economic globalization the country has over the last decades opened more to the world through our immigrant citizens and through young people's involvement through Internet and traveling over the world. This is slowly changing the Swedish identity. In a worldwide investigation called World Values Survey, Sweden was described as one of the most different cultures of the world considering family patterns, the stressing of being independent, supporting political decisions into the everyday life decisions, and concerning the division of roles between the sexes. In areas like this, it is our immigrant citizens who carry the dominant and typical attitudes and life patterns of the world not the majority population of our country. The question of national identity is therefore fast changing.

In our time of growing global interdependency, we all need to challenge closed definitions of identities. We need to look upon identity as more plastic and as a place that invites change and multiplicity. This challenges traditional definitions of belongings and established categories. In a situation like this, more than ever the concept of the hundred languages, which we connect with the preschool experience in the Italian city Reggio Emilia, seems to be useful. It suggests simply a tool for orientation in a globalized world. In the process of redefining humankind, that our time forces us to handle, safe and traditional ways of thinking are challenged. In this perspective we need to understand our potentials to change from one "intelligence" to another from one language to another. Not firstly as a potential within each human being but firstly through our potential to enrich our knowledge and our subjectivity through receiving the meaning and theories of others. We simply more than ever need the listening to others—the strangers—and being open for changing ourselves, or with another word—being open to learning.[4]

To formulate the local challenge today is more and more to be aware of all the relations and interdependencies that tie us together in a risky time for our globe. Today to be a Swede has more and more to become a practical answer to the question of thinking global but acting local. To be a Swede is to become "a glocal."

Probably the Swedish as well as the European identity has to develop in to a project identity: an identity to look for and to project for. It has to be constructed and invented more than discovered looking backwards. It has to be created as something opening up for diversity both within and in relation to the outside. This is the challenge for us all, and it needs tools such as schools. And it needs tools such as research as an attitude to foster. It needs tools for making group learning the highest form of supporting individual learning. This is a normative position that of course has to be questioned.

The Challenge from Reggio Emilia: Schools as Democratic Meeting Points—Is This Possible to Share?

This takes us to the question of citizenship. This takes us into the question of how a globalized democratic society shall survive and develop in relation to political, cultural, ethnical, religious, and economic diversities as well as to gender and different ways of defining the concept of family. This takes us into the role of what kind of learning should and could be supported for all children and families in a diverse and democratic society. This takes us into our image of children, childhood, learning, schools, and families. This takes us to our image of the role of preschools in a democratic society open to and in solidarity with childhood worldwide.

This challenges our preschools as well as our schools to support an intercultural and moveable identity as something necessary in a world where strict definitions of culture, class, ethnicity, and discourses are challenged and where we need to develop strategies to live and develop together. It also stresses the idea of education as the fostering of citizens and the concept of knowledge as something negotiable and expanding. Therefore education should be looked upon as a meeting place where the skill to learn together is a basic goal that is needed in a democratic society and therefore one of the most important challenges for every teacher but still more to every didactical organization. The primary goal of education should be to support the development and the redefining process of a society that supports diversity but still supports community. This is more necessary than ever. This needs a choice of image of democracy that does not support that each group should have their own preschool. This is only understandable when minorities are refusing schools only defined by the dominating majority.

I think that this challenge is the most important contribution that Reggio Emilia can give to our time: a challenge to see schools as tools for developing and fostering a new global democratic and intercultural citizenship. Not schools as mainly a place for research as value neutral processes but researching as processes for constructing hope for the future as the postpragmatists like Rorty[5] still are arguing. This means that we in Sweden as well as other friends in the rest of the world have to accept the inspiration from Reggio Emilia as not merely a pedagogical, but firstly a political, social, and cultural challenge. And therefore I feel good seeing that the dialogue with Reggio Emilia has created almost a modern social global movement. Not without risks, but with huge possibilities.

As being a friend among friends in an international network I often have the possibility to visit other countries. When meeting other countries, I can see that the importance of this focus is more understood in countries with poverty and unequal thinking of distribution of wealth than in our country where our fairly equal distributed social and educational welfare services easily is taken for granted. Perhaps is this one of the most important questions to bring into focus discussing Reggio Emilia in an international context: the question of so many children lacking schools or with only poor schools? To focus on the rights of all children is necessary to build a descent city, not a perfect but a good enough community.

This is what networking is about—sharing values but acting them in different contexts. Surely value is a slippery word and therefore we need to resist finding final answers. We need a community of learning where we are not only guided by but also investigating critically our own guiding values. This challenges us to identify new questions and provisory answers accepting contradictions but still go on acting. This is networks that invites and believe in dialogue with the other, not exclusion of the other. This is a network that relies on dialogue as a winner over autocracy and dictatorship. This is a belief in democracy as firstly a matter of being dependent on my opponent. And this is a base for a belief in that schools can become micropolitical places to make a difference.

This is a normative position that of course can and must be examined in practice and through critics. But this is still standing up for a modern thought of mutual sense and of hope. This attitude is often seen as problematic in the postmodern critics of big storytelling. This is a fruitful and healthy examination of science and dominating discourses. But this critical position has to resist the possibility and risk of only creating irony, relativism, or even nihilism. But instead, it can open for an ethical choice of references.[6] Then it calls for reconstruction, if not of big storytellings, but on an ongoing act for small defining of meaning in small communities: as preschools and schools. So what are the challenges for the Swedish ECE context: what is the image of what should motivate schools in Sweden and what are they tools for?

The Swedish Educare System in Short

The Swedish system has a history of a rather consequent development even if there have been changing in governmental policy over the last 30 years.[7] Earlier you can find similarities with other countries. In the beginning of the twentieth century, collective childcare was disapproved and seen as a matter for philanthropic activity, which later was opposed by the labor movement. The social democrats that early could influence the policy were puzzled even into the 1950s. Should they support a welfare system that enabled the working class families to live on only one income or should they support a childcare system?

In the late 1950 and early 1960, a feminist faction of the labor unions and the social democratic party strongly argued for a general childcare system based on a democratic pedagogy. In a good economic situation, a broad parliament majority voted for a new legislation that from 1975 gave the communities responsibility to plan for a big expansion of preschools. In five years, almost 100,000 new places were built all over the country through big state subsidies to the communities. The state's part grew from 9 percent in the 1950 to 45 percent in the 1970. You can see this as a turning argument: money. In fifteen years the state invested ten times more money in the system than before.

The most important criteria's according to OECD[8] for a successful educare system are accessibility to all children, an integrated system for care and pedagogy for all early childhood ages and a cooperation between state, community, and local level and at last a stabile financing system mostly supported by taxes.

In summary, the Swedish system[7] parents have legal right to childcare from their home community within 3 months. Childcare is since more than ten years administrated within the National Board of the educational system.

The preschools have been since 1998 supported by a 16-page curriculum decided by parliament formulating a democratic task supporting the integration of learning with play and care as well as projects and arts. The parents pay a maximum fee and for children from 4 years old, there is no fee for 15 hours a week. The argument is that the economy benefits from taxes and dynamic factors. Therefore you can keep your child in preschool during unemployment and studies. The educational level of the staff is now increasing but it differs between communities. Out of 500,000 children between 1 and 5 years more than 450,000 children were participating in preschool activities during the year 2005. Almost all 6-year-olds attend special preschool activities within the ordinary school system.

Connected to the system parents have got an insurance that guarantee them most of their salary for 15 months. Added to this some months are for encouraging fathers to stay at home with their newborn child. Parents have right to stay at home when children are ill and have special days to use in connection with the start of the compulsory school at 7 years. Most parents choose to let their child start in the elementary school when the child is six years old. There are no tests for children to admit them to start school.

The Swedish Encounter with Reggio Emilia

The Swedish encounter with Reggio Emilia could be a story made in many ways. The most obvious is to refer to the meeting between my colleague Anna Barsotti and Reggio Emilia in late 1970s. This led to the first presentation of the exhibition "The Hundred Languages of Children" at the Museum of Modern Art in Stockholm as early as in 1981. The exhibition returned to Sweden in 1986.

Through the initiative of Anna Barsotti together with seven other colleagues in different positions with early childhood education in Sweden, we created a group for studying what we could understand of the Swedish challenges by looking closer at the experience of Reggio Emilia. This group started to cooperate with Reggio Emilia and with Loris Malaguzzi in 1989.

In Reggio Emilia, we met not a celebration of beautiful principles and declarations of children. We met a local society experiencing the idea of preschools as a democratic force that inspires the development of the identity of a city. It was an idea that inspired not only teachers but also local political thinking and acting, as well as empowering a new citizenship by a developed participation of families in the preschools everyday life. Here we could see and touch a practice that showed that democracy is not fulfilled by the pure right of voting. It demands that the most important role for a school is to support the possibility to formulate and respect your own viewpoints. But it also to put your viewpoints into negotiations with your peers so you can learn together and also learn strategies for negotiations that turns conflicts into energy.

By comparing Reggio Emilia and Sweden we could analyze problematic issues. Our analyses of the Swedish system gave us the understanding that it is not enough with national policy and legislation defining accessibility, curriculum, standards, and a supporting financing system. There is a need to find more close support to involve all local participants—politicians, administrators, educators, teachers and parents—in the process of defining, building, and organizing the development of a not only legal but also legitimate preschool system. We understood a need both a top-down and bottom-up strategy. We felt that we lacked the latter. We needed to engage many in a revitalization of the pragmatic inspiration Swedish teachers had got from the John Deweyian pragmatic thinking in the 1930.[9] This is thinking that in a democratic society with big differences in culture, economy, religions, and political thinking we need a school where we can experience how to learn together but still being different. A school built on diversity and participation as democratic values that each generation has to discover and revitalize.

In the ambition to expand quickly the quality of the everyday activities for the children in Swedish preschools was not stressed either in politics or in the society as a whole. The expansion also meant that the staff consisted of few experienced teachers and many employed lacked necessary education. This opened for a risk that preschools should be defined firstly as a compensation for the family as the mothers and fathers were off to work. Seen in this way the matter of preschools was discussed mostly as a labor market issue or as a family support issue and of course also as gender issue. The arguments for why children in a democratic society should meet with other children seen as complementing institutions to the families were weak.

This idea that schools should be equal for all children was an important part of the post–World War II discussion in Sweden on the topic of which responsibility also education, childcare, and family upbringing had in the breakdown of a civilized and democratic society opening for the belief in authoritarian political philosophies.[10] A broad majority of the Swedish parliament then reformed the Swedish school system inspired by pragmatism and John Deweys thinking. The first new curriculum aiming for a school system for all children from 7 to 16 years was often referred to as *A school for all children*. This ideological base has successively been weakened—or worse—never been broadly understood and topic for systematically local approach. Luckily it still lives in many individual teachers' and politicians' ambitions.

This approach to learning and schools seems less obvious in the United States or also in Sweden today where much of educational research on learning more often is discussed as neutral in value issues or is turned into general methodological advice. In this aspect group learning only will be looked upon as a method instead of being seen as a basic aim for the learning process. This is what we—together with colleagues over the world inspired by Reggio Emilia—saw as one of the main future challenges.

To Formulate Challenges for Sweden: What Can We Learn from Reggio Emilia?

What were our initial considerations in the encounter with Reggio Emilia? We shared our mutual reflections in a report called Child-Oriented Management.[11] These reflections gave us some eyeglasses to look on differences between Reggio Emilia and our Swedish context.

Firstly we were again reminded of the necessity to define educational challenges not by interpretations of traditions and principles but by relating to the issues that surround the modern childhoods and our understanding of these in Sweden in our time.

This made us aware of the need for an ongoing critical discussion on the dominating discourses within our organizations and ways of thinking and acting. This created a need for confronting our reflections not only with Reggio Emilia but with the international discussion about early childhood as a matter of dominating discourses. Our efforts were aimed at confronting these with different theoretical positions. In this the group was challenged by the participation of Professor Gunilla Dahlberg at Stockholm University (see endnotes 2 and 6).

It soon became obvious for us that the political decision-making had been increasingly influenced by an international trend to criticize public services and financing social rights through taxes. This had opened for a development toward the neoliberal tendencies we have followed over the last decades all over the world. Reggio Emilia pointed toward a reverse way of thinking and acting while focusing on the qualities of life and citizenship of childhood and out of this discuss the responsibility of a school for all children. We could start asking what type of organization we need to build: what its costs would be and then to make priorities when resources is lacking or not yet legitimate.

Another thing that became obvious was that organizational matters and educational stand points had to be kept together within the same political and didactical philosophy. For me as working with management development in communities, this gave a possibility to create a challenge. Reggio Emilia has thrown a glove of challenge to our local communities—how can we relate the identity of our city and our city name to a discussion of renewal of the rights and gifts of children and childhood?

In Reggio Emilia we found that all answers on organizational matters was given with reference to its importance to how it supported the quality of participation and exchange in the relational triangle: Child–Teacher–Family. In Sweden, organizational matters as opening hours, size of groups as well as questions of age mixing or not was mostly related to purely economical and organizational considerations separated from didactical issues. This made us formulate a challenge: How can we encourage foras and strategies to develop the relation between parents and teachers and between teachers and politicians and the surrounding society. What should and could we mean with participation?

In Sweden, we often have a child-oriented view on the relation between children and the surrounding society but our encounter with Reggio Emilia gave us questions of what image of children this was based on. We found that the reflections in Reggio Emilia on what should define the preschool originated from questions of children's rights more than of their needs.

In Reggio Emilia they used a metaphor that the preschool should be placed on square with the wall torn down to show the importance of giving society visibility to the children and vice versa. This made us formulate the challenge of how to bring the issues of the complex and provocative issues of society into the reflections and learning processes of children.

The Reggio Emilia Institute

The challenges we formulated also took us into a reflection on who is responsible for change and development in a society? We had to confront that this is mainly a question of formal roles and appointments. We became aware that we had to take responsibility for our viewpoints and create arenas for discussions and for actions. In 1992 members of the group that studied Reggio Emilia opened the Reggio Emilia Institute in Stockholm. This initiative was not an official initiative but was due to our analysis that there was a need to strengthen the ideological and pedagogical basis for the development of the fast expanding childcare system in Sweden, but also for the renewal of education in broad.

Our answers of what to do was not easy to formulate from the beginning and perhaps they have become more and more clear through the actions we started to "projettazione." Projettazione is the concept used in Reggio Emilia more as an attitude to learning as a looking for, creating of, than of a project method guided by clear goals and steps. I once heard a colleague in Reggio Emilia say that we need a strong idea—an idea of humanity, of knowledge, and of the role of a teacher—more as a torch than as a map.

Our strategy was to start walking "on two legs": firstly we tried to finance a project where we could work together with teachers and preschools that also had been inspired by Reggio Emilia. Together with the Institute of Education in Stockholm we created a project, the Stockholm Project, to try by actions to find what was possible to develop with inspiration from Reggio Emilia in a Swedish ECE context. This effort has been described in many different ways but in English firstly in Beyond Quality: Postmodern Perspectives on Early Childhood Education.[2] The second leg was to create conferences, courses, and to start the publishing of a magazine that today is financed with subscription for 4 issues a year. Today we have celebrated the 15th anniversary of this journey and now the institute has to be renewed in a time with new challenges to be formulated and constructed.[12]

The Reggio Emilia Institute became a hybrid of ideological and commercial efforts. We had to finance to be able to act. We wanted to become a support for networks and for cooperation between top-down strategies and bottom-up movements.

The question of economy is although always problematic: What is commercial and what is having resources to be able to act? The Reggio Emilia Institute has a rather free position to act based on our financing through our own activities. This makes us work on a market but our aim is to support networks and cooperation that contradict a strictly economic position. This hybrid identity of the Reggio Emilia Institute is always accompanied by risk and possibilities. This is always a matter of balance.

In the construction of new challenges for the Reggio Emilia Institute, we do it being a strong voice in our own context when our country as well as most of the world more and more is focusing on measurements and tests of very small children. We are also doing it being a part of an international community as we are part and also responsible for the building of an international center in the name of Loris Malaguzzi in Reggio Emilia. To formulate the local challenge today is more and more being aware of all the relations and interdependencies that tie us together in a risky time for our globe. Perhaps this is the largest challenge for Reggio Emilia inspired people all over the globe: We have to listen to the experiences from Reggio Emilia as a call for international thinking and acting.

We have to take into consideration what Carla Rinaldi from Reggio Emilia and chairman of Reggio Children said while ending the first international network meeting outside Reggio Emilia in Stockholm 2007: "We do not simply believe in building schools; we believe in the necessity to build a renewed global democratic citizenship; schools are just tools for this." So what could that mean in Sweden?

What Can a School for a Global Democratic Citizenship Mean?

A democratic education can never be practiced as indoctrination aiming for consensus. Supporting each child and each human being in her right to be unique in relation to others and surrounding context is necessary in democratic education. But it does not stop with the individual perspective although it values subjectivity.

As well as our colleagues in Reggio Emilia, we, in our work in some preschools in Sweden, have been able to document small children's skills to cooperate. Carla Rinaldi writes in Making Learning Visible[4] that very small children show us that they wish to give voice. But still more they already know how to listen and to wish to be listened to. Social ability does not have to be taught; small children are from the beginning social species. This is the foundation of the image of humankind on which Reggio Emilia build their image of a society and of the role for an empowering preschool and hopeful also a postmodern school. This we can share as I have done together with other international voices relating to the beautiful story The Diary of Laura.[13]

Schools should be places to formulate your own opinion and construct meaning in confrontation with diverse perspectives. Differences represented both by peers as by the different theories introduced by the teacher that has been formulated outside those experiences that belong to the children's and pupils' own world of experiences. This is the real value base for a democratic school built on listening, welcoming the other—the stranger—and solidaric action. This is a school that does not lecture and talk about democracy but practice these values. In everyday life, these values should be seen in how we organize the environment and how the children's time is organized. It is a preschool and school that every day offers children the possibility to play and work in small groups. In projects and other activities, differences and similarities between eyes, noses, trees, small birds, and people are observed and focus on discussions, and thinking and acting. It is an ongoing inquiry of the concept of "learning by doing" where you have to think to create belief that makes it possible to act, but when you act it always creates doubt that makes it necessary to think again and vice versa. And perhaps not as in steps and sequences but probably in a more messy way—a more rizomatic way.

This gives us motivation for the preschool as being a meeting place supporting these values—subjectivity, diversity, mutual interdependence, and learning—so often stressed in Reggio Emilia. Only with these values you can talk about a shared value base for a school in a democracy that aims to engage all social classes and cultures. A citizen's upbringing cannot be a simple matter for every family. It is neither a biological need for children; it is a necessity for a democratic society.

Our motivation is built on an image of democracy where we in spite of diversity are mutually dependent and have to share some decisions. Today we see that other images of democracy is built on the right to stand outside the general solutions. This supports an acceptance of a society more built on rights than on duty to contribute. This promotes the creation of profiled schools based on similarity instead of the idea of schools as meeting places. This attempt is as said before understandable when minority groups experience that their voices is neglected. At the same time, this excluding strategy seems to be extremely dangerous in our world after the 9/11 tragedy and the actions the dominating power of the world has chosen after that. More than ever we need to find strategies to create schools for finding ways to coexist. But this normative activity-oriented position has to be tested through experimentation and challenges from critical friends. It has to become a political and didactical shared project.

The Reggio Emilia Influence on the Swedish Context

In different encounters with colleagues internationally I have been asked to write about the Swedish relation to Reggio Emilia.[13–15] As I earlier discussed we have looked upon Reggio Emilia not as something to copy but as something that can make us look at our own context with different eyes. Our efforts have been to try to make other people in our context listening to us even if our perspective has been critical toward our own traditions and definitions of actual burning points.

During the 1990s, Sweden made many new decisions concerning Early Childhood Education. As a described above, a new law guaranteed the rights for families to childcare in their community within three months and the first curriculum was decided by the parliament in 1998. Through our work and all the networks all over the country, many references in the Swedish curriculum are made to the philosophy of Reggio Emilia. The Ministry of Education has edited a report concerning a retrospective on the last 30 years policymaking in the area of early childhood education. They especially stress the importance for curriculum of the encounter with Reggio Emilia.[7]

A curriculum always is a compromise between different traditions with different theories and images of children and the role of preschools in the society. Still the curriculum takes clear standpoints on some issues that have given teachers in our networks a strong position both in their communities and in their schools.

The first meetings with Reggio Emilia were for many educators and teachers a confirmation of their own ideals. Some felt provoked and frustrated even hostile not finding confirmation of their Swedish everyday practice. At the same time, many said that they felt a home—some said at last—but they found a mastery in how the spoke about and documented their work. Many teachers were inspired by the professionalism in "these strong women." Some argued that they share the same images of children, knowledge, and preschool but understand Reggio Emilia as being better in mastering documentation.

By the contribution of Professor Gunilla Dahlberg and her research group we could meet and even accept that this was a too easy way to go; it also easily created an attitude of finding the problem in others in directors or in colleagues or in to little budget or to poor environment. But by going back and studying the origins of theories that has constructed Swedish education of and practice of preschool staff, we could understand that Reggio Emilia had some other standpoints for their preschools than the Swedish. They had made other choices and used different arguments. Through Professor Dahlberg's work of trying to challenge different possible images of children and learning and schools we could use our networks for relating our starting pedagogical documentation to our tradition not as the only tools for interpretation.

This helped us to create a new "gaze" on what the children were doing; it started a period of bathing in observations and interpretations with diverse tools. Today this has helped us to create many different arenas as new courses and networks of pedagogistas <Au: "pedagogists"?> and teachers. There the meaning of richness of children and other sayings as "all children are intelligent" are being critically reflected in relation to the teachers' own constructed documentations. This has helped us making the gathered documentation into pedagogical documentations connected to visible theoretical and value-based tools of interpretations.

This has also turned the terminology from the concept of theme work in the direction of inquiring strategies and project thinking. It has also helped us understand the crucial use for pedagogical documentation as a tool that makes it possible to share and negotiate about how phenomena and experiences could and should be interpreted.

The Reggio Emilia inspiration has a strong impact on many places and societies in Sweden but big challenges are still to be met to really support a new image of the child, childhood, and a reconstructed democratic society.

The building of more than 100 networks of teachers related to the Reggio Emilia Institute all over the country has supported a bottom-up movement to also have some influence on top-down strategies both at national and community levels. Many communities have invited the institute to participate in their in-service training as well as being hosts for national network meetings. Often local politicians participate in local network meetings making these to new arenas for sharing and discussing a necessity to create new political and educational initiatives in the community.

In this way, the meeting with Reggio Emilia has made many teachers aware of the necessity for them to involve also in formulating and arguing for new local policies. It has also given a possibility for politicians to deepen their understanding of pedagogical everyday situations through the frequent use of pedagogical documentation as a tool for mutual reflections and multiple interpretations.

This has also created a hope for many teachers all over the country to believe that it is possible to contribute to a new type of preschool. Over the years, the question of preschools as possible democratic meeting points has become increasingly possible to raise as related to the pedagogical projects that are taking place. Even the participation of families is slowly developing from a position of buying services to being involved in citizenship activities.

A conclusion could be that Reggio Emilia has helped us to develop a new tribune for a new voice of childhood and democracy in Sweden—a voice inspired by the dialogue with but not the voice of Reggio Emilia. Still with all this said, this is only one of many tribunes <Au: Do you mean "tributes"?> being built in a market-oriented society. Our cause is to revitalize the idea of "a school for all children."

Challenges or Risks for Our Reggio Emilia Inspiration

I will conclude this chapter by discussing some problems connected to our inspiration from Reggio Emilia that we still have to face.

Firstly I see that when we expand and reach more and more contexts we risk being captured and integrated into the dominating discourses. The diversity disappears; the challenge is becoming accepted not only as just a matter of language. The language changes but under the surface, the same old image of children resists and survives. This gives us challenges to become more clear and provocative.

This also has to make us aware of that big impact is doing something with a strong idea. Perhaps it will become more superficial or perhaps it will become only a label on what is possible to see on the surface. To say that our inspiration just have been supporting renewal of culture is to close our eyes for how different messages transform when traveling to new times and new contexts.

Another problem is that our society with long hierarchical traditions is looking for definite answers from above. The debate in our society relating to democracy is often focusing on rights more than on sharing responsibility and on the necessity of mobilization and participation. This challenges us to be more clear about the risks and possibilities in closing the dialogue between *top-down* and *bottom-up* strategies for development and cultural reconstruction. Our idea is that only by dialogue contradictions can be discovered and problematized. This calls for meeting places for dissemination and confrontation with other concepts of thinking within education but also with other fields of society.

In this situation we also have to be aware that the Reggio Emilia inspiration can become a good market label—something to sell and to purchase. Suddenly we can turn up with reducing the efforts of Reggio Emilia to simply a matter of everyday methods and ways of working without connecting to the political aims of citizenship that is the main reason for preschools in Reggio Emilia. This is a real challenge as we face growing tendencies toward concurrence and market thinking that needs labels and profiles. The branding of Reggio Emilia to become a commodity to be sold on the market is obvious.

Often our work meets a wish for fast answers as the everyday practice is not a forum for formulation and critical reflections in the way we find in Reggio Emilia. Our only way to face this is to create arenas for reflection using pedagogical documentation to develop a culture of multiple interpretations and close the gap between the concept of theory and practice.

Our position is to support weak and not definite definitions built on our belief in deconstructive analysis—also of Reggio Emilia. We believe in deconstructive analysis as a strategy to avoid the risk to develop into a method or a cargo. We wish to invite other perspectives in constructive and investigating dialogue and we wish to take part in international dialogue and resist to define ourselves as "belonging" to our context. Such a dialogue can challenge the understanding of Swedish culture and identity and transgress into a global orientation of the local—think global and act local. This can help us create expanding cultural constructions of what is possible to become as a preschool in Sweden and in Reggio Emilia.

The Global Voice of Reggio Emilia

For us, all the challenge with our strong inspiration from Reggio Emilia is to turn our focus toward our own didactical and political context. The question is: what is possible to agree on and what has to be contextualized? Most didactical concrete questions have to be contextualized but although "value is a slippery thing" as postmodern critique often argues, we can agree on, be guided of, and inquire the same value areas in all countries. The values of subjectivity/singularity, diversity/alterity, mutual interdependence, and learning can be looked upon as a matter of constructing cooperative temporary "truths," knowing that they always have to be challenged.

To avoid a cargo or a methodological rigidity, we have to develop an international culture of mutual sharing. We also need to use diversity in contexts and theoretical discourses as tools in interpretation of what in our own different contexts creates a risk for developing cargos of methods? Aware of both risks and possibilities we always most look for a balance. This is mainly the challenge for us—the inspired—not firstly the challenge for Reggio Emilia. They should go on relating to the world, only being aware of their risk to be captured or ending up with experiences that change their aims to contribute to a global democratic and perhaps trans-cultural citizenship.

Of course, the crisis of modernity changes Europe and United States into problematic voices in the global dialogue based on listening and invitation to "the other" as we carry a history of problem to accept "the other." This challenges us Europeans to create a new European identity build on multiplicity within and outside the continent.

This is the challenge for all the international network surrounding Reggio Emilia: to look for supporting strategies all over the world to create theories and an everyday practice aiming toward "a children's international," supporting schools and preschools for a global democratic citizenship.

Notes

1. Gothson, H (1991). *Från gamla svar till nya frågor—Torget* (From old answers to new questions—The Fora). Stockholm : Socialstyrelsen 1991:30.
2. Dahlberg, G, Moss, P. and Pence, A.(2006). *Beyond Quality on Early Childhood Education and Care: Postmodern Perspectives* (2nd ed.). London: RoutledgeFalmer.

3. Johnson, R. (2000). Colonialism and Cargo Cults in Early Childhood Education: Does Reggio Emilia really exist? *Contemporary Issues in Early Childhood* 1(1).61–70.
4. Reggio Children, Project Zero (2001). *Making Learning Visible: Children as Individual and Group Learners.* Reggio Emilia: Reggio Children.
5. Rorty, R (2003*). Hopp I stället för kunskap* (*From Philosophy and Social Hope*), Uddevalla: Daidalos.
6. Dahlberg, G, Moss, P (2005). *Ethics and Politics in Early Childhood Education.* London: RoutledgeFalmer.
7. Martin Korpi, B. (2007). *The Politics of Pre-school—Intentions and Decisions Underlying the Emergence and Growth of the Swedish Pre-school.* Stockholm: Ministry of Education.
8. OECD (2006). *Starting Strong II.* Paris: OECD.
9. Dewey, J (1916). *Democracy and Education.* New York: Macmillan.
10. Arvidsson, S (1950*). Indvid och grupp i den nya undervisningen* (The individual and the group in the new way of teaching). Malmö: Arbetartidningen.
11. *Ledning med barnet I centrum* (Child oriented management—AREA report; only in Swedish) (1993). Stockholm: Reggio Emilia Institutet.
12. Modern Barndom Om (2008). *Reggio Emilia Institutet 15 år* (Reggio Emilia Institute 15 years; only in Swedish). Stockholm: Reggio Emilia Institutet.
13. Gothson, H (2008). Tell Laura I love her , tell Laura I need her. in *The Diary of Laura,* St. Paul: Redleaf Press.
14. Gothson, H (2008). *To Develop a Pedagogy for a New Global Citizenship in Dialog with Reggio Emilia; a Challenge for the Swedish Political and Pedagogical Context* (documentation in connection to the exhibit; A hundred languages of children). Seoul: Karea
15. Gothson, H (2009). *In dialog mit Reggio Emilia:Pädagogik fur eine neue Identität als Weltburger.* (In dialogue with Reggio Emilia: a Pedagogy for a new identity as a citizen of the World, chapter in Knauf, H; Fruhe Kindheit gestalten). Stuttgart : W. Kohlhammer.

CHAPTER TWENTY-TWO

Childhood and the Construction of Critical Research Practices

MAGGIE MACLURE, LIZ JONES, RACHEL HOLMES AND CHRISTINA MACRAE

Abstract

Contemporary engagements with children continue to be over-determined by discourses that 'frame' children in simplified and banal ways. This chapter considers the ways in which children are framed in research texts, and attempts a partial deconstruction of the authors' own framings. Organised around one key example of a child's writing, together with data fragments from an ethnographic project, we try to bring forth questions. What is produced and concealed in the practices through which children become 'data' and 'text'? How does the child exceed the frames that are erected around her? Where 'is' the researcher in the writing that she produces 'about' the child? What are the ethical obligations of researchers who write (about) children?

Introduction

Across the domains of policy, practice and public expectation, children continue to be defined, measured and judged according to psychological notions of normal development and the humanist ideal of the 'proper' child. Such notions tend to deny cultural, social and economic consequence to young children, and fail to address the specificity and the opaque complexity of their lives. The result is often marginalisation and social injustice for children and their families.

Research in early childhood often fails to challenge these prevailing constructions of the child, since it generally shares the same discourses of modernity and normal development. As qualitative researchers who, with one exception, were once classroom teachers, we are aware that our own engagements with children have often failed to disturb the frames of familiarity and illusory immediacy afforded by the discourses of research, policy and professional practice. Working the early years classroom as ethnographers, we have often found ourselves strangely blind to insight, perplexity and cultural nuance. Incapacitated by our customary ways of seeing and apprehending them, children have often been rendered monochrome and deceptively familiar: simultaneously exposed and invisible.

We do not think that this condition merely reflects our particular (in)capacities as researchers. The aggressive lethargy of the ethnographic gaze, as it strikes yet glances off 'the child,' is a more pervasive phenomenon. It is difficult to evade even under the auspices of methodologies that are explicitly devoted to rupture, provocation and defamiliarization, such as those informed by critical theory, poststructuralism, psychoanalysis or deconstruction. Our work is informed by such approaches (e.g., Brown and Jones, 2001; MacLure, 2003); but we also argue that special measures are needed to tackle the methodological ennui induced by the discourses of early childhood. This chapter explores a critical practice for research, in the attempt to reinvigorate ways of seeing, representing and engaging young children. Research, we argue, has a critical role to play in expanding the constituency of children who are 'recognizable' in the abstractions and ambitions of policy and practice, while protecting them from the specious clarity of others' views of them, our own included.

While the chapter engages with theoretical and methodological issues, it also remains firmly lodged in empirical practice and sustained ethnographic work in early years classrooms in the United Kingdom. Organised around one key example of a child's writing, together with data fragments from an ethnographic project (MacLure et al., 2008) we aim to provide an instance of critical practice in action.[1]

'Dissimulation, Ruse and Perfidy': The Frame of Writing

> It is as if a catastrophe had perverted this truth of nature: a writing made to manifest, serve and preserve knowledge—for custody of meaning, the repository of learning, and the laying out of the archive—encrypts itself, becoming secret and reserved, diverted from common usage, esoteric....[A] writing becomes the instrument of an abusive power, of a caste of "intellectuals" that is thus ensuring hegemony, whether its own or that of special interests: the violence of a secretariat, a discriminating reserve, an effect of scribble and script. (Derrida, 1979: 124)

We begin by addressing the writing of ethnography and its inevitable work of 'framing' its subjects, taking our title from Derrida's discussion of 'scribble' and the power, privilege and secrecy that are necessarily 'encrypted' in writing (1979: 133). The chapter works the borders between reality and writing, and the alchemy that translates, or transfixes, children in the documents of research. The problematic of writing and its fraught relation to the lives and interests of subjects is a venerable topic in ethnography (Clifford & Marcus, 1986; Lather, 1996). Yet while researchers often express remorse when their writing inevitably ends up by 'framing' their subjects, qualitative research still continues to favour realist genres that deny the knots and holes in the relation of writing and world. Research often continues, then, to veil its own 'written-ness' (MacLure, 2003), even though that status—as 'mere' writing—is routinely exposed by policymakers and other critics who consider themselves to be champions of a real world of action and experience. From such a viewpoint, researchers can only misrepresent the world through their arcane texts. Academics are charged with operating as a priestly caste with a vested interest in veiling their own power and prestige through a secret (hieroglyphic) language that preserves their control over knowledge and their unique prerogative as 'interpreters'

(Derrida, 1979).

This chapter sets out from that familiar, yet often submerged, anxiety of writing that continues to haunt research and policy discourses, producing shame and antagonism. Such anxiety produces a recurrent desire to free the subjects of research from the framing of texts. Derrida writes of this move in Lautréamont's surrealist *Songs of Maldoror*, as the attempt to '*exit* from a certain text *into the real*' (1981: 42; OE). Lautréamont's figure for this escape from the text into the clear light of the real is the spider emerging from its hole in the ground—out of a 'corner of the narrative' into 'extratextual reality.' But the textuality of writing will always return to haunt the attempt to hook it up with some 'reassuring outside' (43).

With Derrida, we assume that power and violence inhabit writing from the beginning: there is no 'innocent' language that could be rescued from the 'abusive power' of researchers, or indeed policy-makers, and attached securely to a 'reassuring outside.' Something will always have been veiled, forced underground ('scrypted'), or pushed to the outside of the frame.[2] Therefore there is an obligation to question what, in any given instance, has been veiled or forced undergound, even if, as Derrida argues, something *else* will always have been occluded in that attempted decipherment. We are interested here in the ways in which children are framed in research texts, and attempt a partial deconstruction of our own framings. We do not hope, of course, to provoke an unframed emergence of the child into the real, or to evacuate our writing of prejudice. Our aim is to release some of the *excess* of meaning and matter that always threatens to overflow the frame of writing. By picking at the borders of some textual examples, we try to bring forth questions. What is produced and concealed in the practices through which children become 'data,' and 'text? How does the child exceed the frames that are erected around him or her? Where 'is' the researcher in the writing that she produces 'about' the child? What are the ethical obligations of researchers who write (about) children?

Stephen's Story

We begin with a fragment of 'data,' in the form of a piece of writing by a 4-year-old boy, Stephen, 'collected' by Liz Jones during her doctoral studies several years ago.

Liz was studying her own teaching, so the text already sits at the intersection of at least two worlds: it is a piece of writing that was elicited for the immediate purposes of teaching literacy to a child in a nursery classroom, and also potentially for use as 'data' for Liz's Ph.D. But the fragment never made it into Liz's Ph.D., nor, until now, into any other research text. In other words, Stephen's story never realised the promise that it held to become 'data,' to be rewritten or framed in a research text, though as we shall see, it was rewritten (at least) twice at the point where it was originally inscribed on that scrap of lined paper that Liz has kept over the years in her folder. First it was rewritten by Liz as a transcription of Stephen's *spoken* story, a familiar pedagogy of early writing in which the teacher acts as scribe, so that children may practice authorship and composition, even if their handwriting and skills of mark making are still rudimentary. The paper also records a possible 'fair copy' of the transcribed story, written by Liz. There are also traces of Stephen in the marks he has put on the page, which may themselves comprise one or more writings of the story. There are for instance pictorial elements that seem to represent the scene, episodes and actors—a house, stairs, a small and large figure who may represent the baby and the policeman, seemingly in pursuit diagonally across the page. Rudimentary letters may be discernible, top left, and a kind of linear 'scribble' across the bottom of the page may or may not represent the flow of joined-up writing. A string of circles linked by a horizontal line, and incorporating a figure in a box, appears along the top edge of the page.

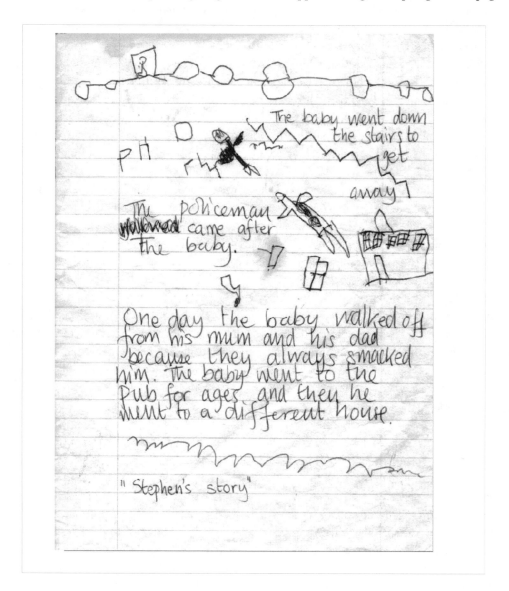

'Stephen's story' already contains not one, but several rewritings therefore, in two different 'hands,' both of which have marked the page. It is a palimpsest, to which our further rewritings in this paper contribute. Like all writing, it cannot be traced back to a definitive origin: we have referred to a 'first' story spoken by Stephen, but that story probably unfolded, haltingly, through questions and formulations by Liz, and was therefore partly coterminous with the written version, rather than preceding it—more in the manner of taking a witness statement perhaps, than of transcribing a single-authored narrative. And of course, whatever the ontogenesis of that spoken 'story,' it is itself an inscription (encryption; scryption; transcryption) of something 'unwritten,' folded into the ongoing weave of Stephen's life. Nor is it clear, in any case, that the spoken story was necessarily the 'first' one. If we follow the conventions of reading/writing, starting at the top left of the page, and going from left to right, we would read first the string of 'o's, which may be letters, or wheels. Liz has always thought of those squiggles at the top of the page as being part writing and part machine/car. In this case, it is the writing that will have come 'first,' suggesting that Stephen already 'knows' the power of writing before he 'has' a writing system in the strict sense—one which does not have to pass 'through' the spoken word (cf. Derrida, 1976). Moreover, the repetitions of the letter/wheel as they spool across the page suggest that Stephen may have written *duration* into his text, in a neat way. The succession of circles would trace both the movement through time of the car as its wheels revolve, and the duration that is stored, yet usually concealed (encrypted), in the tracery of marks that the writing hand makes on the page. Then again, if Stephen did begin by dictating 'The baby went down the stairs,' we might construe the continuous marks at the top and bottom as an adornment, 'embroidered' later to give the piece its own frame.

Time flows within and through the story too, cutting it and connecting it: the time of the making of the marks on the page; the duration that these marks conceal, and partly reveal; the time of the people that it evokes, and the duration of the event that they are/were caught up in; the unfolding time of the interaction between Liz and Stephen that produces the fair copies; the time of Liz's doctoral work, which Stephen's story haunts as absence, as we discuss below; the time of our collective project meetings, during which Stephen's story bobbed up like a message in a bottle sent by Liz to herself, connecting with other children's stories, our own childhood memories, and stories of children in film, hoarded and deciphered by Liz and the other priestly interpreters on the project team; the time of the writing and the redrafting of this account; the future-perfect time of its publication, and the unpredictable times at which it will be read by others. Stephen's story is already dispersed across and folded into versions and deployments.

The Scripting of Stephen's Story

One of the things that interests us about this example is its half-submerged status: a kind of silence or gap surrounds it, in that Liz never 'used' it for the academic (priestly) purposes of her PhD. Yet she did not entirely forget it. She kept it in a folder, from which she was able to retrieve it. Some kind of thread still attaches Liz to Stephen, his writing, and the classroom life in which she and Stephen were immersed.

Perhaps one of the most obvious questions that issues from a re-reading/writing of Stephen's story is the relationship between text and reality. After it had been torn from its original context of appearance, cut from the whirl of classroom activity in which it was written, and reframed years later, it seemed to us to demand questions about the possible relationship between the story Stephen had written/dictated and events in his life. Could Stephen have been writing about real people, places and events—a real baby (himself? his twin brother?), policeman, and mum and dad; an actual pub; regular smacking ('they always smacked him')? Might the 'different house' relate to a wish on Stephen's part to be somewhere else?

These questions cannot be answered definitively, precisely because texts cannot deliver up reality in any direct sense. Nor, we would argue, could they be answered through the occult sciences of interpretation practiced by researchers. Instead, they pose further questions including the question of why such questions were not asked at the time when Stephen wrote his story. Why, in a climate, and in a school, where careful attentiveness to children's safety was an obligation shared and practiced by all adults, might Stephen's story have 'passed' without being treated (as far as Liz recalls) as a text with some possible thread to Stephen's life at home? There are, in turn, a number of possible answers, or at least speculative responses, to this question, none of which is definitive or the last word.

Firstly, we might wonder whether there is a pedagogic imperative that overrides ethicopolitical relations. Does the technology of literacy teaching induce a kind of blindness to possible relationships between children's writing and their experiences, by concentrating the focus on the text as if it had no 'extensions' to children's worlds? On the one hand, this seems unlikely, since the pedagogy of early writing development tends to assume, and/or insist on a *mimetic* relationship between children's first attempts at writing and the events or objects to which they refer. Writing instruction at the early stages of schooling often involves the practice of writing 'captions' to children's own drawings or paintings, which often in turn refer to familiar objects and events within children's experience: 'This is my dog'; There are some trees and a house'; 'I like watching television' etc. One of the versions of Stephen's story (top right of the page) could be read as two such captions: 'The baby went down the stairs to get away.' The policeman came after the baby.' Each of these potential captions is placed near the picture to which it seemingly refers.

However the 'experience' that is so highly valued in early years practice as the ground of children's development is itself an idealised, and often sanitised construction, built out of a stock repertoire of objects, likes, dislikes and activities that young children are 'expected' to have. Children are taught, therefore, to 'have' the kinds of experiences that will be writeable in school—or at least to select those that will be appropriate candidates for storying. These might not usually include pubs and policemen (except perhaps of the 'nice' kind who help children to cross the road). Children may therefore stand in a rather oblique relationship to their 'own' experiences as these are constructed and pre-selected in school. In our more recent work, for instance, Liz observed Hamid enter his classroom with an extremely angry expression and almost immediately proceed to shove Shahed—a girl that he was normally on good terms with—out of his way. But when it came to selecting his written name card so as to put it on one of the four mood charts that were displayed at the front of the classroom he opted to place his name on the 'happy' face. Indeed during the twelve months that Liz spent in the classroom the children were only observed to pick the 'happy' face. Hamid's teacher however employed the activity of aligning her name to a mood as one of several mechanisms for regulating the children: she would sometimes attach her name to the 'sad' or 'angry' face because aspects of the children's behaviour had 'made her very sad/angry' (cf. MacLure et al., 2008). Thus neither the teacher nor we ourselves necessarily expected the constructed 'experience' that is encoded in school writing to carry the traces of 'real' experience.

The sanitised pre-selection of 'experiences' that are writeable/readable in school, and the consignment of other experiences to the crypt of unvoiced material, are given by the meta-narrative of the developing child afforded by developmental psychology. Stephen's story may have failed to issue questions about his home experience partly because it is *'illegible'* as a story within that other, already written story of the typical experiences and abilities of the Piagetian or Rousseauistic child. It resists interpretation. A comparable example of illegibility, not connected this time to writing, can be seen in the following field note from our recent research project (MacLure et al., 2008):

[The class is discussing 'Postman Pat's Windy Day']
Assistant: who likes to get a letter through the door?
Chelsea: as long as you don't have to pay some money [GH11.1.07]

Chelsea's understanding that some letters may be unwelcome (i.e. bills) is not reflected in the Postman Pat stories, where letters are generally welcome. Her experience may not be anticipated therefore in the generic 'script' implicit in her Teaching Assistant's question, which expects that children like to get letters. As in Stephen's story, Chelsea's experience may not be legible within the narrative of normal development.

Another example centres on Daniel when he attempts to help an adult:

> In the art area, Ms S is trying to wind up a stick of glue. 'Why don't you wind it that way?' suggests Daniel to Ms S. 'Instead of telling me what to do, why don't you concentrate on your own work. Turn around and get on' she replies. [Limefield, 7.3.07]

Daniel, while showing initiative and apparently wanting to help, has nevertheless stepped out of a boundary or crossed a line. It seems that by making a suggestion drawn from his own experience, one moreover which could be read as being kind and helpful, he has nevertheless destabilised Ms S. She appears to ignore his suggestion while simultaneously implying he has erred. Daniel's offer is not 'legible' as helpfulness, despite the fact that the latter is one of the cardinal virtues that are promoted in early years classrooms (MacLure et al., 2008). Ms S's admonishment to 'turn around and get on' could be understood as a timely reminder to 'turn' in terms of 'revert,' where he should turn back again to being a child, one moreover who does not tell adults what to do. Following Douglas (1966), we can perceive both Chelsea and Daniel as unsettling 'patterns' and 'systems of ordering':

> from all possible materials, a limited selection has been made and from all possible relations a limited set has been used. So disorder by implication is unlimited, no pattern has been realised in it, but its potential for patterning is indefinite. This is why, though we seek to create order, we do not simply condemn disorder. We recognise that it is destructive to existing patterns; also that it has potentiality. It symbolises both danger and power. (Douglas, 1966: 94)

Returning to Stephen's story, its illegibility vis-à-vis the 'limited selection' afforded by the patterned plot of normal development not only renders it resistant to interpretation, but potentially opens it onto an *excess* of meaning. It seems to harbour danger, in Douglas's sense. For instance, thinking back, Liz wondered whether she feared she might have faced a kind of 'overwhelmingness,' if she had posed to herself the question of possible links between the story and Stephen's home life: a spilling out of the story from its frame to demand actions and responsibility which could not be accommodated within the burden of classroom routine. Ultimately this might have included the involvement of other adults and professionals, the prospect of error and further misinterpretation, stretching out rapidly to the possibility of extreme consequences for the child and his family. Once it is recognised that children's texts may produce 'difficult knowledge' (Britzman, 2000) and experiences that are not prewritten in the innocence narrative of normal development, there is a risk that those texts may open onto a chain of unforeseeable events and demands.

The narrative of the 'proper' child embarked on the plot of normal development limits pedagogy and ethical responsibility to what can be 'read' within this already-written story, and thus renders teaching manageable, and perhaps even possible. What would an early years practice look like, and how would it work, if educators tried to abandon the pre-scryption of children's experience, and attempted to attend to all the nuances and variety of experiences of every child? This would not of course be merely a question of pragmatics because the political imperative to script children in particular ways is bound up on both sides of the Atlantic in a set of Utopian longings. Such longings make the young child into a metaphor, 'a kind of ground zero for the edifice that is adult life…a fantasy of a preferred future' (Bruhm and Hurley, 2004: xiii).

Returning again to Stephen's story it is possible to perceive how in detailing the flight and plight of the baby Stephen effects two significant disturbances. First he positions one of the most potent symbols of innocence—'the baby'—as a knowing strategist who can affect its own escape from what might be a toxic environment. Second he renders fragile normative notions associated with 'the family.' In looking back at this text, Liz finds it possible to imagine herself undergoing something akin to an 'ontological shudder' where Stephen's story serves to destabilise her familiar and habitual ways of 'knowing' young people. Read from the present we can perceive it as holding power and agency: as threatening to the divide that is placed between adult and child in their interactions. When children confound our expectations we may retreat to corrosive practices, insisting that they conform to a mythical or stereotypical notion of what constitutes the child.

Liz now wonders whether the very fact that she held onto Stephen's story might have been an 'effacement,' or interment, of its power. Why did she still have the paper in the first place? It was the usual practice in her school to hand over to parents at the end of the day work that their children had produced, such as paintings, models and drawings. Some things would have been put in the child's portfolio, as 'evidence' of progress (for 'custody of meaning' as Derrida writes in the opening quotation above). And there was a designated space in the 'writing corner' of the classroom where children often stuck up such scraps of 'emergent writing.' The fact that Liz kept Stephen's story in these circumstances adds another layer of veiling. It may 'simply' be that she had struck a deal with Stephen, his teacher and his parents that she might retain some of his work for incorporation in her Ph.D.[3] However as evidence of progress, perhaps the 'worldliness' of Stephen's story would have pointed to *too much* progress, in terms of the staging points erected along the path of normal development. As the examples of Daniel and Chelsea above suggest, children who are considered to be progressing too rapidly along the developmental path may be judged a 'problem.' We have noted elsewhere that children may need to veil their own knowledge and wisdom in order to simulate the innocent, 'proper' child expected and produced in early education (MacLure et al., 2008). Might the same considerations have led Liz to hide Stephen's knowledge, or her own knowledge that Stephen 'had' such knowledge? And even to hide it from herself?

'Writing does not come to power,' writes Derrida. 'It is there beforehand, it partakes of and is made of it.' For that reason, 'struggles and contending forces permeate writings and counter-writings,' setting them against one another (1979: 117). One such struggle might involve Liz's attempt, on the one hand, to 'stay true' to Stephen's own language (notice how she erased 'followed,' in favour of 'came after') and respect the integrity of his story even though its characters and plot departed from the 'canonical' narratives of pre-school children. Yet on the other hand, and under licence of early years pedagogy, she takes words from his mouth to write a story which unavoidably muffles his voice, frames his experience and holds (encrypts) meanings which immediately become unintelligible to her.

We have struggled with other contending forces in our writings as researchers, each struggle producing its own interments and its own shame. We have promised to 'write accessibly,' and thereby buried some of the complexity and nuance that prevents us from lapsing into easy solutions (while *still* failing to be accessible). We have failed to share everything with the participating teachers in our research, allowing our gaps and silences to protect us from responsibility for the offence, shame or paralysis that our own 'difficult knowledge' might have produced in others. We have exercised, then, the priestly prerogative that Derrida describes as 'the hoarding of codes, of archival matters' (1979: 118). And is so doing, we have replayed the acts of omission that held and withheld Stephen's story, preventing it from circulating beyond the classroom. Protectiveness towards others changes places indiscernibly with self-protection in the cryptic economy of writing.[4]

Derrida writes that this is the unavoidable displacement that writing effects, operating as a crypt which 'hides as it holds' (1986: xiv). We know therefore that it is impossible to share or communicate everything, since something must always remain unwritten and unintelligible for any act of writing to take place. But this does not absolve us from responsibility to others and to the other in our self. Dawson, after Derrida spells out the terms of this responsibility:

> [All] inscription and encryption is both the burial and the trace of another. If all inscr(i/y)ption becomes the opportunity to give place to, repress, deny, recognise, preserve and love the other, then all inscr(i/y)ption becomes a question of responsibility to the other and to otherness. (2009: 3)

Conclusion

If there is any excuse for having disinterred Stephen's story only to reframe it, and him, once more, it will have been to counter the myths of the generic 'innocent' child that frame individual children; to press the recognition that young people may have wisdom and experiences that lie beyond (whether in advance of, or outside) the anticipations laid out in the trajectory of developmental psychology and early years pedagogy. Such recognition is the precursor for a critical practice that seeks to establish different relations or interactions between adults and young people. Qualitative research has its own obligations in this respect: it is only by destabilising our own framings and representational practices that we may hope to avoid colluding with other framings that hold and encrypt children, and thereby contribute to a process of opening up alternative futures. Additionally, we would hope that something of Stephen's voice has echoed across the years and the veils of writing. That voice is not pure, but something of its power can still be heard, faintly....

Notes

1. This chapter draws on a paper presented to the Annual Meeting of the American Educational Research Association: Jones & MacLure (2009).
2. We wander among a variety of words that 'stand for,' or stand in the place of, writing in this paper: including *frame*, *veil* and *crypt* (and its etymologically dubious derivations, *scrypt* and *scryption*). We are taking our lead from Derrida here, who used, and discarded, and used again these words amongst others in his writing of/on writing.
3. We can note in passing that '*incorporation*,' as a psychic process of mourning, is equated with loss of the other and consignment to the crypt (cf. Derrida, 1986).
4. There are other silences and 'contending forces' that have set other writings against one another, which we cannot fully address here. For instance there are the acts of 'secretarial violence' that Liz has inevitably experienced, in delivering herself and her writings up as 'data' for us all to 'interpret.' Alongside the satisfactions and camaraderie that this collaboration has enabled, there is also, inevitably, risk and discomfort. And the 'remains' of our interpretive violence still lie more-or-less undisturbed in this text (crypt).

References

Britzman, D.P. (2000) Teacher education in the confusion of our times. *Journal of Teacher Education*, 51, 3: 200–205.
Brown, T. and Jones, L. (2001) *Action Research & Postmodernism: Congruence & Critique*. Buckingham: Open

University Press.

Bruhm, S. & Hurley, N. (2004) Curiouser. On the queerness of children: a simple story, in Bruhm & Hurley (eds) *Curiouser: on the Queerness of Children*. Minneapolis, MN: University of Minnesota Press.

Clifford, J. and Marcus, G. (eds) (1986) *Writing Culture: The Poetics and Politics of Ethnography*. Berkeley, CA: UCLA Press.

Derrida, J. (1976) *Of Grammatology*. Trans, with an Introduction by G. Chakravorty Spivak. Baltimore: Johns Hopkins.

Derrida, J. (1979) Scribble (writing-power). *Yale French Studies*, 58: 117–14.

Derrida, J. (1981) *Dissemination*. Trans, with an Introduction by B. Johnson. London: Athlone Press.

Derrida, J. (1986) Fors: the Anglish words of Nicolas Abraham and Maria Torok, trans. B. Johnson, in N. Abraham and M. Torok, *The Wolfman's Magic Word: A Cryptonomy*. Minneapolis, MN: University of Minnesota Press.

Douglas, M. (1966) *Purity and Danger: An Analysis of Concepts of Pollution and Taboo*. London: Routledge & Kegan Paul.

Jones, L, & MacLure, M. (2009) 'Dissimulation, ruse and perfidy': the frame of writing. Paper presented to the Annual Meeting of the American Educational Research Association, San Diego, 13–17 April 2009.

Lather, P. (1996) Troubling clarity: the politics of accessible language. *Harvard Educational Review*, 66: 525–545.

MacLure, M. (2003) *Discourse in Educational and Social Research*. Buckingham: Open University Press.

MacLure, M, Jones, L, Holmes, R. & MacRae, C. (2008) *Becoming a Problem: How Children Acquire a Reputation as 'Naughty' in the Earliest Years at School*. End of Award Report to the Economic and Social Research Council (RES-062–23–0105). Manchester: Manchester Metropolitan University mimeo. (Project outline and downloadable copy of report at: *http://www.esri.mmu.ac.uk/resprojects/project_outline.php?project_id=1*)

CHAPTER TWENTY-THREE

Using Material Molecular Politics in Early Childhood Education

LISELOTT MARIETT OLSSON

Opening Narrative

Within the research project "The Magic of Language—Young Children's Relations to Language, Reading and Writing," children, teachers, teacher students, and researchers have during two years been experimenting with and engaging in a learning of language, reading, and writing based on the idea of an unexplored creative dimension of language. The theoretical sources come from French and Italian philosophers Gilles Deleuze, Félix Guattari, and Adriana Cavarero, but also social semiotics researcher Gunther Kress. The project aims to investigate very young children's relations to language, reading, and writing in times of globalization, multicultural concerns as well as the possibilities of the continuously growing visual language. The purpose of the project is to, through the gained knowledge of very young children's relations to language, reading, and writing, add something to the formalized teaching of language, reading, and writing through supporting children's own ways of making sense through using language as a creative and pragmatic feature.

Within the project a group of 4- to 5-year-olds had during a semester explored and experimented with letters and more specifically the features of one's proper name. When spring semester started, the teachers' and researchers' intention was to continue the project in which the children had taken great interest. However, in the beginning of the semester, it stood clear to teachers and researchers that something was not going right in the group. There was a weird and restless ambiance in the group with lots of conflicts, little activity, and overall a very stressful situation for everybody involved. Teachers and researchers gathered together to try to figure out how to handle the situation. After analyzing what was taking place in the class it seemed that one reason for this ambiance full of conflicts was the state of the pedagogical environment. In fact, in the analysis we could see that most of the activity stations and the material had gone dead and that they were not challenging enough for the children. The children had gone through all the material presented in the classroom and seemed to sort of be done with it. Another identified reason for the ambiance in the class was that the focus last year had been very much on the written and spoken language and less on all the other languages, such as for instance body and sign language but also engaging in the creation with different materials such as clay, painting, drawing, etc. that children have access to and use in order to think and communicate. It seemed that there had been too much focus on only one dimension of language; the spoken and written alphabetical code—rather than engaging in all of the other possible languages at stake and above mentioned. These are languages that also break with the image of a thought that is organized and progress in a linear way, and where there's a clearly defined hierarchy and cause–effect relationship. On the contrary, in for instance, a drawn picture or in a three-dimensional sculpture, this linearity, hierarchy, and cause–effect logic can be broken. Things can happen simultaneously and in many different directions, it is a nonhierarchal surface that connects events in a different way than a told or a written story. During the first year of observation within the research project, we have seen that children's spoken language develop in close relationship to these other languages and the creation of sense connected to these. Constructing with clay, for instance, is one of the identified moments where we can see that children at the same time as they are struggling with technical problems and construction techniques, very often develop interesting conversations and explore spoken language. Our experiences within the research project also show that it is when children have interesting things to do together and when they get deeply involved in trying to construct problems together, that feelings of solidarity and friendship automatically build among the children.

So in order to work for a more interesting, friendly, and language-rich environment, a decision was made to start renovating the different activity stations, starting with the clay construction corner.

The first occasion at the new clay table starts off with four children exploring the clay through making what they call "tracks" all over the table, they seem to work individually although the tracks slowly take shape in what seems to be collective effort of covering the whole table and make each individual track finally conjure up with the others to create a loop. But strangely enough the children never speak to each other about this and they, at least as far as we can see, do not in any particularly intense way study each others' tracks, each seems to be preoccupied with his or hers own track. But then Adam's father comes to pick Adam up and go home. Before leaving the table, Adam turns around to Victor sitting on the opposite side of the table and he says: "So Victor you'll finish my part of then?" Victor answers "Ok" and then Adam walks out in the hallway with his father to go home. We are astonished by this as it becomes clear to us that the children again have given us a proof of a way of communicating without words that they have access to and that we as adults seem to have somewhat forgotten. Victor continues building the track and he then takes a car to try the track out. At one place in the loop, two tracks do not completely meet and there is therefore a little gap in the loop. Victor jumps with car from one side to another several time and says: "Hmm, the loop was supposed to be whole." We see an occasion to go in and suggest to Victor and his friend Lucas who is constructing next to him the constructing of a bridge over the gap. We see that this could present an interesting challenge and a situation where the children will have to face many technical problems such as stability and different techniques for constructing with clay. So we say to Victor: "Maybe you could construct a bridge over the gap?" "A bridge?" Victor and Lucas say with one mouth. "Yes a bridge, would you like to do that?" "Yes, but how do we do that?" Victor says. We suggest to the children to go into the construction corner and se if they can find a bridge that they can study in order to get some ideas of how to build their bridge. They run off and come back with a wooden bridge that they put on the table, next to this bridge they start building a big heap of clay, they go on for a long time and the heap just grows bigger and bigger, eventually Lucas drifts off and starts constructing something else at the other end of the table. Victor also changes places and starts to build something else. We decide that it is the moment to remind the children of the bridge, have they forgotten, is it not interesting, is it to hard for them? "Have you abandoned the idea of the bridge now?" we ask. Both Victor and Lucas say: "The bridge?" In order to support the children and make them think about what needs to be worked out with the bridge they have tried to do by making a big heap of clay, we ask them if they could find a way of making it possible for the cars to also drive under the bridge. Victor immediately hooks on to this proposition and he starts digging out clay from underneath the big heap. He stands up and is working very hard moving his whole body around the table saying with an enchanted voice: "We will have to work all day!" He keeps digging for twenty minutes or so and gets more and more frustrated, all of a sudden he turns around to us and he says: " Hey guys, really, this was actually your idea!" We answer him: "Yes, it was, are you finding it hard?" Victor says with force: "Yes, I do!" We then ask Lucas to help Victor out and he comes over to join in. Both boys now frenetically dig out clay from underneath the bridge; they stand up, work with their whole body and encourage each other, they lift up the upper bridge part with their hands and then after another half hour or so the bridge is finally finished: "Yes, it worked!" "Finally, we made it!" they exclaim with great joy. The children have now been working for almost two hours and there is a great intensity in the room, a group of six other children have gathered around the table observing what is taking place with great interest. Victor then turns around to us and he says: "You can give us another idea now!" We understand his commentary as a confirmation of the fact that they want us to engage and be part of their processes, but nevertheless feel the need to say: " But we can see that you also have plenty of ideas when you are working," and to this Victor answers: "Yeah, I have all my ideas in my hands, they come along as I am working, I think with my hands."

Introduction: Where Has Materiality Gone?

The situation evoked above shows how engaging in work for change can be quite a messy and complicated story. On a very concrete and everyday level, teachers and researchers are faced with challenges like the one above; how do you get a group going; how do you create a friendly and creative atmosphere in a place where many different people, with as many different experiences, meet everyday? The situation tells about a numerous amount of choices to be made every day at every moment in order to work for change. These are choices that carry with them a certain amount of responsibility and a lot of complexity. But the situation also tells about how you could work with change through experimenting without trying to control all parameters as well as any expected outcome. And, it turns out that this can be a very joyful and interesting affair in that it highlights and uses what could be considered a different image of thought. Victor, with his very intelligent comment on ideas and thinking, encapsulates a different image of thought that could show to be productive when it comes to the question of change; change is not something you control through thinking, ideas and thinking are bodily concrete and material affairs and they take shape as they go along. Victor's way of explaining thought and ideas has its equivalence in the philosophy presented by Deleuze and Guattari, Roy, and Cavarero; thinking is not separated from bodily experience; thought is not the great organizer of experience. Before thought there is life and life is so much stronger and demands so much more than thought. Change could in this perspective be a question of dealing with the materiality of everyday life. Now, one could ask the question if there is, within our field of teaching and research-ing in Early Childhood Education, space for the image of thought that Victor talks about above; a thought that is created and works through the hands as well takes shape as it proceeds? Or have we, in these days where we pay a lot of attention to spoken and written language, for example, discourse, quite lost touch with the material aspects of everyday life? What kind of consequences might that have for our ambitions to work with and for political change and social justice? In this chapter I would like to explore the question and the potentiality of returning to the material aspects of preschool life, both on a level of research and on a level of the pedagogical practice and the consequences that might have for work with political change and social justice. What follows below is a close reading of Manuel De Landa's argumentation for returning to a material politics. Thereafter comes a theoretical section that tries to account for the two French philosophers Gilles Deleuze and Félix Guattari's way of giv-ing consistency to materiality in a way that possibly places them somewhere in between both real-istic and idealistic accounts of materiality. The chapter ends with drawing out the potential of using these theories in relation to research and practice in the field of Early Childhood Education (ECE).

Linguistic Imperialism and Conservative Idealism

In a challenging book chapter, Manuel DeLanda (2008) states that for a long time leftist and pro-gressive politics were anchored in a materialist philosophy that left little space for subjective beliefs and desires about reality. But with the 'linguistic turn' everything changed and what became norm was the ontological standpoint of idealism according to which the world is a product of our minds. The focus turned from a material mind-independent reality to reality as constructed historically, social-ly, culturally, and linguistically. In the field of Early Childhood Education (ECE), this turn has often expressed itself through the use of poststructural or hermeneutic discourse analysis in an attempt to discern and criticise taken for granted assumptions, or linguistically produced discursive regimes, con-cerning young children and learning, in order to open up for change. The French philosopher Michel Foucault has played an important role in these deconstructive attempts.

For DeLanda however, Foucault, from the book *Discipline and Punish* (1977) and so forth paid equal attention to the nondiscursive political practices. According to DeLanda, many scholars con-sider Foucault's contribution to be a highlight of the fact that many material practices, such as pris-ons, schools, the army, are actually linguistic practices. But DeLanda states that this has sometimes turned into a new form of 'conservative idealism' and also that it encompasses a 'bastardisation' of Foucault that must not stand unchallenged. There is an original distinction between discursive and nondiscursive practices that must be upheld:

> To put it in a nutshell: while pairing a certain category of crime, like stealing, with a certain category of pun-ishment, like cutting off a thief's hand, is clearly a discursive practice, the actual act of mutilation is equal-ly clearly a non-discursive one. (DeLanda, 2008: 162)

What is being put forward seems to be somewhat a cry of warning that when focusing too much, or in the wrong way, on practises as linguistically constructed, there is the risk of neglecting the mate-rial aspects of these. If all events in a practice are read as linguistic discourse, we not only miss out on the complexity of Foucault's work and our practices, but also, we might not even be effective in our attempts to work with social and political change, as much of what is going on is falling outside discourse and language. Considering the field of ECE and attempts to work with social and political change, it seems that in order to avoid being trapped within a linguistic imperialism, where all acts are reduced to linguistic expressions, as well as avoiding falling into a new form of conservative idealism, it would be of interest to revisit and reconsider the materiality of nondiscursive practices. In this chapter we would like to depart from and connect our own experiences in the field of ECE practice and research to DeLanda's (2008) reasoning about the need for social justice or any other movements attempting to work with social and political change, to revisit and give consistency to the materiality of the nondiscursive aspects of political practices.

To Conceptualize Materiality Through "Double Articulation of Strata"

According to DeLanda, in order to not let idealism slip in through the backdoor, any kind of coherent materialism must be able to explain how stable identities take shape and maintain over time, or, must be able to create a concept of "objective synthesis, that is of a temporal process that produces and maintains those stable identities" (DeLanda, 2008: 162). The two French philosophers Gilles Deleuze and Félix Guattari have, according to DeLanda, introduced new ideas of how to work with such an objective synthesis.

According to Deleuze and Guattari, all strata, whether geological, biological, or social are formed through a process of double articulation:

> The first articulation concerns content, the second expression. The distinction between the two articulations is not between forms and substances but between content and expression, expression having just as much substance as content and content just as much form as expression. (Deleuze and Guattari, 2004: 49)

What is said in this quote is that all strata, all stable identities that evolve, and maintain over time, are being formed through an articulation of content and an articulation of expression, where both processes harbour both substance and form. Deleuze and Guattari take as an example the formation of a rock and describe how the first articulation is the choosing or deducting of particle flows and molecular units such as flysch and the succession of sandstone and schist (substances) that are connected into a certain statistical ordering (forms) and the second articulation concerns the establishing and consolidation of more functional, stable, and larger material entities (forms) that effects the passing into sedimentary rock and in which these structures are new actualized (substances). From this then, it becomes clear that there is no cause–effect relationship between content and expression, it is not that the content concerns only substances and automatically and consequently leads to a certain expressivity and form. What is said is that both content and expression have a form and a substance. The process goes in two directions at the same time. In the first articulation concerned with content, the flysch, sandstone, and schist, the substances are gathered together and given a loosely defined form. The second articulation establishes larger material entities, forms capable of forceful expressivity in which the loosely defined structures, substances are now actualized in a different way. In both processes, content and expression, there is both substance and form, but none of them serves as determining the other. Content has got both substances and form, but so has expressivity.

Molecular and Molar Scales

So, material strata are being formed and maintained is taking place, not through a predefined order where content determines expression or expression determines content, but rather, according to

Deleuze and Guattari, it is merely a question of different spatial scales. Where the first articulation concerning content operates with and through molecular compounds and the second articulation concerning expression operates with and through larger molar compounds:

> One type is supple, more molecular, and merely ordered; the other is more rigid, molar and organized. Although the first articulation is not lacking in systematic interactions, it is in the second articulation in particular that phenomena constituting an overcoding are produced, phenomena of centering, unification, totalization, integration, hierarchization, and finalization. (Deleuze and Guattari, 2004: 46)

What we come to see as an expressive molar, defined, and finalized rock, then, is still an entity built on molecular substances, and the content of the rock, the molecular substances in the first instance, before the rock, already have form. It is a question of spatial scales. It gets even more complicated as Deleuze and Guattari insist upon the fact that it is not as simple as if smaller entities are always molecular and larger entities always molar. Rather, smaller entities are always small and large at the same time, as much as larger entities are always large and small at the same time. Moreover, first and second are here not to be seen as one coming before the other. Rather, both processes, both articulations take place at the same time. To be able to understand this, the spatial scales, as well as the two articulations content and expression, must be seen not as absolute, but relative. The focus needs to be on the process of the rock coming about and not on the finalized and already cemented rock. A proper becoming-rock.

Language's Pretensions and Nonlinguistic Materiality

What is not said in the first quotation, but should be understood from the example of the rock, is that, despite the linguistically inspired terms, this idea of the relation between content and expression is not primarily of a linguistic character. What is talked about is content and expressivity as nonlinguistic. Deleuze and Guattari show how language through its specific nonspatial but temporal features becomes independent of its formed materiality. All other strata spatially evolve over time, but language is normally (and especially within language-based theories) treated as disconnected from spatial materiality. It is this lack of spatial materiality that creates the imperialist pretensions of language, where language is thought to be able to encompass all the other strata. Seeing this is important in order to understand the specialized function of language and the power it carries, but at the same time not get intimidated by this. There are nonlinguistic materiality, contents, and expressions that are equally worth paying attention to.

Double Articulation in the Field of ECE

Now, what could these quite complex theories possibly have to do with the question of social and political change in the field of ECE? Well, probably a lot. What is really at stake is the question of change, whether we talk about, rocks, social systems, or language.

If strata (geological, biological, or social) proceed and maintain through a process where there is no longer any cause–effect relationship between content and expression, if this process rather is a question of different spatial scales, and if this process is not primarily linguistic, this opens up for a different way of viewing change in all these strata. Actually, first of all the whole problem must rather be turned around, no longer focusing how to be able to work with change despite the cemented identities of strata. Rather the problem must be posed in a way where we try 'to explain the wonder that there can be stasis granted the primacy of process' (Massumi, 2002a: 8). What is described above is really the primacy of process of geological, but also biological and social strata. It includes turning a too heavy focus away from the product, the already defined materiality, and instead focusing how material formations come about.

> Formation cannot be accounted for if a common form is assumed, whether between content and expression or subject and system. If the world exhibits conformities or correspondences they are, precisely, produced. To make them the principle of production is to confuse the composing with the composed, the process with the product. (Massumi, 2002b, p. xviii)

In relation to our field, the field of research and practice in ECE, taking this focus on process seriously implies a slightly different role for research and for the researcher. In order to work with the becoming aspects of practice and focusing process rather than product, research and work for social and political change must join the ongoing production processes in practice. In several different projects, we have struggled with establishing a research approach that joins practice in a collective experimentation in between children, teachers, and researchers. This demands of research to fully admit its productiveness and inventiveness, and it also demands a new kind of empiricism no longer associated with the epistemological features of logical empiricism, where atomistic sensations are seen as in need of being organized and systemized by abstract thought. What is needed is a more "wild" kind of empiricism that no longer positions thought outside or above practice, an empiricism that harbors the complexity of life and experiments with that which is coming about.

The thesis of double articulation could be used in relation to the field of research and practice in ECE through developing carefulness about treating the different contents and expressions in practice as obeying any simple laws of correspondence. For instance, the preschool as content has both form and substance; the form is the preschool and the substance the children, teachers and parents that are there. But the expressions concerning preschool have also got a form and a substance. For instance, the form could be the theories put forward in the name of developmental psychology and the substance would be "the developing child" and the strategies coupled to this in shape of surveillance, monitoring, and intervening with the right "developmental help."

But even if the architecture of a preschool can be seen as a molar, cemented, and finalized unit, it can be totally overturned by tiny little gestures and actions from the people inhabiting it, or phenomena affecting it from the outside such as construction work seen from the window or even the weather's changing features. Or, it could be more dramatically overturned through introducing new furniture or material into it. The content "preschool" is at the same time form and substance, but most of all it is vibrantly alive and changing. And just as expressions of preschool through linguistically produced discourses on children coming from developmental psychology are giving preschool a stable and cemented identity or a form, the actual acting in these practices must be considered as nondiscursive and molecular substances. Within the expressions of a preschool there are always intensities, forces, loopholes, and—to discourse not corresponding—actions and passions that both children and teachers make use of. The thesis of double articulation could also be used in relation to how very young children use language. Through our research we have been able to see how children use language in many more ways than solely as a mediating tool within a system of representations. Children when using language seem to find themselves most of the time in a proper reinvention of the thought of correspondence in between content and expression in the alphabetical code. In one of the projects the children constructed their proper alphabet, in both two- and three-dimensional material. They reused and reinvented alphabetical signs as well as inventing signs never before heard of, but that still had their proper use in the children's own context. They were creatively changing the corresponding relations of content and expression in the alphabetical code but were still able to, at least within their group, to make sense. When one child was asked why they were inventing new letters and signs, the child answered: "At least these ones I understand the other ones I simply can't get a grip on."

Molecular and Molar Scales in ECE

The insistence on relative rather than absolute scales and the importance of the relation between molecular and molar scales can be used by the field of ECE to describe the materiality of practices as being constituted by material overcodings, finalizations, unifications, and cemented phenomena (stereotyped ways of thinking, being, speaking, acting, as well as the rooms and the tools assigned architecture and purposes). But equally it is important to realize that these are just one part of the materiality at stake. There are, as said above, also and at the same time, molecular becomings that are as much, and to the same extent, constituting the materiality of these practices. The scales affect every level of the preschool; even the relationship between children and teachers are affected by the scales. Teachers are seen as molar decision makers but anybody who has worked with (or even been nearby) very young children knows that, again, a tiny little gesture from the children can completely overturn the whole situation. Molecular and molar scales can also be used to say something about the relationship in between individual and society in contexts of learning. Generally, this problem is posed either from the point of view of a realist philosophical perspective where an mind-independent reality is asserted and where individual psychological or cognitive theories stress a learning that depends upon each individual student's capacity to adapt to and identically represent and reproduce (or not) this reality. Or the problem is posed from the opposite philosophical perspective of idealism where social constructivist or poststructural theories insist on focusing the impact and formative aspect that society has on individual students. This never-ending dualism could through the idea of molecular and molar scales be reconsidered. Within the perspective of relative spatial scales, an individual as well as a group or an entire society is no longer thought of as fixed entities affecting each other through cause–effect logic. Rather the molecular/molar definition can bring forward a learning that is seen as taking place within complex networks or assemblages where it would be possible to work with education as well as with social and political change through the unpredictable and intense experimenting with the 'here-and-now events' in practices. This is what we see in the opening narrative where teachers and researchers try to carefully experiment with how to join the children in their process. They try to understand what in the precise moment needs to be challenged in order to hook on to children's desires or make them hook on to theirs. Children want us to play with them they are sensitive to us calling them to join us; "Give us an idea!"…This must be met by teachers and a focusing on the right scale for ones interventions might help us to neither take for granted nor get intimidated by the power normally ascribed to the teacher.

Extralinguistic Forces in ECE

Concerning the relation of language and materiality, it seems important to analyze what is taking place in ECE practices with a great deal of carefulness in seeing these practices as solely linguistically shaped practices. There is a need to be aware of the nonspatial and therefore imperialist pretensions of language. We must see that "reading," "deconstructing," and "interpreting" reach can have a value in relation to, only one part of the practice, its temporal, nonspatial features. Linguistic discourses or expressions do not completely determine the materiality of the content of practices. Practices harbor loads of non- or extralinguistic contents and expressions that must be treated as having both substances and forms. This seems to be of utmost importance especially when taking into account that our practices concern very young children who very often have not yet adapted to the system of language as we know it. Not only do these very young children use a lot of extralinguistic expressions such as mimics, gestures, sounds, looks, etc., but also, they seem to be constantly activating a dimension in language that must be considered to be nothing less than the creative dimension of language. Deleuze and Guattari write extensively on the truly open-ended, creative, and pragmatic dimension of language, where content and expression as well as sense and nonsense find themselves in coproduction of new material events, rather then being each other's opposites (Deleuze & Guattari, 2004). In the research project "The Magic of Language" and in the opening narrative, it becomes clear that children activate precisely this creative and pragmatic dimension of language. When rhyming, singing, inventing new words, changing the first letter in a word, or inventing alphabets never before heard of, they activate a relationship between content and expression as well as between sense and nonsense that is far from being a dualistic or contradictory one. Paired with the highly complex analysis Deleuze and Guattari make of language, it turns out the children are the ones who have got it all right. As Victor says: "I've got all my ideas in my hands, they come along as I am working, I think with my hands."

Conclusion: A Material Molecular Politics in ECE

The move away from realism's pretensions to represent and reproduce real truth about the world has for sure been very beneficial for our practices. Not the least in relation to the fact that individual children in this perspective were always treated in an essentialist way and as the ones having everything wrong in relation to the order of things and words. But it seems equally important to acknowledge that there is no need to lock ourselves up in the opposite corner where it turns out we make the same essentialist claims, although now in the name of society, power, or language. I join Deleuze and Guattari in their refusing to believe in structure: "it is an illusion to believe that structure is the earth's last word" (Deleuze and Guattari, 2004: 46). For them, structures, whether social, administrative, or linguistic, are in the first instance leaking, overflowing and uncontrollable. To believe this is truly a political choice and a theoretically inevitable choice when discovering how change actually happens. It is not enough to say that everything is "socially or linguistically constructed," it leads us nowhere further than crying out "long live the multiple!" Multiplicities, intensities, transformations, and change must be made and produced. In this chapter I have tried only opening up for a few possible roads to take in such a process of production and work with social and political change. It seems that current work on social and political change within social constructivist and post-structural perspectives could benefit from being complemented by a reconsidering of language's pretensions and the material aspect of nondiscursive practices as well as a focus on the right scale. I believe that there is a great deal of space and work in front of us in producing and experimenting with a material and molecular politics within the field of ECE.

References

DeLanda, M (2008) 'Deleuze, Materialism and Politics' in I. Buchanan, and N. Thoburn, (Eds). *Deleuze and Politics*, Edinburgh: Edinburgh University Press.

Deleuze, G. and Guattari, F.(1980) Mille plateaux. Capitalisme et schizophr nie 2, collection "Critique", Paris: Les ſditions de Minuit; trans. Brian Massumi (2004, 2nd edn) *A Thousand Plateaus: Capitalism and Schizophrenia*, London: Continuum.

Foucault, M. (1975) Surveiller et punir: Naissance de la prison, Paris: ſditions Gallimard; trans. Alan Sheridan (1977) *Discipline and Punish: The Birth of the Prison*, London: Allen Lane.

Massumi, B. (2002a) (ed.) *A Shock to Thought-Expression after Deleuze and Guattari*, Routledge: New York.

Massumi, B. (2002b) *Parables for the Virtual: Movement, Affect, Sensation*, Durham, NC: Duke University Press.

CHAPTER TWENTY-FOUR

Kia mau ki te wairuatanga[1]

Countercolonial Narratives of Early Childhood Education in Aotearoa[2]

JENNY RITCHIE AND CHERYL RAU

Introduction

In this chapter, we use our particular national milieu of Aotearoa, New Zealand, for a focus on indigenous childhoods in the twenty-first century. In order to establish this contemporary context, we firstly provide a historical and cultural location for Maori childhoods, including some key indigenous constructs, before briefly outlining some of the impacts of colonization over the past two centuries. In this country, as elsewhere, education and religion have been particularly implicated as instruments of colonization (L. T. Smith, 1995). Injustices of land alienation and economic redistribution facilitated by settler majoritarianism led to the erosion of the promised self-determination for Maori (Walker, 2004). This in turn resulted in an inability to maintain the vitality of the language and of the spiritual values and practices inherent within Maori childhoods (Pere, 1982/1994, 1991).

We then draw upon kaupapa Maori (L. T. Smith, 1999, 2005) and other indigenous critical theory (Meyer, 2001), alongside postcolonial (Loomba, 2005; Young, 2001) and alterity critiques (Levinas, 1987, 1988) to further a countercolonial theoretical positioning with which to frame an analysis of our recent research in early childhood care and education in Aotearoa. Western worldviews predominate in institutions including early childhood education, forming the basis for "the construction of the default category of the universal," which is then assumed as valid and imposed normatively, positioning "other" experiences and knowledges as deviant (Bhambra, 2006, p. 36). Western universality, as seen for example in child development theory, is insidious in its taken-for-granted "invisibility" of pervasiveness, is in fact, culturally specific, representing "the Anglo-US, white, middle-class, masculine subjectivity of the twentieth century" (Burman, 2008, p. 164). Globalization, the "new" colonization, means that young children are increasingly exposed to western popular culture, complicating efforts by early childhood educators to provide children with access to local

Indigenous histories and knowledge. In our final section, we draw upon data from our recent studies, in order to illuminate some discourses which offer countering possibilities to the denarrativization, which has resulted in the othering, silencing, and invisibilization of Maori and other indigenous childhoods (Martin, 2007; Rose, 2004).

Historical and Cultural Context for Maori Childhoods

In this section, selected traditional Maori beliefs and values[3] are highlighted to articulate a te Ao Maori[4] educational foundation. Much of this knowledge has been drawn from the writing of recognized Maori authorities such as Makereti Papakura, Rangimarie Rose Pere, Mihipeka Edwards, Tuki Nepe, Ranginui Walker, and Linda Mead/Smith. Some significant contexts which guide the education of the mokopuna[5] in a traditional Maori paradigm are underpinning premises that embody the values, beliefs, and processes of wairuatanga (spiritual interconnectedness), whakapapa (genealogical interconnectedness), whanaungatanga (family interconnectedness), intergenerational links, all positioning the child as a learner within the context of a whanau, hapu, and iwi setting.[6]

Wairuatanga or Maori spiritual beliefs are derived from Ranginui (Sky Father), Papatuanuku (Earth Mother) and nga Atua (Deities), indigenous origins depicted in cosmological ancient moteatea (chants and songs) describing Maori as "direct descendants of the heavens" (Mead, 1996, p. 210). This holistic worldview embodying Ranginui, Papatuanuku, and nga Atua is inclusive of tangata (people), the environment, and wairua (spirituality). As Mihipeka Edwards explains, "wairua emanates from the beginning of time and never changes. Everything and every person has wairua and mauri—your spirituality and your life force—they are something you are born with" (1992, p. 55). Spiritual links to the animate world and the inanimate world are embedded within the Maori language, and expressed through karakia (spiritual incantations) korero (talking), embodying ways of knowing and values.

Whakapapa is a Maori paradigm that articulates te Ao Maori origins as ancestral narratives (Walker, 2004). Layers of whakapapa narrate the herstories/histories of people, places and landmarks, knowledge of whakapapa establishing one's turangawaewae (ancestral geographical connection) to hapu, iwi, whenua (land), awa (rivers), and the universe. Whakapapa positions individuals within an interconnected animate and inanimate world, mokopuna ancestry inclusive of mountains, rivers, and landmarks: "We are linked through our whakapapa to insects, fishes, trees, stones and other life forms" (Mead, 1996, p. 211).

Whanaungatanga highlights the relevance of being a whanau member, an individual who at birth arrives already deeply embedded in ancestral and geographical connections, with their concomitant reciprocal obligations (Pere, 1982/1994). Whananaungatanga requires allegiance to hapu and iwi, complementary responsibilities reliant upon mokopuna knowing who they are and where they come from.

A Maori worldview inculcates individual selflessness, mokopuna encouraged to show aroha (commitment to kin), respect, and reciprocity for others before themselves. This personal quality epitomizes whanaungatanga as integral to Maori society, the well-being of the collective prioritized. Makereti Papakura's narrative affirms this value:

> When a child is old enough to understand what is being said they are taught chores and customs. One such custom is that of unselfishness. They are taught from an early age to share, no matter how little they have, to care for their elders and those younger than themselves. (Papakura, 1938/1986, p. 113)

Selflessness is a strongly ingrained value highlighting the expectation of every child to act accordingly to strengthen the whanau, hapu, and iwi.

Mokopuna were upheld and valued as unique descendents of grandparents, of tupuna (ancestors) and as precious links between the ancestors and the future. A recognition of the privileges and responsibilities of the mokopuna included the right to access knowledge of their whakapapa, to receive support, love, and tikanga Maori attributes from kaumatua (elders), grandparents, whanau, and extended whanau. In return, mokopuna were expected to honor and respect their parents, kaumatua, grandparents, and extended whanau by listening, sharing, and contributing. Traditional Maori pedagogy accords the mokopuna the birthright of learning and sharing of tupuna (ancestral) knowledge and experiences.

The commitment of kaumatua and grandparents toward mokopuna in this educative process saw children immersed in an interactive early childhood environment nurtured by parents, whanau, and elders. Mokopuna enjoyed a learning framework reliant on the input of grandparents:

> I slept, ate, played, worked and learnt alongside four generations, and was never excluded from anything my grandparents were involved with, including attending celebrations, tangihanga (ceremonial mourning), and many other gatherings. (Pere, 1982/1994, p. 3)

Implicit within the traditional forms of Maori learning was a pedagogy where mokopuna experienced and learned through observing and participating. Kaumatua were valued for their knowledge and wisdom as they helped to guide mokopuna in their understandings of the domains of nga Atua:

> The old people were never put aside. They were the professors, te tohunga of Maori education in all fields. At a very tender age we would be taught about the sea and its many functions. We learnt to be in awe, to respect, to honor and to be very grateful. (Edwards, 1990, p. 12)

Maori pedagogy applied te reo Maori (the Maori language) alongside a process of learning and teaching that reflected tikanga, the ethical base of Maori philosophy and practices. Maori knowledge is not constricted to something static or isolated but can be seen rather as being open-ended with limitless boundaries constantly evolving and interacting. Interwoven in this was oral herstory/history, applied through pedagogy by kaumatua to encourage the enthusiasm and interest of mokopuna for learning. Knowledge transmitted to mokopuna varied from iwi to iwi, dissemination of information drawn from the spectrum of Maori realities. As Rangimarie Rose Pere relates, the "older generations taught their mokopuna history, mythology, tribal and local legends, tribal sayings, waiata (variety of chants and songs), genealogy, karakia (invocations), various crafts, hand-games and other leisurely pursuits" (Pere, 1982/1994, p. 55).

Kaumatua were acknowledged as repositories of knowledge; noted kaitiaki (guardians) of hapu and iwi tikanga, and teachers adept in ensuring Maori lore were ascribed a special passage in the exchange process to mokopuna. The role of the grandparents was to ensure that the mokopuna learnt about their links to Ranginui, Papatuanuku, and nga Atua. Korero of whakapapa helped strengthen the mokopuna understandings of their connections within te ao Maori.

Maori pedagogy was inclusive of an oral learning tradition, which maintained continuity through the intergenerational model practiced. Mokopuna learned by observing, listening, and committing to memory traditional chants that were often complex and lengthy. Kaumatua and grandparents are recognized for their applied teaching process of making education interesting and meaningful through informal learning situations:

> In pre-European contact Aotearoa, the imparting of knowledge, Maori knowledge was an everyday occurrence from the elder to the child. There was no artificial distinction between the care and education of the Maori child; both were interwoven into the child's learning, an integral part of the child's development. (Cooper & Tangaere, 1994, p. 86)

Viewed as integral to the whanau, hapu, and iwi education system, kaumatua were treated with the utmost respect and care and held in high esteem for their knowledge, wisdom, skills, and experience. Kaumatua and mokopuna existed within a distinctive relationship of reciprocity and co-construction, which upheld an intricate, complex, and effective educational system.

Pervasiveness of Colonization

Western imperialism around the globe has generated many and various histories of the impact of colonization, each story resonating with the pain of "extraordinary suffering" and the devastation of indigenous languages, knowledge systems, and traditions, including those surrounding the nurturing of future generations (Young, 2001, p. 6). As Robert Young explains, "Colonial discourse never just consisted of a set of ideological (mis)representations: its enunciations always operated as historical acts, generating specific material effects within the coercive machinery of colonial rule, its enunciative sites and formations of power simultaneously inciting material and psychological effects upon colonised subjects" (Young, 2001, p. 410). However, the interwoven effects of the "discursive formation and its relationship with the non-discursive (i.e., the field of visibilities which is seen as socio-economic forces, political activities and institutions)" (Poddar, 2006, p. 195) are possibly beyond disentanglement, as one considers, for example, the impact of poverty on well-being (Ministry of Health, 2006).

The impacts of colonization on Maori childhoods are so pervasive as to be incalculable. The imposition of the colonizer's systems of government, education, and religion were instrumental in the denigration of tino rangatiratanga (self-determination),[7] reo (language), and wairuatanga (spirituality). In Aotearoa, as in other situations worldwide, colonization operated through means of "guns, guile and disease" (Tiffin and Lawson, cited in Loomba, 2005, p. 83). Maori were demoralized and decimated by introduced illnesses, by land wars instigated by the Crown in breach of their Treaty of Waitangi commitments, and by a multitude of legislation in breach of the Treaty, which not only facilitated alienation of lands but also undermined traditional practices such as that of the tohunga, or spiritual expert. The enormity of the significance of the loss of lands and language, while tangibly visible through maps showing the paucity of lands remaining in Maori ownership,[8] or by comparing the percentages of native speakers[9] is overlaid by the more subtle and less measureable impacts of colonization through discursive means, a process of de-narrativization.

While colonization initially may have been overt, through guns or mission schooling, it was then maintained more subtly but not less dangerously through being discursively institutionalized. "Guns and disease, as a matter of fact, cannot be isolated from ideological processes of 'othering' colonial peoples" (Loomba, 2005, p. 85). As Julie Kaomea has recently written, "it is useful to view the power of colonialism and colonial discourse as operating rhizomically rather than monolithically—like a root system that spreads across the ground rather than downwards, and grows from several points rather than a single tap root" (Kaomea, 2006, p. 334). Maori activist lawyer Moana Jackson has written that:

> Destroying the world-view and culture of indigenous peoples has always been as important as taking their lives, because the actual process of disempowerment, the key purpose of any colonisation, has to function at the spiritual and psychic level as well as the physical and political. (Moana Jackson, 2007, p. 178)

The colonizers' drive to dominate others was justified by white supremacist self-righteousness, the legacy of which continues to be evident today. We see most obviously the overtly expressed racism, such as in the British Prince Harry's recent remarks (BBC News, 2009), while simultaneously and more insidiously, we can ignore the more covert forms of racism that lie below the surface. Joyce King has described as "dysconscious racism" the tacit acceptance of dominant white norms and privileges, linking it to "impaired consciousness," which produces distorted and "uncritical ways of thinking about racial inequality" that perpetuate "certain culturally sanctioned assumptions, myths, and beliefs that justify the social and economic advantages that white people have as a result of subordinating diverse others" (King, 1994, p. 338). Even well-intended "conscious egalitarian attitudes" are overridden by "nonconscious negative attitudes," enabling people to condone discriminatory behavior (Kawakami, Dunn, Karmali, & Dovidio, 2009, p. 278).

Interestingly, there is recent British evidence that despite "a generational shift in the social acceptability of admitting to racial prejudice" and of "a genuine increase in the social acceptance of British ethnic minorities," "British racial prejudice is becoming an increasingly male phenomenon among the young" with "significant levels of hostility to ethnic minorities remain[ing] even in the youngest cohorts" (Ford, 2008, pp. 632–633). Notions of empire and white supremacy continue to be utilised by European media, with these "processes of advertising and the articulation of stereotypes as part of a wider narrative of selfhood." David Wall explains the powerful salience of stereotypes and advertisements in that they "target our deepest human emotions such as fear and desire, and they appear 'real' because they are part of a political, cultural, and aesthetic landscape—the separate spheres of which touch and merge at crucial points—that reinforces their believability" (Wall, 2008, p. 1048). The persistence of racism within our communities can be linked to these racial stereotypes reflecting colonialist binaries, as they define and narrow the subjectivities available to children. Racism then sits hand in hand with colonization, as a product and process of modernity's need "to account for, to know and to control 'Otherness'" (Carter & Virdee, 2008, p. 673), perpetuating binaries of superiority/inferiority associated with European and Indigenous people. This masking of complexities and specificities limits the capacity for respectful participation, since social belonging "is highly dependent on socio-cultural recognition and respect" (Yuval-Davis, Kannabiran, & Vieten, 2006, p. 11). Contemporary childhoods feature immersion in globalised popular culture offering "'bus tickets to identities' that children use to move in and out of networks of association and knowledge" (Nespor, 1997, p. 184, in Eisenhart, 2001, p. 21). Positionality is generated in relation to an interactive set of social practices, meanings, and agency (Anthias, 2006). How are these narratives of selfhood generated by popular culture and the advertising industry informing Indigenous children's identity formation?

Resilience through Rangatiratanga

For Maori, the past 200 years of colonization have been characterized by ongoing and persistent efforts to resist the racist onslaught of colonialist breaches of Treaty agreements, and reassert the tino rangatiratanga (absolute right of self-determination) that had been assured them in the Treaty. For Moana Jackson, self-determination is having the control, "'the power to define' what knowledge is created and how it is created/defined" (cited in Bishop, 1996, p. 24). "The struggle for the power to name oneself" is an integral aspect of decolonization, so that concerns with language are emblematic of "an investigation into the depths of the political unconscious" (Kiberd, 1995, p. 615, in Loomba, 2005, p. 88). Languages are central to cultural meanings and identity. As Ngugi wa Thiong'o explains,

> Culture embodies those moral, ethical and aesthetic values, the set of spiritual eyeglasses, through which they come to view themselves and their place in the universe. Values are the basis of a people's identity, their sense of particularity as members of the human race. All this is carried by language. Language as culture is the collective memory bank of a people's experience in history. (Ngugi wa Thiong'o, 2005)

This is reinforced by the profoundly simple statement by Simon Ortiz who states that, "To me as an Indigenous person, language is my land, culture, and community. I cannot look at the matter of Indigenous language any other way" (2004, p. 145). A key strategy of colonization has been to delegitimize indigenous languages, devaluing them, and punishing those who resist by attempting to retain them. "Children are systematically stripped of their integrity, independence, freedom, and voice in this form of linguistic colonisation. This form of educational violence and slaying of the soul functions to perpetuate social control" (Soto & Haroon, 2006, p. 5). This de-legitimizing of indigenous languages is a core component of the de-narrativization process.

In the final decades of the twentieth century, Maori, despairing at the failure of the state to protect their language (Waitangi Tribunal, 1986), reclaimed their right to educate their children establishing settings utilizing their language and traditional values, and gained funding for Maori radio and television. These have had some impact on reversing the demoralization of Maori, reclaiming some spaces where Maori identities are promoted and valued, but much more needs to be done (Stavenhagen, 2006). As Moana Jackson has written, pathways beyond the pain of colonization are being paved by Maori "now seeking to reclaim the validity of our own institutions, the specifics of our own faith, and the truths of our own history" (Moana Jackson, 1992b, pp. 9–10).

It is interesting to note that New Zealand is one of only three governments refusing to sign the United Nations General Assembly Declaration on the Rights of Indigenous Peoples (United Nations, 2007), which advocates protection for the rights and well-being of indigenous peoples, that has been endorsed by 143 countries. This leaves us searching for an understanding as to how this supposedly left-wing Labour-led government could uphold this stance. However, this stance is in keeping with its passing of legislation that "'replaces' (extinguishes) all previous tikanga, legislative, and common law definitions" of Maori rights in relation to customary ownership of the foreshore and seabeds (Moana Jackson, 2004, p. 1). The New Zealand government appeared fearful of the backlash of "middle New Zealand" voters. Furthermore, the notion of the collective rights of tino rangatiratanga as outlined in Te Tiriti o Waitangi is deeply in opposition to the ideology of western individualism (Feldman, 2001), threatening the absolute control, or sovereignty of the state. "Where indigenous endeavours are directed toward transcendence or transformation through creative engagement, states work toward subordination and hierarchizing, and through avoidance, distancing and deferral. Where indigenous peoples strive to articulate, to name and to be present, states refuse to recognize them or even to speak the names they have chosen for themselves" (Feldman, 2001, p. 165).

Maori have contributed to international resistance to colonization, with kaupapa Maori[10] education initiatives as key examples. For Maori, and for many other Indigenous peoples, colonization continues as the ongoing reality of living in a "toxic environment" (Bamblett & Lewis, 2006, p. 92) in which they continue to be patronized and disempowered. "It is clear that "the unjust destruction or fragmentation of Native cultures and communities, through colonial genocide and subjugation, has not eradicated the need, desire or ability to recover and/or maintain those traditions" (Feldman, 2001, p. 153). The revaluing and retrieval of indigenous knowledges are central to much postcolonial scholarship (Young, 2001), as well as the work of critical pedagogues, such as Joe Kincheloe:

> As we understand the compelling perceptions of indigenous peoples, we can gain new vantage points on the sentient and mysterious life force that inhabits both our being and the cosmos surrounding us. The insights peoples from diverse cultural and historical locales in the web of reality have accessed about this life force in unconscious and other states of consciousness should be a source of fascination and study by scholars from a wide variety of academic domains, critical pedagogy being merely one of many. (Kincheloe, 2008, p.6)

Issues arise however, when we consider that in Aotearoa, only 6.58 percent of registered early childhood teachers are Maori (Ministry of Education, 2007), with 14.6 percent of New Zealanders identifying themselves as Maori in the 2006 census (Statistics New Zealand, 2007). However, only 1.6 percent of the majority of New Zealanders, those with European ancestry, speak Maori.

Our early childhood curriculum Te Whariki stipulates that "New Zealand is the home of Māori language and culture: curriculum in early childhood settings should promote te reo and ngā tikanga Māori, making them visible and affirming their value for children from all cultural backgrounds" (Ministry of Education, 1996, p. 42). This highlights the challenge for the vast majority of educators who are not speakers of the language, in representing Maori language, values, and culture in order to provide Maori children with experiences validating of their subjectivity as Maori, or more specifically, of their individual subtribal allegiances.

Pitfalls are evident, of essentializing, of selectivity, of inauthenticity. These can easily be positioned as rationalization for replicating the status quo. However, this perpetuation of colonization is unacceptable. Alternative pathways must be pursued, utilizing tools such as the repositioning of indigenous and postcolonial theorizing as central to our praxis. In seeking to critique the insidiousness of colonial discourses and foster decolonizing alternatives, postcolonialism can be viewed "as an aspirational project, intent on pursuing the hopefulness" (Lavia, 2006, p. 281). Respectful relationships are fundamental to accessing local Indigenous understandings and stories, with elders the repository of traditional knowledges. Sue Atkinson has suggested that "as more non Indigenous early childhood practitioners position themselves as learners around local Indigenous cultures the Elders' voices can help them rethink Indigenous inclusion in the early childhood curriculum and open up a space to reflect on whom and what has survived colonisation" (Atkinson, 2008, p. 38). The other key voices that must be integral to re-narrativization, alongside those of their parents and elders, are those of the children themselves, grounded in their own lived realities.

> One's natural environment is the world within which one is rooted. In this environment, one encounters on a daily basis issues related to economic, political, cultural, and psychological survival. To make sense of these issues, one needs a language, a voice, a means of communication by way of which one is able to articulate one's condition. In the context of multilingual societies, this voice cannot be that of the oppressor, the coloniser, or the dominant. This voice ought to be one's own voice, one's own natural tongue that is rooted in one's own natural environment. (Asgharzadeh, 2008, p. 350)

In as much as there are multiple histories of colonization, from these sites will emerge many different pathways towards decolonization (Rose, 2004). For educators committed to transformational pedagogies key tasks are clearly to create relationships enabling of Indigenous involvement, generating spaces for their voices to be heard and responded to with honor, allowing for new narratives to emerge and be shared.

Indigenous Theorizing of Countercolonial Possibilities

Countercolonial discourses seek to address the injustices of the past and embrace dialogue between indigenous and nonindigenous early childhood educators. Deborah Bird Rose builds on the work of Hannah Arendt in a call to reject the failed monological master narratives of the colonizer, instead generating alternative recuperative projects that draw upon past wisdom, utilizing dialogical webs of stories woven from our "historically grounded experience" (Rose, 2004, p. 24). Re-narrativization, in facilitating movement toward decolonization, upholds this form of dialogue, which reflects an assertion of ethical relationality against domination, mutuality against control, and connectivity against hyperseparation (Rose, 2004). Decolonizing re-narrativization acknowledges the specificities of dialogical approaches as always being located and open, therefore one cannot presume fixed outcomes.

Anticolonial theorizing has recently been viewed as a way of troubling dominant discourse. We now propose, however, the notion of generating countercolonial theorizing (Rau, 2008). Countercolonial dialogical encounter invites a shift from "anti-" with its associations of being reactive, negative, and binary toward the proactive dialogical openness of "counter-ing" colonized thinking with alternative narratives reflective of hope, regeneration, and transformational shifts. This approach both fosters the liberating of Maori psyche from enforced colonial constructs as well as mobilizing Tauiwi/Pakeha thinking beyond their own Eurocentric mindset. Incorporating Freirean notions of praxis, countercolonial thinking requires internal work, since, "As a nation, for groups and individuals to truly shift towards a post-colonial era we will need to undertake journeys of introspection" (Lang, 2005, p. 560).

In Aotearoa, Maori draw wisdom and inspiration from Te Ao Maori philosophy and theories that are her/historic, authentic and indigenous. The teachings offer a myriad of potentialities toward generating openness and responsiveness to Te Ao Maori. In articulating what is specific to Maori, it is necessary to explore, share, and experience universalities that open channels toward deepening dimensions of clarity and truth. Manulani Meyer, an Indigenous Hawaiian scholar, acknowledges the existence of the "spiritual truth within ancient streams of knowing" (Meyer, 2008, p. 217). Maori, in re-constructing narratives are articulating those truths from the centre and not from the periphery, speaking to a Te Ao Maori existence and rejoicing in the affirmation of indigeneity. Maori have had "to decolonise our minds, to recover ourselves, to claim a space in which to develop a sense of authentic humanity" (L. T. Smith, 1999, p. 23). Amidst this urgency toward reshaping, consciousness needs to be directed toward an articulating of the stories of the tupuna/elders, sharing deeply embedded values and beliefs of whakapapa/ancestry and our ecological interconnectedness. In reaffirming our indigenous links to Ranginui (Sky Father) and Papatuanuku (Earth Mother), we celebrate our holistic world, one in which we come to know and be integrated beings within the universe.

Maureen Jehly, a Maori kuia/educator, of Te Arawa /Ngati Whakaue, Tuhourangi/ Ngati Wahiao, Ngati Pikiao, Ngati Raukawa and Aitanga a Hauiti descent, recently boldy positioned Te Ao Maori as central to tino rangatiratanga and decolonization, stating in her keynote speech,

"Nothing about us without us" (Jehly, 2007). Re-narrativization calls upon indigenous people to be the sages, storytellers, and narrators of their dialogue while also inviting others into the conversations. Re-narrativization requires an ethical stance from nonindigenous educators to engage respectfully with indigenous narratives alongside indigenous peoples, ensuring spaces are created in which Maori assertions of tino rangatiratanga are celebrated, affirmed, and supported.

An Ethics of Alterity—"A Thinking Which Thinks Otherwise"

In countries such as Aotearoa/New Zealand, where everyday activities take place under the shadow of the palpable cloud of histories of colonisation, in theorizing countercolonial possibilities, we are hampered by the language of these historicized colonialist discourses. Even as we struggle to name and define ourselves we are caught up in tensions, and binaries which while acknowledging the very real and painful history, can also simultaneously be limiting and essentializing. The notion of countercolonial possibilities is freeing, in that we are acknowledging the complications of our history, yet seeking to offer pathways that emerge from the cloudiness of the oppressive, essentialized binaries of coloniser/colonized, working instead as allies in a process of dialogical praxis. The acknowledgment of being part of a historical process is useful, and relevant to our use of language to reflect upon who we are in the light of where we have come from and where we may be heading.

The potential trap of re-emphasizing binaries of Western/Indigenous has been a focus for many anticolonial and postcolonial critiques, with recognition of the ways in which both have contributed to molding the identities of each other, generating complex identities, requiring in-depth analysis of the cross-pollinating hybridities rather than retreat into the protective comfort of simplified essentialization (Loomba, 2005). "Alterity, or a binary opposition between coloniser and colonised, is an idea that has enormous force and power in the construction of anti-colonial narratives, by subjects who are themselves complex, mixed-up products of diverse colonial histories" (Loomba, 2005, p. 153). Attempts to present oversimplified binary oppositions between "colonisers" and "colonised" deny the reality of the wide-ranging differences within each of the categories as well as the overlapping shared histories and cultural cross-overs and the historical and contemporary reality of the interdependence of colonized and colonizer. "Colonial identities—on both sides of the divide—are unstable, agonised, and in constant flux" (Loomba, 2005, p. 149). Lourdes Dias Soto, asks us to consider, "How might we heal and end the madness as we move beyond the binaries of power in solidarity toward critically biliterate and multi-literate communities of compassion?" (Soto & Haroon, 2006, p. 14).

Healing the schisms created by binary polarities of oppression requires new ways of thinking as well as new processes. Emmanuel Levinas proposes moving beyond western positivistic secularity and individualistic endorsement of egocentrism, to a more collectivist approach whereby we accept "responsibility for the Other," which he classes as "ethics." Levinas considers that this understanding of ethics validates the primacy of the well-being of the Other, in that "the other's right to exist has primacy over my own, a primacy epitomized in the ethical edict: you shall not kill, you shall not jeopardize the life of the other" (Cohen, 1987, p. 24). "Justice," for Levinas, is "taking on the Other's responsibilities" (Cohen, 1987, p. 24). Our focus becomes that of "*my* responsibility for the other person, without concern for reciprocity, in my call to help him gratuitously, in the asymmetry of the relation of *one* to the *other*" (Levinas, 1988, p. 165). A disposition of generosity and goodwill toward the Other, provides a release from the grasping, controlling, striving to know the Other:

> The relationship with the other is not an idyllic and harmonious relationship of communion, or a sympathy through which we put ourselves in the other's place; we recognise the other as resembling us, but exterior to us; the relationship with the other is a relationship with a Mystery. (Levinas, 1987, p. 75)

For Levinas, the opportunity to come to know the Other comes with reciprocal responsibility. One is obliged "not only to know the Other, or to share an understanding of the world which the Other also shares, but is responsible to respond to the very alterity of the Other," an elusive alterity "which is always on the verge of presence" (Levinas, 1987, p. 18). This orientation involves "a thinking which thinks otherwise…suffering the inversion and election of being for-the-other before itself" (1987, p. 25). Integral to this ability to be open to the Other, is the humility of on-going self-critique. "The putting into question of the self is precisely a welcome to the absolutely other" (Levinas, cited by Peperzak, Critchly, & Bernasconi, 1996, p. 17, in M. Smith, 2001, p. 189).

Knowledge of the "Other" involves far more than mere acknowledgment of difference, since this is usually framed as "their difference from us" (Bhambra, 2006, p. 39). What is imperative, is that we learn to "*think* differently about ourselves and even, perhaps, redefine who we consider 'ourselves' to be," thus shifting the locus from the binary formulation of 'us and them' to a wider, more inclusive "us" (Bhambra, 2006, p. 39). This is not an assimilative paradigm of simply adding "them" to "us," but a collective reconfiguring of who "we" are, as a complex range of overlapping cultural identities, which respects the integrity of each (Kannabiran, 2006).

For Alice Feldman, "ethnicity, and the rearticulation of ethnic identities, constitute a *process*, a process of collective learning" (Feldman, 2001, p. 147). However, she warns of the potential pitfall that, "We speak of process, yet continue to typologize and pigeonhole in ways that delegitimize and silence Other discourses and expressions of identity" (Feldman, 2001, p. 148). In order to counter this potential re-colonization, Feldman advocates that teacher education scholars attend to:

1. the conscientization of those involved in related areas of scholarship and practice and the cultivation of critical literacies;
2. dialogic processes of inquiry that emphasize active engagement with those who may be the "subjects" of study as opposed to theorising about or for them; and
3. an analysis that goes beyond critique to develop co-created, mutually informed principles and courses of action. (Feldman, 2001, p. 149)

It may also be helpful to view "identity as a matter of 'becoming' as well as of 'being,'" rather than romanticizing precolonial traditional ways of being, since there are "no pure or fixed origins to which peoples or cultures can return" (Loomba, 2005, p. 152), although undeniably, "The past continues to speak to us" (Hall, 1994, p. 395, cited in Loomba, 2005, p. 152). With the acknowledgment that this past has since been overlaid, irretrievably in some respects, by the impacts of colonisation, what is required is more than recalling the past, but a re-narrativization of countercolonial possibilities, re-inscribing meanings and understandings through "an imaginative recognition of both what existed and what we continually create" (Loomba, 2005, p. 153).

This generation of countercolonial narratives is a process cognisant of the unhelpfulness of remaining locked into essentialized binaries, instead acknowledging and building upon the everyday reality of the interdependence of colonized and colonizer, and the complexities of hybrid identities and shared experiences and responsibilities. Yet countercolonial pathways can only be envisioned from a positioning that is ever mindful of the ongoing legacies of colonization, and with attention to careful, respectful watchfulness of the ongoing power effects of the historical duality of colonizer/colonized. As Julie Kaomea explains, "in the teaching and writing of indigenous history and curricula across the globe, we need more counter-genealogists to seek out and uncover indigenous voices and perspectives, and call into question the dominant colonial narratives that are so prevalent" (Kaomea, 2006, pp. 345–346). Knowledgeable Indigenous elders are integral to providing guidance and sanction to countercolonial possibilities.

Re-narrativization

Our sense of being is related to our narration of our daily experiences, according to Ngugi wa Thiong'o (in Sander & Lindfors, 2006). Our stories inform our lives, our sense of self, our possibilities. The stories accessed by young children in turn inform their subjectivities, enabling realization of their self-determination. As early childhood educators, we are faced with the awesome responsibility of offering children this sense of possibilities, of validation, of affirmation of their histories and trajectories. Our recent research[11] has utilized narrative and indigenous methodologies (Clandinin, 2007; Clandinin et al., 2006; L. T. Smith, 1999) as a pathway for the re-narrativization of early childhood experiences that are validating of indigeneity in Aotearoa.

Within the Te Puawaitanga study (Ritchie & Rau, 2008), we find examples of teacher, whanau, and mokopuna narratives expressive of ancient knowledge and wisdom promulgating re-connectivity to Maori traditional paradigms. Marae (traditional villages) are representative of whakapapa, whanau, hapu, and iwi. During the research project, teachers from Hawera Kindergarten supported tamariki to visually create all the local marae in their early childhood centre mapping, generating a large mural on the back inside wall of the early childhood center. Cheryl, intrigued, decided to seek some of their deeper understandings and meanings for this activity from teachers Judith and Joy (who are Maori), and Robyn (who is Pakeha, that is, of European descent):

Cheryl: Why all those marae?

Judith: They're the ones Joy and I connect to, we whakapapa through immediate family and my husband's and Robyn through her family connections with my Nan. My Nan spoke highly of Robyn's father-in-law. For Robyn it's a whangai (adopted) relationship through generations past. Community relationships built through time, not our connections but they had already been made.

Cheryl: So what do marae mean for you?

Joy: It's like the core of your family, the images of the marae on the wall transcend energy, light energy, they make you feel like you belong. Even though the marae are a few kilometres away or close, it's the wairua I carry within that connects to those marae. It's the same as the mountain. When I look at the mountain and it's covered in cloud I know the koro (grandfather) is still there. There is a teaching in that. The waters that flow from that mountain provide sustenance for families. It provides a living energy. The maunga (mountain) is a tupuna, he also is our life force. I feel my son's presence in the atmosphere, the mountain, the breeze.

These teachers' insightful dialogical descriptions reflect the tangible and intangible gifts marae represent. Marae in the above context are seen as the heart of whanau, hapu, and iwi; they are respected as places which generate energy and uphold wairua, and encapsulate shared genealogical her/histories. The longstanding relationships and geographical connectedness between Maori and Pakeha residents of this rural New Zealand area are inclusively acknowledged, through the Maori principle of "whangai," which means both adoption and nurture, representing a dialogical movement beyond binaries of colonizer/colonized. The mountain is viewed as a koro, a grandfather, and as a tupuna, an ancestor with life energy. Mokopuna are enriched when they see their whakapapa reflected back to them through their marae and through teacher-enacted values and beliefs.

In exploring tamariki (children's) potentiality to build knowledge and understanding, Judith explains some of the learning evident to her in the marae activity:

> Things I think I know they would learn are about caring for others, the connections you make with each other. Celebrating who they are, how they are, in the ways that they learn about these things, for example, Maori concepts, values, Maori kupu (words) and they build understandings of these. Hopefully they are getting experiences that we got because we went to marae, we went to those gatherings. They are hopefully absorbing some of my Maori knowledges and understandings through how I exist in this kindergarten, how I make this place here.

Judith articulates conceptual contexts critical to mokopuna, the first of these is the importance of collective well-being, which has an implicit responsibility to place others first. Cultural identity is highlighted, access to te reo Maori and tikanga Maori essential to mokopuna building upon their knowledge and understanding. Judith is clear about her role and responsibility as a Maori teacher and what she brings to the center.

In the Whakawhanaungatanga study (Ritchie & Rau, 2006), a Pakeha kindergarten Head Teacher, Penny, explained how through many years of immersing herself with Maori colleagues and friends, she had gradually changed her teaching practice to be inclusive of Maori ways of being, knowing, and doing. Her central philosophy reflects her deep commitment to Maori values, and these are evident in the daily rituals enacted within her center. A morning ritual involves a welcoming circle, where everyone is greeted and shares in the karakia and waiata, honoring both wairuatanga and whanaungatanga. Penny is wary of viewing the participation and contribution of Maori families as a resource that may be drawn upon to supplement the Maori content of her early childhood programme. She values and celebrates the families' willingness to share their precious children with her and the others in the early childhood setting.

> So we share what we have with them. Our joy is just that their children are here and that they're prepared to share their greatest treasure with us, and we want to show them how marvelous their children are, so I'm very wary of being pushy about 'Can you come and do waiata with us?,' 'Can you come and do that?' To me that's the Pakeha grasping and I'm very, very conscious of that. We're trying to do it the other way, "What can we give to people?"

Penny's center provides for daily shared fruit snacks and meals cooked with the children. Those parents with excess produce from their gardens are invited to offer this to others through a kete koha (donation basket). Penny's orientation is one of generosity, upholding a value of collectivity, seeking to contribute to the well-being of others, without expectation of reciprocity. Penny reflects Levinas' understanding of unqualified regard and acceptance of responsibility for the Other.

In our current study (Ritchie, Craw, Rau, & Duhn, in progress), teachers have provided examples of ways in which they are drawing upon the wisdom of Maori elders to enrich narratives pertaining to the care of Papatuanuku. In the following excerpt, teachers from Richard Hudson Kindergarten in Dunedin describe the involvement of kaumatua Huata Holmes, who has been sharing his knowledge of iwi whakapapa with the children:

> We consulted with Huata Holmes, our Kaumatua, for guidance, expert knowledge and inspiration. The Southern Maori perspective or "flavour" is important. Lee Blackie, our Senior Teacher, accompanied Huata

and gave us a practical aspect that could sit side by side with Huata's ideas. In order to add authenticity and depth we arranged for Huata to come and narrate his southern mythology/stories/purakau to the children and whanau as told to him as a child by his grandmothers and great grandmothers. Huata's korero was excellent and by working together we have achieved more of a shared understanding. He told of the great waka[12] of Aoraki coming through the sky down to the South Island. He also used the waiata 'Hoea te Waka' to support his korero. This has become a real favourite. His korero has supported our teaching of the importance of Papatuanuku in our lives.

Huata's reciprocity to the teachers' invitation has enabled intergenerational continuity of ancient stories and songs and the understandings embedded within these. These teachers appreciate and value the need for obtaining expert specific local knowledge:

> One aspect of cultural challenge has been respecting Southern Maori tikanga/traditions against the generic Maori knowledge and understandings that the teachers have been taught and learned through personal and professional education.

The teachers are also supported by Lee Blackie, an experienced Senior Teacher who, working in partnership with Huata, provides a bridge for Huata's wisdom to be pedagogically applied. These teachers from Richard Hudson Kindergarten have gathered examples of children's understandings, as expressed through art and their stories. Here is four-year-old Lily's picture and story relating to the separation of Ranginui and Papatuanuku:

Lily's Story—Rangi is at the top. He is really, really close to the children. You can't see the baby because he's in the ground with his mother. They pushed them apart. The earth mother wasn't close to Rangi anymore. So So So So Sad.

The teachers wrote:

> Lily shows her clear understanding of this story. Her empathy with their feelings of sadness is beautiful. Lily has the ability to write her story down as well as portray it through her art. These forms of communication allow her a depth of expression and creation as she makes sense of her world…

The children have developed deep and valid shared understandings of how we can determine and defend our fertile and fragile earth mother, Papatuanuku.

The children at this kindergarten, including those with Maori ancestry, are recipients of this richness of Southern Maori knowledge and experience, generating a respectful acceptance and openness towards the Indigenous worldviews being offered to them.

Concluding Remarks

Decolonization involves the "unmaking of regimes of violence that promote the disconnection of moral accountability" through an ethical presence that is "relational, connective, mutual and committed" (Rose, 2004, p. 214). Te Ao Maori countercolonial narratives prioritize Aotearoa as a land that is storied, a country with cosmological narratives of the procreative purakau (traditional legends) of Ranginui and Papatuanuku highlighting ancient philosophical values of integrity and relatedness, of existence and connectedness. Maori are intertwined in a spiritual and cultural relationship with nature. In Maori lore, this herstory/history of the devotion and deep love Ranginui and Papatuanuku shared is the foundation upon which Maori trace their whakapapa to all living things. Maori epistemology disrupts colonial discourse and the early childhood interface is a space and place to uphold countercolonial narratives as potential for progressing through the complexities and challenges of today.

Countercolonial re-narrativization in early childhood education can provide pathways toward honoring of histories and wisdoms, respectful recognition of Indigenous children's whakapapa providing foundations for identity and belonging. Children in early childhood education settings in Aotearoa committed to countercolonial re-narrativization are gaining access to deep connectedness with ancient Te Ao Maori knowledge, values, and ancestral wisdom. These narratives offer alternative subjectivities to globally promoted Western individualistic competitive materialism, imbued as they are with spiritual interconnectedness, ethical responsibility, and a valuing of relatedness and collectivity.

> Kia whakapapa pounamu
> te moana
> kia teretere
> te karohirohi e.
> …
> May the days ignite—
> as sunlight
> on greenstone waters.[13]

Table 24.1 Glossary of Maori terms

aroha	commitment to kin
hap	sub tribe
iwi	tribe
kaitiaki	guardians
karakia	spiritual incantations
kaum tua	elders
kaupapa M ori education	education through the medium of the M ori language, and with M ori philosopy as its foundation
kete	flax basket
koha	gift giving
k rero	talking
koro	grandfather
kupu	words
maunga	mountain
mauri	life force
mokopuna	grandchildren
m teatea	traditional chants and songs
ng Atua	deities
Papatuanuku	Earth Mother
p r kau	traditional narratives
rangatiratanga	self- determination
Ranginui	Sky Father
reo	M ori language
tangata	people
tangihanga	ceremonial mourning
tamariki	children
Taonga	artefacts or items of value
te Ao M ori	the M ori world, or M ori world view
Te Tiriti o Waitangi	treaty signed in 1840 between M ori chiefs and the British Crown, which allowed for British settlement, alongside protection of M ori self-determination, lands, and everything of value to M ori.
tikanga	what is 'tika' or correct from a M ori worldview, traditional beliefs, values, customs, practices
tikanga M ori	traditional M ori values, customs, practices
tino rangatiratanga	absolute right of self-determination
t puna	ancestors
turangawaewae	ancestral connection to a particular place
waiata	songs
wairua	spirituality
wairuatanga	spiritual interconnectedness
waka	canoe
whakapapa	genealogical interconnectedness
wh nau	family
whanaungatanga	family interconnectedness
wh ngai	adoption and nurture

Notes

1. In this chapter, we are choosing to honor our commitment to counter-colonial re-narrativization by privileging the use of Maori terms, which are then explained on the first usage, either in brackets or footnotes. A glossary is also provided at the end of the chapter. "Kia mau ki te wairuatanga" means to retain spiritual interconnectedness.

2. Aotearoa is a Maori name for New Zealand.

3. These were previously discussed in *'Te Ahutanga o Toku Whanau'* (Rau, 2002).

4. Te Ao Maori is the Maori world, or worldview.

5. Mokopuna are grandchildren.

6. Whanau is family, hapu is sub-tribe and iwi is tribe.

7. Rangatiratanga can be defined as the right of political authority that enables Maori to exercise self-determination in relation to people and resources (Moana Jackson, 1992a, p. 175). For a detailed explanation of the meaning of tino rangatiranga see Mere Skerrett (2007).

8. See for example, Maori land loss 1860–2000, *http://www.nzhistory.net.nz/media/interactive/maori-land-1860–2000* (New Zealand History Online, 2009).

9. In 1913, 90% of Maori school children were fluent Maori speakers. By the 1970s only 18 to 20 percent, Maori were fluent speakers, and these were mostly elders (Te Taura Whiri o te Reo Maori. The Maori Language Commission, 2009).

10. Kaupapa Maori education is conducted by Maori, through the medium of the Maori language, and with Maori philosophy as its foundation.

11. We gratefully acknowledge funding support from the Teaching Learning Research Initiative (TLRI) administered by the New Zealand Council for Educational Research. Reports from the two studies completed to date are available on the TLRI website (Ritchie & Rau, 2006, 2008).

12. Waka, canoe.

13. "Greenstone, or pounamu, is New Zealand jade. Here it is used descriptively for shining seas, which in turn express a wish for bright futures" (Grace & Grace, 2003, p. 30) .

References

Anthias (2006). Belonging in a Globalising and Unequal World: Rethinking Translocations. In N. Yuval-Davis, K. Kannabiran & U. Vieten (Eds.), *The Situated Politics of Belonging* (pp. 17–31). London: Sage.

Asgharzadeh, A. (2008). The Return of the Subaltern: International Education and Politics of Voice. *Journal of Studies in International Education, 12* (4), 334–363.

Atkinson, S. (2008). Victorian Indigenous Elders as Teachers. *International Journal of Equity and Innovation in Early Childhood, 6*(1), 26–41.

Bamblett, M., & Lewis, P. (2006). Speaking up, not talking down: Doing the 'Rights' thing by strengthening culture for Indigenous children. *International Journal of Equity and Innovation in Early Childhood, 4*(2), 91–103.

BBC News. (2009). Prince's racist term sparks anger. *BBC, Retrieved 30 January, 2009, from http://news.bbc.co.uk/1/hi/uk/7822883.stm.*

Bhambra, G. (2006). Culture, Identity and Rights: Challenging Contemporary Discourses of Belonging. In N. Yuval-Davis, K. Kannabiran & U. Vieten (Eds.), *The Situated Politics of Belonging* (pp. 32–53). London: Sage.

Bishop, R. (1996). *Collaborative Research Stories: Whakawhanaungatanga.* Palmerston North: Dunmore.

Burman, E. (2008). *Developments. Child, Image, Nation.* London: Routledge.

Carter, B., & Virdee, S. (2008). Racism and the sociological imagination. *The British Journal of Sociology 59*(4), 661–679.

Clandinin, D. J. (Ed.). (2007). *Handbook of Narrative Inquiry.* Thousand Oaks, CA: Sage.

Clandinin, D. J., Huber, J., Huber, M., Murphy, M. S., Orr, A. M., Pearce, M., et al. (2006). *Composing Diverse Identities. Narrative inquiries into the interwoven lives of children and teachers.* London and New York: Routledge.

Cohen, R. (1987). Introduction. In *Levinas, Emmanuel. Time and the Other [and additional essays]. Translation by Richard A Cohen*. Pitttsburgh, Pennsylvania: Duquesne University Press.

Cooper, D., & Tangaere, A. R. (1994). A Critical Analysis of the Development of Early Childhood Education in Aotearoa. In E. Coxon, K. Jenkins, J. Marshall & L. Massey (Eds.), *The Politics of Learning and Teaching in Aotearoa-New Zealand* (pp. 82–111). Palmerston North: Dunmore.

Edwards, M. (1990). *Mihipeka: Early Years*. Auckland: Penguin.

Edwards, M. (1992). *Mihipeka: Time of Turmoil*. Auckland: Penguin Books.

Eisenhart, M. (2001). Educational ethnography past, present, and future: Ideas to think with. *Educational Researcher, 30*(8), 16–27.

Feldman, A. (2001). Transforming peoples and subverting states: Developing a pedagogical approach to the study of indigenous peoples and ethnocultural movements. *Ethnicities, 1*(2), 147–178.

Ford, R. (2008). Is racial prejudice declining in Britain? *The British Journal of Sociology 59*(4), 609–636.

Grace, P., & Grace, W. (2003). *Earth, Sea, Sky. Images and Maori Proverbs from the Natural World of Aotearoa New Zealand*. Wellington/Nelson: Huia Publishers/Craig Potton Publishing.

Jackson, M. (1992a). JUSTICE: Unitary or Separate. In D. Novitz & B. Willmott (Eds.), *New Zealand in Crisis. A debate about today's critical issues* (pp. 171–183). Wellington: G.P. Publishers.

Jackson, M. (1992b). The Treaty and the Word: The Colonisation of Maori Philosophy. In G. Oddie & R. Perrett (Eds.), *Justice, Ethics, and New Zealand Society* (pp. 1–10). Auckland: Oxford University Press.

Jackson, M. (2004). *Foreshore & seabed—Moana Jackson's latest analysis of government policy*, Federation of Maori Authorities. Me Uru Kahikatea. Retrieved January 9, 2009, from *http://www.foma.co.nz/archive/MoanaJacksons LatestAnalysisofGovtPolicy.htm*.

Jackson, M. (2007). Globalisation and the Colonising State of Mind. In M. Bargh (Ed.), *Resistance: an Indigenous Response to Neoliberalism* (pp. 167–182). Wellington: Huia.

Jehly, M. (2007). *Keynote Presentation*. Paper presented at the 9th New Zealand Early Childhood Convention. Pakiwaitara—Stories of the Land, Energy Events Centre, Rotorua, New Zealand, 23–28 September.

Kannabiran, K. (2006). A Cartography of Resistance: the National Federation of Dalit Women. In N. Yuval-Davis, K. Kannabiran & U. Vieten (Eds.), *The Situated Politics of Belonging* (pp. 54–71). London: Sage.

Kaomea, J. (2006). Na wahine mana: a postcolonial reading of classroom discourse on the imperial rescue of oppressed Hawaiian women. *Pedagogy, Culture & Society, 14*(3), 329–348.

Kawakami, K., Dunn, E., Karmali, F., & Dovidio, J. (2009). Mispredicting Affective and Behavioral Responses to Racism. *Science, 323*, 276–278.

Kincheloe, J. (2008). Critical Pedagogy and the Knowledgem Wars of the Twenty-First Century. *International Journal of Critical Pedagogy, 1*(1), 1–22.

King, J. E. (1994). Dysconscious Racism: Ideology, Identity, and the Miseducation of Teachers. In L. Stone (Ed.), *The Education Feminism Reader* (pp. 336–348). New York: Routledge.

Lang, S. (2005). 'Decolonialism' and the Counselling Profession: The Aotearoa/New Zealand Experience. *International Journal for the Advancement of Counselling, 27*(4), 557–572.

Lavia, J. (2006). The practice of postcoloniality: a pedagogy of hope. *Pedagogy, Culture & Society, 14*(3), 279–293.

Levinas, E. (1987). *Time and the Other [and additional essays]* (R. A. Cohen., Trans.). Pitttsburgh, PA: Duquesne University Press.

Levinas, E. (1988). Useless Suffering. In R. Bernasconi & D. Wood (Eds.), *The Provocation of Levinas. Rethinking the Other.* (pp. 156–167). London & New York: Routledge.

Loomba, A. (2005). *Colonialism/Postcolonialism.* (2nd ed.). London: Routledge.

Martin, K. (2007). Making Tracks and Reconceptualising Aboriginal Early Childhood Education: An Aboriginal Australian Perspective. *Childrenz Issues, 11*(1), 15–20.

Mead, L. T. T. R. (1996). *Nga Aho o te Kakahu Matauranga: The Multiple Layers of Struggle by Maori in Education*. Unpublished D.Phil Thesis, University of Auckland, Auckland.

Meyer, M. A. (2001). Acultural assumptions of empiricism: A Native Hawaiian critique. *Canadian Journal of Native Education, 25*(2), 188–198.

Meyer, M. A. (2008). Indigenous and Authentic: Hawaiian Epistemology and the Triangulation of Meaning. In N.

K. Denzin, Y. Lincoln & L. T. Smith (Eds.), *Handbook of Critical and Indigenous Methodologies* (pp. 217–232). Los Angeles, London, New Delhi, Singapore: Sage Publications.

Ministry of Education. (1996). *Te Whariki. He Whariki Matauranga mo nga Mokopuna o Aotearoa: Early Childhood Curriculum.* Wellington: Learning Media.

Ministry of Health. (2006). *Decades of Disparity III. Ethnic and Socioeconomic Inequalities in Mortality, New Zealand 1988–1999.* Wellington: Ministry of Health and University of Otago.

New Zealand History Online. (2009). *Maori Land Loss,1860–2000.* Retrieved January 9, 2009 from *http://www.nzhistory.net.nz/media/interactive/maori-land-1860–2000.*

Nespor, J. (1997). *Tangled Up in School: Politics, Space, Bodies, and Signs in the Educational Process.* Mahwah, NJ: Lawrence Erlbaum.

Ngugi wa Thiong'o. (2005). *Decolonising the Mind. The Politics of Language in African Literature.* Oxford: James Currey and Heinemann. .

Ortiz, S. (2004). Our language: poetry, story, community. *Postcolonial Studies, 7*(2), 143–147.

Papakura, M. (1938/1986). *The Old-Time Maori.* Auckland: New Women's Press.

Pere, R. R. (1982/1994). *Ako. Concepts and Learning in the Maori Tradition.* Hamilton: Department of Sociology, University of Waikato. Reprinted by Te Kohanga Reo National Trust Board.

Pere, R. R. (1991). *Te Wheke.* Gisborne: Ao Ake.

Poddar, P. (2006). The power of mantras': postcoloniality, education and development. *Pedagogy, Culture & Society, 14*(2), 189–220.

Rau, C. (2002). *Te Ahutanga Atu o Toku Whanau.* Unpublished Master's Dissertaton, University of Waikato.

Rau, C. (2008). *Manaaki to Whakapapa: Indigenous Maori Origins—A Paradigm Repositioned.* Paper presented at the 18th European Early Childhood Education Research Association (EECERA) Annual Conference. Reconsidering the Basics in Early Childhood Education, Stavanger, Norway, 3–6 September.

Ritchie, J., Craw, J., Rau, C., & Duhn, I. (in progress). *Titiro Whakamuri, Hoki Whakamua: We are the future, the present and the past: caring for self, others and the environment in early years' teaching and learning.* Wellington: Teaching Learning Research Initiative. New Zealand Council for Educational Research.

Ritchie, J., & Rau, C. (2006). Whakawhanaungatanga. Partnerships in bicultural development in early childhood education. Final Report from the Teaching & Learning Research Initiative Project: Teaching Learning Research Initiative. Retrieved January 22, 2009, from *http://www.tlri.org.nz/pdfs/9207_finalreport.pdf.*

Ritchie, J., & Rau, C. (2008). *Te Puawaitanga—Partnerships with Tamariki And Whanau in Bicultural Early Childhood Care And Education. Final Report to the Teaching Learning Research Initiative.* Wellington: TLRI/NZCER. Retrieved December 18, 2008, from *http://www.tlri.org.nz/pdfs/9207_finalreport.pdf.*

Rose, D. B. (2004). *Reports from a Wild Country. Ethics for Decolonisation.* Sydney: University of New South Wales.

Sander, R., & Lindfors, B. (Eds.). (2006). *Ngugi wa Thiong'o Speaks. Interviews with the Kenyan Writer.* Eritrea: African World Press.

Skerrett, M. (2007). Kia Tu Heipu: Languages frame, focus and colour our worlds. *Childrenz Issues, 11*(1), 6–14.

Smith, L. T. (1995). The Colonisation of Mäori Children. *Youth Law Review, August/September/October,* 8–11.

Smith, L. T. (1999). *Decolonizing Methodologies. Research and Indigenous Peoples.* London and Dunedin: Zed Books Ltd and University of Otago Press.

Smith, L. T. (2005). On Tricky Ground: Researching the Native in the Age of Uncertainty. In N. K. Denzin & Y. S. Lincoln (Eds.), *The Sage Handbook of Qualitative Research* (3rd ed., pp. 85–107). Thousand Oaks, CA: Sage.

Smith, M. (2001). *An Ethics of Place. Radical Ecology, Postmodernity, and Social Theory.* Albany, NY: State University of New York Press.

Soto, L. D., & Haroon, K. (2006). A Post-Monolingual Education (United States). *International Journal of Educational Policy, Research and Practice, 1*(1), 1–17, Retrieved January 12, 2009, from *http://www.articlearchives.com-/population-demographics/demographic-groups-children/1601797–1601791.html.*

Statistics New Zealand. (2007). *QuickStats About Culture and Identity.* Wellington: Statistics New Zealand. Retrieved January 22, 2009, from *http://www.stats.govt.nz/census/2006-census-data/quickstats-about-culture-identity/quickstats-about-culture-and-identity.htm?page=para008Master.*

Stavenhagen, R. (2006). *Mission to New Zealand. Report of the Special Rapporteur on the situation of human rights and fundamental freedoms of indigenous people*: United Nations Economic and Social Council.

Te Taura Whiri o te Reo Maori. The Maori Language Commission. (2009). *History—A History of the Maori Language*, Wellington. Retrieved January 9, 2009 from *http://www.tetaurawhiri.govt.nz/english/issues_e/hist/index.shtml*.

United Nations. (2007). *United Nations Declaration on the Rights of Indigenous Peoples. A/RES/61/295*: General Assembly.

Waitangi Tribunal. (1986). *Te Reo Māori Report*. Wellington: GP Publications: Waitangi Tribunal.

Walker, R. (2004). *Ka Whawhai Tonu Matou. Struggle Without End* (revised edition). Auckland: Penguin.

Wall, D. (2008). It Is and It Isn't: Stereotypes, Advertising and Narrative. *The Journal of Popular Culture, 41*(6), 1033–1050.

Young, R. (2001). *Postcolonialism. An Historical Introduction*. Malden, MA: Blackwell.

Yuval-Davis, N., Kannabiran, K., & Vieten, U. (2006). Introduction. Situating Contemporary Politics of Belonging. In N. Yuval-Davis, K. Kannabiran & U. Vieten (Eds.), *The Situated Politics of Belonging* (pp. 1–14). London: Sage.

CHAPTER TWENTY-FIVE

Constructing Critical Futures

Projects from the Heart

LOURDES DIAZ SOTO

The contributors to this volume have taken us on a fascinating journey including, but not limited to the complexities and multiple layers of childhoods. This has been no easy task to deal with the historical, global, critical, indigenous, countercolonial, neoliberal, postcolonial, postmodern, feminist, racial, psychological, transnational, international, continued spectacle of violence, new and increasingly changing technologies, ethnic, linguistic, silencing, numerous literacies, play, assessment, and role of social services and social justice. The chapters in this handbook taken together challenge the reader to consider present, past, and future possibilities in research and praxis (including policy) as the latter relate to childhoods.

In spite of the fact that the impact of neoliberal policies and global capitalism has been well documented, the impact to the daily-lived reality of children and families is rarely expressed. Even more discouraging is the continued lack of implementation of compassionate scholarship, praxis, and policy on behalf of children and families. In this chapter, I will dare you, my dear reader, to continue to tap the imaginary and consider how we can implement projects with ameliorative intentions.

1. What difference has our scholarship made in the daily-life realities of children and families?
2. Can we implement projects from the heart with ameliorative intentions?
3. Is our profession strong enough to have a vision of solidarity?

Patti Lather (1991) in her work embraces the idea that social and educational inquiry can have ameliorative intention so that as inquirers we can contribute to improving people's existing and future lives. It may be that we can continue to argue and critically analyze the types of scholarship we can find liberating for ourselves, children, families, and communities. Is our work designed for professionals speaking to other professionals only? Is our work intended for dissemination to a very few selected scholars? Does our work need to be coupled with ethical dimensions in light of the continued needs of children and families in a neoliberal post-postmodern global context? *Is there room for compassion, humanity, and love in our scholarship?* Can our field pursue projects with ameliorative intentions? What would such projects look like?

The work several scholars presenting at the American Educational Research Association (AERA) in 2009 was carefully framed in order to contribute to improving people's existing and future lives. These projects include, but are not limited to, the work of Valerie Polakow (2009) who continues to passionately challenge United States as a nation with her continued commitment to documenting how child poverty in the country is a violation of human rights. She reveals the *shame of the nation* as the United States has the highest child poverty rates among 19 wealthy industrialized nations. She documents how child poverty has become a *"state-sanctioned public violence."* Among her points are the following:

- The United States has failed to ratify The International Convention on the Rights of the Child (CRC), which is an important document that can affirm children's human rights.
- The United States fails on almost all indices of child and family well-being from a cross-national comparative perspective.
- The United States has no platform of social and economic rights for children.
- The United States has failed to create a national high-quality childcare system that serves working families.

Valerie's voice rings out that "poverty in a land of plenty is a moral disgrace." Yet she sees hope and possibility at this historical moment so that we can organize to end child poverty. This is a critical moment to build a grassroots campaign to ratify the CRC. President Obama's campaign ran on "hope"; let's hope that his administration will see this as a crucial priority.

In her piece, Erica Miner (2009) tracked how sex offender registries and community notification laws contribute to culture of fear of "stranger danger." Erica Miners highlights how "stranger danger" functions to displace the responsibility from patriarchy for violence against children and women. The maintenance of stranger-danger takes responsibility off the construct of the family *or patriarchy* as Miners documents the following:

- More than three women are murdered by their husbands or boyfriends in the United States every day.
- Seventy percent of all reported sexual assaults against children are committed in the home.
- Sexual offenders are more likely than the rest of the prison population to be "representative" of the U.S. population being white, middle-class, and married.
- Persistent white supremacy has delayed our ability to *transform* our conceptions of what makes us secure.
- Miner sees the need for public dialogues about sexual and other forms of intimate violence in order to shift our collective ideas about *health* and *safety* in homes and communities.
- Miner sees the need to move conceptions about *childhood, sexuality, family*, and to implicate patriarchy.

Miner concludes that "in a nation with no adequate or affordable childcare system, no universal healthcare, expensive to prohibitive costs for higher education, and a minimum wage that is not a living wage, we have no registries for the officials, and employers, that routinely elect to implement policies that actively damage all people, including or even *particularly* children." And, what is the "greatest" enemy of childhood? "Poverty is the single greatest risk factor for almost every 'life-smashing' condition a kid might be at risk for" (Levine 2002, 220, cited in Miner). Just as drug-free zones around school do not reduce youth's drug usage but instead criminalize entire communities, and "tough on crime" laws and the "war on terror" don't make us any safer. Expanding the Sex Offenders Registry does not reduce persistent, often state sanctioned, "violence."

Christopher Robbins (2009) documented how zero tolerance and other transformations of schooling erode the social and political rights of youth, especially poor youth and youth of color. Robbins described how

- there has been a historical shift causing the hidden curriculum to remain not so "hidden,"
- there are no public commitments to ensure that learners will be given basic competencies,
- the public is supporting the rupture of the social contract between adult society and youth, and
- Robbins demonstrates "zero tolerance" repositions youth (of color) from the "slow" track to the "prison" track as it helps to institutionalize neoliberalism's broader agenda of suspending citizenship.

Robbins cites Randall Beger (2002) who states, "Ironically, children are unsafe in public schools today not because of exposure to drugs and violence, but because they have lost their constitutional protections under the Fourth Amendment."

Based upon our decades of experience with childhoods, there appears to be a need to pursue newly evolving qualitative and experimental paradigms in order to emphasize decolonizing models as well as research capable of ameliorating oppressive dehumanizing situations. Projects that are improving the lives of others, pursuing related issues of social justice and equity, human rights, children's rights and families' well-being are truly "projects from the heart." Such projects exemplify the possibility that we have as scholars to improve oppressive dehumanizing conditions. Projects that give voice to children and families' daily-life reality are examples of what I would like to term "projects from the heart."

We have a choice to continue to pursue the critique of what we are seeing and experiencing based upon our privileged existence or to pursue avenues that address human rights and children's rights. Several areas are ripe for exploration:

First, self-conscientization; Freire talks about conscientization for learners but what about self-conscientization for scholars where we examine our perspectives, privileges, and our own world view, not as a naval gazing activity but as an intention to better understand our co-researchers/our participants.

Second, ethics is another important issue for childhood scholars to consider. As just one example is the continued demonization of immigrants in the current political climate where ministers and representatives in very public arenas threaten even our president.

And third, how do we struggle with ideology, place, and historical context as scholars? Is our intent to better the human condition or our own privileged condition?

As we continue to pursue alternative paradigms, postpolitical possibilities, and projects with ameliorative intentions I would like to share two theoretical possibilities for extending projects from the heart based upon recent work with graduate students in two institutions of higher learning. These theories include solidarity and social action in liberating collaborative spaces.

First, relying on a piece (Soto, 2009) published elsewhere, I call on teacher educators to extend social action projects that include community within a framework of participatory action research. More specifically, it shares the evolution of what I term "critical emancipatory mezcla praxis" as well as accompanying examples of several hope-filled projects students and I have pursued over a span of eight years. The idea of mezcla (hybrid) can also be related to Kincheloe and McLaren's (2005) descriptions of bricoleurs as we carefully chose a mix of methodologies and analytical tools to make sense of our work. "In the active bricolage, we bring our understanding of the research context together with our previous experience with research methods" (p. 317). This is a reflexive process that includes not only looking at ourselves in the roles of researchers and practitioners but also in an equitable dialogue with community.

Affording opportunities for the practice of freedom within the context of higher/teacher education can lead to a pedagogy that is humanization while at the same time affording learners/participants/co-researchers concientization (consciousness raising). Our inspiration comes from our continued, consistent, persistent praxis helping us to realize that educational-social action projects can emerge from decolonizing perspectives that respect existing linguistic-cultural-socio-economic traditions of our co-researchers (participants, learners) and community members.

The second possibility relies on a piece pending publication (Soto, Cervantes, Perales, Campos; in press) entitled "The Xicana Sacred Space: A Communal Circle of Compromiso for Educational Researchers." For us, the *Xicana sacred space* functioned as a decolonizing tool capable of displacing patriarchal and Western linear notions of research. We found the ability to reclaim indigenous ways of knowing while working in conjunction with the Mestiza consciousness (Anzaldúa, 1999). The piece explains how the *Xicana Sacred Space* evolved in a higher/teacher education context and holds possibilities as a method or tool in participatory action research. Our experience taught us about the importance of Freire's (1970) notion of conscientization (consciousness raising) and Delgado Bernal's (2000) notion of cultural intuition.

We also learned about the importance of examining positionalities/standpoints as well as how to strengthen scholarship among those of us interested in conducting decolonial, emancipatory, and feminist research. Anzaldúa's call for new theories with new theorizing methods was the starting point for our journey.

> Necesitamos teorías that will rewrite history
> using race, class, gender and ethnicity as categories
> of analysis, theories that cross borders, that
> blur boundaries—new kinds of theories
> with new theorizing methods. (Anzaldúa, 1999, p. 25)

This feminist epistemology examines the influence of issues on immigration and migration, language, and power. It validates the mestiza consciousness of living in hybrid cultures, races, languages, and spiritualities while navigating competing powers. In the same way, scholars interested in working with immigrant groups can place the immigrant at the center as expert of their own experiences. Our society can no longer continue to choose stereotypical children's identities, as hybridity becomes the norm. My youngest grandchildren, having parents of differing ethnicities, are Puerto-Indian and Puerto-Polish. Recalling how my youngest son (now a father himself) asked me long ago, how do we fill in those racial questions?

Returning back to our theoretical piece we began to identify and recognize what we term as "Xicana Sacred Space." We propose that our *Xicana sacred space* can be utilized by others as a collective pedagogical tool or research method. Inserted into projects with emancipatory and decolonial intentions the *Xicana sacred space* may lead to powerful possibilities. Resembling indigenous circles (Smith, 2005) displaces androcentric and Western linear notions of research, reclaiming indigenous and organic ways of knowing. This is our idea of a collective *third space* that can have ameliorative intentions. Gloria Anzaldúa and Cherrie Moraga (1981) elaborated on the emergence of a third space feminism, in which there is a "diversity of perspectives, linguistic styles, and cultural tongues" (p. xxiv). This third space has a decolonizing goal capable of raising conscientization (a la Freire), embracing hybridity and uniting forces against oppression.

bell hooks noted: "The moment we choose to love, we begin to move against domination, against oppression. The moment we choose to love, we begin to move toward the freedom to act in ways that liberate others and ourselves. That action is the testimony of *love as the practice of freedom.*"

If your work is more interested in improving the lives of others, issues of social justice and equity, human rights, children's rights and learner's well-being, then perhaps the idea of projects from the heart will appeal to you as well. The current state of our field and the future of childhoods are what is at stake. Are we up to the challenge of becoming living testimony of "love as the practice of freedom"?

References

Anzaldúa, G. (1999). *Borderlands, la frontera: The new mestiza* (2nd ed.). San Francisco, CA: Aunt Lute Books.

Anzaldúa, G., & Moraga, C. (1981). *This bridge called my back: Writings by radical women of color.* Watertown, MA: Persephone Press.

Delgado Bernal, D. (2000). Historical struggles for educational equity: Setting the context for Chicana/o schooling today. In C. Tejeda, C. Martinez, and Z. Leonardo (Eds.). *Charting new terrains of Chicana(o)/Latina(o) education.* Cresskill: Hampton Press, pp. 67–86

Freire, P. (2000). *Pedagogy of the oppressed* (M. B. Ramos, Trans.). New York: Continuum International. (Original work published 1970.)

hooks, b. (2000). *Feminist theory: From margin to center.* Cambridge, MA: South End Press.

Kincheloe, J. & McLaren, P. (1994) Rethinking critical theory and qualitative research. In N. K. Denzin and Y. S. Lincoln (Eds.). *Handbook of qualitative research.* Thousand Oaks, CA: Sage, pp. 138–157.

Lather, P. (1991). *Getting smart: Feminist research and pedagogy within the postmodern.* New York: Routledge.

Lather, P. (1993). Fertile obsession: Validity after poststructuralism. *Sociological Quarterly,* 35, 673–694.

Lather, P. & Smithies, C. (1997). *Troubling the angels: Women living with HIV/AIDS.* Boulder, CO: Westview Press.

Miner, E. (2009). Never innocent: Feminist trouble with sex offender registries and protection in a prison nation. Presented at the American Educational Research Association, San Diego, California.

Polakow, V. (2009) Child poverty in the U.S.: Violating human rights. Presented at the American Educational Research Association, San Diego, California.

Robbins, C. (2009). Suspending Citizenship: The social contract, the hidden curriculum, and the not-so-hidden curriculum of punishment and disposability. Presented at the American Educational Research Association, San Diego, California.

Soto, L.D., Cervantes-Soon, C., Villareal, E., and Campos, E. (Winter 2009) The Xicana sacred space: A communal circle of compromiso for educational researchers. *Harvard Educational Review* 79(4), 755-775.

Soto, L.D. (2009). Toward a critical emancipatory mezcla praxis. In B.B. Swadener, C. A. Grant, S. Mitakidou, & E. Tressou (Eds.). *Beyond pedagogies of exclusion in diverse childhood contexts.* Hampshire, England: Palgrave Macmillan.

Contributors

MARIANNE N. BLOCH is Professor of Curriculum and Instruction and Women's Studies at the University of Wisconsin-Madison. Her publications include *The Child in the World/the World in the Child* (Palgrave) and *Governing Children, Families and Education: Restructuring the Welfare State* (Palgrave). With Gaile Cannella, she also co-edits the online public knowledge publication, *International Critical Childhood Policy Studies Journal*.

SUE BOOKS is a professor in the Department of Secondary Education at the State University of New York, New Paltz, where she teaches courses in the social foundations of education, comparative education, and action research. Her scholarship has focused primarily on issues of equity in U.S. schooling, especially school funding and poverty as an educational issue. She is the editor of *Invisible Children in the Society and Its Schools*, 3rd edition (Erlbaum, 2007) and the author of *Poverty and Schooling in the U.S.: Contexts and Consequences* (Erlbaum, 2004). In recent years, she has enjoyed conducting research and teaching in South Africa as a visiting scholar and in Iceland as a Fulbright scholar.

MARIE BOUVERNE-DE BIE is head of the Department of Social Welfare Studies at Ghent University. In her research, she underlines the necessity to study social work as a historical understanding of the interrelationship between social politics, social policy, and social work practices; specific attention is given to the relationship between social work and social welfare rights.

ERICA BURMAN is Professor of Psychology and Women's Studies at Manchester Metropolitan University in the United Kingdom. As a feminist developmental psychologist and group analyst, she has written extensively on the role of psychology in international development policy and practice, on the politics and affects of representations of children (both remembered and depicted), on relationships between women and children, and on transnational issues such as violence and migration as they affect state responses to women and children. Her most recent books, *Deconstructing Developmental Psychology* (Routledge, 2008) and *Developments: Child, Image, and Nation* (Routledge,

2008) reflect these themes.

STEVEN P. CAMICIA is a white male who grew up in the San Francisco Bay area of the United States. He earned his bachelor's degree at San Francisco State University in Classics. After 20 years as a carpenter, he returned to the classroom as an elementary school teacher in Reno, Nevada. As an elementary teacher, he became interested in the ways that certain speech is privileged while other speech is marginalized in classroom discussions. He earned a Ph.D. at the University of Washington, where he pursued his research interest in this area. He is currently an Assistant Professor of Social Studies Education in the School of Teacher Education and Leadership at Utah State University. His research focuses on curriculum and instruction in the areas of perspective consciousness, social justice, global education, and democratic decision-making processes. His work has been published numerous times in most of the top-tier social studies research journals.

GAILE S. CANNELLA is Professor and Velma E. Schmidt Endowed Chair of Early Childhood Studies at the University of North Texas in the United States, the largest higher education institution in the Dallas metropolitan area. Her books include *Deconstructing Early Childhood Education: Social Justice and Revolution* (Peter Lang); and *Childhood and Postcolonization* (Routledge) with Radhika Viruru. Her work has been translated to Spanish and Korean. She is a charter member of the newly formed Society of Critical Educators. Currently, her work includes the exploration of critical qualitative research methods as avenues for counterimperialism and for challenging oppressive childhood policies and discourse practices. This work is reflected in the contemporary Velma E. Schmidt Critical Childhood Policy Studies Research Initiative at the University of North Texas that currently supports research projects related to migrant worker young children (reflecting the Initiative's support for cultural and linguistic diversity) and childhood and critical disaster studies (reflecting the Initiative's focus on critical examinations of childhood and globalization). These projects represent the Initiatives overall mission to inquire into, collaborate with critical researchers, and disseminate research that focuses on critical childhood policy studies that recognize the construction of privilege and oppression.

SANDRA CHANG-KREDL is a lecturer in the Department of Education at Concordia University, in Montreal, Quebec, Canada, and is completing her doctorate in curriculum studies in the Department of Integrated Studies in Education at McGill University. Her research interests include studies in the discursive formation of childhood in literature and film, children's symbolic play, and the use of memory work with early childhood teachers. She has contributed publications in the areas of curriculum inquiry, media studies, and childhood studies.

DONALD R. COLLINS is an associate professor at Prairie View A&M University in the United States. He has over 25 years of professional experience in education and psychology that spans teaching, counseling, assessment, and administration. He has worked in the public, private, and corporate sectors. Dr. Collins has taught at the graduate and undergraduate levels and worked as an educational consultant for 56 school districts in the Houston area. He has published academic articles that focus on the education of African American children and on institutional effectiveness.

IRIS DUHN is a senior lecturer in the School of Critical Studies in Education at the University of Auckland. She teaches education studies, with a particular focus on childhood and globalization. Her current research focuses on pedagogy, curriculum, and ethics in early childhood education in Aotearoa/New Zealand. She is particularly interested in theorizing childhood in the interstices between power, subjectivities and ethics, and in using interdisciplinary perspectives in early childhood research.

HAROLD GOTHSON has a masters in political and social sciences, completing studies of education at the University of Stockholm in Sweden. He has served as director for large kindergartens and as the head director of all preschools in a suburb city outside of Stockholm. In 1987, he was appointed by the Ministry of Education to lead a project with ten communities concerning pedagogical management and leadership. Further, he has lectured and supervised headmasters and pedagogues. In 1992, he joined with colleagues to initiate the Reggio Emilia Institute in Stockholm and served as the director and chairman of the Institute until 2006. Today he is a board member, senior consultant, and International Coordinator at the Reggio Emilia Institute.

SUE GRIESHABER teaches and researches at the School of Early Childhood, Queensland University of Technology, Brisbane, Australia. Her teaching and research interests are framed by equity and diversity and include early childhood curriculum, policy, assessment, and families. Sue co-edits the international, refereed online journal *Contemporary Issues in Early Childhood* and her latest research projects include (with Allan Luke) a quantitative sociological study of family literacy practices, pedagogy, and achievement in the first year of school; and with Carmel Diezmann, a project about understanding the achievements and aspirations of new women professors in Australia. Her work has been translated to Spanish, German, and Chinese.

CLARE HITE is an associate professor in the School of Education at Dalton State College, Dalton, Georgia in the United States. Her primary teaching responsibilities are literacy and ESOL courses for teachers. Clare holds a bachelor's degree in English from the University of Florida, masters and specialist degrees in Reading also from the University of Florida, and a doctoral degree in Curriculum and Instruction with and emphasis on Language and Literacy from the University of South Florida. She has published articles on reading comprehension, teachers' knowledge of working with English learners, and teacher education in several journals, including *Reading Research and Instruction, Teacher Education Quarterly*, and *Journal of Educational Research*.

SHARON L. HIXON previously taught first and second grade in Baltimore City Schools. At the college level, she has taught Developmental Reading at Frederick Community College and Dalton State College. Currently, she is an associate professor in the School of Education at Dalton State College in Dalton, Georgia.

RACHEL HOLMES works in the Educational and Social Research Institute at Manchester Metropolitan University. She is a senior lecturer and researcher within the Centre for Cultural Studies of Children and Childhood. Her research interests are among the interstices of applied educational research, social science research, and arts-based research within the field of childhood. She also has interests in notions of childhood territories such as ways childhood becomes imag(in)ed through fictional, documentary, and ethnographic film; children's child(self)hood, identities and objects; and ways to (left) field childhood via opening up off-center research methodologies.

LIZ JONES is Professor of Early Years and Childhood Education in the Education and Social Research Institute at Manchester Metropolitan University. Her research interests span poststructuralism, feminism and postcolonialism. Much of her work is located within mainstream UK early-years settings. A key concern centres on children's identities. Here the task is to reinvigorate existing canons of thought so as to break with systems that are increasingly incapable of grasping the complexities of young children and the cultures that they create.

DEVORAH I. KENNEDY is an assistant professor in Early Childhood Multicultural Education at the University of New Mexico. Her work includes a focus on the mobilizations of the "universal child"—a construct that relies on difference and exclusion, while appearing to include everyone.

I-Fang Lee is an assistant professor in the Department of Early Childhood Education at the Hong Kong Institute of Education. Her research interests include postmodern theories of early childhood education policy, curriculum reforms and changes, educational philosophy, and global educational discourses. Her theoretical interests focus on critical, poststructural, and feminist theories of childhood and families as well as education and care.

Maggie MacLure is Professor of Education in the Education and Social Research Institute at Manchester Metropolitan University. Her research interests include qualitative methodology, especially discourse analysis, deconstruction, and poststructuralist approaches. She is the author of *Discourse in Educational and Social Research* (Open University). See: http://www.ioe.mmu.ac.uk/research/res-ppl/m-maclure.shtml

Christina MacRae has 16 years of experience as an early years practitioner and more recently as a researcher into early years practice. Her Ph.D. offers a critique of normative ways of interpreting children's representations in the early years classroom where it examined the practice of child observation and how it serves to frame what we see when we look at young children. Additionally, Christina has been involved in research into children's learning in museums and art galleries. Alongside her research interests, Christina is an artist whose practice is interested in the connections that people make with the objects that they collect.

Melinda Miller is an associate professor in the Department of Language, Literacy, and Special populations at Sam Houston State University in Huntsville, Texas in the United States. She teaches in the reading program area and serves as assistant chair of the department. Her research interests include literacy and diverse populations, assessment, English language learners, and emergent literacy.

Greg Neal is a senior lecturer in the School of Education at Victoria University in Melbourne, Australia. His research interest areas include the use of ICT in education to improve teaching and learning, social inclusion, action research, and innovative pedagogies in primary schooling. Greg has been involved in a number of research projects, for example, the inclusion of Tablet technologies in classroom practice, improving students' digital literacies, exploring relationships between ICT literacy and pedagogical practices in various school settings as a means of engaging students in their learning. Integral to his research is the use of student voice to capture rich qualitative data.

A. Bame Nsamenang is associate professor of psychology and learning science at the University of Yaoundé 1 (ENS, Bambili campus) and founder/director of the Human Development Resource Centre, a research and human services facility. His research explores lifespan human development, with keen interest in local understandings of Africa's next generations—children and youth—as the knowledge generated there meshes with, or stands to extend or enrich, the frontiers of developmental science. He has published influential Africentric theoretical and applied research. He is an avid advocate of African voices and strategizes to niche them into developmental science discourses and publications. In 2009, he started an initiative to publish Africa-centric teacher education textbooks and tools. His first edited volume to be published in 2010 and authored by African and Africanist scholars—*African Educational Theories and Practices: A Generative Teacher Education Textbook*—is sponsored by the Jacobs Foundation.

Liselott Mariett Olsson began her work as a preschool teacher in 1990. She served as project leader for "Pedagogy in a Changing World" from 1993 to 1998, then as headmistress for preschools in Trangsund, a community outside Stockholm from 1998 to 2001. Her dissertation in educational work was published by Routledge as *Movement and Experimentation in Young Children's*

Learning: Deleuze and Guattari in Early Childhood Education. She is currently a teacher educator at Stockholm University and coordinator of the research project "The Magic of Language—Young Children's Relations to Language, Reading, and Writing."

VERONICA PACINI-KETCHABAW is Associate Professor and Coordinator of the Early Years Specialization in the School of Child and Youth Care at the University of Victoria in Canada. She teaches and conducts research on issues related to poststructural, feminist, and postcolonial theory-practice in early childhood education. She is currently directing a multiyear participatory action research project with a group of early childhood educators in British Columbia, Canada. Aspects of this work will be published as a book in 2010 by Peter Lang.

MICHELLE SALAZAR PEREZ is an assistant professor of early childhood education in the Department of Curriculum and Instruction, Southern Illinois University in Carbondale. She conducted her dissertation research in New Orleans, Louisiana, which examined discourses of power surrounding young children, charter schools, and the privatization of public education post-Hurricane Katrina. Her current research interests include using marginalized feminist, critical, postmodern, and poststructural perspectives to examine structures of power that exist socially and institutionally and oppress/privilege/other individuals and groups based on constructions/representations of race, class, gender, sexuality, age, and ability.

CHERYL RAU, Te Tari Puna Ora o Aotearoa, New Zealand Childcare Association, Wellington, is of Tainui, Kahungungu, and Rangitane descent. Her educational and research focus has centered on Te Tiriti o Waitangi partnerships in Aotearoa, Maori educators articulating strategies which nurture tamariki Maori potentiality across the early childhood community. From 2004 to 2007, she completed two research studies funded by the New Zealand government's Teaching and Learning Research Initiative (TLRI) centered on prioritizing Maori (indigenous to Aotearoa) ways of knowing, doing, and being, and transformative praxis within the sector. She is at present codirecting a further two-year TLRI project, which explores kaitiakitanga (ecological sustainability) utilizing an ethic of caring for self, others, and the environment from both indigenous and western perspectives. Cheryl's 30-year background in education has been across sectors, including Primary, Secondary, and Tertiary. For the past 16 years, she has been an early childhood educator and coordinator/director of Ngahihi professional learning programmes, a Maori organization facilitating learning that is funded by the Ministry of Education.

JENNY RITCHIE is Associate Professor in Early Childhood Teacher Education, Te Whare Wananga o Wairaka–Unitec Institute of Technology, Auckland, New Zealand. Jenny's teaching and research have focused on supporting early childhood educators to enhance their practice in terms of applying an awareness of cultural and social justice issues. She has completed two-year studies funded by the New Zealand government's Teaching and Learning Research Initiative (TLRI), focusing on the implications of honoring the indigenous culture and language within early childhood education and teacher education in Aotearoa. She is currently co-directing a further two-year TLRI project exploring ecological sustainability utilizing an ethic of caring for self, others, and the environment from both kaupapa Maori and western perspectives. With Sandra Morrison of the University of Waikato, she recently began a Ministry of Education–funded longitudinal research and evaluation project of a Ngati Whakaue-initiated early childhood service, exploring benefits of participation for both tamariki and whanau. She has a background as an educator and whanau member in a wide range of early childhood services, and 20 years as a teacher educator.

ARACELI RIVAS received her Ph.D. in Educational Psychology Foundations from Texas A&M

University and a BA in Psychology from the University of Notre Dame. She is an independent scholar with interests in critical research methodologies, indigenous education, educational leadership, and social justice advocacy. Her scholarship has been greatly influenced by living on the southwest border where globalization's multiple visages are reflected every day in the community life—for example, from the impoverished colonies, the border wall, bilingual education, to the local indigenous groups' revival of traditions and knowledge. Currently, her expertise in applied educational psychology involves the systemic evaluation of programs in border town school districts.

RUDI ROOSE is senior researcher in the Department of Social Welfare Studies at Ghent University and assistant professor in the Department of Criminology in Free University Brussels (Belgium). He is involved in courses and research on children's rights, child protection and welfare, social work theories, and forensic social work.

CINTHYA M. SAAVEDRA is a first-generation immigrant from Nicaragua. In the early 1980s, her family moved to Texas in the United States because of the Nicaraguan civil war. She was raised in south central Texas and earned her Ph.D. from Texas A&M University. She worked as a visiting assistant professor in early childhood education at the University of North Carolina, Greensboro and is currently an assistant professor of ESL/bilingual and diversity education at Utah State University. Her research interests include Chicana/Third World/Transnational critical perspectives and methodologies of early childhood education, immigrant childhoods, and critical teacher education. She has published critical examinations of language diversity, teacher linguistic diversity training/research, and on transnational childhood experiences in the curriculum (with friend and colleague Steven P. Camicia). She has also co-authored a chapter on borderland-feminist mestizaje in the *Sage Handbook of Critical and Indigenous Methodologies*. Her most current co-authored publication, "Weaving Transnational Feminist(s) Methodologies: (Re)examining Early Childhood Linguistic Diversity Teacher Training Research" is featured in a special issue on methodologies in the *Journal of Early Childhood Research*.

SADAF SHALLWANI (MSW) is pursuing her Ph.D. in Developmental Psychology and Education at the Ontario Institute for Studies in Education, University of Toronto. She also currently works with the Aga Khan Foundation (based out of Geneva, Switzerland), supporting programme implementation, evaluation, and research for community- and school-based early childhood programmes, mostly in majority world countries in Asia and Africa. Sadaf's research interests are clustered around human development, particularly early childhood development in diverse cultural contexts. Her scholarly work includes an aim to deconstruct mainstream (primarily Western) conceptualizations and theories of human development, and reconceptualize them from different perspectives and contexts. In particular, Sadaf's doctoral research explores the conceptualization of school readiness and quality in early primary education in Pakistan.

LOURDES DIAZ SOTO is the Goizueta Endowed Chair in Teacher Education at Dalton State College in Georgia in the United States. Some of her publications include *The Praeger Handbook of Latino Education in the U.S.* (Greenwood Publishing Group); *The Politics of Early Childhood Education* (Peter Lang); and *Making a Difference in the Lives of Bilingual/Bicultural Children* (Peter Lang). She has taught diverse learners in Puerto Rico, New York City, Pennsylvania, Texas, and Georgia. She teaches critical pedagogy and has published numerous refereed articles and book chapters viewing how issues of social justice and equity impact children and families.

MICHEL VANDENBROECK is assistant professor in the Department of Social Welfare Studies at Ghent University (Belgium), where he teaches family education and early childhood care and education. His main areas of research are diversity, early childhood education, and parent support. He is a member of the editorial board of the *European Early Childhood Education Research Journal.*

RADHIKA VIRURU is Associate Professor and Coordinator of the B.Ed Program in Primary Education at Qatar University, Doha, Qatar. She teaches courses in early childhood curriculum, research methods, and qualitative research. Her research interests are international early childhood education and postcolonial theory.

CORRINE M. WICKENS is an assistant professor in the Department of Literacy Education at Northern Illinois University. Her research interests examine the intersections of sexuality and schooling, adolescent literacy, and young adult literature. Recent works have explored homophobia and heterosexism in a college of education, social regulation in LGBTQ-themed young adult literature, and censorship challenges in the Midwest region of the United States.

NICOLA YELLAND is a professor at the Hong Kong Institute of Education. Over the last decade, her research has been related to the use of new technologies in school and community contexts. This has involved projects that have investigated the specific learning of students in computer environments as well as a broader consideration of the ways in which new technologies can impact on the pedagogies that teachers use and the curriculum in schools. Her multidisciplinary research focus has enabled her to work with early childhood, primary, and middle school teachers to enhance the ways in which new technologies can be incorporated into learning contexts to make them more interesting and motivating for students, so that educational outcomes are improved. Her most recent publications are *Rethinking Learning in Early Childhood Education* (OUP) and *Rethinking Education with ICT: New Directions for Effective Practices* (Sense Publishers). She is the author of *Shift to the Future: Rethinking Learning with New Technologies in Education* (Routledge). Nicola has worked in Australia, the United States, the United Kingdom, and Hong Kong.

Index

RETHINKING CHILDHOOD

GAILE S. CANNELLA, *General Editor*

A revolution is occurring regarding the study of childhood. Traditional notions of child development are under attack, as are the methods by which children are studied. At the same time, the nature of childhood itself is changing as children gain access to information once reserved for adults only. Technological innovations, media, and electronic information have narrowed the distinction between adults and children, forcing educators to rethink the world of schooling in this new context.

This series of textbooks and monographs encourages scholarship in all of these areas, eliciting critical investigations in developmental psychology, early childhood education, multicultural education, and cultural studies of childhood.

Proposals and manuscripts may be sent to the general editor:

Gaile S. Cannella
c/o Peter Lang Publishing, Inc.
29 Broadway, 18th floor
New York, New York 10006

To order other books in this series, please contact our Customer Service Department at:

(800) 770-LANG (within the U.S.)
(212) 647-7706 (outside the U.S.)
(212) 647-7707 FAX

Or browse online by series at:
www.peterlang.com